Splendour & Squalor

MARCUS SCRIVEN read history at Oxford before becoming a journalist, first at the *Sunday Telegraph*, then at the *Evening Standard*. He was a leading contributor to Channel 4's documentary on Victor Hervey, 6th Marquess of Bristol, which broadcast in spring 2009. *Splendour & Squalor* is his first book.

Splendour

&

Squalor

THE DISGRACE AND DISINTEGRATION OF THREE ARISTOCRATIC DYNASTIES

Marcus Scriven

ATLANTIC BOOKS

LONDON

For my parents, and in memory of
'The Rev' Jonathan Peel, 1962–2009

First published in Great Britain in 2009 by
Atlantic Books, an imprint of Grove Atlantic Ltd.

This paperback edition published in
Great Britain in 2010 by Atlantic Books.

1 3 5 7 9 10 8 6 4 2

A CIP catalogue record for this book is available
from the British Library.

The illustration credits on pp.xi–xiv constitute
an extension of this copyright page

ISBN: 978 1 84354 125 7

Printed in Great Britain by Clays Ltd, St Ives plc

Atlantic Books
An imprint of Atlantic Books Ltd
Ormond House
26–27 Boswell Street
London WC1N 3JZ

www.atlantic-books.co.uk

Contents

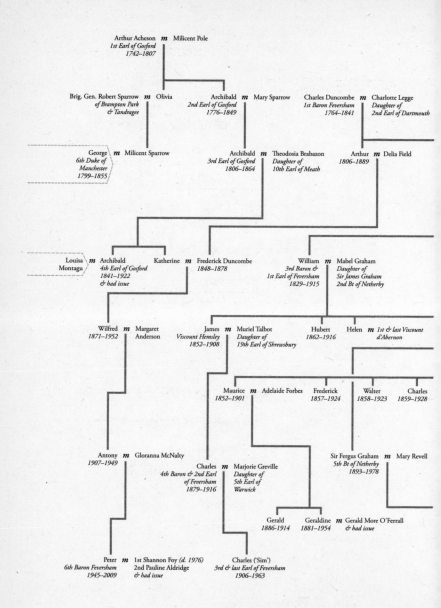

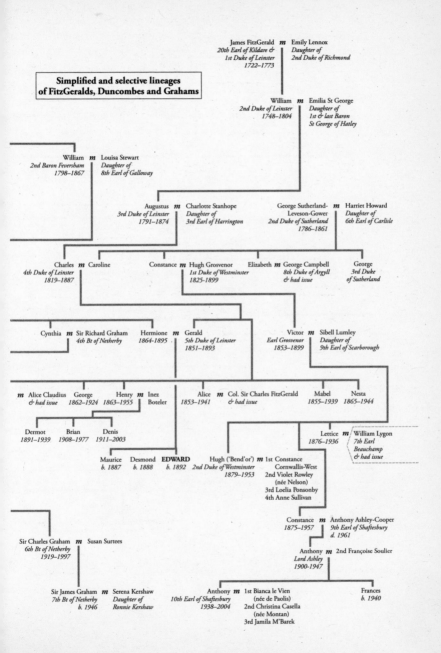

Simplified and selective lineages of FitzGeralds, Duncombes and Grahams

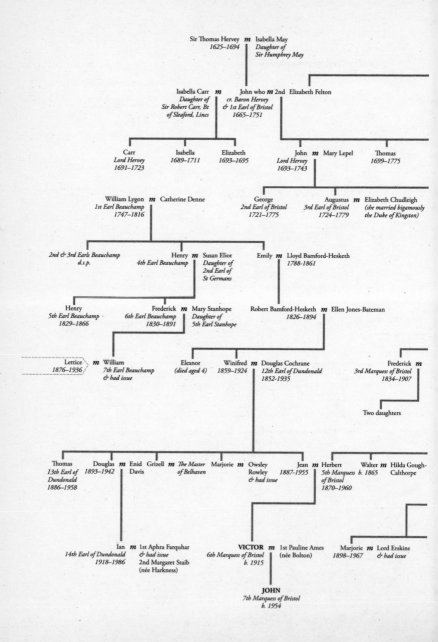

Sir Thomas Hervey *m* Isabella May
1625–1694   *Daughter of*
             Sir Humphrey May

Isabella Carr *m* John who *m* 2nd Elizabeth Felton
Daughter of   *cr. Baron Hervey*
Sir Robert Carr, Bt *& 1st Earl of Bristol*
of Sleaford, Lincs   *1665–1751*

Carr   Isabella   Elizabeth   John   *m* Mary Lepel   Thomas
Lord Hervey   *1689–1711*   *1693–1695*   *Lord Hervey*   *1699–1775*
1691–1723   *1693–1743*

William Lygon *m* Catherine Denne   George   Augustus *m* Elizabeth Chudleigh
1st Earl Beauchamp   *2nd Earl of Bristol*   *3rd Earl of Bristol* *(she married bigamously*
1747–1816   *1721–1775*   *1724–1779*   *the Duke of Kingston)*

2nd & 3rd Earls Beauchamp   Henry *m* Susan Eliot   Emily *m* Lloyd Bamford-Hesketh
d.s.p.   *4th Earl Beauchamp* *Daughter of*   *1788-1861*
                                          2nd Earl of
                                          St Germans

Henry   Frederick *m* Mary Stanhope   Robert Bamford-Hesketh *m* Ellen Jones-Bateman
5th Earl Beauchamp *6th Earl Beauchamp* *Daughter of*   *1826–1894*
1829–1866   *1830–1891*   *5th Earl Stanhope*

Lettice *m* William   Eleanor   Winifred *m* Douglas Cochrane   Frederick *m*
1876–1936 *7th Earl Beauchamp* *(died aged 4)* *1859–1924* *12th Earl of Dundonald*   *3rd Marquess of Bristol*
          & had issue   *1852–1935*   *1834–1907*

                                                                                      Two daughters

Thomas   Douglas *m* Enid Grizell *m* *The Master*   Marjorie *m* Owsley   Jean *m* Herbert   Walter *m* Hilda Gough-
13th Earl of *1893–1942* Davis   *of Belhaven*   Rowley *1887–1955* *5th Marquess* *b. 1865* Calthorpe
Dundonald   *& had issue*   *of Bristol*
1886–1958   *1870–1960*

            Ian *m* 1st Aphra Farquhar   VICTOR *m* 1st Pauline Ames   Marjorie *m* Lord Erskine
14th Earl of Dundonald 2nd Margaret Staib *6th Marquess of Bristol* (née Bolton)   *1898–1967* *& had issue*
1918–1986   (née Harkness)   *b. 1915*

                                    JOHN
                                  7th Marquess of Bristol
                                       b. 1954

Sir Thomas Felton **m** Elizabeth Howard
4th Bt   *Daughter of James*
3rd Earl of Suffolk &
3rd Baron Howard de Walden

**Simplified and selective
Hervey lineage**

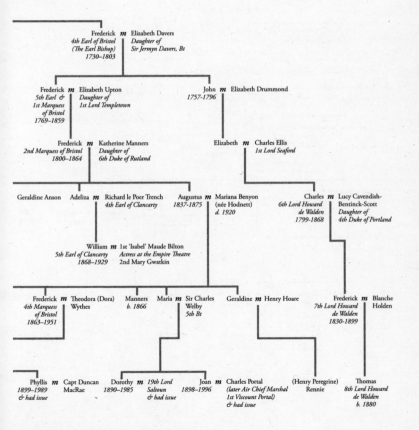

Captain William
1699–1776

Frederick **m** Elizabeth Davers
4th Earl of Bristol   *Daughter of*
(The Earl Bishop)   *Sir Jermyn Davers, Bt*
1730–1803

Frederick **m** Elizabeth Upton   John **m** Elizabeth Drummond
5th Earl &   *Daughter of*   *1757–1796*
1st Marquess   *1st Lord Templetown*
of Bristol
1769–1859

Frederick **m** Katherine Manners   Elizabeth **m** Charles Ellis
2nd Marquess of Bristol   *Daughter of*   *1st Lord Seaford*
1800–1864   *6th Duke of Rutland*

Geraldine Anson   Adeliza **m** Richard le Poer Trench   Augustus **m** Mariana Benyon   Charles **m** Lucy Cavendish-
    4th Earl of Clancarty   *1837–1875*   *(née Hodnett)*   6th Lord Howard   Bentinck-Scott
                                 d. 1920   de Walden   *Daughter of*
                                                 1799–1868   *4th Duke of Portland*

William **m** 1st 'Isabel' Maude Bilton
5th Earl of Clancarty   *Actress at the Empire Theatre*
1868–1929   *2nd Mary Gwatkin*

Frederick **m** Theodora (Dora)   Manners   Maria **m** Sir Charles   Geraldine **m** Henry Hoare   Frederick **m** Blanche
4th Marquess   Wythes   *b. 1866*   Welby   7th Lord Howard   Holden
of Bristol   5th Bt   de Walden
1863–1951   *1830–1899*

Phyllis **m** Capt Duncan   Dorothy **m** 19th Lord   Joan **m** Charles Portal   (Henry Peregrine)   Thomas
1899–1989   MacRae   *1890–1985*   Saltoun   *1898–1996*   *(later Air Chief Marshal*   Rennie   8th Lord Howard
& had issue   *& had issue*   *1st Viscount Portal)*   de Walden
                                                       & had issue   *b. 1880*

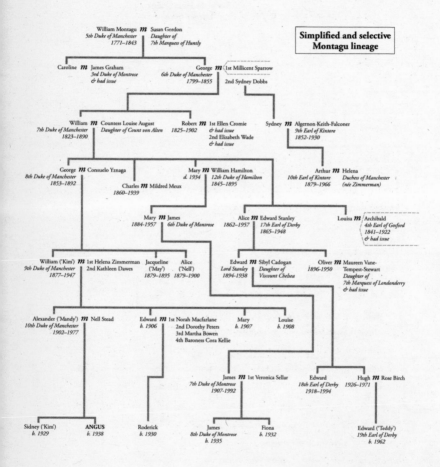

Simplified and selective Montagu lineage

List of Illustrations

Edward

87 St. George's Drive. The final residence of 'Mr Fitzgerald'. Courtesy of Express Newspapers.

Victor

Ickworth. *Country Life.*

The Earl Bishop. '4th Earl Of Bristol and Bishop Of Derry 1790' by Elisabeth Vigée-Lebrun 1755–1842, Ickworth, The Bristol Collection © NTPL/Angelo Hornak

Gwrych. Gwrych Castle Preservation Trust.

Douglas Cochrane, 12th Earl of Dundonald.

Winifred Bamford-Hesketh. Courtesy of Gwrych Castle Preservation Trust.

Herbert Hervey. National Portrait Gallery, London.

Jean Cochrane. Gwrych Castle Preservation Trust.

Victor and John Rowley. Gwrych Castle Preservation Trust.

Sandhurst group and Victor, inset. Royal Military Academy, Sandhurst.

Victor in white tie. Mary Evans Picture Library/Illustrated London News Ltd.

Eton College group and inset. Eton College.

Victor and associate. Associated Newspapers.

Victor lighting cigarette. Associated Newspapers.

Headlines. Associated Newspapers.

Victor and Pauline. Associated Newspapers.

Victor and Michael Havers. Associated Newspapers.

Victor and Juliet. Getty Images/Hulton Archive.

Victor and Yvonne. Associated Newspapers.

Victor and Yvonne at Frederick's Christening. Associated Newspapers.

Victoria and Isabella. Richard Stonehouse/Camera Press, London.

Angus

Kimbolton. Courtesy of Kimbolton School.

Edward, 2nd Earl of Manchester. Courtesy of Kimbolton School.

'Mandy', 10th Duke of Manchester. Private Collection.

Nell Montagu. Private Collection.

'Lord Edward Montagu – Lord of the Jungle'. Express Newspapers.

Louise Montagu and biplane. Private Collection.

Angus and grandfather, 9th Duke of Manchester. Private Collection.

Angus and Kim. Private Collection.

Angus, childhood photo montage. Private Collection.

Squad 911 and inset. Private Collection.

Angus on the water polo team of HMS *Loch Fyne*; at the beach; on the green. All Private Collection.

Angus and first wife, Mary. *Herald and Weekly Times* Ltd. (Australia)

Angus and second wife, Diana, with friends. Private Collection.

Angus and third wife, Louise. Private Collection.

Angus and fourth wife, Biba. *Daily Mail.*

Angus and Jane. Private Collection

Cheesemans Reunited. *Luton News*, 1981.

Angus and Kerry. Private Collection.

Louise, Duchess of Manchester, visiting Angus at Petersburg Federal Correctional Institution. Private Collection.

Angus, Louise and Patsy Chilton. Private Collection.

Angus playing swing ball, July 2002. Private Collection.

Times & Citizen article, 2002. Bedfordshire *Times & Citizen.*

The Unknown Montagu. Private Collection.

'The Frog' playing cricket. Private Collection.

John

John on horseback and Teddy Lambton. Private Collection.

John in second year at Harrow. Harrow School Archive.

John as a young boy at Harrow. Harrow School Archive.

John as a young man with Nick 'Nick-Knack' Somerville. Private Collection.

David 'Grigglet' Grigg and Nick-Knack. Private Collection.

John, Gabrielle Coles and Peter Gieger. Tatler IVM Company Ltd.

Rupert Everett aboard the *Braemar*. Private Collection.

John with Tim von Halle and Nick-Knack. Private Collection.

John with Nick-Knack on the *Braemar*. Private Collection.

John and Marianne Hinton with Jonny Ruane. Private Collection.

Lord Nicholas Hervey, founder of the Rockingham. Private Collection.

Andy Pearce and Maria Rawlinson (née Garton). Both Private Collection.

John and Francesca. Both Private Collection.

John and Francesca on wedding day. Courtesy of the Norman Parkinson Archive, London.

John Aston Martin. *Jersey Evening Post.*

John with Pauline in Jersey. *Jersey Evening Post.*

John leaving St. Mary's Paddington. MirrorPix.

John leaving Ickworth. Assignments/Rex Features.

David Cholmondeley at State Opening of Parliament, November 1999. Getty Images.

Acknowledgements

Only with the cooperation of innumerable people (some of whom prefer to remain unacknowledged) has the compilation of this book been possible. To all of those listed in the Sources and References, I offer my thanks. One or two answered very specific questions (sometimes just a solitary question), amongst them undertakers (at J. H. Kenyon and G. C. Northwood), prison warders (at HMP Camp Hill), firemen (in Bedford), crematorium spokesmen (at Golders Green), staff at the HMS *Conway* Association, the House of Lords, the Maritime Archive & Library, the Merseyside Maritime Museum, the Law Society. So did Charles Mosley, former editor-in-chief of *Burke's Peerage*, whose expertise was invaluable. Others tolerated repeated inquiries, amongst them staff at the British Library, Colindale; at Kensington Library; the Imperial War Museum; the National Archives; the Royal Military Academy, Sandhurst; Edda Tasiemka ('the human Google') and her team of helpers at the Tasiemka Library. Penny Hatfield and Rita Boswell, Archivists at Eton and Harrow respectively, allowed me to intrude on their establishments, as did Lieutenant Colonel R. J. S. Bullock-Webster, formerly Regimental Lieutenant Colonel of the Irish Guards, Nora Butler, who showed me around Kimbolton and unearthed 'the Kimbolton three', Peter Lord, who welcomed me and two guests to the Ickworth Hotel, and Conor Mallaghan, who twice sanctioned visits to Carton, as well as answering my questions with charm and patience. The late David Williamson, co-editor of *Debrett's*, giggled eloquently as he recalled Monarchist League dinners and told anecdotes about each of the primary families under scrutiny; the late Hugh Massingberd, whose enthusiasm was and remains a source of inspiration, made ripe disclosures from the obituarists' treasury, most of which suggested intriguing lines of inquiry. The late David Erskine dredged his memory for vignettes from his childhood at Ickworth. He and his wife Caroline had me to lunch, as did Brian and Kiloran Murrell, the latter displaying immense generosity in putting family photograph albums at my disposal, a kindness in which they were emulated by George Lambton, Brian Joyles, Maria Rawlinson, Lucy Warrack, Serena Graham and Kerry Cheeseman. Gerald Howson, Mark Baker and Nils Jensen-Eriksen were equally munificent when sharing their expertise (in, respectively, arms trading during the Spanish Civil War, nineteenth-century north Wales society and post-war Anglo-Finnish trade).

Sally Shalam, Alison Tyler (both of them when at the *Evening Standard*), Cath Urquhart (*The Times*) and Tom Otley (*Business Traveller*) commissioned articles which enabled me to complete research which would have otherwise been impossible; Sadler and Co., Charlotte Doherty PR, Mango PR and Pippa Isbell, Vice President-Corporate Communications at Orient Express, facilitated arrangements, whilst Katie Benson, formerly managing director of the Langham Hotel, Melbourne, and Patrick Griffin, managing director of the Observatory Hotel, Sydney, were astonishingly tolerant of 'the loitering Pom'. Closer to home, Orchid Communications and the staff and management of The Club Hotel, and of L'Horizon Hotel and The Royal Yacht Hotel, ensured that research in Jersey was a particular pleasure. Back in England, Jonah Weston, director of *The Real Pink Panther* (for Channel 4), offered valuable and inventive advice about photographic and other sources.

The library staff, past and present, at Associated Newspapers have for years (beginning long before the idea for this book was conceived) responded to my requests for esoteric information with apparent equanimity and cheerfulness; they continued to do so throughout the time that it was being written. Jackie Tarrant-Barton, Secretary of the Old Etonian Association, forwarded letters and rootled through records on my behalf. Charles Kidd, editor of *Debrett's*, answered unending questions with habitual courtesy and every simulation of interest as, in the concluding months of research, did Professor Bill Rubinstein. I am highly indebted to them all, as I am to Charlie Glass, who opened doors that would otherwise have remained closed if not ignored.

Then there were those whose connection to the subject was not scholastic but intimate. One or two lied calmly and coolly (evidence, perhaps, for the contention by Robin Cook (see Introduction, p. 6), that 'the psychopath is the furnace that gives no heat'). These exchanges were, in their way, instructive, although not as conducive to progress as those who talked with generosity of spirit and often astonishing patience and candour, of whom Angela Barry, Kerry Cheeseman, the late Patsy Chilton, Ian Codrington, Mary Fox, Peter Geiger, Imogen von Halle, Tim von Halle, Robin Hurlstone, Louise Manchester, Kiloran Murrell, Simon Pott, Maria Rawlinson, Betty Stafford, the late Caroline Tahany, Paul Vaughan and James Whitby are content to be publicly acknowledged. Almost all of them read a part, or parts, of the manuscript, as did Richard Grosvenor, the late Peter Gwatkin, Selina Hastings and Dr Alan Sanderson. The wisdom of their comments improved its accuracy and tempered its judgements. My thanks to them is immense if inadequate.

Throughout this protracted process family and very good friends provided regular infusions of encouragement and nutritional support (and, in the case of Sam and Jeannie Chesterton, a few days of almost annual refuge), whilst Alexandra Gray additionally introduced me to Toby Mundy, a publisher with whom discussion is unfailingly stimulating. My thanks to him, and to all his staff at Atlantic Books, especially to Mathilda Imlah, Sarah Castleton, Caroline Knight and Sachna Hanspal. I am similarly indebted to my agent, Andrew Lownie, whose good sense and good humour were always welcome. Finally, my thanks and admiration go to Jane Robertson, my editor, who plunged into a pool from which she had previously kept a healthy distance but through which she swam with determination, ignoring the toxic matter which occasionally fizzed in front of her, pausing only to purify grammatical inadequacy and to remedy structural deficiency. Surviving infelicities of style (and errors of fact) are, in consequence, mine alone.

'The upper classes in every country are selfish, depraved, dissolute and decadent.'

Major Denis Healey,
at the Labour Party conference, May 1945

Introduction

Many staked claims for inclusion in this book, which spans the twentieth
century (with glimpses of the final years of the nineteenth and the opening
decade of the twenty-first). There was, for example, the marquess who
insisted that his wife ('stunningly beautiful, with pale green eyes and bright
red-gold Titian hair') should undress and stand naked in front of him, while
he loaded her with emeralds, rubies and diamonds. He required nothing more;
the marriage was annulled after two years on grounds of non-consummation.

There was also the earl who sought a more conclusive embrace. By the
time he was in his sixties, he searched for it among 'the sad creatures who
make a business of love', preparing himself by undergoing surgical treatment
(a face-lift: the operation performed in Mayfair, the result paraded in the
Barracuda, Le Carré Blanc and other playpen bars of Cannes).

It might seem perverse that neither Henry Cyril Paget, 5th Marquess of
Anglesey ('The Dancing Marquess', born in 1875, succeeded in 1896), nor
Anthony Ashley-Cooper, 10th Earl of Shaftesbury (born 1938, succeeded
1961) is treated to sustained scrutiny hereafter. Until his disappearance in
2004, however, Shaftesbury had not impinged on the public's consciousness,
other than for his presidency of the Hawk and Owl Trust and his vice-
presidency of a butterfly charity. If his marital record (three wives, with his
eye on a fourth) was poor, it could not be considered particularly exceptional
by contemporary standards. It is true that a capacity for kindness (a house
placed at a friend's disposal at a moment's notice, for as long as it was needed,
little rent to be paid) appeared to be allied to moods, or moments, of callous-
ness (informed as he left a lunch party that he had just crushed two dogs
beneath his wheels, he managed the briefest acknowledgement – 'Oh... oh,
yes I have' – before driving on without apology). But only posthumously, as

the barbarity of his death became known (murdered by his Tunisian-Moroccan brother-in-law, acting in collusion with Shaftesbury's wife), was he dragged to national, indeed international, attention. He bequeathed a pitiful legend and 9,000 acres of Dorset, which he had planted with more than a million trees.

The Dancing Marquess ensured that his claim for attention is less easily dismissed. With an inheritance of just under 30,000 acres, he developed his wardrobe without inhibition (crocodile leather boots, grey suede shoes, silk slippers, 260 pairs of white kid gloves, a sable overcoat 'with twenty tails and ten heads hanging from it', and a suit cut from bird's-eye cloth, 'each bird's-eye a diamond'), whilst maintaining interests in walking sticks (his collection, the world's largest, included many 'thickly encrusted with diamonds, rubies, amethysts and emeralds'), jewellery (he had 200 gold scarf pins and innumerable individual stones) and yachts and cars (the latter invariably subjected to bespoke redecorative treatment involving dark red Morocco upholstery and Wilton carpets). Sensing fresh potential for the family chapel, he converted it into a theatre and commissioned a London company to stage a production of *Aladdin*, for which he pioneered 'the Butterfly Dance', a solo which he alone performed (to choreography teased from his own imagination). Later, he paid for the company to go on tour, extending its repertoire as it did so (though he was especially fond of *The Ideal Husband*). The tour reached Dresden, where a German observer adjudged Henry 'a most interesting personality... an English Marquess... with a seat and a vote in the House of Lords'.

By 1904 there were few servants left at Plas Newydd, the ancestral seat on Anglesey, besides which the Dancing Marquess owed creditors £544,000 (perhaps £340 million today), a cataclysm made no easier for the family to bear given the doubts about his legitimacy. Trustees intervened, authorizing the sale of Henry's belongings; the auction lasted over forty days, three of which were devoted to the disposal of his clothing (almost none of which had ever been worn). The Dancing Marquess died the following year, from pleurisy, at the Hotel Royale, Monte Carlo. He was thirty.

James Francis Harry St Clair-Erskine, 5th Earl of Rosslyn (born 1869, succeeded 1890), lasted longer. Opting to invest most of the income from his inheritance – 3,310 acres in Fife and Midlothian, and £50,000 in securities – in a string of racehorses (which he backed lavishly) and in the Stock Exchange, as well as in the clubs of Cannes and London, he racked up personal debts of £125,000 by 1893, by which time the family estates were mortgaged for £100,000. Four years later, he was declared bankrupt. He responded by taking to the stage, trimming his name to James Erskine for professional purposes. Although his bankruptcy was annulled in 1902, he resisted the chance to reform: by 1907 he had divorced for the second time, was gambling with renewed vigour and had taken to drink. In 1923 the family collieries were sold; two years later, Rosslyn fled abroad with his third wife. A bankruptcy petition was served on him in Madeira. He died in 1939.

It was as calamitous a life as the Dancing Marquess's had been. There are, however, few if any alive today to bear testimony to Rosslyn's descent (and none to Paget's); hence their omission from the pages that follow, which, although drawing on documentary and other written sources, attempt to resurrect each primary character via the memories of those who knew them, lived with them and (in many cases) loved them. All the leading roles are assigned to men because they – rather than women – were (and continue to be) the putative beneficiaries of primogeniture. However, the parts women played in the disasters that unfold are given significant (and, I hope, adequate) attention, perhaps more than is usual in studies of aristocratic families, in which the patronymic tends to hold almost hypnotic sway.

If sections of the backdrop inevitably shift as the action moves from the 1890s to the 1990s, one aspect remains constant: the diminished standing of the aristocracy. At times, especially during the pre-war decades, that diminution might have seemed difficult to credit. The coming of age celebrations for Bernard Fitzalan-Howard, 16th Duke of Norfolk (1908–75), held in 1929, for example, were unrepentantly feudal. Driving from his Sussex seat, Arundel Castle, Bernard (who had succeeded to the title at the age of nine) passed through streets crowded with onlookers, heard the local mayor make a deferential speech in his honour, then continued to Littlehampton (most of which he owned), this time in an open carriage. People lined the length of the route; the town band was in place to greet him on arrival. Shops in Arundel (where the celebrations lasted three days) closed at noon, and a public holiday was declared. A month later, 20,000 people joined in similar festivities at Norfolk Park, Sheffield, his Yorkshire seat.

Hugh Lowther, 'the Yellow Earl', 5th Earl of Lonsdale (born in 1857), favoured a more populist style. Educated for a year at Eton and thereafter by his father's old batman from The Life Guards (a former regimental heavyweight boxing champion) and then by Jem Mace (the last bare-knuckle champion of England), he unexpectedly inherited his brother's title in 1882 and, with it, annual revenues of between £80,000 and £100,000 (£73.4 million and £91.8 million today). These he invested in mistresses and sporting entertainment – hunting, racing and boxing – and in swaddling his footmen (and many of his possessions, squadrons of cars included) in yellow livery. 'Almost an emperor, not quite a gentleman' (in the words of his brother-in-law, Gilbert Henry Heathcote-Drummond-Willoughby, 1st Earl of Ancaster), the Yellow Earl blazed on for decades, eventually dying in April 1944, though not before writing to his niece: 'Life has been such lovely fun.'

Herbrand Arthur Russell, 11th Duke of Bedford (1858–1940), derived less obvious pleasure from possessions or status, had 'very little time for human beings and rarely spoke', but found consolation in a daily cup of beef consommé, made from nine-and-a-half pounds of shin of beef (always by the same kitchenmaid, employed specifically to prepare it) and in insisting that the routines of the stage-coach age should prevail in that of the internal combustion engine. Setting out from the duke's London houses (he had a pair in Belgrave Square), his chauffeurs were instructed to drive as far as Hendon, where guests dismounted and joined cars which had been sent from Woburn, his Bedfordshire seat. Luggage was loaded into separate vehicles, it being considered unseemly that anyone should travel in too intimate proximity to their belongings.

The Pagets adhered to less antediluvian standards. Nevertheless, thirty-one years after the Dancing Marquess's death, his cousin and successor, Charles Paget, felt it right to feed his dog Cheekie on steak, and to commission Rex Whistler to begin his masterpiece, a 58-foot mural, painted on canvas, later installed in the Plas Newydd dining room. By 1976, however, the family had relinquished Plas Newydd to the National Trust.

The surrender had been a long time coming, and owed less to the Dancing Marquess's shopping expeditions than to changes which were beyond the scope of the Pagets or or any other aristocratic family to control. The Fitzalan-Howards had sanctioned the sale and demolition of Norfolk House in the 1930s; even the Yellow Earl had seen Lowther Castle closed, its contents shrouded in dustsheets, and had suffered the sale of two of his lesser seats. None of this had been conceivable in 1876, when two thirds of the British Isles had been owned by 11,000 people (or, according to a bolder, quite possibly more accurate, estimate, just 7,500). This was land which nourished the world's richest nation (or alliance of nations); the rents paid by the tenants who farmed it had, broadly speaking, risen in real terms continuously since 1800. 'Land,' in consequence, 'was wealth: the most secure, reliable, and permanent asset.' The rewards for those with the most – or the most productive – were stupendous. In about 1880, the 9th Duke of Bedford, father of the consommé drinker, enjoyed an annual income of about £225,000 (£222.7 million today); the 4th Marquess of Anglesey, father of the dancer, was indisputably comfortable on £111,000-a-year. Many grandees 'did not know how rich they were, how much land they owned, how many titles they possessed'.

It scarcely seemed to matter. Even the succession of a scapegrace eldest son did not necessarily presage irretrievable disaster. Mortgages could be raised without difficulty and the resulting interest payments borne without strain. Comparatively limited retrenchment was invariably enough to ensure recovery within a generation, possibly two. Pre-eminence seemed assured, change unthinkable. But from about 1875 onwards the first refrigerated ships were built in Britain; in America, Canada, Argentina, Australia and New Zealand, prairies and grasslands were farmed more extensively than ever before. New World grain began to pour into Britain – the amount swelling from 30 million hundredweight in 1870 to 70 million by 1900 – at a price which conclusively undercut that of domestic competition. Similarly, meat which once would have rotted during a transglobal voyage now arrived in good condition.

Tenant farmers could not in consequence sell their produce and could not, or would not, pay existing levels of rent, which began to plunge, down by a quarter in England between the mid-1870s and the mid-1890s, and by a third or more in Ireland. Suddenly, interest payments on mortgages and other loans consumed a frightening proportion of disposable aristocratic income, rising – in the case of the Duke of Devonshire – from 17 per cent in 1874 to 60 per cent by 1880. Aristocrats whose circumstances were already far more constrained than Devonshire's inevitably found new mortgages almost unobtainable. Land no longer equated to money but to millstone. Governments, which were aristocratic in composition and leadership, whether Liberal (Rosebery) or Conservative (Salisbury), passed a series of Land Acts making taxpayers' money available to tenants who were thereby able to acquire the property they farmed. Some 9 million acres changed hands between 1903 and 1909. The process continued in the decades that followed, as grandees sold up, either for purposes of investment or for the maintenance of status, the latter path being preferred by William Selby-Lowndes, of Whaddon Hall and Winslow Hall, both in Buckinghamshire, who disposed of fourteen outlying farms in the 1920s thereby allowing him to retain his position as Master of the Whaddon Chase. Such disposals helped to ensure that, by 1950 (the year in which the price of agricultural land 'recovered' to what it had been in 1880), probably half the farms in England and Wales were owner-occupied.

As if territorial contraction were not humiliation enough, landed families were simultaneously shunted further into the margins by the ferocious, irreversible rise of the new plutocrats – ironmasters, railway contractors, textile manufacturers, brewers, financiers, arriviste Americans – who bought their way into the peerage as never before, diluting and devaluing the class they now nominally joined. At the end of the seventeenth century, there had been only nineteen dukes, three marquesses and a total of 152 earls, viscounts and barons; by 1900, the number of British peers had risen to 673, a figure which soared unchecked as Liberal and Conservative parties sold titles to fund party political operations, a further 312 new peerages being created between 1911 and 1940. The quality of recipients was not consistently good. Sir Archibald Williamson, ennobled in 1922, 'was widely thought to have traded with the enemy during the First World War', whilst Sir Joseph Robinson 'was a publicly convicted swindler, whose appeal [against conviction] had been dismissed by the Judicial Committee of the Privy Council' only a few months before his elevation to the Lords. The baronetage was not spared contamination. In 1921, for example, the baronetcy conferred on Rowland Hodge recognized his 'public services, particularly in connection with shipbuilding', but ignored his conviction, three years earlier, for hoarding on an epic scale (1,148 lbs of flour, 333 lbs of sugar, 168lbs 6 oz of bacon and ham, 29 tins of sago, 25 tins of sardines, 10 jars of ox-tongue and nineteen tins of salmon).

Some of the 'new men' preferred to graft themselves to the nobility a little less crudely. Among them were the descendants of William Cook, seventh son of a 'peasant farmer' from Norfolk (the phrase is that of his great-great grandson). By the time of his death in 1869, William's fortune was sufficient to ensure that his family had 'started going to Eton, bought commissions in smart regiments, bought houses, built a castle in Portugal' and had begun buying its way 'into the aristocracy by marrying its plain or half-witted members'. Two generations later, in 1931, as agricultural depression deepened, William's grandson Ralph Cook called in tenants from farms which the family had acquired over the previous sixty years and announced that there would be 'no more rent paid till further notice'. It was as authentic a demonstration of noblesse oblige as any belted earl could have managed.

Two further generations on, Ralph's grandson Robin Cook (more formally Robert William Arthur Cook, 1931–94) emerged as the most astute of guides to the down-escalator of life (a phrase he favoured; a route he took). Young Robin had early intimations of his destiny. He and his brother devised a game called Tom and John, 'one of whom was a very good person, the other a very bad one'. The former guise proved inimical to Robin, who thumped his brother when it was his turn to assume it, just as, at prep school, in games enacting captured British spies resisting German interrogation, he opted, unhesitatingly, for a Gestapo role. At home, his grandmother's lament, in

1940, that she had only 'nine in the house' ('she meant nine servants') left him unmoved; at Eton, he failed to imbibe the prevailing ethos ('Cricket is supposed to be a game, Cook. You are supposed to play the ball, not the man'). He left early, never thereafter to wear an Old Etonian tie ('except when out on a scam: an Eton background is a terrific help, if you are into vice at all').

An obituarist, though acknowledging Cook's criminal activities, noted his other work as 'pornographer, organizer of illegal gambling, money-launderer, roofer, pig-slaughterer, mini-cab driver and agricultural labourer', as well as his five ill-fated marriages, and his accomplishments as a novelist – the French made him a Chevalier des Arts et des Lettres in 1991 – and as the author of acclaimed memoirs, in which, amidst much else, he offered a description of madness as 'that lethal room occupied by people who do not realize it has no floor'.

His achievements and self-awareness, if not his notoriety, were beyond those who appear subsequently here. In as far as they developed talents, it was to misapply them; in as far as they were aware of their own deficiencies, it was to ignore them, just as they ignored those in their families who occupied 'the floorless room'. Theirs was, in consequence, a journey of dynastic destruction, completed in single or successive generations. There would be no return, no temporal redemption. Yet each of them could echo the epitaph composed by John Knatchbull, fourth son of a baronet, shortly before his execution in Australia in 1844: 'For some part I am to be blamed; for the rest I am to be pitied.'

PART ONE

'The basic romantic notion that we can always "liberate" ourselves is corruptly optimistic.'

Jim Harrison, *Off to the Side*

Edward

It took only two or three minutes for the ambulance to wail through the Monday afternoon traffic. A futile race: by the time it reached Horseferry Road and turned into Westminster Hospital, Mr FitzGerald was dead. His exit – angular bones splayed on a stretcher, a lock of lank white hair falling over his face – might have been suffered by any of London's genteel poor. Only two details – fuel for the subsequent inquest – betrayed his utter wretchedness: the breath of alcohol on his lips, contending with the sour scent of old skin; and the barbiturates, a fistful of them, which had gone down with the drink.

There was no note of explanation or apology in his Pimlico bedsit; nor was there a will, though that scarcely mattered. Mr FitzGerald left little more than the watch on his wrist and the clothes that flapped from his body. Five days later, on 13 March 1976, his widow, wrecked by grief, sobbed continuously, obliviously, in the West Chapel at Golders Green. Few were there: her stepson, step-grandchildren, almost no one else. The service was brief, a necessarily clinical business, one of more than twenty processed there that day. Yet there was one indication of the dignity, and grandeur, that the eighty-three-year-old had once known: the funeral arrangements were entrusted to J. H. Kenyon, London undertakers to the Royal Family for generations.

* * *

Today, about fifteen miles west of Dublin, as suburbs and ribbon development grudgingly yield to open country, traffic begins to fight its way around five miles of eighteenth-century wall which encircle 1,200 acres of parkland. Guided by the gatehouse on its southern side, visitors take a drive which leads through the park, past estate offices, up to a Palladian house of austere splendour. To its south, a little way from the parterre separating the portico from the ha-ha and the land beyond, a yew of profound antiquity screens a discreet Victorian cemetery. Mr FitzGerald's parents lie here, as do one of his brothers (whose grave is unique, in that it alone is marked by a Celtic cross) and three FitzGeralds of an earlier generation who did not survive infancy. It would have been pardonable if, during the course of Mr FitzGerald's life, members of his family had occasionally allowed themselves the luxury of reflecting on what might have been, had he too been good enough to die in childhood. Until his intervention, the house was the seat of the FitzGeralds, Dukes of Leinster. Today, hemmed in by two golf courses, it is reduced to hotel use, though its name – Carton – remains unchanged.

Mr FitzGerald was less fastidious about what he was called. At times, he chose to be known as Mr Taplow; at others, Mr Gay (before the word assumed its contemporary connotation). To intimates, he was variously 'Fitz', 'Ed', 'Eddie', 'Boy' (to the first of his four wives) and 'My Imp' (to the second). To members of the peerage, he was – unpalatable though they found it to acknowledge – one of them. More galling still, he could not be dismissed as an ermined parvenu. His family had not grubbed its way into the aristocracy a couple of generations before, in the manner of the Tennants or Pearsons, nor greased its way to favour with gross, well-judged bribes to Liberal or Tory governments, nor had it wheedled to preferment three or four hundred years earlier, like those sixteenth-century upstarts the Cecils, as a reward for sly and dexterous statecraft.

The FitzGeralds were, instead, an emblem of ancient nobility, securing status and privilege by shedding blood on the battlefield over the course of nine hundred years. At the time of the Domesday Book, they held land from the king in what were to become Berkshire, Buckinghamshire, Middlesex and Surrey. In succeeding generations, they nudged their way westwards, first to Wales, where Henry I appointed one of Mr FitzGerald's ancestors Constable (and, later, Keeper) of Pembroke Castle; then, in 1169, to Ireland, where Maurice FitzGerald and his half-brother Robert FitzStephen offered their services to Dermot MacMurrogh, King of Leinster. Their intervention proved effective, restoring Dermot to his throne and helping him to take Dublin, prompting Henry II to conclude that it might be prudent to co-opt the brothers for his own uses. He made Maurice Keeper of Dublin, and granted him land in County Kildare and County Wicklow. It is testimony to FitzGerald durability that the same lands were still held by the family when Mr FitzGerald was born on 8 May 1892; at the time, and for several years afterwards, he was known as Lord Edward FitzGerald, as was accurate, since he was a younger son of Gerald FitzGerald, 5th Duke of Leinster (pronounced 'Linster'), premier Duke of Ireland, and of his wife Hermione.

Under Edward, the family was to progress to unexpected territory: to Brixton and to Streatham, to a bedsit in Birchington, Kent, to a flat in Sliema, Malta, and to another in Brighton; and, three times, to the bankruptcy court. It was no accident, given the remorseless downwards trajectory of his life, that his friends were to include Lord Castlerosse, later the 6th – and last – Earl of Kenmare (1891–1943). Castlerosse, it has been magisterially asserted, 'lacked brains, looks, charm, or prospects. At university, he was idle, unambitious, gluttonous, ran up many debts, and had many affairs'. In maturity, 'he weighed eighteen stone, was constantly in debt to tradesmen, and depended on money-lenders for survival'. He died two years after inheriting his father's earldom, but not before acknowledging: 'I dissipated my patrimony; I committed many sins; I wasn't important.'

Yet Edward did not lack looks, charm or money; nor – impressively though his behaviour could argue to the contrary – was he without brains. Leanly athletic all his life, he was blessed with (arguably cursed by) phenomenal physical stamina. His more benign passions included ornithology, lepidoptery and music; once his feckless youth was behind him, he was usually sweet-natured, which endeared him to his web of well-intentioned, well-connected relations, who included three of his fellow dukes[1], as well as the British Ambassador in Germany[2], and ensured that – for a time, at least – he was welcome in several aristocratic houses. His younger son was not peddling a myth when he remarked that Edward might have been 'the black sheep of the family, but he was genuinely kind and understanding'.

Unfortunately, however, he was also driven by an incendiary wilfulness which eliminated any danger that his would be a life of dutiful predictability. Longevity gave him the opportunity to leave an indelible mark on his family: he seized it, establishing a pattern of behaviour which he endlessly repeated, even though he was excruciatingly aware of his deficiencies and the pain he caused others. He married regularly, procreated twice (though not on each occasion with the woman to whom he was married at the time) and increasingly preferred the comforting fiction that he was a victim – of life, of fate, of an unforgiving financier – rather than someone with the rare twin gifts of squandering his (enviable) birthright and rupturing one generation of his family from the next. He spent most of his eighty-three years on the run from creditors, gambled insatiably, if secretly, developed the habit of betraying and deserting those who loved him, lost Carton, thereby effectively severing the FitzGeralds' ties with Ireland, and provoked the sale and dispersal of four fifths of the family paintings, silver and heirlooms. His wives, and other women, usually died unhappily – variously overdosed, drowned or demented.

Initially outraged, then numbed by Edward's behaviour, the FitzGeralds were speedily reduced to spectators in their own dynastic downfall. There, thanks to a single decision taken by Edward in obstinate defiance of their advice, they were fated to remain, locked into their seats while the grandstand burned. No resurrection of the FitzGerald fortune has followed. 'We meet at funerals but not otherwise,' reflects one of Edward's granddaughters. 'We are not a lucky family to belong to, in any way.'

* * *

Little could have warned them of impending conflagration, even though, from early adolescence, Edward offered occasional indications of his intractable character. Amongst the personal possessions he kept in the ottoman in his room at Eton were a number of live snakes; at home, he disturbed his family – assembling for breakfast on an austere winter morning – with the sound of repeated gunfire, which was seemingly coming from the rookery at the side of the house. 'Everyone rushed out and saw Eddie shooting into thin air. They said, "What the hell are you doing?" Eddie said, "I'm just keeping my hands warm."' The nonchalant reply, so at variance with the manic blaze of action, was an early indication of the tension that already simmered within; Edward was about sixteen at the time.

But it would have taken exceptional powers of prophecy to have predicted the consequences this combustible temperament was to have for the FitzGeralds. When, in his mid-sixties, he reflected on what he called his 'turbulent life', Edward admitted that there was a special place in his heart for Gerald, the 9th Earl of Kildare, who burned down Cashel Cathedral in Tipperary (asked to explain his actions, Gerald is said to have replied: 'I thought the bishop was inside'). Buoyed up by Gerald's example, Edward suggested that it had been 'natural' to behave as he had, when his ancestry was taken into consideration. This was a convenient, as well as a romantic, fiction. The family had survived several unruly forebears, those who had perished by evisceration, imprisonment or hanging, as a consequence of rebelliousness or ill luck. But for many generations before Edward's birth, the FitzGeralds had lapsed into decent conformity. They paid their servants well, took a significant interest in their tenants' welfare, and served as Commissioners for National Education in Ireland; some sat as MPs, either for Kildare or Dublin; one, Edward's great-great-grandfather, had been

Ireland's Master Freemason. Their younger sons had been similarly dutiful, also becoming MPs (one being rewarded with a peerage in his own right), serving in the Royal Household, or in decent regiments or the Royal Navy. None was noticeably profligate, none debauched.

One of Edward's great-great-great-grandmothers did not, however, conform to this quiescent type. Lady Emily Gordon-Lennox, daughter of the 2nd Duke of Richmond, married James FitzGerald, 20th Earl of Kildare, later 1st Duke of Leinster, and gave birth to nineteen children. Much of the time her playful spirit was sublimated in the embellishment of 'dear sweet Carton', which she ensured was worthy of her husband's newly elevated status, even if he periodically squealed at the cost. A year after James's death in 1774, she married William Ogilvie, her children's tutor, a choice which society considered offensive (Ogilvie was ugly, as well as Scottish).

Edward was particularly proud of his namesake, Lord Edward FitzGerald (1763–98), Emily's fifth son, a figure who enjoys an iconic place in Irish folklore. Lord Edward's conversion to republicanism was partly intellectual, a consequence of 'immersion in the works of Rousseau, Voltaire and English radicals like Priestley and Paine', and partly emotional (following his service in the British army in the War of American Independence, he became bewitched by the simplicity and honesty of the Indian 'savages' who, he concluded, were what 'nature intended we should be'). In 1798, he played a doomed role in the Irish uprising, was wounded, and then incarcerated in a Dublin prison, where he died from blood poisoning, thereby securing himself posthumous glory in the name of the rebel cause, and enduring reverence within his family and beyond it.[3]

But if the younger Lord Edward owed a genetic debt to anyone in his family, it was perhaps less to Emily or any of the FitzGeralds than to one of his mother's brothers, Hubert Duncombe, an outwardly stolid, walrus-faced Englishman, who reconciled his duties as Tory MP for West Cumberland with two extra-curricular interests: soldiering (he was awarded the DSO whilst commanding the 14th Battalion Imperial Yeomanry in the Boer War) and relentless, illegitimate procreation.[4] As the third son of the 1st Earl of Feversham, the head of an old established (but recently ennobled) Yorkshire family, Hubert had, in his youth, proved a disappointment to his father, straying across the United States and marrying a music-hall artiste soon after he was twenty-one. An enraged Lord Feversham reputedly retaliated by 'stopp[ing] the young man's allowance, which until then had been very liberal'. Since neither Hubert nor his bride was 'of a saving disposition', they 'ran heavily into debt, landing in the bankruptcy court'. Feversham then agreed to give his son an allowance of $2,000 a year on condition that he remained abroad. For a while, the couple complied but then returned to England, 'when the lady went back to the stage and behaved in such a manner as to enable Hubert Duncombe to obtain a divorce'. If uncle Hubert had been intent on providing a template for Edward's early adulthood, he had done quite well. But his nephew was never a creature of formulaic predictability, a caricature rogue of the mess or clubland.

Somewhere near the heart of his contradictory character lay a fascination with his mother, Hermione. Edward had no memory of her or of his father; both died before he was three. But Hermione seems to have impressed herself on his subconscious to such an extent that his reverence for her was always devout, often suggestive of emotional instability. Born Lady Hermione Duncombe, she was the eldest of the first Countess of Feversham's four daughters (each, allegedly, of a different father), a forthright woman refreshingly indifferent to Victorian social convention, given to voicing her distaste for the Viceroy in Ireland, Lord Houghton (despite the fact that he was her cousin), and capable of earning a rebuke from an aristocratic contemporary, Lady Zetland, for 'unladylike behaviour' (Hermione had whistled a tune for the orchestra they were about to listen to). Her friend, Lady Fingall, who frequently stayed at Carton, wrote admiringly of Hermione's talent not only for gardening but also for music and sculpture.

She was also considered a beauty, notably by Churchill, who told Edward she was the most beautiful woman he had ever met.[5] Twenty-first century opinion might not be so rapturous: photographs of Hermione show a solid woman with a robust rather than decorative chin. Nevertheless, Churchill could not have said anything that would have delighted Edward more. During a trip to Ireland in 1936, Edward's second wife – aware of how her husband, in her words, 'worshipped his mother' – was obliged to help him at Carton, while he 'spent many dark nights with a candle, rummaging in a secret cupboard he remembered in the old nursery, looking for photographs of his mother'. Several years after they had parted, Edward visited her in Grosvenor Square. 'He saw his mother's miniature lying on a small table and went to it as though she had spoken. His eyes filled with tears as he picked it up and said: "Could I take her with me for a little while? I promise to return her."'

His father, Gerald FitzGerald, 5th Duke of Leinster, who died when Edward was only one, occupied a less exalted place in his affections. Lord Lieutenant of County Kildare in the year of his premature death, Gerald seems to have been a diligent, sensible man, who, like many late Victorian aristocrats, was fearful of the future, his overriding concern being to prepare his family for an abruptly changing world. The task was far from negligible. In 1878, the FitzGeralds' 68,000 acres yielded £47,646-a-year – too little for a family which had lived beyond its means for generations. Gerald's father, Charles, the 4th Duke, had had fourteen children, ten of whom survived to adulthood. All the while, the agricultural crisis intensified. The fools' paradise was coming to an end. In 1881, the Leinster tennants burned their leases at a public demonstration; when Charles offered to let them buy their land, they snubbed him. By the time of his death in 1887, the estate's debts were a fearful £292,000. Fortunately, Gerald later succeeded in selling 19,200 acres in County Kildare for £240,400 under the terms of the 1881 Land Act. It was an important step in securing the FitzGeralds' future.

A still more significant move was made by Gerald's brother, Lord Frederick FitzGerald, who became custodian of Carton and the family estates when Gerald died suddenly (albeit conveniently before the introduction of death duties a few months later) in December 1893, aged forty-two, after contracting typhoid whilst staying with his cousin, the Duke of Argyll, at Inveraray. Gerald's eldest son, Maurice, succeeded to the dukedom aged six. Lord Frederick seized the opportunity, which arose a decade later, under Wyndham's Land Act of 1903[6], to sell the rest of the FitzGeralds' Kildare estates for £786,000 (£487 million today). Edward, who was only eleven at the time of the sale, was to give a slightly inaccurate account of this process in the 1950s. 'In case the word estate has conjured up visions of vast lands in Ireland, let me disillusion you,' he wrote. 'There had been vast lands but they were sold and the money invested during my father's life'. This rather melancholy summary neglected to mention the circumstances in which the family inheritance had been so dispassionately converted into cash; it also failed to explain that it had enabled the FitzGeralds to secure the future of Carton, with a rump of what was then 1,500 acres, and their other property, Kilkea, reputedly Ireland's oldest occupied castle. Any attempt to cling on to their ancient lands would have antagonized an already volatile tenantry, and caused the family to suffer a relentless decline in income. Edward's father and uncle had saved the day.

Although the FitzGeralds lacked the gross riches of some ducal families, such as their cousins, the Sutherland-Leveson-Gowers, or the Russells, Grosvenors or Percys,[7] they now, thanks to Gerald and Frederick, had an income of a 'very substantial character', derived from investments worth approximately £600,000 (£367 million today). They were admirably well placed for the new order, with its nauseating plutocrats, its tasteless death duties (introduced in 1894 by the Liberal Chancellor Sir William Harcourt, and levied at 8 per cent on estates valued at £1 million or more), and its depressing enthusiasm for extending the franchise to the common man. But, as it turned out, nothing could have insulated them from the activities of Gerald's third son – if, that is, Edward was Gerald's child.

Adultery was invariably a useful antidote to the inexpressible boredom of so much aristocratic life; Hubert Duncombe had frequent recourse to it. So, in all probability, did his sister Hermione. Gerald gave her ample excuse. Less assured as a husband than as a financial strategist, he was 'small, like most of his family[8], and homely in character', and, in Lady Fingall's words, a good and kind man, but not the man for Hermione, who wanted someone 'she could look up to and fear a little, as well as love'. Hermione confided in her favourite sister, Helen, Viscountess d'Abernon (Edward's favourite aunt), that Gerald, while admitting there was no love or sympathy between them, 'still insists upon trying to force me to become something different to what I am, or to what it lies in my nature to become'.

Other women might have consoled themselves with Carton (Queen Victoria stayed there, sleeping in the Chinese Room; amongst its luxuries was a shower, whose water-supply came from the floor above, a manservant pouring jugs of hot water down a sluice, its spiral design preventing the jug-bearer from seeing his monarch in her full majesty) or sublimated their restlessness in childbirth and bursts of landscaping and redecoration. Perhaps Hermione tried her best: she had three children in quick succession (a daughter, who was born and died in 1886, and two sons, Maurice, born in 1887, and Desmond, born in 1888), and designed new gardens for Carton (which remain much as she left them). But by the time Edward was born in London, four years after Desmond, Hermione had learned how to avoid the marital bed (according to Lady Fingall) in favour of a 'small white room with a narrow bed like a girl's'. At other times she might have taken refuge elsewhere in the house: in April 1891, just over a year before Edward was born, she concluded a letter to her sister Helen by remarking: 'One helping hand has been unexpectedly stretched out to me, and in your absence, till your return, to that hand I will cling'.

The hand to which Hermione clung so fondly probably belonged to Hugo Charteris, Lord Elcho, later the 11th Earl of Wemyss and March – Edward's real father, according to one enduring theory, seemingly based on more than inventive spite. Elcho's grandson, the 12th Earl, acknowledged that Elcho was 'a great friend' of Edward's mother, though how fruitfully that friendship was expressed he was uncertain. 'There is a portrait of her at our house at Stanway, Gloucestershire,' he reflected towards the end of his life. 'Whether she ever had a child by him, I know not. He went to her on her death bed, and his wife, my grandmother, raised no objection to his doing so.' Hermione died in Menton, at the Hôtel des Iles Britanniques, on 20 March 1895, a victim of tuberculosis. The Prince of Wales, who was staying at the hotel at the time, sent a wreath to Carton, which he had visited a decade earlier. She was buried in the yew-shaded cemetery, next to her husband.

Her death had two immediate consequences – both of far-reaching effect – for Edward and his two brothers, Maurice, who had celebrated his eighth birthday three weeks earlier, and six-year-old Desmond. Responsibility for their upbringing would henceforward be shared between their uncle, Lord Frederick FitzGerald (who had been living at Carton with his sister Nesta since Gerald's death), and the second youngest of Hermione's sisters, Cynthia. In practice, the boys' home became Netherby, in Cumberland[9], the family seat of Cynthia's husband Sir Richard Graham, Bt (who was also her first cousin). Simultaneously, Edward ceased to be the youngest child of the family, becoming the third of four – and, in due course, of six[10] – being a year older than the Grahams' first son, Fergus Graham, who was to prove a lifelong friend. Edward's connection with Ireland now also faded rapidly. Near the end of his life, Sir Fergus Graham recalled that his FitzGerald cousins were rarely at Carton during childhood or at Kilkea, where another uncle, Lord Walter FitzGerald, lived in the company of a clutch of his plain, unmarried sisters. They were still there forty years later, when Edward's second wife met them for the first time; they watched her, she recalled, 'with concern', through thick-lensed glasses.

Edward – or Eddie, as he came to be known in the Graham household – had the rather more sympathetic figure of his Aunt Cynthia to contend with. Some years later, when Maurice fell seriously ill, she became precariously distraught, reacting as a mother would, rather than as a reluctant guardian. She appears to have been similarly protective towards Edward, especially when he was hurtling into his first marriage, aged twenty-one. During his courtship, largely conducted in fashionable restaurants, Edward found that his evenings were prone to a pattern of sabotage, with Cynthia sending notes to him from another table. Later, on his return from a voyage to New Zealand and Honolulu (intended, by the family, to distract him from his unsuitable fiancée), Cynthia was waiting for his ship to dock in Liverpool. Assisted by Desmond, she marched him straight on to a train, before he could see his fiancée or his friend, Captain 'Whisky' Cole, both of whom had also been waiting for him.

Edward betrayed no sign of being grateful for her efforts (although, much later, he was to concede that his first marriage was a disaster). By then, it was doubtful that quasi-maternal love, or any amount of material comfort, could ease the friction between the gentleness and charm with which he invariably faced the world, and his insistence that he would do as he damned well pleased. He was, as his second and third wives recorded (and as his step-granddaughters remember), a man of ineradicable shyness – a trait painfully twinned with an exhibitionist streak.

Documentary clues about his upbringing are elusive. There is not a single letter from his aunt Cynthia, for example, voicing her disquiet about her third adopted son, nor a postcard to him from either of his older brothers. The void – a direct and inevitable consequence of Edward's life of semi-vagrancy – is keenly felt. 'We are a family without history, in the immediate sense,' acknowledges his elder granddaughter. 'There have been no handing on of family stories or traditions or personal stuff because we weren't constructed like that. You didn't learn anything at anybody's knee. It is an extraordinary story that can only be pieced together from nothing.'

An unpublished memoir, written by the third of Edward's wives, refers to the letter in which Edward proposed to her ('sheet after sheet... a wonderful letter') and recounted the unhappiness and disappointments he had experienced, notably his upbringing at the hands of an apparently unsympathetic uncle and a poisonous nurse. (The letter does not appear to have survived.)

Such scant knowledge as the current generation of Grahams possesses was passed on by Sir Fergus Graham shortly before his death in 1978. As far as the family knows, Edward had a 'normal' childhood at Netherby, the Grahams' seat since about 1600, a house – incorporating a fifteenth century Pele tower – clad in the accretions of successive centuries. With more than twenty bedrooms, it was not quite the barracks manqué of Carton but still expansive enough to remind its occupants of their status.

At Eton[11] (which followed an Eastbourne prep school, Warren Hill), there was little – aside from the snakes he kept in his ottoman – to mark Edward out from contemporaries who arrived each Half (term) in a chauffeur-driven car (in Edward's case in the company of his brother Desmond and, latterly, their cousin Fergus Graham, with the Grahams' chauffeur, Robert, at the wheel). Desmond, who played the Field Game vigorously (returning to play with scratch sides after he left), was 'beloved from the first for a certain sunny simplicity and directness which made him free from variable moods, clear in his choice of duty and unswerving in his loyalty to any friend or cause or institution to which he had once given his heart... To be with him was to sit in sunshine.'

Edward sought the shadows. Academically undistinguished (though not disgraced), he became a member of his House debating society (an unexceptional achievement) and indulged in acts of routine delinquency (drinking whisky, for example, in his room with Oliver Lyttelton, nephew of the Head Master). But unlike Lyttelton, who subsequently became Secretary of State for the Colonies and was ennobled as Lord Chandos, Edward never quite outgrew his taste for adolescent transgression. Staying in New York during Prohibition, he was intrigued by the development of speakeasys and by the mild subterfuge adopted by more conventional establishments. Several restaurants, he noted, served drink with meals, 'even though it was against the law and even though there was a policeman in the room at the time. A favourite was whisky and ginger ale, so you could say it was just ginger ale.'

The same vein of arrested development may partly explain the energy he devoted to having affairs, selecting inappropriate wives (then deserting them) and evading creditors. At the age of seventy-three, he was asked why he had married so often. 'Four? It's not so many for my age,' he replied, still the schoolboy hoping to shock. Visiting Woburn in the 1950s (by which time one of his stepdaughters had married Ian Russell, 13th Duke of Bedford), Edward sat through a slide show given by an ornithologist, who, his talk over, asked if there were any questions. 'Suddenly,' remembered one of Edward's step-granddaughters, Caroline Tahany,[12] 'Fitz piped up from the back: "Do you have blue tits?"' He was always, she added, very childlike. A girlfriend (later his fourth wife) was made aware of this when Edward took her out for dinner on her birthday in the 1950s. The restaurant staff, noticing his unkempt appearance and tired suit, had initially been disinclined to believe that he was a duke; he retaliated by ignoring his plate and eating his food straight from the serving dishes.

Towards the end of his life, he assured an interviewer that he had always been something of a rebel. After leaving Eton, however, he followed Desmond into the Irish Guards (not generally considered as the opening gambit for the dedicated insurrectionist). Although he would eventually disengage from aristocratic life completely, in his youth he contentedly ricocheted from St James's Place to Stoke D'Abernon (the London and country residences of his aunt Helen and her husband, Viscount D'Abernon), from Netherby to Kirkdale (where another aunt, Lady Marjorie Beckett,[13] lived). When he married for the second time, he chose to have his wedding at the Savoy Chapel, a traditional refuge for divorced members of the upper classes;

his cousin Sir Fergus Graham (by then MP for North Cumberland) was his best man, one uncle, D'Abernon, gave his bride away, while another, Lord Henry FitzGerald, was among the guests.

He did, however, supplement conventional company with street acquaintances, among them Gaby Deslys, a woman whose talents had developed in a Marseilles slum (to lucrative advantage; her lovers included King Manoel of Portugal). Whilst heiress-hunting in America in the 1920s – a trip organized, and sponsored, by a London bookie called Tommy Dey – he was accompanied by a Mr Gilbert Marsh, a man of definite if often misapplied talent (he had, Edward later discovered, been sentenced to five years' imprisonment for his part in a racing fraud). Marsh, Edward concluded, was 'fine company', a man with 'a way of dealing with any attractive girls who were not wealthy enough for our plans. He just made friends with them on his own account. He had a good time. In fact, all Marsh wanted in life was a good cigar, a pretty girl and a speakeasy.' For much of the time, Edward gave the same impression. His second wife noted that he 'seemed as at ease in the pantry as with his own kind. Bookies, hooligans and money-lenders flattered him, as did their women.' He tended to dress like them, too. He looked like a gamekeeper, said the same wife; he favoured 'filthy old corduroys and a sloppy old jersey', and was often, remembers one of his step-granddaughters, 'mistaken for the gardener'. By the 1950s, he occasionally varied his 'terribly scruffy' appearance by favouring 'hideously old fashioned clothes, double-breasted [suits] with huge lapels'.

But, as a newly commissioned officer, Edward appeared clean-cut enough. Like many others stationed in London, he had little intention of wasting much time soldiering,[14] and was soon offering evidence that, like his unconventional uncle, Hubert Duncombe, he was not of a 'saving disposition'. By his own account, he 'liked a good time and pretty women, and was fond of good wines'. His priority, as always, was to find somewhere where he could be free to express himself. He found it in the 'Elinor Glyn', a beautifully proportioned, white-panelled room with an Adam fireplace and Sheraton and Hepplewhite furniture, in one corner of which was an endless expanse of sofa, big enough for four people to sleep on in comfort, 'piled high with lavender, apple-green and rose-pink cushions'.

This was the heart of the Cavendish, the Piccadilly hotel owned and run by Rosa Lewis,[15] whom Edward later described as one of the most interesting women he had ever known. Besides Edward VII, who was permitted to maintain his own private cellar at the hotel, Rosa's most indulged guests were the American polo team and the Irish Guards. She also had weaknesses for those with titles and for those who bought – and shared – 'cherrybums' of champagne. Edward learned that the hotel was a place where he could misbehave, and get away with it, reassured by one of the aphorisms which Rosa snapped out in untamed cockney: 'No letters, no lawyers and kiss my baby's bottom!' It was, noted Daphne Fielding, 'particularly fascinating that she knew who really were the fathers of one's friends.'

Edward was not alone in finding the Cavendish agreeable territory. Whilst fastidious characters like Lady Dorothy Nevill were bitterly lamenting what she described as the 'mob of plebeian wealth which surged into the drawing room', the Prince of Wales, later Edward VII, was keeping company with financiers and stage girls. The aristocracy was in an unprecedented state of flux; red-blooded 'men about town' appreciated the Cavendish's patrician-louche style, its excellent food, and the chance it offered for unbuttoned relaxation.[16] Amongst them was Sir William Eden (father of Anthony Eden), an abrasive baronet who insisted that a wall be knocked down so that he could enjoy his own private entrance. It was from men like Eden and the 'Yellow Earl', the 5th Earl of Lonsdale, that Edward now increasingly took his cue.

He took up sparring, became a member of the National Sporting Club (co-founded by Lonsdale) and did his best to unsettle his trustees in the company of cronies like Castlerosse, 'Whisky' Cole and Horace de Vere Cole.[17] During the course of the next few years, the trustees heard that his French mistress had given birth to his child at a racecourse in France; that he had formed an inappropriate attachment to a Gaiety Girl; that he spent money he didn't have and drove – at manic speed – cars he couldn't afford. He had bought fifteen monkeys, a lemur, a score of snakes; he was living at the Buckingham Palace Hotel, then in a flat in Barons Court. He was leading a convoy of three Rolls Royces across England, en route for Scotland and Ireland, and had been obliged to resign his commission in the Irish Guards. Most of this was true (he did not have a child by a French mistress).

But not only was Edward spending freely, he had also begun to gamble. It was the vice that was to shape his life; one which he, like most addicts, was only ever able to acknowledge in the most oblique and inconsequential of terms. Years later, for instance, he admitted that, while walking down Haymarket in the West End, he had accepted a bet from de Vere Cole, who claimed that he could lie down in the street without attracting a crowd (Edward lost: de Vere Cole curled up under a parked car). One of his step-daughters from his third marriage recalls Edward's weakness in starker terms, describing him as a compulsive gambler. It was a deficiency he shared with at least one of his relations, again a Duncombe rather than a FitzGerald. Charles William Slingsby Duncombe (always known as 'Sim'), the 3rd and last Earl of Feversham, was Edward's first cousin once removed. A one-time director of the Midland Bank and chairman of the National Association for Mental Health (now Mind), he was, like Edward, capable of captivating charm (he had, it was said, the 'gift of making everyone he talked to feel that they were the only person in the world'). He also backed horses at 'impossible odds', was a regular at the Mayfair *chemin de fer* parties organized by John Aspinall in the 1950s; and, in the 1960s, travelled to London several times a week to unload more of his inheritance at the Clermont Club. Whilst on family holidays, he was frequently unable to pay his bills 'because he had gambled everything away… the previous night'. There were predictable consequences for his Helmsley estate which, between 1876 and 1976, contracted from 39,300 acres to 12,500, some of it clawed away by death duties, but much of it – like the village and Abbey of Rievaulx – forfeited at the racecourse or on the roulette wheel.

Edward's addiction was just as punishing, as all his wives would discover.

* * *

The pre-cinematic years before the First World War proved to be the heyday of the Gaiety Girls, chorus girls so named because they were selected – as much for their decorative value as for their histrionic talent – to appear at the Gaiety Theatre. Generating the same sort of raw appreciation – and distaste – as lap-dancers in twenty-first-century London, they employed more subtlety than their latterday successors, though that did not prevent them from being regarded, like most ladies of the stage, 'as little better than prostitutes'. By 1912, May Etheridge had graduated from the Gaiety to the Shaftesbury Theatre, a regular haunt for Foot Guards officers, where she was appearing with a rival troop of chorus girls, the Arcadians. Neither the fact that her mother lived in Brixton nor that her late father had been a travelling salesman improved her status.

It was at the Shaftesbury that Edward first saw her.[18] Here, he sensed, was a girl to break rules with. He sent her a note, inviting her to supper and suggesting that she should bring a friend along. May accepted. Sheila Hays, one of May's fellow Arcadians, joined the two young officers at the Savoy Grill. 'That first evening with May was one of the happiest in my life,' Edward recalled, more than forty years later. 'I was twenty, easily impressed and ready to enjoy the company of any pretty girl. May was more than pretty. She was tiny, dark, and looked like an angel. Other people envied my being

with her, and that pleased my vanity. I saw her again and again. I was fond
of her, she liked me. Her interest flattered me. She was gay, too, and adorable.
But,' he added, 'I was not in love with her.'

Nevertheless Edward wooed her with determination, as he did all the
women in his life. His aunt Cynthia, who had already been humiliated when
her brother Hubert had married (or co-habited with) his 'music hall artiste',
led the family's fight to keep him (and themselves) out of the mire. To
Edward's mind, this explained why what should have been an agreeable diversion became, instead, the start of an unruly marital career. 'I would probably
not have married her,' he explained, 'if my family had not acted as they did.'
Edward's reasoning was desperately straightforward. Had his family indulged
him with May, his appetite for her would have soon waned. But they did not;
worse, they had the temerity to intervene (intruding on him in restaurants,
exiling him to New Zealand and Hawaii) and so they, not he, were responsible for the episode that messily unfolded. Edward clung resolutely to this
thread of argument throughout his life, extending it well beyond the marital
field, as an explanation for all he did. 'There is nothing,' he explained, 'which
will make me want to do a thing so much as someone trying to stop me.'
Bolstered by this justification, he invariably struggled to make passable judgements on advice he was given. To his way of thinking, his appetites and
desires tended to be validated by the very fact that they were his, in much the
same way that 'My Way', Frank Sinatra's signature tune, is so regularly named
by prison inmates as their favourite song.

On his return from Honolulu, Cynthia was at Liverpool to escort him
down to London; May was aboard the same train. Edward appeared briefly
in her compartment and assured her that he would see her that night. He
kept his word, arriving at her house in dishevelled state after dark; he had, he
said, been locked into his bedroom at the FitzGerald house in Belgravia, but
had escaped by shinning down a drainpipe. On subsequent nights, he doled
out a cascade of jewellery, not to May, but to the programme girls at the
theatre, considering this an appropriate way to reward them for taking billet
doux to May backstage. The charm of the technique was slightly lost on the
FitzGeralds when they learned that Edward's gifts were family jewels. May
retrieved them – and kept them, together with the ring which Edward had
said was his mother's as he slipped it on to her finger.

After resigning his commission (marriage to an actress being considered
incompatible with the dignity required of a Guards officer), he 'made plans
for the wedding', which was not overly lavish. He and May married on 12
June 1913 at Wandsworth Registry Office, chosen, Edward later explained,

because May lived in Streatham. The marriage accelerated Edward's divorce from aristocratic society and his disengagement from his own family. When, in 1930, Lord Henry FitzGerald was required to give evidence in court (May had tried to commit suicide), he admitted that he very rarely saw his nephew, and was unaware of his whereabouts. But there was less deliberate antagonism in Edward's decision than self-indulgence: he married for his own amusement, exhilarated to be breaking the rules, in this case, of endogamy, devoutly practised by the FitzGeralds for generations.[19]

During the brief, hopeless marriage that followed, Edward showed himself at his worst: callow, selfish, inconsiderate. The honeymoon in Canada, for example, was arranged solely with his interests in mind – an amalgam of property deals, fishing and moose-shooting. Most of it was spent at a lakeside hut of spartan purity, almost unfurnished except for an iron bed marooned in a room with wooden floorboards and wooden walls. Supplies were brought in periodically by motor-boat. These proved inadequate for May's requirements (she later acknowledged that she wanted a drink 'very badly'), while Edward exuded impatience, perhaps because no moose were shot, or because he lost (so May thought) something like £4,000 on his property deals; or because he was already resenting his mistake in marrying her.

He seems to have known that disaster beckoned. According to what turned out to be May's posthumous account, Edward announced, moments before they were due to leave for the registry office on their wedding day, that he couldn't go through with it, offering the explanation that it would 'absolutely kill' his eldest brother, Maurice. But Maurice, as usual, was nowhere to be seen, nor were any of the FitzGeralds, which was unsurprising as, aside from Edward's best man, Whisky Cole, there were to be no guests. The press, however, newly invigorated and vulgarized by the Harmsworths and the Astors, was out in force. Edward was not a duke, but he was, indisputably, an aristocrat, a member not only of the richest class but of what was still widely seen as the ruling class,[20] notwithstanding the agricultural crisis, the Parliament Act of 1911 (emasculating the powers of the House of Lords), and the emergence of middle-class men like Asquith and Bonar Law as party leaders. His choice of bride was sensational.

There was, though, the consolation that press attention could be neutralized by mildly delinquent behaviour. 'We had to climb two walls to get into the street,' said Edward, recalling how the registrar had let them out by a side door. 'May was game for anything. She clutched her bouquet in one hand, her handbag in the other while I called her over.' The couple's taxi shook off a press car by doing a U-turn in Bond Street; at the Carlton Hotel, Lady

Edward FitzGerald soothed her nerves with two large brandies. It was to be the limit of her wedding celebrations. Edward declined to waste money by taking rooms at the Cavendish, and had no intention of spending the night in Streatham. He returned, instead, to his family's house in Belgravia, while May headed back to 76 Amesbury Avenue. For the next two days, she didn't see him. In desperation, she telephoned the FitzGeralds, remote in alien Belgravia. The butler took her call: Lord Edward was out; no, regrettably, he did not know when Lord Edward would return. As she prepared for a third night alone, Edward knocked at the door of number 76 and shouted: 'Come on, I've got the tickets. We're going.' It was an apposite precursor to the honeymoon and, indeed, for all four of Edward's marital excursions.

Back in England, the bravado of his courtship gave way to insecurity. He told May that he had got into 'enough trouble' by marrying her without also having to introduce her to his family. He yielded only once. During an exquisitely brittle afternoon at Netherby, Lord Frederick FitzGerald (who happened to be staying) remarked that May must be finding her visit 'altogether different from the stage'. 'Yes,' said May, in an exemplary reply, 'it is rather a rest.' In London, whilst they were living, briefly, at the Buckingham Palace Hotel, she asked, with pitiful innocence, if she would soon be taken across to Buckingham Palace to be presented to the Royal Family. Edward again betrayed his vulnerability, replying that he had made 'sufficient fool' of himself by marrying her without needing to give anyone the opportunity to comment.

His sensitivity to social decorum was less acute when his own amusement was at stake. Spasms of expenditure were followed by crises of indebtedness, which were in turn momentarily relieved by further borrowing. After the Buckingham Palace Hotel, there was a fortnight opera-going in Paris, a stint in a furnished flat in St James's Court (where Edward retained the services of a black butler), then enforced sanctuary at May's grandmother's house in Brixton (when, in May's artless words, 'we found we had spent all our money'), a few giddy weeks in a house in Fawley, outside Southampton (after Edward had borrowed more from Whisky Cole), during which Edward acquired two yachts, then Brixton again, followed by Stanhope Gardens – all within a year.

A pet-shop was discovered off the Waterloo Road, whose owners proved gratifyingly accommodating. They produced a lemur for Edward whilst he and May were at the Buckingham Palace Hotel, and fifteen monkeys in time for the move to Fawley. Unfortunately for May's grandmother, the monkey phase, although beginning to peter out, continued when May and Edward took refuge with her for the second time. The Brixton bathroom coped as well as it could with eight monkeys (seven having been returned to the pet-shop), but was eventually not equal to the struggle, and was abandoned. 'The smell,' May recalled, 'was simply terrible.'

A chimpanzee, procured for £50, followed. Edward dressed it in red trousers, jersey and hat, and insisted that it ate with them, whether in Brixton (where it had its own high-chair) or at the hotel or restaurant where they were having dinner. It, in turn, was succeeded by snakes – his old Eton favourite – which were given the run of the couple's rooms at Stanhope Gardens, and then a fox cub which, at Edward's insistence, May carried under her arm when walking down Regent Street.

Ownership of inappropriate animals was quite fun: like marrying inap-propriate women, it was part of the liberating business of transgression. It had an advantage over marriage, of course: the foxes, the chimps, the lemurs could all be traded in. May couldn't be, at least not immediately, so Edward did what he was to do all his life – he fled. His desertion followed the birth of his son, at six o'clock on the morning of 27 May 1914. (The night before, Edward had decided that his wife should accompany him to the boxing at the Ring in Blackfriars Road.) The baby was christened Gerald, as so many FitzGeralds had been down the centuries. It was, though, one of the very few respects in which Gerald's early life adhered to family tradition. His home was not Carton, not even Carlton House Terrace, but a flat in Barons Court which his parents shared with May's mother. It was, in May's words, a 'dismal existence'. Gerald's clothes came from Brixton, where they were made by one of his maternal great-grandmothers; his doctor and nurse were paid for by his mother, who found the money by pawning the FitzGerald diamonds which 'Boy' had given her as a wedding present.

Within months Edward felt the need for refuge elsewhere; he chose India. It was the end of the marriage, although he and May were not to divorce until 1930. She saw her husband off at the station, returned to her flat, alone with her baby, and cried herself to a standstill. Their final parting came at the end of the war, in the offices of the FitzGeralds' family solicitors. It was then that Gerald was taken to live in Ireland at Johnstown Castle, County Wexford, with his great-aunt Adelaide, widow of Lord Maurice Fitzgerald. The four-year-old screamed as he was led from his mother.

According to May, Edward assured her that it was 'all for the best'. It might have been more precise to say that things could have been worse. Adelaide was an affectionate woman, who almost certainly gave Gerald a more stable upbringing than he would have experienced with his mother, who gambled as enthusiastically as she drank, but who was nevertheless made welcome at Johnstown whenever she felt able to visit. But Gerald saw nothing of his father. Edward's second wife recalled how, when she insisted on meeting his son, she learned that he had 'not seen or heard from his father, except once when he had been ill, for many years. They seemed complete strangers and rather stiff with each other.' The rupture was never healed, with the inevitable consequence that Edward never knew either of his grandsons beyond social superficiality.

He found better things to do than worry about Gerald – like driving, an activity from which he derived unusual pleasure, perhaps because of his impregnable indifference to the terror of his passengers. Two of May's aunts and May's mother were given a taste of this after a visit to Fawley. On the day of their return to London, Edward volunteered to drive them home. May followed with her sister in another car, driven by Wright, a chauffeur who had been recruited despite Edward's parlous financial circumstances. It was a wet day, but Edward had no intention of reducing his speed. After about ten miles, he flew off the road and buried his car in the verge, ripping his mother-in-law's suitcase from its place on the side of the car. Mrs Etheridge and her sisters, their clothes scattered in a rain-sodden ditch, decided to complete their journey by train.

As an act of youthful idiocy, it was unremarkable. But this was only the beginning of a lifetime spent driving with race-track fervour. As far as Edward was concerned, driving offered a chance for self-assertion – a gamble, but a better one than most, since he tended to set the odds. His second wife later recalled that he would drive 400 miles in a day, without strain (she said that he had 'the nervous energy of a racehorse'), at up to 113 mph, a terrifying speed for the narrow roads of the 1930s. 'He could not bear any car to pass him. He must be ahead and stay ahead, which was very tiring and frightening indeed.' He attacked the road whatever the circumstances, even if these included having a child in the passenger seat beside him, as it would in the 1950s when he occasionally drove one of his step-grandchildren to school. 'I was absolutely frightened out of my wits,' says Sir Gavin Lyle,[21] recalling 'Uncle Fitz' at the wheel of 'a massive great Jaguar. He always thought he was in a grand prix... everything was done on the wrong side of the road. He used to terrify my grandmother, too; [it] led to endless rows.'

Decades beforehand, Edward's family had the consolation of knowing that there was little prospect that he would succeed to the dukedom or inherit Carton and the FitzGerald fortune. But the outbreak of the First World War caused them a tremor of disquiet.

* * *

Craighouse is a Victorian building of almost intimidating scale, standing in its own parkland, aloof from the modest terraced housing of the surrounding Edinburgh district of Morningside. Seagulls coast in from the Firth of Forth. By day, wrote one student of FitzGerald history, it 'is forbidding; by night it is frankly ominous, with its long and intricate neo-Gothic façade, its helmet-shaped cupolas, its high rectangular chimney-stacks and row upon row of narrow, barred windows. Its function is unmistakable: Craighouse is an asylum for the insane.'[22] Ever since June 1909, the FitzGeralds had lived in its shadow.

Nothing in the unremarkable boyhood of Maurice FitzGerald suggested that swift disintegration would follow. He had, it was true, suffered bouts of ill-health at Eton (where he preceded his brothers in the Reverend H. T. Bowlby's house), especially, it seems, each Lent Half, when he was invariably absent. But he performed perfectly respectably in class and (like his youngest brother) became a member of the house debating society. Once his school-days ended in 1904, however, his horizons clouded over. According to Robert, the Grahams' chauffeur at Netherby, 'Leinster was never the same after he left Eton'. When, four years later, his coming of age was celebrated at Carton on 1 March 1908, marching bands preceded a torch-lit procession through the neighbouring town of Maynooth (designed and created by the 2nd Duke). Former tenants joined estate staff around an immense bonfire; beer was drunk by the barrel. But Maurice was absent. 'It was with feelings of very great regret,' the *Kildare Observer* reported a few days later, 'that the people of the district heard of his protracted illness.'

Maurice's medical records disclose that he was suffering from epilepsy and 'delusional insanity' – a form of schizophrenia suggests one of his great-nieces, Edward's granddaughter, Rosemary FitzGerald. Scraps of information contained in solicitors' or doctors' letters suggest that she is right. As his problems worsened, it was accepted that he needed the companionship and care which only a full-time doctor could provide. The family secured the services of Donald (later Sir Donald) Pollock; his duties were very nearly to cost him his life. On 11 June 1909, while holidaying in Berwick, Maurice succumbed to overwhelming paranoia. By the end of the attack, which seems to have lasted five days, he had tried to kill Pollock, his own valet and himself. Extreme action was now inevitable.

Six days later, on 17 June 1909, the 6th Duke of Leinster was brought – bound, tied and dragged by servants – to Craighouse. He never left. Known as Mr FitzGerald, he lived at the Bungalow, 153 Morningside Drive,[23] a semi-detached villa in the grounds, about fifty yards from the monolithic mass of the main house but connected to it by an underground passageway. In return for £2,500-a-year, Maurice had this to himself, together with 'special board, the service of a doctor [not Pollock, although he moved to Edinburgh so that he could be on call], the exclusive service of five attendants, one of whom was the Duke's recently assaulted valet, and the use of a carriage and pair'.

As soon as Lord Frederick FitzGerald heard of Maurice's attempt on Pollock's life, he sent a Dr Clouston to examine his nephew. Clouston's report made frightening reading. Explaining that it was his belief that Maurice was suffering 'insane delusions', he wrote: 'He is also seriously suicidal and homicidal, having inflicted a serious wound on his throat and several other wounds on his chest and arm, as well as having seriously assaulted Dr Pollock.' Pollock, for his part, foresaw a wretched future for his patient, one which was likely to conclude abruptly. Writing to the FitzGeralds' solicitor, Mr Johnson, on 27 July, he said: 'I may tell you that the medical impression is that he will sooner or later commit suicide wherever he is but that the chances of his doing this are very much less where he is than in an outside establishment. Poor boy, it's a terrible ending for a short and sharp life's tragedy [sic].'

Pollock's faith in Craighouse was justified. Maurice spent the rest of his life there, remaining 'moody and unpredictable, given to long periods of total silence, when he would not eat, alternating with bursts of manic activity'. There were moments of relief. He enjoyed having his portrait painted. He tried his hand at curling. He played hockey. He was provided with a piano fitted with organ pedals (nourishing the harmless delusion that he was playing the organ at Carton). But there could be no recovery.

His aunt Cynthia took the news of his incarceration badly. Edward's reaction is not known; at the time of the crisis, he was in the throes of leaving Eton. There can be no doubt, though, that he knew the seriousness of the situation as well as the rest of his family did; and, like them, found it difficult to accept. Neither he nor Desmond is believed to have visited their brother before the First World War.

* * *

War gave Edward an opportunity. Although there was no question of rejoining Desmond in the Irish Guards, nor of emulating his cousin, the Duke of Westminster, who had his Rolls-Royce armour-plated (with a Hotchkiss machine gun mounted on the rear) and formed his own brigade, there was no reason why he could not serve in a regiment of the line. Returning from his self-imposed exile in India, he was commissioned into the 8th Service Battalion of the West Riding Regiment. If his family nurtured hopes that he might die gallantly, as many a FitzGerald had done before, they did so in secret. Pollock, Maurice's doctor, probably voiced their unspoken desires a little later when, hearing that Desmond had been wounded, he remarked in a letter: 'I am glad that Desmond's wound is no worse. Personally I feel thankful that he is not in the middle of it and may be kept out of it for good. With Ed as successor things would be too dreadful.'

On 2 July 1915, the 8th Service Battalion embarked on the SS *Aquitania*, sailing from Liverpool the following day, destination unknown. At 5.45 a.m. on 4 July, the alarm sounded: the *Aquitania* was under submarine attack. 'Troops ordered to boat stations,' recorded an officer, in one of the first entries jotted into the battalion's war diary. 'Torpedo missed by about eight feet.' Three days later, there was a further alarm, but it too was safely negotiated. By the 22nd, Edward and the rest of the battalion had disembarked at Imbros, their first, deceptively straightforward step into the Gallipoli campaign.

May later remembered that her husband returned home 'very badly wounded'. Edward's step-grandson, Sir Gavin Lyle, recalls his unusual walk, 'with one foot splayed out', which he thinks might have been a legacy of his injuries. But Edward's records suggest otherwise.

The battalion embarked for Suvla Bay, Turkey, on 6 August. The war diary entry for 7 August amounts to a few words: 'Heavily engaged in night and during day. Heavy losses.' At some stage in the early morning of 8 August, before the battalion was pulled back to the beach, Lt Lord Edward FitzGerald was hit in the right arm, about two and a half inches above the elbow. The bullet made a one-and-a-half inch exit wound; more significantly, it caused severe damage to the musculospiral nerve, which controls movement of the wrist, fingers and thumb, leaving him incapable of gripping a rifle butt, still less of squeezing a trigger.

Rudimentary treatment in a field hospital presumably followed but did little good. It might, in any case, have been days before Edward received attention. During the next three months, the battalion rattled between front-line duty and time in reserve, repelling occasional Turkish attacks but constantly trapped, vulnerable to shell and sniper fire: a demoralizing, spasmodically terrifying experience which ended on 19 December, when the battalion pulled out. If Edward had been evacuated earlier, it went unrecorded. In either case, his war was effectively over. It did nothing to jolt him towards domesticity or persuade him to moderate his behaviour. 'Even when he was invalided home,' recalled May, 'I found it was impossible to effect a reconciliation with him.'

The army hierarchy now also discovered that Edward could be a hard man to contain. In February 1916, he was traced to the Grosvenor Hotel on Buckingham Palace Road but either disappeared or ignored the orders that followed. 'Notice was posted this officer to attend here 10th inst.,' recorded the colonel in charge of the medical board Edward had been due to attend, 'but he did not do so... two wires, copies of which are now sent, were despatched to the officer on the dates stated thereon, but he has not attended, nor has any intimation been received that the wires have not been duly delivered.' Battle-shock, described as 'overstrain of the nervous system', was almost certainly more to blame than wilfulness, though army doctors found it difficult to determine the proportionate influences of front line and domestic experiences on this unusual subaltern. 'The present worry about his private affairs,' noted one of them, 'may be one of the contributory causes of his state of health.' Edward's arm began to heal but there was no commensurate improvement in his frame of mind. He started to lose weight. In July 1916, he was judged 'still unfit to resume military duties', though the doctor concluded that 'a further rest of six to eight weeks will probably be sufficient to effect a cure'.

It could not have helped that, by then, fresh disaster had befallen the FitzGeralds. Desmond had already been awarded the MC and twice been mentioned in despatches; promotion to major was imminent. When on leave, he spent most of his time visiting the families of Irish Guardsmen killed in action, yet 'was never morbid, never tiresome, never censorious... Always he swung true like a compass.' The panegyric appeared a few months after his death at the Front on 3 March 1916.[24]

In his will, he left £25,000 (£8.69 million today), with bequests (each of £5,000 or £2,000) totalling £16,000 to his uncles and aunts. Understanding rather than despising Edward's weaknesses, he left money in a protective trust, stipulating that his younger brother should receive the income from the remaining £9,000 for the rest of his life. But this was not unconditional: a clause made it plain that if Edward went bankrupt, or borrowed against his life interest, any further payments were to be made only at the discretion of Desmond's trustees.

There is no record of how Edward responded. He was almost certainly, as the current Duke of Leinster believes, as distraught as the rest of the family. In a less volatile state, he might even have spied a glimmer of salvation through his grief. He was – honourably – out of the war, and had just become heir presumptive to Ireland's premier dukedom, to a seat in the House of Lords (thanks to the viscountcy created for the 2nd Duke), to Carton and Kilkea, and to a fortune worth at least £400-a-week. Now, though, he sought solace in Hampshire (Tyrell Lodge, Lyndhurst), in Barnes (49 Melville Road) and in Aberdeenshire (Park House, Drumoak), a route march seemingly of his own devising, and much more appealing than returning to May and their son in Barons Court. But most of all, he later recalled, he turned to the Cavendish Hotel. Rosa Lewis had greeted hostilities by moving a portrait of the Kaiser (one of her old favourites, for whom she had occasionally cooked by special request) to the gentlemen's cloakroom ('That's the only throne for old Willy'), and by becoming more munificent than ever to those she considered deserving causes. Edward had always been appreciative of the quirks of her book-keeping. 'She had a pleasant habit,' he noted, 'of adding a bottle or two of champagne to the bills of the richer clients and deducting it from the accounts of the less wealthy.' Officers on leave or convalescing were now treated with particular generosity, their bills frequently 'forgotten', so that, at the end of the war, Rosa had a drawer full of uncashed cheques, tied up with red, white and blue ribbons.

After Gerald was born, Edward had hidden the newspapers from May to prevent her from seeing that he was threatened with bankruptcy. Now unchained from her company, he found it easier to enjoy himself, encouraged by Rosa's soothing, if doubtful, maxim that 'great men are poor husbands'. Edward was massively and catastrophically in debt, to the tune of £15,000, a phenomenal accomplishment for a twenty-five-year-old who had spent months on a cruise to New Zealand, months more in India and five months on active service. In these circumstances, Desmond's bequest was of marginal consequence. So, too, was Edward's army pay which, in any case, came to an end in March 1917, when a medical board relinquished him of his commission 'on account of ill-health caused by wounds'.

Edward now contrived to make the crisis far, far worse. He had already approached the family trustees, with what he considered to be modest proposals. They could, he told them, buy him a small estate in Scotland for about £20,000, and supply him with an annual allowance of £3,000 or £4,000. They would also presumably (though Edward never mentioned this irksome detail) pay off his creditors. Understandably, the trustees declined to comply. Clinging to his habitual reasoning, Edward argued that it was their refusal to do so which 'forced' him towards the money-lenders – amongst them, a solicitor's clerk called William Cooper Hobbs – who lent at rates of interest of up to 400 per cent. This solved his short-term problem, allowing him to repay cronies like Whisky Cole. 'The world,' Edward remembered much, much later, 'was as rosy as the pink champagne I drank at the Cavendish Hotel.' But immediately and inevitably his debts quadrupled, to more than £60,000. When the effects of the pink champagne wore off, he was prepared to resort to desperate measures to expunge them – even, it seems, a visit to Craighouse.

Throughout his life, Edward rarely mentioned Maurice to anyone, not even to his wives; he limited his public pronouncements to an assertion that his eldest brother suffered from a condition 'similar to shell-shock' (a condition, he added, which prevented Maurice from having children). But a letter, found by Edward's son Gerald in 1980, 'suggest[s] that Edward may have visited his brother in Scotland, and that an unpleasant scene took place between them'. Not long after this, however, he found someone who was only too willing to come to his assistance.

* * *

Sir Harry Mallaby-Deeley has been variously described as a 'charming, rich parvenu', an 'avaricious money-lender' and a 'vigorous raiser of war loans'. His obituary opted for 'philanthropist and racehorse owner, as well as financier', adding that he had been a Conservative MP (first for Harrow, then for East Willesden) and a recipient of a baronetcy (for his immense financial contributions to the war effort), but would be especially remembered 'for his spectacular deals in "slices" of London involving millions'. The most gratifying of these had been his purchase of the Russells' Covent Garden estate from the 11th Duke of Bedford. 'Mallaby-Deeley,' Edward reflected later, 'was reputed to have made nearly £500,000 from the deal, but I think this was an exaggeration.'

Edward never disclosed whether he knew how adroit an operator Mallaby-Deeley was. In a way, it was irrelevant, since he was in no mood to listen to well-informed advice (unless it was to act against it): in 1918 he was declared bankrupt for the first time. The two men met through the appropriately dubious offices of a character called Fraser, who, according to Edward, was a gillie's son from the Highlands, 'a strange individual who delighted in meeting young men in trouble... whose business was to introduce them to money-lenders and then collect a nice commission'. Mallaby-Deeley, Edward recorded many years later, was 'a shrewd but charming man, a delightful conversationalist, well dressed, with curly white hair and a red face'. He was also a barrister, educated at Shrewsbury and Trinity College, Cambridge, who left little to chance. The details of the agreement he eventually made with Edward make it clear that he was fully acquainted not only with Edward's parlous position – one authority on the FitzGerald affairs[25] suggests that he was one of Edward's creditors – but also aware of the situation at Craighouse.

But Edward didn't act in hot blood: first, he returned to the trustees, to let them share the good news. '[I] told them what I proposed to do if they did not make suitable provision for me.' They listened, 'aghast, mesmerized', as he outlined details of the intended agreement: Mallaby-Deeley was to pay off all his debts – by then amounting to £67,500 (£16.4 million today) – and pay him an annual allowance of £1,000 for life. In return, Mallaby-Deeley (and, in due course, his heirs) would receive all income from the estates entailed with the dukedom, worth roughly £50,000 a year, as well as the use of Carton and Kilkea, from the moment Edward succeeded Maurice, until the day of Edward's death.

'It was a gamble,' Edward reflected. 'If my brother lived for another fifty years I would come off best. If he lived for only a short time I would lose.' Described like that, the deal sounded like an even-money bet. But Edward knew that it wasn't, so much so that he later admitted that he felt 'uneasy'.

The estate trustees presumably felt appreciably worse. The shrewdness of Edward's father, and of his uncle Frederick, had safeguarded Kilkea and Carton. The latter's restrained, even sombre, exterior masked a dazzling interior, especially the dining room and saloon which Emily had had emblazoned with stucco work by the Swiss Lafrancini brothers, Paulo and Filippo, 150 years earlier. Now this restless, intractable younger son, with his perverse choice of bride, his adolescent exhibitionism, his destructive bloody-mindedness, threatened to wreck everything, even before his ailing brother died. Edward, as ever, attributed his behaviour to their attitude. 'They said that it was impossible, that no one would make such a purchase. I went straight off and did it.'

Yet Edward was not incapable of calculation. Realizing that he faced an unforgiving future, he appears to have made attempts to extricate himself from the agreement not long after signing it in January 1918, bringing an action against Mallaby-Deeley, 'claiming among other things that the Principal and other hereinbefore recited Agreements should be rescinded and cancelled'. But Sir Harry, aware that Edward was unable (and his trustees unwilling) to repay the £67,000 that had been handed to his creditors, stood firm. The action failed. On 14 September 1920, a final agreement, summarizing all previous ones, came into force. Within six months, Edward was scrabbling around for more money, applying to the army to recompense him for the cost of his passage home from India in 1914. 'I should be pleased,' he wrote (on 31 March 1921), 'to obtain [my expenses] as soon as possible as I need the money urgently.' The reply explained that the final date for claims had been 31 December 1920.

Courtesy would be all he could expect from Mallaby-Deeley, who had been scrupulously careful, insuring Edward's life for £300,000, and peppering the agreement with clauses curbing his capacity for self-destruction. There was also a proviso allowing Edward to buy back his life interest, assuming that he could find the asking price of £400,000 (£75.2 million today).

Sir Harry's appetite for detail, and his willingness to exploit opportunities offered him by the atrophying aristocracy, make him a tempting figure to demonize. But he was not as brutish as other men on the make. Rosemary FitzGerald points out that Sir Harry and his son, Sir (Antony) Meyrick Mallaby-Deeley, behaved 'most honourably throughout the entire history [of the agreement]'. The evidence bears this out. Years later, when Edward's son Gerald wanted to make his career in the aviation industry, it was the Mallaby-Deeleys who guaranteed his overdraft. Similarly, they proved wholly sympathetic when, after the Second World War, the FitzGeralds sought to minimize the drain on their (by then hugely reduced) income by selling Carton. The bald truth was, as Gerald was later to say, that Mallaby-Deeley had made a good deal and Edward a bad one.

Quite how bad became apparent less than seventeen months after Edward signed the final, binding agreement. At ten minutes past midnight on 2 February 1922, Maurice FitzGerald, 6th Duke of Leinster, died at the Bungalow, 153 Morningside Drive. Fergus Graham and Dr Pollock accompanied his body from Edinburgh to Carton; it was interred a few feet from his parents' graves, beneath a Celtic cross. Edward, who was holidaying with a girlfriend in Italy at the time, treated the news of his brother's death as a rather tasteless distraction, declining to return for the funeral, subsequently explaining that there 'was no point'.

It was a useful indication of his future intentions. Desmond's death had not stung him into reform; nor would Maurice's. Instead, that July, in a mammoth gamble, he accepted a £3,000 wager – or three years' income – that he could drive from London to Aberdeen in under fifteen hours. A seemingly modest challenge to twenty-first-century thinking, it demanded significant stamina and skill on 518 miles of single-track roads. Driving an open-top Rolls – and accompanied by a wolfhound – Edward took two wrong turns and drove a total of 557 miles, but managed them in thirteen hours, earning himself vehement condemnation in the House of Commons for recklessness, as well as attracting the attention of at least one local constabulary. Summonsed for failing to produce his licence, he notched up two speeding fines the following week (when his licence was 'eventually tracked down, it showed convictions dating back to 1914').

But his London–Aberdeen triumph was all the encouragement he needed; he now accepted a challenge from an American yachtsman, William Nutting, to race across the Atlantic. He had already visited New York, where the city's yacht club was to offer a trophy to the winner, and had put down a £1,000 deposit with a firm of Long Island boat-builders, who were to make his 36-foot ketch, when Mallaby-Deeley intervened, pointing out that their agreement allowed him to veto any activity which might cut short Edward's life. The race was off. (Mallaby-Deeley's anxiety was well-founded: on Nutting's next Atlantic crossing, the American sailed into oblivion; his body was never found.) Edward lost his £1,000 deposit and, worse, learned to what extent he had forfeited his freedom. It was this, much more than the loss of Carton, Kilkea and the FitzGerald fortune, which was to prove intolerable to him in the years ahead.[26] He now faced an existence of enforced tranquillity, utterly inimical to his temperament. The prospect seems to have stoked his internal rage, fuelled his fury behind the wheel and, quite probably, explained his frequent disappearances – escapades during which he could achieve anonymity and shrug off the need for restraint or caution.

The following year, in September 1923, he was briefly detained following an attempt to obtain credit without disclosing that he was an undischarged bankrupt. There was to be no solace in work. Bankruptcy detached him from the novel arenas of employment (as well as traditional ones like the army) into which other impoverished aristocrats were gingerly lowering themselves. Some were embracing the City, with wildly varying degrees of enthusiasm and expertise – and consequences. Many more had, figuratively if not literally, decided to 'go out and govern New South Wales'. Others had begun to try their hand in trade, amongst them the Hon. C. S. Rolls, younger son of Lord Llangattock, who, before joining forces with Frederick Royce, had supplemented his annual £500 allowance as a salesman and demonstrator of the horseless carriage.

Given his addiction to fast, luxurious cars, Edward would have seemed well placed to try to emulate Rolls or another motoring pioneer, John Douglas-Scott-Montagu, 2nd Lord Montagu of Beaulieu, founder and editor of *Car Illustrated*. But although he was later to prove willing to tackle the most humdrum and menial of tasks – accepting a job polishing brass stair-rails on the Cadogan estate in the 1960s – he had yet to tear up his dynastic script and, with it, any ambition to live an aristocratic existence. Decades later, when he did so, he experienced rare moments of contentment, living alone in a small, white-washed cottage in Kent, where he designed hand-knitted children's clothes. By then, forty years after his agreement with Mallaby-Deeley, it was much, much easier to let go; a further decade on, in the mid-1970s, half a dozen ducal families would be authoritatively described as 'invincibly middle class'. In the 1920s and 1930s, though, Edward lacked the rebelliousness of spirit necessary for such a renunciation of status. Consequently, in as far as he sought or accepted employment, it was only of the most ornamental kind.[27]

This was entirely understandable, for it was neither the purpose nor the function of the aristocracy to work. A nobleman's *raison d'être* was to lead wherever his duty took him, traditionally to death (or glory) on the battlefield. He continued to accept deference as his appropriate due, even though his place in the chain of command was slipping fast. Little wonder that Americans, weaned on strictly commercial hierarchies – as Edward's second wife, Rafaelle van Neck, had been – were immediately enchanted. On honeymoon in the 1930s, staying at Kirkdale Manor, Rafaelle noted that her own maid 'went into meals first and sat on the right of the butler wherever we went'. No under-servant was allowed to address her or enter her room, even to lay the fire; and only the head servants could serve her and Edward. 'It was very fashionable to be a duke and a duchess,' added Rafaelle, 'the Connaught and the Dorchester Hotels were anxious to have us stay with them at nominal rates'. Similarly, show-room salesmen were only too eager to arrange favourable terms for Edward, who continued to acquire cars – for truncated periods – on hire purchase.

But perhaps more important than fawning members of the motor trade or servants slavishly adhering to etiquette was the influence of Edward's family. Despite Edward's accusations, they had neither 'forced' him into his marriage with May nor his agreement with Mallaby-Deeley. They were, however, guilty of nursing his belief that he would, in due course, redeem his inheritance. This disastrous through well-intentioned attitude encouraged Edward in the smug assumption that everything would be put right at some stage, until which time he could spend money in his usual uninhibited manner. He did so with gusto. Following a brief stint in custody shortly after succeeding to the dukedom (when he owed £58,900), he busied himself in accumulating fresh debts, which the surviving FitzGeralds of his father's generation – now living at Carton and Kilkea on Mallaby-Deeley's sufferance – decided to eradicate by selling four-fifths of 'the family jewellery, most of the silver, many paintings, including Old Masters – as well as tapestries, porcelain and furniture' in December 1925. Much of it – filling twenty-one pantechnicons, according to one account – disappeared overseas, bought by William Randolph Hearst, who had it delivered to San Simeon.[28]

It was an exercise in futility: by 1936 Edward had notched up his third bankruptcy, owing £139,233. As usual, he was borrowing at fearsome rates of interest. One creditor lent £50, but later claimed £3,075; another demanded £10,000 in repayment for a £2,000 loan. As one of Edward's solicitors observed much later, 'This was not normal money-lending.'

Nevertheless, the family persisted with its efforts to redeem the estate on Edward's behalf. Mallaby-Deeley's price of £400,000 was immense, but it seemed reasonable to assume that it might be negotiable. The FitzGeralds offered him £250,000, a very attractive proposition since it amounted to nearly four times what Sir Harry had paid Edward. But he proved unwilling to negotiate. In the mid-1920s he had attempted to dominate the market in men's cut-price suits. Demand was huge – the phrase 'not in these Mallaby-Deeleys' temporarily entered the language – but for once Sir Harry's financial acumen deserted him. After three years, during which his factories turned out 5,000 suits a week, he abandoned the experiment, saying that it had cost him £60,000. It might have been because of this setback that he mortgaged his rights to the FitzGerald estate to the Legal and General Assurance Company, although by the time he died, in 1937, his fortunes were very much recovered, despite the distractions of his new wife, his former secretary, Miss Edith Maude Shoebridge, whom he had married in 1935.

Edward could have interpreted this as evidence that Sir Harry had emerged, belatedly, as a kindred spirit. He preferred not to do so. Writing in the *Sunday Dispatch* in 1957, he claimed that Mallaby-Deeley's refusal to accept his offer had 'ruined' his life. It is difficult to know if Edward really meant that. Eight years later, he showed himself in a more attractive and convincing light when he acknowledged: 'I've made every mistake you can.' The assessment displayed a degree of self-awareness absent during much of his life. In his final decade, it ebbed away completely. Less than a year before his death in Pimlico – by which time he had irretrievably lost Carton, been reduced to hiding from creditors hammering at his door, and done his utmost to alienate himself from his only legitimate son, accusing him of being the offspring of a Piccadilly money-lender called Witkowski – he turned angrily on his fourth wife when she described him as a black sheep. He had, once more, come to see himself as Mallaby-Deeley's victim, rather than the author of his own misfortune.

In the 1930s, though, the blinkers had yet to descend; the night before Rafaelle, his second wife, had her appendix removed, Edward visited her at her Park Lane nursing home. He gave her a toy black lamb. 'Hold fast to this little black sheep,' he said, 'because I am the black sheep.'

By then he had become public property, a cherished figure in a novel public forum, the gossip column, one of which was written by his old friend Castlerosse, whose figure was ballooning gratefully, and fatally, on Beaverbrook's expenses. Edward's vulnerability was palpable. His book-making acquaintances sensed possibilities; so, too, did a gentleman with offices at 38 Parliament Street. This was the lair of Maundy Gregory, a char-latan in whom greed, venality and chutzpah fruitfully coalesced. The son of a clergyman, he had gone down from Oxford without a degree, had been fined £5 whilst a theatrical manager for employing an under-age dancer (she was seven), and served ingloriously in the First World War (unspecified 'intelligence work' kept him in London). A charity performance in aid of earthquake victims had taught him, however, that parvenus would pay unhesitatingly to bracket themselves with the aristocracy. Backed by Jack and Harry Keen-Hargreaves (their father, John Keen, a clerk, had died in the Sick Asylum in Poplar, east London, though that did not prevent Jack from styling himself 'Baron J. C. Keen-Hargreaves'), Gregory founded and edited *Mayfair*, a weekly magazine in which, he explained, 'business and society could rub shoulders'; business paid for the privilege, just as it did after the war, in Gregory's new magazine, the *Whitehall Gazette* (men on the make paid between £50 and £500 for the honour of being profiled). By 1918, it was unsur-prising that Gregory should have been introduced to Freddie Guest, one of Winston Churchill's favourite cousins, Liberal Chief Whip in Lloyd George's Coalition government. Guest put Gregory in charge of selling titles and honours, an illegal practice in which both political parties had freely indulged for more than thirty years but which now became an industry with 'a recog-nized tariff: £10,000 for a knighthood, £30,000 for a baronetcy, and £50,000 upwards for a peerage'.

Edward's ancient dukedom and complete penury made him irresistible for Gregory's purposes. The latter proposed that if Edward married the woman to whom he was introduced, he would be paid £100,000. Edward did not dismiss this out of hand. Nor, though, did he immediately accept, despite Gregory's insistence that the marriage would be one in name only, allowing Edward full scope to amuse himself elsewhere. 'Gregory,' Edward later remembered, 'tried so hard to get me to marry the woman... that I think he had already received payment from her.'[29]

Edward eventually decided against the deal: having once sold himself, he was marginally more circumspect about doing so again. Another plan to snare an heiress, concocted by a London bookie, Tommy Dey, was much more tempting. Dey and his fellow bookies noted that the 5th Earl of Carnarvon had made himself half a million pounds richer by marrying an American (Alfred de Rothschild's illegitimate daughter) and that other noblemen had followed suit. 'Lord Curzon – with the prospect of Kedleston to keep up – married the daughter of a millionaire shop-keeper from Chicago... The 4th Earl of Strafford married the widow of Colgate's soap. One New York heiress successively married the 2nd Marquess of Dufferin and Ava and the 4th Earl Howe... The prizes were out there, for those with the nerve to take them.' When Dey offered to put up £3,000 (paid in instalments, a necessary precaution) to enable Edward to travel to America, accompanied by the engaging fraudster Gilbert Marsh, Edward agreed.

The scheme was blissfully simple. Marsh would ensure that the Duke was never short of appropriate company – women who were rich, eager and vulnerable to the unique appeal of the British peerage. After Edward was profitably married to one of them, he would pay Dey £10,000. This was an infinitely more agreeable arrangement than the one he had made with Mallaby-Deeley. At the very worst, it meant several months loitering in America, being drip-fed cash. Edward even felt bound to point out that he was quite likely to meet and marry a pretty stewardess, rather than find a wealthy woman whom he found acceptable.

As it was, he was offered an assortment of prospective brides. There was an Egyptian woman with a weakness for all-in wrestling (happily as a spectator, rather than participant); there was Margaret Brown, a widow who was much older than him, whose late husband – a 'coal man', according to Edward – had left her $120,000 (he had, he added, known Mrs Brown for years, could have married her, and perhaps should have done); and there was Mildred Logan, another widow (this time of a stockbroker), who had seven Rolls-Royces – one for each day of the week. Edward was captivated. He didn't mind Mrs Logan either, considering her 'an attractive woman, dark, though greying a little and very vivacious'. He proposed, and was accepted.

The engagement lasted several months, during which time Edward stayed with Mrs Logan at her house on the Hudson, playing golf each morning, while she went riding. The arrangement might have seemed unimprovable: Rollses, golf, an attractive wife who, given a certain amount of luck, might predecease him. But Edward sensed that intolerable curbs on his freedom lay ahead. Mrs Logan talked incessantly about horses; worse, she obliged him to attend horse shows. 'We even went down to Kentucky to see one,' he wrote. 'That was too much for me.' Retreating to New York, Edward spent much of his time entertaining an English girl – 'pretty, fair; her mannerisms were a nice change from the Americans' – called Barbara. But he didn't marry her. He reserved that privilege, instead, for a handsome brunette who was already married and had no money of consequence. Ignoring these impediments, Edward proposed whilst they were sightseeing from the top of the Empire State Building, three weeks after they first met.

According to one of her surviving acquaintances, Rafaelle van Neck was 'a honey'. She also had the necessary reserves of self-delusion to accept Edward's proposal. Though she had experienced five years of lukewarm marriage to an English consumptive, Clare van Neck, she retained a weakness for what she called 'the elegance of rank', remaining in thrall to the British upper classes, who 'spoke so beautifully, and had such good manners, and a type of quality and breeding the like of which I had never known before'. Edward she saw as a 'rather wistful young man', rather than a forty-year-old divorcé who was warming up for his third bankruptcy, and Ireland as a 'timeless, dateless, gentle land', despite the fact that most of its country houses were freshly charred shells. Kirkdale, where they spent the first three weeks of their honeymoon, was 'a most lovely house in Yorkshire' – an unusually generous description for what is, in the words of the grandson of its then owner, 'the sort of dump put up [at the turn of the nineteenth century]'. Even when, in due course, Edward deserted her, she did not abandon her faith in him, seeking out his creditors, pleading for their tolerance and patience.

Her tractability was not exceptional: young and old proved susceptible to Edward's charm. So did the Duchess of Windsor, though the intensity of their friendship may never be conclusively proven. Even his aunt Nesta – noted by Rafaelle for her 'disapproving manner and spinster chill' – was not immune, reputedly remarking: 'All he has to do is smile, and you forgive him for everything'. When not quelling disapproving relations, Edward turned the gulf between his pedigree and circumstances to romantic advantage. His last three wives recalled how he poured out versions of his life story – the death of his adored mother, his eldest brother's illness (imprecisely specified), his impetuous marriage to May, Desmond's fatal accident in the trenches, the agreement with Mallaby-Deeley. Each performance was delivered in a gentle, almost bemused manner – he always seemed vague, remembered one of his step-granddaughters – which guaranteed him sympathy. Once that sympathy had been engaged, women became aware of Edward's other qualities. He was, remembered one of his step-daughters, an 'amusing, loving man, wonderfully well read, highly intelligent, [blessed with] an inquiring mind... [but] no pride'.

Nevertheless, his second wedding, in December 1932, was followed by what Rafaelle would describe, in an echo of May Etheridge, as a nightmare of a marriage. She had had a partial preview of what was to come when, soon after they met, Edward rang her from his hotel room at the Ambassador to say that he wouldn't be able to come to lunch. He was, he explained, being held by detectives until he paid his bill. Would she come over with some money? Rafaelle hurried to the Ambassador, offering a diamond brooch in lieu of payment; Edward was released, though a sympathetic hotelier declined the brooch. (Rafaelle later said that she believed that Mallaby-Deeley settled the bill.)

Once married, Edward allowed her to assume control of every aspect of their domestic arrangements (just as he would with his third and fourth wives). Rafaelle coped admirably – too well, in fact, since her resourcefulness prolonged Edward's misconception that he could continue as before. Supplementing Edward's allowance from Mallaby-Deeley with about the same amount again from her mother, and helped by the minimal wages then paid to domestic servants ('five in England cost little more than the price of a couple in the United States'), Rafaelle employed a staff of cook, butler, housemaid, tweenie (a junior servant whose duties were typically split between kitchen and bedroom), chauffeur, lady's maid and part-time secretary, and paid 'the rent, living expenses, doctors, dentists, clothes, entertaining and so on.' 'We lived,' she recalled, 'in comparative style and comfort. It was not as grand as other dukes, but I could make a shilling look like a pound [and] clothes off the peg look like models.'

But she could do nothing to eliminate Edward's debts, many of them contracted at impossible rates before his trip to America. Nor could she cool his scalded mind. They moved seventeen times in three years. There was a flat in Portland Place, momentary refuge at the Connaught, a house in Hertford Street, a grey stone lodge on Mull, lodges in Ireland, manor houses in the Cotswolds; even Wales was considered. Each time Rafaelle signed the lease (a duty which Edward, an undischarged bankrupt, could not perform), and each time Edward commanded a change. Occasionally, Rafaelle recalled, Edward would receive notes whose contents he declined to disclose but which invariably caused him to disappear. 'Off went Edward to London where he stayed for several weeks,' she remembered of one desertion, which left her stranded in Ireland. 'God knows where, or with whom and why. I waited and waited with the dogs, until finally he came back and we settled down again to a temporary lull before the next storm.'

By now, Edward's only friend of any social standing was the man they knew as 'The Priest', the Reverend H. B. Allen,[30] vicar of Didbrook in Gloucestershire, 'a monument to the preservative powers of whisky and a firm believer in free love'. Rafaelle dignified him as Edward's old tutor, adding that most of his pupils (whom he took for Latin and Greek) were 'gay blades and peers of the realm', one being Michael Hicks-Beach, 2nd Earl St Aldwyn; another, an unusually tall aristocrat whose cast-off overcoats the Priest would wear when in London. A Didbrook villager, Hilda Archer, remembers Allen's appetite for early evening cricket ('when they were supposed to be doing lessons'), his five-minute sermons (delivered 'so quickly you could never understand a word he said') and his alliance with Bert Edwards, a Londoner and First World War shell-shock victim who acted as his handyman-chauffeur whilst operating a sideline as village barber (sixpence-a-time, in the vicarage kitchen), although, as one of Bert's customers, Glyn Wright, remembers, 'shell-shock and hair cutting was not the best combination', a fact confirmed when Bert cut 'a large bit out of [a] neighbour's ear'.

When not enjoying solo adventures or receiving the Priest's tuition or risking cranial damage from Bert's scissors, Edward found time for jaunts, jointly undertaken with Rafaelle, to New York, Jamaica, and even, soon after their wedding, Carton. It was the first time Edward had been back for many years. Locals massed around the Maynooth Gate: at the house, a hundred estate staff waited beneath a 'Welcome Home' banner and a band prepared to play 'America, my America' in Rafaelle's honour. Edward ordered the chauffeur to stop the car soon after it had turned in past the gate; he suggested to Rafaelle that they walk the rest of the way, so that he could show her the glories of the park. A few moments later, their car swept up to the house. Family retainers raised their hats, and were about to cheer when it dawned on them that their new Duchess appeared to have arrived without the duke. The 'new Duchess' was in fact Marden, Rafaelle's companion. 'I hadn't a clue then how like "My Imp" it was to avoid things,' Rafaelle later wrote, remembering how, even after they finally reached the house on foot, Edward had slunk behind a pillar, leaving her to stand alone under the 'Welcome Home' banner, acknowledging the crowd and the band, which played the 'Londonderry Air' and 'Home Sweet Home'.

Edward's taste for avoiding things, combined with his appetite for pepping himself up with new female acquaintances, soon finished off the marriage. Over lunch one day, Rafaelle asked him if he was sure that it was all right for her to sign yet another lease, this time for Inverawe House in Argyllshire. Edward assured her that it was. Later that afternoon, she was at home when a letter came by hand. It was from Edward, telling her that he had taken the dogs and car and fled. 'Only an hour before his letter came he had told me to be happy and send off the lease, knowing, as he must have done, that he was going to run for it,' Rafaelle remembered. 'I had no roots, no real friends... they had drifted away when I married my black sheep. I had no need or reasons to stay. The only thing to do was to ring down the curtain and go home.'

As an example of unadulterated selfishness, it equalled anything Edward inflicted on May. Yet Rafaelle hung on, until a trip to Kitzbühl, where it became blindingly apparent that she was being traded in for the remarkable Denise Wessel. Like May, Denise Wessel had done a stint as a Gaiety Girl. But there the resemblance ended. Born seven years before Edward, she grew up as Jessie Smither, the daughter of bohemian parents, both of them musicians, although her father earned his living as a judge's clerk. Whilst in her teens she had taken the stage name Denise Orme, in which guise she attracted the attention of a Guards officer known as 'Yardie', John Yarde-Buller, then ADC to the Duke of Connaught, subsequently the 3rd Lord Churston, charmer and reckless gambler (his losses had already precipitated the sale of the family's Cornish estates). They married in secret at Kensington registry office in 1907. The future Lady Churston bore her husband two sons and four daughters, later offering her girls the advice: 'If you marry well, darlings, love will come later'.[31] Familiarly known as Jo, she had an indisputable talent for making male pulses quicken. Even at the end of her life, remembered one of her granddaughters who saw her naked ('by mistake – the doctor was visiting'), she 'still had the most startling figure'.

By 1928, she had wearied of 'Yardie', who, heedless of his reduced circumstances, insisted on living in the manner to which his family had long been accustomed. She defected to Theodore 'Tito' Wessel, a Dane whose looks, she reflected, 'were too striking for an Englishman to admire', who had been left 'an enormous fortune at an extremely early age and had become... a law unto himself', a trait he partially expressed by keeping two monkeys and a lion at his house at Winslow. Their marriage proved short-lived, ending in Tahiti, Wessel deciding that he preferred the talents of a native dancer to those of his wife. By then Jo had borne him a son, and was as at ease with members of the Danish and other continental royal families as she was with the conventions of aristocratic British friends, like the Marquess and Marchioness of Headfort.[32]

Rosemary FitzGerald, Edward's granddaughter, who was only sixteen when she met Jo for the first time, describes her as a wonderful, very dramatic character, while one of Jo's sons-in-law, the 13th Duke of Bedford, wrote that she was 'one of the most enchanting and fabulous characters' he had ever known, someone who had 'never really left the stage', who needed, and secured, an audience wherever she went. Astute with money ('she looks frightfully vague,' noted Bedford, 'but the first thing she does in the morning is to pick up the *Financial Times* and juggle with stocks and shares with fantastic insight'), she had, at the time she met Edward, a London house, in Hamilton Terrace, as well as Beech Hill Farm in Sussex. More importantly, she possessed a self-assurance that none of his other wives – or lovers – would ever match. Whereas Rafaelle, a talented pianist, had felt too intimidated to play her Steinway when Edward was around, preferring to listen with him to his recordings of Wagner's *Ring Cycle*, Jo performed whenever the mood took her. Before being lured to the stage, precocious talents as both a violinist and a vocalist had won her scholarships to the Royal Academy of Music and the Royal College of Music respectively. During the war, when Beech Hill lay on the flight-path of London-bound doodle-bugs, she thrilled her grandchildren – and, quite probably, the paying guests she took in to defray household costs – by 'rush[ing] out into the garden with a frying pan on her head, to fire [a flare]', thereby alerting the nearest airbase that an enemy rocket was en route.

Those who saw Edward with Jo at Beech Hill could have been forgiven for concluding that he had finally conquered his tendency to self-destruction; if they were meeting him for the first time, they would have been hard pressed to guess his past fecklessness. 'Uncle Fitz was the opposite to her but they were happy,' recalled one of Jo's granddaughters, part of the wartime gang of children at Beech Hill. '[There were] six children in the house, if not eight, at all times. [We were] nothing to do with him. But he was always utterly charming. He was a very gentle, kind person, a magical person for children – gentle and sweet and thoughtful. He was incredibly well read and very interesting. If we were ill or it was a nasty day or one of us was away from school, he used to read to us – poetry which was slightly over our heads, but he did read incredibly well. He used to take my brother off looking for butterflies and things.'[33]

Edward's new extended family included Jo's third daughter, Lydia. At the time, she was married to Ian Lyle, heir to a Scottish baronetcy (and a scion of the Lyle sugar suppliers), who was serving in the Black Watch. Their son Gavin (later to experience Edward's driving skills as a schoolboy in Jersey) was seven months old when news reached Beech Hill that his father had been killed at El Alamein. In these most wretched of circumstances, Edward came into his own. 'We all wept buckets,' remembered Lydia, four years before her death. 'Then there was Fitz. Hugging my little son every evening while my mother played Chopin… He worked at all the hateful jobs round the house, like wood-cutting, coal fetching, dust-bin emptying, garden jobs of the unpleasant side [sic], pruning, turf laying, sweeping up, pulling brambles! All this without a murmur of dismay.' Edward's capacity for work even impressed itself on one of his step-grandchildren. 'He was very thin, but very energetic,' she remembers. 'We, as children, did not treat him as an old man. He wasn't old looking.'

At the outbreak of the Second World War, Edward was forty-seven, twice married, thrice bankrupted. He had failed as a father, beggared the family fortune, and disgraced the FitzGerald name. But in wartime Sussex, some kind of serenity, some kind of redemption – a chance to prove himself the man he intended to be – seemed to be within his grasp.

* * *

At the end of October 1960, the Yarde-Bullers and their cousins gathered at Burrow Hill Farm, on the edge of Chobham common, for Jo's funeral. It was raining hard, 'a hideous day', remembered Caroline Tahany. 'The entire family was there, even my uncle Dickie [the 4th Lord Churston]. We hadn't seen him for years.' The ever-vibrant Jo had died in her bath at her Chelsea flat. Although she was seventy-five and had suffered a minor stroke earlier in the year, her death was unexpected, so much so that most of those at Chobham found it difficult to accept that she had gone for good.

But a more intense shock awaited them. Before the family set off for Chobham church, another mourner arrived, glasses misted with rain, hair smeared over his face, a grim macintosh clinging to his frame: an 'appalling looking figure, absolutely soaking wet'.

Edward had materialized without warning. 'Nobody had seen him for some years,' Caroline Tahany recalled. 'I don't think Granny had; in fact, I know she hadn't. He'd vanished. Nobody knew where he was. One of [my cousins] grabbed his coat off him, and shoved it into the boiler room to dry out.'

Now sixty-eight, Edward had walked from London, a distance of thirty miles. Epic though such a trek would have been for almost any other man his age, it had become almost a matter of routine to him. Nevertheless, he was in evident distress, not because of his forced march but because, in the words of his step-daughter Lydia, he was 'full of unhappiness and regrets'. Caroline

Tahany agreed. 'When we were all saying goodbye to each other, my brother or somebody offered to give him a lift home to London. He said, "Don't be so stupid; I've walked here, and I'm walking back".' For a moment or two, Edward dithered, unable to remember what had happened to his mackintosh. Then it was retrieved, and he began the march back to London.

Jo had made no mention of him in her will (preferring to leave her money to two of her grandchildren, who needed constant care), although this could not have surprised him. His apparent reformation – seemingly dignified by his eventual marriage to Jo in 1946 – had proved illusory. By the early 1950s his conduct had become as disturbing and hurtful to her as it had been previously to May and Rafaelle.

Most of Jo's younger grandchildren, who came to know Edward in the south of France (where he and Jo had decamped after the war), remember him as 'a very weird little man', unlike the avuncular story-teller familiar to their older siblings and cousins from wartime Beech Hill. 'One just saw him, in the distance really. It was extraordinary. [He was] a little figure that appeared and a little figure that disappeared. You never questioned, as a child, why he was there or not; he appeared with a smile on his face, a pair of glasses and grey hair, and never spoke an awful lot to us.' Edward's appearance also made an indelible impression on Caroline Tahany. 'He had very long hair, lots of it. He wasn't over in love with soap and water. He wasn't in love with the razor-blade either. Sometimes he wouldn't shave for days on end. I was really quite shocked as a child. Just after the war, everybody dressed fairly well, and washed, and shaved.' Erratic behaviour mirrored 'Fitz Pop's' untamed appearance. 'Even in the south of France he would disappear for days on end. Nobody knew where the hell he was. He would always arrive, totally unexpectedly, looking slightly confused – he wore quite thick spectacles… He used to walk in through the door, his shoes and coat always filthy dirty. He must have slept rough.'

Perhaps in a miscalculated attempt to compensate for his haphazard desertions, Edward now resorted to petty theft. 'He always had the most amazing presents for my grandmother. This enormous, very exciting parcel from Paris [would be] unwrapped. It was usually some sort of fur garment.' But it had not been bought. 'Unfortunately, under closer inspection, the lining was always creased and it always had a collection ticket in the pocket.' Many women would have blanched when presented with someone else's dry-cleaning parcel but Jo took Edward's unexplained disappearances – and the resultant harvest – in her supple stride. 'He was renowned for doing that sort of thing. Where he got [them] wrapped was always a mystery. Granny was wonderful. She would say, "Oh, Fitz, not again". She was frightfully good with him, very forgiving.'

Even the war, with its irksome petrol rationing and black-outs, had done little to curtail Edward's adventures. Not long after the outbreak of hostilities, by which time he and Jo were living together, he arrived at Netherby, alone, in a caravan, which he insisted on staying in, even when his cousin Sir Fergus Graham implored him to move into the house. Later, he explained his absence from Beech Hill by pointing out that he was serving in the Argyll & Sutherland Highlanders, recording in *Who's Who* that he had retired as a captain in 1942 (when he reached the age of fifty). Although Edward's age and marginal military usefulness would have ensured he was far from the front line, he might well have concluded, as so many patricians instinctively did, that he was required to do his bit, whatever that was, besides which, minimal though army pay was – in 1940, a newly promoted captain received 16s 6d a day – it offered a financial bonus. His success in securing a commission in the Argylls seems likely to have owed something to the influence of his second cousin, the 10th Duke of Argyll, who, from 1914 to 1929, had been Honorary Colonel of the regiment's 8th Battalion.

Jo loyally recorded in her memoirs that Edward had been 'quartered in a tent near Stirling'. Yet his duties appear to have been less orthodox than that, to the extent that the Argyll & Sutherland Highlanders have no record of him. What is known, within the Graham family, is that he stayed at Netherby for several weeks, if not months, during which time he managed to stray on to the Duke of Buccleuch's land, where the gamekeeper caught him shooting a pheasant. The ensuing dispute – Edward insisted that he thought he was still on Graham land – was recorded in a local paper.

Despite that contretemps, Netherby always remained open to him. Elsewhere, though, old refuges fell: Stoke D'Abernon had been requisitioned for use by the diplomatic corps (Edward's favourite aunt, Helen, took refuge in a converted stable), Duncombe Park became a school, as did Kirkdale. In 1949, Carton was sold – with the Mallaby-Deeleys' permission, and with Edward's blessing. (According to his eldest grandson, Maurice FitzGerald, 9th Duke of Leinster, Edward 'wished to sell everything but [the family] were able to stop him selling the chattels'). Carton fetched £80,000, some of which was used to renovate Kilkea Castle, where Edward's son Gerald and his family lived until 1960. Then, again with the Mallaby-Deeleys' permission, Kilkea was sold; Langston House, in the Oxfordshire village of Chadlington, was bought in its place.

By the 1950s, the last surviving relations of Edward's parents' generation had died, so that he could no longer rely on the web of support which had bolstered him during his periodic crises. He did, though, have Jo, whose resourcefulness extended to her property deals. She bought Château de Pigranel (which boasted a drawbridge, despite lacking a moat) between Grasse and Mougins, running it, like Beech Hill during the war, as the grandest sort of boarding house, open only to her friends and then, in the mid-1950s, a house called Lyndhurst overlooking St Aubin's Bay in Jersey.

Edward's life in the south of France was comfortable, a hybrid of café society – golf with the Duke of Windsor, dinners with expatriate plutocrats holed up in villas outside Cannes, parties with American film mogul Jack L. Warner – and of boarding-house host (on at least one occasion, the Yarde-Bullers remember, he was tipped by guests whose suitcases he had carried upstairs at Château de Pigranel). But comfort came at a cost. 'My grandmother was a fairly dominating woman,' says one of Jo's granddaughters. 'I'm absolutely convinced that she controlled the purse strings. I think she used to be quite strict with him.'

This was never likely to agree with Edward for long. He had probably been at his happiest when at the wheel of their Ford V8, as he and Jo made their way down through France, with what Jo described as a luxurious, two-bedroomed caravan in tow. Stopping each day at 6.30 p.m., they went for an evening walk, allowing them to see the surrounding country and, just as importantly, give Jo's maid, Annie, time to make up their bed, lay the table and cook supper. 'We would come back for a cocktail before dining,' remembered Jo, who recorded that Edward carried a pistol at all times (there had been unfortunate incidents of roadside banditry) and filled the hip bath in which they washed each morning. 'It was a wonderful life... both Fitz and I loved it.' Nevertheless, even this idyll came at a price, Jo insisting that a shovel and sack were to be kept in the V8's boot. 'Horse manure was the prime target,' remembers Richard Grosvenor, one of her grandsons, explaining that Edward was expected to scoop it into the sack ('come rain, shine or dinner jacket') for subsequent use in Jo's flowerbeds.

Shovel duty continued once they had settled at Pigranel, where Edward found his routine more precisely choreographed than ever before. When not playing assistant guest-house manager – visitors included the Duke and Duchess of Leeds, Lady Diana Cooper, Lord and Lady George Cholmondeley, and assorted displaced continental princelings – he helped entertain the Windsors and other friends on what Jo liked to call her yacht, a boat bought with an unexpected windfall 'of a few thousands'. The Windsors reciprocated with regular invitations to dinner, at one of which their hostess asked Edward if he thought Jo would sing for them. He assured her that she would, suggesting 'My Love is like a Red, Red Rose' to Schumann's setting. Jo complied, just as she did to further requests from another of the Windsors' guests, Sir Winston Churchill.

From time to time, Edward broke free from these parades, either on one of his unscripted solo 'shopping' expeditions, or to Woburn, seat of the Dukes of Bedford, where his stepdaughter Lydia was now living with her husband.[34] But soon these safety valves were not enough. Edward, who later wrote appreciatively, perhaps wistfully, about Jo's 'lovely daughters', felt it was about time that he had a lovely girl of his own. 'He was', reflected Lydia, 'a very energetic, young-thinking man; this sent him in another direction.'

* * *

He met Miss Yvonne Probyn at a cocktail party which she was giving at a house in Belgravia, 85 Eaton Terrace. The attraction was mutual and instantaneous. Although he had only quite recently married Jo, Edward was soon entertaining Miss Probyn whenever possible (she is said to have described him as a 'wonderful lover'), wooing her with a generosity that he could not afford (dinner at the Ritz was a particular favourite), much as he had wooed May forty years earlier. Agreeable though this was, Miss Probyn was eager for a more formal arrangement. Unlike the adaptable Jo, she was a conservative woman of thirty-four, whose family had distinguished itself in the services and the medical profession.[35] According to one account, Edward was sufficiently taken with Yvonne to ask Jo to divorce him; when she refused, he suggested to Yvonne that they should 'try for a child... [Jo] would never stand in the way of a child'.

Compared with most of Edward's plans, this one was at least partially successful: on 17 October 1952, at a private nursing home in Blackheath, Yvonne gave birth to a son, christened Adrian. Edward put his name on the birth certificate, gave his occupation as peer of the realm, and paid the fees at the nursing home. But that was the end of his contribution to Adrian's upbringing. Despite his insistence that he was a 'rebel', he lacked the stomach for eloping with Yvonne; nor, though, did he revel in his betrayal of her. Faced with the choice of abandoning his lover or his wife, he chose to jettison both. The twin disengagements, falteringly effected, were vintage Edward, inflicting pain on, and causing lasting damage to, everyone involved, himself included.

Miss Probyn, who had changed her name by deed poll to FitzGerald before Adrian was born, left London with her son to live in Ireland, but returned, hoping that Edward might marry her. Jo was not in the mood to concede. Her memoir recalls her unhappiness, though not its cause: 'France was becoming too much for me in every way... We had intended motoring home... but Fitz's affairs had made this impossible... I am afraid I was very sad and depressed on arrival [in London].' Nevertheless, although profoundly hurt by Edward's behaviour – 'I think,' says one of her granddaughters, 'that [Adrian's birth] was when my grandmother reckoned she'd almost had enough' – she was, as Caroline Tahany put it, a 'tough cookie'. She refused to allow Edward a divorce, apparently concluding that being a duchess was one of the little luxuries that she had earned by putting up with him for so long.

By 1956, though, Edward had reached the opposite conclusion: he abandoned his marriage and the new house on Jersey, and with them his struggle to be the Duke of Leinster, although not before raiding Jo's funds, apparently to finance investments on the turf. Jo was wrecked. 'I had never seen her so upset,' remembers Richard Grosvenor, who happened to be staying with his grandparents at the time.[36] Edward appeared not to care. Installing himself in a service flat off Baker Street, he now embarked on life as 'Mr FitzGerald'. First, though, he decided to wring one last advantage from his ducal status. Still an undischarged bankrupt (as he had been for the past twenty years), he sold a version of his life story to the *Sunday Dispatch*. The payment, probably around £5,000, could have bought him a London pied à terre, where he might have fashioned a life of modest bachelor comfort on his £1,000-a-year. Edward, though, continued to prefer feast and famine. Still leaking money with the incontinent profligacy he had displayed as a twenty-year-old, he ensured Miss Probyn enjoyed dinners at the Ritz, made his usual attempted investments on the pools, and lunched regularly with an old friend – Rafaelle, now living in Grosvenor Square.

Entitled 'My Forty Years of Folly', his story was serialized in the paper for six successive weeks. It was not an era given to analytical introspection. Edward chose, instead, to recall youthful adventures, such as an evening of excess presided over by Ahmad, Shah of Persia, at a restaurant in Paris, at which seven dancing girls emerged from a grotesquely large pie (the Shah then plunged his hand into the pie and dragged out baubles – a piece of jewellery for every woman and a gold cigarette case for every man). When remembering May, he was contradictory, in one instalment saying that he had never been in love with her; in the next, claiming that she was one of the loves of his life, and insisting that they were still friendly at the time of her death. Just before the serialization began, Edward regaled Rafaelle with his latest plans to redeem his life interest, then asked her to remarry him, seemingly indifferent to Miss Probyn, and apparently forgetting that he was by then also enjoying an association with Vivien Conner, the caretaker at his block of flats. But this was not indifference or forgetfulness; Edward was on the verge of disintegration.

A few days after the first instalment of his story appeared, he took an overdose. It was, he claimed on the front page of the next edition of the *Sunday Dispatch*, the result of a misunderstanding, a case of mistaking a bottle of sleeping pills for painkillers prescribed for rheumatism in his knees. This was a face-saving fiction. He had left a letter for Rafaelle, telling her that, by taking his life, he would be able to leave her better off than if he lived. To Vivien Conner, who found him unconscious on his bed, he offered a different explanation. That evening, during dinner, she had told him that their affair was over, explaining that she was no longer interested in being just another of his women. According to Vivien, Edward then persuaded her to return to his room, where he produced a bottle of pills, threatening to take them if she left him. Vivien told him to go ahead, assuming that he would not. On the bus home, she realized that she had left her briefcase in his room. She returned to collect it. When there was no answer at the door, she turned the handle and went in. Edward lay, grey and motionless, on his bed: a copybook preview of his eventual demise at 87 St George's Drive, nearly twenty years later. A telephone call, an ambulance cutting its way through Saturday night traffic, five days in the Middlesex Hospital – Edward was saved, in body if not spirit. Dismal years as the 'bedsit duke' awaited him.

Soon he was trying to supplement his annual £1,000 allowance by polishing stair rails on the Cadogan Estate. 'I believe that my father gave him a bedsit in Lower Sloane Street, and a job polishing brasses at various blocks of flats in Chelsea,' remembered Caroline Tahany. 'He was highly unreliable, but he did it quite beautifully when he did it.'[37] Still in a distressed state of mind, Edward found some consolation in a new hobby. He took up marathon walking with masochistic zeal, inspired by Dr Barbara Moore, a Russian-born woman of disturbing intensity ('ungenerous, driven and unaffectionate'). Her achievements were remarkable, however. In the late 1950s, sustained by a diet of wild grass and honey, she walked 3,000 miles across America; in subsequent years, she tackled Canada and Australia. Edward did his best to emulate her, frequently walking thirty miles in a day, and attempting to win a walking race from John O'Groats to Land's End, only to be thwarted when his companion, Vivien, could not keep pace with him.

Perhaps these exertions helped Edward to re-establish some kind of emotional equilibrium. By the early 1960s he was installed in a white-washed cottage in Kent, designing children's clothes, and selling them – as well as afternoon tea – in a shop called Jour et Soir. Anonymity delivered freedom, which he was anxious to preserve. A reporter traced him to the shop. 'How is your Grace?' asked the journalist. Edward replied blankly that he was 'Edward FitzGerald'.

Unfortunately, his fourth wife was stimulated by the idea of achieving aristocratic status. Born Vivien Felton, her upbringing had not prepared her for exalted rank: her father had been an impoverished accounts clerk. In 1956, when she first met Edward, she was 'unused to wine' – in fact, had never drunk it. She was also married to George Conner, by whom she had a son, Tony, who was later to display uneven talents as an entrepreneur (he established a gallery in Cork Street after making an unsuccessful foray into one of the service industries). Initially unaware of Edward's title, Vivien, who was twenty-eight years younger than him, thought that he might be a professor; she allowed him to borrow milk from her fridge. These marginal beginnings eventually led to marriage on 12 May 1965 at Brighton register office. 'I was worried by Fitz's girlfriends,' Vivien said later, acknowledging her anxieties. 'I wanted to be the only one, not one of five or six.' As soon as her position had been dignified by matrimony, she liked to stand in front of a mirror and practise saying – in an accent stranded between Belgravia and Battersea – that she was the Duchess of Leinster, for which Edward teased her very gently. Together, the couple began a steady, irreversible descent into poverty.

Like Jo and Rafaelle, Vivien was resourceful, though in a lower key. She prodded Edward back to the Bankruptcy Court in 1964, where he was finally discharged ('Some of the creditors,' observed the registrar, 'would have to come accompanied by the fanfare of trumpets'), and eventually, in 1975, to take his seat in the House of Lords for the first time, fifty-three years after he had inherited his title. She had already helped him establish his dual businesses in the cottage in Rye, but success in these proved elusive. Eventually, there were scores of disgruntled creditors, some of who made fruitless attempts to pursue the duchess for bankruptcy. For a time, Edward was splendidly indifferent to his reduced circumstances. According to Vivien (who mimicked her husband by selling a version of her life with him to the *News of the World*), he was a frequent visitor to the pawnbroker, accepting half a crown for a tiepin, or a pound for his overcoat. As at Beech Hill during the war, he seemed to revel in adversity. When he and Vivien took part in a *World in Action* programme examining the lives of Britain's non-royal dukes, he appeared agile, healthy and contented – utterly unlike the bedraggled depressive who had shambled on to Chobham Common for Jo's funeral or the would-be suicide of nine years earlier. Once again, he seemed to be enjoying breaking the rules: he avoided creditors by crawling across the floor at the cottage at Rye, and fed the electricity meter with bottle tops.

He and Vivien moved frequently: from Rye to Brighton, to Ennismore Gardens in Knightsbridge, to Malta, where they had an agreeable five-roomed flat in Sliema. But the pace began to take its toll. Edward's kinsman, Peter Duncombe, 6th Lord Feversham, occasionally encountered him in the late 1960s, including once at a cocktail party, when Edward struck him as 'thin, nervous and somewhat haggard with... a somewhat more robust wife in tow'.

At about the same time, Edward's behaviour assumed an edge of calculation that he had not displayed before. He apparently began making, and keeping, copies of the letters he wrote, including the one to his son Gerald, in which he alleged that Gerald's real father was the money-lender Witkowski.[38] In January 1967, a few days before sending this letter, he and Vivien paid an unscheduled visit to Langston House, Oxfordshire, home of Gerald and his second wife Anne. Arriving by chauffeur-driven van from Brighton, they told Anne that they intended to reclaim some of the remaining family chattels, including a Joshua Reynolds portrait of Emily, Duchess of Leinster, and an immensely valuable Beauvais tapestry. A brittle exchange of words followed, before Anne telephoned Gerald and the police, who escorted Edward and Vivien from the house, empty-handed. Three months later, Edward placed an advertisement in the personal column of *The Times*, seeking a financier with £130,000 capital who 'should approach British duke to acquire life interest worth annual income of £23,000 net, use of priceless heirlooms and stately home, plus superb reinvestment possibilities'.[39]

The letter to Gerald, the attempted raid on Langston House and the advertisement in *The Times* were wholly out of character. Edward could be – and frequently was – cavalier towards creditors, and to dry-cleaning establishments in France. But whatever his inadequacies as a husband or a father, and however irresponsible he was with money, he rarely, if ever, went out of his way to hurt people with the viciousness that he now displayed. His previous conduct towards Gerald was a case in point. Though content to abandon him during his boyhood, Edward had made a significant effort to attend Gerald's (first) wedding in 1936 (to which he wore not a morning coat but a six-year-old suit), travelling third class to Ireland for it, shortly after being declared bankrupt for the third time. During the 1950s, he invited Gerald to visit him in the south of France and Jersey, invitations which Gerald and Anne accepted.

In the 1970s, he even moved to Oxfordshire for a while, so as to be close to his son. 'He lived briefly in the same village as father,' says Gerald's older daughter, Rosemary FitzGerald, who remembers that Edward would often have Sunday lunch at Langston House. 'We knew him as quite a quiet old man with a small dog. [My father was] terribly pleased when Ed was close by, and it was all sort of more normal. He liked that, and valued that.' So, too, did Edward, who, near the end of his life, stayed with Gerald and Anne, who converted part of their house into a flat for him, whilst Vivien remained at Ford Manor, another rented house, near Lingfield in Surrey, where she took in paying guests. At Langston, Edward was photographed with Gerald, Gerald's older son Maurice, and Maurice's son, Thomas. 'It was frightfully notable because that was the only conceivable time, in any of those lifetimes, when those four males could have been in the same room at the same time,' says Rosemary. 'It was a great event, really.' It is also potent evidence that Edward was at peace with his son, and his family, which makes his earlier spasms of venom all the more puzzling.

* * *

Throughout his life, Edward had been almost uniquely vulnerable to outside manipulation, a prize to be captured and exploited, whether by successive money-lenders or by Mallaby-Deeley or, latterly, by the press. Oddly, though, as Rafaelle had found when she strove to eradicate his debts in the late 1930s, the money-lenders were remarkably fair-minded. Similarly, though it is easy to vilify Mallaby-Deeley, he and his heirs behaved impeccably, as several of Edward's family acknowledge. But in the last years of his life, it appears that Edward did finally fall into the clutches of a singularly venal chancer, a character who feigned concern for his plight whilst milking the old man for whatever small advantage he could deliver.

Edward's illegitimate son, Adrian, may have understandable suspicions that this culprit was Vivien; he points out that she intercepted letters which his mother, Yvonne Probyn, wrote to Edward, begging him to honour his promise to marry her, if Jo died. 'Dear Fitz [Yvonne wrote, in 1963], You always made me a solemn promise that if this were made possible, you would legitimize Adrian [legitimizing a child after birth became possible in 1959, following a change in the law]. I do beg and implore you to do so, as he will soon have to go to public school. He is an unbelievably handsome boy, brimming with health and always happy. He is also very intelligent, quick on the uptake and very interested in birds and animals – a son to be proud of.'

Edward did not reply.[40] According to Adrian, Vivien ensured that he never saw the letter, nor others that his mother wrote. But if Vivien were capable of cruelly overstepping the mark when safeguarding her relationship with Edward – and, with it, a significant advance up the social scale – she seems unlikely to have possessed the malign flair to suggest that Gerald was the son of a Piccadilly money-lender. In September 1967, by which time she and Edward had taken refuge from creditors by settling in Malta under the name Taplow, a solicitor described her as 'utterly feather-brained' – not, in other words, the sort of person equipped to mount a campaign of organized malevolence against her stepson. That, at least, is the opinion of Edward's legitimate family, who believe instead that someone else wormed his way into Edward's favour, persuading him and Vivien that they were somehow being cheated by Gerald. The same creature, says Rosemary FitzGerald, continued to do damage after Edward had died. 'He took to visiting [Vivien] and saying, "They're mistreating you".'

In his final decade, Edward found it increasingly difficult to elude the press, who invariably found a 'friend' on hand to comment about the latest misfortune of the 'Bedsit Duke'. After Edward's death, just such a 'friend' remarked that the duke had had an 'insatiable love for both [money and women] and not a clue as to their value'. Yet, despite his restless, consistently faithless behaviour, Edward was not a conventional womanizer, indifferent to the consequences of his actions, but a man riddled with regret. By the same token, he had no insatiable love for money or for the trappings of aristocracy, and had adjusted to the new, staffless post-war order – the age of Hooper, as Evelyn Waugh stigmatized it – without demur. Nor did he need to be bolstered by cronies. In 1965, he told *World In Action* that he and Vivien didn't really see anyone apart from each other. It was no exaggeration. When, a decade later, he finally took his seat in the Lords in July 1975, he said that he knew only one or two peers, adding that most of his contemporaries were dead.

Edward had cut himself adrift from them many years before, however, as Rafaelle had observed during their marriage. The 2nd Earl St Aldwyn, a former pupil of the Priest, and a guest at Edward and Rafaelle's wedding, was alive and flourishing in 1975, enjoying his eighteenth year as Conservative Chief Whip in the Lords, but he never mentioned Edward to his son, Michael Hicks Beach, 3rd and current Earl St Aldwyn. Edward's first cousin and trustee, Brigadier Denis FitzGerald, said that he seldom saw Edward, who remained similarly aloof from another cousin, Edward More O'Ferrall.[41] Edward's granddaughter, Rosemary, says that, immediate family aside, she has never met anyone who knew her grandfather.

Nevertheless, Edward seemed grateful that his belated arrival in the Lords promised to ameliorate sixty years' vagabond existence. Announcing that he would speak occasionally – 'whales, porpoises, animals, that sort of thing' – he said that he would attend two or three times a week, noting 'There is some money in it, isn't there? Not much, but it will help.' He was unsure what 'the going rate' was. In the event, he never made a maiden speech[42] or even attended the Lords, except for the State Opening of Parliament that November, when he was photographed disappearing beneath the family coronet (last worn, said a note on the box in which it was found, for George III's coronation in 1760), which was several sizes too big for him. (FitzGerald ermine had proved less durable: the robes had disintegrated. Edward was reported to have hired replacements from Moss Bros for £8.50.)

Press photographs reignited television companies' interest in his story; there were suggestions that he might write his memoirs. Regrettably, how-ever, after spending Christmas at Langston, Edward was lured away by a trip to America, intended to raise money for a short-lived charity to which he had been persuaded to lend his name, the All Ireland Distress fund, founded to aid the victims of Irish terrorism. The expedition was a fiasco. Even before Edward and Vivien set off, aboard the *QE2*, they had been advised to leave Ford Manor by the police after receiving a number of what Vivien described as 'peculiar telephone calls', which had preceded the unsolicited arrival of two men who drove up outside the house and remained watching it from their car.

On arrival in America, they were told by the British Ambassador in Washington, Sir Peter Ramsbotham, that their tour was an embarrassment to the British government. The FitzGerald coronet, only recently retrieved from the bank vaults, and brought across the Atlantic to excite American sensibil-ities, went missing. Edward and Vivien returned wretchedly to England on a Polish steamer. Debilitated and humiliated by the trip, they resigned from the All Ireland Distress fund and took refuge in a bedsit at 87 St George's Drive. A Press Association reporter visited them. He recorded that their soli-tary room (15 ft by 20 ft) housed a two-ring stove, two single beds, a coffee table, a fridge, a chest of drawers, a wardrobe and a 'broken tubular easy chair'. Within three months Edward was dead.

Only a decade earlier, his annual allowance of £1,000 had been enough for one man to live on comfortably enough; by the mid-1970s, it meant inescapable poverty. Three years before his death, he made a fruitless attempt to sell 25ft square parcels of land in Sussex to credulous Americans. By 1976, confused and distressed by his predicament, he had come to believe that he was being denied money that was rightfully his. According to Vivien, he was particularly depressed on 8 March 1976. He was, she said, convinced that a letter containing good news was going to arrive that day. While waiting, he grew restless. Twice or more, he took his dog out for the briefest of walks. When the letter did not appear, he drank some whisky. Later on, in the afternoon, Vivien emerged from the bathroom to find him sitting on his bed. An empty bottle and two sleeping pills lay on the floor. He told her, 'I have taken some', but was unable or unwilling to say how many.

A desperate 999 call and a futile chase through the traffic to the Westminster Hospital followed. His last words, reported by Vivien, were not of regret, just a plea: 'Oh, for the peace of Ford Manor.' In the days that followed, his elder son Gerald weathered a storm of abuse from his stepmother, who announced that she did not want him or any of the FitzGeralds at Edward's funeral. He had to contend, too, with the emergence of a claimant to the dukedom – a retired school teacher from California who said that his father had been Maurice, the 6th Duke, who had not died at Craighouse in 1922, but had emigrated after 'abdicating his title' in favour of Edward.[43] It was an aptly vaudevillian climax to Edward's public career. The private business was concluded in secret. Only those who had been closest to him attended his funeral, which was discreetly organized by Gerald so that its whereabouts eluded the press. Of Edward's wives and lovers, only Vivien was there. Adrian, Edward's younger, illegitimate son was not invited.

May was long since dead. After Edward abandoned her, she lived on a small allowance from the FitzGeralds (who obliged her to style herself 'May Murray'), took destructively to drink, was profligately and indiscriminately generous, and died of an overdose in 1935.[44] Her mother, a widow, spent her savings on her daughter's funeral, remarking that she didn't give a damn for the FitzGeralds. Edward attended the service nevertheless. Yvonne Probyn, who never married, had died in 1973, a victim of cancer. She was only fifty-nine, but almost certainly broken, as her son Adrian argues, by unhappiness.

Rafaelle fared better, although she too died in distress. Declining the Earl of Southesk's enduring entreaties to marry – reputedly because she preferred to remain a duchess – she lived for several years at the same flat, 15 Grosvenor Square, where she kept a portrait of Edward, and from where she trotted out for lunch at Claridge's with friends like Dame Barbara Cartland. In the end, though, her talent for making a shilling look like a pound deserted her. Her telephone was cut off after she failed to pay a bill for £577.74; then a number of her cheques bounced at Claridge's. 'Rafaelle has no money at all now. She kept turning up at Claridge's, wearing galoshes and with holes in her stockings, demanding to be given lunch,' reported Barbara Cartland. 'She made a terrible scene each time they turned her away.' The hotel did what it could in mitigation. A former employee recalls how the general manager, alerted to Rafaelle's arrival by the light system on his desk, would ring the duty manager to ensure that the duchess was given a plate of sandwiches and was seen by the hotel doctor. Another friend, Sir James Cayzer, witnessed similar acts of charity. 'I remember her,' he says, 'sitting in the hall, being fed by the waiters for nothing. She would sit by the fireplace with a bow on the back of her head. Pathetic.' In November 1993, she was finally removed from Grosvenor Square and admitted to the psychiatric wing of St Luke's Hospital, Muswell Hill; then, shortly afterwards, to Athlone House Hospital in Highgate. She died a month later.

Although unlikely to have been aware of it, Rafaelle had outlived Vivien, who remained in London for several years after Edward's death in a flat provided for her by Gerald, until in 1987 she decided to return to Brighton, where she took up once more with her first husband, George Conner. She died in 1992. Rosemary FitzGerald and her half-brother John (Gerald's younger son by his second marriage) attended her funeral, and were, says Rosemary, 'made extraordinarily welcome by her family'.

There was another consolation for the FitzGeralds. Catastrophic though Edward's financial legacy was, it could have been worse: had he inherited everything on Maurice's death in 1922, he had had the appetite and temperament to have run through it within years. Perversely, the Mallaby-Deeley agreement offered the family a form of protection from Edward, although understandably they did not see it like that at the time. When he died, there was no question of repurchasing Carton; on the other hand, the few treasures not dispersed in the 1926 sale, which had been in Gerald's safekeeping for decades, first at Kilkea, then at Langston House – as well as what remained of the family fortune – reverted to FitzGerald ownership.

The Mallaby-Deeleys, oddly enough, fared little better. Sir Harry had not formed his association with Edward for the sake of immediate pleasure or momentary advantage. His was a calculation made for the long-term: one which, he could have been forgiven for thinking, would ensure that the Mallaby-Deeleys – newly hyphenated, recently raised to the baronetage – would prosper for several generations, invulnerable to all but a Bolshevik revolution. But none now bears the Mallaby-Deeley name, intensely though that would have pained Sir Harry. Anna Cull, one of his four great-grand-daughters, his only surviving descendants, lives in comfortable but modest circumstances in Sussex. Neither she nor her three sisters is rich, partly, she thinks, because Sir Harry's son, Sir Guy Mallaby-Deeley (known in the family by his second name, Meyrick), spent freely, in a manner of which Edward might have approved.

When Sir Harry died, the press confidently asserted that he had left the bulk of his fortune – estimated to be between £1 million and £2 million – to his young second wife. But Sir Harry died without making a will (in England, at least); probate records show that he left £488,863 gross, but a net figure of only £178,789.[45] Meyrick, on the other hand, who did make a will before dying in 1946, left the comparatively unprincely sum of £8,495 12s 6d. Yet, even so, the Mallaby-Deeleys should have benefited from the FitzGerald estate for another thirty years. Anna Cull, who was brought up by her stepmother, heard only a fragmentary account of her great-grandfather's agreement with Edward. Bizarrely, the family solicitor, Gordon Allan, said that it had damaged the Mallaby-Deeley fortune. 'We were told that it cost us money – that Edward lived too long,' she remembers. Regrettably, it is not possible to ask Mr Allan why he reached this perverse conclusion. Anna Cull recalls that he was ejected from his own company, F. R. Allan & Co.; a few years later, he and his wife drove into Epping Forest, and gassed themselves on the fumes from their car's exhaust.

It was an appropriate postscript to Edward's life story: simultaneously pathetic and apocalyptic. He had been born when aristocrats defined themselves purely by birth, rather than by bourgeois notions of accomplishment or conduct. By the time he died, Carton was arguably better known for its brief association with Marianne Faithfull – a tenant, for a time, in Lady Emily's Shell Cottage – than for the centuries during which it had been the seat of the FitzGeralds. But if his descent into oblivion was emblematic of a ruling class in irreversible decline, his march to damnation was uniquely his own. The *Sunday Dispatch* had been right when, introducing his 'Forty Years of Folly', it had called him 'one of the strangest characters alive today'. So was Caroline Tahany, when describing him as 'a very nice, very, very hopeless man'.

PART TWO

'From time to time he disappeared from the civilized area and returned with tales to which no one attached much credence – of having worked for the secret police in Bolivia and advised the Emperor of Azania on the modernization of his country. Basil was in the habit, as it were, of conducting his own campaigns, issuing his own ultimatums, disseminating his own propaganda, erecting about himself his own blackout… he was used… to a system of push, appeasement, agitation, and blackmail, which, except that it had no more distant aim than his own immediate amusement, ran parallel to Nazi diplomacy.'

Evelyn Waugh, *Put Out More Flags*

Victor

By June 1940, the air raid warnings were incessant, the nightly scramble for the dug-out a familiar routine. The Luftwaffe's ripest targets lay a few miles away, in the docks at Southampton and Portsmouth, but there always seemed to be a spare stick of incendiaries for the Isle of Wight, perhaps especially for Albany naval barracks. Over the next two months, the bombs ploughed fairly harmlessly into the surrounding fields, but on 16 August – the start of the Battle of Britain – there was an impromptu change of tactics. About a dozen Messerschmitts came in lower than ever before, diving to only fifty feet, then machine-gunning the village and the buildings beyond, a good burst hitting the hospital (but missing the Roman Catholic chapel next to it). Astonishingly, no one on the ground was killed or even wounded. Not a single shot was fired in retaliation... these were inmates of HMP Camp Hill.

The inadvertent attack on the prison was the sort of mistake that any pilot flying for Führer and Fatherland could have made, which might partly explain the restrained tone in which the details were jotted into the Governor's logbook. Then, as now, Camp Hill was a structure of colonial dignity – the governor's block colonnaded, the prison entrance gates embellished with circular finials, all entombed within a siege-withstanding wall (much the same sort of wall, in fact, as surrounds the neighbouring barrack block of Albany,[1] which the Luftwaffe presumably believed it had been taking on); then, as now, Camp Hill's cells measured approximately 6ft by 9ft, although today a pool table, darts board, payphone and colour television offer some diversion to the misfits and inadequates of St Patrick's wing. In 1940, their predecessors experienced a more abrasive regime. If ever addressed by prison staff, it was to hear a name, number or command barked out, perhaps when being paraded for morning inspection (their sheets and blankets already folded into bed blocks), drilled on the square, marched to chapel (attendance compulsory), or when cleaning boots, making mattresses or mail bags (eight stitches to the inch), or working outside in the potato fields.

From the day it opened in 1912 until 2 September 1939, Camp Hill served as a borstal, each of its wings taking the name of a saint, rather like houses at a boarding school. But wartime exigencies saw it pressed into the prison service: on 4 September, two days after closing as a borstal, it reopened to admit 100 inmates from Wormwood Scrubs, a further 133 arriving the following day. Almost certainly amongst them was Victor Hervey (pronounced 'Harvey'), son of Lord Herbert Hervey, and nephew of Frederick Hervey, 4th Marquess of Bristol.

A couple of months earlier, on 6 July 1939, at the conclusion of an Old Bailey trial – chronicled under headlines about 'Mayfair Men' and 'Crime under the Cloak of Friendship', and watched from the public gallery by Douglas Fairbanks Senior and the former King and Queen of Siam – Victor had been sentenced to three years' penal servitude. 'It is said,' reflected the Recorder, Sir Gerald Dodson, as he singled out the twenty-three-year-old aristocrat from his three fellow defendants, 'that for every man there is a high way and a low. You have chosen the low way of living, and it has led you into the shadow and doom of this disaster. How low you have stooped, you alone know.' Victor's father, a gentle man who had retired from the Consular Service a decade earlier, broke down and wept.

In later life, Victor barely acknowledged the two years that followed,[2] certainly never discussed or dissected them with his eldest son and heir, John, or, seemingly, with any other member of his family. Nor did he offer an explanation for the events which led to his conviction. 'Victor never spoke about anything connected with that time,' remembers the second of his three wives, 'and I never asked him.' But on his release in June 1941, Victor did briefly speak to a newspaper reporter. 'For a year,' he said, 'I have been in the prison hospital with bone trouble following strain whilst I was working.' He did, indeed, suffer from a chronic bone condition, yet he emerged from prison 'fit and sun-burnt', according to the reporter, whose description matched the newspaper's accompanying photograph, suggesting that Victor might only have been briefly in the Camp Hill hospital, if at all.

As others learned, his recollections – often entertaining, always vividly recounted – rarely approximated to the truth. Later in life, he rescripted his military record, uninhibited by the fact that an inadvertent Luftwaffe attack on Camp Hill was the closest he had come to seeing action. To his son, John, he said that he had been awarded the Sword of Honour at Sandhurst; to

Gerald Howson, author of the definitive account on arms dealing during the Spanish Civil War (in which Victor claimed to have played a vigorous part), he insisted that it had been 'the Monarchists who won the war for Franco'. Their troops, Victor explained, were far better disciplined and determined than the rest. 'Several ex. British officers on the correct side all Guardsmen (including myself) led charges on foot in the customary manner with Pipers and buglers and as at Narvik[3] the opposition were so confused at these amazing apparitions that they mostly ran away.' The truth was less illustrious. Victor had, in fact, been removed from Sandhurst late in 1934, having failed the junior course – judged 'temperamentally unsuited' for a career as an officer, according to a police statement read out at his trial. Nor does it seem likely that he set foot in Spain during the Civil War, still less commanded men in battle, though his attempts at arms dealing might have provoked the occasional fracas in his personal front line, the bars of Cannes.

But if his army days were nipped in the bud, and his glimpses of the battlefield were confined to the weekly Pathé news reel, his taste for firearms was real enough. A couple arriving for a shooting weekend in the 1960s at Ickworth, the Herveys' Suffolk family seat, noticed Victor leaning from an upper window. As they drove nearer, he opened fire (whether with a revolver, rifle or shotgun, his guests were uncertain. 'We didn't stay to find out. We practically had to run for cover'). During his marriage to his first wife, Pauline, Victor usually favoured a revolver, using it, on at least one occasion, in unorthodox manner, in London. A family friend recalls passing the Bag o' Nails, a pub on the Buckingham Palace Road, in the company of Pauline and John, her son by Victor. 'That,' Pauline said to John, gesturing at the Bag o' Nails, 'is where your father emptied a revolver into the ceiling.' It is possible that some of Victor's other targets were not inanimate. He assured a friend, Moira Lister,[4] that he had shot two men in a mutiny whilst treasure-hunting on Cocos Island, 360 miles off the coast of Costa Rica. According to one of John's friends, the claim might have been uncharacteristically modest. 'We found a packet of photographs,' he remembers. 'One of them showed Victor standing with his foot on four dead bodies.'

But the picture was inconclusive proof of Victor as cool-headed marksman, homicidal maniac or accidental bystander, since without third-party corroboration even his photographs offered imprecise clues to his past accomplishments. This one did, though, capture a profounder truth: it showed Victor doing what mattered – striking the right pose, one which reassured him, during his lifelong shriek for attention, that he was where he believed he belonged, at the top of the heap.

Known as 'the Reptile' by some of his family, equipped with what one apologist described as a 'splendidly villainous appearance', the subject of a Black Book diligently maintained by various of his cousins, he was, says one relation (admitting that he is influenced by family prejudice), 'a nasty, creepy' boy who tore wings off flies, who continued to use violence – sometimes the threat of it, to be administered by others – as a means of youthful self-assertion, before maturing into a fantasist, a charmer, a raconteur, a relentlessly generous host, a drunk. By then, he was quite frequently likened to an eighteenth-century eccentric, an assessment that probably consoled him. He knew, however, that others still spoke of him as the last man to have been publicly flogged in Britain and, worse, bracketed him with his eldest son, John, Earl Jermyn, many of whose excesses were being exuberantly performed on the public stage.

* * *

No other aristocratic family has been, or is, so glibly dismissed. The Herveys, it has been confidently and repeatedly asserted, are genetically destined for damnation: programmed for lives of cruelty, self-indulgence, untamed lust and ultimate self-destruction. But their recidivist gene is unpredictable: it may lie dormant for several generations, only to resurface centuries later. It is a seductive theory, suggesting that, no matter how long the poison has previously remained inert, a couple of drops of 'Hervey' will be enough to pervert an unborn child in its mother's womb. Just as beguilingly, it links Victor and his progeny with the vibrant narrative of their eighteenth-century forebears, who, between them, inspired the remark – often attributed to Voltaire – that there are three sexes: men, women and Herveys. Of these restless ancestors, Carr Hervey (1691–1723; known, following his father's elevation to an earldom, by the courtesy title Lord Hervey) was relentlessly promiscuous, even by the demanding standards of the eighteenth-century court, entertaining scores of maids of honour, as well as Catherine Walpole, wife of William Walpole, generally considered to be Britain's first Prime Minister, very possibly impregnating her, and so becoming the father of Horace Walpole, belletrist and novelist, whose posthumously published correspondence helped crystallize posterity's opinion of the Herveys.

It was Carr's half-brothers – John (devout bisexuality), Thomas (exhibitionism of a specialist kind) and William (profound cruelty) – who really established the family's credentials. John (1696–1743; who after Carr's death became Lord Hervey, and, until his own early death, heir to their father's earldom) was, according to William Pulteney, Earl of Bath, 'such a nice composition of the sexes, that it is difficult to tell which is the most prae-dominant' – a quality which earned him a number of sobriquets, among them 'Lord Fainlove', 'Lord Fanny' and, courtesy of Alexander Pope, 'Sporus', the boy whom Nero had castrated, then married. Thomas, by comparison, was notably single-minded, running off with Lady Hamner, the young second wife of Sir Thomas Hanmer (Thomas Hervey's father's oldest and most loyal friend). During the rest of his seventy-seven years, Thomas rescued himself from anonymity by writing noxious open letters (one of which Walpole described as 'beat[ing] everything for madness, horrid indecency and folly, and yet [having] some charming and striking passages'), several of them addressed to the luckless Hanmer, others to Pitt the Elder. William's sexual predilections went unrecorded, but the report precipitating his dismissal from the navy found that he had treated his officers, 'particularly Lieutenant Hardy, with the most unmerited and unwarranted severity, and the crew in general with a rigour bordering on barbarity'.

The next generation yielded Augustus (1724–79, 3rd Earl of Bristol), a vice-admiral whose relentless sexual energy went unchecked by scruple,[5] and Frederick, Victor's direct forebear. Although untroubled by a vocation or much discernible religious belief (according to one acquaintance, he 'treat[ed] even the immortality of the soul as an article of doubt and indifference'), Frederick was ordained, appointed a chaplain to the king, and subsequently became Bishop of Cloyne, then of Derry, thanks to the intercession of his eldest brother George, 2nd Earl of Bristol, and Lord Lieutenant of Ireland. By 1779, Frederick had succeeded as 4th Earl of Bristol. Known thereafter as the Earl Bishop, he was disinclined to fritter time on his wife (though she had borne him five children) or the church, and devoted most of his energies to touring the Continent,[6] often for years at a time, collecting art and antiq-uities as he did so. Although frequently distracted by women – in particular, Emma Hamilton, wife of his lifelong friend Sir William Hamilton, and mistress of Nelson – his trophy-hunting was so successful that he soon lack-ed space for his collection at his Irish seat, Downhill Castle, which he had begun building in 1776. The solution, he decided, was to build two additional residences, one, Ballyscullion, in Ireland, and the other in place of the Tudor hall which stood at Ickworth, Suffolk, where the Herveys had settled in the 1400s.

Increasingly obsessed by his art – his visits to Ireland were rare but not easily forgotten[7] – he verged on complete disintegration when Napoleon's troops seized a trove of his acquisitions, which were being stored in Rome. Detained for nine months in Milan at the Castello Sforzesco, he was released in February 1799; during the last four years of his life, his unkempt appearance and unsteadiness in the saddle ensured that he became a creature of fascination. 'His figure is little, and his face very sharp and wicked,' recorded an Irish girl, Catherine Wilmot. 'On his head he wore a purple velvet night cap with a tassel of gold dangling over his shoulders and a sort of mitre in the front; silk stockings and slippers of the same colour, and a short round petticoat, such as Bishops wear, fringed with gold about his knees... The last time I saw him he was sitting in his carriage between two Italian women, dress'd in white Bed-gown and Night-cap like a witch and giving himself the airs of an Adonis.' Three months later, he died on the road from Albano to Rome.[8]

Several years earlier, he had heard that his nephew, George Fitzgerald (son of his older sister Mary), had been hanged for murder. He knew, too, that his second daughter, Elizabeth, known as Bess, was enjoying an uninhibited menage à trois in the company of the Duchess of Devonshire (née Lady Georgiana Spencer) and her husband, William Cavendish, 5th Duke of Devonshire (whom Bess in due course bore an illegitimate son, finally marrying him after Georgiana's death).

The 'Hervey Germ', as the family's 'bad blood' has been described, had potently expressed itself for the third successive generation; according to popular theory, it then lay dormant for the next two hundred years, before being revived once more in Victor (and, subsequently, his eldest son John).

But there had been no evidence of the 'Hervey Germ' in several preceding centuries. Of French extraction – Hervey is an Anglicization of 'Herve' – the family had been established as prominent landowners in East Anglia since the Conquest. During the sixteenth and seventeenth centuries, they were periodically knighted for their services to the Crown, and one of them ennobled (though the title died with him when his two marriages produced only one daughter between them).[9] The 'bad blood' then erupted, without precedent or warning, following the second marriage of John Hervey (successively 1st Lord Hervey, and 1st Earl of Bristol) to Elizabeth Felton, a granddaughter of the 3rd Lord Howard de Walden. Together, they produced the ungodly trinity of John, Thomas and William, as well as thirteen other children, some of whom survived to sane and conventional adulthood.

The Earl Bishop's eldest son, Frederick, was advanced to a marquessate in 1826, ushering in an era during which the Herveys were invariably as dutiful as their predecessors. Discordant notes were few. Some of the family's Irish cousins had a tendency to emigrate to Canada; one of them founded and edited *The Rambler*.[10] Otherwise, they were very nearly the embodiment of aristocratic virtue: benevolent to their tenants, philanthropic to the deserving poor of Brighton[11] (where, in 1831, the 1st Marquess bought 19–20 Sussex Square), steadfast in their service to church and state. Some exhibited intellectual brilliance; according to his mother, the 1st Marquess passed his examinations at Cambridge with 'such wonderful credit and éclat that he was declared first of his year in every subject'. If that assessment owed something to maternal hyperbole, there was no disputing the abilities of Lord Arthur Hervey, the 1st Marquess's fourth son. After taking a First in Classics at Cambridge, Arthur studied Hebrew, Arabic and Sanskrit, helped revise the Authorized Version of the Old Testament and became Bishop of Bath and Wells (and a tennis champion).

Above all else, these Herveys' personal lives were models of orthodox contentment. The 1st Marquess married for love, much to the disgust of his father, the Earl Bishop, who had an illegitimate daughter of the King of Prussia in mind for him. Successive generations followed his example. They displayed no carnal appetite for their own kin: the only instance of members of the family marrying each other dated from the seventeenth century. Even then, the couple were third cousins; and they were childless.

Perhaps the bad blood – or a certain susceptibility to misanthropy – simply needed the right conditions to trigger it into fruitful expression. Towards the end of the nineteenth century, one of the Earl Bishop's great-great-great grandsons was delivered into exactly such conditions – a marriage so loveless that the child produced by it once remarked that he had been conceived out of spite. His father, who drank to excess, greeted the birth of his son and only child by leaving home 'not to return or be seen for months to come'. It was one of many such desertions, some of them lasting for years at a time. Most of the boy's first years of infancy were spent alone. Shy, short-sighted, intelligent, he was then consigned to Cheam prep school, whose headmaster's sadism cauterized those who suffered it. Eton proved little better. When he was just nineteen, his father died, bequeathing him an ancient title and a fortune that could only be described as immense.

It was as if the 'Hervey Germ' were being lovingly stimulated in laboratory conditions. But it failed to stir. The Earl Bishop's great-great-great grandson wrote poetry, medieval epics and Byzantine plays; he bought the Haymarket Theatre, befriended Bernard Shaw, G. K. Chesterton, Hilaire Belloc and Max Beerbohm; he bought two ancient, ruined castles and painstakingly restored them; he took up fencing, and was good enough to be selected as Britain's reserve at the 1908 Olympics. He was a bibliophile of such distinction that his advice was sought by experts from abroad. At thirty-one, he married, and remained married to the same woman until his death.[12] He was the 8th Lord Howard de Walden – one of Victor's fourth cousins – whose son devoted a chapter of his own autobiography to the remarkable life which his father had been too modest to record.

The contrasting lives of Victor and his kinsman indicate how facile it is to attribute Victor's flaws and inadequacies solely to his Hervey bloodline. Herveys, whether male or female, did not self-replicate: they married and procreated in conventional fashion, refreshing – or muddying – but undoubtedly extending the gene pool with each generation. But if precise genetic analysis is elusive, the broader influence of the eighteenth-century Herveys on their descendants is indisputable. Whereas similarly aberrant, lewd behaviour would have gone unrecorded if perpetrated by a less prominent family, theirs was observed and lovingly chronicled, by Voltaire, Horace Walpole and Samuel Johnson: a battery of anecdote, jotted into letters or diaries, ensured that the reputation of the Hervey/Felton era survived, super-charged, through the coming generations of unwavering decency.

There was, however, more to the legacy than an extensive lexicon of delinquency; there was Ickworth. Though the Herveys were soon parted from both the Earl Bishop's Irish houses,[13] they kept hold of his most extraordinary creation, or at least its foundations. Described by the Earl Bishop's wife as 'a stupendous monument of folly', Ickworth extends 600 feet from the end of one wing to the end of the other. Impressive its scale may be, but it is its central Rotunda, embellished with friezes of the ancient Olympic games and with others inspired by Homer's *Iliad* and *Odyssey*, which liberates the building from convention. The Earl Bishop intended to live in this immense lozenge, whose height – rising to 104 feet at the centre of its dome – would allow him to enjoy rooms with thirty-foot high ceilings on the ground floor. His lungs, he explained, 'always played more freely' and 'his spirits spontaneously rose much higher in lofty rooms than in low ones, where the atmosphere is much too tainted with… our own bodies'. The wings to the east and west of the Rotunda, each of them, as his biographer noted, 'the size of a substantial country house', would shelter his pictures and sculpture. But by the time the Earl Bishop expired, the Rotunda was still a shell, and the wings of the house rose barely three feet out of the ground. It was left to the 1st Marquess to complete his father's vision, which he did in diminuendo fashion, deciding that he and his family would live in the East Wing, dividing the Rotunda into a number of grander rooms, and completing the exterior of the West Wing – an aesthetic necessity – though it would house nothing more than an orangery.

Nevertheless, Ickworth was, and remains, a mesmerizing architectural oddity, its impact redoubled by its position in the heart of a seemingly endless park. According to Robert Erskine, a grandson of the 4th Marquess, structure and setting exert a discernible influence on Ickworth's occupants. 'Living at Ickworth is a pretty peculiar thing to do because it's such a strange house. My own grandfather was fairly peculiar. I concluded that this was the result of somebody living in the middle of a park which is nine miles in circumference.' Erskine and his parents moved there when they returned from India in 1940,[14] at which time Victor was experiencing the more constricted accommodation of Camp Hill. But he had spent much of his childhood at Ickworth, often alone, save for the Hervey art collection (which included a memorable portrait of the Earl Bishop, his eyes lit with a playful expression, Vesuvius simmering in the background) and his resolutely feudal uncle, the 4th Marquess, and aunt Dora (née Wythes), a railway contractor's daughter who had brought the Herveys an immense (and badly needed) fortune.

Neither of Victor's parents was in evidence. They were described by one relation 'as two of the worthiest and dullest creatures you could imagine'. That assessment seems half right. David Erskine, who lived with his grandparents at Ickworth for the first thirty years of his life, described his great-uncle Herbert, Victor's father, as 'a very nice chap' who used to come to stay two or three times a year. There was never, he added, any sign of his wife, nor any mention of her. One of Herbert's acquaintances, Tessa Montgomery[15] recalls him as 'a rather sweet old boy who lived in a very gloomy flat in Basil Street'. It is probably as good a summary of Herbert's character and circumstances as any.

Born in 1870, Herbert's upbringing (and that of his older brothers, Frederick, Walter and Manners[16]) was overshadowed by the agricultural crisis. Unlike the FitzGeralds and others who levered themselves out of the quagmire via the Land Acts, the Herveys declined to sell any of their 32,000 acres. Indeed, the boys' uncle, the 3rd Marquess of Bristol – nearly 6'4", handsome, 'deservedly respected amongst the County families of Suffolk', successively Tory MP for West Suffolk, then Lord Lieutenant – continued as before, entertaining in London, visiting Scotland and Brighton, and proposing to give each of the local unemployed an acre of land to till for themselves. Some detected the influence of his wife, Geraldine, née Anson ('very pretty, petite but extravagant'). But far from being able to make philanthropic gestures, Lord Bristol was forced into humiliating economies. At Ickworth, many of the cattle were sold; the shoot was let; so, too, was the kitchen garden, and, finally, the house, to a Mr Wood.[17]

The 3rd Marquess's difficulties inevitably affected his younger brothers and their families, who were, to varying degrees, sustained by the family estate. One of them reputedly died of starvation at his lodgings in the King's Head Hotel in Bungay, proof, perhaps, that in one instance at least, plummeting rents were literally fatal to the aristocracy.[18] Herbert's father, Lord Augustus Hervey, avoided starvation but died, aged only thirty-eight, in 1875 (when Herbert was not quite five), leaving his widow, Mariana, less than £800 (£765,000 today) and seven children to support. Spirited, sharp-tongued and half-Irish, Mariana (née Hodnett) was, however, a practical woman. She had been widowed once before and was prepared to dispense with convention for survival's sake, mining her friendship with the Prince of Wales (the future Edward VII) for financial reward, accepting 'a consideration' from any acquaintance seeking an introduction to him. Far from objecting, Edward rewarded Mariana with a blue and gold snuff box (inlaid with pearls forming the letters 'ER'), and very possibly helped secure her a grace and favour apartment at Hampton Court. In old age, she equipped her grandchildren with pea-shooters when they visited her there, encouraging them 'to attack... any too inquisitive visitor'. She died when Victor was four.

Herbert, her fourth surviving son, had not revived the family fortune. After schooling at Clifton, he had entered the Consular Service. Most of his subsequent career was spent in South America (Chile, Uruguay, Columbia, Peru and Ecuador). But in October 1914, on one of his rare trips home, he married Lady Jean Cochrane, daughter of the 12th Earl of Dundonald. Herbert was forty-four; Jean, twenty-seven; and the marriage, Herbert later said, a mistake. The Herveys agreed: within the family he came to be known as 'P.O.H.' – Poor Old Herbert. Just under a year after the wedding, on 6 October 1915, the couple's only son was born. Christened Victor Frederick Cochrane Hervey, the baby lacked a courtesy title of his own, but had Queen Victoria Eugenie of Spain as a godmother. More pertinently, he had a father who had come late to parenthood, and who was disinclined to lay down the law to his only son.

If Victor's father was indulgent, his mother was indifferent, even negligent. Few of the current generation of Cochranes have ever heard of Jean; those who have know little of her, though one very elderly widow 'remembers being sent out of the room by her mother when the name of Jean Alice Elaine Cochrane was mentioned. Perhaps an indication of her character.' Although she secured herself a job working at the Foreign Office during the First World War – an indication of some level of independence and competence – Jean is variously described as 'not a maternal woman', 'a bolter' and 'flighty', and possessor of 'the best Scotch medicine cabinet in London'.

Her great-grandfather, Thomas Cochrane, 10th Earl of Dundonald, was both hero and villain, the most remarkable of 'the Fighting Cochranes'. In 1809, he played a crucial role in the defence of Rosas, Trinidad's fortress, when others considered it indefensible; five years later, he abetted his uncle in a stock market fraud, for which both were imprisoned. Thomas was additionally stripped of his knighthood and flung out of the navy, but later found alternative employment with the governments of Peru and Chile, secured a pardon and returned to the service as a Rear Admiral.[19] He lived long enough to see his son, also Thomas, later 11th Earl of Dundonald, marry Louisa Mackinnon, daughter of William Mackinnon of Mackinnon, 33rd Chief of Clan Mackinnon. The union is considered by some Cochranes to have been a mistake: Louisa, argues one of them, was 'as mad as a hatter; it's always said that she brought very bad blood into the family – from the 11th Earl downwards there's peculiar...'

The unfinished sentence finds tangible expression on the north Wales coast. About seven miles east of Colwyn Bay, a mass of towers and crenulated, limestone, ivy-clad walls loom over the A55. Roofless, gutted of its marble by New Age travellers, ringed with municipal signs warning visitors to stay out, Gwrych Castle has manifestly seen better days. Yet as a symbol of the follies of dynastic pretension it can hardly be bettered. Jean's mother, Winifred, owner of Gwrych, was tall, assertive,[20] financially independent, far better educated than most other women of the day (fluent in German, proficient in French, authentic in Welsh) and unburdened by beauty; by the time Victor, her first grandson, was born, she was also diabetic, overweight and – in consolation for her abysmal marriage – gripped by fervent religiosity. Her husband, Douglas (son of the 'mad as a hatter' 11th Countess of Dundonald), was almost a caricature of the unflinching Victorian army officer. Good-looking (though shorter than his wife), extensively moustached, the inventor of a Wedgwood teapot, bloody-minded and endlessly brave, he was mentioned in despatches six times in the Boer War, during which he commanded the 2nd Cavalry Brigade, earning national acclaim for the relief of Ladysmith in 1900, and eventually retired in the rank of Lieutenant General. They had married in 1878, when Winifred was eighteen and Douglas twenty-five. The bait for the bridegroom – who, like successive generations of Cochranes, lacked both land and money – was a settlement promising him £2,000-a-year.[21]

It would not be quite true to say that the newly-weds lived unhappily ever after: Douglas was cheerful enough when on active service overseas (which was as often, and for as long, as he could contrive), periodically returning to 'do his duty', as a member of the family puts it, with the result that Winifred bore him two sons and three daughters. By the early 1900s, however, the marriage was over. Winifred took solace in the company of Dr George Alfred Edwards, Bishop of St Asaph (subsequently Archbishop of Wales), a frequent visitor to Gwrych, whom she gave, amongst other things, a frock coat with a collar of lamb beaver fur.[22] On 11 November 1905, Dr Edwards also accepted her invitation to replace her husband as principal trustee of their marriage settlement. The following year, Winifred celebrated her altered circumstances by banning Douglas from Gwrych for good;[23] her involvement with the church, notes Welsh historian Mark Baker, increased significantly thereafter.

It was in these volatile, if diverting, circumstances that Lady Jean Cochrane grew up, her time being divided between Gwrych and London where her mother maintained a residence, first at 34 Portman Square, then at 5 Cadogan Square. The family holidayed in Biarritz and Bayonne, Cannes and Le Touquet; they knew Jack Warner, the film tycoon, and held 'motor gymkhanas' at Gwrych for friends like the Knollyses, Sykeses, Grosvenors, Bowes Lyons, Naylor-Leylands and Llangattocks (whose younger son was making such a success with the horseless carriage). By comparison with the Herveys, the Cochranes were moneyed, metropolitan, unconventional. Jean and her sisters may also have been unusually restless: Marjorie, the youngest – an intelligent, artistic woman – divorced messily and never remarried; the younger of her two sons succumbed to alcoholism. Grizel, the eldest, widowed for nearly sixty years, was an enchanting figure, who displayed a life-long taste and tolerance for alcohol and her Hervey nephew.[24] 'I remember everybody saying how good she was,' recalls a member of the family who met Victor once or twice at Grizel's house in Wilton Crescent, 'the way she had him to tea, when nobody else ever did much for him.' Victor repaid her with unfaltering devotion.

Photographs of Jean show a poised, dark-haired young woman. Her husband was never to see much of her, however: she walked out whilst Victor was in infancy. When in 1932, many years after her desertion, she sought a divorce, Herbert did the decent thing, shuffling off to a hotel in Cliftonville for the night, so as to provide 'evidence' of his adultery. Poor Old Herbert had no lover; nor did he have any money: he drove an Austin and spent most of the rest of his life alone in London at No. 5, Washington House, Basil Street. Jean chose a younger, more vigorous, less impoverished replacement: Sir Peter Macdonald, seven years her junior, a friend of Douglas Bader and Unionist

MP for the Isle of Wight. Jean spent most of the rest of her life on the island, decreeing that her ashes should be interred there after her death, which came in 1955. By then, she seems to have almost completely expunged Victor from her life, making no mention of him in her will, even though he was her only child from two marriages. For his part, Victor rarely, if ever, spoke of her, though in due course he appears to have grown fond of his step-father.[25]

Whilst a boy, Victor had begun to suffer from osteomyelitis, an inflammation of the bone marrow, which, according to his second wife, necessitated surgery. His cousin David Erskine never heard the condition identified, but could vouch for the effect it had. 'I remember him lying on the sofa – when I was about ten or eleven – having his legs straightened. They were bad, for some reason.' Periods of prolonged treatment might explain why Victor spent a year at home being tutored by a governess before going to prep school – Heatherdown in Ascot – and why he was absent from Eton during the Lent Half of 1931. The illness left him with intermittent problems with his back, as well as a slight limp, apparently causing him pain throughout his life. Jean seems to have been stoically indifferent to his plight; perhaps, as some suggest, because motherhood revolted her, or because the little boy was too palpable a reminder of her first husband and her failed marriage.

Winifred may have tried to bring her own brand of consolation to her first grandchild. Towards the end of the First World War, she became much taken by a Mrs Bain, a spiritualist whom she credited with healing her younger son Robin, whose war wounds had proved impervious to conventional treatment. Regrettably, Mrs Bain was able to do very little for Winifred, who was prescribed a diet of bread and milk as an antidote to diabetes and ballooning weight. It was to no avail: she died in 1924 when Victor was eight. Daunting in stature, almost intimidating in piety, she had not been a grandmother to forget. Yet Victor was determined to do just that, preferring to airbrush Winifred and Gwrych from his personal history, even suggesting that his mother's formative years had been spent on a Cochrane estate in Scotland. (There was no such estate: Lochnell, the Cochranes' current seat, was not bought until Jean was twenty-five.)

The instructions in Winifred's will, all of them bitterly precise, ensured that memories of her were not quick to fade. Gwrych was to be offered to George V, as a permanent residence for the monarch and the Prince of Wales; if it were declined (it was), it should become a priory for the Order of St John of Jerusalem; or, if that was considered impractical (it was), it was to be sold, and the proceeds divided between the Order of St John and the Church of Wales (it was; they were). Her estranged husband was bequeathed nothing (but was reminded instead that any of his wife's belongings should be returned to her trustees). Dr Edwards did rather better, receiving £1,000-a-year, tax-free, for as long as he remained Archbishop of Wales, as well as much of Winifred's jewellery.[26] Douglas fought a futile High Court battle to have the will declared invalid. Later, he indulged himself in the Pyrrhic victory of buying Gwrych back, reputedly for £70,000; thought of turning it into a hotel and health hydro; was opposed by his daughter Grizel and abandoned the idea, dividing his final decade between Lochnell and his London house, Wimbledon Park.

* * *

Ickworth and its occupants were marginally easier for Victor to acknowledge. Victor's uncle, Frederick William Fane Hervey, 4th Marquess of Bristol, was a diehard who argued that Britain needed a much larger army and navy 'in order that this country might wipe the floor with any nation which had the temerity unnecessarily to come into collision with it'. Eager to propagate his views, he had interrupted a successful naval career to become Tory MP for Bury St Edmunds in 1906, only to have his time in the House of Commons abruptly curtailed by the death of his uncle, the 3rd Marquess, the following year. After the twin impertinences of the 1911 Parliament Act and the middle-class capture of the Conservative Party, he adapted, as many shrewder aristocrats did, by asserting himself at local level, becoming leader of West Suffolk County Council in 1915, in which position he remained for the next twenty years, sustained by impregnable indifference to whether or not his proposals proved popular.

Uncompromising in all that he did, he considered the water closet a needless luxury for estate cottages, abominated the telephone, and cycled to and from Bury for council meetings until he was well over eighty. His frugality was unsparing and extraordinary. According to one unpublished account, 'He wore his clothes until they were in worse condition than those worn by his labourers... mended his own gloves so often that it was difficult to see which was the original material... made Lady Bristol patch his coats and trousers until they were more patch than coat... [and] never allowed [his daughters] to have both cake and jam for tea, just one of them. This was not meanness, but a matter of principle.'

It was certainly not a matter of enforced economy. Like his youngest brother Herbert, Frederick was brought up in genteel, if not grinding, poverty but had irrevocably altered his circumstances by marrying Theodora Wythes (always known within the family as Dora), who, following her father's death

The Saloon at Carton, the FitzGerald family seat.

Left: Hermione with Maurice and his younger brother Desmond. By the time Edward was born, Hermione had learned how to avoid the marital bed.

Gerald, 5th Duke of Leinster, Edward's father – or was he?

Edward's uncle, Hubert Duncombe: soldier, Tory MP and father of numerous illegitimate children.

Netherby, Cumberland, seat of the Grahams, where, from the age of three onwards, Edward experienced a 'normal' childhood.

Maurice FitzGerald, 6th Duke of Leinster: 'Never the same after he left Eton.'

Craighouse, Edinburgh.

Desmond in 1916: 'To be with him was to sit in sunshine.'

Young Edward: found diversions in a lemur, fifteen monkeys and three Rolls Royces.

Lady Edward FitzGerald: 'Formerly Miss May Etheridge,' noted Tatler, 'the charming little actress.'

Harry Mallaby-Deeley (*right*) golfing in Cannes: he made a good deal; Edward a bad one.

Edward with his second wife Rafaelle. 'It was very fashionable to be a duke and a duchess,' she recalled, 'the Connaught and the Dorchester Hotels were anxious to have us stay with them at nominal rates.'

With his third wife Jo, Edward initially found some content-ment. *Above*: with Jo, her daughter Lydia and grandson Francis. *Left*: with Jo's son, John Yarde-Buller.

With Jo and her son-in-law, Lord Ebury.

Left: Edward, on the verge of disintegration, in 1957. *Right*: on the road with his fourth wife Vivien.

Edward at the House of Lords for the first time, July 1975. The family coronet had last been worn in 1760, for George III's coronation.

Four generations: Edward (sitting, right), his grandson Maurice (standing), his son Gerald (sitting, left) and on Gerald's knee, great-grandson, Thomas.

a servant's job says bedsit Duchess

The Leinster arms. The late duke was the 7th in a line.

87, St George's Drive, March 1976, the final residence of 'Mr FitzGerald': 15ft by 20ft, a two-ring stove, two single beds, a coffee table, a fridge, a chest of drawers, a wardrobe and 'a broken tubular easy chair'.

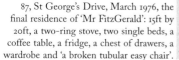

had been made a Ward of Court, dependent on trustees who had ensured she had little money whilst growing up. Theirs was a love-match – the spell reputedly cast over a plate of macaroons Dora had made at cooking class – yet it is not over-stating it to say that their marriage, in 1896, saved Ickworth, a fact immediately anticipated by the Earl of Wharncliffe, Frederick's third cousin, who sent his congratulations referring happily to 'the large fortune which your fiancée has, and will inherit',[27] adding that it would be 'a very good thing indeed' if further charges on the Bristol estates could be avoided. Frederick needed no prompting: by July 1897, he and Dora had pumped £16,000 into the 3rd Marquess's bank account, enabling him to make a critical mortgage payment. Frederick, though, had no intention of allowing his wife's money to gurgle away in one extended futile gesture. Neither his uncle nor his Hervey cousins – George, the estate's ineffectual agent, and John, a vicar – nor those labouring away in the estate office were left in any doubt about Frederick's willingness to speak his mind. There were disputes over interest payments and demands by Frederick for assurances that he would not subsequently be subject to death duties on property which he was effectively buying. The assurance was given and, with John Hervey acting as an intermediary, an agreement reached. The 3rd Marquess was to receive £2,500-a-year (paid into his personal account), in addition to which Frederick would make good any annual loss sustained by the estate up to £10,000. In return, the 3rd Marquess made Frederick the heir to the unsettled estates (the settled estates would, in any case, devolve on Frederick on his succession), as well as to almost all his personal property.

In practice, Frederick and Dora did more than the agreement required them to, feeding the estate with £9,000 in the first half of 1902 alone, for example, whilst also paying off a mortgage to the Wythes Trustees and simultaneously increasing the 3rd Marquess's allowance. The following year, when Frederick became one of the estate's trustees, Dora lent him £310,000 – a staggering amount, about £192 million today – enabling the Herveys to redeem thousands of mortgaged acres.[28] Dora's munificence continued throughout her life, much to Victor's ultimate benefit. Following her husband's succession as 4th Marquess in 1907, she paid for extensive alterations to the house, installing electricity and new bathrooms, and making substantial improvements to the staff quarters. Furniture and objets d'art were restored; sculpture and paintings once owned by the Herveys but dispersed over the years were reacquired. Even in 1950, seven years before her death, Dora took advantage of the demolition sale at Downhill to buy back works which the Earl Bishop had commissioned but bequeathed to his cousins, the Hervey-Bruces.

Together, Frederick and Dora embodied Gladstone's belief that possession of landed property was inextricably associated with duty to the less fortunate. In thrall to neither Celtic prelates nor London spiritualists, their lives revolved around their family, the Church of England, and the county. Far from seeking to repel visitors, they ensured that Ickworth's park was open to all, as Pam Potter, whose father went to work as Ickworth's dairyman in 1939, remembers. 'People used to draw up just on the side of [Ickworth's drive], and take their picnic baskets under a tree nearby. I think the Bristols were really pleased that people enjoyed it. Everybody seemed to like [Frederick]. He never interfered.' Those villagers of Horringer who did not own cars (most of them) were welcome to bicycle or walk through whenever the gates were opened, a task which Frederick reserved for himself on Sundays, when, says Mrs Potter, he invariably 'put his hand out for a tip'.

Never 'socially inclined', as one resident of Horringer put it, Frederick took pleasure in philately, heraldry and working in the park, when 'he would talk with anyone who passed while he was at his favourite occupation of "spudding thistles"'. Dora, according to the same authority, verged on the beatific. 'Nothing was too small for her attention... There was nothing pompous or overbearing about her.' In later life, her clothing tended towards the ordinary, if never quite the scarecrow style her husband favoured. 'She could have been the cook,' recalled John Knight of his first visit to Ickworth after becoming Town Clerk of Bury St Edmunds in 1949. Frugality never developed into parsimonious reclusion, however. Twice a year, the Bristols held parties at Ickworth for the children of Horringer. At Christmas, their young guests received presents from Dora; in the summer, when trestle tables were laid out in the servants' quarters, they were each given half a crown (about a day's pay for Pam Potter's father), after which Frederick took them 'to the top' – the top of the 104 ft Rotunda, from where they could see Ely Cathedral over twenty miles away. He was still leading the way up until the year of his death in 1951, by which time he was within a fortnight of his eighty-eighth birthday.

By dint of unyielding character – helpfully underpinned by immense wealth – Frederick had ensured that the rhythm of life at Ickworth remained unaltered for fifty years. As one of his grandsons reflects, it could be said that he never got beyond the First World War. It might be more precise to say 1900. Life inside the house was utterly without ostentation – self-denying high Victorian, not sybaritic Edwardian – while the estate, though not comparable with Woburn or Chatsworth, was run in a manner which fewer and fewer aristocrats could still emulate. Even in 1940 and 1941, the shoot was maintained by a head gamekeeper, four or five under-keepers, and half a dozen warreners. A further sixteen men or so worked in the woods, whilst many more of the villagers, most of whose houses were owned by the Herveys, depended on the estate for their livelihoods. Frederick was proud to say that he had never raised the rent for any of his sitting tenants; in return, he did not expect to hear requests for building improvements. He also expected to see them in Ickworth church, where his brother Lord Manners Hervey, Rector of Ickworth-cum-Horringer, delivered sermons of testing erudition and length. The family sat on sofas installed in the upper gallery; their servants were seated in specially reserved pews below; the remainder fitted in where they could. 'People would go because they thought they might get the sack,' says Pam Potter, adding that similar considerations came into play at election time. 'I suppose that most of the people voted Conservative because they daren't vote anything else, in case [the Herveys] found out.'

Victor could not help but notice his family's place in the social hierarchy and, despite his absent parents, his own exalted place within the family. In 1915 (the year of his birth), his uncle Frederick was almost fifty-two and Dora forty; the younger of their two daughters was already sixteen. The heir presumptive to the marquessate, Frederick's second brother Walter, was fifty and had been married for twelve childless years to Hilda, by then thirty-four, daughter of the 6th Lord Calthorpe; next in line came Frederick's third brother, Manners, forty-nine and unmarried,[29] on whose lawn the villagers danced after the annual July flower show, and finally Herbert, Victor's forty-five-year-old father. By the time Victor reached Eton thirteen and a half years later, none of these uncles had produced an heir. His destiny was clear: he would, barring his own premature death, succeed one of them – or his father – as Marquess of Bristol; and with the title would come the entailed estates, unencumbered (thanks to Dora) by even a ha'penny of debt.

One family acquaintance, Guy Sainty, an art dealer who met Victor in the early 1970s and subsequently offered him advice about his paintings, believes that the situation was formally recognized soon after Victor's birth. 'There was a new settlement,' says Sainty, explaining that its purpose was to avoid the double death duties which would otherwise be inescapable if Frederick's death were followed in quick succession by that of Poor Old Herbert. The solution, adds Sainty, resulted in Victor supplanting his father as Frederick's heir. This was not especially unusual: estates, like titles, were frequently inherited by nephews, grandsons or cousins. There was, however, a profound gulf between Victor's boyhood status – the only son of an indigent youngest son – and his ultimate position as a senior peer of the realm who would be spared financial anxiety. In the 1920s, the gulf mattered – more than it had fifty years earlier when the aristocracy's pre-eminence had seemed secure (despite the spectre of democracy raised by the 1867 Reform Act). Since then, the landed classes had seen their wealth eclipsed by the breathtaking accumulations of a new plutocratic elite, and had been sidelined in both Houses of Parliament. In these embattled circumstances, the consolations of rank and antique lineage assumed renewed significance.

Etonians of the day, with their acute antennae for social nuance, were especially appreciative of this; sixty-four of them were peers or sons of peers (which Victor, it should be emphasized, was not; nor was he a baronet, of whom there were ten in the school). Still worse, unlike more than half his contemporaries, he was not even the son of an Old Etonian. He had arrived at Eton from Heatherdown in the summer of 1929. Three of his O'Neill cousins,[30] related to him through the Cochranes, were already there, but, bearing in mind that his mother had bolted from view, he could have been unaware of them (and they, older and in different houses, disdainful or ignorant of him). He was not the sort of boy to attract other allies; he was untitled, exhibited no special talent at games or in the classroom, was troubled by an unusual illness (osteomyelitis) and, to an even greater extent than the rest of his class and generation, had been brought up alone, by a nanny. Only the most secure of Etonians would have shrugged off these handicaps without difficulty; Victor was not one of them.

It was at about this time that David Erskine, then three or four, had his first encounter with Victor at Ickworth. It proved brief but disagreeable, for both of them. 'He is alleged to have covered me with something, I don't know what, some muck,' remembered Erskine, 'and was soundly beaten and sent upstairs.' The episode might have been a misjudged prank, or early evidence of the vein of aggression which pulsed, unabated, until petrified by imprisonment. 'Not a skilled player but he goes hard,' a Field Game report noted approvingly in 1929. 'He goes into his man well and is a dangerous player to play against.' But Victor Cochrane Hervey had little inclination to limit his fighting instincts to legitimate arenas. Very quickly things began to go wrong; within two and a half years, and when still only sixteen, he was obliged to leave.

Had he had a more conventional Head Master than Dr Cyril Alington, Victor's departure might have come earlier. Known as 'Creeping Jesus' by many of the boys, Alington was a disciplinarian, but an erratic one. He had reintroduced birching (a practice abandoned by his predecessor, Edward Lyttelton), and was 'ready to dismiss boys from the School, particularly if they

added lying to an initial offence', but occasionally inflicted group punishments (even when he had already identified the miscreant) and sometimes
delegated the exercise of retribution to the President of Pop or the Captains
of the School and Oppidans[31] when it was singularly inappropriate to do so.
Such a lapse in judgement occurred in 1929 when he decided that, rather than
expel two boys who had indecently assaulted another, he would allow them
to be dealt with by the Captain of the Oppidans.

There is no evidence that Victor suffered assault, indecent or otherwise;
he also avoided being consigned to the care of two of Eton's more sadistic
housemasters, H. K. Marsden, known as Bloody Bill, and Sam Slater, who
enjoyed beating boys with their trousers down. Amongst those experiencing
Slater's regime was a diminutive boy, two years Victor's senior, who might
have hoped that school would offer a degree of stability that his home life
had not always been able to provide. If disappointed that it failed to do so,
Gerald FitzGerald, Marquess of Kildare, son of the 7th Duke of Leinster,
did not show it, but concentrated instead on becoming a member of Eton's
shooting VIII, perhaps picturing Slater in the cross-hairs as he squeezed the
trigger, though it was a mountaineering accident which cost Slater his life –
an event poignantly remembered by another member of the house as the
happiest day of his childhood.

Victor's housemaster, A.H.G. Kerry, was neither mountaineer nor sadist,
but an avuncular character, 'dear old "Cyrus" Kerry', in the words of one of
his charges, Alfred 'Freddy' Shaughnessy,[32] who arguably knew Victor as well
as anyone at Eton, 'messing' with him for his first year at school. Victor's
activities (Shaughnessy told his wife and sister) ranged from the casually
pyrotechnic (collecting any newspapers he could find, heaping them into a
pile in the middle of his room and setting fire to them) to the painstakingly
malevolent (electrifying the door-handle to his room, in the hope of delivering a nocturnal shock to the Dame[33] as she did her rounds). But Shaughnessy
seems to have made no mention of the most contentious incident in Victor's
school career, one which, shortly after his death in 1985, provoked a letter
to *Private Eye* magazine. This claimed that a boy called John Dyer – 'an
extremely harmless citizen' – had been selecting a tie at Devereux's, a hatter
and outfitter in Eton High Street, when Victor leaned over and said, 'I want
that'. Dyer objected; Victor thumped him, hitting him so hard that Dyer was
knocked unconscious – the result, added the letter-writer, not so much of the
speed of the punch but the fact that Victor was wearing knuckledusters. 'Why
the Headman, Dr Cyril Alington, did not sack him on the spot we shall never
know. Both boys were swiped for causing a fracas in a public place.'[34]

Victor came close to making a confession of sorts to his oldest son, John, one of whose friends asked why he had not been sent to Eton. 'John said: "Oh, my father didn't like Eton, so I went to Harrow." I asked why Victor didn't like it. [John] said: "When he was there, he almost killed someone – left under a bit of a cloud".' Yet, as Victor's Eton contemporary noted in his letter to Private Eye, randomly inflicted violence was deemed insufficient reason to earn expulsion. Victor was thrown out, instead, for a comparatively humdrum offence. 'He was keeping a book,' recalled David Erskine, adding that Victor was '"asked to leave", which is different from being sacked.' His departure came at Christmas 1931; in 1932, Alington issued a warning to the school: 'Boy bookmakers must not be surprised if they are told that they must carry on their pursuit elsewhere.'

It was fitting that denouement at Eton should have involved money. Of the many destabilizing aspects of Victor's upbringing, the most perplexing is the grotesquely excessive allowance he received whilst at school, generally believed to have been £1,000-a-year (£269,000 today).[35] The money came from Frederick and Dora, an attempt – suggested their grandson David Erskine – to prepare Victor for the flood of riches which would, in due course, come his way. Their reasoning was almost certainly influenced by the dismal fate of Frederick's first cousin, the 5th Earl of Clancarty (1868–1929), who inherited when only twenty-three, was twice declared bankrupt within the following seventeen years, and thereafter consoled himself by running up hotel bills which he could not pay. Yet this ignored an example closer to home – that of Dora herself, who, though brought up almost austerely, had been in a position to lend the Herveys £310,000 in 1903, when she was only twenty-eight, and who was still sane and unspoiled when Victor left for Eton in 1929. Indulging Victor with a huge allowance was a strategy whose success depended on his ability to emulate Dora's self-restraint. Unfortunately, as so many were to discover, Victor defined himself by self-advertisement, a trait which flourished in the years after Eton, but never quite luridly enough to persuade Frederick to disinherit him.

The 4th Marquess adhered to the principle of primogeniture with characteristic rigidity. It was, he believed, inconceivable that an estate could pass down the female line, even as a temporary, defensive measure lasting just a single generation. Perhaps, just as importantly, Frederick was reluctant to think the worst of Victor, whatever his transgressions. Whenever the name 'Hervey' was mentioned, the 4th Marquess of Bristol was ready to ignore, if not wholly to forgive, just as others, a generation later, would immediately condemn. Neither reflex was rational. 'It was very difficult to convince [my uncle otherwise],' recalled David Erskine, 'because he thought, "My heir must be a nice chap", and he wasn't. He rather blinded himself to what a crook Victor was, hoped he would turn out a bit better.'

Last-ditch attempts to extend Victor's schooldays proved unsuccessful. 'He got sacked from two crammers, as well,' remembered Erskine. 'One crammer left him on the doorstep at Ickworth, in the very early morning. He was found there by the chap who opened the front door.' One of the few – perhaps the only – ally Victor had at home was Arthur Lainson, whose parents lived nearby at Horringer House. 'Probably neither of them was allowed to play with the village boys, so they were together quite a lot,' says Lainson's daughter, Diana. 'I don't know that they had that much in common but they bought a car together and drove around, probably before they were [legally] allowed to.' She adds that her father, who died in 2001, periodically remarked that Victor had been a very neglected child, even by the particular standards of the pre-war upper classes. This was the impression also formed by Guy Sainty, to whom Victor spoke of a largely unregulated upbringing during which he had progressed from persecuting governesses to keeping a motorbike (rather than a car), on which, he said, he had roared along the Ickworth cellars.

The abbreviated education, coupled with the deluge of cash received so young, seems to have had lasting consequences. Although undoubtedly possessing an inventive, fertile mind – one which impressed those whose academic training, like Sainty's, had been far more rigorous than his own – Victor never developed the discipline, patience and tact needed to bring his ideas to fruition, just as he lacked the stamina to read a book or experience the rigours of the opera house or concert hall, his preferences respectively being for newspapers and magazines, musicals and jazz. Restlessly commercial, his tastes encompassed offshore schemes, massive developments, small-scale wheezes. The problem lay, says Carol Havers, a close friend for the last three decades of his life, in 'putting them into action. He was full of ambition and good ideas, [but] they never seemed to materialize into anything, as far as I know'. Michael Chappell, whose father Roy was Victor's accountant, agrees. 'Victor thought he'd got a good business brain but I don't think he had,' says Chappell, who later became accountant to Victor's eldest son, John. 'He had lots of promising ideas but none of them were money-spinners.'

After his involuntary departure from Sandhurst (he lasted ten months), Victor became a broker in the City but soon abandoned it when distracted by the Spanish Civil War, a conflict which guided him towards his *métier*: the arms trade. By the time he was twenty-one, his activities were provoking questions to the Foreign Secretary in the House of Commons. Far from recoiling in dismay, still less shame, Victor gave an interview to the *Daily Express*. Energized by the attention ('flashes of remembered fun lighting his dark eyes', noted the reporter), he revealed that he had survived attempts on his life ('He just fired, twice. Yes, point blank'), was a pivotal figure in negotiations ('an armoured car, with escort, was put at my disposal'), who had almost pulled off an astonishing deal ('there was £2,500,000 in it – and half a million would have been mine') and was on the verge of a new, clandestine adventure ('a government – mustn't say which one – are [*sic*] probably giving me a job... something diplomatic'). The traits of a lifetime were on full view: the self-inflationary fantasies, the obsession with big money – unconventionally, if not immorally, made – and what David Erskine categorized as an appetite for telling 'the most appalling lies'. Here was abundant evidence that Victor was, in Erskine's phrase, 'a very difficult person'. His aunt, Dora, recoiled, and stayed away; so, too, did her two daughters, Lady Marjorie Erskine and Lady Phyllis MacRae. But Frederick kept faith, as did Herbert who, almost incredibly, was present throughout Victor's interview, given whilst lolling on a bed in Grosvenor House. In Herbert's defence, it can be argued that he was doing his rather ineffectual best to support his son who was facing significant trouble. Despite Victor's nonchalant manner – he displayed, said the *Express* reporter, the self-possession of a man of twenty years older – he had just been declared bankrupt with gross liabilities of £123,955, although only £6,668 was 'expected to rank against the estate'.[36] It was the first, and perhaps most extreme, example of how Victor's business affairs tended to end in failure.

That was not how Victor saw it. He preferred, instead, to blame his misfortune on the Marquess of Donegall, Hereditary Lord Admiral of Lough Neagh – gossip columnist on the *Sunday Dispatch*. On the 18 April 1937, Donegall disclosed an 'an almost unbelievable tale of spying, counter-spying, bribery, trickery and corruption'. After inveigling his way into their confidence, he had accompanied Victor and his associate, Christopher Lonsdale, a twenty-three-year-old 'man about town', to Finland where they were trying to complete a deal for 140,000 rifles, bayonets and cartridges (valued by Donegall at £2 million, and by Victor at £2.7 million). As intermediaries, Victor and Lonsdale stood to make £50,000 each ('between £50,000 and £150,00,' insisted Victor; £12 million and £36 million today).

The publication of Donegall's story sank the deal, according to Victor. (He was probably right: Donegall made the unhelpful allegation that, though

Victor and Lonsdale were buying the consignment for the Republicans, they were intending to alert Franco's Nationalists when it neared Spain – a betrayal which would earn have earned them an additional £30,000.)

Towards the end of Victor's life, Gerald Howson engaged him in sporadic but detailed correspondence about his role in the arms trade; Howson concluded that, despite obituaries which described him as 'the man who sold arms to both sides in the Spanish Civil War', there was 'good reason to doubt that he ever succeeded, despite many attempts, in selling any arms to either side' – before or after Donegall's intervention. Decades earlier, Victor had done his best to ensure that history recorded a different verdict, asserting that his lucrative new career had begun when he supplied five planes to the Republicans in mid-July 1936. It was, he implied, breathtakingly easy, assuming that you could hold your nerve. One night, in a bar in Cannes, he had been approached by a drunken (or apparently drunken) Spaniard who was looking for aircraft for the Republic; Victor offered him five, at a cost of £5,000 each. The Spaniard was keen, but for reasons best known to himself insisted on paying £10,000 per plane. Victor naturally accepted, and hurried to his contacts, with whom he had options to buy planes (as well as a couple of submarines, had they been required). Within five minutes, he had completed the deal: 'Outside, on the tarmac, were the five 'planes, screws ticking over, all ready for the 20-minute hop to Spain.' Victor paid five pilots £40-a-head to fly them over, and pocketed a profit of £6,300 (£1.5 million today). It was a remarkable coup. Or would have been, had it happened. 'His tale seems a fantasy,' Gerald Howson recorded drily, 'for no group of five French civil aircraft crossed to Spain at this period.'

Other claims splintered under Howson's scrutiny. Victor said that he had ensured that a consignment of Czech planes, Avia 534 fighters, reached the Nationalist forces in Seville. The planes had arrived in Spain in crates; he had personally seen to their unloading, before smuggling them through Republican lines – still in their crates – in a Red Cross convoy 'after a little hubbub waving white flags etc'. In fact, none of them made it to Spain – 'not one,' emphasizes Howson. 'They all got stopped in Poland.' Had they reached their intended destination, he adds, the notion that they could have crossed the lines without being inspected was an 'absurdity'. Victor also remembered a gripping flight in a Spartan Cruiser ('had to come down at Barcelona due to my co-pilot being full of Pernod and the compass not working properly'), which culminated in the plane being put into a double roll. Had this happened, Howson points out, the Spartan's wings would have sheared off.

Victor's memories of the war's dramatis personae were less easily shot down, though he did a pretty good job of it, casting himself as a figure of almost mythic invincibility, a sort of Richard Hannay/Biggles amalgam. Of Agustin Sainz, a Republican airman, he wrote: 'Had submachine gunners at the Gard du Nord to bump me off... His people were panicky and missed. I got them both with a .48. This was all suppressed by the French police.' Turning to one of the Nationalists' most brilliant pilots, Joaquin Morato, he assured Howson: 'I flew with Morato. He never panicked. Even when an engine cut. No radio. No radar and jammed machine guns.' Victor, Howson concluded, was mad. On the other hand, he might only have been drunk: by the early 1980s, he was initiating his daily routine with a 10 a.m. slug of vodka. Even so, Howson did not dismiss everything that Victor claimed out of hand. He had no doubt that Victor had a thorough knowledge of aviation, and had been on familiar terms with a number of arms dealers, fences and sharks; it was more his effectiveness that was questionable.

Victor's chosen trade did, though, offer twin consolations. It established his name in the public mind; little matter that it did so in a manner that would have made others cringe. Learning that the newspapers would take him at his own estimation, he used them to refashion his achievements. He reminisced fondly about Eton, omitting mention of his enforced departure, said that he had made money not only in the City but also at Sandhurst (chartering buses, on which he offered fellow cadets cut-price fares to London), had decided not to take his commission ('having thought it over very seriously'), and celebrated the launch of his own film production company with a party costing £3,000 at 6 St James's Square, the Herveys' London house – 'Seven hundred people. We drank 1,000 bottles of champagne... a trifle too lively for... uncle!' Following another party, a three-day jamboree, he 'drove a car into a row of taxis, just to see whether or not they would buckle up like a concertina.' The legend of 'Mayfair Playboy No 1' was born: no longer could Victor be neglected.

Just as gratifyingly, the arms trade allowed him to fraternize with what might be called the knuckleduster classes, from whose activities he derived both vicarious pleasure and business inspiration. Congratulating himself on his 'knack of collecting odd characters', he had, he said, 'got to know any number of the "boys", and become persona grata with the racing "spivs" and the "con" men, the small timers and the big timers in the twilight world of Soho', and 'found as much amusement in knowing what you might call the low life as... in knowing the fashionable set'. Amongst his acquaintances was Michael 'Mick' Corrigan, born Kenneth Edward Cassidy in the workhouse at Youghal, Ireland, who was sentenced to five years in prison for fraud in 1930 yet managed to establish himself in a flat at 4 Park Lane by 1936. Corrigan's sources of income included jewellery-running, supplying (or trying to supply) aircraft to the Spanish Republicans, and swindling his former customers. His luck ran out a few years later; he hanged himself whilst in Brixton prison.

Absurd and objectionable as Victor already appeared to many of his family and his contemporaries, he nevertheless seemed enviably sophisticated to another stratum of society – the young men who, though veneered with a public school education, were neither aristocratic nor especially rich, who survived the 1930s slump 'living by their wits' (a phrase often heard at the time). Rootless, directionless, some eked out an existence on modest allowances from their fathers. Many of them, noted a commentator at the conclusion of Victor's trial, 'were bred in an atmosphere of uncertainty, of feverish pleasure, of "getting-what-you-want-at-any-cost"… Is it likely that parents driven temporarily reckless by the topsy-turvy world into which they had suddenly been plunged could possibly instil… those principles of self-control so necessary to the growing child?' Others, lacking even the most modest of allowances, were all the more susceptible to ploys for speedy enrichment, especially if expressed fluently, plausibly, by Victor, who treated money with reckless indifference, drank freely and had rooms at 31 Upper Berkeley Street (£2-a-week, breakfast included). One of his fellow lodgers was Ronnie Kershaw, who had been three years his junior at Eton. Although differing routines and friendships almost always kept them apart – Kershaw remembered meeting Victor only once – the younger man received occasional bulletins from their landlady, an indefatigable smoker called Mrs Harlow. One morning she came into Kershaw's room 'in a frightful fuss' and announced that Mr Hervey had returned home in debilitated condition, 'throwing money around', his tailcoat 'dripping £5 notes'. Bearing in mind that 'millions survived on a weekly wage of around £3 10 shillings', her distress was understandable.

Victor's essentially nocturnal regime did not inhibit – indeed, might have stimulated – the almost cinematic presence which he sought to cultivate. It was one which never wholly deserted him, even long after his taut, youthful good looks were lost beneath a mask of what one acquaintance remembers as 'white, etiolated, waxy skin'. When it came to convincing his three accomplices of his plan for the Bank Holiday weekend of 1939, Mr Hervey – so at home in Mayfair and St James's, so assured with Corrigan and associates – proved irresistible. Many of those who, years later, enjoyed Victor's hospitality – even admitted to friendship with him – refer to 'the hotel robbery' or 'that business with the jeweller'. Sir Eldon Griffiths, who, as MP for Bury St

Edmunds, came to know Victor in the 1960s, says Victor could never elude the consequent notoriety. 'That was one of his problems: every time he wanted to do anything, people remembered that he had been one of the few people to have been publicly flogged.' The episode inevitably fascinated Victor's son John, to whom he never recounted more than the most inadequate details. 'People used to say, "My, God, you should see Victor's back – still bears the marks",' remembers one of John's friends. 'We used to try to see him without his shirt on.' Their opportunity usually came when Victor went to a 'sort of study' at Ickworth where he would sit, shirtless, with 'chains and medallions around his neck. John and I used to find some excuse to go round the back to have a good look.' They were intrigued to see that Victor bore no scars.

Lord Hewart, the Lord Chief Justice, who heard the Hyde Park Hotel case, was not a flogger by appetite or instinct, but felt that the events described obliged him to order that two of the defendants should receive twenty and fifteen strokes of the cat-o'-nine tails respectively (as well as significant terms of imprisonment). It was the only time in his judicial career that he passed a sentence of flogging; it is not too taxing to understand why.

One afternoon, Etienne Bellenger, a Cartier director, had received a telephone call at the firm's New Bond Street headquarters; it was a Mr Hambro,[37] ringing from the Hyde Park Hotel, to say that he had become engaged to 'a woman of position' for whom he wanted to buy a ring. Could Mr Bellenger bring a selection – ranging in value from £1,500 to £4,500 – to room 305? At about 3.15 p.m., Bellenger arrived, with rings worth a total of £16,000 (£3,648,000). A few minutes later, he was inexpertly but savagely beaten unconscious, sustaining six fractures and nine jagged wounds to the head. Had his skull not been unusually thick (the jury was informed), he would almost certainly have died.

Details of the case – and Lord Hewart's uncompromising sentencing[38] – inflamed emotion. Soon after the trial, a well-connected woman, meeting Hewart socially, upbraided him for sentencing public school boys to the cat. He was having none of it, arguing that the defendants had been lucky. 'They might easily have been on a capital charge. The fact that they are public school boys makes their crime all the worse. They should have known better.'

The headlines, about 'Mayfair Men', and the 'London Jewellery Robbery', lingered in the public consciousness, as Victor was to discover, though details soon slipped from memory. Before long, people – Sir Eldon Griffiths amongst them – became convinced that Victor had been amongst the defendants. But that detail is as mythical as his claims to have flown with Morato or to have led an infantry assault with pipers and buglers.

Confusion is understandable. Victor's trial was in 1939, a year after the Hyde Park case. Like its predecessor, however, it involved four young defendants (three of whom had been at public school), and inspired headlines about 'Mayfair Men' and jewellery. At both trials, one of the country's most eminent barristers, Norman (later Lord) Birkett, KC, acted for one of the defendants (for Wilmer, one of the pair sentenced to the cat in the Hyde Park case, and for Victor the following year). John Lonsdale, Victor's arms-dealing ally, was one of those convicted in the Hyde Park trial. And there needed only the shortest sequence of Chinese whispers to lead people into one further error: in the Hyde Park case, in 1938, the ring-leader had been Harley; in 1939, it was Hervey.

Though Victor's case may sound inconsequential now, to those weaned on a diet of twenty-first century, narcotics-fuelled crime, in the 1930s, it was a sensation. Members of the aristocracy occasionally came to grief, but when they did so it was usually in the bankruptcy courts or for unorthodox business practice, as had the 6'7" Lord Kylsant, sentenced to a year's imprisonment in 1931 for publishing and circulating a false prospectus.[39] Victor's story was far more compelling: the son of Lord Herbert Hervey, and nephew of the Marquess of Bristol, was accused of being a common criminal, a jewellery thief. At the committal proceedings, late in April 1939, the Marlborough Street Police Court became stiflingly crowded; policemen had to be posted at each of its entrances. The defendants were refused bail. Victor, who had worn suede shoes to court, remained in custody for more than a fortnight, until Herbert pledged two sureties of £2,500. His son was required to report to the police twice a day.

There was the same feverish interest when the trial began three months later, on 3 July. In the same week, the *Daily Telegraph* noted that the Milton Abbey estate was up for sale, while, from Lords, *The Times* cricket correspondent commended the Gentlemen for dismissing the Players 'for the reasonably quiet score of 270'. But neither paper could ignore events at the Old Bailey, which was packed with 'expensively-gowned social women, film celebrities, prominent figures in London's night-club life and Eastern potentates,' (reported the *Daily Mirror*, which later told its awed readers that Victor had worn a different suit on each of the trial's three days).

The principal prosecution witness, twenty-year-old Michael Walter, was not impressive; indeed, the prosecution acknowledged that the jury might conclude that he had been the defendants' accomplice. He had no occupation, lived in Ebury Street in Belgravia, courtesy of his father, who paid his rent and gave him an allowance of £3-a-week, his only income. Still less promisingly, he admitted that he had known three of the four defendants, including Victor, for some time. He had been at a café near Marble Arch with two of them, Victor and George Hering, on Good Friday when they began discussing which of their friends and acquaintances might have left jewels or other valuables in their flats while they were away over Easter. Later, he had been out for a walk with Hering when they bumped into Pauline Daubeny and her brother, Prince Galitzin, who mentioned that they were going to spend the weekend in the country with Hering's sister. By the time Mrs Daubeny and Prince Galitzin returned to the flat they shared in Queen Street, Mayfair, the following Tuesday, jewellery worth £2,500 was missing.

From today's perspective, elements of Walter's evidence have an almost Wodehousian tone; he had, he said, been introduced to Mrs Burley, the second victim, on Boat Race day. (A carefree evening, during which Mrs Burley admitted drinking rye whisky and passing out during the cabaret at The Nest nightclub, had culminated in the removal of £2,800 worth of jewellery – a ring from her handbag, and her watch and her dress clips, which were detached from her as she danced.) But other elements might have been scripted by Graham Greene: Walter had been told that unless he kept quiet he would get the broken end of a bottle in his face (or, as the *Daily Mail* put it, he 'was threatened with violence if he "squealed"'). The threat had come from one of three strangers to whom he was introduced, 'Alf', 'Bill' and 'Mo', one of whom was the getaway driver, another a specialist at scaling buildings, the third a lock-picker. Birkett, on Victor's behalf, savaged Walter's version of events. 'If it is not lies,' he told the jury, 'it is evidence you cannot trust.' But the jury found Victor even less convincing. After deliberating for an hour and twenty minutes at the end of the third day, they concluded that he and another defendant, William Goodwin, were guilty on both counts: conspiring to steal and stealing jewellery from Mrs Daubeny and Mrs Burley. The two other defendants, Hering and Geoffrey Coop, had already pleaded guilty to their respective charges, which was taken into consideration when Sir Gerald Dodson passed sentence.

Sir Gerald had not troubled to disguise the distaste that he felt for all involved – defendants, witnesses and at least one of the victims, Mrs Burley. Nevertheless, he reserved his severest censure – and longest sentence – for Victor, who, he concluded, was 'the mainspring of the conspiracy'. Inspector Berry, the police witness, described Victor as 'an associate of persons in the West End who live by their wits and exist on people who have money', adding that there was no doubt that he had been the ring-leader of the gang, over whom he had exerted 'a peculiar domination'; nor, Berry insisted, was there any doubt that Victor had 'for some time past indulged his criminal tendencies'.

None of his co-defendants was remotely his equal in wealth, connections or apparent self-assurance. Coop, twenty-four, who had been educated at public school, had met Victor at Sandhurst, and was subsequently commissioned into the Durham Light Infantry but was later obliged to resign for bouncing cheques. Hering, though only twenty-three, had a wife, from whom he was separated, and a three-year-old child. After public school, he had gone into the 'commercial side of journalism', then worked as a laboratory apprentice on a dairy farm from which he was sacked. He then emerged as a casual reporter and freelance writer with the pen name 'Peter Proud', in which guise, noted the *Daily Mail*, he could pick up odd items of society gossip in the West End, 'associate with people far above his station... and give the impression of ease and plenty', though in fact 'practically living by his wits'. Goodwin was different: a thirty-year-old silversmith who preferred crime to conventional employment. Adept at picking Yale locks, he 'associated with very bad characters, including blackmailers', had four previous convictions, including one for stealing, and had last been in prison in 1937. Sir Gerald decided that he should return for two more years; Hering was sentenced to eighteen months and Coop nine months. Victor received three years' penal servitude.

Sir Gerald appears to have concluded that although no violence was meted out to Mrs Burley or Mrs Daubeny, Victor had used the threat of it to keep Walter silent, and to influence Hering, whom he visited in Brixton when Hering was on remand, a trip which Victor explained by saying that he had gone 'in order to find out whether [Hering] was going to tell any further lies'. Dodson disagreed. 'I only hope,' he said, as he passed sentence, 'that all of you, certainly those of you who have the advantage of birth and education, will have sufficient manhood in you when this punishment is over that you will redeem the past. There is no reason why you should throw up [sic] the sponge.'

* * *

The E-type Jaguar was white and unadorned; the Rolls black and embellished with both the Hervey mascot (a snow leopard, finished in gold, bolted to the bonnet) and coat of arms (hand-painted on the Rolls's doors by H. R. Owen of Mayfair). Guests arriving at Ickworth in humbler vehicles could console themselves that, by the time the weekend ended, their cars would at least be cleaner – washed by hand, courtesy of estate staff. Other staff would carry suitcases to rooms, and unpack them, then serve at dinner – white-gloved, one standing behind each chair – under the direction of Jenkins the butler.[40]

Even thirty years earlier, entertainment on a similarly expansive scale had been rare amongst the aristocracy. By the mid-1960s, it was almost unthink-able.[41] This put Victor in self-congratulatory mood. 'One hears about the problems of finding staff, but we have not found it that difficult,' he assured a reporter, late in 1962. Traditional standards could be maintained, he explained, if one were pragmatic and progressive enough. 'We have modern-ized our homes to cut out much of the hard work. We find that a 20-line intercom… is worth about two-and-a-half staff. It cuts out the running up and down stairs.' The system was intended to have other advantages, remem-bers Guy Sainty, who stayed at Ickworth a decade later. 'There were the printed names of all the other guests, so you could call [them] if you wanted to.' Sainty was appreciative of his host's attention to detail, which was in some respects influenced more by the hospitality industry than country-house tradition. 'Victor had completely redecorated the house. All the bedrooms had an intercom telephone and a bathroom, and each bathroom had every kind of aftershave and bath oils and everything else, rather like a fancy hotel.'

Another occasional visitor recalls a bold emphasis on 'glitz and pomp': a style which correctly reflected the difficulty that Victor – always happiest in London or on jaunts abroad, Marbella being a particular favourite – experi-enced when trying to reconcile himself to East Anglian life. A lasting impression was made, even on those who stayed only once, like Tessa Montgomery, who accompanied her first husband, Peter de Zulueta, to an Ickworth shoot. 'They lived in very grand style – butlers and what have you. We even had to take somebody with us to act as a loader.' Crisp white cards, crowned with the Hervey arms (picked out in gold), were placed by objets de vertu, detailing their provenance in copperplate script ('if something had been given by the King of Prussia,' recalls another visitor, 'so much the better').

Weekends were congenial, comfortable, leisurely, largely undemanding affairs, though requiring a degree of digestive and alcoholic stamina from those, like Carol and Michael (later Lord) Havers,[42] who were frequent visi-tors. 'You arrived on Friday evening, and left on Sunday evening or Monday morning. Breakfast [was] brought up on trays,' recalls Carol Havers, who emphasizes that the running of the house was left to the owner of the white E-type – Juliet, Victor's second wife. 'Juliet went round [the evening before] and said, very quietly, to guests, "What would you like on your tray in the morning?" I never got up [for breakfast]. When one wandered down, if it wasn't a shooting weekend, it would to be in time to go for a walk or look at a particular piece. [Victor's acquisitions included Bluebird, in which Donald Campbell had set the world land-speed record.] Then it was straight into things like Bloody Marys and champagne and a long, long lunch. Then everyone retired for a siesta, before it all started again. Each evening, another long frock was brought out. It was all laid out for you.'

Conversation at dinner never paused.

'Will I see you in Le Touquet?' (asked Victor)

'Oh, Victor, can you afford to go to Le Touquet again?'

'I can't afford to stay away.'

Or their host might turn the subject towards an area of his expertise: 'I was in Columbia/Peru/Brazil/Uruguay. I said, "I'll give you three days to put your country in order. I can't spare any more than that".'

Members of Victor's court – an arresting bunch – included displaced royals, treasured specimens of the Monarchist League, amongst them King Simeon and Queen Margarita of Bulgaria,[43] their presence an important consolation for Victor who, as Sir Eldon Griffiths puts it, 'never got the time of day out of the British Royals'. There were one or two titled locals, like the 8th Lord Abinger, who, years later, would give the address at Victor's funeral, and the Milford Havens, as well as aristocrats from slightly further afield, like Lord Masserene and Ferrard,[44] and, on at least one occasion, Brigadier Denis FitzGerald, whose first cousin the Duke of Leinster had been causing his family distress for several decades. From time to time, there were also junior ministers from foreign governments, especially the Finnish government, whose defence minister, for example, met his British counterpart at Ickworth in 1961, and ambassadors, lured down for a weekend's shooting.[45] The shoot, remembers Carol Havers, was a good one. 'Victor didn't shoot himself, just had the parties, drank a great deal, drove about in a Roller, from drive to drive. It was beautifully run, huge number of birds.'

An occasional guest, Viscount Davidson, also remembers it keenly. 'We were given a loader, which was quite something for me. There were high birds except in the last drive before a late lunch. I once stood next to an ambassador on that drive. He swung his gun right through the middle of my pelvis aiming at a cock pheasant that was running out of the rhododendrons.'

Victor's closest friends remained undaunted. Aside from the Havers, there were the Merrivale Austins, Leroux Smith Leroux, a South African who, though of uncertain provenance, managed to become director of the Tate

Gallery (though his new-found status held little sway at Christie's. 'We eventually refused to deal with him,' remembers Brian Sewell, then working at the auction house, 'because we thought that he was actually stealing things; it was impossible to guarantee that anything he brought in belonged to him') and Sir Hugh Trevor Dawson, a 6'4" Old Harrovian baronet who, during his days as a captain in the Scots Guards, had made a point of scrutinizing potential officers' pedigrees in *Burke's* and *Debrett's*. 'Trevor was an absolutely wonderful character,' recalls a member of a younger generation. 'Whatever one says about Victor, or thought about Victor, I can tell you he did attract and make friends with very amusing people. If you can have friends around you who can make you laugh, who gives a damn whether they're a bit dodgy?'

Victor's relationship with alcohol gave an impetus to much of the action. He contrived to lock himself in the electricity cupboard, he mounted the stairs on all fours, shouting 'rissoles, rissoles, rissoles' ('It started off, I think, "Arseholes, arseholes",' says Carol Havers, 'but it changed to "rissoles"'), invariably after being dragged 'from the downstairs loo on a wonderful rug, across the marble floor', he played endless rugby songs on the gramophone, to which 'he knew all the awful, dirty lines' and, sometimes, he played little jokes. Awaking one morning, Carol Havers realized she had no recollection of how she had reached bed, only of Victor insisting that she and another guest, Peggy Dunnet, should have a final glass of brandy. When her husband, Michael Havers, awoke, he filled in the gaps. Peggy Dunnet, he said, had got on to a chair and started dancing, before being led away by her husband; Carol's own performance had begun on a table in the drawing room. In the middle of the table there was a substantial figurine ('either Meissen or Chelsea, heavily decorated with cherubs and leaves and flowers'), standing confidently above which Carol had also started to dance. 'I'd taken off my skirt, which was fastened with Velcro, tore it off and, just wearing tights, done high kicks over this piece.' The Meissen survived. When rebuked later that morning, Victor said nothing, but gave his usual, high-pitched, tinny, little laugh. 'He just had that look in his eye [that said], "I got you". Wicked. We could both have been in hospital.'

For Sir Eldon Griffiths, those days remain a time of some enchantment. 'When not tipsy, Victor was an exceedingly good host. He ran the place with enormous elegance. There was a large staff – must have been fifteen, eighteen, that number. They all dressed [in Hervey livery]. You dined in black tie; it was done in huge style, in the eighteenth-century manner, the candles, the gold. Outside the front door [there was] the beautiful flag of the Monarchist League and, alongside it, the Hervey banner. I remember having the very decorative Marchioness of Milford Haven on one arm and Juliet Bristol on the other, and going out to see the Bluebird.' Others found the experience a little rich. Viscount Davidson recalls waiting in the receiving line at the annual Christmas party, and 'spotting in an alcove, a floodlit coronet, together with other marquessate accoutrements, as I supposed they were. I felt like turning round and walking out – but I didn't'.

Perhaps it was Juliet's presence that persuaded him to stay. Much as Victor enjoyed his friends, no one mattered a fraction as much to him as Juliet did. It was Juliet (née Lady Juliet Fitzwilliam), whom he had married (as his second wife) in April 1960 in the teeth of her family's opposition, who dignified his existence and – he fervently hoped – legitimized his place in society. It was Juliet who had given him a second son, Nicholas, as well as mothering his elder boy, John; Juliet, whose splendid Palladian ancestral seat, the 365-room Wentworth House, was the largest house in the country,[46] who ensured that weekends at Ickworth flowed blissfully to their conclusion; Juliet who went on the County Council; who, when in Venice, helped him choose the beautiful pieces of glass given to house guests at Christmas. But even Juliet could never quite reprieve him from memories of Hering and Goodwin, Coop and Camp Hill.

* * *

Scraps of anecdotal evidence suggest that fallen pre-war grandees – plutocrats as much as aristocrats – sometimes received preferential treatment in prison. It might not have been unreasonable for Victor to have hoped that a degree of deference might also be shown to him; after all, at his trial's conclusion, his father had been given special permission to spend a few minutes with him before he was carted off to begin his sentence. His transfer to Camp Hill might have sparked further optimism, since his stepfather, Sir Peter Macdonald, was MP for the Isle of Wight. If so, Victor's hopes were short-lived: nothing suggests that his term of penal servitude was leavened by favouritism. Among the few terse entries from the Governor's Journal for 1939–41 is the assertion that a prison inspector had declared himself 'agreeably surprised by the prison diet'. Victor was unable to share his enthusiasm: following his release, he claimed that 'a lot of rubbish' had been written about convicts being over-fed, adding that he had eaten more butter (or margarine; he was uncertain which) in one meal in the restaurant car on his train journey back to London than he ever had in a whole day in prison. He did not go into further details about the diet or, indeed, anything else. But the bleakest moments of Camp Hill life – and death – were recorded in the Governor's

Journal: on '4/2/41', Walker 'met with an accident in the carpenter's shop'; on '19/2/41', McCabe was forcibly fed; and one of their fellow prisoners expired in custody, apparently of natural causes. Of Camp Hill's most patrician prisoner there was no mention.

After a fruitless appeal against both verdict and sentence in 1939, Victor appears to have decided to do whatever was necessary to minimize his time inside. 'There was a marvellous statement by a prison officer,' David Erskine remembered, 'who had been nabbed by the press or something, saying "Hervey is a model prisoner, reads his bible every day". I wonder what was in the bible. Drink, I should think.' Victor's efforts to find favour with the authorities may have gone beyond displays of piety, to the extent of acting as prison nark.[47] If so, his technique was sufficiently adroit to avoid alienating all of his fellow inmates, as a post-war acquaintance, Branko Bokun, would discover. Arriving in London in the early 1960s as a foreign correspondent, Bokun and his wife, Princess Francesca Ruspoli, met Victor a number of times and invited him to dinner at their flat. When Victor arrived, Bokun was taken aback to see his guest hugging the porter (a man with a discernible limp of unspecified provenance). After dinner and Victor's departure, Bokun made his inquiry. 'I said, "You know the Marquess? How did you know him?" He said, "We spent time in jail together...".'

Released, with a year's remission, in 1941, Victor expressed his hope of joining the RAF but, failing that, emphasized his willingness to help the national effort in other ways. 'I speak French, German, Russian and Spanish,' he announced. (He did nothing of the kind, having no languages other than 'reasonable French', though even this seems to have deserted him in his twilight years in Monte Carlo.) 'I acted for the French Deuxieme Bureau in many capacities in Germany and Czechoslovakia,' he added, 'and I am going to publish some sensational revelations to show how Nazi espionage has worked. I was named in a secret Nazi document, drawn up by Himmler, as one of the enemies of the Third Reich.' No Nazi espionage document was forthcoming, but there were further promises to his family, as David Erskine recalled. 'He wrote a splendid letter to my grandma, saying, "I shall try and recoup some money and see what I can do for my country".' It was authentic Victor. By that stage, however, the country had learned to expect very little of him. Worse, as David Erskine's brother Robert explains, the bankruptcy, the tireless self-promotion and, above all, the prison sentence had taken their toll on his family. 'He became a sort of joke; anything terrible in the newspapers was [dismissed as] the sort of thing Victor would do.'

Family legend suggested that his wartime contribution to his country was limited to fire-watching duty, negligently performed. The disparity between his military service and that of the rest of his family was inescapable and humiliating.[48] Other deficiencies, fresh or retrospective, real or imagined, were entered against his name, among them an alleged injustice to 'old Moley, the man who lived on the estate somewhere and caught the moles', whose perk was the right to sell the skins of any moles he trapped; Victor allegedly insisted that the money should go to him instead.

Even Frederick, with his reflexive, feudal loyalty to primogeniture, was ready to inflict a measure of public humiliation on his nephew, though still declining to disinherit him completely. Not long before his death in 1951, he decreed that Dora would remain in situ at Ickworth for the rest of her life,[49] rather than move (in Victor's favour) sedately to the Dower House, which was, instead, given to their daughters, Marjorie and Phyllis, neither of whom had any time for Victor. It was not coincidental that one of Phyllis's daughters, Merelina (known as Merri), became custodian of a 'Black Book' chronicling Victor's misdeeds.

Even Robert Erskine, Marjorie's youngest son, who was only eleven at the time of Victor's release, imbibed the mood. At a party given by an Egyptian friend of his in the 1950s, Erskine met his cousin for the first time. Learning that Victor wanted to ingratiate himself with their host before visiting his country, he intervened. 'I thought to myself, "I don't think this is very useful to [my friend and his family]", because they were much spied upon, pursued by Nasser, and, as I understood it, Victor had had some connection with Egypt for gun-running. So I warned them: "Don't touch him with a barge-pole". They put up the shutters, as it were.' Returning from what proved to be an unsatisfactory trip, Victor wrote to Erskine, berating him for his interference. Erskine replied promptly: 'I always advise anyone who goes to Egypt to take their sense of humour with them.' He never saw Victor again.

On the Cochrane side of the family, the shutters were also going up, though not quite quickly enough to prevent Victor from paying a visit or two to his great-uncle, Thomas Cochrane, 1st Lord Cochrane of Cults, who lived at Crawford Priory in Fife. 'Victor was extremely unpopular there,' says the current (4th) Lord Cochrane, who remembers rare but painful meetings with his cousin. 'My grandfather found it hard to stay in the same room as him.' It was the Cochranes, he adds, who christened Victor 'the Reptile'. 'When asked what it was like [to meet him] in later years, I've said he had the look of a prisoner. I've done a certain amount of prison work, so I might know.'

Another kinsman, Lord Rathcavan, recalls his grandparents being appalled by the connection. 'It was never spoken of, except when my grandmother used to refer acidly to "cousin Victor", probably intending to wind up my grandfather.'[50]

Victor did little, if anything, to soothe his relations' ill-feeling. There was no remorse, no display of new-found humility, no acceptance that a period of self-abasement or immersion in good works was necessary or helpful in a spirit of *reculer pour mieux sauter*. Only one of his cousins, Douglas Cochrane,[51] a more forgiving character than most, ever heard him apologize for the events of 1939, at a ninetieth birthday party given by Victor for his aunt Grizel at Ickworth in 1970. 'He made a few remarks in her honour, and said he was very sorry for all the trouble he'd caused. That's the only time I heard him refer to it.' There was almost no one there to notice – just Grizel, Juliet, Douglas and one other person, whose identity Douglas Cochrane could not, towards the end of his life, remember.

On his release from Camp Hill, Victor's choice of business associates suggested that he intended to resume not far from where he had left off. He and a gentleman called Moss Goodman became joint proprietors of a Mayfair drinking club (dignified as the International Club, 4 Hertford Street), employing as its secretary Frank Cheeld, who in October 1938 had been sentenced to four years' penal servitude for forgery. By December 1943, the club's licence had been revoked by Bow Street magistrates, although by then Victor and Goodman (whose brother Michael also had a criminal record) were ready to redirect their energies elsewhere. Indeed, it was an application from Empire Film Productions for permission to establish a radio station on the Isle of Man early in 1944 which assured Victor of renewed attention from Scotland Yard. Routine wartime checks on the company's status and personnel disclosed that it was a subsidiary of Radnor Films Ltd; Radnor's proprietors were, in turn, Moss Goodman of Shoot up Hill, NW2, and Victor Frederick Cochrane Hervey, Criminal Record Office number 19440/41. The company secretary was Frank Cheeld.

Any chance that the authorities might accept that this was a legitimate business proposition evaporated when they were reminded of Victor's Old Bailey conviction and, just as damagingly, his pre-war claims to supremacy in the arms trade. Detective Sergeant Cornish noted that he had been 'notorious as one of a number of men, known as Mayfair Playboys, with some of whom he was convicted', had been involved in 'suspected fraud in respect to the sale of arms' during the Spanish Civil War and, allegedly, in 'dope trafficking'. Although conceding that 'no evidence was forthcoming' in support of either area of suspicion, Cornish pointed out that Victor was, and continued to be, 'an associate of persons of doubtful character, and a frequenter of night clubs in the West End of London'. He concluded with the information that Victor had just paid a deposit on a Thames houseboat called *Dilkhusha*, moored at Thames Ditton.

His report set the tone for what was to come. Over the next three years, memoranda fizzed between Scotland Yard, the Home Office (Aliens Department) and London police stations, with recurrent references to Victor's 'history in gun-running' and his involvement in the 'notorious "Mayfair" affair in 1939', a phrase made all the more potent for its imprecision. The years since the two Mayfair trials had been crowded with the suffering and dislocation of war: as 1944 turned into 1945, there were more urgent things to consider than the respective composition of the Cartier gang, who had so nearly cost Etienne Bellenger his life, and the team of burglar-thieves who had abstracted jewellery from the Galitzin/Daubeny flat and from Mrs Burley.

The Isle of Man application (which mutated into a request to make a propaganda film) was vetoed; so, too, was one the following year, in which Victor and Goodman sought permission to travel to France ('our idea,' wrote Victor, who hoped to make a propaganda film, 'is to show the public how flying routes are operated from this country to the South of France'). The Met was confident that it had made the right decision. 'Hervey's recent conduct does not appear as though he were reforming, and his past history in gun-running during the Spanish Civil War, together with the allegations that he was a drug trafficker should not be lost sight of,' concluded an Inspector Callaghan in February 1945. A senior officer agreed. 'Neither of these oily scoundrels should be granted an exit permit,' he noted. 'They are quite unreliable and untrustworthy, and, in fact, capable of anything bad.' The discovery that Goodman, who gave his date of birth as 27 December 1893, had been declared bankrupt in 1931 heightened police interest, as did Victor's displays of public belligerence. On 11 January 1945, he was fined £7 at Kingston magistrates' court for failing to comply with black-out regulations at his houseboat (now renamed *Dry Martini*) and for the persistent use of obscene language from its deck. This was the prelude to a busy summer, during which he was convicted of seven motoring offences – all between June and August – four of them for speeding, two for obstruction, and finally one for reckless driving, which culminated in a year's disqualification and a £25 fine.

Nevertheless, the Met's interest might have ebbed away, had it not been for an anonymous letter which arrived at Scotland Yard in mid-August 1945. 'If you are not already aware of the fact,' it began, 'it might be as well to inform you, so that you can advise those under you who are responsible, that behind almost every jewell [sic] robbery which takes place in the Metropolitan area, and within areas outside London, is the Hon. Victor Hervey. You are probably aware that this villain is one of the most unscrupulous, calculating and cunning criminals at large.' After warning that Victor was a danger to the public ('he is usually armed'), the letter continued: 'Seldom does he take part in the actual robberies. He employs crooks to work for him, and they enter premises which he has previously gained particulars about. He meets his accomplices in a public house on the corner of Chester Row and Eaton Place, and also in another public house called the Antelope... Some of his arrangements for burglary are made over the telephone. If he has not already disposed of it, a large supply of stolen whisky and gin, as well as stolen cigarettes may be found in his office at Empire Film Productions, as he is also the instigator of large scale thefts of these goods... No effort should be spared in ridding this ghastly parasite from our midst. He stops at nothing, and nothing is too low for him to stoop to in order to satisfy his lust and greed.' The unidentified informant correctly pointed out that Victor was 'the leading light of a concern which styles itself Empire Film Productions Ltd'; he also asserted that Victor drove 'a luxurious Rolls-Royce Car... purchase[d] from the proceeds of some of his robberies'.

Scotland Yard's interest moved up a gear. Victor and Moss were watched; Inspector Robert Fabian, later the inspiration for a 1950s television series, was put on the case, assisted by a colleague from CID, who soon confirmed that Victor was the owner of a black Rolls, registration number DUV 26. Fabian reported that Victor still lived aboard *Dry Martini*, moored off Palace Estate, Thames Ditton, where he was a regular at the Swan Hotel. 'Local gossip has it that he is contemplating... a big game hunt in Africa. He is looked upon... as a general nuisance, but on account of his spending propensities is well tolerated.' Explaining that Victor commuted, almost daily, to an office at 93 Regent Street ('which sports the business name of Empire Film Productions'), Fabian added: 'When in town Hervey frequents most of the so-called better-class establishments. He is always immaculately dressed and usually in the company of a number of ne'er-do-well sons and daughters of married parents. I have visited him at his office but could see no signs of business and certainly no signs of any property which might be stolen. Although vicious to almost a sadistic degree, I am certain he would not be fool enough to carry firearms.' Fabian's conclusion did not, however, suggest that he believed that he was on the tail of a master criminal. 'I am in touch with a person who keeps me informed, within reason, of the activities of Hervey. Should anything of real interest occur I will submit a further report.'

The inspector's coolness was justified not only by his own findings but arguably by the tone and style of the anonymous letter. It might, initially, appear that an Old Etonian contemporary, newly back from the war, had been repelled by Victor's propensity for spraying money around, just as he had before imprisonment – and had decided to silence him. But a trio of misspellings ('jewell', 'enquirey', 'Mirabell' rather than Mirabelle), the incorrect designation of Victor as 'the Hon' and the gauche description, 'a luxurious Rolls Royce Car' all appear to betray the informant as one of Victor's former professional associates or rivals, however eager the correspondent might have been to disguise the fact. The police would receive one more anonymous tip-off, this time by telephone, on 14 May 1947. The caller was male; his message brief: if the police investigated the owner of a car with the number plate DUV 26, they would uncover information about the Hever Castle robbery.

Once again, it was a lead the police could not ignore. More than a year earlier, shortly after 3 a.m. on 21 April 1946, a number of masked men had arrived at Hever Castle, Kent, seat of Colonel John Jacob Astor,[52] overwhelmed the night watchman, whom they had trussed up in a tablecloth, and helped themselves to a discerning selection of irreplaceable treasures – Elizabeth I's prayer book, Anne Boleyn's psalter, a gold hexagonal ring worn by Henry VIII, snuff boxes of royal provenance, a gold Tudor chalice, a miniature of Lady Hamilton. The raiders departed as they arrived – in a black Rolls-Royce. Despite the offer of a £2,000 reward, nothing was recovered and no one charged.

At about the same time as the telephone tip-off, 'discreet' police inquiries were yielding potentially intriguing information. Victor was said to be shielding Alick Kostanda, on the run since escaping from Wormwood Scrubs where he had been serving four years' penal servitude for burglary and assault with intent to resist arrest. The police placed Victor under close observation throughout June and July 1947. He had by then left *Dry Martini* in Thames Ditton in favour of what the police described as his yacht, the *Cochrane Hervey*, moored at Garrick's Lawn, Hampton. Learning that he intended to sail to Ostend, they ensured that Customs boarded the *Cochrane Hervey* when Victor set off downstream on 1 August. The search that followed was predictably thorough, but fruitless, 'no trace was found of Kostanda', acknowledged the police report, 'nor of any property likely to be connected with the Kent crime'.

About a fortnight later, the *Cochrane Hervey* returned to Hampton; observation was resumed, albeit in a lower key. 'Nothing suspicious was seen,' recorded the police when the case was written up in December 1947. By then,

Kostanda had been rearrested at 17 Rosslyn Hill, Hampstead, where he had been living as 'Dr Canning'. In the ensuing house search, police found nothing to link him to the Hever Castle break-in (or any other), though they unearthed 'a knotted, webbing climbing rope' which suggested that he had not entirely renounced his profession. 'We have failed to establish any connection between Kostanda and Hervey... Reviewing the facts and the vague information – anonymous – implicating Hervey, I suggest that it would be imprudent to obtain a search warrant to search Hervey's yacht. Should there be any developments, a further report will be submitted.'

No further report was forthcoming: nothing more – no subsequent review or comment, no memo concerning tip-offs by letter or telephone – was added to Victor's files for the rest of his life, which suggests that he was either brilliant enough to elude police interest (let alone detection) or that he became, as his second wife Juliet argues, a reformed character. The first proposition is difficult to sustain. Between 1944 and 1945, there was 'a formidable surge in almost all types of crime, particularly those involving violence', led by gang leaders like Jack Spot and Billy Hill, men who were unsqueamish about the use of the razor or blunter instruments (at Ascot in 1946, a member of an Islington gang was pursued down the course by one of Spot's men, who brandished a hammer, 'in full view of the occupants of the Royal Enclosure'). Admittedly, there remained room for the gifted solo operator, like jewel thief Barry Fieldsen, who, following a minor, youthful conviction, spent subsequent decades masquerading as 'Barry Redvers Holliday', owner of a Bentley, a Mercedes, a motor boat, a flat with a mirrored cocktail bar, a house in Chelsea, and a turreted villa on Friary Island at Old Windsor. Victor, however, lacked the finesse to emulate Fieldsen or the muscle to take on Spot and Hill, nor did he have the temperament to avoid attracting Messrs Spot and Hill's attention. In fact, it is difficult to see how Victor – in the persona of a toxic Mr Toad – could have made himself more conspicuous.

Cronies knew the *Cochrane Hervey* as 'the Punt'. A former Royal Navy escort vessel (of 156 tons) converted to provide five bedrooms, two bathrooms, a saloon (with walls of pale lavender and green satin-covered chairs), a study and a cocktail bar, the Punt was occasionally taken for cruises in the Mediterranean. Generally, however, she was securely moored, as the police had noted, near Hampton Court. It was there, and elsewhere, that Victor began to cultivate his reputation for eccentricity. The obscenities which had attracted the attention of the magistrates at Kingston could, acknowledged his friend Johnny Kimberley,[53] 'be something of an embarrassment'. 'He would get on his feet in some smart London restaurant and shout out: "Fuck 'em all. Fuck 'em all…" He also gave way to this temptation when aboard his boat… He would bellow through a loud hailer his expletive order to the world around him, often while indulging in another of his curious habits, which was chucking the family silver into the swirling muddy river… As far as I know, no one has ever sent a frogman down there. There should be quite a little hoard waiting to be collected.' Kimberley, an alcoholic, took this all at face value, although it seems more likely that Victor arranged for his silver to be surreptitiously retrieved, so that the stunt could be endlessly repeated.

* * *

For a while, his first wife might have found this amusing. According to one acquaintance, she was drawn to him 'because he held out the prospect of a lot of laughs and adventures'. She was not alone in finding Victor attractive, as a much younger male acquaintance, who saw him in action at Ickworth, testifies. 'He certainly had a big appeal to the ladies; whether that was just the chat, I don't know.' When only twenty, and reliant on good looks, a brash, ebullient manner, and a useful allowance, Victor had been fleetingly engaged to Diana Seton,[54] whose beauty had begun to attract the interest of film directors. In 1935 an unnamed friend was quoted in a newspaper as saying that Diana and Victor 'met two years ago at May Week when he was still at Cambridge', which suggests that Victor had decided that his pursuit of beautiful women – a recreation later listed in *Who's Who* – need not be impeded by the truth, any more than were his other avenues of endeavour.

That seems to have been the experience of the woman who became his first wife. Pauline Ames was not aristocratic – she described her father, Herbert Bolton, as a managing director – and, by the time she was twenty-three, already had one marriage behind her (a brief, wartime liaison with Robert Ames). But Victor – viewed with distaste by most of the aristocracy – was lucky to be next. No fortune- or title-hunter, Pauline was memorably attractive – a 'very luscious looking blonde', in the approving assessment of Victor's best man, Johnny Kimberley, who had decided at the age of 21 to 'lay every girl he could get his hands on' (he would marry six times). (Other observers usually considered her a redhead). She was also noticeably kind, remembers Tessa Montgomery, 'very sweet to old Herbert, used to take him around, came to my wedding with him'.

Pauline and Victor married at Middlesex register office in 1949. Five years later, she had their first and only child, a boy called John. There is no evidence that these five years gave her cause to share Inspector Fabian's belief in Victor's 'sadism' (of which Fabian supplied no details); on the other hand, she had discovered that the inspector had been over-confident when asserting that Victor would be reluctant to carry firearms. By then, she had tired of Victor, largely (she would later say) because he became insufferably pompous after becoming Earl Jermyn (on Frederick's death, and Herbert's succession as 5th Marquess) in 1951. According to Kimberley, however, she had begun an affair with one of her husband's closest friends, Derek Le Poer Trench,[55] within two or three years of her marriage, though it was not for Trench but for another Old Etonian, a Newmarket trainer called Teddy Lambton,[56] that she jettisoned Victor. Pauline did not contest their divorce in 1959, which was settled unequivocally in Victor's favour, the judge granting him custody of their five-year-old son, John, and directing that, although Pauline was to have access to the little boy, 'in no circumstances should [the child] have any contact with Mr Lambton'. It was a condition which Victor had insisted on, explaining that he was determined to prevent John from succumbing to the corrupting influences of the 'Newmarket racing set'. Costs were awarded against Lambton.

A year later, Victor remarried, this time choosing Trench as his best man, either out of ignorance or gratitude. But it was his success in snaring his new bride which staggered his family (but appalled hers). Lady Juliet Fitzwilliam, only child of the late 8th Earl Fitzwilliam and his widow 'Obby' (née Plunket), was twenty-five; Victor was forty-four. She had read English at St Hilda's College, Oxford; of more interest to potential suitors, she was heiress to an immense fortune, one which dwarfed anything that Victor had inherited. (Her great-grandfather, the 6th Earl, had left £2.8 million on his death in 1902, about £1.7 billion today.) But money, Juliet had learned, could do little for the sudden fragility of aristocratic status; nor could it insulate her from her family's sudden tendency to self-destruction.

Both Juliet's parents had always been easily bored, an affliction which, before the war, Obby Fitzwilliam had tended to tackle by orchestrating 'spur-of-the-moment trips... the house party decamping by private plane to Le Touquet or Paris'. Juliet's father Peter welcomed these excursions but by 1946 needed further diversion. He found it in Kathleen 'Kick' Hartington (née Kennedy), widow of Billy Hartington.[57] In May 1948, he and Kick boarded a privately chartered De Havilland Dove at Croydon aerodrome, bound for Cannes, intending to spend Whitsun at a villa in the south of France before returning to Paris to meet Kick's father, Joe Kennedy,[58] who, they hoped, would give his consent to their marriage. After breaking their outward journey at Le Bourget, they flew into a storm 'of quite exceptional strength' above the Rhône Valley. Later that day, the De Havilland's wreckage was found strewn over the mountainside of the Ardeche; four crumpled bodies lay in the fuselage – the pilot, co-pilot, Peter and Kick.

Juliet, who was thirteen, returned with her mother to Ireland, to County Wicklow. By then, some of Wentworth's 365 rooms housed a teacher training college for sports mistresses, and its Park was being steadily desecrated by open-cast mining, by order of Manny Shinwell,[59] Minister for Fuel and Power. Peter's first cousin once removed, Eric Fitzwilliam, a sixty-five-year-old divorcé known as 'Bottle by Bottle', succeeded as 9th and penultimate Earl Fitzwilliam. Obby Fitzwilliam never remarried; according to Juliet, 'no other man really mattered to her'. Juliet's own fatherless adolescence helps sustain one theory about why she was drawn to Victor. 'She was married to people who were older than herself,' says Carol Havers, 'father figures.'

This hypothesis failed to console, or occur to, the Fitzwilliams. The family escutcheon was blotched with alcoholism and flecked with obvious indiscretion. None of it, though, remotely compared with Victor's criminal record and dismal reputation. 'Every member of the family is opposed to the marriage,' Juliet's kinsman, Tom Fitzwilliam, the 10th (and, as it transpired, last) Earl Fitzwilliam, assured the press, a week after the engagement was announced in February 1960. Obby was similarly distressed, though preferring to express her anxieties in private. She eventually agreed to attend the wedding (held on 24 April, at the Crown Court Church of Scotland, Covent Garden), something which Tom Fitzwilliam pointedly refused to do.

The Fitzwilliams remained on their guard long afterwards. 'They took jolly good care to make sure that [Victor] wasn't going to get hold of her money,' remembered Viscount Colville of Culross, a friend and contemporary of Juliet at Oxford. He adds that he was 'surprised' by her choice of husband. So was Victor's cousin, David Erskine, who remained perplexed for the rest of his life. 'Very, very odd. I think she had a mission to reform him, but it didn't work.' Others agree, including a friend of Victor's son John. 'There's a Somerset Maugham quote – "No stronger emotion, or no greater emotion, to affect the heart of man than that of self-sacrifice". [Maugham] wasn't talking about going to war [but] saving another human soul. I think she thought, "I can do it, I can change him, I can make him feel loved".' Juliet makes no such claim for herself, saying only that she found Victor 'a very entertaining character, a good raconteur, with an excellent sense of humour and a sharp wit'. Whilst describing her old friend as 'a saint', Carol Havers acknowledges that, for most of their marriage, Juliet seemed happy enough with Victor. 'She had a very busy life, used to ride in those days, then she went on the district council. [She was] quite cross when she couldn't find him or something. Very bright. Very loyal. Stood by her man.'

It was with Juliet at his side that Victor tackled Ickworth. He had first descended on Suffolk in 1957 when his aunt Dora died, aware that she had come to an arrangement with the Treasury, but far from reconciled to that fact. Half the Herveys' 30,000 acres were sold; 6 St James's Square (owned by the family since 1677, the longest tenure in the square) had gone in 1955. More galling still, from Victor's perspective, Ickworth, together with most of its pictures, sculpture and silver and 1,1792 acres, had been consigned to the National Trust in lieu of death duties. In return for an endowment of £185,000 (£11 million today), the largest the Trust had ever received, the family was granted a ninety-nine-year-lease on the East Wing.

The arrangement spurred Victor into sporadic tussles with the Trust and the Treasury over ownership of certain paintings, including a Lely of Charles II, which he was eager to exchange for Giordano's *Death of Seneca* which remained in his possession; the Trust agreed to loan the Lely but would not sanction its transfer. A portrait of Don Balthasar Carlos, which had been in the 1st Marquess's collection, caused him far more pain. Acquired by the Treasury (and subsequently loaned to the Trust) as 'studio of Velázquez', it had been valued in the 1950s at £1,000. By 1962, however, cleaning had disclosed the picture, which had hung at Ickworth for 130 years, to be by Velázquez himself – and its value, as Victor's solicitor noted in a letter to the Inland Revenue, around £150,000. The temptation was more than Victor could resist. He instructed his solicitor to inform the Revenue that, at the time Dora had drawn up the list of what was to be sold to the Treasury, it had been 'with his agreement [that] this particular picture was excluded'. Thereafter, a mistake had obviously been made: '[the Velázquez] appears in some way unknown to him to have been transposed from the list of objects to be retained to the list of those to have been included in the sale... the error is most unfortunate from Lord Bristol's point of view... he asks that the Treasury should kindly put the matter right by handing back the picture to him in exchange for an article worth about £1,000.' The ensuing detailed investigation by the Treasury found that there was 'not a shred of sensible evidence' to support Victor's claim.

The fate of the estate, not just the Velázquez, still made him simmer a decade later. 'I remember him asking me to look at the paintings in the Rotunda, including West's *The Death of Wolfe*, which is a seriously valuable painting,' says Guy Sainty, who by the mid-1970s was establishing himself as an art dealer. 'The sense that [Ickworth] wasn't his gnawed away at him.'

Awareness of his late uncle's approach to financial planning only intensified Victor's resentment. The 4th Marquess had treated all mention of tax as a personal affront. 'The estates were decimated by death duties because he refused to have anything to do with it,' recalls his grandson Robert Erskine. 'He used to boot the poor accountant he hired out of Ickworth: "WHAT TAX? GET OUT!" The estate was ruined by all sorts of things that could have been got around.' But if Victor's regret was understandable, it also showed a failure to acknowledge that, without the entirely fortuitous infusion of Wythes money sixty years before, Ickworth's contents – and, quite probably, the house in its entirety – would have been lost decades earlier.

There was, in any case, something which tormented him even more. Away from 'the Punt', or West End restaurants where he could perform on terms of his own choosing, he was aware that his name was routinely greeted with derision.[60] In the country, trapped in a shallow pool of fellow grandees, there was no escape. '[Victor] was very shy at the beginning; you could see he was nervous,' remembers Betty Stafford (née Shaughnessy), who, by the late 1950s, was living near Ickworth with her second husband, Berkeley Stafford, one of Victor's Eton contemporaries. It was not from Berkeley, however, that she had first heard of Victor, but from another Old Etonian, her brother Freddie, witness to Victor's pyrotechnic and electrical experimentation three decades earlier.

The Staffords might have kept their distance, had it not been for Betty's alliance with Obby Fitzwilliam, one of her oldest friends. Meeting Juliet by chance in Bury St Edmunds, Mrs Stafford established that Juliet was staying at Ickworth. 'I told my husband, "If they marry, you can't bar the house because I've got to have her here: I'm very fond of her". Then, of course, they did get married. We became good friends; we couldn't help it.' Initially, however, Victor held back. 'He didn't come for months, if not a year. Juliet used to come for tea, bringing [Victor's son] John. Then one day I said, "We really must have Victor, it's too awful", because they kept on asking us over there.' The Staffords found that they enjoyed the Ickworth performance. 'We'd drive in and wonder which flag we were going to see over the front door: there was *always* an ambassador staying.' Others in East Anglia began to capitulate, their resistance eroded by an appetite for entertainment, for shooting, for a generous table and impressive cellar. Robust hypocrisy helped. 'Every year more people came, more wilted. You can imagine country life after the war wasn't all that exciting. It gave people things to talk about. People used to say, "Are you going for dinner with the Borstal boy tonight?" Awful things were said.'

Arranging reciprocal hospitality had its pitfalls. After inviting Victor to dinner for the first time ('a biggish party, about fourteen people'), Betty Stafford realized too late that 'all the men, every single one, had been at Eton with him'. The prelude to the Bristols' arrival was difficult: a hot summer's evening of stage whispers ('Betty, I think you should put those silver boxes away') and inadequately suppressed sniggering. 'I could see what they were all going to be like. I said, "You've all got to behave, for goodness sake". I felt quite sorry for Victor coming in. He looked so... he saw all these men, who he knew...'

In London, the House of Lords offered little respite. 'It was the sort of place where people would get up and walk out [if he appeared],' says Guy Sainty. Victor attended just once a year, never made a maiden speech, preferring instead to use the Lords as the setting for an annual drinks party, the summer counterpart to an even more lavish Christmas beano at Ickworth when flares lit the length of the drive. On these occasions, choreographed to his own designs, Victor performed as showman, eccentric and munificent host,[61] just as he did at weekends in Suffolk or at dinner parties at the Mayfair house he bought in the mid-1950s, 15 Chapel Street, or at banquets for the Monarchist League. Each expressed his desperation for social redemption; each was an opportunity to place a notice in *The Times* or the *Daily Telegraph*, as was his attendance at any party or event, whatever its insignificance. 'Every time they went anywhere, they put it in the Court Circular. Every single day, there was "The Marquis[62] and Marchioness of Bristol attended..." They did it one day and the wedding – it might have been a memorial service – had been cancelled.' Obby Fitzwilliam begged a friend to intercede in the hope that the blizzard of announcements might end. The appeal had limited success. 'It quieted down a bit: they didn't put all the things they were doing – funerals, [for example].'

The craving for acceptance, and Victor's willingness to try to buy his way towards it, inevitably left him vulnerable, not least to the hundreds who trooped into Ickworth for the annual Christmas guzzle, when the dazzle of the 'marquessate accoutrements' was teamed with limitless good champagne. Hearing a guest belittling him, Carol Havers intervened. 'I said, "How dare you. You come in here, drink yourself into a stupor on champagne and then say the most horrible things about him". [He was] a local big-wig type who just went to try and nick something, or certainly drink everything, and then tear [Victor] to shreds.'

Staunch friends though Michael and Carol Havers were, Victor did not have many allies like them. A continental aristocrat remembers his father being 'extremely critical' of Victor, despite agreeing to become godfather to one of his children; Obby Fitzwilliam accepted Victor's hospitality in a spirit of more or less open subversion, as a guest at an Ickworth dinner party remembers. 'The butler came in with a tray, not with a drink on it, but [Victor's] coronet. He put it on a table, on a sort of little cushion, looked frightfully embarrassed about it, then went out.' The Dowager Countess Fitzwilliam plucked the coronet from its cushion, 'plonking it on her head' and began 'prancing around the hall'. The performance would have earned approval in Horringer. When, in 1963, two hundredweight of silver, valued at £20,000, was stolen from Ickworth – a burglary carried out for the Russian market, said Victor, assuring the press that Lloyd's had 'paid out in full' – the village, remembers Diana Lainson, had no hesitation in concluding that it was 'an inside job'.

Ostracism sharpened Victor's already keen appetite for reinvention. Practising a rigid code of *omertà* about his past, he tried to reinvent himself as a maverick cruelly born into the wrong era, his intention being to persuade people that he was a 'jolly old card' rather than a jailbird. He wrote blimpish letters to *The Times* and the *Daily Telegraph*, and became a master of the 'eccentric gesture' (choosing, when staying with his old friend Johnny Kimberley, to go shooting in a pinstripe suit). He had enjoyed recounting that, before conversion of the *Cochrane Hervey* could begin, live canon shells and machine-gun rounds had to be extracted from the hull; now he ran the Ickworth shoot on quasi-military lines and referred to his valet as his 'batman', the first intimations of the fantasies which would culminate in claims of heroism in the Spanish Civil War. It was a performance, relentlessly sustained, which yielded equivocal rewards. Whilst Victor remained silent about his trial and imprisonment, others inaccurately reminisced: very quickly, he came to be remembered for a crime he did not commit – an oddly appropriate fate for this most delusional of men. But he also became a prize exhibit, acclaimed far beyond his immediate circle, as his cousin Douglas Cochrane came to appreciate when Victor, driving from London to Suffolk after a demanding lunch, fell asleep at the wheel and steered into another car. Douglas, who had been Victor's only passenger, hurried to placate the victim; there proved to be no need. 'He said, "Good heavens, do you mean to say I've been run into by the Marquess of Bristol?" "Yes," I said, "you have".' The driver, evidently enchanted, excitedly asked if he could be introduced to Victor, which he was.

It was the Monarchist League which allowed his imagination freest rein. According to Juliet, Victor was amused by dressing up. He took full advantage, appearing at the League's dinners in frock coats, lace cuffs, buckled shoes, Ruritanian sashes, the ensemble being completed by 'a sword hanging at his side, a collar badge and an assortment of medals'. These decorations were of Victor's own creation, one of them (possibly the Order of St Edmund) 'look[ing] remarkably similar to the Garter'. No seven-year-old could have raided the dressing-up box to more telling effect. Better still, the League offered an antidote to reality, a refuge which treasured the accident of high birth above any professional or personal accomplishment (or, most helpfully, criminal conviction). Founded in 1943 by the Revered John Bazille-Corbin, a barrister-rector-delusionist whose career transcended Church of England convention, its *raison d'être* was 'to uphold the principle of monarchy against the disintegrating forces of Bolshevism and socialism'. In subsequent decades, it also developed a reputation for providing good dinners for supporters and members of exiled royal families, a trumpet fanfare greeting each arriving guest, who was then seated according to hereditary status. Often held at the Savoy, these were gratifying if expensive occasions for Victor, who almost certainly bore much of the cost himself.

The League never failed him: whether at Ickworth or the Savoy or at its headquarters (then in Belgravia, today displaced to Paddock Wood), it afforded him a degree of respect and deference – and a form of fellowship – which proved elusive elsewhere. In 1976, after a number of years on the League's Grand Council, Victor emerged as its Chancellor. Thereafter, his letters were headed: From The Most Hon. The Marquis of Bristol, GO. St. A., GCLJ etc. His Excellency The Chancellor – The Monarchist League. The same formula was repeated at the end of the letter, beneath Victor's signature. As his cousin Douglas Cochrane remembered, 'he appeared to take it seriously'. It had taken time for Victor to graduate to the League, however. The date of his enlistment is uncertain, though he might have thought it prudent to wait until his uncle Frederick had died, if only so as to be able present himself for membership with a courtesy title, Earl Jermyn, rather than as plain Victor Hervey.

In the interim, he concentrated much of his energy on commercial projects. Radnor Films had led neither to Hollywood nor the Isle of Man, just the production of a stream of obscure promotional films. A slightly earlier enterprise – an attempt, in 1942, to become a registered money-lender – had been similarly starved of success. However, neither setback daunted Victor, who would always give a convincing impression of being thoroughly in tune with the pre-war credo, 'out of land and into business'. Undistracted by notions of traditional aristocratic paternalism, he appeared likely, if presented with an appropriately lucrative opportunity, to stifle sentiment and, say, bull-doze a building of beauty and distinction, perhaps pausing to retrieve its fireplace for installation in a penthouse.[63]

In the early 1950s, Richard Innes, whose mother lived at Horringer Manor, was flabbergasted when Victor, a guest at Sunday lunch, handed him a business card, and asked for his. A few years later, the rest of Horringer also learned quite how different the new Marquess was from the old.[64] Victor was eager that Ickworth should, as far as possible, pay its way. After lavishly redec-orating the East Wing (the first renovations since Dora's improvements of 1908), he got cracking. Late in 1961, a row of slot machines was installed outside the post office, beneath 8ft signs ('Fruit Pastilles', 'Spearmint Chewing Gum', 'Interesting Books'; the last included the work of American author Mickey Spillane, whose 1947 bestseller, I, the Jury, had shocked readers with its sadistic eroticism). The machines were, Victor alleged, 'a non-profit-making amenity for the village of Horringer'. The 'amenity' was removed after vehement objections from Horringer Parish Council and, perhaps more importantly, from Victor's cousin Phyllis MacRae.

Christmas trees were sold by mail order; the shoot was put on a rigorously commercial footing: every bird – sometimes as many as 10,000 brace a season – pre-sold to a firm of food exporters, and days let. A newspaper article, 'Out with Britain's Most Expensive Guns', noted that sixteen days' shooting at Ickworth cost £1,700, which, it pointed out, was more than most Britons earned in a year. A museum, a magpie's nest of often macabre miscellanea (exhibits included a 12,000-lb bomb and a dagger with which the Moroccan Prince Abd el Krim was said to have killed 10,000 Spanish soldiers), was lodged next to the stables, with Donald Campbell's Bluebird as its showpiece. There was a plan to sell Shetland ponies, and another to create landfill sites in Lincolnshire and Essex; a fragment of a Suffolk acre, just a quarter of a mile from Ickworth's gates, was divided into 4ft-square plots, and offered for sale (with accompanying illuminated scroll signed by Victor, and a refer-ence to Magna Carta) to unwary Americans. 'To all who purchase a piece of this most historic old England, held by my family for many hundreds of years,' Victor declared in the conveyancing notes, 'I confer the dignity of belonging to the High Steward Association of the Liberty of St Edmund because of my faith in multiple world membership of the birthplace of Magna Carta (Bury St Edmunds) as a means of preserving peace and free-dom also encouraging communication amongst peoples'. By 1970, he was claiming to have sold 40,000 of these plots, at £3 16s 8d apiece.[65] The claim was roughly 40,000 out, says Michael Chappell, who came to know the details of estate affairs when he became accountant to Victor's son John four years later.

Although some of Victor's schemes would seem routine today, there was an unusual hunger in his approach, typified by his enthusiasm for talking up his plans in the press, as though he were heading a corporation in which he had an appreciable stake. (It was characteristic that, later in life, when he handed Ickworth over to his eldest son, he frequently warned him – often by telegram – against 'depleting the resources of the marquisate'.) Late in 1966, tenants at Ickworth, immunized against the twentieth century by Frederick's conservatism, were jolted by a series of advertisements in the personal columns of *The Times*. These offered their cottages for sale, explaining to potential buyers, in unusual detail, that the sitting tenants would not be there for ever – or, in some cases, for very long at all, the most encouraging being one who was 'crippled, currently in hospital, and may not ever return home'. Following the ensuing and inevitable outcry, Victor claimed that the advertisements had appeared without his knowledge, although a reference to a tenant as 'one Grimwood' (which caused particular offence) seems a vintage Victor phrase.

It was proof, he might well have concluded, of how irksome estate business was. His preference was for grand-scale projects whose success he could proclaim well in advance of completion. In the 1950s he had led the hunt for what he said was £14 million worth of treasure buried on Cocos Island, in the Pacific ('the expedition yielded anecdotal and photographic riches, if nothing else');[66] by the 1960s he was striking a generally less adventurous, but more authoritative pose. He proposed the creation of a 75-acre industrial estate at Sleaford in Lincolnshire (where the Herveys retained 11,000 acres) and a 120-acre housing development just outside Bury St Edmund's. Both schemes were rejected.

But they were inconsequential by comparison with the marina and power-boat harbour Victor had announced he was building at Shotley in 1963. Costing between £1,000,000 to £1,500,000 (£64 million today), it would almost certainly be the largest in Europe, with initial berths for 1,000 boats, rising to 2,000, then to 3,000. At least one newspaper was caught up in the enthusiasm, reporting that the Marquess of Bristol, owner of the magazine *Watersport and Motor Cruising* (circulation unknown) was 'to introduce hydro-karting – an aquatic form of go-karting – to the new million-pound yacht marina which is being built at Shotley'. However, it wasn't being built: it was never started, still less finished, much to Victor's fury. Unenlightened official-dom thwarted the final planning bid for the marina, submitted in 1968 by one

of Victor's companies, the opaquely named Estates Associates, which, according to the *Daily Telegraph*, was 'acting on behalf of the Oakdale Company, of
Nassau, Bahamas'. It had not helped, recalled Viscount Colville, that during
the planning process Victor had invited the minister responsible to spend a
weekend at Ickworth.

Victor's interests extended beyond the Bahamas, recalls Sir Eldon
Griffiths, who was invited to fly by seaplane from Miami to the Dominican
Republic, where Victor had invested 'sight unseen' in some 'seafront acreage'.
(According to press reports, Victor had divided this into plots, offering them
for sale at £6,000–£10,000 an acre). 'I don't think he had ever set foot there,'
says Sir Eldon, who soon understood why: Victor's investment was 'mangrove
covered swamp' interspersed with 'strips of sand and rock'. 'At the only the
open section of beach,' adds Sir Eldon, 'we saw a white man on crutches,
waving.' Victor identified him as his 'agent'. More intimate acquaintance was
never made: with heavy surf preventing a sea-landing, they vainly scoured the
coastline for a landing spot, until the pilot, eyeing the fuel gauge, refused to
stay any longer. 'That was the kind of thing Victor was doing. One could
admire it, in a way.'

He claimed to be a director of twenty companies, as though that alone
were proof of commercial effectiveness. Turnover and profits were never
mentioned, despite his relish for talking about money, though there was
always a purpose to his schemes. Peter Geiger, who went into business with
his son John in the mid 1970s, remembers Victor's enthusiasm for sole trader-
ships 'because if they made a loss, it could be offset against investment
income'. And if neither the Bristol Publishing Company nor the Dominica
Enterprises Company nor any other of his enterprises delivered the booty
that Victor dreamed of, they allowed him a grandiloquent flourish in
Debrett's, *Burke's* and *Who's Who* – a significant consolation for a man whose
self-esteem was precariously dependent on titles and position.

Esoteric business interests also allowed for adventure, especially overseas
where they might be conducted in a hearteningly buccaneering manner. By
the late 1950s, Victor was enjoying success in Cuba, selling arms and equip-
ment to the Batista government – and then to the Castro regime which
ousted it. This was dexterity of the sort to which he had baselessly laid claim
twenty years earlier, yet this time there were no proclamations, no press interviews. His capacity for learning from past mistakes was not unlimited,
however: by February 1961, the Foreign Office was remarking on the 'dubious
reputation' of one of his companies, a reputation arising from 'its arms deals
in Cuba and elsewhere'.

By then, as Whitehall was aware, Victor had switched most of his energies from Cuba to Finland, scene of his difficulties with the Marquess of Donegall in 1937 but now a territory whose non-aligned status and frontier position in the Cold War demanded his attention. He was, he assured the *East Anglian* in March 1961, chairman of the de Jersey Group of Companies, one of which had a 'fully Finnish board', as well as offices in Helsinki. 'We operate in Finland under a special treaty,' added Victor.

Con O'Neill, appointed British ambassador in Helsinki in December 1960, knew that the prominence of de Jersey & Co. (Finland) Ltd in Anglo-Finnish trade could not be ignored. In consequence, when invited to a de Jersey reception in London – to be held in his honour at the Institute of Directors, and attended by senior staff from the Finnish Embassy – he accepted. So it was that he came face to face with 'Cousin Victor', quite probably for the first time in his life (notwithstanding their time at Eton together). The accident of kinship would, very quickly, generate significant embarrassment for the ambassador, for reasons which those lacking access to official files would find difficult to fathom. As far as Juliet was concerned, for example, Victor's Finnish enterprises involved a perfectly innocuous, if unspecified textile industry. Like the rest of Victor's friends and acquaintances, she neither spoke Finnish nor was she privy to Finnish Foreign Office records or the memoranda and minutes compiled by various British government departments whose contents would be declassified only some years after Victor's death.[67]

Although there was notable versatility about the de Jersey group (they handled exports to South America and provided financial services to anyone who was interested), its Finnish company achieved success in a field dear to Victor's heart. In 1960, it sold the Finnish government thirty-five Charioteer tanks at £5,000 apiece. What made this especially impressive was the fact that, three years earlier, the Finns had bought three Charioteers direct from the Ministry of Supply in London for just £3,500 each – the same price, in fact, that de Jersey was paying the Ministry for the thirty-five tanks to which it was adding an agreeable £1,500 mark-up before offloading them to the Finns. It was difficult to see the advantages of this from a Finnish perspective, and not only because the Finnish Ministry of Defence agreed to pay transportation costs, which (at roughly £500–£600 a tank) were significant.

Nevertheless, de Jersey's involvement in Finland's defence procurement programme continued, indeed intensified. In the summer of 1960, for example, the Finns paid the company £213,000 for five gun barrels and other hardware (bought by de Jersey from the War Office for £191,000); a few months later, in November, Finland bought forty Comet tanks from another de Jersey company, de Jersey & Co. AG of Switzerland. The tanks were not new, a detail which explains why de Jersey had been able to buy them from the War Office for £1,250 apiece, but not why the Finns were prepared to pay twice that (£2,500 apiece) to acquire them from de Jersey, especially since the Finns again paid for transportation (£27,000).

Had Victor ever been quizzed about this dazzling run of success, he could have pointed to impressive boardroom talent. By 1961, the directors of de Jersey & Co. (Finland), though not 'fully Finnish' as Victor had claimed, included a rear admiral, Victor's cousin, Ian (the Earl of) Dundonald, and an MP – Victor's stepfather, Sir Peter Macdonald. The firm's managing director was Major B. G. Merivale Austin, who, like Dundonald, had served in the Black Watch during the war. It was a team which 'helped to create a highly respectable façade'.

The board's Finnish contingent included Major-General Lars Melander, a director since 1945, but now held in flatteringly high esteem (a 'Finnish war hero,' de Jersey assured the War Office in London, 'who has entrée to the Army purchasing staff at top level and who can influence budget allocations'), and Kullervo Killinen, a former naval captain who had been Finland's military attaché in London, 1958–60 – two years during which de Jersey made gratifying inroads into the Finnish arms market. Understandably, de Jersey rarely struggled to arrange meetings with ministers and other influential Finnish public figures, amongst them General Paavo Lammetmaa, Permanent Secretary at the Finnish Ministry of Defence, who argued hard in favour of the Charioteer deal, eventually quelling protests ranged against it by the Commander of the Finnish Defence Forces. When Lammetmaa was obliged to resign his post in 1961, he too was recruited by de Jersey in the twin roles of 'military adviser' and 'transport adviser'.

In London, a War Office official asked the Assistant Finnish Military and Air Attaché why Finland 'was the only country to use an agent as intermediary when buying weapons from the UK'. De Jersey's intimacy with senior members of the Finnish establishment, coupled with the lucrative deals which it repeatedly pulled off, caused similar disquiet to Sir Douglas Busk, Con O'Neill's predecessor as ambassador in Helsinki, who had categorized de Jersey as 'efficient but far from scrupulous', warning Whitehall that the company was not to be trusted. Nevertheless, Victor and his directors enjoyed a productive relationship with the Ministry of Supply (later the Ministry of Aviation), which kindly authorized de Jersey to sell tanks to Finland without first troubling to consult the Foreign Office or, indeed, the British Embassy in Finland. The Foreign Office, noting that the letter of authorization 'was written at high level in the MOS against officials' recommendation', pointed out that de Jersey had, in effect, been given 'a blank cheque'. The Embassy in Helsinki braced itself for the worst. 'The arrangement could provide a trouble-making journalist with a very nasty story of how HMG and the British Embassy in Helsinki allowed the Finnish Government to be over-charged in order that de Jersey might make their profit,' read one report. 'There is obviously room for hints that people in high places – in the Finnish Ministry of Defence, for example – may be making a good thing for them-selves out of this arrangement.'

As far as Victor was concerned, that was someone else's problem. Encouraged by his tank engagements, he advanced fearlessly into what became known as Finland's 'Locomotive War', which had erupted in 1957 with a vote by the Finnish Parliament to begin modernizing the country's railway system, a decision which alerted manufacturers in France, Germany and Britain that immense contracts would soon be at stake. In the ensuing scramble, the allegiance of some senior Finnish politicians – and even whole political parties – seemed to owe more to their own pecuniary advantage than to Finland's national interest. 'There is a good deal of talk here of possible corruption,' reported the Commercial Counsellor at the British Embassy, '... businessmen talk openly about the more than lavish hospitality offered by the French and the Germans to such people which apparently includes the entire spectrum of pleasant human experience'.

This was a quagmire from which many would have recoiled; Victor had already plunged in. On 21 March 1961, he had written to Frederick Errol, Minister of State at the Board of Trade.[68] He had good news. 'The Finnish Minister of Communications and his Delegation went home last Friday morning after having been in our hands since Tuesday. [He] agreed to buy 40 English Electric locomotives at £52,000 each (just over £2 million, which, with spares etc., will be nearer £3 million).' Although conceding that this required Finnish parliamentary approval, Victor added that the deal enjoyed the support of the Defence Minister, Leo Happola, 'who is well known to us'. He concluded with a request. 'We were wondering whether you could cable our Ambassador on an official basis, to help as far as he is able. The Hon. Con. O'Neill happens to be a cousin of both Lord Dundonald and myself, and we know that he would be only too glad to assist!'

Notes jotted on to the folder containing Victor's letter to Errol reflected the dilemma that the Foreign Office now faced. 'This would be a fine contract to bring off,' read one, 'a pity it will probably go to de Jerseys';

another – 'Already invoking the family ties!' – had an uncomfortable reso-
nance for Con O'Neill, especially since, by December 1961, it had emerged
that the company was trying to secure a further arms deal, this time on a scale
dwarfing all previous ones, by offering the Finnish government a loan of
between £5 million and £6 million.

O'Neill's misgivings about de Jersey's operational techniques were known
across Whitehall. However, there was an acceptance that trading with
foreigners was an occasionally squalid business, a state of affairs which could
be tolerated if there was a cordon sanitaire between Her Majesty's
Government and malodorous firms like de Jersey. 'So far as we know, de
Jersey's UK principals are not positively acting as pacemakers in the bribery
of Finnish politicians,' reflected Sir Richard Powell, Permanent Secretary to
the Board of Trade. 'It may not, therefore, be too much to hope that, if and
when some scandal occurs, the mud, or most of it, will attach to the Finns
and/or to de Jersey's.' Subtlety, however, had never been Victor's forte. When,
earlier in 1961, he had learned that the Finnish President, Urho Kerkkonen,
planned to visit London, he alerted the Foreign Office that the President had
expressed an interest in visiting Ickworth. Whether this was true or not,
officials set about thwarting the plan, urged on by Con O'Neill. Victor,
presuming that his cousin would be 'only too glad to assist!', nevertheless
wrote to O'Neill as well, offering a vivid description of the hospitality to
which he had recently treated Leo Happola, during the Finnish Defence
Minister's trip to Britain.

Victor's luck held for one more year. By the spring of 1962, however, the
Finnish military attaché in London had concluded that de Jersey was a 'bad
firm' which had grossly overcharged Finland in a succession of arms deals, and
had contrived to do so by falsely claiming that Charioteer and Comet tanks
could not be bought directly from the British government. The mud which
Sir Richard Powell hoped would stick only to the Finns and de Jersey now
spattered O'Neill: the Finnish military attaché in London, having received
confirmation that O'Neill and Victor were related, suggested that de Jersey
was a company which enjoyed a 'position of special influence' – special
enough, it was soon rumoured in both London and Helsinki, to have secured
O'Neill the ambassadorship. O'Neill could only lament that the firm was
'a confounded nuisance', not least because of his 'relationship with some of
their directors and suspicions of the firm's honesty', but also because of its
capacity for incompetence.[69]

Later that year, General Lammetmaa demonstrated the vigour of the
company's approach, remarking to a visiting representative from English

Electric that he had been 'trying to soften up the [Finnish] Minister of Trade' by offering him shares in a small company that he and de Jersey's local manager had recently floated. English Electric promptly alerted the British Embassy in Helsinki, where a report noted that de Jersey had done 'untold harm' to the reputation of the British companies it represented, categorizing its sales methods during the previous two years as 'little more than stratagems and intrigues'. As a summary of Victor's approach to business, it was difficult to better, although Victor had resigned a few months earlier, both from the de Jersey chairmanship and the board. He had lost an invaluable ally at the end of 1961, following the death of his stepfather, Sir Peter Macdonald, whose parliamentary status had done much to veneer the company with authenticity and to secure access to government ministers.

By then the Board of Trade was urging British firms to do without de Jersey's representation. English Electric needed little encouragement: its successive attempts to win a locomotive contract had ended in failure. In fact, there had been only one British beneficiary from the 'Locomotive War' – de Jersey & Co. In September 1960, it had secured an order, worth £361,000, to supply Finnish State Railways with train wheels. There may be no incontrovertible proof that Victor and de Jersey were guilty of bribery, but the circumstantial evidence is resistant to alternative interpretation. The recruitment of a succession of senior Finnish officers to de Jersey's board might, by itself, have been unexceptional, but not in the light of a sequence of lucrative contracts and General Lammetmaa's remarks about 'softening up the Finnish Minister of Trade'. It is also instructive that Victor spent £70,000 on the redecoration of Ickworth at this time, according to someone later intimately involved in the management of the estate. In addition, 'it was never clear,' as his eldest son's solicitor puts it, 'how Victor made his money'.

Away from the blurred morality of post-war Finland, there were indications that he had emerged from Camp Hill not a reformed character but a shrewder one. In yet another enterprise, a gold prospecting expedition, he claimed to have contrived his escape after realizing that the costs threatened to overwhelm him. 'During the night – this is what he told me, he'd already told John several times,' remembers one of John's friends, 'he rubbed his signet-ring up and down the drill. Then he left, legged it.' The next morning, the prospecting party found that Victor had abandoned them without warning, but before they could decide whether to go after him, they were distracted by the discovery of traces of gold on the drill.

Even in maturity, small-scale deceit permeated Victor's life. Almost all the paintings at Ickworth, for example, purported to be Old Masters. 'There was

"Van Dyck" or "Titian" everywhere,' remembers John's friend. 'I said, "It certainly doesn't look like a Titian to me".' John seemed unruffled; he knew, his friend soon realized, that Victor had deliberately misattributed almost all the family pictures. The same inventiveness could yield financial reward, explains Peter Geiger: 'Victor used to book a villa holiday in the sun – in the days before people did [as a matter of course] – have the holiday, come home and then write a letter listing everything which was wrong with it, then sue and not pay. According to John, he was always suing.'

Friends understood these to be Victor's little jokes, rather like his claims to have assisted central American governments (a little joke which Victor paraded each year in *Who's Who*).[70] But the little jokes sometimes had a purpose, as Selina Hastings learned when, in 1965, she spent her long vacation from Oxford looking after John, then aged ten. Interviewed for the job by Juliet at 15 Chapel Street, she was told that she would spend most of the summer at Ickworth, but would also be required to accompany John to Italy: did she have an international driving licence? 'I said, "I have but it's expired, but I've only got to take it to the AA and pay five shillings and get a new one".' The remark prompted her introduction to Victor. He made an immediate impression, partly because he wore dark glasses and highly polished co-respondent shoes, but more because of the advice he offered her in a steady, earnest voice: 'Don't take it to the AA. Give it to me. I've had a stamp made that exactly replicates that of the AA, and it will save you five shillings.' Miss Hastings – as Victor referred to her – was transfixed.

Her routine was soon established. She and John spent each week at Ickworth, alone except for John's younger half-brother Nicholas, and Nicholas's nanny. On Friday evenings, Victor and Juliet arrived from London by chauffeur-driven Rolls-Royce, returning to Chapel Street on Sunday night. In the summer months there were, of course, no shooting weekends; in fact, Selina Hastings noticed no visitors at all. Nevertheless, even the simplest food was served in stately manner – 'incredibly grand meals, with footmen, often with a silver chafing dish being passed round [yet] when the lid was lifted up, there was [just] sausage and mash.' Stilted conversation was occasionally initiated by Victor.

'Why has John got dirty fingernails, Miss Hastings?'

'I'm terribly sorry, Lord Bristol. I will see that they are cleaned.'

In adulthood, John would claim that he had been terrified of his father. His fear was already apparent in childhood, says Selina Hastings, adding that, even to an adult, Victor seemed a disquieting figure, who progressed – 'sort of glided' – almost noiselessly from room to room. But shortly before the trip to Italy, her own relationship with Victor markedly improved. 'He was very grand with me. It was, "Miss Hastings do this, Miss Hastings do that". Then he saw my passport, and saw, "Lady Selina Hastings" on it.'[71] She laughs. 'There was a definite change in Victor's attitude towards me after that. He was quite sort of gracious then, very stiff but gracious. He would make dreadful little jokes when he was trying to be jolly.'

In the company of friends, Victor's attempts at jollity were invariably when he was drunk. The phrase 'off his trolley' probably ought to have been invented for him. Carol Havers has an abiding image of a stooped, round-shouldered man, dressed in a smoking jacket and slippers (embroidered with the Hervey coat of arms), leaning over a bottle on a trolley. 'He was very keen on trolleys with booze on,' she says. The trolleys, says Peter Geiger, were not things of beauty. 'They were frightful – brass plate and formica. Victor had a slight penchant for the naff.' But they fulfilled their purpose, enabling Victor to refresh himself wherever he was in the house, as another of John's friends remembers. 'John used to say that they bred when the lights were off. Victor was trolley mad, absolutely trolley mad. I can visually remember his study; there were at least three trolleys in it. They were *everywhere*.'

Juliet has commented that Victor 'enjoyed a drink, only occasionally drinking perhaps rather too heavily when upset – as on one occasion when a friend was killed in a car accident'. As a demonstration of loyalty this was admirable, since Victor seems to have been ceaselessly 'upset'. At a Monarchist League dinner, it was announced that the Marquess of Bristol was unwell. He looked it, lying face down in his soup until being carried out unconscious. A dinner at the Eccentrics Club proved similarly challenging; Lord Montagu of Beaulieu, the club's president, was rather surprised to hear that Victor was to be the guest speaker, and rather less surprised to see him being stretchered out (though only after he had collapsed into his pudding, Baked Alaska, 'splosh, head first into it'). To Sir Eldon Griffiths, Victor appeared 'very addicted to the bottle'. Isla Abinger found him a demanding dinner guest, consistently drunk, frequently embarrassing. John Knight, who became mayor of Bury St Edmunds in the 1960s, remembered going to Ickworth with his wife to have dinner with Victor and Juliet in the Chinese Room; by the time they arrived, Victor was obviously tight. Janet Milford Haven says that he was invariably 'on his way' by lunchtime.[72]

There was, she remembers, a particularly testing night when Victor and her husband, David Milford Haven, remained downstairs long after everyone else had gone to bed. 'I was about to run down in my night clothes and tell David he should damn well come to bed when I heard Juliet.' A yelled command followed. 'She said, "Leave him alone! Leave him alone!"' David Milford Haven, who had been helping Victor make the perilous ascent to his room, joined his wife moments later, leaving their host, face-down, moaning into the stairs.

But it wasn't Victor's drunkenness, or his dreadful little jokes, or his rendition of rugby songs, or his Finnish affairs, or his forgeries that wore Juliet down. Five years after giving birth to their son Nicholas in 1961, Juliet had a daughter, Ann, who died the day she was born. She also suffered a number of miscarriages. Victor seemed incapable of articulating concern for his wife and it was then that their marriage, in Juliet's words, 'did rather begin to fray at the edges'. Members of staff noticed. 'I think she was having a very, very difficult time,' recalls one of them. 'We'd hear that when Lady Bristol called in the morning, she was crying and had a black eye, and there was a broken glass on the floor. I think it wasn't terribly easy for her.' The thrice-married Conservative MP Somerset de Chair was a more alluring prospect. Juliet became his literary executor in 1968 and his wife in 1974.[73]

The desertion redefined the remainder of Victor's life. With Juliet at his side, he could convince himself that he had clawed his way back to social respectability. Without her, that comforting fiction evaporated. Carol Havers recalls the moment in 1971 when Victor learned that Juliet had gone for good. 'He rang up, crying on the phone in the middle of the night, desperately upset. [She] left a letter on the fireplace: "By the time you get this, I shall be somewhere in Italy". It completely unsettled him. We had the same doctor, Brian Piggot. Mike [Michael Havers] rushed over to Chapel Street, to their house, so did Brian Piggot.'

After the initial shock, a sort of logic seems to have asserted itself in Victor's head: Juliet, an aristocrat with an Oxford education, had been his salvation; therefore he must find another Juliet. He began to subject Selina Hastings, whom he had last seen about six years earlier at Ickworth, to a relentless and extraordinary courtship. She was in her early twenties; Victor in his mid-fifties. 'Three times a day I would get hand-delivered letters with the stamp on it saying, "Special Delivery From The Most Honourable The Marquis of Bristol".' There were presents, too – wine and trinkets – and intimate dinners at the Monarchist League headquarters, enriched one evening by dining *à trois* with King Simeon of Bulgaria. When, after a few months, Victor proposed, he did so indirectly, writing a letter to Selina Hastings' parents, the Huntingdons, enclosing an additional sheet of paper. 'On one side, he listed one-to-ten why I would make a suitable chatelaine of Ickworth; then, on the other page, one-to-ten why he would make me a good husband.

My mother wrote back – it's like something out of a Jane Austen novel – "I'm afraid my daughter's affections are engaged elsewhere" or a phrase like that. He took absolutely no notice; the letters and presents kept arriving. Finally, my father said, "This has got to stop. We'll come up to London and tell him".'

Victor accepted an invitation to lunch at Lord Huntingdon's set in Albany. On the appointed day, Selina, then working at the *Daily Telegraph*, returned home from Fleet Street in good time. At one o'clock, the bell rang. 'There was the porter in his top hat and uniform supporting an obviously terribly drunk Victor.' After being introduced to her parents, Victor whispered to her to look out of the window. 'He said, "you'll see I've brought you a little something". I looked out of the window and there was a lizard green Daimler, with a chauffeur in a lizard green uniform. I suddenly thought, "Oh, am I doing the wrong thing?"' Although laughing as she says this, she adds that the lunch that followed was '*extremely* sticky', with Victor almost drinking himself to a standstill. 'He could hardly speak. At about ten to three, I said, "I'm terribly sorry, I've got to get back to the office". When I came home at about half past six, my parents were in the last stages of exhaustion. My mother said, "You realize he's only just gone?" But that was the end of it.' Victor, says Selina Hastings, 'was a terribly, terribly lonely man. He was incapable – at least incapable with me – of unbending. I don't know whether I even dared call him Victor. It was always extremely proper – he never laid a finger on me – but I think he liked me because I teased him a bit. I felt terribly sorry for him, I didn't like or dislike him.'

Though his pursuit of Selina Hastings proved fruitless, Victor did not despair but embarked on an energetic search for other targets, who were invited to dinners at Ickworth, where the less exalted members of the Monarchist League were described on their place settings as 'delegates'. His attention settled on someone who today is still remembered with immense affection by those who met her years ago. Sanchia, says Carol Havers, was 'a very big girl, a very statuesque girl, very beautiful, with glorious hair, just a picture'. A younger (male) regular at Ickworth remembers Sanchia as 'a darling: very, very glamorous – dark hair, great figure, very much the sort of sex symbol', adding that Victor, not usually a tactile man, allowed his hands to wander over her, publicly and appreciatively.

Originally employed as a chauffeuse, Sanchia's duties had gradually become more extensive as Victor's marriage disintegrated. 'She was so efficient and wonderful with Victor, coped an awful lot with his problem with drink.' After Victor had crawled upstairs howling 'rissoles, rissoles', it was often Sanchia who put him to bed. 'Sometimes she would go to Cyprus, not

Juliet; that was sort of accepted,' adds Carol Havers. 'Juliet was up, up and away with Somerset. Didn't care two hoots.' When Juliet finally left, Sanchia appeared to have been installed in her place, remembers Peter Geiger. 'Sanchia was the hostess,' he says. 'It was a Charles and Camilla thing.' Victor dared to list her name in *The Times*, among the guests attending a lunch at Ickworth, held in honour of Yehudi Menuhin in April 1972. Another visitor to Ickworth says that, in Sanchia, Victor had found a rare and extraordinary person. 'I met her probably twice, thirty years ago. You know how some people leave a very positive impression, a kind of aura of sweetness and genuineness? She was adorable, outstandingly sweet, charming, loyal, lovable; she really loved Victor. John wouldn't have minded at all if she had married Victor.'

Victor married Yvonne Sutton.

* * *

'I think she really wanted to make a completely fresh start, which I can well understand,' remembered Douglas Cochrane, whose convivial weekends at Ickworth, and refreshing evenings at Chapel Street, fell victim to the regime change instituted by Victor's third marriage on 12 July 1974.[74] Victor was on the brink of his sixties; his new bride was twenty-nine. Like Sanchia, Yvonne was attractive (though cut from a narrower mould); like Sanchia, she had been a member of Victor's staff, working as his secretary. She was determined, clear-sighted, protective.[75] John Knight clearly remembered his first meeting with her. 'I was sorry that Juliet wasn't there [but] this was the Marchioness now, the new order. She struck me as being a young woman with quite a presence; I got the feeling that she was going to handle Victor all right.' It was a shrewd assessment. Few, if any, could have handled Victor in his final decade as adroitly as Yvonne did.

Victor's snobbery and pretentiousness – which, some of his friends assumed, had always had an element of self-parody to it – now seemed in earnest. 'He suddenly took himself incredibly seriously,' recalls one of his much younger acquaintances. 'I remember saying, "Victor, that car – a Rolls – is so beautiful…" [He said], "It's a very good town carriage". You'd think, "*What?*"' An inquiry about the flags on the Rolls' bonnet brought the rebuke that they were not flags but pennants. Some of Victor's other pronouncements suggested not affectation but derangement: asked about the provenance of a pair of candlesticks, he replied that they had been given to him by George III. 'He just became very odd.'[76]

The change did not escape the notice of Arthur Lainson, with whom

Victor had kept a car in adolescence. The two men rarely saw each other in maturity, when Lainson, at 6'4", dwarfed Victor, who shrank to about 5'8" in his dotage. Periodically, however, Lainson and his wife were invited to Ickworth. On one of the last occasions their daughter Diana accompanied them. The Lainsons were given champagne and shown to three chairs; Victor also took a chair, the only difference being, remembers Diana, that his was placed on a dais, raising him from the floor by between six and nine inches. Victor betrayed no sign of finding the arrangement anything other than entirely normal; the Lainsons managed not to laugh until later.

Yvonne never let her husband's furniture arrangements trouble her, proving a punctilious and tireless chatelaine, as Viscount Davidson noticed when he and his wife had dinner at Ickworth. 'While we were having coffee, she went round asking the people who were staying what they wanted for breakfast, taking notes.' Juliet's tradition was being maintained, albeit in slightly different style. More remarkably, Yvonne rekindled Victor's interest in having children (by 1982, she had given birth to two daughters and a son), an accomplishment that startled Juliet and those, like Sir Eldon Griffiths, who felt that Victor's enthusiasm for the bottle precluded further stabs at procreation. There were, though, casualties along the way, notably Sanchia, whom Victor had gracelessly erased from his life. 'I don't think he even told her he was marrying Yvonne,' says one frequent visitor to Ickworth. 'I think she read about it.' If so, Sanchia finds the episode too intense for comment, saying that, even now, she 'can't handle' talking about it. Carol Havers voices her sympathy: 'Sanchia is the one we all thought Victor might marry.'

Victor did not trouble to invite his heir to the wedding either, or even let him know when it would be. His aloofness during John's childhood made it unlikely that theirs would be an especially rewarding relationship when John reached adulthood. When drugs edged ahead of drink in John's affections, and when his bisexuality – with a preference for men – became apparent, their estrangement was very nearly complete. Carol Havers and others attempted to intercede, but were brushed aside. 'We'd say, "John's not that bad, Victor, you really ought to patch it up". [He'd say] "No, never". That was all very sad.'

Soon after his marriage to Yvonne, he decided to move permanently to London – always his preferred territory, remembered John Knight, certainly if no jaunt abroad was in the offing. This entailed handing Ickworth over to John, who was still only twenty-one. His son arrived to find every stick of furniture – every lamp, every chair, every picture – and almost every fitting (even the doorknobs) being stripped from the East Wing, in readiness for auction. 'He hired 26 removal vans,' remembered John, fourteen years after-wards, 'four cranes, two horse boxes and 30 men. The two hunters, one of them given by him to me as a Christmas present, were loaded and driven away to be sold as dog meat.' The episode, remembers one of John's friends, came to be known as Victor's £100,000 joke, so called because that was reput-edly the cost in solicitors' fees and storage payments needed to secure the furniture's return.[77] Peter Geiger, John's one-time business partner, believes that Victor was motivated by unspoken resentment. 'He wasn't that old [he was fifty-nine] but he was clearly in poor health. I just had this feeling that he was jealous of John, because John would soon inherit, without having to do any hard work, without having to redecorate [Ickworth] as he had done.'

Four years later, early in 1979, Victor made his final move, opting for tax exile in Monte Carlo. Inviting reporters to Chapel Street to record his depar-ture, he claimed to have paid between £15 million and £20 million in tax[78] during the previous fifteen to twenty years, all of it earned through his own endeavours. However, it was not tax alone that had forced him to leave but crime. 'It is no longer safe to walk the streets with one's girlfriend or wife any more,' he said. 'Not that I am at all unnerved to go out alone, because I have a black belt in karate. But I wouldn't dream of taking my wife for a stroll – even in Belgravia. There is no crime rate in Monte Carlo, or it is negligible, and one has much more security and peace of mind there...'

England was deficient in other ways, too. 'People will really have to get down to work and earn a living,' Victor advised. 'Take the Civil Service and all those pen-pushing parasites at Whitehall. We could do with 80 per cent less of them because they are all no-goods who got the job because they couldn't get a job anywhere else.' It was a vintage performance, blimpish in tone, laced with self-delusion, preposterous in detail. One or two newspapers made arch comments about Victor's trenchant distaste for crime, though none mentioned his time in Camp Hill. No one challenged his claim to have paid taxes equal to over £400 million in today's money, nor asked him which of his 'endeavours' had generated such a fabulous sum. It was, though, the deferential acceptance of Victor's claim to be a karate black belt that showed how far he had succeeded in his aim of self-reinvention. Slightly stooped, palpably frail,[79] alcohol leaking through tired, very white skin, here was a man fit only to break wind. Yet he was taken at face value. Context helped: in a decade that delivered the Three Day Week, the Bay City Rollers and the Winter of Discontent, Victor could masquerade – frequently in silk sashes and decorations of his own devising – as an antidote to egalitarian banality.

Regrettably, perhaps, no class warriors stumbled into the christenings he choreographed for Victoria and Frederick, his first daughter and only son by Yvonne. Nominally Catholic occasions, though notable for their impressive indifference to doctrine (Victor had a tendency to select Muslim prince-lings[80] as godparents), they were quite unlike the conventional ceremonies he had considered appropriate for his two elder sons by earlier marriages. 'My husband was told to wear his medals,' remembers Margaret Dundonald, adding that nearly all their fellow guests were crowned heads, or displaced royals. Ian Dundonald was of the opinion that medals should not be worn at a christening, so he complied with his cousin's request but concealed them beneath his overcoat.

Nevertheless, these essays in folie de grandeur did have a certain enchant-ment, as Margaret Dundonald acknowledges. 'We started at the Berkeley Hotel with photographs, then had six Rolls-Royces to take us, I think it was to Farm Street. It was quite fun.' A volley of trumpets greeted their arrival. 'Then we went in procession, with somebody carrying the baby on a pillow at the front. Princess Astrid of the Belgians and myself were the only two Christian godparents; the others were arab princes [who] weren't allowed to go up to the altar.' Even Victor was not immune to the excitement of the occasion, as Margaret Dundonald's stepson Douglas, 15th Earl of Dundonald, remembers. 'Victor was wearing a morning coat with a sword. He tried to put the unsheathed sword through the morning coat. That was when my father decided that he [Victor] had had enough to drink and put his head in a bucket of water.'[81]

* * *

In Monte Carlo, Victor and Yvonne installed themselves in the Square Beaumarchais in a monochrome building with a glimpse of the sea. Any aesthetic inhibitions that Victor had had when decorating Ickworth now vanished. Carol Havers remembers their apartment as 'sumptuously decorat-ed', but Victor sensed that he could do better. 'They moved to another,[82] even more sumptuously decorated, [with a] huge garden on the terrace.' Guy Sainty recalls it well. 'It was flash beyond all belief, [filled with] over the top, French eighteenth-century furniture and what we call pompier pictures – extravagantly painted costume dramas from the 1860s and 70s, technically very well painted but somewhat vulgar.' If visitors, adds Sainty, had been told that the apartment 'belonged to the most nouveau riches of nouveau riches', they would not have demurred. There was certainly no shortage of them, as far as Carol Havers could tell. 'They used to have a lot of parties. [There

were] ex-pats, and a lot of French, though Victor never spoke a word of
French.'

His new acquaintances might have thought that their host was set for a
contented old age: he had abundant money, a slim, energetic and attentive
wife, and two young children.[83] But an article he contributed to *The
Monarchist*, shortly after the move to Monte Carlo, offered a glimpse beneath
the surface. Attacking what he styled 'The BLOODSUCKER Department'
– the Inland Revenue, whose employees he characterized as 'throwouts [*sic*],
dropouts, drugouts, long-haired morons, idiots' – Victor asserted that 'this
great Monarchy of ours has been debased in Government to a fifth-rate
third-world Republic'. Adding that he was writing from a 'beautiful balcony
at the Chancery [i.e. his flat]', from where he had a view of the 'upper midriff
[*sic*] of the Hotel de Paris', he concluded by praising the Monte Carlo police,
simultaneously noting that 'anyone with any psychology' knew that 'a squat
fellow with a flat bulgy nose, little beady eyes and a pig-like expression' was
someone to be avoided. The Monarchist League decided that, henceforth, all
articles, including the Chancellor's notes, should be submitted for scrutiny
before publication.[84]

Gerald Howson received Victor's jottings in unexpurgated state. The
letters conformed to unvarying pattern: casual asides ('Being a Monarchist I
stopped the plot to kidnap Haile Selasse'), double and triple exclamation
marks, hand-written addenda almost incoherently jammed down beside the
fields of type, Victor's signature spattered across the page in a climb of thirty
degrees.

Carol Havers, who twice stayed in Monte Carlo with Victor, sensed
desperation, if not disintegration. 'He just missed England, he missed
Ickworth. He went [to the English Pub] every day, just out of the block and
down the steps.' But Victor began drinking long before reaching the pub. 'I
remember walking [around] the apartment at about 10 o'clock in the
morning. He was in dressing gown and pyjamas, with a bottle of vodka,
standing in front of the mirror and saying, "God Save the Queen" – and
having a great slug out of the bottle.'

Trips home offered the prospect of fun in London: lunches in Claridge's,
dinners with friends. Towards the end, however, even these pleasures were
diminished by infirmity and bereavements. In November 1983, Victor was
admitted to the London Clinic (afterwards, he chose to recuperate at
Claridge's, rather than at Chapel Street). Earlier that year, in February, his
ebullient friend Sir Hugh Trevor Dawson had drunk half a bottle of champagne in his flat in Eaton Square, then pulled a plastic bag over his head. He

had been facing probable fraud charges arising from his role as head of the unit trust division of his merchant bank, Arbuthnot Latham;[85] Michael Havers had been amongst his unfortunate investors. Dawson thereby became the second of Victor's closest allies to take his own life: five years earlier, Derek Le Poer Trench, best man at his wedding to Juliet, had shot himself in the head after selling his family seat, Woodlawn House, in Co. Galway.

* * *

But the cause of Victor's instability may have lain deeper than depression and physical deterioration. One of his second cousins, Henry Hoare, mentions his own grandmother – Lady Geraldine Hervey, Herbert's younger sister and, consequently, Victor's aunt – who was, he says, 'slightly dotty'. By the 1920s, it had become evident that she was unable to be a 'satisfactory mother', so her son – Hoare's father – spent much of his time with his cousins, often at Ickworth, whilst she remained at home under supervision.

Elsewhere, 'slight dottiness' was eclipsed by mental illness. Near the centre of York, there is a handsome eighteenth-century building set in its own grounds. From within its passageways comes the sound of quizzical chatter and squabbling (generally good-natured). Founded at the end of the eighteenth century by a Quaker merchant, who named it the Retreat, it became and remains one of Britain's finest psychiatric hospitals. It was, for some time, home to John Rowley, elder son of Victor's aunt, Lady Marjorie Rowley (née Cochrane), by her marriage to Owsley Rowley, a Huntingdonshire landed gentleman. Marjorie's photograph album shows the two boys – John and his first cousin Victor – on the beach together near Lochnell; they briefly overlapped again at Eton, John arriving there in 1931. Later, John went up to Trinity College, Cambridge. By 1941, Victor was in prison; John an inmate of St Andrew's Hospital, Northampton.

According to Eton's records, John undertook no military service during the war. Ian Dundonald (another of John's first cousins) and Peter Rowley, his half-brother, knew otherwise. John's was a pitiful and appalling story. Although wholly unfitted for military service (as subsequent clinical study would make apparent), he had been commissioned into a cavalry regiment, courtesy of some effective string-pulling by his father, Owsley, whom he then attempted to kill (using a ceremonial sword). He suffered a complete breakdown during the retreat to Dunkirk, was medically discharged from the army and admitted to Northampton mental hospital, only to be released (considered 'cured') shortly afterwards. Soon he faced repeated questions about why he was not in uniform; the girl he hoped to marry rejected him. John slunk home, and shot himself in the mouth with a .22 rifle. He did not die, but lived for almost another forty years, blinded in one eye, the bullet still lodged in his skull.

So began incarceration in a series of psychiatric institutions, at one of which, in Ticehurst, he was said to have nearly killed a nurse. By the late 1950s, he had been moved to the Priory, Roehampton, where he was visited by Ian Dundonald and, once, by his much younger half-brother Peter, who lived in New York. On that occasion, John, wearing a three-piece suit, sat in an armchair and did not speak. He never did; nor, whenever the dentist visited, would he open his mouth. His teeth had, in consequence, long since been reduced to putrid brown stumps. As Peter and his wife took their leave, John began to roar. The roars grew louder as the door was locked behind them. John had first turned his back on the world in adolescence. 'You could hardly get him to say anything,' remembers one of his contemporaries. 'He was very odd.' In fact, he was schizophrenic. He choked to death on 26 December 1979.

Unlike Ian Dundonald, Victor seems never to have visited his cousin, nor to have mentioned his name or that of his younger brother George, born in 1922, educated at Stowe and Magdalene College, Cambridge, and, by the late 1950s, living in a serviced flat at 20 Hyde Park Place, Paddington. Clever, myopic (unable to drive), huge (over 21 stone), more comfortable in the company of servants (his accent approximating to theirs rather than that of his peers), George sustained himself on alcohol, nicotine and prostitutes (visiting his favourite each Friday evening). When told that his flat at Hyde Park Place was required by its landlord, he marked his final night there by ordering seven puddings, each of which he returned uneaten but speared by half-smoked cigarettes. He spent the remainder of his life in a flat in Artillery Mansions, Westminster, dying there, unmarried, in 1976.

Victor expunged both brothers from his life completely and utterly, just as he had expunged Gwrych and Winifred, Camp Hill and Coop, so that Juliet did not know of their existence, just as she had remained ignorant of their mother, Marjorie. Another Cochrane relation, Denzil Cochrane-Newton, asserts that Marjorie was 'a bit odd'. Peter Rowley, who when visiting England usually saw his half-brother George, never dared ask for details: Marjorie was 'a forbidden subject – a black hole of anger', who lived for 'much of the time as a voluntary patient in nursing homes'. Following her divorce in 1933 from Owsley Rowley, she undoubtedly preferred spinsterish anonymity, living alone in Dorking and seeing out her final years at 61 St George's Square, Pimlico. Only her will – a brief document, written in

December 1945 – offers a trace of evidence for the Cochrane-Newton thesis. Decreeing that her property and chattels were to be divided equally between her two sons, Marjorie added that it was her 'earnest desire that they join either The Life Guards or the Navy or Brigade [of Guards]'. Yet by then John was already twenty-seven; rather more importantly, he had been in a psychiatric hospital for four, perhaps five, years.

* * *

Victor never joined his cousin at the Priory, much though he might have benefited from treatment. Those whom he charmed or entertained or flattered are prone to say that his problems were caused by drink; that, if deprived of alcohol, or rationed to a sane amount, Victor was capable of decency and sense. To an extent, this is indisputable. Unlike Churchill, however, Victor never managed to get more out of alcohol than alcohol got out of him, but adhered to a regime which would have tested even Churchill's stamina: vodka at 10 a.m., the English Pub until lunch, something from the trolley – whichever trolley, the nearest one to hand – and a little more in the afternoon, then more again (legitimized by the approach of dinner) until nightly oblivion.

But while drink exacerbated Victor's paranoia, and fuelled his insecurity and vanity, it was not their cause. That was buried deep within him. Victor did not care to look, preferring instead to blot out the possibility of sober analysis, whose conclusions, as his old friend Johnny Kimberley found, were not necessarily comforting. 'I didn't analyse my actions at the time,' Kimberley finally admitted in his memoirs. 'If I had done so, I knew I would not have liked the analysis. The truth [is] that really I am not a very nice person.'

At the end, Victor demonstrated that he had unusual reserves of venom. On one of his final visits to England in 1984, he placed an advertisement in *The Times*. 'The Marquess and Marchioness of Bristol,' it read, 'will not be able to attend the marriage of Earl Jermyn to Francesca, daughter of Mr & Mrs Douglas Fisher, on 14th September owing to a prior engagement in London.' John's attitude towards Yvonne – or the under-secretary, as he persisted in calling her – deserved rebuke; unfortunately Victor, who had done so much to inculcate the snobbery that underpinned it, was ill-qualified to deliver it. His notice in *The Times* was contemptible and brilliantly effective. John was making an immense effort to do the right thing – to forsake drugs, to marry, to father an heir, to preserve Ickworth, for all of which he sought blessing from the man who terrified him. Victor lacked the dignity and grace to give his blessing, and so did not hear his son's wedding speech, in which John referred to him as 'a cantankerous old bastard', but added: 'I still love him'.

Six months later, on 10 March 1985, the old bastard was dead. Unlike the Earl Bishop, Victor was not posthumously repatriated. Only his immediate family attended his funeral in Monte Carlo, following which there were testing scenes in the Bristols' flat, whose floor John reputedly coated with cigarette ash.

It is perhaps appropriate that Victor remains in exile. He was, says Michael Chappell, son of Victor's accountant Roy Chappell, a man who 'knew about incomes and trying to live within them'. It was a useful but limited achievement. Victor displayed none of the modesty or frugality of his uncle Frederick; too little of his father's sweet nature; none of the Earl Bishop's erudition or of Lord John Hervey's altruism or the cerebral Christianity of Lords Arthur and Manners Hervey. If the pain of osteo-myelitis diminished his inhibitions and partly explained his extravagant behavior, it did not excuse his tendency to criminality or his taste for wounding the vulnerable. To Kay Fisher, one of his younger relations who knew and loved and saw the potential for goodness in his eldest son John, he was and remains 'an appalling man'. But to those, like the enduringly loyal Carol Havers, who experienced his generosity and charm, he will always be 'dear Victor'.

PART THREE

'I can't understand,' said Daniel, 'how you're so caught up with these people... who are so used to being on top.'

'That's the thing,' said Whittington. 'They aren't on top. Not any more. I mean take this poor devil the Duke of Radley...' He pulled a yellowing newspaper cutting out of a file he carried around with a view to preparing a collection of his obituaries... He started to read. '"Convicted on eight charges of cheque fraud and two of theft, Radley was working as a washer-up in a Reading hotel where he was dismissed for stealing teaspoons shortly before he perished by his own hand. He will be remembered for his bold and innovative interpretation of the Radley family motto: Death before Dishonour." Do you know,' he added, 'that, at the time of his death, he was living in a numbered house in Leatherhead?'

Robert Chalmers, Who's Who In Hell

Angus

Silence in the saloon, with its fluted Corinthian pilasters and columns, its portraits (the best by Lely), its marbled fireplace by Galilei; silence beneath the staircase ceiling, its murals by Pellegrini (cherubs toying with coronets, flautist and Negro trumpeter picked out against a Mediterranean sky, Caesar adorned with bay-leaf crown); silence in the chapel, remodelled by Vanbrugh and Hawksmoor. Outside, the scent of summer; sun on Ketton stone.

Thursday, 25 July 2002.

There would be few better days that year to pay court to Kimbolton, for centuries the seat of the Montagus, first Earls then Dukes of Manchester. But visits to the Castle, as it is known in the village, were, and remain, by appointment only. None had been arranged for that Thursday.

In Bedford, however, thirteen miles south, a knot of bystanders gathered in the sunshine outside a low-rise block of flats. The building – its façade a melange of black fish-scale tiles and horizontal and vertical strips of white and blue – had been erected in the 1960s, in brave juxtaposition to the mock-Tudor timbers of the Embankment Hotel, overlooking the River Ouse. It was not, though, the jangle of architectural styles which gripped the onlookers' imagination but the presence of the local fire brigade.

A little earlier, a man at number 15, Broadreach – a flat on the third floor – had dialled 999. He was suffering chest pains, he explained, and needed help. Only once the ambulance men were inside his flat did they sense that this would not be a routine job. The flat's internal configuration was unusual. A kitchen had been remodelled as a bar (an improvement which a previous visitor had felt unable to applaud: 'It was made of dark brown plastic; mock oak, possibly'). The stricken man lay in a bedroom which could only be reached by a staircase whose modest width was further cramped by acute corners at top and bottom: use of a stretcher to aid his descent was out of the question.

Other casualties might have been eased down the stairs with an ambulanceman at either shoulder, but not this one. Though only about 5'8", he was of formidable bulk, seemingly a prize-fighter gone to seed: big-boned, square-built, generously fed, weighing in at over 20 stone, though still capable, at sixty-three, of defeating all challengers when arm-wrestling at Bedford Rowing Club or when pumping out press-ups on one arm or fingertip. The bedroom's balcony window alone offered hope, as the ambulance service subsequently told a local paper. 'The only way we could get him into an ambulance,' explained a spokesman, 'was to crane lift him.'

Helen Eldred, of the *Times & Citizen* newspaper, arrived just as the fire engine's hydraulic platform lowered its cargo to the ground. Moments later, a white-haired figure, almost totally obscured by blankets, was lifted into the waiting ambulance. Before filing her report, Eldred telephoned Bedford Hospital to check on his condition. Told that there was no news, she limited herself to noting that the sixty-three-year-old had led a chequered life, adding that his fourth wife had divorced him the previous year, after just seventeen months of marriage. He had been, she noted, a car salesman, crocodile hunter, cattle-train driver and Hollywood stuntman.

His death that night prompted John Mingay, Bedford's deputy mayor, to pay a remarkable tribute: it was, asserted Mingay, 'a tragedy that he is no longer in our lives'. Yet it would have been difficult for the uninitiated to have intuited the dead man's status or accomplishments. When casually dressed in brown leather jacket, his appearance was suggestive of a local minicab driver; when favouring white shirt, club tie, blazer and dark grey flannels, he might have been taken for a stalwart member of the local British Legion. Neither guise betrayed the unlikely truth: Angus Charles Drogo Montagu had been born at Kimbolton on 9 October 1938, an event celebrated (so he later claimed with uncharacteristic accuracy) by the flying of the Montagu standard. By the time of his death, he had been 12th Duke of Manchester for seventeen years, most of which had been spent at 15, Broadreach.

He was, he rightly remarked, a very un-noble noble. His knowledge of, and interest in, even his most recent antecedents was minimal, his appetite for aping the more illustrious of them non-existent. His grandfather had regularly entertained Edward VII at Kimbolton, as well as at the Montagus' secondary seats in Ireland; in his father's day, the Duke of Kent was a frequent and welcome guest. Angus's familiarity with royalty was restricted to the recurring possibility that he might be detained at Her Majesty's pleasure.

Though enduringly fond of his paternal grandmother, he had no inclination to emulate her by dividing his time between a country seat and a London residence in Eaton Square, nor did he seek out the dukes, marquesses and earls to whom, with varying degrees of intimacy, he was related. A bedsit in Victoria, a house in Kingston-on-Thames, his carefully remodelled flat at 15, Broadreach – these would do for him as well as any. Nevertheless, though disinclined to keep in step with most of the aristocracy, he revelled in his ducal status, which he expressed in idiosyncratic fashion. He believed, explains a Bedford friend, that 'a duke must be seen to behave like a duke. That means, when you arrive at the Inn on the Park, you take out a five-pound note, preferably a ten-pound note – "Your Grace, thank you" – and walk in. The door is always held open for you; when you come out, your car is swept up for you, and in you get and drive off.'

Acquaintances, to whom Angus was indiscriminately generous, were treated to prolonged and frequent binges, not only at the Inn on the Park but also in the dining room at the House of Lords, and at Bedford Rowing Club where he was a very active social member. 'He always spent,' reflects one beneficiary, 'as though money were no object.' It was a simple routine, but an expensive one for a man of Angus's limited means, which partially explains why, as his solicitor Ian Codrington puts it, 'his great god was money'. Uninterested in its potential for regilding the House of Montagu, he viewed it, instead, as a means by which to achieve self-expression in front of an eclectic court of admirers. His final, impressively full address book was democratically studded with Christian names like Reg and Keith, Kerry and Gerry. Many of these acquaintances lived blameless professional lives; a number didn't. It was invariably with the latter that Angus – whose solo efforts at self-sufficiency were ill-judged, short-lived, frequently still-born – chose to collude in what he called 'a bit of business', a characteristically impenetrable phrase, uttered as an index finger was raised in magisterial manner.

By the early 1970s, Angus's bits of business had attracted the attention of Scotland Yard. In subsequent decades, they led him to appear in the dock at the Old Bailey, to become the subject of protracted surveillance by the FBI and eventually – via the Federal Court, in Tampa, Florida – an inmate of the Federal Correctional Institution, Petersburg, Virginia. Simultaneously kind and sly, fastidious and obdurate, he frequently reduced those of his friends who had his best interests at heart to irritation, exasperation and despair. Often estranged from his father (and always from his only brother), he deserted his first wife when the youngest of their three children was barely a week old, and induced unease and distaste in his fellow hereditary peers, whose continued presence in the upper house was already imperilled by threats of unspecified 'reform'.

It was understandable that a newspaper should describe him as 'a one-man argument against the hereditary rights of peers', and rather more perceptive of another to conclude that 'there was always something dysfunctional about the man'. Those intimate with the Montagus' twentieth-century conduct would not have expressed surprise: theirs was a Gadarene plunge unequalled in the peerage. As a Kimbolton man who knew Angus in childhood puts it: 'What I'm wondering is, where are the white sheep in this family?'

* * *

The question would have affronted Angus's sixteenth- and seventeenth-century forebears, who, in the course of three generations, had elevated themselves from Northamptonshire yeomen to courtiers and statesmen, their earliest known forebear being William Ladde,[1] of Hanging Houghton; his son, Richard, changed his name from Ladde to Montagu (possibly to secure an inheritance). In their new incarnation, the family thrived. Richard's grandson, Sir Edward Montagu, became Chief Justice, a Privy Counsellor and an executor of Henry VIII's will; he was also responsible for drafting that of Edward VI, by which he attempted to settle the Crown on Lady Jane Grey. Queen Mary consigned him to the Tower immediately after her accession in 1553. The extinction of the fledgling Montagu line was a distinct possibility, but Sir Edward pleaded his case adroitly enough to avoid decapitation; after two months' imprisonment, he secured his freedom, in exchange for an appreciable payment of land and money. In the twentieth century, three of his direct Montagu descendants – besides Angus – were to follow him into custody, though none could be described as a political prisoner.

The Tudor and Stuart Montagus did not squander the reprieve, establishing a dynasty which at times seemed likely to rival the extent and influence of that of the Cecils. Sir Edward's son, also Sir Edward, held no high office but bred productively.[2] The privilege of being Angus's direct ancestor fell to his third son, Henry, who, towards the end of his life, was routinely drunk with every meal, but who, though 'hardly in the front rank, either as a lawyer or as a statesman', had been Chief Justice (securing Sir Walter Raleigh's execution), Lord President of the Council, Lord Privy Seal and, crucially, Lord High Treasurer, a position which, though he held it for less than a year, entitled him to a barony and a viscountcy. His purchase of

Kimbolton,[3] a fortified manor house originally built by a family called Mandeville in about 1200, inspired him to style himself the 1st Lord Kimbolton and 1st Viscount Mandeville. Six years later, he made a further advance, becoming the 1st Earl of Manchester.[4] The Laddes were doing well.

Henry's eldest son, Edward, 2nd Earl of Manchester, though emerging as a leader of the Puritan party (initially as MP for Huntingdon, then in the House of Lords) during the Long Parliament of 1626–42, was a man of moderation and compromise, which explains why, at different times, both Charles I and Cromwell wanted to do him fatal damage.[5] Despite that, and despite his subsequent unequivocal opposition to Charles I's trial (and execution), he survived, withdrew from public life during the Commonwealth, emerged after Cromwell's death to play an instrumental part in the restoration of the monarchy, outlived four wives (but not the fifth) and sat in judgement on the regicides (he favoured leniency, to no avail). Durability was the abiding characteristic of the Montagus for at least the next two centuries. Charles, the 4th Earl, who was blessed with 'more application than capacity', was Lord Great Chamberlain, twice ambassador to Venice (and once to Paris), as well as Lord Lieutenant of Huntingdonshire. He became the 1st Duke of Manchester (in 1719), though, as has been remarked, 'it is not at all easy to see why'. He did, however, instigate the great rebuilding of Kimbolton, transforming it from a Jacobean manor house into something altogether more inspired: only a minor example of Vanbrugh and Hawksmoor's work, perhaps, but still a building which almost any family would treasure (with the exception, it transpired, of the twentieth-century Montagus).

In the eighteenth century, and for much of the nineteenth, Kimbolton's custodians served dutifully in limited capacities, usually as Lord Lieutenants of Huntingdonshire or sometimes, when young, as MPs; in one case as Colonel of the militia; later, after the acquisition of an Irish estate, Tandragee, as a Deputy Lieutenant of Armagh. None hungered for high office, although the family name remained renowned for a while, thanks in part to Charles Montague [sic], one of the 1st Earl's grandsons, whose financial genius was instrumental in creating the Bank of England, as well as securing him the post of 1st Lord of the Treasury, a viscountcy and an earldom (both of which expired with him); and to John Montagu, 4th Earl of Sandwich, who became 1st Lord of the Admiralty and gave his name to the Sandwich Islands, as well as to the sandwich, dying from a digestive disorder in 1792.[6] Though the 3rd and 4th Dukes[7] came through their marriages unscathed, William, the 5th Duke (1771–1843), an enlightened governor of Jamaica (he exempted women from flogging and prohibited whips from being carried in the streets), was less fortunate, despite being considered by one female admirer to be 'the most beautiful statue-like person that ever was seen in flesh and blood'. His wife left him in favour of one of their footmen, which might explain why William distanced himself from their eldest son, George, Viscount Mandeville, seeing him as too palpable a reminder of marital humiliation.

Despite paternal rejection, George (1799–1855, 6th Duke of Manchester) enjoyed what appears to have been a contented marriage (to Lady Olivia Acheson, daughter of the 1st Earl of Gosford), the last Montagu to do so until Angus's father, four generations later. George's eldest son, William Montagu (1823–90, 7th Duke of Manchester), married the spirited and (according to contemporary accounts) intoxicatingly beautiful Countess Louise Frederick Auguste, an indefatigable member of the Prince of Wales's set and a daughter of Count von Alten of Hanover. Louise proved to be ardently and enduringly in love; not, unfortunately, with her husband – a 'well intentioned bore' – but with Spencer Compton Cavendish, 8th Duke of Devonshire.[8] William and Louise's uneasy marriage produced three daughters, all of whom married satisfactorily, and two sons, the younger of whom, Lord Charles Montagu, not only reached the traditional limit of Montagu accomplishment (becoming a Deputy Lieutenant of Huntingdonshire, and the Commandant of the county) but also displayed some understanding of money (he was a partner in what seems to have been his own stockbroking firm, Montagu & Co). Resisting marriage until he was seventy,[9] he had, by 1920, moved from his London house, 44 Grosvenor Square, to Kimbolton, where he gave a convincing impression of being 'a splendid, upstanding person'. He was still alive when Angus, his great-great nephew, was born at 'the Castle' in 1938.

Lord Charles's financial acumen was badly needed, his return to Kimbolton being prompted by pleas from family trustees. Though never as rich as the great ducal houses, like the Cavendishes or the Russells, the Montagus had 15,000 acres in East Anglia and 12,000 in Armagh. Until the 1870s, these produced over £90,000 a year; following the collapse in rental income in the 1880s, this slumped to £25,000, barely enough to meet the interest payments on mortgages cheerfully raised by previous generations. The situation demanded self-restraint and stoicism, qualities difficult to detect in Lord Charles's elder brother, George Montagu, 8th Duke of Manchester, Angus's great-grandfather. The electorate had resisted the temptation to return George as MP for the family seat in 1880, a decision handsomely vindicated nine years later when, at the age of thirty-six, he was declared bankrupt, owing £100,000. He invested heavily in Bessie Bellwood, a 'notorious music hall singer', with whom he spent most of his married life (which had begun in 1876), succeeded his father in 1890, and died in 1892 aged thirty-nine. The only son amongst his three children was William Angus Drogo Montagu, 9th Duke of Manchester – Angus's grandfather – always known to his intimates as Kim, a diminutive of his first courtesy title, Lord Kimbolton.

At the time of his death in 1947, *The Times* argued that Kim had displayed 'personality and a certain ability', adding that 'his firm mouth and jaw betokened qualities which might have brought him distinction had he not also been curiously lacking in judgement'. This neglected Kim's self-confessed preference for sport over what he called 'brain work', and ignored the decades he had spent successfully sabotaging the family's (already frayed) reputation for stolid probity, during which he 'exhibited symptoms of genius as an amateur bartender'. His memoirs (*My Candid Recollections*) disclosed that he was 'unrepentantly addicted' to gambling, but omitted any reference to his strenuous infidelities, his three bankruptcies, his court appearance in 1916 (on a charge of trying to obtain credit without disclosing that he was an un-discharged bankrupt) or to James McClelland, who gassed himself in a flat off Ladbroke Grove, west London, in 1930 after claiming that the Duke owed him money. It was disappointing, too, that the memoirs were published three years before his time in Wormwood Scrubs in 1935, to which he was consigned after receiving a nine-month sentence for defrauding a firm of London pawnbrokers.

But although, as one of his obituaries noted, Kim was 'frequently in financial difficulties', at other times he had a great deal of money. When his mother died, in 1909, she left £500,000 (£272.2 million today), a fortune entirely separate from the Montagu estates; one which, even now, has not been entirely dissipated, despite the sustained efforts of Kim and Angus. Remarking that he did not 'understand finance or the intricacies of accountancy', Kim pinned the blame on his father, whose mistake, he said, had been to give him too little pocket money (6d-a-week, 3d of which went in the church collection). 'To keep a child short of money,' argued Kim, 'is not the best method to teach that child the true value of it; by far the better course is to give the child money and show him how to spend it wisely and to keep a proper account of income and expenditure.'

This neglected the fact that Kim had inherited when he was only fifteen and ignored both his determined approach to his own amusement and the apparent burden of his status ('a duke is expected to give a higher contribution and to spend more than other people; if he fails to fulfil expectations, he is called a mean fellow, or worse'). He managed a year at Cambridge, where his allowance was £400 p.a., before going down with debts of £2,000. Thereafter, he jaunted through Central and South America, luxuriating in the hospitality of American millionaires and Porfirio Diaz, President of Mexico; he fitted in time for China, where he saw pirates beheaded, and India, where he went tiger shooting with Maharajahs. In enthusiastically adopting this existence, he was in the vanguard of an aristocratic set whose 'social life [was] essentially plutocratic', differing little from that of 'a Vanderbilt or an Astor or a Morgan'.

Kim had no objection to being bracketed with arriviste Americans. His father had married one of them, with the result that Kim's life had been 'intimately bound up with America' from childhood. He counted William K. Vanderbilt among his godfathers (a role which his mother reciprocated as godmother to Consuelo Vanderbilt, later to be contracted to the 9th Duke of Marlborough in an unremittingly loveless marriage) and another Vanderbilt amongst his aunts. Here was proof that his father, whatever his moral deficiencies and the futility of his financial ventures, had triumphantly married for money. It was one of the few lessons that Kim really took to heart.

By the time he inherited in 1892, the estates' income was entirely 'gobbled up in jointures and interest payments on extensive debts'. The situation was critical.[10] There were various redemptive possibilities. Kimbolton or Tandragee – or both – could be let; or redundant acres could be converted into capital via the terms of the Land Acts. By 1901, the first of these solutions was adopted when Kimbolton was let. But Kim decided that he could only be sure of financial salvation by marrying an American heiress, a conclusion being reached by more and more aristocrats.[11] Kim's father (then Viscount Mandeville) had met Consuelo Iznaga, a Cuban-American, in 1875, at a ball in Saratoga, California. Their wedding in New York the following year was attended by 1,400 people. The bridegroom's family was not, apparently, amongst them, the 7th Duke reputedly being 'almost heartbroken at the thought of "a little American savage" becoming his daughter-in-law' (his wife Louise also 'deeply grieved'). The Manchesters' pain probably abated when they realized that the little American savage might inherit a fortune, albeit one which was prone to disquieting fluctuations. Consuelo's parents had owned a Louisiana cotton plantation, with 300 slaves, which paid for a house in New York, on 37th Street, just west of Fifth Avenue. Later, both the plantation and the New York house were lost, as were Mr Iznaga's Cuban estates, obliging the family to live for a time at New York's Westminster Hotel.

Consuelo was undismayed. An attractive character, who 'thought nothing of picking up a banjo and singing minstrel songs in a Mayfair drawing room', she made herself available to the Prince of Wales, just as her mother-in-law, Louise, had done a few years earlier, and was indulgent towards her children. A friend, visiting her at Kimbolton, noticed Kim – then about eight years old – rolling on the floor beneath his mother's bed, playing with her chamber-pot. 'It seems to be the only thing that amuses him,' Consuelo acknowledged, leaving Kim 'to play on, unreproved'.

Ensnaring an heiress would allow him to play on in adulthood, but his prospects were helped neither by his first bankruptcy nor by unhelpful cover-age in the New York press ('Britain's poorest Duke seeks our richest heiress'), which explains why the Vanderbilts and Astors eluded him. Helena Zimmer-man, daughter of Cincinnati railway magnate Eugene Zimmerman, was less worldly; she and Kim married, secretly, in London in November 1900.[12]

Kim was fortunate, his bride proving an aristocrat in style and spirit, if not pedigree. The couple had two sons and two daughters before divorcing in 1931, the year in which Kim married Kathleen Dawes, a superannuated actress; in 1937, Helena also remarried, becoming the wife of the 10th Earl of Kintore, with whom she lived in Scotland (dying there in 1971). Long before the divorce, however, Eugene Zimmerman had paid off Kim's debts of $135,000, settled what was described as a large income on him and Helena, and bought the couple an estate in County Galway, Kylemore Castle, for £70,000, where 'half the aristocracy' stayed (undismayed that it was 'in the worst Victorian style').[13]

Kim's hunger for easy money never diminished. Kimbolton boasted both a golf course and racecourse, though it was London's gaming tables which made ferocious demands on his finances. His triumphs were occasionally spectacular (and, on one occasion, legendary[14]), but never frequent enough for his requirements. Besides letting Kimbolton, he put land up for sale during the First World War, converted the Irish estates into cash, courtesy of various Land Acts (though keeping the castle at Tandragee and the golf course which his wife had designed around it), and, in 1920, disposed of much of the Huntingdon property. It was in these testing circumstances that his uncle, Lord Charles Montagu, agreed to return to the Castle.

Freed from traditional responsibilities, Kim embarked on a number of money-making ventures. Briefly a journalist (receiving a $1,000 advance from Randolph Hearst in 1899), he prospected for gold in Canada, developed an interest in cinema, and invested in a cure for tuberculosis whose lack of success he blamed, in part, for his accumulation of debts of £129,656 when, in

1928, he applied for a discharge from bankruptcy. The Registrar could not agree. 'I regard this case as one of unjustifiable and reckless extravagance,' he said, suspending Kim's discharge for another three years. Eventually, already demeaned by frequent public exposure, Kim wrote his memoirs, using the pages of the Daily Express as his confessional. He died in 1947, still mired in bankruptcy.[15]

His infrequent appearances at Kimbolton would not easily be forgotten. 'My mother always talked about being in the Castle with Miss Franks [the cook],' recalls Dawn Gooderham, daughter of Alma Waite, one of the Castle maids. 'The bells would go in the middle of the night, and they would have to open the doors for the Duke because the clubs had been raided in London.' The morning after one of the duke's nocturnal arrivals, Alma knocked on the door of his bedroom, said, 'Good morning, your Grace', and went in to open the curtains. A voice filtered its way from under the blankets ('I will need four more cups'). Turning towards the bed, Alma saw 'two women either side of him, one being Tallulah Bankhead'.[16] In those circumstances (she explained many years later), 'you just got on with it'.

In May 1935, the villagers of Kimbolton learned of the duke's nine-month jail sentence; a month later, they heard that it had been quashed; they heard, too, disquieting things about the duke's younger son, Lord Edward, and glimpsed his younger daughter, Lady Louise, energetically entangled with relays of local men. Nevertheless, under the benign direction of Lord Charles Montagu, life at the Castle followed a pattern of hierarchical good order. A year before the outbreak of the Second World War, the shoot still required seven keepers, and almost every Kimbolton family worked for the estate or was indirectly dependent on it. 'They always said that you could walk from here [Kimbolton] to St Ives without getting off the duke's land,'[17] remembers John Mayes, whose parents ran the village greengrocer's. 'If you put a step out [of line]... you were for it.'

In 1939, seemingly endless renovation at the Castle (until then candlelit) was finally completed. Carried out by builders and decorators from London, it had included the installation of a mirrored bathroom, and had cost £14,000 (£2,960,000 today). The duke's elder son, Viscount Mandeville, footed the bill. Few doubted he could bear it, any more than they doubted the Montagus' pre-eminence would continue when Mandeville succeeded. A former naval officer of reputable character, refreshingly unlike his father, he and his attractive Australian wife had had a son, born in 1929. The Montagu dynasty was secure; the birth of their second boy, nine years later, seemed almost inconsequential.

* * *

'I bloody well shan't, I bloody well shan't.' The yelled retort – inexhaustibly
repeated – came from the roof of the newly built Scout hut, on which a small
boy – his fair hair a mass of long, corkscrewing curls – was running helter-
skelter. On the ground, fifteen feet below, scampered Aubrey Butler, Scout
Master, in woggle, lanyard, blue shorts and naval hat. Known as 'Skipper',
Aubrey had become a popular figure in Kimbolton since arriving at the end
of the war.

That did not diminish the glee of the watching village children, who were
fascinated by the roof-top fugitive, who spoke English oddly, as if it were
somehow foreign to him. They knew him as Lord Angus, though none of
them really knew or cared why. They did notice, though, that he seemed to
have no parents; instead, he lived with Skipper at Park Lodge, a substantial
house of red Victorian brick, about half a mile from the village; there was no
Mrs Skipper.[18]

The Castle now verged on dereliction. The Queen's Room, on the East
Front, was locked; the ceiling of the Green Drawing Room (its walls once
hung with green Italian damask) was propped up by telegraph poles; some of
the best furniture had been moved to Park Lodge but much more had been
heaped into the chapel and stables. The rides through the woods were over-
grown, the lawns uncut – all familiar evidence of leisurely army vandalism.
The one man who might have curbed it, Lord Charles Montagu, had died
on 11 November 1939, at Derby House,[19] the London residence of his
brother-in-law, the 17th Earl of Derby. When his body was returned home
for interment in the family crypt, the witnesses to his funeral included
soldiers from the Royal Army Medical Corps, the new custodians of
Kimbolton.[20] Once they had seen Lord Charles safely buried, the men
hacked holes in panelled doors, used portraits as dartboards and rummaged
through wardrobes until they found what they presumed were the duchess's
clothes, which they enjoyed wearing as they cleared the Castle's rooms. No
member of the family intruded on them for the rest of the war.

* * *

Angus liked to say that his father had been a senior colonial figure in Ceylon
(perhaps even its governor), and that, as a boy, he, young Angus, had been
sent to a Roman Catholic school, run by nuns, from where, over the school
wall, he could see Ceylonese boys riding past on log-bearing elephants.
In time, he had managed to befriend the elephant boys and, with their

assistance, had escaped from school. At the end of the war, his parents had been able to trace him only because they heard a rumour about a white elephant boy. 'He said he didn't speak English when his parents came to collect him,' remembers an acquaintance, Charles Lousada. 'He didn't know he [even] had parents, because none of the elephant boys had parents either.'

During National Service, Angus had returned to the island. 'His ship, which I think was *Britannia*, put into Ceylon. He got to the [elephant] encampment [but] they said, "No, no, your elephant is now king – he'll kill you if you try and go near him." He said, "No, I know my elephant, he won't."' Insisting that he be allowed to approach, Angus 'walked into the compound, and this elephant... saw who it was, and lifted him up onto his back with his trunk'. Lousada concluded that the story was so improbable that it might be true. His counter-intuition was not absurd: Angus's English was woefully poor when he returned to England; he was in Ceylon for part of his national service; his father had been living there at the beginning of the war. On the other hand, the 10th Duke was never in the colonial service, still less had he been Ceylon's governor; Angus served on a frigate, HMS *Loch Fyne*, not *Britannia*; he knew people in even the most obscure parts of the island but they were not former elephant boys but tea planters and others of similar colonial ilk. His national service contemporaries heard no mention of a child-hood spent with elephants.

The story was like many others, including a claim that he had been at Suez, where his best friend in the Royal Marines – identified only as 'Brian' – had been killed. 'In retaliation, Gus always claimed, he went out and did something,' recalls Jane Bishop, a girlfriend during the 1960s. 'He didn't describe it; one assumed that [he] shot a few arabs.' By the time of his third marriage, to Louise Bird, the retaliation attack had been edited from Angus's military recollections, though Louise remembers Angus saying that his best friend had died at Suez. Angus, however, did not leave school until July 1956: his only military experience before the Suez crisis (which broke in November) seems to have been a two-week Royal Marines training course that September, details of which were mentioned in a letter from his father to Gordonstoun's headmaster. At some stage, he suffered an injury, with the result that he did not start his basic training at Lympstone until 28 January 1957, passing out with the rest of Squad 911 on 10 May – six months *after* Suez.

It took time for Louise and others to learn that, though there could be threads of truth in Angus's stories, most were highly embroidered; others unadulterated fantasy. Whilst on national service, he had, he said, been presented with a pair of silver chopsticks by Chairman Mao, and had seen the Terracotta Army (not unearthed until 1974); he claimed that he had been sent to school at HMS *Conway* (there is no record of his attendance there, and the claim is flatly denied by a friend of the headmaster of the prep school he did attend); and that he had played rugby for the marines (he had not, though he was a useful member of HMS *Loch Fyne*'s water polo team). Returning home late one afternoon, he assured Louise that he had just had tea with the Queen. 'I said, "Don't be ridiculous, of course you didn't". He said, "How do you know? You weren't there".' To Angus, Louise realized, assertion equalled validation: 'Once out of his mouth, [his words] were true.'

No period of his life was subjected to such insistent reinvention as his wartime childhood. Not long before his death, he claimed that whilst in Ceylon he had spent 'five or six years' in the wild; his elephant had been called Raja. When his parents eventually returned for him at the end of the war, he had been unable to recognize his mother, who had handed him a toy tin car as a present. This he had hurled back at her (hitting her in the face, the result-ant wound causing a tiny scar), before running away, only to be recaptured and soundly thrashed by his father. Even the nuns, to whose care he had initially been consigned, had treated him contemptibly. 'They weren't very pleasant people,' he said. 'They used to make these dummies of the baby Jesus and because I had blond curls they used to cut them off and use them for the dummies, so most of the time I was bald. I objected to that.'

Twelve Montagu family photograph albums chronicling the 1920s to the 1960s, most of them meticulously annotated by Angus's father, present a different picture: Angus is in Singapore with his father in October 1939; in Colombo, the Ceylonese capital, in January 1940 (frequently photographed with his ayah 'Missy', but also with his mother); back in Singapore in 1940, then in Egypt. By 1942 he has returned to Ceylon, this time to Kandy, where he is pictured – an unmistakable figure with streams of fair hair – cuddling his mother, who is in nurse's uniform, with his father alongside them. In an undated photograph, he is a five- or six-year-old dressed for a party of cowboys and Indians, again with his mother at his side.[21]

This does not disprove Angus's claim that he spoke Tamil and Ceylonese far better than English, but it does reveal that he saw much more of his parents than did many of his contemporaries. Regrettably, this was not neces-sarily to his advantage, even though his father was the most promising of the Montagus for at least three generations. The 10th Duke of Manchester was brought up in what seems to have been the Montagus' traditionally abrasive manner. Kim, the 9th Duke, explained that he had wanted to 'make him manly' (a quest arguably made more pressing by the fact that the boy was known as 'Mandy', a diminutive of Mandeville). This had been accomplished, said Kim, by not offering sympathy when Mandy fell over, but by 'mak[ing] him take a second tumble' instead.

After Hawtreys prep school, he attended the naval colleges of Osborne and Dartmouth. Thereafter, Mandy never seemed likely to perpetuate Montagu inadequacies into a third generation. Thick-set, good-looking, unimaginative and cheerfully philistine, an improbable member of the Eccentric Club, he played rugby for Blackheath, was self-assured enough to enjoy needlework and competent enough to enjoy a steady naval career before retiring to Brampton Park in 1930.[22] If there was a blemish on his record, it concerned his motoring, but even in fatal accidents[23] he retained an impressive sangfroid, which helps to explain why arguably his finest hour came with his recall for wartime service. In August 1940, he was aboard HMS *Eagle* when an explosion in the hold killed fourteen of the crew and seriously injured nine others. Although wounded, Mandy continued the search for those unable to move; the citation for his OBE spoke of his 'outstanding courage and enterprise' and 'persistent devotion to duty'.

Patsy Chilton, whom he and his wife befriended in the early 1950s, remembered him as 'great fun, very normal'; younger acquaintances recall a 'very nice old boy' and a 'nice, easy person'. Even his butler-valet considered him 'a grand chap'. Hugh and Saffron Duberly, Mandy's neighbouring landowners on the Cambridgeshire/Bedfordshire border, agreed. His was the sort of charm, says their daughter Grey, Mandy's frequent pre-war golf partner, that 'you only encounter two or three times in a lifetime'.

He was also admirably free of illusions about his family, as Patsy Chilton discovered when she suggested that he write a history of the Montagus. 'He screamed with laughter and said, "It doesn't bear thinking about. My brother is in jail in Mexico, and my sister is in a loony bin in New York, and my father died in a jail in Newcastle."' Mandy's father, released from Wormwood Scrubs in 1935, did not in fact return to jail, nor die in Newcastle. On the other hand there is anecdotal evidence that Lady Mary Montagu, the older of Mandy's sisters, did need clinical help. A physically unprepossessing woman, grossly overweight and reputedly burdened by a narcotics habit, she left Kimbolton in her youth, married in 1949 – a Mr Fendall Littlepage Gregory – and died, childless, in 1962, three weeks before her sixty-first birthday.

The younger sister, Lady Louise Montagu, was quite different, 'extremely attractive – in an ugly way – and charming... very exciting indeed. She flew aeroplanes and drove about at Brooklands.' Like Mandy, Louise favoured a Stutz motor car. The marque soon developed pleasurable connotations for a roll-call of Kimbolton men, whom she drove to London where she entertained them in a flat retained for the purpose.[24]

Mandy's only brother, Lord Edward Montagu, four years his junior and a godson of Edward VII, was educated at Harrow, was thwarted in an attempt in adolescence to marry a Ziegfield Follies girl in Paris and was packed off to a ranch in Canada where, according to his father, he was 'enthusiastic about the life'. Months later, Edward abandoned farming in favour of a Hollywood career. This was not a success, though when resuming cinematic work the following decade he was given a bit part in a film called, *The Rich are Always With Us*. Despite receiving an allowance of more than £1,000-a-year, he became a taxi-driver in Alberta, a hot-dog seller, and a crew member of a yacht called *Karma*.[25]

He returned to England in 1934, intending to join the Foreign Legion. 'I know,' he acknowledged shortly before heading to Marseilles, 'the life will be very hard indeed but there is no going back.' Within weeks, he had opened a coffee-stall in Maidenhead. 'I think this is much better,' said Edward, who nevertheless again felt the pull of the Legion the following year, this time successfully enlisting. His service was brief (possibly a fortnight, after which he was rescued from Marseilles by his sister Louise, flying in on her plane, a Puss Moth). Later in 1935, he secured employment as secretary to a Mrs van der Elst (a campaigner against capital punishment); in September he was convicted, at the Old Bailey, of forging a cheque (for £17 5d) in her name, and sentenced to nine months' imprisonment. Louise picked him up from Wormwood Scrubs the following April. During the war, he took American citizenship and, in 1944, enlisted as a GI. His service ended abruptly and appallingly: driving an army car in Pennsylvania, he crashed, killing one of his companions and severely injuring himself. His subsequent suit for £62,000 damages was dismissed.

In 1942 he had generated the headline 'Lord Edward Montagu's Rubber Cheque Holiday', much to the distress of his kinsman, Lord Montagu of Beaulieu, then a schoolboy waiting to return to England from New York aboard a warship. 'He had been had up for bouncing cheques. There I was, as far as the Americans were concerned, Lord Edward Montagu, and I had no money. I was absolutely terrified.' On that occasion, Lord Montagu was able to leave America without explaining the nuances of the peerage to a sceptical audience; he was less fortunate on his return in 1953, when he 'was rung up by an irate lady demanding alimony'.

Edward by then had two ex-wives living who were shortly to be joined by a third (another wife had died). In 1954, he married, aged forty-eight, for a fifth and final time, at the Mexican home of his elder sister, the elusive Mary. Soon afterwards, he plunged into the jungle to film the Lacandon Indians in the ruins of Yaxchilan, accompanied by his new bride, twenty-six-year-old American Roberta Joughlin. On the morning of 4 May 1954, he was unusually hungry: by noon, he had eaten three large bowls of oatmeal, a bowl of black beans, a bowl of macaroni and pheasant, and, by way of slight variation, a bowl of beans and macaroni, as well as several bananas. He died that evening.

Once or twice, Angus mentioned his uncle's name but never referred to the career path which had similarities to his own. His reticence might have been partly born of ignorance; more probably of lack of interest. Family ties – excepting, later in life, those with one or two of his children – were only of consequence if they promised the delivery of fresh funds or booty which could be speedily converted into cash. 'He was not,' remembers his third wife, Louise, 'remotely interested in his relations.' In fact, no relationship was sacrosanct to Angus. 'He used people,' reflects a Bedford friend, 'and was used by people.'

He would not have found his father especially tractable, which arguably explains why their relationship was 'not ok' during Angus's time at Gordonstoun, and why by the mid-1960s it had deteriorated further. Mandy undoubtedly had his limitations: a certain rigidity of outlook, notably his faith in high birth (a triumph of faith over lavish family experience) and a corresponding reluctance to adapt to a changing world. He was, however, a comparatively approachable figure, known to his sons (as to his intimates) as 'Mandy'. One incident suggests that Angus held him in some affection. Brian Joyles, a fellow Royal Marine aboard HMS *Loch Fyne*, recalls a chance night-time encounter with a cruise liner in the Indian Ocean. '[Angus] was aware of the fact that his father was on board that ship, [so] he arranged for our signals people to send a message, saying something along the lines of, "Hello, daddy, this is Angus. Hope all's well".' This was not the action of someone brimming with filial loathing.

When troubles between father and son unfolded later, they did so because Angus never developed Mandy's moral equilibrium, nor tolerated his willingness to impose discipline – a concept wholly alien to Mandy's wife. 'Mandy,' reflects Grey Duberly, 'would have been splendid if he'd married an ordinary woman.'

* * *

The airmail letter is thin and faded; the handwriting that sprawls across it childishly exuberant, its punctuation minimal, its capital letters generously strewn through sentences ('on the Ship the Captain a mad play Boy... B. awful no Boy no food and whats more no water the place stank'). But more striking than its grammatical deficiencies is the uninhibited opening line. Even today there may be only one or two duchesses who would begin a note to a friend, 'Well Kid how is your sex life' – the flourish with which Nell Manchester greeted Patsy Bowles (subsequently Chilton) in December 1954.[26]

Such directness evidently appealed to Mandy. He met Miss Nell Stead at a swimming pool in Colombo, whilst serving in the navy. A brunette (blonde after the Second World War), Nell was twenty-one, apparently rich, definitely playful and completely Australian; her engagement to Viscount Mandeville was announced a week after their poolside encounter. They married on 5 May 1927. Newspapers noted that her father was a millionaire 'with great estates and important mercantile and financial interests in Melbourne'. Unlike his father or his paternal grandfather, however, Mandy married for love, not money, and remained in love with his wife – obsessed by her, says Mary Fox, who met the couple in the early 1950s – until her death. '[He] was a one-woman man all his life,' agrees Grey Duberly. 'Never looked at anybody, except Nell; it was extraordinary.'

At the beginning, it was also entirely understandable. 'She was very beautiful,' adds Grey Duberly. Nell's behaviour was unconventional, hedonistic, exhibitionist – and it appalled and thrilled Cambridgeshire society, bewitching not only her husband but also her brother, the charming but feckless David Stead, who had joined her in England. 'He was sort of slave to Nell. He lived with them and drove over to fetch things all day long.'[27] But it was invariably Mandy who drove Nell to London for excursions to the Four Hundred, in Leicester Square. When not dancing, Nell shared her father-in-law's enthusiasm for illegal gaming clubs, once being bound over by magistrates after a police raid on a Piccadilly establishment.

Country life at Brampton Park (or at Tanderagee,[28] the Montagu seat in Armagh) held less obvious appeal for her, but she enlivened it by wearing trousers to Kimbolton village ('terribly shocking in 1930') and by giving a succession of house parties. Guests included the most dazzling of the Bentley Boys, Babe Barnato, who had inherited his father Barney Barnato's diamond fortune in unusual circumstances,[29] and the Duke of Kent, ever alert for new

tastes and experiences with which to reignite a jaded palate. Local landowners Hugh and Saffron Duberly were about a decade older than Nell and
Mandy, and were 'quite respectable'. Both handicaps were negotiated with
Nell's encouragement. 'I think they went a bit mad with the Mandevilles,' says
their daughter, Grey, recalling that it was at their house, Staughton Manor,
that Nell proved most adventurous. 'One exciting night she came to dinner.
She had on a dress made of, I don't know, mink or something. After dinner,
she dumped it and stepped out naked.' Saffron Duberly decided that she and
her husband should stop trying to keep pace with the Mandevilles.

Nell hurtled on. When, a few years before the war, she and Mandy moved
into the Castle, she took the opportunity to combine two of her interests in
a single stroke, converting the chapel into a bar and stocking it with glasses
decorated with 'pornography of the most interesting kind'. The chapel was
now placed out of bounds to young Grey Duberly, which served only to
heighten her fascination with a woman whom she unhesitatingly describes
as 'extraordinary, amazing'. Nell was expensive, too. What little of Mandy's
money remained after paying bills for the Castle's restoration was easily
consumed by the cost of house parties and metropolitan diversions. Until he
succeeded his father, Mandy was frequently – and publicly – broke. 'When
he came shooting, he didn't give a tip to whoever cleaned his gun,' remembers Grey Duberly, 'someone always wanted to anyway because they adored
him.' Perhaps financial distractions prevented him from noticing his wife's
propensity for sharing her body as well as displaying it. Although Patsy
Chilton believed that Nell was 'completely faithful to Mandy', Grey Duberly
had been unable to reach the same optimistic conclusion twenty years earlier.
One favourite apparently perished in Lord Duncannon's fatal car crash of
1934. ('It was an exciting life then, thrilling.')[29]

An attempt to interest Nell in breeding and showing Pekinese misfired
('she just got off with other people at the sales'), whilst a proclamation by
Kimbolton's vicar, Canon Frank Powys Maurice, that his daughter Evelyn
could make her into 'a proper countrywoman' proved ill-advised ('Nell would-
n't have her in the house'). Two decades later, in Africa, Mandy adopted more
successful tactics. Nell remained 'very attractive and extraordinary, [with] a
very good figure, very well dressed but [was] totally spoilt, totally used to
being serviced, so to speak'. Norman 'Knockie' Marsh became central to Nell's
servicing, with Mandy's full agreement. 'Knockie was used as a sort of handler
to keep Nell quiet,' remembered Patsy Chilton. 'I don't mean sexually, in any
way; he was just a good chum, a courtier, a Brit, very charming.[30] Mandy
appreciated Knockie because it meant he could go off fishing and shooting.'

Knockie sometimes accompanied Nell and Mandy on rare trips to London, jaunts which enabled Nell to parade the family jewels in public – 'the most amazing piece of jewellery, with big drop pearls and emeralds and diamonds' – as Patsy Chilton noted at a dinner at the Savoy in the mid-1950s. 'She was never allowed to [wear it] unless there was a detective in sight.'

Other London outings proceeded less decorously. One began with Nell enjoying a drink in the bar at the Ritz, then commandeering a taxi to cross the street to the Berkeley ('which in those days was opposite'), where she joined Knockie, Patsy Chilton and Mandy for another drink, then 'went to the loo and didn't come back' – locked in by a broken sliding bolt on the door.[31] Mandy, Knockie and Patsy Chilton were soon in the ladies, where there was 'quite a kerfuffle. The loo attendant said, "I've sent for the plumber". A voice from inside the loo said, "I want to come out through the door, not down the ****ing drain".'

Rawness of language, delivered with vestiges of an Australian accent, was part of Nell's repertoire. Other habits were messier. 'She wet her pants from time to time,' recalled Patsy Chilton. A scene aboard a passenger ship remained vivid. 'She said, "Oh, Patsy, I've peed all the way to the cabin". I said, "Oh, you can't do that, you're a blooming duchess."' The reprimand had no effect. 'She said, "Yes, I did. Look." And she started doing it again. I was furious with her. I said, "You really must behave better than this, this is simply ghastly." It didn't register.'

But nothing was to have as destabilizing an effect on her younger son as her disconcerting passion for little boys. 'She adored [them],' remembered Patsy Chilton. 'A friend of mine had a son aged about ten; Nell wanted to buy [him] and bring him up as her son. She offered the mother money. Then she wanted to borrow my freckle-covered son. She had a thing about little boys; I don't think in any salacious way. She liked to have a court round her.' Babies – inadequate courtiers – were of no interest to her, so that, initially at least, Angus was completely eclipsed in her affections by his older brother Kim, 'until Kim got to the age where he adored other women, then she didn't like [him] at all, and loved Angus, and spoilt him very much. The poor little darling didn't have to go to school because he didn't like it. In some extraordinary way, [Nell] was in love with her children.' Aileen Dickens, widow of Frank Dickens, one of the Kimbolton gamekeepers, recalls that Angus was 'very much spoilt by his mother'. Mary Fox agrees. 'She would always say Angus was so wonderful, Kim was so useless. It was always, "Angus, darling, do you like what I'm wearing? Do you approve?"'

The consequences were corrosive and predictable. Another acquaintance recalls that Kim was jealous of the fact that his brother 'somehow got the attention of his parents more easily than [he] did'. Angus saw it differently, as Jane Bishop remembers, insisting that 'Kim was the favourite'. With Mandy, Kim undoubtedly was, though this did not persuade father to suffocate elder son with money or attention. But no one doubted where Nell's affections lay. In her will, she left everything to Angus; Kim went unmentioned.[32]

Although during his national service Angus boasted about his older brother, especially his rally-driving exploits, thirty years later he acknowledged that they did not get on, sometimes attributing their differences to the influence of his sibling's second wife. Shortly after the end of the war, the two boys were seen on a tractor together, with Kim, then sixteen, at the wheel; Angus was seven. It was effectively the first time they had met. In some inescapable respects, they would become very alike: massively strong, highly charming (when the mood suited them), intellectually undistinguished and woefully under-educated.[33]

Kim, however, appeared more aristocratic than Angus, spending his adulthood in a manner his paternal grandfather would have recognized: rally driving, deep-sea fishing, womanizing (entertaining Ava Gardner, for example, whilst she was married to Frank Sinatra), looking plausible in black tie or morning coat (when back from Kenya for Ascot), and shooting in Dorset with Fido May or in Hampshire with Lord Montagu of Beaulieu. Kim was also scrupulously honest. 'He borrowed several times from me and was meticulous about paying it back,' remembers Mary Fox. 'There wasn't a dishonest bone in his body.' Unfortunately, this did not equip him to take a detached view of Angus's blundering progress through adulthood. According to a friend from Kenya, Jenny Coreth, he 'absolutely couldn't stand' his younger brother; Lord Montagu of Beaulieu remembers that Kim and his second wife Andrea 'disapproved of Angus enormously'; Mary Fox describes relations between the two brothers as 'awful'. Kim, she adds, 'never talked about [Angus]. Never, never.'

* * *

Unusually for a traditionalist like Mandy, he employed a woman, a Mrs Carter, as his agent at the Castle. No bulletin she sent him during the war would have prepared him for what the Royal Army Medical Corps had accomplished. Wiring and plumbing, installed at almost ruinous expense in the 1930s, were still in place. Little else was. Restoration would easily consume another fortune.

Mandy's response, in 1946, was to buy farmland in Kenya, where he and Kim renovated and extended the existing farmhouse.[34] This was not a renunciation of England, still less of Kimbolton, but an attempt to keep options open. At home, skilled labour was in short supply, building materials were almost unprocurable and, even if both could be found, wartime restrictions remained in force: it was, for instance, illegal to spend more than £100 on a single property within a year, without a special licence. In 1941, the top rate of income tax had been raised to 19s 6d in the pound (97.5 per cent). Death duties followed cripplingly upwards, increasing to 75 per cent on estates valued at £1 million or more. Resulting land sales were extensive, despite the fact that, even in 1950, land values languished at their 1880 level. Everywhere, country houses were being demolished, 400 disappearing between 1945 and 1955.

Mandy had no appetite for Attlee's new Jerusalem; Kenya seemed a far more attractive prospect, a colony whose administration had what to his mind was the advantage of having been shaped by the 3rd Lord Delamere and the 22nd Earl of Erroll; a place where the Montagus could live in ducal style on the residue of two generations of American money. He would return home to shoot, leaving Frank Cowlard, the head keeper, to keep an eye on his interests and report on insubordinate comments overheard in Kimbolton's George Hotel.

He entrusted his younger son, then nine, at Park Lodge, to the care of Aubrey Butler. Angus did not go to school with fellow cubs like David Whiteman, nor accompany them to Wales where 'Skipper' presided over summer camp on Lord Gibson-Watt's estate. Yet the village boys knew him well enough. Even before he conquered the Scout hut roof, his wayward, intractable behaviour, his misfit English and long curly fair hair, had set him apart. 'Today you would call him hyperactive,' says David Whiteman. 'He was always... a bit scatter-brainish... would never do anything correctly.' This was particularly apparent when Skipper took the cubs to swim in the moat at Major Reuben Farley's house, Wornditch Hall. 'Angus wouldn't go in the water proper. He would just have a mud bath, just roll about in the mud to get as ridiculously filthy as he could. He did seem to be a penny or two short of a shilling at times.'

Neil Sclater Booth agreed. He was seven when, in 1946, his American mother brought him to England, determined that he should have an upbringing in keeping with his lineage.[35] Initially they lived at Park Lodge, with David Stead, who soon developed an enthusiasm for Neil's mother (known admiringly as 'Snakey Legs'), and Angus, who became Neil's frequent companion. Neil did not find this an agreeable experience. 'I could never know what he would do next,' he remembered, suggesting that Angus might today be diagnosed as suffering from Attention Deficit Disorder. It was not a condition recognized in post-war Cambridgeshire: Olga Welton, who read to him in bed for hours on end when he was ten or eleven, thought him a 'horrible kid'; Grey Duberly, who returned to England in 1948, describes him as 'a beastly little boy'.[36]

By then, the Sclater Booths had renovated Kimbrook, a house on the Kimbolton estate; David Stead soon joined them there. Angus remained at Park Lodge with Skipper, his tutor as well as his guardian, though he appears to have struggled in both roles, confiding in John Mayes that he found Angus impossible to control. Young John was more interested in Angus's collection of birds' eggs, kept in cotton wool in drawer after drawer. The contrast with his own horde – two dozen eggs crammed into shoe-boxes – was dazzling, as was the impression made by Angus's train set, laid out to fill most of a room. 'It was absolutely fantastic. I'd just got a little figure of eight.'

Angus, however, seemed indifferent to his enviable possessions, his enthusiasm sparking into life only when he and John careered down Park Lane in home-made carts. Away from the house, he usually remained attached to Neil Sclater Booth and sometimes to Neil's friend Bill 'Tiddler' Ewens, whose fighter pilot father had been killed in the war, or even to Frank Cowlard. Bill Ewens's mother pitied him. 'I remember her saying something to the effect that the poor boy needs a bit of looking after,' says Ewens, adding that Angus was frequently hungry. 'He seemed to be almost ignored. [My mother] would feed him.' Angus, he adds, 'always looked the poorest' of their trio, who shot moorhens and rabbits, played bicycle polo or pedalled to the cinema in St Neots or Bedford. 'He had the worst bike of all, tied up with string and rubber bands and God knows what.'

His education was shoddier still. His first, fleeting experience of the classroom was in Kenya, where he attended 'the village school [and] hated it'. According to Angus, most of his fellow pupils were Afrikaners, who bullied him. In England, under Skipper's brittle supervision, he showed no signs of progress. This might have been because, as an Old Bailey judge would later assert, he was 'absurdly stupid',[37] or because, as his solicitor Ian Codrington believes, he was an undiagnosed dyslexic, or because of a combination of the two. In adulthood, he was unable to 'read fluently' (though he derived some pleasure from Wilbur Smith thrillers and cowboy books) and could barely spell, with even the names of old friends sometimes proving beyond him.

Without the intervention of a family friend, Edmund Alington, heir to a

Cambridgeshire estate and, more pertinently, the headmaster of Trearddur House, a prep school on Anglesey, he might have remained completely illiterate. 'No other school would take him,' says Angela Wood (married to Reuben Farley's nephew and heir), who heard of Angus's challenging character from Alington himself. Until then – by which time he was eleven or very nearly eleven – he had had no formal education. The Trearddur regime seems to have been effective: by the time he reached Gordonstoun, he was (at least when at school) a presentable boy, civil and apparently tractable.[38] Nevertheless, it had again required the intervention of a family friend, this time his godfather, Reuben Farley, to ensure his acceptance there. 'Reuben Farley knew the headmaster, and got [him in],' remembers Angela Wood, 'despite the fact that he could only just read and write.' It helped, as a Gordonstoun man explains, that the school adopted a pragmatic attitude to less gifted pupils: 'He might pick up something, he might not – it doesn't matter, he's paid for, and that's the end of it.'[39]

Angus's recollections of Gordonstoun fluctuated. In the mid-1960s, he insisted that he had not enjoyed it; decades later, when married to Louise, he was full of enthusiasm for the place. His contemporary Fergus Rogers suggested that Louise was treated to a closer approximation to the truth. 'I never remember seeing him depressed or down or grumbling. He was always immensely polite, and always cheerful.' Most impressive of all was Angus's gentleness, especially apparent on his arrival in 1953. 'He was already the size of an eighteen-year-old, a big lad, heavy – much larger than us little shrimps – but he was never a bully, always very kind. Nobody had any trouble with Angus. He was liked.' Their housemaster, Roy McComish,[40] was master in charge of art as well as the cadet force. Like many of Gordonstoun's staff, he had served in the war. 'He was a lovely man, a charming man. They were fantastic, those guys, tough ex-soldiers,' remembered Rogers, adding that one of the masters would always be prepared to rise at 5 a.m. each Sunday to drive them to the Cairngorms for rock climbing or mountaineering.

Angus wasn't built for the mountains but revelled in weight training, the fire service ('if the siren went, he would be first out of bed and running up the road'), rugby and putting the shot. He was also 'immaculately turned out, terribly neat'. So he remained. Allan Warren, an acquaintance from the 1980s, recalls a 'very clean, meticulous person', a description echoed by a female visitor who accompanied her late husband to 15 Broadreach, where she noticed Angus following her dog around the flat with a Hoover. This fastidiousness – impressively at odds with his frequently chaotic private life – extended, says a Bedford friend, to his clerical arrangements. 'He was meticulous in his filing; [he used] one credit card to pay for another, always kept his plane tickets and everything, so he could prove when he was somewhere else.'

But clean fingernails and a crisply ironed shirt could not disguise the fact that he was, as Fergus Rogers put it, 'remarkably academically stupid'. Patsy Chilton reached the same conclusion when Angus – then aged about sixteen, with a leg in plaster – stayed with her in London while his parents went to New York. 'He was extremely kind and very courteous, quite a giggle, but so stupid it was painful – innumerate and inarticulate. I felt sorry for him. You had to ask his advice to pump up his ego. The advice, of course, was quite useless. But to make him feel happy, you made him feel big.' This, she suggested, is why he later fell into the hands of 'extraordinary people', the sort, in the words of his third wife Louise, who could be guaranteed to 'butter him up'.

The Gordonstounian system[41] spared him much of the classroom humiliation which he would have experienced elsewhere. There was no orthodox marking or form order, no end-of-term exams, still less school prizes. He left in summer 1956 without an 'O' level to his name. Yet the school had done its best to inculcate its values in him via its pedagogic peculiarities, which included 'early morning run, training plan, morning athletic break, trust system, rescue services, projects, after lunch rest groups'. Foremost amongst these was the trust system. 'You went through a training programme that you did every day, [for example] five press-ups, fifty skips, two hot washes and two cold showers,' remembered Fergus Rogers. Progress was recorded by each boy in his own notebook, which was 'divided up into squares for every day for the rest of the term. If you put a plus when it should have been a minus, this was lying to yourself.' The system extended to the enforcement of discipline. 'Nobody was allowed to beat. You had walking punishments – number one, two or three. You had to go for a walk a certain distance and back again in your spare time on Saturday afternoon. You were trusted to do those walks, and you did them.'

Admirable though this was, it seems to have washed over Angus almost without trace. According to one longstanding associate of the Montagu family, he was 'a completely amoral man, [for whom] right and wrong had no meaning'. Others suggest that Angus preferred not to make the distinction between the two, especially where money was concerned. 'He didn't see why he had to repay loans,' says a friend who once lent him several thousand pounds. It was an attitude which Angus fearlessly extended to banks, as a female acquaintance remembers: 'It was their honour to be allowed to lend to him.' Angus's solicitor, Ian Codrington, inevitably became familiar with what he describes as 'a marvellously cavalier attitude: "If you've lent me money, I'll pay you back when I feel like it".' Even when there was no prospect of repaying what he already owed, Angus had no qualms about borrowing more.[42]

His sense of entitlement owed nothing to Gordonstoun, which, in the 1950s, was a 'wonderfully mixed establishment' of only 140–50, predominantly sons of professionals, with a 'sprinkling of the aristocracy' and boys from local fishing villages on merchant navy scholarships. 'Nobody had money at Gordonstoun,' remembers Fergus Rogers, adding that Elgin, the local town, offered fish and chips and a cinema, nothing more. Angus, however, was indulged during the Christmas and Easter holidays, spent at Keith Hall, Aberdeenshire, home to Riggs the butler, Brooch the chauffeur and, most importantly, his paternal grandmother Helena, and her husband, Lord Kintore. 'When Angus was small, she doted on him,' says a longstanding acquaintance, who remembers being told by an ancient family solicitor that Helena had given her grandson a gold watch which, when lost, she had immediately replaced with another.

In Kenya, where he spent each summer, Angus experienced the distorted and distorting twilight of Happy Valley. His father farmed 10,000 acres at Kapsirowa, their estate in the hills of the Cheranganis district, employing a staff of 187, fourteen of them houseboys and twenty gardeners – a retinue 'no more than a couple of dukes could match [at home]'. His chattels – three railway carriages' worth, remembered Patsy Chilton[43] – reputedly included Holbeins, Van Dycks, an Aubusson carpet and a library of 13,000 books, 'a library you would die for, first editions of *Alice in Wonderland*, that sort of thing,' says Giles Remnant, whose parents were part of the Manchesters' set.

Although everyone knew Mandy by his lifelong nickname, only an inner circle would ever address him by it, adds Remnant: 'He still liked to be referred to as "Your Grace".' While Mandy fished off Malindi, Nell enjoyed her garden ('white flowers only') and embroidery and her status as the colony's only duchess (seeing Bridget Portsmouth[44] at the Muthaiga club, she gestured to Patsy Chilton and said, 'Dreadful fat woman; she's only a countess'). Both drank enthusiastically. 'The oldies used to go from pink gin to pink gin,' says Remnant. 'It was a way of life out there, "from bottle to throttle".' The regime seemingly left Mandy unaffected; Nell, according to Patsy Chilton, 'got a bit shhtupid'. As the gin drip took its toll, she became an increasingly raddled, if still compelling figure, encased within a leopard-print plastic raincoat ('she lived in it'), with a shamelessly large emerald decorating one finger. Three Maltese terriers, each with a purse around its neck, each cloyingly named ('Peach Blossom' or 'Passion Fruit' or similar), were in attendance as she was chauffeured around Nairobi. Angus invariably accompanied her.

Steaks were flown in from England for his barbecue parties, even though (as their butler later recalled) there were thousands of cattle on the farm. By adolescence, Angus's build and manner seemed at odds with his noble status, as far as contemporaries in Kenya were concerned, who likened him to 'a butcher's boy'. He was a little younger, probably twelve, when Mary Fox first met him, as she accompanied her father (a Dartmouth contemporary of Mandy's[45]) and stepmother to the New Stanley Hotel for drinks with the Manchesters. 'In those days, we all drank gin and orange,' she remembers. So, it transpired, did Angus, 'a revolting little spotty thing', who drained her glass. There was no rebuke from Nell or Mandy. 'He [had] a terribly smug and happy look on his face. He was horrible but it wasn't his fault. I remember being absolutely amazed [seeing] this very objectionable boy being dragged around by Mummy, being brought into the dress shop we all used in Nairobi.' Though the move to Kenya allowed Mandy to perpetuate a version of patrician existence, it also perversely accelerated the process begun by his father's graceless, self-pitying behaviour – the family's marginalization from the rest of the nobility. By the mid-1970s, it was claimed, probably fairly, that Mandy and his second cousin, James Graham, 7th Duke of Montrose,[46] were viewed with a degree of disapproval, born of a residual belief that 'it was unthinkable that any peer of the realm, especially a duke, should live anywhere but on his land' and of an accompanying conviction 'that they ought to have stayed when times were bad, their ancestors having reaped handsome rewards from the good times'.

This is unlikely to have troubled Mandy, who had an authentically aristocratic indifference to the opinions of others. What he did mind, however, were the grievous, if inadvertent, consequences of his self-imposed exile. Although the library, carpets and pictures at Kapsirowa were magnificent, they represented only a fraction of what had been stacked in the chapel and stables at Kimbolton during the war. The rest had been sold in 1949. Given that, at the time, the 'international art market was not yet restored', and that 'there were fewer millionaire collectors in America willing and able to buy' – not to mention the fact that the great transatlantic museum purchasers had yet to emerge – the sale can, in retrospect, be seen as one of his worst decisions. In the late 1940s and early 1950s, however, people throughout Britain – not just members of the vanquished upper class – were jettisoning belongings, often because they 'hadn't any money, or else the articles reminded them of someone dead'. In this impoverished buyers' market, 'bent individuals set up as dealers, their rooms crammed with anything that took their fancy... reproduction Millais and Winterhalter jumbled up with a real Picasso, a moderate Lely, a probable Greuze back-to-back with a fake Watteau'.

The Montagus' collection was dispersed with almost scornful cheapness during a four-day sale in July 1949.[47] Nell was at the Castle for it, scribbling prices into the margins of her catalogue; the figures were dismal. 'A portrait of Cromwell 8ft high in its frame sold for £11 11s, though it was attributed to Lucy,' recorded one report. '[A] picture of a military Duke of Manchester went for £10 10s – £1 1s a square foot. Two portraits believed to be by Van Dyck fetched £31 10s each... *Descent from the Cross* [attributed to Rubens] was knocked down for £11 11s.' Only once 'did the bidding rise out of the slough', when a Rubens of more certain provenance – *Prometheus, chained to a rock*, in the Montagus' possession since the seventeenth century – fetched £3,045 (£316,692 today). Eighteen months later, the painting was resold, this time for £30,000, to the Philadelphia Museum of Art. Kimbolton villagers sensed that, once again, the Montagus were mishandling their inheritance.

Though no longer indecently rich, the family was not destitute. There was, however, a logistical need for the sale – the impending loss of Kimbolton, a disaster which, Mandy later admitted, nearly broke his heart and which resulted from Olympian incompetence even by the competitive standards of the Montagus. After Mandy's return to Kenya in October 1947, Canon Frank Powys Maurice, Kimbolton's vicar since 1899, had enquired if the Castle might be adapted for use by Kimbolton School, an ancient grammar school which had recently assumed direct grant status, and which consequently required additional buildings for boarders and house masters. Mandy was far from hostile, though negotiations stalled over the length of the lease (the trustees' consent being needed for anything longer than fifty years) and the scale of rent (the school governors, chaired by Powys Maurice, suggested £105 per annum; Mandy's trustees sought £500). The introduction by the Attlee government of compulsory purchase orders, in February 1949, reinforced the governors' hand. Nevertheless, chaired by Powys Maurice, they emphasized that they would not seek to enforce such an order if offered the chance to acquire a long lease (or buy the Castle outright). The trustees were given until 21 March to devise a sensible response. Incredibly, they failed to do so.

From then on, the sale of Kimbolton became inevitable.[48] It was completed in 1951 for £12,500 (£1,122,754 today), an amount, suggested Pasty

Chilton, that Nell seemed capable of 'spending on gin in two or three days'. When Angus's parents now appeared at Kimbolton, they did so as visitors, motoring down from Claridge's, rather than staying at Park Lodge. In Northern Ireland, Tandragee was locked up, and its golf course leased to the local club. Ties were being cut, responsibilities delegated, status diminished.

Regrettably, Mandy's attempts to exert long-distance control of his estates – only fifty acres had been sold with the Castle – were undermined by his choice of Prince Nicholas Galitzyn as Mrs Carter's successor. 'Mandy,' reflects a family adviser, 'would have liked the idea of having a prince: if he was a prince, he must be all right.' Others, including Dawn Gooderham, soon learned that he wasn't. Assisted by Mandy's brother-in-law, David Stead, Galitzyn, she says, 'robbed the estate blind'. Grey Duberly agrees. 'Nick was a great shooting friend of everybody's [but] of course he didn't know how to be an agent. He and David drank all the drink, and used all the money having a good time at Newmarket.'[49]

Angus's uncle, David Stead – memorably good-looking, 'very elegant', invariably dressed in a navy blue blazer, but not 'rolling in money', despite allegedly being heir to a Melbourne fortune – is remembered by Grey Duberly as immensely charming, more or less penniless and always thirsty, which was unfortunate for the beguiling Jean Sclater Booth. 'They drank themselves to death, really.' Jean Sclater Booth succumbed first, dying in 1957; Stead a year or two later, in a London taxi, apparently from a heart attack, en route to the Savoy for dinner with Mandy. In the interim, he had sustained himself as barman at a pub near Kimbolton.

Later in his life Angus would make proprietorial references to his ancestral seat. He seems rarely, however, to have blamed anyone for its loss, nursing no grievance against trustees, still less against his father, perhaps because, as a second son, he had had no expectation of inheriting it. As it was, the sale of the Castle and (most of) its contents offered a helpful precedent. When, subsequently, Angus inherited furniture and silver, and hungrily converted them into cash, he was – he could remind himself – following family tradition. The loss of the Castle, together with the Montagus' disengagement from Cambridgeshire, also presented him with an opportunity for reinventing details about his past. Charles Lousada, who invited him to a charity dance at Kimbolton in the 1990s, was treated to a full disquisition. 'He showed me where he used to sleep, how they lived in the house, how his father was happiest when he was with the estate workers, perhaps down in the pub. He told me his father [said] of the estate workers, "These are your real friends, this is your family, you look after these people".'

* * *

Near the end of his life, Angus gave a remarkable interview during which he described his life as an elephant boy and made a tantalizing reference to his military career: 'I never talk about my service life. Let's just say I'm not very proud of some of the things I had to do.' At the House of Lords, one of the doorkeepers, who, like all twenty-two of his colleagues, had a distinguished service record, was intrigued by a tie which Angus occasionally favoured. Eventually, he allowed curiosity to get the better of him. 'Forgive me, your Grace, am I right in thinking that that's a Combined Operations tie?' Angus's reply was unhesitating. 'He said that it was, and that he'd been in the special forces.'

Usually, Angus said only that he had progressed from the ranks of the Royal Marines to become an officer, omitting all mention of his special forces role. Brian Joyles can testify that Angus opened fire, remembering, in particular, an incident involving a 3.5-inch rocket-launcher whose back-blast demanded respect. 'You had to lay virtually at right angles to it, otherwise you'd get a scorched arse.' Marine Lord Angus Montagu, adds Joyles, got a scorched arse.

This didn't detract from his popularity. 'Monty', as he was known, had never attempted officer selection. 'I gained the impression he wasn't academically qualified,' says Joyles, who remembers Angus as someone who 'liked to have a run ashore, have a few pints with the lads'. It did him no harm that he was noticeably strong, 'a bloody good water polo player, [with] a hell of a throw on him: he had a good physique, always in very good shape.' Bill Green, a fellow recruit in squad 911 at Lympstone in January 1957, acknowledged that Angus was 'physically up to it: quite a hefty lad', but found his intellect less impressive and his manner unendearing. 'He wasn't as quick on the uptake as he could have been; with his background, he should have made a commission. A bit of an arrogant bugger, I thought. He once offered me something like 1s 6d to press his khaki and his two blue uniforms; I turned him down.'

Another member of the squad, in the same hut, remembers 'Monty' flourishing a £5 note. 'That was a rarity to me. I'd been brought up in south-west London in a very modest family. We recruits were earning 26 shillings one week and 24 shillings the next. Most of it went on cleaning kit and a little bit of nutty [chocolate].' He was grateful, however, that he did not share Monty's surname. 'In those days, Montagu did mean a few things,' he adds, an oblique reference to the difficulties which had by then engulfed Angus's distant kinsman, Lord Montagu of Beaulieu.[50]

Angus appeared unperturbed by this or by the parade ground attention of Corporal Morley, a combative Geordie ('Does Daddy have a big yacht, Monty?') or by conditions in the hut ('cold, wet and horrible'). Instead, it was in his dealings with his fellow public schoolboys that he seemed to struggle. There were forty-seven recruits on squad 911; only three others were public school-educated. Attitude, as much as accent, marked them out. 'You could tell they were used to working till eight o'clock at night,' said Bill Green. '[They] just buckled down.' But there was a definite gulf between Angus and the rest. 'They spoke to him but they didn't pal up with him. They didn't want to know him as a serious friend.' Recent Montagu history could not have helped: the 9th Duke's abbreviated stint in Wormwood Scrubs; the vibrant behaviour of Lady Louise Montagu; the sale of Kimbolton and the death in the Mexican jungle of Lord Edward Montagu. Lord Montagu of Beaulieu's imprisonment helped to keep the brew fizzing.

Just as importantly, Angus didn't fit in: he lived abroad, had attended a small, strange school, founded by a rather odd German, in Scotland,[51] and didn't know their friends. The 'butcher's boy' didn't really seem to be one of them at all. For his part, Angus was all too aware that his academic quali-fications were less than paper-thin. The consequent vulnerability never left him, partly explaining why he felt uncomfortable in the company of people from his own background, even those within it who had achieved only modest classroom success, particularly Old Etonians, whom he openly resented.

There was no danger of meeting them aboard HMS *Loch Fyne*. Angus was, predictably, the only one of the marine detachment who had been to public school and, of course, the only one with a title. Just as encouragingly, he discovered that the ship's captain, Bertie Pengelly, had been in the navy with his father. These were the sort of conditions in which Angus would be happiest throughout his life, ones in which his aristocratic lineage assured him of attention without any risk of being subjected to erudite or patrician scrutiny. Shedding the defensive arrogance evident during basic training, he emerged, says Brian Joyles, as 'a most affable person, absolutely charming, great fun', his background a subject of mild interest to his fellow marines, but never a source of resentment. 'We were on a mess deck of our own, of about fourteen, sixteen people. He took his turn as what they call mess-deck dodger, scrubbing the deck floors and things like that. He was jolly good at it. You'd see all these elaborate envelopes addressed to Marine Lord Angus Drogo Montagu [but] he was just Monty, one of the crew.' For the first time in his life, Angus found that he could not only do what was required of him but could help others, in particular a fellow marine who, in Joyles's words, had a 'heavy domestic problem'. 'Monty was very forthcoming in financing the chap. He was very well liked.'

HMS *Loch Fyne* docked in Mombasa, the Seychelles and Colombo. 'Everywhere we went, Monty seemed to know someone. He always got sort of special leave, and off he went for a few days. Somebody would pick him up in a car.' Angus's popularity was sufficiently well established that this inspired admiration, not envy. 'He used to enlighten us [about] the food and wine he'd had. Nobody held it against him.' Nowhere was Angus's network of contacts more extensive than in Ceylon. 'It was quite amazing. Even when we were at this village called Yetawawa, Angus disappeared and was put up at places owned by various people.' His hosts, adds Joyles, were exclusively drawn from the chauffeured classes. There was little or no opportunity to blow money (whether on board ship[52] or off it), and no especially arduous duties to perform. It was an idyllic if humble existence.

After HMS *Loch Fyne* returned to Plymouth at the end of 1958, Angus headed to London whenever possible. Joyles formed the impression that 'he used to be a bit of a lad for the girls. There was one starlet at the time I think he had a crush on, Lisa Gastoni.[53] He used to speak about her quite a lot.' The following year, Neil Sclater Booth was invited to a May ball at Cambridge. To his surprise, he bumped into Angus, who did not seem to be going to any of the balls but was loitering with intent – 'chasing skirt', remembered Neil Sclater Booth.

* * *

A flight of stairs led to the agency's offices. The outer room, Jane Probyn was encouraged to see, was large and clean. The advertisement in the *Evening Standard* had promised television work to models or other girls with appropriate potential. Jane, a petite, twenty-two-year-old brunette, was keen to see if she had what was required. A receptionist told her to take a seat. A little while later, a man appeared. He was in his late twenties, broad, clean-cut, and wearing black-framed glasses. Sideburns jagged across his cheekbones in fashionable mid-sixties manner. He told Jane to follow him into the adjoining room. Once there, he began closing the curtains, issuing a brief instruction as he did so.

'Take your clothes off.'

'WHAT?' Jane's half-stammered, half-howled reply halted the screen test.

The man from the agency remained completely unabashed. 'Oh, alright then, if you don't want to, let's go for a drink.'

Her association with Angus, says Jane Probyn (now Bishop), went from there. It led to an informal engagement, followed by a friendship which was ended only by Angus's death nearly forty years and three wives later. 'I think it was that night that we drove to Windsor,' she says. 'We had a few more drinks, and he drove back at a phenomenal speed. It wasn't a very smart car – a blue Ford.'

Jane soon learned that there was very little which was smart about Angus. She learned, too, that he was very fond of his mother, but she remained in ignorance – as did all Angus's adult acquaintances – of Nell's remarkable character, her interest in extra-marital activity and her intense feelings for her younger son, all of which had left their mark.

As a child, Angus displayed a precocious interest in sex utterly at odds with his stalled educational development. 'He was telling me how babies were made when he was seven,' remembered Neil Sclater Booth, adding that, at the same age, the word 'do' – when used by adults – caused Angus enormous excitement. The excitement endured. One of Angus's female friends, who crafted a career supplying company to gentlemen in need, describes him as 'women mad', adding that he had 'no hang-ups' about prostitutes. Bill Ewens witnessed Angus's familiarity with the escort industry when joining him and Neil Sclater Booth on a trip to London in the 1950s. 'I was seventeen or something like that, terribly innocent. Angus set me up with one of his girl-friends; I didn't realize she was a whore. [Later] it was a question of finding me a place to stay for the night. [Angus] said, "Don't worry, you can stay with Frangipan" or whatever her name was. The bed was about twenty foot wide and draped in velvet from head to floor. I was given a cot at the foot of it.' Angus would have been fourteen at the time, though his bulk was that of a bruising eighteen-year-old.

A few years later, he drove down to Kimbolton in a sports car, dropping in on the Ewenses' cottage when he did so. 'He had a whore on the bonnet, her legs astride, waving her garter belt in the air,' remembers Ewens. 'I can't remember if she had any drawers on. Quite pretty, heavily made up.' Ewens' mother drew on a useful reservoir of experience. 'My dad had been in the air force; she just said, "One lump or two?"' In adulthood, Angus's attitude to women contrived to be both chivalrous and clinical. His enthusiasm was frequently reciprocated. A family trustee who attended Angus's second wedding, to Diane Plimsaul in 1971, remembers being struck by the qualities of the bride, who was obviously intelligent, sane and remuneratively employed. She was also, he adds, 'a good-looking girl'. Finding it perplexing that she should see her future with Angus, he sought enlightenment from a fellow guest, Tom Gilchrist, an American lawyer in charge of the Montagus' US trust. 'Tom, who'd had about four wives, said, "You mustn't underestimate his sexual attraction".'

Although neither Jane Bishop nor Angus's third wife, Louise, found Angus unusually attractive, both enjoyed a sense of complete security in his company. Jane Bishop mentions a Christmas drive through snow. 'We skidded; he put his left arm out to stop me shooting forward onto the dashboard. I thought, this is a man who would always fight for you.' Still immensely powerful if not quite as lean as he had been during national service, Angus reinforced this impression by remarking that he had some expertise in judo or karate, though no demonstration of his proficiency was forthcoming. Nor was it during his marriage to Louise, though Louise felt that all his strength would, if necessary, have been put at her disposal. 'He was the kind of guy who would have killed for the woman he had with him. He would have protected you at all costs; and he was *very* charming.'

Ready to devote his attention to whomever he was with, Angus nevertheless betrayed little sign of dismay when these relationships faltered. A Bedford acquaintance, who knew him from 1985 onwards, gained the impression that he 'would marry at the drop of a hat', a judgement supported by his swiftly arranged fourth marriage and, after its speedy failure, his determination to remarry Louise. During fallow periods between marriages, however, Angus was content to form less exclusive attachments, and was never especially fastidious about methods of introduction – as his father had discovered.

In September 1966, a telephone call had disturbed the orderly routine at a firm of solicitors in Upper Brook Street, Mayfair. The caller was Mandy. 'Will you come to the Ritz, and ask for Lady Kintore's suite, straightaway? Don't speak to the press.'

A young solicitor hurried to Piccadilly. Inside Lady Kintore's suite he was greeted by Mandy and a medley of accountants and Montagu family trustees. Mandy began to recount the events of the night before. He, his mother (Helena Kintore) and the family doctor, Tom Creighton, had been having dinner at Quaglino's, when the head waiter had approached and asked if he would leave the table for a moment. Mandy had followed the waiter into the hall. A pram had been pushed into a corner. Inside it were a five-month-old baby and two envelopes addressed to the Duke of Manchester. '[One said], 'This is your grandson. Angus won't look after him so you must.' The other [gave] directions for feeding the baby.' After delivering this resumé, Mandy asked those present for their advice. It was soon agreed that blood tests should be conducted as soon as possible, to try to establish the baby's paternity.

The attempt to minimize press coverage was initially successful, although the 'Quaglino's baby' later became the subject of a cartoon in the *Evening Standard* and of a brief report in *The Times*, recording that a Mrs Montagu, formerly Miss Trixeena Hudson,[54] had served an affiliation summons against Angus, alleging that he was the baby's father. Shortly after the boy's birth on 14 April, Angus had gone to Marylebone Register Office and signed the register, seemingly acknowledging paternity.[55] A month later, Trixeena had issued a writ demanding repayment of £9,000 (£315,058 today) which she claimed to have lent him. But the blood tests, remembers the solicitor who was summoned to the Ritz, put Angus in the clear. Years later, Angus 'swore blind' that he was completely unacquainted with Trixeena. Louise Manchester was unconvinced. 'I find it very difficult to believe that a woman could say she had a child by him, if she had never known him.' Three decades earlier, Angus had been comparatively candid with Jane Bishop. 'I think he called her Stella. He told me about [her] fairly early on in our relationship [but] he denied that [the baby] could be his.'

The solicitor (now retired) who attended Mandy's emergency conference at the Ritz says that there is little if any doubt that Angus knew Trixeena really rather well; no one, he suggests, was more surprised by the negative blood test than Angus, who, he adds, might have first become acquainted with Trixeena in Australia. Whether or not that was the case, they definitely formed, or intensified, their association in London, where Trixeena lived in Piccadilly. 'Quite distinct from this case, we acted for the landlord of the building, who was concerned that it was being used for immoral purposes. An inquiry agent was instructed to investigate. The inquiry agent had a jolly time. It was obviously being used... [for] various types of massage. He mentioned in the report that Lord Angus Montagu was often seen there.' Details of Angus's involvement with Trixeena never emerged publicly, but that did not deter his first wife from using the Quaglino's incident as grounds for divorcing him when she belatedly instituted proceedings in 1970.

* * *

Mary McClure was part of the past that Angus liked to consign to oblivion. Towards the end of his life, however, he acknowledged that his marriage to her had been his 'first big mistake', a remark which suggests that his judgement was not uniformly flawed. They had met at a party in Yarra, a Melbourne suburb, in the summer of 1961. That September they announced their engagement, explaining that it would not become official until the Duke and Duchess of Manchester, then on a world tour, returned to Kenya. After

Nell and Mandy had been informed, Angus and Mary married at All Saints Church, Newtown, near Geelong, on 22 November. 'The reason I didn't marry an English girl,' the groom reflected, 'is because they are too blasé and put on too many airs.' His bride – indisputably a plain-speaking sort, employed as a £15-a-week typist – bore him two sons and a daughter in swift succession (Alexander in December 1962, Kimble in October 1964, and Emma in September 1965).

Mary's father, Walter McClure, was said to be the first Australian to have become a director of General Motors Holden; her mother's family, the Stintons, owned extensive nurseries in Geelong. But neither the McClures nor the Stintons had any intention of subsidizing their son-in-law. Nor, it became apparent, were Angus's own Australian relations, the Steads, capable of doing so. Their house in Geelong had been sold and there was no evidence of their previous affluence; in fact, there was very little evidence of Nell's family at all, except for her sister Ginty, who had appeared at Kimbolton, been briefly engaged to Reuben Farley, but was now married to an Australian, John Grimwade, and living in Melbourne.

A trickle of Montagu money – the interest from a £10,000 trust which had been settled on him in about 1953 – reached Angus, who since leaving the Marines, had supplemented it by working on Texan oil fields as a £2-an-hour roustabout, offering his services as a water-skiing instructor in Florida, shooting sharks in Sydney harbour, rally-driving with Gelignite Jack (whose nickname paid tribute to his tendency to lob explosives at other drivers), steering cattle wagons across thousands of miles of scorched outback, and securing unspecified employment, courtesy of family connections, with a state governor. His admiration for Lisa Gastoni had not been rewarded by artistic collaboration with her but he had, he claimed, appeared as an extra in a film starring Esther Williams,[56] on whose behalf he had grappled with a crocodile. Unfortunately, by the time of his engagement, Angus was shifting from reliance on muscle to faith in his brain, studying business methods and salesmanship – and reputedly selling trousers in the menswear department – at Myer, a Melbourne department store.

A combination of modest income and trust dividends could have supported a young family in civilized conditions, given appropriate self-restraint. The restraint enforced on Angus at Gordonstoun and during service with the Marines had not, however, become habitual. Left to his own devices, he sought out avenues of amusement; one of these led to the gaming tables. Although he never enjoyed the resources which the 9th Duke had (intermittently) had at his disposal, Angus's inclinations were indisputable.

Playing roulette in Las Vegas in the early 1980s, he placed mounds of chips with familiarity – 'on the corners, on the sides, all that,' recalls his companion from the trip. 'He knew exactly what he was doing. It stunned me.'[57] Thirty years earlier, Angus's modest trust fund had provided him with the occasional fistful of cash or, when necessary, an inch or two of credit. It was all the encouragement he needed. 'He used to go to quite a lot of the gambling clubs before he met me, before he went to Australia, while he was in the Marines,' says Jane Bishop. 'He always claimed he owned one.'

It was not a claim he repeated to Fergus Rogers, his Gordonstoun contemporary who, by the 1970s, was a chartered accountant whose clients included Le Cercle, a casino above Les Ambassadeurs, a Park Lane dining club. 'I think he was a member [of Les Ambassadeurs]. He would ask if I was in when he came in for lunch.' Rogers saw no sign that Angus was gambling, adding that he would have been worried if he had. Yet that was exactly what he was doing, combining it – in the mid-1970s, at least – with other recreational activity. 'It was just [an] extraordinary existence, where he'd throw all this money around, going to incredibly expensive venues and chucking it on the gaming table,' remembers a girlfriend from that era. 'He'd invariably end up gambling, which I hated.' In the second half of the 1980s, he only once allowed Louise to accompany him to a newer casino, the Colony Club, a few yards from Les Ambassadeurs, though she was convinced that this was a world of which he was a regular – if low-rolling – member.

Even an occasional small-scale loss would have been enough to kick the scaffolding away from Angus's perennially unstable finances, which might, in part, have been why his first marriage foundered. Although Angus usually managed to remain on good terms with former wives and girlfriends, he was rarely able, or willing, to do so with Mary.[58] His former wife handsomely reciprocated his feelings. 'If they had cause to speak, it was just a shouting match, just dreadful,' says Louise. Trustees often bore the brunt of Mary's fury: one of them uncharitably referred to her as 'Mad Mary'. A member of the family attempts to achieve a degree of neutrality by saying that both Angus and Mary were 'hot-headed'.

In the early 1960s, however, observers tended to sympathize with Mary. 'Everybody was talking about him as rather a ne'er do well,' says Lord Montagu of Beaulieu, remembering a trip he made to Melbourne in 1964. The timing of Angus's defection from Mary did nothing to undermine this view: he abandoned her in 1965, days after she had given birth to their daughter Emma (who eventually met her father nearly twenty years later).

Mandy flew to Australia to console Mary. The visit was not a success. 'He said he went up some slum, about sixteen floors [up], and found [Mary] with these children,' remembers Grey Duberly. 'He said that as he left, she picked up the eldest one and threw it at him, and said, "Take the bugger".' Mary's sense of grievance never diminished. Two years after divorcing Angus in 1970, she flew to New York to try to secure the services of Melvin Belli.[59] Her intention, she told a British paper, was to sue Mandy for more money; her divorce settlement – entitling her to £15-a-week – was inadequate. Describing her living quarters as an 'upholstered sewer outside Melbourne'; she said that she and her children were obliged to use an outside lavatory, that the roof over one of their two bedrooms leaked, and added that she didn't eat a 'full meal' when they were all at home together to ensure that her children were properly fed.

Though the approach to Belli generated excitement, it was a futile gesture. 'She had no possible claim against [Mandy],' explains a family trustee. Nor, as Mary herself acknowledged, did she have the slightest chance of extracting anything from Angus. When Jane Bishop first encountered him in the mid 1960s, he was living in Shepherd Market, in a 'grotty bedsitter' which seemingly lacked a kitchen if not a bathroom. He did, though, have the consolation that his title (dropped lightly into conversation) was enough to interest some employers, who tended to retain him for 'about six weeks; then, when they found he wasn't capable of very much, they moved him on.' Angus claimed to have brought Edmundo Ros[60] to England to play in a nightclub, though Jane Bishop remembers less dazzling assignments: a stint with a design company and another with an encyclopaedia publisher. Later, they worked together at a Kensington hotel, just off the Cromwell Road, Jane waitressing, Angus helping in the bar. He seemed to enjoy himself.

Given his familiarity with – and capacity for – alcohol, a career in the drinks trade might have appeared appropriate. A friend from Bedford says that Angus 'had hollow legs, could drink forever'; a girlfriend from the 1970s remains awed by his capacity ('he'd order incredibly expensive stuff, I remember it very nostalgically'); Mary Fox says that once he had embarked on a binge it was impossible to stop him; Paul Vaughan, an ally during the last twenty years of his life, recalls that, when Angus drank, it 'never touched the sides'. Like his strength, it was a trait which the uninitiated underestimated at their peril. Casualties included P&O, whose management were prevailed upon to allow him to drink without charge during a cruise from Kobe to San Francisco (via Hawaii) in the 1980s. 'The bar bill,' reflects Paul Vaughan, who negotiated the deal on Angus's behalf, 'made the accountant's eyes water.' But even Angus had not achieved this single-handed. 'He was not a solitary drinker,' explains Vaughan. 'He felt that his job was to go round and tell everyone how wonderful P&O was, and say, "Oh, come and have some champagne".' If it was the sodality of drinking that mattered more than any alcoholic kick, it was, however, always as consumer rather than salesman that Angus seemed more convincing.

His prospects elsewhere were equally limited, for reasons that Kurt Hahn, Gordonstoun's founder, had identified years before. 'The individual,' Hahn had asserted, 'becomes a cripple from his or her own point of view if he is not qualified by education to serve the community.' Angus embodied the dictum. 'He wasn't qualified to make a living at anything,' acknowledged Fergus Rogers, though suggesting that, in the right firm where his title would have done no harm, Angus might have made a go of it as an estate agent. The guarantee of mild acclaim for his hereditary status was one of the reasons, remembers Jane Bishop, why 'he liked people from not quite the same background as himself'. His sole Montagu connection was with Tom Creighton, the family doctor. When he took Jane to Kimbolton, it was not for a weekend's shooting or cricket but for tea 'with an old girl in the village: he felt more comfortable with that'.

Soon after meeting Jane, Angus had abandoned his Shepherd Market bedsit in favour of her flat in Victoria, then followed her to Aylesbury for six months, before they both headed to Bedford, to stay with a friend of his who had bought a flat in a newly built block of flats called Broadreach. When Jane began working for the BBC, travelling the country with an outside broadcast unit, Angus came too. 'That got a bit awkward. Eventually one of the chaps said, "Does he have to come everywhere with you?" [Angus] was most put out. He was a very lost little soul, definitely wanted to be loved and wanted.'

The hunger for companionship, for cosseting, never diminished. In the early 1990s, learning that friends of his, a Bedford couple, were going on a Caribbean cruise, Angus announced that he and Louise would like to join them. His friends murmured their approval, and later regretted it: whenever they docked in port, Angus would be loitering at their side. 'He'd follow all day. He'd no brain of his own. We hid.' At parties back in Bedford, Angus frequently looked awkward and lost. 'If he didn't know anybody, he stood in a corner; he did not work the room. He hung onto you. You couldn't get rid of him.'

When amongst a handful of familiar faces, he fared better. 'He would sort of go with the flow,' remembers Jane Bishop. 'He liked playing cards.' To her astonishment, he liked the theatre too. With minimal expectations she

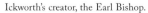
Ickworth's creator, the Earl Bishop.

Gwrych.

Ickworth: 'a stupendous monument of folly'.

Right: Winifred Bamford-Hesketh, the owner of Gwrych, ('proficient in French, authentic in Welsh'). She married Lord Cochrane – later 12th Earl of Dundonald (*left*) – in 1878, and lived largely unhappily ever after.

Left: The Earl Bishop's great-great grandson, Herbert Hervey, Victor's father, known in the family as P.O.H. ('Poor Old Herbert'), partly due to his marriage to Jean Cochrane.
Right: Jean, possessor of the 'best Scotch medicine cabinet in London'.

Victor and his first cousin, John Rowley, the son of Jean's sister Marjorie, at Lochnell, the house the boys' grandfather, the 12th Earl of Dundonald, bought to 'escape from his wife'.

Left: Victor in white tie, around the time that he was living at 31, Upper Berkeley Street. His fellow lodger, Ronnie Kershaw, remembered Victor maintained a nocturnal regime.

Sandhurst: Victor assured the younger generation that he had been awarded the Sword of Honour; the truth was less illustrious.

Inset: Victor's cousin John Rowley at Eton. His contemporaries included Ronnie Kershaw (back row, fourth from right). The world would turn its back on John, as would Victor.

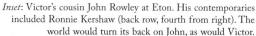

Cultivating an almost cinematic presence.

As Victor pointed out, he 'got to know any number of the "boys".'

Below: Victor with Pauline aboard the Cochrane Hervey, Victor's 156-ton house-boat (and a former Royal Navy escort vessel), in 1947. The 'luscious' Pauline was later to become his first wife.

COURT STRIPS 4 MAYFAIR MEN OF GLAMOUR

BY A SPECIAL CORRESPONDENT

FOUR more young men, whose lives centred on Mayfair cocktail bars and night clubs, are now behind prison bars with time to reflect on the words of the Recorder, Sir Gerald Dodson, when he sentenced them at the Old Bailey yesterday for stealing £3,100 worth of jewellery.

"The way of the amateur criminal is hard," he said, " but the way of the professional is disastrous."

Resplendent evening Mayfair suits, satin evening dress shirts and heavy silk rolls...

Unsurprisingly, Victor's career failed to find family favour.

MARQUESS BAILS NEPHEW

y Freed from Gaol

YEAR IN HOSPITAL: "THEY WORKED ME VERY HARD"

S 28 JUN 41

Exclusive to "The Star"

VICTOR FREDERICK COCHRANE HERVEY, son of Lord Herbert Hervey, nephew of the Marquis of Bristol, and godchild of Queen Ena of Spain, returned to-day to the West End, after serving a sentence of penal servitude, mostly at Camp Hill Prison, in the Isle of Wight.

He was convicted, with others, in July, 1939, for conspiracy and theft of jewellery, valued at £3,500, from two women.

At the time of his appeal against the sentence he was 23. Prison life appears to have touched him lightly.

When a "Star" reporter interviewed him he was fit and sunburnt. Convict life had not taken the wave from his hair. He was debonair, in a striped blue suit.

GOOD CONDUCT

He said: "I carried full remission for good conduct, having a year and a fortnight taken from my three-year sentence. I was at Brixton, Wormwood Scrubs, Maidstone and Camp Hill.

"For a year I have been in the prison hospital with bone trouble following undue strain whilst I was working. They worked me very hard.

"A year ago I registered voluntarily, and I would like to join the Air Force. Failing that I am willing to help in the national effort in other ways.

Victor Hervey in London after leaving prison.—" Star " photograph.

With lawyer Michael Havers, a future Attorney General and Lord Chancellor, outside Marlborough Street Magistrates' Court, where Victor was convicted on a drink-drive charge in 1970. Havers explained that Lord Bristol usually had a chauffeur.

Right: Victor marries Juliet, 'a saint', on 24 April 1960.
Far right: Victor marries Yvonne, 'a young woman with quite a presence', on 12 July 1974, signing the register as 'Victor Frederick Cochrane' and fictionalizing his father's name as 'Robert Arthur Cochrane'.

Left: Victor and Yvonne at their son Frederick's christening, 1980. Victor had earlier experienced some difficulty returning his sword to its scabbard.
Below: Victoria and Isabella Hervey – young women both admirably equipped for the celebrity arena.

'dragged him' to see Olivier as Othello at the National. 'I thought, he'll last ten minutes and then he'll be bored to death.' She was wrong. 'He was mesmerized, didn't move a muscle.' About two months later, by which time she and Angus were no longer living together, he rang and asked if they could go to the theatre again. 'I said, yes, of course, I'll look something up.' Angus had a very specific request. 'He said, "I would really like to see that black man again".'

There had been surprises elsewhere: a visit to his solicitor, a Welshman called Derek, from whom Angus extracted £5 'to get home' (the money was invested in supper at a roadside hostelry); a telephone call to the Home Office explaining that he was unable to retrieve his passport ('it was locked in somebody's house and they were abroad' – which Jane knew to be untrue); and a mortifying evening with a colleague, a BBC engineer, when Angus very quickly ran out of money. The engineer footed the bill; Jane subsequently repaid him but bade farewell to Angus.

* * *

By October 1968, Angus was thirty, homeless and penniless, and no longer able to turn to his mother, the source of endless, unqualified adoration. Blitzed by alcohol and nicotine, Nell had died, aged sixty-two, the previous month, just before the Quaglino's affair. If Angus expected financial consolation – he was the principal beneficiary of her will, drawn up in 1956 and never amended – he was to be disappointed: Nell left just £2,345 and six shillings.

Mandy appears to have forbidden him from attending her memorial service, held at Kimbolton church on 29 September,[61] and when, in February 1969, he became engaged to Elizabeth Crocker, widow of an American banker, he insulated his fiancée from contact with his younger son. 'I've never even met Mrs Crocker,' said Angus, when asked for his reaction to the engagement, 'or heard of her.' His vulnerability was palpable. Just as the bookies and chancers had closed in around Edward FitzGerald fifty years earlier, so their descendants now sniffed out Angus.

There were, however, two people who had Angus's best interests at heart. One of them was his closest and oldest friend. Angus used to say that he had known John Lickfold since confronting him as a boy in the Castle grounds at Kimbolton and telling him to leave, with the warning, 'I own this place'. Lickfold, whose family had been the Montagus' solicitors for generations, had not complied. A trustee suggests that the friendship really began a decade or so later when Lickfold 'was given the job of meeting Angus off the train. They got on like a house on fire.' It was, outwardly at least, an unlikely alliance. Always his own man, Lickfold joined his family firm only to leave to become a 'brilliant computer programmer'. A few years older than Angus, he remained the quintessential bachelor, one of his many girlfriends being remembered by a male acquaintance as 'ravishing, the most beautiful girl I've ever seen'. In the mid 1960s, he bought a flat in a newly built block of flats called Broadreach, overlooking the river Ouse in Bedford, though he had proved himself the staunchest of Angus's friends long before then. 'Johnny bailed him out several times while he was in the Marines,' says Jane Bishop. 'He was very good to Gus over the years.' He was also candid, repeatedly telling Angus that he was stupid, and making it plain that, though prepared to shelter him during emergencies, he was not running a charity. 'He just one day said, "I do get fed up keeping him. I can't go on".'

It was apparently through John Lickfold that Angus met the other stabilizing influence in his life, Diane Plimsaul, who, on 5 March 1971, at Westminster Register Office, became his second wife. Mandy did not attend the wedding, possibly deterred by the site selected for the reception (a room above a café in Ealing) but mainly because he judged Diane to be socially unacceptable. 'He used to turn his nose up,' remembers a family trustee, 'used to say her father was a porter. I don't think [Diane's father] was quite as lowly as that but he certainly didn't come up to ducal expectations.' Had he quelled his prejudices, Mandy might have been pleasantly surprised. Fergus Rogers found Diane – a former colleague of John Lickfold – a level-headed, intelligent woman with a good job at one of the clearing banks. 'She was a bright, working-class girl. I was delighted to find he had somebody so clever. They lived halfway up Kingston Hill in a nice, quite modern house.'

Diane's professional success continued during her marriage to Angus. 'I always had the impression that [she] supported him,' says a female acquaintance, adding that the second Lady Angus Montagu eventually became customer liaison director of the Midland Bank. But financial dependency on his wife threatened to stifle Angus's scope for action. The remedy, he decided, lay in the West End. Never a creature of clubland,[62] certainly not of White's, he did, nevertheless, befriend the man who is now the barber there, Ivor Edwards, who remembers him as 'a great chap and a character'. Another West End acquaintance, Willie Wong, took him to Chinese restaurants 'for chow'; Angus reciprocated with tea in Kingston, where Mr Wong met John Lickfold. Fergus Rogers encountered two other associates at Les Ambassadeurs, one from Kenya, the other an Australian called Tindall; he cared for neither. It was in Tindall's company that Angus outlined some projects. 'He muttered something about offshore stuff. Well, I was meant to be an accountant [but] I couldn't follow what he was talking about, I really couldn't.'

Before temporarily losing touch with Angus, Jane Bishop heard that he had teamed up with a gentleman who, though Russian, liked to be known as Larry Taylor, with whom Angus shared further interests. Their firm might have been what Angus later described as a cheque guarantee company, which was apparently 'sold off to Barclays', or the 'export business' which Angus liked to say he had established; which might, in turn, have been the 'Import Deposit Scheme', whose raison d'être was to help small import and export companies which, under the Labour government of Harold Wilson, were obliged to pay a 50 per cent deposit on the value of all incoming goods. In 2000, Angus acknowledged that the scheme had attracted the attention of the Fraud Squad. 'I turned over £6.35 million, but it all came to an end after eight months when the Government reversed the policy. I had to spend two weeks sending back money, which hurt.'

Some of Angus's new associates did rather better, perhaps none more so than Michael Whitear, who, in the early 1970s, was making his mark in what he describes as 'the banking business, money-lending, financing'. He met Angus in unusual circumstances. 'He'd had an accident on the Hammersmith fly-over,' says Mr Whitear. 'Some guy had come across the road, his car had taken off, gone through the air and ended up going through the front of [Angus's] car, so he was taken off to the hospital in a pretty broken state.' The accident, adds Mr Whitear, was reported in the press.[63] 'When I read it, I felt very concerned.' He traced Angus to his hospital bed, 'just to make sure he was OK'. It was the beginning of a relationship which was characterized by 'warmth, happiness and friendliness' and which ended only in 1996 when Mr Whitear declined to fly to America to give evidence on Angus's behalf.

Uniquely amongst ex-wives, lovers, friends, contemporaries or relations, Whitear describes Angus as 'a bright spark'; he recruited him to his firm. Starting 'not as a tea boy but pretty much watching and learning what other people did', Angus remained with Whitear for two years, at the end of which he accepted an offer 'from somebody in the property business'. Before then, however, Whitear had received a telephone call from Mandy inviting him to lunch. 'He sent the family chauffeur round to collect me. I met him at his family home, Eaton Square. He greeted me and said, "I can't believe you've done what you've done and I thank you for doing it because it's turned out an amazing success: he's a different person."'

Perhaps Mandy was right and Angus did become a different person during the early 1970s. Besides extending the range of his acquaintances, he seems to have developed a new sense of purpose, a misplaced belief in his own abilities and a talent for manifesting unexplained moments of prosperity which caused unease to one of his girlfriends, who sensed that 'whatever money he had was coming from some dubious source'. He also met the Cheesemans. Mr Keith Cheeseman, like Mr Whitear, employed Angus in the early 1970s,[64] though he, like Whitear, found that their relationship did not survive beyond Angus's imprisonment in America. His ex-wife Kerry, by contrast, was in touch with Angus to the very end. She believes, with good reason, that she was his closest woman friend. 'He would phone me at least once a day, very often twice a day,' she says, adding that Angus was a fairly frequent visitor not only to her current residence in Essex but also to her previous one, a council flat in the East End. Whilst there, he relaxed, had 'no airs and graces', constructed and consumed substantial raw onion sandwiches, chatted to members of her family (her 6'5" grandson was a particular favourite) and went to the pub for lunch. She knew him as Aggi or, occasionally, the Duke; he responded by calling her the Queen ('because I was the Queen of the East End'). 'I saw a side to him that other people didn't. He was happier being around me and my friends, even [though] some of the people I know may be a bit notorious.' Both the Cheesemans would stand shoulder to shoulder with Angus when he appeared in the dock at the Old Bailey in 1985.

* * *

One of Mandy's last requests was that his coffin should lie in the Castle chapel the night before his funeral; the wish was granted. Four days after his death on 23 November 1977, coffin and corpse were brought by hearse from London.

His final years had been marred by throat cancer, an operation reducing his voice to 'a sort of forced whisper', obliging him to speak through an electronic box or to scribble on a pad of paper. He bore it with characteristic stoicism, remembers Mary Fox, who saw him shortly before he died. The diminution in Mandy's abilities suited Angus, not because he bore him any malice but because, for the first and only time, he was able to come to his father's assistance. Ian Codrington, who became Angus's solicitor in the 1980s, heard of a rapport between them quite unlike the fractious relationship Angus habitually described to friends in previous decades. 'He said he got on very well with Mandy, said he would go and see him, and was the only one who would take him out, so that he could have a cigar which he wasn't supposed to have.'

If true, the improvement in his relationship with his father followed in the wake of the rupture between Mandy and Kim. Although Mandy liked his elder son, and believed that he could rely on him,[65] he had not intervened when Kim had been repeatedly and vociferously belittled by Nell, nor had he ever offered him the slightest financial support. Kim's impecuniousness, says Mary Fox, whose first husband, Michael Cunningham-Reid, was evacuated to America with him during the war, had been evident since adolescence. 'Michael said [Kim] never had any money, never had any clothes.' Back in Kenya, after the war, he ran up debts with the duka,[66] experimented with Russian roulette whilst staying with Patsy Chilton ('I said, 'Don't be a bloody fool, Kim'... The next thing I knew there was a bullet through the ceiling. It was as near as damn it he killed himself') and was publicly humiliated by his mother at the Rift Valley Club in Nakuru where she harangued him for owing Patsy money. 'I don't know how she found out. It embarrassed him dreadfully. [She] made him go to the bank and give it back, then and there.'

Whilst Angus's diet was being boosted with steaks flown in from England, Kim was expected to make his own way, even though his qualifications for doing so were very nearly as meagre as his younger brother's would be. Pathetically dependent on others for food and lodging, he took refuge with Lord Delamere.[67] 'He had no money, nothing, never a penny piece to his name,' recalls Mary Fox. 'It was extraordinary.' Once, in the 1950s, Kim disappeared whilst escorting children from Tanzania to Australia (it was said, in Kenya, that he had sold the children to a circus), only to be 'rediscovered' at Keith Hall, with his grandmother, Helena Kintore, the only member of his family for whom he really cared. He was also glimpsed at Kimbolton – 'living on borrowed money', remembers Bill Ewens, who noted that Kim was accompanied by 'gorgeous blonde debutantes' – but returned to Kenya, competed several times in the East Africa Rally and served as a member of D Force during the Mau Mau emergency, running a police station in the Ngong Hills with Michael Cunningham-Reid. 'Michael would listen to the racing; then it was Kim's turn: he would listen to motor racing.' Mary Fox's father, who lived nearby, found it difficult to have complete confidence in D Force's Ngong command.

Nevertheless, Kim survived, embraced the motor trade, lasted a week in his first job (requiring him to retrieve cars from customers who had defaulted on payments; all were friends of his), then found work with film companies needing mechanics and drivers for location work. Although periodically distracted by some of Hollywood's leading ladies, he married on 5 February

1955, his twenty-sixth birthday, when Angus was in his final Easter term at Gordonstoun. His bride, Valerie 'Val' Christie, 'a very lovely person', had 'the bluest eyes – total sapphire' and a dependency on the bottle, although it was her adoration of her new husband which antagonized her mother-in-law. 'Nell was horrid to her,' says Mary Fox. 'A bolt of lightning went through the church as Kim said, "I do".'

The couple's failure to procreate inspired different theories. 'Kim was hit in the balls by a cricket ball when he was a child,' says Lord Montagu of Beaulieu. Angus preferred to say that Kim 'had had his balls cut off in a car accident'. That, happily, was not the case, but Val's alcoholism, coupled with Kim's tendency to drink with characteristic Montagu enthusiasm, and his penchant for chain-smoking large Cuban cigars, stacked the odds against them.

Although Mandy had removed the Manchester Papers from the Public Records Office in 1967 – they were found to include a hitherto unknown manuscript poem 'in the hand of John Donne' – and auctioned them at Sotheby's, and sold Tandragee (retaining its golf course), only part of which had been rescued for progressive commercial use ('there was a potato crisp factory in the stables'), he nevertheless lived in hope of perpetuating the Montagus' association with dynastic territory,[68] now embodied by Park Lodge and a rump of 3,000 Cambridgeshire acres.

He did not have Angus in mind. 'Mandy knew [Angus] was completely unreliable; he had no patience with him,' explains a family trustee. 'I remember [Mandy] being furious because [Angus] had painted the Manchester arms on the door of his car, or had a transfer done.' He had no hesitation in handing the remaining Kimbolton land and Irish property to Kim in 1972. By then, Kim's marriage was disintegrating – and Val with it, largely because of her drinking problem, which worsened very publicly, not in Kenya but in Kimbolton. Living at a house called the Chestnuts, she sometimes crawled home from the pub along the road; at others she climbed the Castle wall. A few years later she moved to Fishguard in south Wales, dying soon afterwards. Before leaving Kimbolton, however, she redecorated Park Lodge, a final act of devotion to Kim, who let it for shooting parties. Unfortunately, he removed the running of the shoot from Reuben Farley's nephew, Pat Wood, and handed it to his own nominee. When it failed to prosper, he felt little incentive for staying on.

With the exception of a few months after the end of the war and an occasional visit thereafter, Kim had not lived in Kimbolton since he was ten. Unlike his father, he felt no compelling sentimental ties to the place nor had social bonds with neighbouring landowners; nor, unlike Angus, had he ever developed a particular affinity for those employed on the estate. Worst of all, he seemed unlikely to have a son and heir to whom to bequeath his inheritance, which would, instead, fall into the lap of his younger brother, from whom he was by now irrevocably estranged. In 1975, he made his decision, selling everything – the Kimbolton estate, as well as the golf course and clubhouse at Tandragee.

Mandy could conceive of no more flagrant act of betrayal. Perhaps for the only time in his life, he began to look favourably on his younger son. A member of the family suggests that he even toyed with the idea of making Angus the primary beneficiary of his will. If so, he thought better of it, leaving the small sum that was not tied up in trust funds to his wife. He did, however, take an increasingly close interest in his grandchildren, especially in Angus's elder son, Alexander, insisting that the boy be sent to school at Kimbolton. The experiment required Alexander and Angus to become reacquainted with one another, for which they proved unwilling (the young nobleman's visits to his father and stepmother in Kingston ended in mutual recrimination and allegations of violence).

By then, the cross currents of bad blood flowed invigoratingly between the generations. Those who attended Mandy's funeral and the wake lunch afterwards noted the animus between the new Duke of Manchester and his American stepmother. 'Kim infuriated Elizabeth,' remembers a surviving guest, 'by plonking himself at her table at the reception.' The antagonism, which was mutual, would in due course lead to the law courts, generating a useful income for solicitors and barristers for the best part of a decade, though this did not mean that Elizabeth[69] was suddenly enamoured of Angus, of whom there was no sign at the Cambridge crematorium or the wake lunch.

As soon as Mandy's ashes had been interred in the family crypt, Kim abandoned England. His disposal of the Tandragee golf course (for £39,380; about £499,532 today) and the last 3,250 acres at Kimbolton, which included six farms, eighteen cottages and the newly renovated Park Lodge (for about £1 million; £12,694,913 now) offered persuasive evidence that he shared his father's gift for relinquishing assets at inopportune moments. 'He didn't get enough money for them,' acknowledges a trustee. Nevertheless, with one of his trust funds boosted by £1 million, Kim had an income of about £100,000-a-year – comfortable enough, since 'he was domiciled in Kenya, so it was all tax-free'.

The year after his father's death, on 25 August 1978, he married for a second time, aged forty-nine; his new wife, Andrea Kent, a colonel's daughter, was thirteen years his junior. Their union might have been formalized sooner – they had lived together since the early 1970s – had it not been for Mandy, who voiced doubts about Andrea, who had three children from two previous marriages. She was robust enough to weather the delay and to tolerate Kim's tendency to talk about his ex-wife – almost the only person from his past whom he ever mentioned. 'He seemed entirely disconnected from his family,' remembers Joss Kent, the younger of his stepsons. No Montagus visited Kim's farm in the Sabukia valley or, later, his house in Nairobi. Of Angus, Joss remained completely unaware.

With the years of penury behind him, Kim bought a second property, a ranch in Tennessee, an E-Type Jaguar for Andrea and a Range Rover for himself. His life now was not onerous – smoking cigars, shooting in England, deep-sea fishing in Kenya. Though he suffered from asthma (and had experimented with blood transfusions) he was as muscular as his father had been, and seemingly as robust. Even if he and Andrea did not have children, they could confidently expect many more years together.

* * *

Life was becoming altogether more eventful for Angus. Until July 1974, few had heard of Dunstable Town, a Southern League football club. Then a new owner arrived, an ebullient character who drove a Lamborghini, enjoyed flying by executive jet and persuaded George Best to turn out for the club. His name was Keith Cheeseman; he appointed Angus to Dunstable's board of directors. Despite his new responsibilities, Angus did not put his expertise exclusively at Cheeseman's disposal, remaining close to Michael Whitear, whom he would introduce to friends as 'my business partner' during the course of the next two decades.

It is, nevertheless, Keith Cheeseman rather than Michael Whitear who reminisces more persuasively about Angus's commercial value. They met in 1970 or 1971 (almost exactly the same time that Angus encountered Whitear) and found they had much in common. Like Angus, Cheeseman was, and is, a big man (his weight fluctuating between sixteen and twenty stone), who enjoys female company (he now has four wives behind him); like Angus, he has a remarkable capacity for alcohol (one of his former employees remarking that he had 'never seen anyone who could take their drink like him') and is capable of brazenly effective charm (he could, in the words of the third Mrs Cheeseman, 'charm crocodiles from mud').

But Mr Cheeseman is not, as far as is known, of aristocratic descent. Born in 1942, the second son of a Luton shopkeeper, he left school at sixteen, joined the Royal Artillery, leaving five years later as a bombardier. His 'short neck and cannonball head' subsequently appeared in the scrap-metal business and building trade, though his true *métier* was never in doubt. As Ian Codrington, Angus's solicitor, puts it: 'He's a crook – and proud of it.' Cheeseman considered his protégé to be as 'silly as a bag of nuts' – a quality which, he realized, when combined with Angus's noble pedigree, endowed him with real potential. Nominally employed at one of Cheeseman's two companies, Angus and, more especially, his title lent tone to proceedings. High birth was particularly potent in their initial zone of operations ('Luton: they didn't have too many lords').

By the mid-1970s, Angus was living an increasingly schizophrenic existence. Although married to Diane, his desire for extra-curricular activity was beginning to take him far beyond the West End. 'He lived in Kingston but he was always around Bedford,' explains Cheeseman, who preferred not to leave Angus unsupervised but to take him under his wing and bolster his self-esteem, much as Patsy Chilton had twenty years earlier. Cheeseman's technique did not risk over-complication. 'I'd bring him into the conversation, get a couple of drinks down him – brandies and cokes and what have you – get him performing. I made him confident.'

Only once, though, did he risk using Angus in an ambassadorial role – in Birmingham. 'You send him into a council building – Lord Angus Montagu – [and] they all automatically thought he was the other Montagu – Beaulieu. It was useful.' Angus's title, he found, also had noticeable advantages when travelling by air. 'The times we've been on the piss and the plane needs to be held up... We used to get glared at when we come on. Fortunately, we always used to go business class or first class.'

Angus was grateful for the money, the drink, the attention. But he found an additional attraction in working for Cheeseman. 'He met quite a few characters from the East End. He enjoyed that.' Having no acquaintances of similar standing, Angus responded as best he could, telling his employer about Gordonstoun, the *Britannia*, his friendship with the Duke of Edinburgh and his familiarity with Esther Williams and Marlene Dietrich. 'You let him get on [with] it because it always sounded good.' Sometimes it was convincing, too. Cheeseman, for example, learned that Angus had been an officer during his national service. ('Wasn't he? He told me he was a captain, a captain in the marines.')

Usually, though, there was little doubting that Bombardier Cheeseman outranked Marine Lord Angus Montagu – certainly in financial planning, such as the 'simple but gigantic fraud' perpetrated at the expense of the

Beneficial Finance Company, to which Cheeseman had applied for a personal loan. This was granted so easily that he decided to continue: abetted by two of Beneficial's employees, he obtained 318 further loans, all of them bogus, many in the names of Dunstable Town footballers or employees at his building firms, raising £287,000 (£3,071,786 today) which he invested in a Rolls-Royce (number plate KC 25), a light aeroplane, a six-bedroom house (equipped with two bars and a swimming pool), as well as a Jensen and the Lamborghini. His players, important if unwitting participants in this success story, were not ignored, enjoying a 'champagne celebration' at a nightclub (the evening's entertainment cost £7,000, only £4,000 of which was ever paid).

An audit at the Beneficial's Luton branch led to Cheeseman's exposure. On 10 January 1977, at Bedford Crown Court, he pleaded guilty to a charge of conspiracy to defraud and received a six-year prison sentence. Angus's name did not appear in the following day's newspaper reports; few, other than those privileged to be connected with Dunstable Town FC, knew of his association with Cheeseman. But the warning had been unequivocal. Here, in the final year of his father's life, was his cue to keep less ebullient company.

* * *

'Fraud Trial Man Becomes a Duke!' A photograph of a thick-set man in profile – his sideburns emphatic, his hair crinkly grey, his spectacles heavily rimmed – accompanied the *Sun*'s headline on 5 June 1985. It was a fitting overture to Angus's public career. Though Kim had not been 'the healthiest guy in the world', he had appeared well enough, certainly to Allan Warren, who had photographed him for inclusion in an illustrated book about Britain's twenty-six dukes,[70] when he had noticed that Kim 'could really put away the booze'. Lord Montagu of Beaulieu had reached the same conclusion, after inviting Kim to shoot at Beaulieu, then watching as he and Andrea accounted for a bottle of brandy during the course of the evening.

If his constitution had thereby been undermined, it was unlikely to have been repaired by his protracted, embittered, self-defeating litigation against his mother-in-law. The heirlooms case, as a longstanding family acquaintance describes it, was 'tremendously expensive', never satisfactorily resolved, and could, with a modicum of diplomacy and tact, have been avoided altogether. At stake were a number of paintings (several reputedly Holbeins), as well as Kimbolton furniture which had survived consignment to Kenya. The Dowager Duchess treated the dispute 'with absolute contempt', according to the same family acquaintance, who has some sympathy for her position. There was only one Holbein, he says, and even that – a portrait of Henry

VIII – was of disputed provenance. 'It was very like a [Holbein] but lifeless.' The nearest the seven-year High Court battle came to resolution was when a judge ordered an inquiry to discover the heirlooms' whereabouts. This was, at best, a Pyrrhic victory for Kim, who did not live long enough to recover even a single painting.

In what proved to be the last weeks of his life, he spoke sourly of his younger brother and the impending Old Bailey case. Joss Kent, then in his mid-teens, and unaware of any of Kim's relations, asked him who Angus was. 'He said, "He is my brother; I'd rather he wasn't".' Shortly afterwards, Kim and Andrea flew to their ranch in Tennessee where Kim suffered a fatal heart attack. Angus, who had seemed destined to spend the next quarter of a century in the shadows – or forever, if Kim had had a son by Andrea – succeeded as 12th Duke, a few months before his forty-seventh birthday. Only many years later, after emerging from the Federal Correctional Institution, Petersburg, would he learn the intensity of his brother's contempt for him; in June 1985, he was simply aware of Andrea's radiant hostility.

So, too, were those of Kim's old friends, Mary Fox amongst them, who attended the funeral, a less formal and infinitely more pitiful affair than Mandy's had been, before which some of the congregation had found solace in alcohol. Angus exhibited more decorum. 'He was standing all on his own. Not one person went up and spoke to him. It was one of the saddest things I have ever seen.' Mary Fox does not exonerate herself from blame. 'He asked if I would go into the funeral with him; I said no, because I knew it would upset everyone.' To others, Angus was a figure of some fascination. 'It was the first time anybody had set eyes on him,' remembers a woman who met him that day. His appearance and manner – 'fat little neck, drip-dry suit, very curly grey hair, slightly belligerent' – made an indelible impression. 'He could have been the grave-digger.' Almost everyone went on to the wake; Angus was not invited.

His second ex-wife was at his side, however. With the Old Bailey trial looming, Diane had faced a decision: to continue an increasingly successful career with the Midland Bank or to enjoy the marital privileges of life as Lady Angus Montagu (or even Duchess of Manchester). She chose the Midland, though always remaining on good terms with Angus thereafter, allowing him, for example, to continue living at their house in Kingston for several weeks after their divorce.

The experience of separation could not have been an incalculable shock to either party. During 1976, Angus had found time to entertain a young woman in London; only once, in the south of France, had he allowed her to meet Diane. Later, after Keith Cheeseman's release from prison in the early 1980s, Angus saw nothing of his wife at all for many weeks, joining the Cheesemans in Las Vegas. 'He stayed for about six months. We used to gamble every night. I limited myself to $50, I just let him get on with it. If you gambled, everything was comp: booze, food, everything.'

A lifetime in Las Vegas would probably have been perfectly agreeable to Angus, but Cheeseman, untamed by prison experience, remained ambitious. He was later intrigued to discover that one of Angus's female acquaintances – a black stripper called Diana McLeary – had formed a friendship with James Burrows, manager of the Streatham branch of NatWest. Burrows enjoyed taking what were described as glamour photographs of Miss McLeary, for whom he arranged a generous loan and overdraft facility. According to Miss McLeary, Mr Burrows was 'terribly excited' when she introduced him to her friend, Lord Angus Montagu. Not long afterwards, Angus and both the Cheesemans – Keith and Kerry – chose to open accounts at NatWest's Streatham branch; they also paid for Burrows to experience a weekend in Brighton in Miss McLeary's company. Very quickly, Angus and the Cheesemans ran up substantial overdrafts. When Burrows said that he required security for these, Cheeseman suggested that Burrows could loan them £38,000, for which Cheeseman offered 145 $5,000 US bonds as collateral. 'I ended up doing anything they asked me,' he said, when Angus and the Cheesemans appeared at the Old Bailey in October 1985. 'I felt threatened and in danger.' Matters were taken out of his hands when the NatWest's security department announced that all 145 bonds were forgeries.

The trial lasted three weeks. The judge, John Owen, QC, unable to agree with Michael Whitear's assessment that Angus was a 'bright spark', pronounced that, 'on a business scale of one to ten, the Duke is one or less, and even that flatters him'. The possibility that Angus could be a company director could 'send shivers down the spines of many investors'; he was 'absurdly stupid… negligent about his own affairs and [had] brought suspicion on himself'. Angus's barrister, Peter Coni, QC, informed the jury that his client had been 'gullible'; Angus was acquitted, as was Kerry Cheeseman. Keith Cheeseman (and two others) were convicted, receiving two-year sentences, six months of which were suspended.

The trip to the Old Bailey was Angus's second warning, shriller than the first. He ignored it, convincing himself that he was, as his counsel claimed, culpable of nothing worse than gullibility. When, a year or two later, Mary Fox re-encountered him for the first time in at least two decades, she discovered that he had developed the con-man's talent of believing his own lies with

Jesuitical conviction. She listened 'dumbfounded' as he poured out fantasies about his time in China ('I don't think he'd ever been there') and his abandonment in Ceylon ('a marvellous story'). His own legal team had been under no illusions. 'Peter Coni said, "Of course, he was extraordinarily lucky to get off, extraordinarily lucky",' remembers Ian Codrington. Roger Peryer, Angus's solicitor at the time of the Old Bailey trial, shared Coni's opinion, Codrington discovered. 'I said, "I don't think he would deliberately do anything that he knew was illegal". Roger said, "My dear Ian, if there was money in it, he wouldn't think twice".'

Succession to the dukedom reinvigorated Angus's capacity for self-delusion, encouraging him to believe that his elevation was some kind of accomplishment. 'It wasn't, "When I inherited the title",' remembers Ian Codrington, 'it was, "When I became a duke", as though it were a metamorphosis. He was a different animal: what he said was right, and [he was] expected to tip the doorman £10 and that sort of nonsense.' Keith Cheeseman was alert to Angus's newly exalted rank and its consequent possibilities. 'For God's sake, you've got to be on such a winner, ain't yer? Every woman's gonna lay down and want to be a duchess.' Kerry Cheeseman remembers her ex-husband intensifying his promotional activities on Angus's behalf. 'Keith flaunted the title. He played the duke. Angus was the under-dog.'

Even when not in Cheeseman's company, however, Angus basked in self-veneration. His old friend Jane Bishop noticed that he had begun to refer to his title, 'if he thought it would impress'. Here was the fulfilment of a dream, the moment when he might once more become the focus of unquestioning, uncritical attention. Although he told acquaintances that he had never expected to succeed his older brother, he had given frequent indications that he would be interested in doing so, erroneously assuring Keith Cheeseman, for example, that, following Mandy's death, he had become Viscount Mandeville.[71] In other company, he began styling himself the Duke of Manchester long before his succession, informing a Bond Street jeweller, from whom he had bought a gold bracelet for a young female companion, that he was a peer of the realm ('He wasn't: he was the son of a duke'). There was also friction with Lord Montagu of Beaulieu, who noticed that Angus was occasionally referred to as 'Lord Montagu' – a transgression, Lord Montagu of Beaulieu now charitably suggests, that was largely the fault of the press.

Following his succession, Angus demanded that a trustee investigate Kim's death (with special reference to Andrea); he took his seat – on the cross benches – in the House of Lords, an institution for which he soon developed an addictive affection; had cards printed ('His Grace The Duke of Manchester'); and convinced new acquaintances that he had 'oodles of money'.

But he hadn't. Unknown to him, or to the cronies who had collected around him since his return to England in the mid-1960s, he would never receive the income that his elder brother had enjoyed. 'On Kim's death, the [English] trust became entirely discretionary,' explains the widow of one of his trustees. 'The same thing applied to the American trust. Angus could never understand [this].' The terms of the trusts had been altered a few years after the Quaglino's incident and the unravelling of Angus's marriage to Mary. 'A good thing,' reflects a trustee. 'We could control how much money he had.'

The 1985 trial ensured that Angus's debts mounted to about £100,000, a situation exacerbated by the judge's decision not to award him costs, despite his acquittal. There was also a bill running into tens of thousands from Roger Peryer, with whom Angus – homeless since his separation from Diane – had taken refuge whilst the case proceeded. Peryer received what he was owed, as did Hoare's bank and other creditors. Angus, however, was emphatically warned by his trustees that his income would be very modest 'for the first two or three years' while his debts were erased.

A residence commensurate with his circumstances was acquired by the trustees – 15, Broadreach, Bedford – in the same block as his old friend John Lickfold. When, a few years later, the neighbouring flat became available, that too was bought on Angus's behalf. The two flats were subsequently linked by an arch, and a bar installed. Elsewhere, there was an upstairs bedroom, an open-plan kitchen, a second bedroom, a dining area (rather than dining room) in which reproduction Regency furniture confronted handyman shelves, and a sitting room with a Laura Ashley sofa, two different sets of curtains, a brace of tables covered by white cloths, a chair, and a huge television.

Unconstrained by his modest domestic and financial arrangements, Angus found solace in expenditure. 'He *had* to spend,' remembers a female acquaintance, citing an occasion when, arriving far too early for a meeting with one of his trustees, Angus was told to go away for an hour or so, and returned carrying a new £600 suitcase. Cars – invariably limousines, though Rollses were not unknown – were ceaselessly hired, no matter how trivial the journey (the Dorchester to the Intercontinental for the Cheesemans; Euston station to Westminster for Ian and Karen Codrington). A trustee and his wife, whom Angus treated to several such rides in New York, were obliged to replicate the experience when accompanying him to the theatre in London. 'We couldn't have a taxi to take us there. It was always a stretch limo. It cost a fortune, £200. We could have walked.'

To Angus, it was an appropriately ducal gesture, one which compensated for the modesty of his own vehicles (successively, a Mini, a silver Volvo and a BMW, which were stationed in one of Broadreach's lock-up garages). 'If he bought anything,' remembers a Bedford friend, 'he'd buy two or three of them, whether spectacles or screwdrivers.' Miserly peers learned to take advantage of this in the bar of the House of Lords, where Angus, besides being incontinently generous when buying drinks, almost always bought three packets of cigarettes at a time, from which he would soon be parted. Far from seeing himself as a victim, he felt reassured. 'Angus,' reflects a female acquaintance, 'always wanted to be the person buying lunch.' Status was maintained in Bedford, where a friend remembers dinner at an Italian restaurant, at which 'various hangers-on were sitting there quite happily ordering another bottle'. Angus delightedly insisted that he would pay the bill, dismissing his friend's objections that he couldn't afford to, insisting that he, a duke, *should* pay.

In London, Allan Warren was amongst the beneficiaries. They had met when Warren invited Angus to his flat so as to include him in his pictorial book about British dukes. Thereafter, Angus appeared almost daily at 9 a.m.; Warren begged him to delay his arrival until 10. Angus complied but, in return, expected his new friend to accompany him to lunch, invariably at one of two local restaurants, Leonardo's on the King's Road or Glaisters in Hollywood Road, with occasional trips to a pub, the Ifield, by way of variation. Each and every outing was at Angus's expense. 'Anyone who was [in the studio] he'd take off to lunch,' says Warren, who remembers a Leonardo's session at which he and Angus each drank three bottles of Frascati ('and were on the brandies') when one of his assistants appeared, reminding him of a photographic assignment with Britt Ekland at her house in Chelsea (successfully negotiated, thanks to Angus, who propped Warren up by prodding a single finger into his back).

An overseas tour encompassing Alaska, Japan, Hawaii, San Francisco, Los Angeles and Texas was organized by Paul Vaughan, television and literary agent for Lord Montagu of Beaulieu who had explained that his 'cousin,[72] Angus Montagu, needed 'a bit of help'. Then, as now, Vaughan acted as agent and manager for a number of performers, including Larry Grayson and Chris Tarrant. Although rapidly aware that Angus was 'a bear of little brain', he developed the idea of instituting a charitable organization, to be called the Dukes' Trust, which would harness the social standing of all British dukes to philanthropic ends, as well as giving Angus a role as the Trust's figurehead. It seemed providential that P&O had retained Vaughan to supply guest lecturers for its new ship, the *Royal Princess* – particularly aristocrats whose titles, it was considered, would evoke 'the golden era of the liner'. Knowing that Angus was incapable of assuming anything more than an emblematic lecturing role, Vaughan also recruited Allan Warren, to whom he had been introduced by Lord Montagu of Beaulieu, since Warren could 'talk for England' whilst parading his ducal photographs in front of an appreciative American audience. The demands of the tour were not punishing. Time would be reserved for fund-raising for the Dukes' Trust; there would be scope for leisure, and just one lecture whilst at sea. The lecture was not Angus's priority. Flying first class from London to Anchorage, he took such conclusive advantage of the hospitality available that, during the next leg of the journey, from Anchorage to Japan, he required no further refreshment. The bullet train to Kobe and the first leg of the cruise – from Kobe to Hawaii, aboard the *Royal Princess* – revived his appetite. 'You had your own private balcony,' remembers Warren. 'You'd ring the bell and champagne would come.'

There was more champagne on a beach in Hawaii. Then came the lecture. Angus hesitantly took a microphone. A question came from the audience.

'When does your dukedom date back to?'

'You'll have to ask Mr Warren that.'

The hour that followed was a gruelling one for supporters of the hereditary principle.[73] Nevertheless, the American weakness for the peerage, which Angus's grandfather and great-grandfather had so gratefully exploited, was flourishing in San Antonio, Texas, where Vaughan, Warren and Angus were entertained by Bobby and Maggie Sheerin, a generous couple doing their best to divest themselves of their oil fortune through philanthropy and alcohol,[74] who were entranced by a photograph of Angus outside the chapel at his ancestral seat. (Warren had taken it in Brompton cemetery.) Mrs Sheerin appeared especially eager to advance her connections with the aristocracy. 'She would have divorced Bobby at the drop of a hat to become [the Duchess],' reflects Paul Vaughan, 'but Bobby had it all sewn up: if she married before he died, she wouldn't get the money.' Enslaved to certain misconceptions about the English class system (Vaughan tried, fruitlessly, to persuade her that curtseying had had its day), she arranged a lavish lakeside party in conditions of extreme humidity, as well as a lunch of excruciating formality.

Angus, never a willing martyr to decorum, recovered on a fund-raising riverboat cruise that followed. 'People were paying money to come and sit in the boat with [him]. He said, "Look, we can make money out of America, old boy." He was piggy in pooh-pooh. I said, "Angus, don't take this as being the real world".' Further deference was savoured in New York at the 21 Club, where Angus 'obviously knew the staff very well'. He returned to the city with the Cheesemans, following the completion of Keith Cheeseman's second prison sentence. The party patronized the Waldorf Astoria, Cheeseman enjoying the use of one of its larger suites, thanks to the initiative of a member of the hotel staff, awed to be looking after 'a proper Dook'.

At home, Angus's fellow countrymen were less easily conquered, though some, inevitably, thirsted for an introduction. Not all of them were con-men. One was David Kirch, who had amassed many millions through property deals. His former tenants included Allan Warren, whom he now telephoned with an inquiry about the Duke of Manchester. Kirch explained that he had a dinner planned at his house in Jersey, to which he had invited a number of bank directors and various of the island's grandees. It would, he added, 'be nice to have a duke there: would he come?'.

Angus flew in with Warren. Soon after arriving at Kirch's house, his attention was claimed by his host's impressive swimming pool. Minutes later, he had ditched his suit ('light grey') in favour of swimming trunks, and plunged in. Kirch, who had spoken briefly to his guest of honour ('Your Grace, how nice to meet you'), only to receive an unexpected reply ('Just call me Angus. How are you, mate?'), now articulated sudden anxiety ('Allan, I'm a little worried. He doesn't sound like a duke'). The following night, Warren took Angus to a restaurant overlooking the beach at Goory. Alan Whicker and 'the elite of Jersey' awaited them. Warren had tried to placate Kirch by explaining that Angus was 'the working man's duke'; he failed. 'They couldn't wait to get rid of us,' says Warren, adding that the evening was 'an extreme disappointment' to Kirch. The memory moves him to prolonged laughter.

In England, much of Angus's time was bound up with the House of Lords. Although he did not make his maiden (and, as it turned out, only) speech until November 1991, he soon established himself as a familiar figure in the upper house.[75] 'He'd arrive at 11 a.m., then he'd have a "toddy for the body" in the Bishops' Bar,' remembers a Bedford friend. 'Richard Long would have a sherry to "get the liver going" and Barbara Castle[76] would come and have a chat.' Drinks and discussions led into a fairly early lunch which concluded 'sometime between 2 p.m. and 3 p.m.'. Angus then left for Prayers (always held in private), but not before he had issued instructions. 'He'd say: "Watch me".' His guest knew what to expect: after lending his presence to the debate for several minutes, Angus would abandon the chamber in search of supplementary refreshment. He was disconcerted when his friend failed to follow suit. 'Sometimes I was very interested in what was being said,' remembers the Bedford man. 'I wanted to listen.'

Although Keith Cheeseman was unavoidably detained elsewhere during 1986, he was regularly in Angus's company thereafter. The Inn on the Park was 'the watering-hole' ('we knew everybody, slid down the banisters, the normal men bit'), though he and Angus spread their patronage generously ('Simpson's in the Strand, Langan's, a couple of the clubs, the White Elephant on the River, the White Elephant, Curzon Street'), tips pressed into palms on arrival, 'phenomenal' bills generated within hours. Cheeseman was most appreciative of the way things operated at the Lords, particularly the peers' attendance allowance. 'I think he used to pick up about a hundred and eighty quid. If we'd get short, we'd go, "Come on, Angus, let's pop into the House of Lords". We'd get a magnificent meal for no money. You'd have subsidized food, subsidized booze, you'd come out with subsidized fags, whisky and chocolates, all with the portcullis thing on.'

Angus's relentless generosity – Allan Warren felt obliged to 'write a day off' after each visit – ensured that his attendance allowance was usually spent, with interest, in the Lords' bars and dining rooms. Sometimes, the regime of all-day drinking took its toll even on him. 'He came out once and [found] his car parked in front: two policemen drove it home to his house,' says Paul Vaughan, for whom Angus relentlessly ordered 'slippery nipple'. 'He just liked [saying]: "My friend wants a slippery nipple".' Vaughan didn't want it ('a cocktail of the vilest variety') but the performance secured Angus the attention he yearned for, silencing those at the bar. It was, however, the behaviour – and provenance – of certain of his guests that led to his 'card being marked'.

Allan Warren remembers a reprimand from the sergeant-at-arms after Angus had hurled a barrage of House of Lords chocolates and cartons of cigarettes down a busy staircase, but it was 'acquaintances of acquaintances' who caused real disquiet, roaming into bars 'where they had no right to be'. 'There were,' explains Paul Vaughan, 'quite a few young friends [of one of Angus's cronies] going around causing grave embarrassment to [peers] who had no doubt made use of their services at one time or other [in a less gilded setting]. The police and, it was implied to me, Special Branch, were keeping an eye on things.' Days which began at the Lords tended to lead to a full dinner, before being rounded off by a visit to a strip club, often the Stork club in Swallow Street, Piccadilly. The routine afforded Angus satisfaction – or so it might have seemed to those meeting him for the first time. 'Being a peer is very civilized,' he assured a reporter in March 1988, at Warren's publication party, an occasion graced by two of the twenty-four dukes (the Duke of Bedford being the other) and hosted by Mr Peter Stringfellow at one of his clubs.

But the bingeing and the drinking, the limousines and strip clubs were increasingly the consolations of a man stranded between the nobility and the Cheeseman classes. It was lonely territory, as Mary Fox, back in England after many years abroad, realized when meeting Angus by chance at the Maisonette Club, a Shepherd Market drinking den run by Ruby Lloyd.

The once over-nourished boy who had trailed so contentedly in his mother's wake now struck Mary as an incurable fantasist, pathetically lonely. 'Ruby said, "Please, Mary, be nice to Angus because nobody has anything to do with him".' Mary Fox enlisted the help of Patsy Chilton, by then also back in London, who found Angus as charming and courteous as he had been in adolescence. It was evident, though, that the intervening decades had done nothing to improve his judgement. As an occasional guest at the Inn on the Park, Patsy Chilton met a number of his associates, amongst them one who was notable for a propensity to 'flash Russian money about', for the glamour of his female companion and for the fact that he had had a lobotomy. 'He was really quite terrifying. Angus was mad about him.' Mary Fox also met the lobotomised stranger at the Inn on the Park, and others who had not submitted themselves to cranial surgery but who struck her as 'a dreadful lot. You could see they were just running rings round him. He was lying on his back purring.'

The need for company at almost any cost prompted repeated invitations to Allan Warren and Paul Vaughan, to Bedford acquaintances – Rotarians and Rowing Club members – and reputedly spurred him into appointing one of Warren's friends as his chauffeur, a would-be actor known as Sooty (real name Graham White), who had tried his luck as a model for *Playgirl* magazine.

A gap remained where Angus's family ought to have been.[77] Not long after his succession to the dukedom, he heard that his elder son and heir Alexander was experiencing difficulties which could only be resolved in the courtroom. Shared experience did not inspire him to sympathy, nor did any of Alexander's subsequent difficulties, which Angus greeted with an habitual mixture of bluster and contempt, assuring acquaintances like Paul Vaughan that he had disinherited his elder son, not only preventing him from becoming a beneficiary of the Montagu family trusts but also disbarring him from succeeding to the dukedom (an inalienable inheritance which was not in his gift to bestow elsewhere, as Paul Vaughan attempted to explain).

He did, however, establish contact with his two younger children, Kimble and Emma, whom he had not seen for decades. Understandably, however, these relationships were subject to periodic strain. In the early 1990s, for example, when Emma stayed at Broadreach for several months, she was given a key to the flat's secondary entrance, so that she could come and go as she pleased. When, one morning, she remarked that she had seen the milkman on her return home, Angus began barking questions about her nocturnal routine. The outburst did not sit easily with his accomplishments as a father.

'Emma pointed out that he had missed her childhood. She said that she wasn't going to have him tell her what time she had to be home.'

* * *

At the time of their wedding, at Bedford Register Office on 27 January 1989, Louise Bird (née Taylor) was forty-six, twice-divorced and 'very glamorous'. A doctor's daughter from Yorkshire, she had emigrated to South Africa in 1964, returning to England in 1987, with her second marriage, a bruising affair, recently at an end; she was unaware of Angus's appearance, two years earlier, at the Old Bailey, which had not merited inclusion in the South African press. When Jane Bishop, an old friend from drama school, introduced her to him, she knew nothing of the Montagu family or its recent history.

An acquaintance suggests that Louise saw Angus as 'the key to all glamour: to Ascot, the House of Lords, grand houses'. Temperament and circumstances combined to ensure that she was especially susceptible to his charm. Almost without exception, her friends describe her as an actress manqué, with a talent (as one of them puts it) for 'livening things up… a lovely girl but a bad picker of men'. Paul Vaughan says that she was 'absolutely right' for her third husband – a view to which Ian Codrington subscribes, saying that Louise 'was a great attribute to him'. John Lickfold, who also approved of her, acted as best man. A reception was held at Flitwick Manor Hotel. The following night, there was a dinner at Langan's, the London restaurant where Angus and Keith Cheeseman had periodically enjoyed convivial business lunches. Neither celebration, however, was graced by the Cheesemans.

During their engagement – Angus proposed two months after they met in November 1987 – he introduced Louise to a number of his friends, the Cheesemans amongst them. Friendship did not blossom. 'I survived lunch,' remembers Louise, 'and made [Angus] promise never to see them again.' Her fiancé told her that she was a 'terrible snob'. Her initiation into the ways of the British aristocracy continued to be unusual. Amongst Paul Vaughan's clients was Margaret, Duchess of Argyll;[78] he arranged for her to meet

Louise and Angus for lunch at 90 Park Lane, the Grosvenor House restaurant. Allan Warren, who had photographed Margaret (not, admittedly, a unique privilege), also attended. She gave a vintage performance, as Vaughan remembers. 'Margaret would say [to Louise], "Just watch me. Don't smile – you're smiling – don't smile, it'll crease your face, it takes away your beauty".' At times, though, Margaret found herself distracted by Angus, as Paul Vaughan explains. 'She said to me, "Sweetie, the first job is to teach him to be a duke".'

Angus's sartorial and stylistic deficiencies were difficult to ignore. Paul Vaughan remembers 'appalling' Christmas cards, signed 'Angus, The Duke of Manchester', as if someone had 'come into money and [started] living in a stately home'. Other cosmetic details told against him: the shoes with Velcro fastenings and the 'drip-dry blazer' which he wore to Bedford Regatta. Louise did her best to take charge, jettisoning the blazer in favour of a bespoke replacement, complete with buttons reserved for those who, like her husband, had been commissioned into the Royal Marines. When the Savile Row tailor regretted that he was unable to find Angus's name on the list of retired officers, Louise explained that the list was wrong: the Duke of Manchester had undoubtedly been an officer. The buttons were his. Fellow peers and Cambridgeshire grandees remained unconvinced. 'Angus was always treated with suspicion, even before going to prison,' acknowledges Ian Codrington. 'He never got into the county set.'

Angus concentrated instead on expensive restaurants and hotels. 'We used to go off to Paris House [a restaurant in Woburn],' remembers Paul Vaughan. 'He loved that because he was well regarded and liked: he lived in a land of hall porters and maître d's, who would be not toadying but naturally respectful towards him. The occasional "your Grace" did him no harm at all.' Sometimes, though, he found staff insufficiently deferential. 'He could be very abrupt with [them], which was not the mark of an aristocrat, in my opinion or experience,' concedes Vaughan, who attributes this abrasiveness to the arthritis by which Angus was increasingly afflicted. Louise mentions the back pain he suffered from for many years (when, in due course, the American prison authorities subjected Angus to medical examination, they noted that he had had a disc removed from his spine, perhaps as a consequence of his car accident in 1971).

Both could have contributed to Angus's occasional brittle moods, if not the parallel universe in which he had played rugby for the marines and in which his status was unquestioned. 'Louise is going to be kidnapped,' became a frequent refrain. 'He always wanted to pretend that he had security officers around,' remembers Paul Vaughan, who found that the Duke and Duchess of Manchester's trips to the theatre required particularly precise choreography. 'We went through all this palaver of getting him in ten seconds before the lights went down, getting him into seats, [through] side doors, straight out [afterwards], all that sort of business, straight into a car and off to the party or round to the stage door.' A pantomime starring Larry Grayson was a great success, Angus being as overjoyed as a six-year-old, remembers Louise, adding that they both enjoyed watching rugby (local matches involving Bedford and internationals at Twickenham) and Formula 1 racing (at Monza and Silverstone). The cinema was another shared interest, though Angus's tastes were conservative (he managed forty minutes of *Reservoir Dogs* 'under great protest', before walking out).

By then, Louise was familiar with his antipathy towards bad language and manners – as well as to drunken women – though completely unaware of how potently these deficiencies had been embodied in his mother (of whom he spoke so lovingly). She was, instead, aware that her husband desperately 'wanted people to like him'. She recalls him as a 'terribly sweet, very naïve' man, generous and kind, if a little passive, so that it was always left to her to suggest a trip to the theatre or cinema and to make the necessary arrangements (though once, memorably, he managed to book tickets for the ballet for her birthday). In Bedford, the Manchesters entertained frequently at 15 Broadreach, Louise proving to be as accomplished a hostess as Angus could have wished for. Old friends like Jane Bishop marvelled at what seemed, if not a transformation, then at least a redirection. Louise, she says, 'took him out of the mire'.

The process of extraction took its toll, however: Angus could also be abrupt, scornful and selfish. An acquaintance remembers hearing him rebuke Louise because 'she was not behaving as a duchess should'. It was a reprimand which was susceptible to variation, as when Louise tried to cure hiccups by drinking out the wrong side of a glass, 'He said, "Imagine if the Queen were here",' recalls a Bedford friend. 'We said, "Well, she isn't".' Dismissive, even contemptuous in argument, Angus invoked the authority of fellow peers ('Lord Denning told me that yesterday'), robustly disregarding whether he had ever met them or not. Entertaining as well as preposterous though this was, it was only a minor consolation to Louise. 'She told me she would never contradict him in public,' remembers a family acquaintance. 'That is mental bullying.' Paul Vaughan noticed it too. 'He'd bark at her: he was the Duke and she was the handmaiden. She wasn't one for a fight. She'd figuratively shrug and turn away.'

The tactic of not taking too much notice of her husband allowed Angus a similar freedom to that which he had enjoyed during his marriage to Diane. There were disadvantages, however. 'He was,' Louise concedes, 'the most secretive person on earth.' Later, during his trial in America, the prosecution warned the jury that the defence would make the risible claim that 'Mr Montagu' discussed very little with his wife. But, explains Louise, the defence lawyer was quite correct: 'Angus hid everything. Even when bills came in through the post in the morning, he would take them and lock them in a drawer. I didn't see the electricity bill or the phone bill or the anything bill.'

This was not encouraging. Aside from paying for trips to the opera, ballet and the theatre, Angus was ensuring that Louise kept regular appointments at Vidal Sassoon and made additions to her wardrobe. At the same time, he met the punishing cost of entertaining at the House of Lords, Paris House and the Inn on the Park, and adhered rigidly to the creed that 'the Duke must pay', whether he could afford to or not (as when buying a boat for Bedford Rowing Club for £7,000, a purchase made possible only by borrowing £6,000 from a friend who was never repaid). Newer acquaintances were occasionally taken in, perhaps convinced by Angus's frequent references to his 'royal duties' with Prince Philip. One such acquaintance, serving on a local charity committee, insisted that Angus be invited to a fund-raising lunch because he was 'absolutely rolling in money'.[79]

Incorrect though that was, the costs of the Old Bailey trial had been cleared by the end of the 1980s, as had other debts. Potential awkwardness from Australia, where his first wife Mary had begun calling herself the Duchess of Manchester, had been subdued via a modest payment of £15,000. The trustees now allowed Angus £30,000-a-year (£111,000 today), out of which he had no mortgage or rent to pay and which he supplemented by his House of Lords attendance allowances (£60 overnight subsistence, £23-a-day subsistence in 1988–9). More impressively still, he had managed to secure an honorific position with a firm of solicitors then lucratively engaged in recovering debts from Names in the Lloyd's insurance market, a sinecure worth about £15,000-a-year.

Yet it was never enough. Unwilling to curb his spending, he was soon practising the family tradition of selling anything he could get his hands on. Though there was comparatively little left, the value of what remained had never been higher. His stepmother Elizabeth entrusted him with some of the last of the family silver and a substantial amount of the Kimbolton furniture, having received an assurance from him that he would 'keep [it] for ever'; Angus 'sold [the furniture], before he'd even seen it, flogged it on the spot'.

The purchaser, an acquaintance of Angus's who owned a business letting props to theatres and television companies, paid him £50,000. By the time Ian Codrington was aware of what had happened, the deal was done: he insisted that he and Angus visit the warehouse where the furniture was being stored. Angus was allowed to retrieve a number of family photograph albums (which awkwardly punctured his myth about his wartime abandonment) and a Georgian table, but not another smaller table of notably fine marquetry, which particularly caught Codrington's eye. 'That was one thing the chap wouldn't let us have. I'm sure it was worth as much as he was paying [for the lot].'

Angus's fragile relationship with his stepmother – 'she had no time or patience for [him]' – disintegrated completely when one of the London auction houses sent her a catalogue, drawing her attention to two lots which, the auctioneer felt, might be of particular interest. They were, being the silver which she had so recently handed to Angus. She bought it back and, apparently, shipped it to Venice where she was now living for part of the year. Angus received nothing further from her.

There were, however, always other avenues to explore. The most glittering of these emerged from the will drawn up in 1909 by Angus's great-grandmother, Consuelo. The bulk of her fortune had been left in a series of trusts to provide for her grandson Mandy and others of his – and subsequent – generations. One convoluted clause, concerning her finest jewels, furs and laces (and certain portraits of sentimental value), decreed that one of her direct descendants would eventually be able to own the jewels outright. It was simply a question of waiting: first, for the death of the last of certain Montagu kinsmen who had been alive during Consuelo's lifetime (she died on 20 November 1909);[80] and, second, for a further twenty-one years after that.

The jewels were worth waiting for: the 9th Duke's attempt to pawn them had led to his truncated spell in Wormwood Scrubs.[81] They had subsequently been entrusted to the V & A for safe-keeping. Decades later, Kim's fatal heart attack meant that Angus was the likely beneficiary. It was this delicious if tantalizing prospect which nursed him through his bleakest moments. 'Angus's view,' remembers Paul Vaughan, 'was, "There are so many jewels there, we're alright".' Fallow days, recalls Ian Codrington, were pleasurably filled pondering their disposal at Bonham's. 'He said, "They're going to be able to sell them for a lot more than those horrible bastards"' (an apparent reference to the V & A). Then they were to be sold abroad, and, finally, via an acquaintance from the Lanes in Brighton. 'This was Angus's great friend,'

remembers the widow of a trustee. 'Nobody else knew as much about emeralds as he did.' The trustees, however, 'wouldn't let this man touch them', nor
did they ever let Angus know that he was entitled to borrow the jewels, as
his mother and Andrea had done for different occasions (dining at the Savoy
in Nell's case, attending the State Opening of Parliament in Andrea's).

None of this diminished Angus's appetite for what he saw as his dynastic
due. He began raising loans, using the jewels as collateral,[82] a costly business,
since no reputable lender would allow him to borrow until he had also taken
out a life policy, which he did 'at vast expense', thereby further diminishing
the residue of the family fortune. On the other hand, securing life assurance
at any price was fairly remarkable. Although still phenomenally powerful – a
circus strong-man, unconquered arm-wrestling champion at Bedford Rowing
Club – his physique was now severely overburdened, courtesy of an unhelpful diet and an inability to distinguish strength from fitness. An older
acquaintance, hearing his voice for the first time, pronounced a one-word
judgement: 'Heart'. The Bedford couple whom he joined on a Caribbean
cruise would agree with this diagnosis, being convinced that he had suffered
a mild heart attack whilst at sea (and noticing that he was taking pills for a
cardiac condition).

Nevertheless, Angus felt sure that he would live long enough to inherit
the jewels outright. A preliminary investigation was conducted into how to
divide the potential spoils in as equitable a manner as possible. Since this
involved an attempt to reconcile Angus's interests with those of his estranged
elder son Alexander, failure was not unexpected. There was, however, sudden
and very substantial compensation. Not long after marrying Louise, Angus
learned that he was to receive £500,000, apparently in consequence of the
death of a kinsman, who had died without an heir. Here was an opportunity
for true security, a boost to his income of perhaps a further £20,000-a-year
after tax. When added to the annual £30,000 he already received from the
English and Irish Trusts (not to mention the admittedly taxable £15,000
retainer from the solicitors immersed in the Lloyd's debacle), the windfall
income (if cautiously invested) could have assured him of a comfortable life.

Instead, he now attempted to wrestle his income up to a level commensurate with ducal requirements by involving himself in a company which had
hopes of designing a housing estate in Southampton, and by immersing
himself in projects of impressive range (property in Spain and Chelsea
Harbour, golf courses, drag-racing, computers, casinos, hotels, waste disposal
in the Republic of Ireland, development of Heathrow airport, a safety deposit
scheme in the Channel Islands, acquisition of the Caribbean island of

Aruba). He volunteered his services as a PR man to the Four Seasons hotels, sought a post as president of a New York bank, offered advice about currency transactions and passports, continued his involvement with a hire car company, and talked about an association with both Sheik Makhtoum and Bear Stearns. Some of this activity might have been confined to his imagi-nation. Michael Whitear, for example, says that Angus was never involved in the Heathrow scheme. If so, he was undoubtedly involved in *a* Heathrow scheme, applying for a mortgage for three tenanted houses 'in the middle of the land likely to be compulsorily purchased'. His application was rejected; he had failed to acquire copies of the tenancy agreements.

But if some of these projects were imaginary, others were undoubtedly real. When arriving in Bedford in the mid-1980s, he had advertised his serv-ices as a financial adviser in a local paper (a career which did not take off). Now, newly equipped with £500,000, he found that many of his friends were keen to draw his attention to a series of investment possibilities. The trustees learned of his involvement with a sofa-making company whose owner was in an open prison; they also heard of the Firotex venture, about which Michael Whitear wrote to Angus on 30 August 1990. 'I have negotiated to buy this Licence at a Price of £600,000,' recorded Whitear, who, after outlining Firotex's immense commercial potential, concluded: 'I would there for [sic] be grateful of [sic] your indication as to your interest in this project to enable me to proceed without any delay to finalize the transaction.' Today, Whitear emphasizes that the people he does business with 'are all top, top, top organ-izations, the top people', adding, 'I'm represented in various parts of the world.'[83] Angus became a staunch advocate of Firotex. One of the trustees was given a Firotex mitten, whilst Paul Vaughan, though not a recipient of its promotional products, was urged to take this chance of making his fortune. He resisted. Firotex has since vanished without trace.

By the early 1990s, the same fate had befallen Angus's windfall inheri-tance. There were trips to the States, and lunches and dinners with an ever more eclectic circle – a Swiss whom one of Angus's trustees found particu-larly unpalatable and a man christened John but known as 'the Chipmunk', who always needed 'to be found entertainment'. But even frenzied self-indulgence could not account for the almost immediate disappearance of half a million pounds which, as one of Angus's trustees noted, 'was re-settled in some way through the Channel Islands'. Once there, it melted away. 'I said, "Angus, if someone comes up with a scheme, come and talk to me about it",' remembers Paul Vaughan. 'I think he saw Ian Codrington and me as being the right way. But sometimes he was going to be naughty bear and go [the other] way. When there was silence, I knew that he was up to no good.' It was in these silences that he saw his old friends, Keith and Kerry Cheeseman.

* * *

Kerry Cheeseman remembers screaming as the plane landed. In other respects, the flight was uneventful. She, Angus and Keith were due in New York to 'meet people, obviously mafia'. Angus, who had drunk more or less continuously, was lying slumped at her feet in the first-class cabin, complaining of tiredness. 'He said, "You must have something on you to keep me awake". So I gave him one speed tablet.'

The amphetamine worked quickly. Angus left first class and moved towards the cockpit. His precise contribution to what followed is unknown but Mrs Cheeseman says that she has never experienced a landing like it, the plane repeatedly thumping into – and bouncing off – the tarmac, seemingly out of control. When it eventually came to a standstill, Angus reappeared, wreathed in a self-congratulatory smile. 'He told me he'd landed the plane, if you don't mind. He said we were so many hundred kilos overweight. I said the only thing overweight is you, fat bastard. I don't even know if he could fly.'[84]

Similar abuse from anyone else – particularly from any of his four wives – would have outraged Angus; from Kerry Cheeseman, it was accepted without demur. Blessed with glamour that began to wilt only after she was struck down by pancreatitis 1995, Mrs Cheeseman had graduated from an East End upbringing to a West End career, the summit of which was her foundation of an escort agency, 'Aristocats'. She regularly received tokens of affection from admirers, including a bauble from a Bahraini prince ('Tiffany's New York couldn't put a price on it'), though she declined many others so as not to cause her first husband, John Dedman, needless consternation. Dismissive of those of her staff who went further ('the girls going out shopping come back with five hundred quid, plus all the presents; the ones laying on their back got £150'), she nevertheless operated a laissez-faire policy which ensured the agency's success. It did not take her long to gauge Angus's enthusiasms. 'He liked the agency, but he never got a girl from there. I never had my girls entertaining friends. Once you start that, [the girls] think they're special.'

On the night of their arrival in New York – they were staying at the Waldorf Tower – it was evident that Angus was in the mood for company. 'He never slept for two days, kept banging on the door. Keith said to him,

"Go and order some booze". He went and ordered four or five hundred pounds' worth for his room.' Angus had a further request. 'He tells me to go and get him a girl. I go down to the bell-porter and Keith is chasing after me, wants to know where I'm going. Keith done his nut.' The porter found Angus what he was looking for. 'The next minute he'd met a girl. Six o'clock in the morning, he's on our door, [then] whisked us out to this girl's house. Whatever Angus wanted, he got.'

Flights, food, drink, narcotics,[85] girls – Angus relished them all. But more important than any of these was Mrs Cheeseman's affection – indulgent, mothering, unconditional. In England, he telephoned her constantly, sometimes three or four times a day. 'He always used to say, "If you'd've married me, I'd've been alright". You imagine me, rank East Ender, a Lady? He always told everybody, "I would have married her but she would never marry me".' The second half of Angus's assertion was true. "I wouldn't want him as a husband," Mrs Cheeseman acknowledges, 'he could be a sod, [but] I loved him to death, I really did.' For his part, Angus was jealously protective of Mrs Cheeseman. 'He used to come down to me at least every month. He would never bring anyone. In fact he was quite selfish about me: I was his friend. If we was out and you were over-friendly to me, he'd let you know in no uncertain terms.'

Possessiveness did not dissuade Angus from parading Mrs Cheeseman in public, although never at the House of Lords. Instead, they went for drinks in Shepherd Market, usually at Ruby's or a similar establishment called the Little House on the Prairie, and dined at the Inn on the Park, the Intercontinental and, later, the Dorchester. On one occasion, Angus persuaded her to accompany him to a black tie dinner, making only one condition ('I wasn't to call him Aggie. It was, "Your Grace" or something'). Towards the end of the evening, unable to remember the exact phrase ('I'd had a few bevies'), Mrs Cheeseman improvised. 'I said, right across this function, "Oi, Gracie, get your arse over here".' Angus was thrilled. 'He said, "That's my girl. Never change, be as you are".' With Kerry there was no pretence, no need for the bludgeoning criticism casually meted out to Louise for lapses in etiquette; nor, joyously, was much, if anything, expected of him. 'He used to say, "I can do what I want to now". As soon as he come through the door, his jacket would come off, and it'd be shirt and trousers.' Sometimes, shoes would be kicked off, too. 'I said, "I bet you don't do that in [Louise's] bleeding house, sweaty feet everywhere". He said, "No, I don't".'

Aware of the limitations of the Montagu fortune ('he had champagne tastes and lemonade pockets'), Mrs Cheeseman also saw the full extent of

Angus's chameleon talents. Voice ('fruity but nasal' one moment, saloon-bar grunt the next), mannerisms, 'everything' would change, sometimes at a moment's notice, according to the company he kept, which was helpful when Kerry introduced him to pie and mash at Kelly's and to the Duke of York in Hoxton. Visits to the Duke of York and similar hostelries were periodically turned to commercial advantage, particularly in the 1990s. By then, the Cheesemans were divorced, and Kerry was spending more time with her first husband, John Dedman, who became an important member of the pub routine. 'We'd start talking about fitness,' explains Mrs Cheeseman, adding that Dedman would gradually turn the conversation to press-ups, as a prelude to an impressive demonstration. 'John's very good at [them], he's got a good body on him. [Then] they'd all start doing press-ups.' Dedman would acknowledge that he faced competition, but suggest that no one could do many press-ups on fingertips. Money was mentioned for the first time. 'We'd say, "Yeah, how much d'you bet? Round of drinks? Make it a bit better than that".' With the stakes satisfactorily ramped up, a grey-haired man – grossly overweight, hitherto inert – would enter the fray. 'There would be Angus, in the middle of the floor, in a pub in the East End, doing his press-ups on his toes and fingertips.' The bet was never lost.

Much though Angus enjoyed converting winnings into drink, there was something intangible which he valued more. Whilst tramping around Kerry's Bethnal Green flat, shoeless, eating raw onion sandwiches, he heard about her early life ('if you didn't thieve, you didn't eat'); he watched as first Kevin and Karen (her children by John Dedman) and then her grandson, Shaun, grew up. 'He worshipped my kids,' she remembers. Angus had become part of the family, even if his own role within it oscillated between would-be lover, delinquent elder son and wayward grandfather. His 2 a.m. telephone calls were endlessly forgiven; Kevin made him his leather belts. 'An inch and a half [broad], brown one side and black the other. Never cost him nothing, did it?'

One association with Mrs Cheeseman's world would cost Angus dear, however. After his experiences at the Old Bailey, he became slightly wary of Keith Cheeseman, though never enough to curtail their friendship, which was still punctuated by full-scale entertainment at the Inn on the Park and the House of Lords. Over the years, the two men had discussed many business opportunities, amongst them an attempt to redirect part of the Dowager Duchess of Manchester's fortune their way. That proved fruitless, but did nothing to inhibit Cheeseman, who continued to plan projects which, if successfully accomplished, would allow him to live in his preferred, expansive manner. Although in the mid-1980s he and Kerry were obliged to make do with a council flat in Bethnal Green, his aspirational tastes were reflected in his wardrobe – an entire room – which was stocked with his suits and shoes. None, according to his ex-wife, had been paid for. 'Do you know something about Keith? He never paid an electric bill, never paid a gas bill, never paid a mortgage, he's never paid a debt in his life. When he went to prison [the last time], he owed £125,000 [to] American Express alone. Every time he goes down, he owes every credit card a fortune; he comes out and gets a credit card again. And he's still got credit cards in his name. How does he do it? He never owned a property.'

Cheeseman's alleged failure to join the property-owning classes was not for lack of trying. By late 1990, he was the largest shareholder in Link International, a company he had formed with a French-Canadian called Tessier, whose Christian name alternated from Carl to Carroll according to circumstances. Kerry Cheeseman did not take to Tessier, an instinct she vainly tried to convey to Angus, who had agreed to become Link's chairman.

He was in familiar company. Besides boasting Cheeseman as its key shareholder, Link had secured the services of Michael Whitear as chief executive officer. Work promised to be lucrative. On 7 May 1991, the company solicitor wrote to Angus and Whitear to confirm that their salaries would be £152,000 p.a. 'In addition,' added the solicitor, 'you will be allowed expenses reasonably incurred on behalf of the company.'

By that stage, Link was in negotiations to acquire a shopping mall in Orlando, Florida, and to sell spring water to Saudi Arabia. It was also about to make a major investment in the Tampa Bay Lightning, a Floridan ice hockey team. 'It was a fiddle,' remembers Cheeseman. 'We were going to pull a lot of money out.'[86] At a board meeting on 21 May 1991, at 20 Buckingham Palace Road, it was resolved that Whitear, with his experience of dealing with 'top, top, top people', and His Grace, the Duke of Manchester, should travel to the United States on 3 June.

The visit was a triumph. On 4 June, Whitear and Angus joined Tessier, Phil Esposito, president of Tampa Bay Lightning, and the local press at the Sheraton Grand, a Tampa hotel which Angus found perfectly acceptable. Esposito was ecstatic. Scrambling to raise $22.5 million by 15 June,[87] he had found a man with the money, just in time, a man whose company was going to invest $50 million. 'Great, isn't it?' said Esposito. 'We don't now just have all the financing in place, we got us a Duke. Nothing shabby about the Tampa Bay Lightning.'

A brief storm of flashlight followed as Esposito handed Angus an ice-hockey jersey, emblazoned 'THE DUKE'. Fortified by a 'pre-lunch toddy and small cigar', the club's new saviour fielded questions with good-humoured patience, admitting to ignorance about ice hockey but declaring his love for America, for American football and basketball, adding that he would quickly come to love hockey, too. His own sporting credentials, he explained, included playing rugby for the Royal Navy (full back had been his position). Then he indulged his audience's fascination with his aristocratic upbringing, acknowledging that he had been educated at Gordonstoun – the same school as Princes Charles and Andrew – and explaining that his dukedom was connected not with Manchester but with Cambridge. Kimbolton, he added, was 'quite a nice place'. Just in case anyone could have been in any doubt, Whitear publicly acknowledged the duke's 'very real qualities'. These, explained Whitear, 'come from, shall I say, breeding'. Angus, he concluded, was 'exceptionally loyal and a very good leader'. Tessier announced that Link would be opening an office in Tampa very soon.

The following day, under the headline, 'His Grace lends royalty to Lightning', Tom McEwen, sports editor of the *Tampa Tribune*, described the 12th Duke of Manchester as 'robust of build, good of humour, an international investor and businessman beyond managing his own estate'. This fiction unravelled within weeks. The contract, signed by Angus, was worthless. Esposito did catch a glimpse of a $3 million cheque – signed, once again, by Angus, and counter-signed by Durgesh Mehta, the company solicitor – but only a faxed copy of it. The original never left England. No money ever did. Instead, Tessier and another of his associates, Steven Vicory, became highly insistent that the ice hockey club should start paying Link advance fees for the firm's accomplishment in raising $50 million. Esposito paid $30,000, but no more.

By then, the Tampa Bay Lightning was desperately looking for a genuine backer. Whilst it did so, the *Tampa Tribune* delved into Angus's past. On 27 June, the paper published an impertinently detailed account, including Judge Owen's observation that he was 'absurdly stupid'. Traced to New York – he was staying, once again, at the Waldorf Astoria – Angus pointed out that British courtrooms were not air-conditioned. 'The judges get hot,' he explained, 'and take it out on anybody who's there.'

Back in England, there had been a flurry of activity. On 14 June, Whitear sent a fax from his Surrey residence to the company solicitor, a man who had steered clear of the mainstream of his profession. '[Mehta] had two front doors,' explains Ian Codrington, 'depending on who was going to see him, one in one street, which was a sort of better address, the other on the back street, [which] Cheeseman went in and out of.' Whitear's fax explained that he was about to go to Jersey, where his mobile telephone might not work, but offered the assurance that he had 'already spoken to Keith'. A week later, one of Angus's trustees was telephoned by the Canadian Imperial Bank of Commerce. The bank was eager to establish Angus's financial position, explaining that it had received an application from him for a bridging loan for $50 million, to be repaid by the end of the year. The trustee was still digesting this news when, three hours later, the bank rang again, this time to discuss a 1985 *Daily Telegraph* report about a fraud trial concerning Lord Angus Montagu.

By 11 July, Angus had been prevailed upon to resign the chairmanship of Link International. Seemingly unaware of this, Tessier sent him and Whitear a fax on 24 July 1991, requesting that neither of them should discuss 'any issues' with Phil Esposito or Durgesh Mehta. Angus had no appetite for doing so. When, at the beginning of September, the *Mail on Sunday* reported his unhappy dealings with the Tampa Bay Lightning under the headline, 'Mystery as Duke's millions go missing', Ian Codrington responded on his behalf, pointing out that, though Angus had signed the dishonoured contract promising the hockey club $50 million, he had left Link 'because he was not satisfied about [the company's] conduct'.

The situation, already perilous, was now exacerbated by Keith Cheeseman's other professional commitments. More than a year earlier, shortly after 9.30 a.m. on Wednesday, 2 May 1990, John Goddard, a fifty-seven-year-old messenger for Sheppards, a money-broking firm, had been mugged at knife-point by a young black man in Nicholas Lane, close to the Bank of England. Goddard's briefcase contained £292 million worth of bearer bonds – 170 Treasury bills and 131 certificates of deposit. Both types of bond could be converted into cash or used as collateral for loans; all the bonds were highly perishable, the bills maturing on 30 July 1990, whilst the last certificate of deposit was due for payment on 16 November. The next day's newspapers reported the biggest robbery in history. The Bank of England issued a global alert, notifying financial institutions of the relevant serial numbers. Only the most brazen, or over-confident, of characters would now be willing to handle them. Amongst them were Keith Cheeseman and a Texan associate, Mark Lee Osborne, whose conventional stockbroking career had ended in the mid-1980s with ejection from the American securities market. Subsequent events suggested that their faith in their abilities was misplaced.

On 31 July 1990, in New York, Osborne tried to sell ten bonds to a potential buyer called 'Tony' (in fact David Maniquis, an undercover FBI agent attempting to recover $6 million worth of bonds stolen from Salomon Brothers in New York the previous year). Osborne's ten bonds were part of that haul. But his arrest and subsequent cooperation enabled the FBI to monitor the aftermath of the far bigger London robbery and, in particular, Cheeseman's activities. In one of several recorded conversations between the two men, Cheeseman assured Osborne that he could acquire up to eighty of the London bonds, adding the chivalrous warning that they were 'extremely hot'. Three weeks later, on 21 August 1990, Osborne's Lincoln Continental was found parked in a shopping mall off the Houston freeway. His body was on the back seat; he had been shot twice in the back of the head.

The FBI's interest in Cheeseman intensified. He was arrested, at its behest, on 27 November 1990 by the City of London police. Extradition proceedings were initiated. At the beginning of December, however, Cheeseman was granted bail, allowing him to resume discussions with Carl Tessier about Link's business prospects and, in particular, the chance of a successful 'fiddle' involving the Tampa Bay Lightning. Angus's relationship with the American authorities appeared to be on a different footing, as a Bedford couple noted when they flew with him and Louise to America in 1990. To their astonishment, the FBI greeted Angus on arrival, and eased his party through immigration. Unfamiliar with the concept that friendship affords the best and cheapest surveillance, Angus accepted this as appropriate recognition of his ducal status rather than a comment on his longstanding association with the twice-jailed Cheeseman.

Cheeseman did not appear ready for a third spell in custody. Cash kept in the boot of his Mercedes enabled him to patronize Tramp, a Piccadilly night-club, and enjoy repeated infusions of Napoleon brandy and amyl nitrate. There were, however, also regular business meetings at the Black Prince Hotel, just off the A2 near Dartford, from which he would emerge bathed in sweat and order his driver: 'Check we're not being followed and, if we are, lose them.' On 30 August 1991, nearly three months after Angus and Whitear's trip to Tampa, Cheeseman jumped bail.

Back in London, at 5.20 a.m. on 29 December 1991, police arrived at a flat in Brockley, south London, where a twenty-seven-year-old black man was dying from a gunshot wound. Patrick Thomas, whose family specialized in armed robbery, had a series of convictions to his name, ranging from firearms offences to burglary; he had recently been released from Belmarsh prison, where he had been held on remand, accused of possessing a kilo of cocaine. Police were advised that he had also been responsible for the London bond mugging, a theory given credence by the discovery of £150,000 in his bank and building society accounts. Investigations suggested IRA involvement in the mugging he had carried out.[88]

* * *

Serenely ignorant that he was a peripheral figure in the world of organized crime and terrorism, Angus attended to parliamentary business. He intended to make his maiden speech. This required nerve and preparation. 'He was petrified about it,' remembers Paul Vaughan. 'The first two times he chickened out completely.' Eventually – his script (concerning the preservation of British sovereignty) sharpened by the Labour peer Lord Bruce of Donnington;[89] his voice steadied by coaching from Vaughan – he was ready. Rising from his seat at 3.55 p.m. on 25 November 1991, he prefaced his peroration by observing that the last time a member of his family had spoken in the Lords had been in 1903. (In fact, his grandfather, Kim, had spoken as recently as 1914; his maiden speech had been in 1903.) Then he was into his stride, reminding their noble Lordships that their fellow countrymen had fought in two world wars 'with great loss of life to defend this country, our constitution and our monarchy'. Three minutes later, at 3.58 p.m., he sat down, allowing Lord Cockfield, replying for the government, to congratulate the noble duke on his 'most interesting and sincere' maiden speech. The fact, added Cockfield, that it was one of the shortest maiden speeches he had ever heard increased, rather than diminished, its value.

Angus explained to reporters that he had 'kept it short' because he was not a great speaker, though there was 'a lot between the lines' if anyone cared to read it. He declined to discuss the removal of hereditary peers from the House of Lords. There followed, says Paul Vaughan, the biggest celebration in parliamentary history.

Emboldened by his parliamentary performance, Angus gave a talk to the Kimbolton Local History Society, took to attending holy communion at St Andrew's church each Christmas Eve (occupying the Duke's Pew) and treated the Duke and Duchess of St Albans[90] to dinner at the Inn on the Park. On that occasion, deciding that he had had enough for one evening, Angus demanded the bill (no one had ordered, let alone eaten, pudding), hurried out to find a taxi, was unable to find one, halted a car and thrust £10 at the driver, telling him that he was to drive the Duke and Duchess of St Albans home. The driver did as bidden.

The Dukes' Trust had proved less responsive. Advised by Paul Vaughan that it would be prudent to wind it up, Angus handed over the accumulated proceeds ('a few hundred pounds') to a children's holiday farm in the

Midlands. At about the same time, Paul Newman expressed eagerness to set up a children's camp in England along the lines of the Hole in the Wall Gang camps which were well established in the USA. Angus and Louise met him and his wife, Joanne Woodward, in America. Angus insisted that the English camp should be called 'The Duke of Manchester's Ducal Trust Camp'; discussions ended.

He had more pressing concerns. Instead of the £152,000 salary promised by Link International, he had received £5,000 ('immediately spent') and 'some plane tickets and minor expenses', his total reward for exposing himself to the threat of federal prosecution. The sale of family silver and furniture now became the only means of eliminating his debts. When this led to the final rupture with the Dowager Duchess, he responded furiously. Angela Wood, meeting him again in the mid-1990s, found him in vituperative mood, 'slating his stepmother up hill and down dale'.

His acquaintances in the FBI became friendlier than ever. One, Bob Mahoney, presented him with a beer mug shortly before leaving London in 1991; it was inscribed 'Special Agent Angus Manchester'. Mahoney's successor, Frank Wakert, and Wakert's wife, not only enjoyed lunch at the House of Lords but spent three successive Christmases at Broadreach (the Wakerts reciprocated by having the Manchesters to a Thanksgiving party). Just before Wakert's time in England concluded, in July 1995, he too handed Angus a token of his affection – a brace of commemorative plaques.

Days later, Angus was indicted on charges of conspiracy and wire fraud arising from the Tampa deal. Kerry Cheeseman took immediate action, destroying a cheque for $3 million, payable to the Tampa Bay Lightning, which inconveniently bore Angus's signature.[91] Keith Cheeseman was unable to help. Rearrested in the Canary Islands in January 1992, he had received his third prison sentence the following year, in an American court, this time for six and a half years.

Ian Codrington urged Angus to plead guilty. It was a futile task. In the nine months between his indictment and trial, Angus contrived a characteristically contradictory position, continuously protesting his innocence whilst implicitly acknowledging his guilt by denouncing Carl Tessier and Durgesh Mehta, Keith Cheeseman and Michael Whitear. 'He told me how dreadful they were,' remembers Paul Vaughan, 'how they'd taken him for an absolute ride.' Ian Codrington heard much the same. 'He knew it was a scam but just said, "They used my name without my authority". I said, "Angus, when you become chairman of a company, they are entitled to use your name and say you're chairman".'

Louise was not treated to even these limited exchanges. 'He was only telling her a third of the story,' explains Paul Vaughan. 'She said it was like trying to nail jelly to the ceiling. Her attitude was, "Come clean, we'll fight this together". She found herself in a pretty terrible situation.' Louise speaks of 'a very traumatic year, hell on earth for Angus... difficult for everybody. We all tried to support him.' The 12th Duke of Manchester, now fifty-six and heading towards twenty stone, would never have cut a convincing figure on the run. But those closest to him sensed that he had accepted that this was one crisis that he would face.

Two of his fellow defendants took a different view. Neither Carl Tessier nor Durgesh Mehta was in court alongside him when the trial began on 13 March 1996. Tessier jumped bail, fled to Russia, was rearrested in Italy two years later, extradited to America and sentenced to five years' imprisonment in August 2000. Mehta, who operated in Britain, was struck off the Roll of Solicitors by a Law Society Tribunal,[92] maintained a residence in Chalfont St Peter and, in collaboration with three others, amassed £10 million in a VAT fraud between July and November 2003 (the crime for which he was eventually jailed, receiving a ten-year sentence in 2006). The third of the four defendants, Steven Vicory, Tessier's crony, reached a plea bargain agreement with the prosecution.

Angus was on his own. Before flying out to meet his fate, he visited Kerry Cheeseman in hospital, where she would remain, stricken by pancreatitis and dosed on morphine, for eleven months; he told her not to die. Her ex-husband was, inevitably, unable to speak on Angus's behalf, and Michael Whitear unwilling,[93] though both men's names, particularly Whitear's, recurred throughout the six-day trial (in which Whitear faced no charges). Ian Codrington was given special dispensation to sit alongside Angus's attorney, Bill Jung. The only witness for the defence, however, was Louise. Taking the stand on 18 March 1996, she said, in good faith, that her husband had left school at sixteen (he had in fact been four months short of his eighteenth birthday), described the warm relations they had both enjoyed with the FBI in London and pointed out that, far from resisting extradition, Angus had cooperated as soon as indicted.

With very limited ammunition at his disposal, Bill Jung took aim with care. Explaining the structure of the British legislature with great economy – the House of Lords was 'like the US Senate but more ceremonial' – he assured the jury that his client's title was a historical detail, mildly romantic but completely inconsequential. 'It's not a merited thing. It's simply he got to be duke like I got my last name Jung, because that was my daddy's name.'

Jung then laid bare the gulf between Angus's putative status and his slender gifts: 'Angus wasn't very sophisticated... not ever a good businessman... had no regular job other than going to the House of Lords.' His associates, added Jung, 'paid him once to get his attention... [then] they led him around by the nose like the prize bull at the county fair... the perfect fall guy if something happened'. The bull was kept well watered ('every time Angus – Mr Montagu – is involved, you'll hear someone is handing him a drink') and remained the focus of attention, even when others seemed just as intent on lowering their snouts to the trough. 'Michael Whitear, who was a friend of his from England, also signed [the partnership agreement] and was also there,' Jung reminded the jury. 'And as you will see, only one of the two were [sic] indicted. Only one of those two are [sic] a duke.'

The dozen or so Tampa citizens who troubled to come to court learned that the fraud had very nearly succeeded: Phil Esposito, desperate to meet the payment deadline (which had already been extended once by the National Hockey League), sanctioned an advance fee of $2.25 million to Link, only for it to be vetoed by his fellow Lightning directors. Other details tumbled uncomfortably out. Carl Tessier had paraded a list of sixteen NASDAQ stocks, in which, he had said, Link had holdings valued at no less than £74 million. These stocks were awkwardly illiquid so that the company had been obliged to seek help from a succession of banks. The banks, in turn, had struggled to assess Link's financial muscle or, on at least one occasion, even trace its executives, who were tied down by a variety of commitments. 'It was very difficult because the Duke was with the Queen, or something similar to that,' testified a witness. When a letter of credit had eventually been produced by Link, it had been swiftly exposed as a forgery: the company had had the less than formidable assets of £12,000 (held at the Borehamwood branch of Barclays Bank).

In his closing statement, on 19 March, Bill Jung did everything he could to emphasize that Angus had been led astray by men who were either career criminals or creatures of the most dubious credentials. 'You have heard the statement, the guilty flee when no man pursueth and the righteous stand as bold as a lion. Angus Montagu is standing before you now... His life's in your hands.' The jury found Angus guilty on four of the five charges.

* * *

Sentencing was delayed until 6 June. In the interim, Angus was allowed to return to Britain but it was obvious what his fate would be. Ian Codrington had spent the best part of a year emphasizing that, because he was an alien, he would not serve his time in an open prison. The warning finally sank in, remembers Paul Vaughan. 'He was living in permanent dread of going back.' On the 6th, Bill Jung repeated that Angus had been the front man rather the originator of the fraud, had made no money from it, had not waited for extradition and would, if an American, now be sent to 'a camp' (open prison). He added that a letter written by Angus to the Probation Service had been 'from the heart'. Jung's submission had some effect: Judge Ralph W. Nimmons, Jnr, sentenced Angus to thirty-three months – the shortest term possible[94] – and ordered him to repay the Tampa Bay Lightning $51,000. Yet had Angus pleaded guilty, he would, almost certainly, have walked away with a fine and a suspended sentence.

His imprisonment was delayed by three and a half weeks, an excruciating period of limbo spent, electronically tagged, amidst the Picassos and Braques which clothed the Sheerins' house in San Antonio, where, a decade earlier, he had wallowed in Texan adulation.

* * *

Louise Manchester remembers the watch-towers and the armed guards; so does Ian Codrington, though he was also impressed by the lie of the land. 'From the highway you could see it rising in the fields in the distance, surrounded by wire, out in the middle of nowhere.' The Federal Correctional Institution, Petersburg, Virginia, was not a place for ducal pretension. Visits, Louise discovered, were scrupulously choreographed. An armed guard patrolled a line of nearly a hundred prisoners, each of whom sat at one of the small, square, pale tables placed a foot or two apart; more armed guards sealed off either end of the hall. A globular camera trundled continuously along the ceiling. Violation of the no-touching rule seemed ill advised, though there was no physical barrier to prevent it.

Most of the prisoners were black; an exception caught Louise's eye. 'I thought he was a woman. He sat there, tossing his hair like a movie star. He looked just like a woman. It's obvious that that's what he was, really; certainly used by the other prisoners. I know that sounds awful, but that's what happens, isn't it?' Neither she nor anyone else would learn more from Angus. In as far as he ever spoke about his experiences as prisoner 19127-018, it was to liken them to *The Shawshank Redemption*, a film version of a Stephen King story in which a decent, innocent man – wrongfully jailed – survives institutionalized sadism, corruption and coercive buggery.

Angus arrived at Petersburg on 1 July 1996. His first three nights very nearly broke him. They were spent in solitary confinement, details of which he gabbled to Louise when allowed to make a telephone call. 'He said he'd been in permanent darkness, with no furniture – apparently not [even a bed or a mattress] – with food fed through a hole. I think he thought that his whole jail sentence was going to be like that. His documents hadn't arrived, so they treated him as though he was a murderer.' Visiting him a few weeks later, she saw that his hair had turned completely white; more distressingly, he repeated questions which she had already answered, unable to remember what she had told him moments before.

Only once – just after he had been found guilty – had he ever come close to admitting culpability. 'We went back to the hotel, the Hyatt in Tampa,' remembers Ian Codrington. 'We walked in, and he said, "Oh dear. You play with the big boys, you have to pay the penalty, occasionally." That's the nearest he ever came to saying he knew what he was doing.' At Petersburg, Angus retreated to the sanctuary of his imagined world, in which his innocence was incontrovertible. Self-deluding and consistently catastrophic though this had proved for much of his life, it was probably as effective a survival mechanism as any. Letters home were peppered with references to American corruption, a premise (maintained after his release) which encouraged him to reason that he did not have a criminal record, and which the rejection of his appeal as 'meritless' in May 1997 did nothing to undermine.

A fellow inmate, Nick Waycaster – 'a spoilt little rich kid' who had ingratiated himself with a gang of bikers, graduated to amphetamine production, and received a fifteen-year sentence – was treated to Angus's reminiscences. 'They talked a lot about the House of Lords and about Princess Diana, and [Angus's] children,' remembers Waycaster's wife, Carol. Although he had two staunch allies in Waycaster and another prisoner, Randall Smith Peters, and although he secured a job as a clerk in the prison laundry, he remained a prized target in the eyes of most inmates. 'They did not like him because of who he was,' says Carol Waycaster. 'He was an older person, and of course there was the language barrier, that accent.' Predators closed in.

Angus later described what happened. 'There were these hard men who wanted to try me out to prove to their gangs who was the toughest. The only way to make sure they didn't get the upper hand was to fight them. I may be getting on a bit, but I stood up to them and they left me alone after that.' Perhaps for the first time in his life, he had opted for understatement. Unfortunately, shortly after his release, he preferred to say that he had been stabbed in the stomach. This was fantasy: his only admission to the prison hospital (apart for medical assessment on arrival) had been for a check on an irregular heartbeat, not for treatment of stomach wounds, which went unmentioned in letters, telephone calls or any other reminiscence. Yet Bill Jung, who had striven to protect him from what he describes as a 'real prison', saw that, for all his faults, his client had one truly noble quality. 'Angus,' says Jung, 'was brave.' When combined with still formidable strength, it ensured that he was a less digestible proposition than some of his new acquaintances expected.

The fight occurred soon after his arrival at Petersburg. 'One of his teeth was slightly broken but he'd obviously held his own,' says Ian Codrington. 'He was a very strong man.'[95] Kerry Cheeseman describes Angus's difficulties as 'a couple of disagreements'. Few first-time prisoners – certainly not those fast approaching their fifty-eighth birthdays – can have initiated a 'disagreement' as magnificently as the 12th Duke of Manchester did. 'There was a lot of the mob involved in Petersburg,' explains Carol Waycaster. 'Angus had an encounter with one of [them]; he had thrown the man's shoes out the window.'

The repercussions of this action were still being felt two years later, when Angus's locker was broken into and its contents – probably a stash of Hershey bars – removed, triggering another of his regular appeals for money. These were not only, or even primarily, prompted by desire for a treat in the prison shop but by the urgent need to dole out rewards. Perhaps impressed by Angus's unexpected pugnacity, as well as by the belief that he was rich, two substantial black prisoners volunteered to protect him from mob retaliation, in return for appropriate payment. 'He'd have to buy them Hershey bars and so on,' explains Ian Codrington. 'He was desperate for money the whole time. We sent it via someone in America; it had to be in American postal orders. He was left alone.'[96]

There was one other threat at Petersburg that Angus had to see off, however. 'In American prisons, they put you into school, if you have no educational qualifications,' explains Codrington. Panic-stricken, Angus begged his solicitor to intercede on his behalf, which Codrington did, writing to the federal authorities and saying that Prisoner No.19127-018 had received an expensive education at an exclusive public school. But Angus's letters home, written in a cramped, painful hand (frequently splashed with capitals: 'the CORRUPTION is just out this world... the government STINKS'), showed how desperately he needed remedial help. The style and spelling ('HELPFULL... MOMMENT... HAVEING... pappers... any money witch may come to me from the USA') recalled his mother's jottings – as well as her priorities ('when I get back lets all have a big birthday party for your 40th and Ian, Michael and I for our 60th birthdays').

* * *

With Nell long gone, there was no word from the only surviving members of his family, his children, who became the focus of aggrieved belligerence, an emotion which intensified when Angus learned of developments which had been set in train a few months before his trial started. His sister-in-law Andrea, engulfed by grief in widowhood, became confused and querulous, convinced herself that she was short of money, developed cancer, and died in January 1996, aged fifty-three. A memorial service was held at St Andrew's Church in Kimbolton, on 24 February, the address being given by her old friend, Lord Runcie of Cuddesdon.[97] Only then did Kim's detestation of Angus become apparent.

Several years earlier, Joss Kent, the younger of Kim's two stepsons, had been taken to the American embassy in Nairobi. 'I was thirteen, fourteen. I witnessed all sorts of documents, which I was just told to sign as a family member.' He remained in ignorance of their significance during his mother's lifetime. 'I only found out when she died and they released her will: I'd been made the sole beneficiary. I was staggered.' So was Angus. Kim, though powerless to redirect the English and Irish trusts, had been able to dictate the fate of the family's American money (the residue of Consuelo's estate), which, he decreed, would pass first to Andrea and then to Joss and his descendants – 'a terrible thing to do', in the words of one of the Montagus' English trustees.

Angus, in Petersburg, bewailed his fate, though failing to grasp that Kim, rather than his trustees, was responsible for what had happened. What pained him almost as much as his own misfortune was the fact that his children, as well as Joss Kent, would be beneficiaries, very probably for the remainder of their lives,[98] even though they had already received money from their step-grandmother, Elizabeth, the Dowager Duchess, after she sold what Angus described as the 'Henry VIII picture' (presumably the disputed Holbein). 'I get nothing from the US trust and they get it all. When I was their age I got nothing from my father [sic] I had to work for a living and that's a fact.'

This self-serving distortion did not preclude him from drawing attention to hard-earned wisdom. 'I AM VERY VERY WARY OF EVERY THINK,' he wrote in May 1998, 'WHICH I ONLY WISH I HAD BEEN IN THE PAST.' Two months before his release – which came on 21 November 1998 – he remarked that his time inside had taught him 'HUMILITY AND TOLERANCE'. Professional acquaintances, whose advice he had routinely ignored, were repeatedly assured that they were 'DEAR FRIENDS'. Angus, however, had very few close friends indeed. Kerry Cheeseman wrote frequently but her letters never reached him (she declined to use an alias, thereby prompting the federal authorities to divert them). Paul Vaughan's letters got through unscathed, as did those of a trustee and his wife, and – to Angus's joy and astonishment – those of Mike Cobbold, a contemporary from the Marines whom he had not heard from for forty years. But the sense of external support was hardly overwhelming, though Maggie Sheerin, Ian Codrington and, of course, Louise did what they could to bolster him when he telephoned. Twice Louise crossed the Atlantic, first in September 1996 and again in March 1997, on each occasion staying for a fortnight, seeing Angus daily (except Tuesdays when no visits were permitted). He was thrilled to have her with him. 'He just didn't have any visitors. He asked me an awful lot of questions… didn't want to talk a lot [about prison] but about people he knew.'

Louise's reserves were coming to an end, however. At the time of Angus's imprisonment, he had accumulated a familiar range of debts, including one of £9,000 to the National Westminster Bank, which Louise was obliged to pay off at £350-a-month. Recourse to the trustees was no longer possible: the trial had cost $100,000, several thousands had been fruitlessly invested in his appeal and further funds were frittered away in drainingly expensive exchanges between solicitors and trustees, who could now authorize only the smallest of payments on his behalf.[99]

Even Angus's usually blunt antennae detected difficulties ahead. 'I DONT WANT TO LOOSE HER, SO PLEASE DO ALL YOU CAN TO HELP US BOTH,' he wrote to a trustee after Louise's first visit in 1996. After her second trip, it was Louise who made the decision. An attractive woman, never short of admirers, she sought a judicial separation. Ian Codrington urged her to be unequivocal: to remain married or to seek a divorce. She chose divorce. Although receiving the news with apparent equanimity, Angus raged against her in subsequent letters ('[she] has given me hell… out of three wives Diane was the only good one but that's life'), if never quite bracketing her with his first wife, Mary, whom he blamed for his alienation from his children. 'As for them I hope I never see them again. THE CHILDREN HAVE BEEN AND ALWAYS WILL BE UNDER THE INFLUENCE OF THERE MOTHER WHO IS THE BIGGEST BITCH OUT.'

Detestation of Mary aside, his essentially dispassionate approach to women gradually reasserted itself, however, to the extent that, during the course of a long, broad-ranging telephone conversation with a trustee on Saturday, 26 September 1998, he remarked that it was quite likely that he would be taking a new wife. No prospective bride was named, but Angus would prove as good as his word.

* * *

Biba Hiller, a bottle-blonde, once of Bournemouth though reputedly of Swedish extraction, had never expected to snare a duke, certainly not at her fourth attempt, aged fifty-seven. Interviewed on honeymoon in April 2000, she recalled that she had first married at sixteen; she was twenty-two when her husband had killed himself. With two young daughters to support, she had turned, she said, to modelling, starring in the first Allied Carpets television commercial. A second marriage, to Peter Bruell, ended acrimoniously in 1982; a third, to Ivan Hiller, whom she met in California, lasted five days. She had then worked as a West End property dealer: the name Biba Hiller, she insisted, was so well known in the London market that becoming the Duchess of Manchester might be a commercial disadvantage.

Kerry Cheeseman, whom Angus had telephoned as soon as he returned to England, has never been willing to accept this, arguing that Biba closed this, her most important deal, 'in about three weeks flat'. A number of Angus's Bedford friends voiced other misgivings. One, noting that she operated from Shepherd Market, remembers her as 'an absolute tart, a frightful woman'; another, John Lickfold, declined to reprise his role as best man.[100] If Biba moved at a giddy pace, she had good reason to. At about the same time that Angus made her acquaintance, he met another woman who caught his eye. Anna West lived in Exeter, 'and had a good job with House of Fraser'. Angus announced that they were getting married. Unfortunately, remembers a Bedford friend, he 'promptly wanted to know what her earnings were. She dropped him on the spot.'

Biba was both more resilient and munificent, taking charge of the wedding arrangements. The service was held at the Swedish Church in Marylebone, in deference to the bride's Scandinavian roots, and the reception in a Mayfair pub, the Audley in Mount Street. Biba very probably paid for everything; Angus was certainly in no position to do so. The English and Irish trusts, already dented by the cost of his trial and appeal, were further diminished by his divorce from Louise, to whom his trustees now made regular alimony payments. The result was that his income, on release from prison, dwindled to £100-a-week, which he collected in cash from the Bedford offices of Sharman & Trethewy, where Ian Codrington was senior partner.

Although the trusts suffered no further punishing demands during

Angus's lifetime, their recovery was steady rather than spectacular, with the annual income generated limping slowly up to £10,000 by 2002 – intolerably inadequate for a man of Angus's appetites. There was nothing left for him to sell – or almost nothing. On one of his last visits to Kimbolton, he headed to the Castle to remove an ancient leather chest (once, according to probably erroneous family legend, owned by Katherine of Aragon) which Mandy had bought back at the 1949 sale and left, on loan, initially to the parish church and then to Kimbolton School. The chest had cost Mandy £750; Angus sold it, fifty years later, for £350.

He decided to seek credit, difficult though this was. His employment prospects had not been advanced by a conviction for fraud, whilst his primary assets were now limited to a collection of grey flannel trousers, a blazer with Royal Marines (officer's) buttons and a small library of war videos. Within a month of returning to England, he was 'flashing £50 notes around [Bedford]'. Angus put them to familiar use two months later. Accompanied by Mike Green, of *Bedfordshire on Sunday*, and another friend, Clive Coleman, he drove up to London in his Ford Galaxy (its doors emblazoned with the Montagu coat of arms), kept a rendez-vous with a Mr Vernon Legge, fortified himself with a couple of drinks (probably at Grosvenor House), paid the bill ('well over £50 [for] two bottles of beer and two gins') and headed to the Lords.

On arrival, he made for the bar. The barmaids were affectionate and some of his fellow peers reassuringly friendly, notably a Labour peeress who embraced him. After further refreshment, Angus led his guests into lunch. Later, his appearance in the chamber prompted a 'satisfying number of "hear, hears".' But initial success was illusory. The *News of the World*, learning of Angus's intended return, had carried a curt editorial headed 'Crook of Manchester'. More damaging than that, however, was the prevalent mood in the upper house – nervy, defiant, wary – as it awaited reform at the hands of the new Labour government, whose influence, a peer informed Angus, had already manifested itself by the installation of double-glazing and 'a lot more breast-feeding'. In these attritional circumstances, an oafish if generous scapegrace could only be distressingly conspicuous.

Angus affected not to notice. He assured members of Bedford Rowing Club that reform was no longer on the agenda ('it'll never happen, dear boy'); that he would survive the cull of hereditary peers ('I was asked to be one of the 100') and, finally, that he could return whenever it suited him ('I've always been asked whether I'd like to come in'). His attendance record unlocks the truth. Desperate though Angus was to collect his allowances (£80.50

overnight subsistence, by 1999, with £35.50 day subsistence, and 50.1p per mile travelled by car), he ventured back only three more times after his return that February, an unprecedented spell of absenteeism (even in the parliamentary year leading up to his imprisonment in 1996, he had attended forty-two times, whilst in 1992–3 he had chalked up a personal best of 135).

Before experiencing Petersburg, Angus would almost certainly have ignored whatever opprobrium was heaped upon him, much as he had once scorned strictures about his House of Lords dining companions. But the Federal Correctional Institution had left its mark. Ian Codrington who, at Angus's insistence, flew to America to accompany him home, noticed the change immediately, even though he saw periodic, almost reassuring glimmers of the Angus of old. When Codrington contacted the Marines archive at the behest of the probation authorities, Angus eagerly asked what he had found. Codrington diplomatically told him that there had been 'very little' (there had been 'absolutely nothing'). Angus, who had finally conceded that he had not been an officer, expressed satisfaction, 'tapped his nose and said: "You see, I was on secret missions".' He took a similarly idiosyncratic view of his relationship with America, insisting that he could return at any time because he had 'diplomatic immunity'. Yet the defiance was superficial: faith in his own myth of ducal invulnerability had been irrevocably damaged by his conviction and subsequent incarceration. 'He was a different man: a worried man.'

Angus nevertheless managed to present a brave face to Kerry Cheeseman, whom he continued to telephone at least two or three times a day and visit once a month. 'He quite enjoyed [prison], believe it or not,' she says. Those, like Paul Vaughan, who received his letters or telephone calls from Petersburg, knew differently. 'I think it destroyed his health,' says Vaughan, who has a number of his scrawled notes, including one written in August 1997. Angus recorded that temperatures were over 100, on one day reaching 110, accompanied by almost intolerable humidity ('HELL'). 'Quite a few of the inmates have had to be taken to the Hospital suffering from too much heat, and one had brain damage because of the heat... only one more year and a few weeks and I will be home thank God.' Even allowing for exaggeration, these were uncomfortable, even perilous conditions for a man with a heart condition, burdened by six or seven stone of superfluous flesh. It was the severest price to pay for involvement in 'a fiddle' about which he 'didn't,' in Keith Cheeseman's words, 'know too much'.

Denied alcohol during his twenty-eight months in Petersburg, Angus emerged three stone lighter but rapidly replaced this, with interest, in the consoling binges which followed, though – in further evidence of his bruised confidence – these were shifted from the Inn on the Park to the Dorchester. A London acquaintance remembers the extreme struggle he now experienced in reaching her fourth-floor flat. 'He came staggering up the stairs. My husband said, "Oh, I thought you were going to lose a lot of weight". He said, "Oh, no, this is all muscle".' Kerry Cheeseman, listening uneasily to the messages Angus wheezed into her answering machine, became increasingly concerned. 'It was just awful, awful. He was going like a balloon.' In the end, she remembers, Angus began to talk about going to WeightWatchers but, characteristically, said he would only go if Kerry, ravaged by pancreatitis and needing to gain weight not lose it, came too.

Unnerved by the collapse in his income, embittered by the comparative enrichment of his children, bedevilled by failing health, incapable of coping with solitude, Angus grew desperate for companionship. He had renounced both Whitear and Cheeseman (to whom he was so antipathetic that he begged Kerry Cheeseman to change her name), whilst a new-found sense of shame inhibited him from making contact with longstanding, if less intimate, acquaintances like Fergus Rogers, who had telephoned him on his return from America. 'I left a message saying, "It's Fergus here; if you want to talk to me, here's my number". He never did.' Instead, he made transatlantic calls to Carol Waycaster, wife of his fellow inmate from Petersburg, with whom he would discuss castles and ghosts (two subjects which fascinated Mrs Waycaster), or visited or telephoned his beloved Kerry. 'He just had a thing about living on his own, the fear of getting old on his own,' she remembers.

It was in this forlorn mood that Angus decided to marry Biba. Later, Louise would ask him what had persuaded him to do so. 'He said, "Oh, I was lonely and she paid me attention". I thought, yes, he always wanted to be loved.' Despite Biba's commercial skills (she arranged for part of the honeymoon, a cruise, to be paid for by *Hello!* magazine),[101] the auguries for marital success were not encouraging, although Angus's daughter Emma flew over to act as bridesmaid, and the couple's guests – seventy-five in all – enjoyed a lively bus ride from Bedford, during which refreshments were taken. The day ended fractiously, though not before wedding photographs had been taken of Biba – teeth bared in leonine, triumphant manner – with Angus standing beside her, looking trapped and slightly sick.

A journalist, having arranged to interview Angus on honeymoon in Jersey,[102] arrived to find the duchess with her left arm in a sling, her eyes 'bleary with painkillers and G & Ts', and Angus 'nursing a Scotch and Coke and sucking his briar pipe'. Biba, it transpired, had slipped when stepping out of a late-morning bubble-bath; two operations and the insertion of a metal pin had been required. Her accident elicited little sympathy from Kerry Cheeseman. 'I think she was a lush; John [Dedman] said every time he spoke to her she was paralytic drunk.' Angus's allies in the rowing club felt much the same, though they rarely saw her. 'She would come here occasionally,' says one of them, 'he would go up to London occasionally and stay there, but basically he lived here and she lived there.' The difficulties experienced by Biba's son (by her marriage to Peter Bruell) introduced further complications. Whilst still on honeymoon, a fax had been pushed under the couple's door, informing them that Alexander Bruell, a 6'4" London nightclub bouncer (Biba preferred 'security consultant'), was being held in an Italian jail, charged with attempting to smuggle 453,000 ecstasy tablets to America. The haul, valued at £9.5 million, was the largest ever seized.

Angus was instinctively sympathetic to his stepson's plight. 'He's been duped,' he reflected when interviewed. 'He's not dissimilar from me at his age. He's a go-getter, very hard-working. And he's naïve. I was naïve, but I was innocent, too.' Soon, however, even his role as stepfather could not dissuade Angus from seeking sanctuary in East End pubs. There, in the welcoming, undemanding company of Kerry Cheeseman and John Dedman (and sometimes their friend Barry), he bullied his overloaded frame into action, winning £10 or £20 in impromptu press-up competitions. These were treasured times, infinitely more stimulating than his tenuous marriage to Biba (which was formally dissolved, with merciful speed, by September 2001).

Daily routine in Bedford was less rewarding. Teaming up with Clive Coleman, known to members of the rowing club as 'the Welsh wazzack,' he established a coach tour business. Clients were picked up in a Ford Galaxy Tourer, 'driven to the historic site of their choice, regaled with tales of Merrie Olde England, treated to lunch and high tea, then whisked back to London... all for just £250-a-head'. Angus had high hopes of the new venture. 'The guests are honoured to see an English Duke or Lord,' he reflected. 'Once you have put them at ease, they're wonderful people.' Nevertheless, the enterprise was undermined by a degree of imprecision. The company's brochure confused the Chilterns with the Cotswolds; figures showing the costs the business had incurred were apparently being compiled by a friend; they never materialized. The tours ceased; Clive Coleman later disappeared, inadvertently leaving an unpaid bill at the rowing club.

Social life now lacked the spark which Louise had once injected into it. Angus spent Christmas Day 2001 with Jack Pope, a widower, and Tom Williams, an enthusiastic patron of both the Fleur and the George and

Dragon, who had begun to style himself Angus's butler (although allowing Angus to cook Christmas lunch). But the New Year brought fresh hope. Angus revived his friendship with Louise. He began to talk of marriage. Louise listened, although Angus did not intend to limit his options, according to Kerry Cheeseman, who suggests that he had as many as four prospective brides in mind. By the summer of 2002, however, Louise was a clear, seemingly unchallenged favourite. Urged by Ian Codrington to make a fresh start, she and Angus began house-hunting in Devon. The trustees had a modest residence in mind, costing no more than around £150,000; Angus's ideas, nourished by thoughts of Consuelo's jewels, were on an altogether more generous scale. 'They started off looking at houses for £500,000,' says Ian Codrington, recalling that this did not register favourably with the trustees. He fixed a date in early August for a meeting between them and Angus, then headed to Spain for a brief holiday with his wife. 'I saw [Angus] the day before we flew. He was on good form.'

Kerry Cheeseman also had plans for a Spanish holiday, but her anxiety about Angus's health very nearly persuaded her to postpone it. About a fortnight earlier, Angus had joined her and John Dedman at the Treacle Mine, an Essex hostelry, before visiting Mrs Cheeseman's house in South Ockendon. 'It was about a week before I went on holiday. He was running around the garden playing swing-ball, trying to tell me how fit he is. A couple of whacks and of course he's panicked for breath.' She repeatedly begged him to see a doctor. 'The day before I went, I was literally screaming on the phone, saying to him, "I'm going to cancel this bloody holiday unless you go to that doctor because you can't breathe, you're getting on my nerves". Every single word I called him.'

Scarcely reassured by Angus's reply – he acknowledged that he was in 'a bit of pain' but insisted that he would see a private doctor the following day – she flew to the Costa Brava. 'The following week,' she remembers, 'I get a call.' It was Tom Williams; he had bad news.

* * *

The funeral of the Most Noble Angus Charles Drogu Montagu, 12th Duke of Manchester, took place on a bright afternoon on Monday, 5 August 2002 at Bedford crematorium, although days earlier the crematorium authorities had been uncertain that their facilities could cope with someone of Angus's stature. After discussion with the undertakers, A. L. & G. Abbott, they agreed that they could proceed. Six bearers shouldered the oak coffin (its sides 18" deep), whose weight nudged the total burden up to twenty-two stone.

Kimbolton, which almost any family would treasure (except the twentieth century Montagus).

Edward, 2nd Earl of Manchester (by Lely), antagonised both Charles I and Cromwell, but survived.

Far left: 'Mandy' (*left*), 10th Duke of Manchester, with his brother-in-law, David Stead.
Left: Mandy's wife and Angus's mother, Nell, enjoying war work with a friend.

Mandy's younger sister Louise adored their brother Edward, flying in to collect him from the Foreign Legion and eventually picking him up from Wormwood Scrubs.

Lord Edward —of the jungle

The much-married Lord Edward met his death in Mexico in 1954.

WHEN the amazing Lord Edward Montagu died with his wife by his side in the green hell of Mexico's unmapped jungles a few days ago it was a final act of drama in keeping with his fabulous life.

I knew him—this godson of King Edward VII, son of the ninth Duke of Manchester, born to rank and riches who yet lived much of

crashed, killing one of his companions and severely injuring him.

The best medical opinion in the U.S.A. told him he would never walk again. "Nonsense," said Edward—and in less than a year he was back on his feet.

But during the time he was in hospital he became fascinated by the ancient Indian civilisations in the still largely unexplored Mexican jungles.

He decided to devote the rest of his life to discovering

Left: Angus with his grandfather, 'Kim', 9th Duke of Manchester, also once an inmate of Wormwood Scrubs, at Kimbolton, October 1938.
Right: Angus with his elder sibling, also 'Kim', who would later acknowledge Angus as his brother but add: 'I'd rather he wasn't.'

Living wild?
Family photographs stubbornly refused to conform to Angus's memories of life as an elephant boy.

Angus on pageboy duty at a wartime
wedding in Ceylon (now Sri Lanka).

Squad 911 completed training in May 1957
– seven months after the Suez crisis.

'I was on secret missions'. *Above*: Angus at
the beach (back row, second left). *Right*: as
No 2 in HMS *Loch Fyne*'s water polo
team. *Far right*: testing the golf course.

Above left; *above right*: Angus with first wife, Mary; with friends and spouse number two, Diane.
Below left; *below right*: Angus and third wife, Louise; wedding to fourth wife, Biba.
Right: The one who got away – Angus with Jane Probyn (now Bishop).

Cheesemans reunited: Kerry greets Keith on his release from Wormwood Scrubs, 1981.
Far right: Kerry with Angus: an indulgent, mothering and unconditional woman.

The Duchess of Manchester visits Prisoner 19127-018 in the Federal Correctional Institution, Petersburg, Virginia.

With Louise and Patsy Chilton (*right*), who had known him since his teens.

Playing swing-ball with Kerry Cheeseman's grandson in Essex, July 2002.

High society visit

AMBULANCE crews went to new heights to treat a nobleman with a colourful reputation yesterday.

The Duke of Manchester called paramedics to his top floor flat on the Embankment because he had chest pains.

A spokesman said: "Because of the way the building is organised and the weight of the gentleman, the only way we could get him into an ambulance was to crane lift him."

The fire service was brought to hoist the 63-year-old down from his balcony on an aerial platform.

He was taken to Bedford Hospital.

Angus Manchester has led a chequered life – his many jobs include car salesman, crocodile hunter, cattle-train driver in Australia, alligator wrestler and Hollywood stuntman.

In 1996 he was sentenced to 33 months in a high security prison in America for his part in an attempt to defraud the Tampa Bay Lightning ice hockey club of £18 million.

His fourth wife, Bibu Hillier, divorced him after just 17 months of marriage last year.

A hospital condition check was unavailable as the *Times & Citizen* went to press.

Angus's departure from 15, Broadreach, Bedford, 25th July 2002. *The Times & Citizen* was unaware that he was critically ill.

The Unknown Montagu: 'the Frog' (wearing beret, third right) at Staughton in 1930. According to Grey Duberly (second left, front row), he was never seen again after the war.

The Frog, doing his best at cricket.

Angus's daughter, Emma, his younger son Kimble, his stepmother Elizabeth, and two of his former wives, Louise and Diane, were amongst those who crowded into the crematorium chapel for the 3.15 p.m. service. John Lickfold and Ian Codrington and most of the rowing club were present; so was Kerry Cheeseman, wearing a full-length fur coat. She had arrived in a white stretch limousine, accompanied by two friends whose identity was the subject of some conjecture ('one of them, someone said, was with the Kray twins'). Mrs Cheeseman is emphatic that the first of her ex-husbands, John Dedman, was with her, together with a female friend called Anne. 'Everybody did gawp at me,' she acknowledges. It was, though, the sight of Sue Whitear, wife of Michael, which Louise and Emma found much harder to digest.

The mood was not strained for too long, however. As the curtain closed around the coffin, there was 'a spectacular thunderclap' prompting the Revd Ron Frost to remark that Angus's presence was already being felt above. The service concluded, remembers Kerry Cheeseman, with a 'special request for Angus and all his friends. They started playing Colonel Bogey. Everybody sung it. I walked out of there and I laughed.' The mourners progressed to the rowing club for the wake, whose duration and intensity would have given Angus much pleasure. The following day, Louise, Emma and Kimble were present as his ashes were interred in the family crypt at St Andrew's, Kimbolton. His cassette and video tapes (including *Oklahoma* and *The Sound of Music*) were auctioned at the rowing club, fetching slightly under £100,[103] a figure of little comfort to a number of financial institutions. At the time of his death, Angus had an HSBC loan (contrary to the precise instructions of one of its managers), an HSBC credit card, an Amex card, and another credit card. His total debts amounted to £70,000. A friend who had sustained proportionately bigger losses than the banks was handed a bottle of port by John Lickfold. 'He said to me, "You know, dear boy, we were all conned, we all did things for him – and never had a bloody penny".'

These few good friends did not go as far as John Mingay, Bedford's deputy mayor, in describing Angus's death as a tragedy. They had, however, been willing to forgive him his deficiencies, partly because he patently needed help, and very often because they were gripped by a fascination to see what he would do next, just as the children of Kimbolton had been fifty years earlier. 'Everyone,' says Mike Green, 'missed him as a character.' Paul Vaughan and Ian Codrington acknowledge that they still do. So does Kerry Cheeseman. 'I miss him, God do I miss him; I miss him being a pain in the arse at times, to be quite frank.'

It is difficult to avoid concluding that the fate of the ducal branch of the family, already undermined by a series of unsatisfactory marriages, was sealed by a chance meeting at a Colombo swimming pool in 1927. However, those who insist that there is genetic instability within the family[104] could do worse than attempt to trace the fate of the 'unknown' Montagu. In his will, Angus's great-great uncle, Lord Charles Montagu, resisted the temptation to leave anything to his nephew Kim (or anyone bearing the surname Montagu). He did, however, bequeath £15,000 (£3,171,531 today) and any balance in his account with Lloyds & Provincial Foreign Bank, Paris (or any other bank in Paris), to Mademoiselle Suzanne Leonide Renard, of 100 Boulevard Pereire. In addition, Mlle Renard was to receive the income from a £60,000 trust for the rest of her life.

History does not relate when Lord Charles made Mlle Renard's acquaintance, but her existence was known to the Duberlys. They were impressed by the dexterous way in which Lord Charles handled this relationship – one whose potential for complications and misunderstanding was exacerbated by the fact that Mlle Renard had borne him a son. Lord Charles did not deny his son's existence. On the contrary, Edouard (or 'the Frog') frequently stayed at Kimbolton in the 1930s. 'You don't marry those women, do you? [But Lord Charles] made provision for them. Edouard was educated and brought up properly,' remembers Grey Duberly, who has a black and white snapshot of him taken on a summer's day at Staughton. 'He was something like twelve or fourteen when I last saw him, 1932-ish. He played cricket with us [at Staughton]. He was very nice. It was all done properly.' Edouard's surname, she adds, was never mentioned.

It is tempting to think that he was known as Edouard Renard; a clause in Lord Charles's will suggests otherwise. In it, Lord Charles bequeathed £15,000 to 'Edward Macalister of Harvard College and the Villa de Tours, Cimiez, Nice, France (if he shall attain the age of Twenty five years)'. Nowhere in the will, or in four subsequent codicils to it, was Macalister referred to as Lord Charles's son. There can be no doubt, however, that he was in the old man's thoughts to the very end. The last codicil was added on 10 November 1939: the day of Lord Charles's death. In it, he rearranged matters so that his bequest would not pass to Edward Macalister immediately but would instead be held in a trust for him for fifteen years 'from and after my death'.

'The Frog' never returned to Kimbolton, says Grey Duberly, who remembers how the young 'Frenchman' had astounded her by saying that he was a mixture of four, or five, or even six nationalities. He was, however, as much a Montagu as his first cousin, Kim, 9th Duke of Manchester, and his first cousin twice removed, Angus. Perhaps he perished heroically, in the Resistance or at Omaha Beach on D-Day; perhaps, like his English cousins, he had by then embarked on a life of indebtedness and self-indulgence, punctuated by custodial sentences. Until his fate is known, it is inevitable that the Montagus will be judged by Angus's record – and by the progress of his elder son, Alexander, 13th and current Duke of Manchester.

PART FOUR

It's a queer, queer world we live in
And Dame Fortune plays a funny game –
Some get all the sunshine,
Others get the shame
I don't know why but since I was born
The scapegrace I seem to be.
Ever since I was a little boy at school
A name has stuck to me
But I'll try my luck in the colonies.
There I'll rise or fall.
And when I come back
The sheep that was black
Will perhaps be the whitest of them all.

Fred Barnes,
'The Black Sheep of the Family'

John

Nerves had picked away at him all afternoon. They *had* to be on time; *had* to be there by 5.30 p.m.; would *have* to wear suits for dinner. The litany of imperatives was reiterated throughout the drive from London to Suffolk. His passenger, a friend from Yale, was still listening without complaint as they neared the village of Horringer. There, with the church on their right and a cottage – white-washed, thatched – on their left, they thrummed across the cattle grid and onto the drive. A sign, installed by the National Trust, instructed motorists to limit their speed to 20 mph; Lord Nicholas Hervey complied. There was no glimpse of the house ahead, just a landscape of oaks and parkland. The drive led on for three-quarters of a mile. Only then, from behind a screen of cedars and yet more oaks, did Ickworth present itself – a crazed *coup de théâtre*, a frontage of 200 yards, its midriff bloated by the 104-foot high rotunda.

But Nicholas did not relax: he never did at Ickworth or, indeed, anywhere else. Further, urgent instructions followed: they would go to their rooms, shower, change and return to the drawing room, ready to meet Nicholas's older brother John, at 7.30 p.m. precisely. His Yale friend did as asked, heading upstairs, past the massive coronation portraits, by Ramsay, of George III and Queen Charlotte. A while later, as Nicholas's schedule dictated, they reached the drawing room, its walls dressed in yellow silk damask, one of them enriched by a version of 'Charles I' by Van Dyck (so Victor's attribution insisted). A butler appeared; drinks were brought. The two men, both in their late twenties, talked to one another, rather as if awaiting interview. An hour passed. More drinks came. They talked and drank and remained alone. Evening turned to night.

It was around 11 p.m. by the time John joined them. There was little to suggest kinship between the siblings (aside, perhaps, from a similarity in contour of forehead and sweep of hair). Nicholas, a tangle of inhibition, made sense of life from within a straitjacket of etiquette seemingly buttoned down as securely as his blazer (invariably his first line of defence against a world of ineffable informality); John, seven years older and, at 5'11", an inch or so shorter, tended to release himself from the constrictions of decorum and convention. This evening was no different. He did not wear a suit but what the Yale man would later recall as 'a robe'; at his side was a black friend called Cecil.

Dinner began. Wine, then port, was in plentiful supply. Time blurred in alcohol. In the early hours John felt that the moment had come for action. He was taking the helicopter up: everyone was to come with him. The flight seemed unlikely to involve communication with air traffic control.

Nicholas's Yale ally found a spark of self-preservation within him and, with it, the strength to resist the call; so did Cecil. Nicholas lacked similar reserves. He walked into the night, at his brother's heel.

John, still in his robe, managed to climb into the pilot's seat with no more difficulty than might be expected of someone who had just drunk two or three bottles of claret and a pint of port. His younger brother took the front seat beside him. Rotor blades chopped into action. The helicopter – a Hughes 500 Defender – began a groggy, hesitant ascent, then veered forward and up, but not far, nor especially high, hovering no more than 80 feet above the ground. As it did so, a light of immense power, fitted to its underside, cut a jagged pattern through the night sky ('it was one of those things they use on a 747') before coming to rest on a section of the Rotunda: a section, it was about to become apparent, occupied by an employee of the National Trust.

Moments later, a squawking, demented cacophony erupted. Although indecipherable at first, ferocious repetition gradually allowed Nicholas's Yale friend to piece together words, then phrases, all of them being spat through a megaphone powerful enough to penetrate the noise of the helicopter, whose light now locked onto a bedroom window: 'I HATE YOU, YOU BASTARD... YOU BASTARD... I HATE YOU, YOU ****ING BASTARD... WAKE UP, YOU BASTARD.' Another night at Ickworth was drawing to a close.

* * *

Years later, when darkness and silence had once more returned to the night skies of Ickworth, John's will was published, prompting one of his two surviving half-brothers to issue a brief statement to the press. 'You could say the wealth he had was sufficient for him in his lifetime…,' reflected this younger sibling. 'We all know he was quite a flamboyant character and he pretty much lived the way he wanted to. He made the most of his life – he packed more in his forty-four years than most people do in their whole lives.'

Those who, in retrospect, seek to unearth an augury for how John would 'make the most of his life' might settle on 6 February 1955, the day of his christening in Belgravia, conducted at St Peter's, Eaton Square, five months after his birth on 15 September 1954. One of his godfathers, Derek le Poer Trench (friend of Victor, very good friend of Victor's first wife Pauline) had been unable to attend, and so (as *The Times* recorded the following day) Jeremy Lowndes stood proxy. The infant son of Lord and Lady Jermyn was named Frederick William John Augustus. Few have godparents who later shoot themselves in the head (as Trench would do in 1978); no one, perhaps, other than John (as the baby would always be known), also has a prospective murderer lurking by the font as the baptismal water smears the forehead in benediction. (Lowndes's victim would be the third of his wives.[1])

Most critics, however, have had no need for auguries, preferring to see John's life as reassuring evidence of the danger – or evil, as some prefer – inherent in Hervey blood. Explanations for the Gothic story of self-damnation that followed were obviously and comfortably reducible to his paternal genetic inheritance: this, they have argued, could only be Victor's son.

* * *

'You'd better take him and adopt him.' Victor's remark was rewarded with laughter, primarily his own, admittedly, but that didn't matter: the lunch party was going well. John, aged about ten, might have felt otherwise. A solitary child dwarfed by those around him, he sat next to Betty Stafford. She always tried to seek him out, aware that none of Victor's friends would follow suit. 'No one took an interest,' she remembers. 'I felt desperately sorry for him.'

Years later, John remarked that life at Ickworth was very much 'upstairs-downstairs'. He saw Victor only rarely; it was not necessarily a treat when he did. 'My father never did anything with me. He was an extremely cold man… I was terrified of him because he commanded so much authority. He wasn't really a father, he was a demi-god.' Childhood holidays (John later told one of his professional advisers) amounted to solitary confinement in Deauville, with a nanny on guard. An intimate friend heard a variation on the same refrain: 'Victor wanted nothing to do with John – John was an embarrassment, surplus to requirements. He was palmed off to the Isle of Wight.'

Juliet, the first of John's stepmothers, says that John looked forward to his holidays on the island, where he stayed with his step-grandfather, Sir Peter Macdonald, and Macdonald's second wife, Phoebe, a couple who lacked grandchildren of their own. In the years after Macdonald's death (in December 1961), Juliet and Victor took John and his younger half-brother, Nicholas, to 'seaside resorts in France and Italy' for at least part of the summer holidays. When at Ickworth, Juliet drove him to Miss Howe's kindergarten in Bury St Edmunds; if she was unable to do so, Shelagh O'Donnell ('a very pleasant Irish governess') deputized or a chauffeur-groom did (his other duties also included taking 'Lord John' riding). Both boys had friends to stay at Ickworth, and went to stay with those friends in turn. Juliet concedes that Victor was mostly in London during the week – where she often joined him – but explains that she would arrange for the boys to come up 'for dentists, oculists, etc., and also for treats such as pantomimes, theatres and parties'.

To Edward and Henry Wodehouse, sons of Victor's old friend Johnny Kimberley, aspects of John's life seemed enviable, particularly the trainset laid out in the Ickworth nursery. 'Much bigger and better than ours: very superior,' says Henry, who recalls the pleasure John derived from the delight and envy it inspired. The Wodehouses also attended Miss Howe's, from which, at the end of almost every day, they would go to Ickworth or return, with John, to Great Blakenham, their home since their mother's remarriage. Henry, five in 1961, was the youngest of the trio, John being eighteen months his senior and Edward a year older still. Energy was expended running around the garden or channelled into debate over the respective lengths of the drives at Ickworth and Kimberley, the Wodehouse family seat in Norfolk until it was sold in 1958. 'We'd have bets about which was longer,' adds Henry, 'even though we weren't at Kimberley any more.' At tea one afternoon at Ickworth, John devised an alternative wager. 'He had a bet with Edward and me that Bluebird was in one of the garages.' Both the Wodehouses accepted. A few moments later, they were being led to Victor's 'museum' where, to their incredulity, Bluebird was on display. John's exploitation of insider knowledge cost them 6d each, 'one week's pocket money in those days'.

In retrospect, however, Henry Wodehouse senses that (contrary to the impressions formed by cousins who descended en masse on Ickworth[2]), there was not too much to envy in John's upbringing, so much of which seemed confined to the nursery. 'Everything happened there. The television was there; all the meals were served there. He was completely abandoned, had nobody else to play with. We were the only people who were ever there. Of course, we didn't think about it at the time – Edward and I were the youngest of seven – but I remember my mother saying, "Well, he's a very lonely little boy: he hasn't got any brothers or sisters".'

Another of John's cousins, Catherine Rossdale,[3] retains the same impression, remembering him being 'kept away from people, up in the top nursery'. The nursery was recognizably the Ickworth of Frederick, the 'Old Marquess', 'a dingy, very Edwardian environment', in the words of a friend from adolescence. 'One would have expected to find a nursery maid coming round the corner smelling of carbolic soap.' Another friend, an exact contemporary of John, remembers 'one huge corridor running from one end [of the fourth floor] to the other', all of it layered with blue lino. 'It was extraordinary.'

It was, though, less the style or the fabric of the nursery that struck Selina Hastings during her summer at Ickworth in the mid 1960s (see Part Two, 'Victor', p.121) than John's relationship with his father. 'The situation was extremely pathetic. The nursery was on the top floor: it was me and nanny with the new baby, Nicholas, and John. Victor was impossible… so stiff and unbending. He didn't seem to talk to John at all.' Catherine Rossdale agrees, characterizing Victor as 'very peculiar, really cold to John', whom, as far as she could tell, he steadfastly ignored. In these circumstances, the nursery became both cell and sanctuary, as Maria Rawlinson (née Garton) remembers. 'Even when he was older, the one thing he used to do was to go upstairs to where the old nursery had been. He was devoted to [it] in one way, but I think it conjured up all sorts of… I feel like crying, thinking about it.'

They had met as children in the early 1960s, when their parents holidayed in Marbella.[4] John was about nine; Maria two years older. A very small child – Nicholas – completed the party. Juliet alone offered hope that the gulf between father and elder son might be bridged. 'Juliet was divine,' says Maria Rawlinson. Everyone agrees. She was 'tremendously kind to John', remembers Kay Fisher and 'wonderful with him', according to Carol Havers. A Suffolk friend of John recalls that Juliet was 'the closest thing that he ever had to a mother. If somebody ever cared about him, it was Juliet… the only person to take his side, to tell Victor, "No, you can't treat him like that". John was always much more at ease with her around.'

The alliance between new wife and stepson had been dignified two years after Juliet's wedding (at which John had been a page) when she arranged to have his portrait painted, in secret, as a surprise for Victor. The seven-year-old Lord Jermyn[5] was dressed in blue cloak, white socks and silver-buckled shoes. Lessons in the nursery dispelled any lingering doubt about his social eminence, as Selina Hastings discovered during her summer at Ickworth three or four years later. Bicycling through the park, she and John passed a gardener who looked up and said good morning. 'John stopped and said, "Do you know who I am? I'm Lord Jermyn".' She asked him why he felt the question had been necessary. 'He said: "The last governess[6] told me to".'

Armoured by his confidence in the hereditary principle, John was considered ready for his father's old prep school, Heatherdown, an establishment at which titles (amongst the boys, not the staff) were unexceptional. To Rhidian Llewellyn, two years his junior (and merely a baronet's nephew) he appeared 'an extraordinary person. I was rather intimidated by him; he was just so… languid… didn't really talk to anybody whom he didn't really believe worth talking to.' Llewellyn's contemporary, Harry Wyndham, Lord Egremont's younger son, was not intimidated but dismayed by John's vulgarity which jarred with the prevalent mood of sub-fusc patrician restraint. 'He was always being given silver hairbrushes and things like that, [although] it was not an era when displays of wealth and ostentation were well thought of.' A rather crude compensatory mechanism appeared to be in place. 'I think his parents would say, "We'll take you out on a Sunday", and they wouldn't turn up; then a big car would turn up full of toys for him. If I had been asked who was going to go wrong – or get into hot water – in adult life, his would have been the first name that would have sprung to mind.' He adds that James Edwards, Heatherdown's headmaster,[7] who administered corrective treatment with a clothes brush, spoke sympathetically of John, 'saying that he felt sorry for him because he had come from a world which had rather a skewed view of reality. He was certainly sensitive to his situation.'

One of John's masters had fewer anxieties, remembering him as 'an exceptionally nice boy, diffident, hard-working, though not particularly scholarly… [who] went through the school without drama and without any particular distinction… on general good terms with those around him, [and whose] industry took the character of one anxious to please.' Juliet's significance was inescapable. 'I am sure she meant a great deal to him,' the former master adds, describing her as John's 'chief link between school and home'.

There were, however, limits to her powers of salvage back at Ickworth. 'She was very nice to John. She used to take him for rides in her E-Type Jaguar and take him to the stud, to see the horses,' remembers Selina Hastings, 'but she was terribly taken up with Nicholas.' Besides, Juliet spent weekdays in London with Victor. '[They] came down on Friday night in this incredible, chauffeur-driven Rolls-Royce, with the gold leopard on the bonnet and the coat of arms on the front door, and were driven back to Chapel Street on Sunday evening.' In their absence, John remained in the nursery at Ickworth, with his three-year-old brother Nicholas and Nicholas's nanny. 'All nanny's attention was for Nicholas. [John] was a pathetically lonely and unhappy little boy. He never mentioned any [friends from Heatherdown].'

He had lost touch with the Wodehouses, who attended a local prep school; in as far as he replaced them, he did so with girls, Juliet remembering one called Margaret, who had an American mother and stayed at Ickworth 'at least twice'. Selina Hastings devised diversions, like taking him into Bury St Edmunds in her Mini to buy catfish for his aquarium. 'I have a feeling I paid for them: I never remember John having any money at all.' But loneliness had not crushed his spirit. On Sundays, in the hours before the Rolls's departure, he invariably got to work on its bodywork. 'He used to put stickers [on it]: "This car must be constipated – it hasn't passed a thing all day"… "Drive quietly, driver asleep", which they never noticed. I didn't stop him because I thought it was quite funny.'

By then, John knew that he had an ally. 'One of my jobs was to take him down the stairs at eleven o'clock in the morning, and hear his piano practice. The first time I suggested it, he did it very reluctantly, but the second day he said he wasn't going to. I said, "You must". He said, "All right, make me".' The act of self-assertion was well-judged: Selina Hastings could scarcely force him to play nor, as John had accurately gauged, did she have the appetite for inflicting physical punishment or reporting him to Victor. 'I felt terribly sorry for him. We had to have a little pact about it.' There were further little pacts, hatched when she and John headed to Italy, ten days before Victor and Juliet. 'I was supposed to interest him in Italian culture and speaking Italian.' It became apparent that lessons, both cultural and linguistic, were 'a non-starter'.

Instead, they played endlessly on the mini-golf course at their hotel, the Milano Marittima, near Rimini. 'All I could teach him in Italian was the word for ice-cream. He wasn't faintly interested in anything else. I read sexy bits out of James Bond novels, which was all he really [liked]. He didn't want to read himself.' John was making an important discovery: rather than learning to amuse himself, he could, if he applied pressure correctly, persuade others to amuse him instead. The precocious antipathy to effort would prove lifelong.

Matters improved with the arrival of Lois Leroux, wife of the head of the Tate Gallery, and her daughter Ariane, then ten or eleven years old, another of John's childhood allies. '[Mrs Leroux] was terribly nice, and so was her little girl. We had quite a jolly time as a result.' The Bristols then joined the party, in 'an enormous canary yellow Mercedes'. 'They were very nice to me, but we did the sort of things that would make the heart of a ten-year-old boy sink: we'd go into Ravenna and look at the mosaics.' By the end of the summer, Selina Hastings sensed that John had probably come to adore her. 'It was', she remembers, 'terrible when I left.'

* * *

'I think you brought him up rather well.' Pauline's comment to Juliet was premature: John had plenty of growing up still to do, besides which, as one of his closest friends during late adolescence explains, 'he wasn't really brought up by anybody – staff excepted; he was brought up alone, and, for a lot of the time, he brought himself up'. Pauline was being tactful. Accompanied by her husband Teddy Lambton, she had joined the Bristols at Harrow for John's confirmation.[8] She had had little to do with her son since leaving Victor in 1959. 'It was a tricky situation,' remembers another confirmation guest. 'They made the best of it.'

Pauline's absence from John's life was, in part, proof of how completely Victor had trampled over her during their divorce, with its ruling that their son should live at Ickworth, thereby sparing him from the malign, adulterous influences of Newmarket. It was also, to an extent, a consequence of the symmetry in Victor and Pauline's new lives: Pauline and Teddy Lambton, like Victor and Juliet, had had a son (theirs, christened George, being born in March 1962, three months after Nicholas). John rarely stayed with the Lambtons at Mesnil Warren, their Newmarket house, but when he did he learned of a world less gilded than Ickworth – the saying at Mesnil Warren was, 'we didn't have enough money for the dog meat' – but also less constrictive. 'I had to muck out my own pony stable box and clean my own boots,' John remembered many years later. 'My mother's husband was a wonderful stepfather to me... he used to take me hunting.'

George Lambton's memories of his half-brother are 'pretty sketchy' for the first fifteen years of his own life, although he remembers being taken for rides on the back of John's motorbike, 'always at high speed', during the school holidays. He also remembers one Christmas holiday when John joined the Lambtons in Ireland. That was all. Yet it need not have been: Newmarket was just twelve miles from Ickworth.

Pauline's exile from John's life was very largely self-imposed. Later, she acknowledged this rather more explicitly than she had on confirmation day at Harrow. 'She felt remorse about running away,' remembers one of John's friends who frequently joined mother and son for Sunday lunch when John was in early adulthood, as well as holidaying with them – and George – when

Pauline talked candidly about the past. 'She didn't really want [John] because he got under her feet, her new marriage, her new child, George. Pauline and Teddy really were so happy together: such a great couple... That was a real love match. You always think that the mother will want to look after a little boy. But she just wasn't interested; just didn't care.'

Selina Hastings had noticed that John never mentioned his mother during the summer she spent at Ickworth. It was a silence which continued through most of his schooldays. Pauline's absence implicitly condoned whatever role Victor chose to play. He resolved to keep John trapped at arm's length, sparing himself the need for effort or intimacy yet allowing him to exert control which his elder son was, at that stage, powerless to resist. Victor's appearances at Heatherdown had been rare, possibly limited to attendance at a solitary sports day (the sighting of the Marquess of Bristol had been considered of sufficient significance for one master to draw it to others' attention). John was not completely ignored, however. 'Towards the end of his time [at Heatherdown],' recalls a retired master, 'he was deflected from Eton to Harrow, on account, I believe, of his father's connection with the former.' At other schools, and in other circumstances, the switch might have seemed almost incidental, but at Heatherdown – and given Victor's past – it sounded a fanfare. Although one or two boys headed to Harrow, 'more or less everybody went to Eton, almost exclusively via Common Entrance,' remembers Rhidian Llewellyn. 'Scholarships were considered a bit... no one needed the money, after all.'

John approached the Common Entrance exam studiously, although Harrow's pass-mark was set modestly at 50 per cent. He arrived there in January 1968, aware that the path ahead might be obscured by his father's shadow. It had been left to Juliet to tell him of Victor's imprisonment, which she did before his first term. His friends were gradually making the same discovery. Randle Siddeley, whose parents, Lord and Lady Kenilworth, lived in Suffolk and had befriended Victor and Juliet, was intrigued by what he heard. 'He did the Cartier robbery, didn't he? It was gossip that went around.' Maria Rawlinson was similarly enthralled. 'I think Daddy did always mention something rather dreadful, something about Park Lane and the last man to have the cat o' nine tails; it was really rather fascinating.' The fascination was shared by John's Harrovian contemporaries, although, according to Stewart Johnston, who had the neighbouring room for much of their time at school, they did not probe as woundingly as might have been expected. 'We all knew the stories about his father – had been in jail, one of the last people to be flogged and all that – but none of us teased him about it. Which was a rarity.'

If John felt any anxiety about his father's reputation, he did not betray it. Heatherdown had helped inculcate the oldest of prep school lessons: the capacity to disguise feeling.

His housemaster for his first two terms was Charles Lillingston,[9] an Old Etonian member of White's, a gifted teacher of history – and 'an extraordinary misogynist', as well as 'a crashing snob'. Harrow presented him with a glut of opportunity, the school's intake being more variegated, socially and intellectually, than Eton's: a sprinkling of aristocrats; a number of boys from Harrow families – the Peels and the Wheens – who had been continuously associated with the school for generations; and rather more whose parents had made their way in trade, amongst them one, a year older than John, called Thatcher,[10] a gifted rackets player (although, in November 1968, causing the school chronicle, *The Harrovian*, to lament his 'unforced errors'). Lillingston reputedly contrived a system to ensure that the first of these tribes flowed disproportionately and gratifyingly towards his house, Druries. 'Boys who had failed Common Entrance to Eton,' says a former member of the house, 'simply came and sat the exam in Charlie Lillingston's office.' Sensitive invigilation ensured appropriate results. The most recent and authoritative history of Harrow makes no mention of this special service, but its author does describe Lillingston as a 'devious Machiavel'.

Initially, John made little impression. 'He wasn't sporty; he wasn't that bright,' explains Tommy Watson,[11] another boy in Druries, who, like John, lived in East Anglia and invariably travelled back to school with him, chauffeur-driven from Ickworth – a display which caused less unease at Harrow than at Heatherdown, reminding John that his destiny was determined by his status, not as a convict's son, but as Earl Jermyn, elder son and heir of the 6th Marquess of Bristol. 'He was very, very aware of who he was,' remembers Peter Henderson,[12] who arrived in Druries a little later. John chose his friends accordingly, two of his closest allies being Teddy Beckett and Robin Cayzer, elder sons of Lords Grimthorpe and Rotherwick respectively.

Their headmaster was Dr Robert James, an elfin Welshman, a freemason, 'a manager and a manipulator', who accepted that 'boys were interested in sex, drink, and smoking ("one cannot really expel boys for that")', and did not see it as his business to unearth obscured talent, preferring to operate a system of 'selective laissez-faire... disowning responsibility for his own or the school's failings or errors, as if he were merely an observer of the scene not its choreographer'. An extraordinary variation in academic performance resulted. Scholars and other 'precocious intellectuals' took O levels after one or two years, were thereafter 'tested and extended to reach a level of interest and achievement often far beyond the requirements of A level', and ensured that the school's Oxbridge results were better than Winchester's. Most of the rest, however, John amongst them, 'were allowed to wallow in an academic sump'. James's policy, although 'hardly... in the best interest of all his pupils', presented 'the right image of confident unity whatever the reality'.

The world beyond Harrow began to intrude. In John's second year, Lindsay Anderson, whose allegorical film *If...* was thought by many to have done irreparable damage to the public school system, was invited to give a talk in Speech Room (he accepted); a few months later, a nun, Sister Patricia, gave a sermon about drug addiction in Sunday Chapel. Heroin, she warned, was 'the most dangerous'. *The Harrovian* approved of her efforts, albeit with a world-weariness which would have been incomprehensible in the 1950s. 'Few of us have not heard talks given about the effects of drugs,' it reported, 'and this might have detracted from the impact of Sister Patricia's address... However, she did manage to put over fairly effectively to a thoroughly complacent audience the horror, the wretchedness, the misery, the futility and the stupidity of drug addiction.'

Lillingston faced down emerging challenges in conventionally abrasive manner; his successor, John Leaf, opted for liberalism. 'He was the first housemaster on the Hill to say, "OK, I'm not going to beat anyone",' remembers Stewart Johnston. 'That was fine by us but it meant that discipline completely fell to bits.' The change in tone was emphasized when Dr James was succeeded by Michael Hoban, a scholarly, private man of great affability, who lacked the requisite ruthlessness and guile to impose himself as head-master. Piers de Laszlo, an acquaintance of John, though two or three years younger than him, remembers a carefree era during which boys pursued the three interests identified by Dr James, as well as indulging in displays of high camp: de Laszlo and another member of the school swimming team refused, for example, to dive into the pool at Eton, explaining that they did not want to get their hair wet.

John attempted nothing more strenuous than photography, with the result that he successfully developed the soft, sybaritic look – that of an over-larded Regency buck, 'too chubby to be good-looking', remembers one female friend – which lingered until he was over thirty. He took great interest in his hair, variously remembered as 'almost permed' and 'very, very distinct: certainly not done by any barber near Harrow on the Hill', for which he was 'mercilessly teased' and which earned him the epithet 'Poof Jermyn' from some of the younger members of the house.

To Peter Henderson, he appeared to be impeccably dressed, and his room extraordinarily sophisticated, every single wall being clad in silver foil. 'Very cool. He had this great spool-to-spool tape recorder, [part of] a fantastic stereo system. There's still one track… whenever I hear it, it reminds me of Jermyn in the Seventies: "No more speed, I'm almost there. I've been driving all night, my hands hot on the wheel". I always remember hearing it on John Jermyn's machine.'

The enthusiasm for gadgetry, and the desire to evolve a definite sartorial style, would later verge on obsession, but at Harrow both appeared to evolve gradually, almost subliminally. His progress in the classroom was notable only for a decision to take an A level in Business Studies, still something of a novelty at the time. Almost nowhere did John give an inkling of the pyrotechnics ahead. His appetite for transgression appeared, instead, to be confined comfortably within familiar boundaries. Tommy Watson remembers that several of the young gentlemen of Druries enjoyed Sobranie cigarettes and marijuana; he is confident that John was one of their number (he was, he later acknowledged). Peter Henderson found John an amiable character – 'a kind man, actually' – though he enters one caveat. 'There was a boy called Collins in his year, who had a younger brother. [Their] father had obviously scrimped and saved and struggled to get these children to school, and Jermyn – amongst others, but I can sort of hear John [repeatedly saying to] this poor boy… "You ghastly little man". If there was something that was not very attractive, that was [it]. But he was born into this extraordinary world.'

Few from Harrow glimpsed that extraordinary world. One who did remembers its ambiguities: Ickworth's stage-set grandeur in morning room, drawing room and dining room, and John's continued dismal exile on the nursery floor. It is the grandeur that lingers in the memory of Tommy Watson, whose father dropped him there at the beginning of each term, prior to the onward journey to Harrow: 'a big house, shooting with two guns… I was at that age when you are very impressed'. Randle Siddeley, a frequent visitor from the age of fifteen onwards, often in the company of his parents, was similarly awed. 'Everything was so grand, unbelievably grand. The parties were lavish, glamorous, full of fun people. Must have been a footman standing behind every chair.' Young Randle noticed that Somerset de Chair, a guest who was not always accompanied by his wife, appeared to get on extremely well with Juliet. At other times, Juliet's place would be taken by a marvellous woman – all bust and smiles – called Sanchia. Even Sanchia, though, could never completely dislodge attention from Victor. A melange of menace, style and disreputability imbued him with glamour. 'He was the closest we ever got to meeting a convict,' remembers Randle Siddeley. 'We all thought he was rather cool: always immaculately dressed – suit, tie, the tie always with that bit of a bulge. When he barked, everybody ran for cover: we all hid. John was petrified of him.' The adolescent Randle was caught taking pot-shots at rabbits on the Ickworth lawn early on a Sunday morning. A quiet word of admonition was not in Victor's range. '"DON'T YOU REALIZE YOU CAN'T GO KILLING THINGS ON A SUNDAY?" I thought, "I know now". I was petrified of Victor too.'

No longer ignored by his father, as he had been in childhood, John now fulfilled an unenviable role: one part protégé, four parts whipping boy. It made for a distressing spectacle. 'John could never do anything right. Victor was forever castigating him, always coming down on him from a great height, just persecuting him.' It was especially rewarding, Victor found, to have a scapegoat for the deficiencies of guests, old or young. When John acquired what would be the first in a useful collection of motorbikes, he allowed Randle to take it across the park. His friend roared off, hit 'some straw – there was an [equestrian] event taking place', felt the bike go from under him and was 'cut to ribbons', permanently scarring himself beneath his right eye. Victor blazed away at John. 'Although John was nowhere near the scene, it was all his fault for letting me go on the motorbike – he shouldn't have let me.'

On that occasion John was berated in private; more often, laceration was publicly administered, as it was when, late on a weekend morning, Lord Kenilworth suggested that John should join him and Randle for an inspection of the Earl-Bishop's Obelisk, erected in a field on the southern boundary of the Park, about a mile from the house. The trip, Kenilworth decided, should be undertaken in his Bentley. 'Stupid: of course, it got stuck – and this was before lunch,' his son remembers. After a few futile attempts at extraction, the Kenilworth expedition abandoned the Bentley and returned on foot – too late for Victor's pre-prandial drinks, too late for the start of lunch. Randle Siddeley remembers 'the bollocking of a lifetime' being delivered to John as the rest of the dining room squirmed in silence. 'Victor just humiliated John in front of everybody. Cruelty personified.'

The cultivated hedonism of Victor's Ickworth – its hothouse warmth, lavish cellar, liveried staff – made the toxicity of each eruption seem more disturbing: a taste of the sewer corrupting the claret. 'The only unhappy part of the house was the combination of John and Victor,' remembers Randle Siddeley. Yet it was this combination which was yoked together, without fail, in Victor's study for an hour each weekend.[13] 'It was an extraordinary thing. John would be called in, either on a Friday or a Saturday, and would have to sit there for one hour and be lectured, and be given letters to read that Victor had written to various people, saying, "This is how we deal with such and such".'

John unearthed allies during lulls between battle and lectures. By his late teens, he was no longer shunned by Victor's friends, getting on well with Lord Kenilworth and with the Havers family, who were indebted to him one Easter weekend, when Philip, the elder of the two Havers boys, then aged about twenty, enjoyed rather too much liqueur on Saturday night, with predictable consequences. The following morning, Philip's younger brother Nigel 'rushed up to the nursery where poor John used to have to sleep, and said, "John, what are we going to do? This place is ruined, and we have to go to church".' John, who was about fifteen at the time, urged him not to worry. When the Havers, including a green-hued Philip, returned from church, the room was spotless, its transformation overseen (if not single-handedly effected) by John. 'He had stayed behind and checked it all,' remembers Carol Havers, '[so that] no one need ever know.'

Victor's elderly first cousin, Phyllis MacRae,[14] still taking an interest in family developments, also appreciated him. Randle Siddeley remembers that John would 'disappear to see her occasionally'; another friend, visiting Ickworth a year or two after John left school, noticed the pair's rapport when he and John chanced across Phyllis outside Horringer church. 'She said, "Oh, hello, John. How many parents have you got at the moment?"' It was not the sort of inquiry that John would have cared for a few years earlier when Juliet had left for good – an event he would often describe as one of the worst of his life. 'I think his world fell apart then,' says Randle Siddeley. '[She was] the barrier protecting him.'

Trips to visit Pauline in Newmarket, still comparatively rare until John was in mid-adolescence, became more attractive than ever. It was there that he befriended Jonny Ruane, whose parents lived in Ballybrack, the house next to Mesnil Warren. Ruane was being educated at Stonyhurst in Lancashire; his parents – 'a very glamorous mother and a much older father' – remained married to one another; he had no title, nor any expectation of inheriting one. He is variously remembered as 'a lovely, lovely man', and 'a really sweet, rather shy, crazy boy'. His alcoholism would become apparent only much later. By then he was John's best friend.[15]

The friendship sustained John following Juliet's departure, as did holiday alliances with Randle Siddeley and the girls John had known since child-hood: Maria Garton (later Rawlinson), Ariane Leroux and Gabrielle Coles, who became Nicholas's nanny when he was about eleven or twelve. At school

he was able to count on Teddy Beckett and Robin Cayzer. Less prominent –
but still in evidence – were Christopher Nevill, nephew of the Marquess of
Abergavenny; the Earl of Sunderland, who, on his grandfather's death in 1972,
became known by a different courtesy title, the Marquess of Blandford;[16]
and, for a while, a significantly older boy named Somerville, who left Harrow
nearly two years ahead of John.

Although, like Cayzer and Beckett, John had a reputation for generosity
('it was certainly popular to be John Jermyn's personal fag: you got tipped very
well'), he was not riotously rich at any stage during his time at Harrow, from
which Victor remained as aloof as he had been from Heatherdown. Jonny
Ruane noticed John's comparative impecuniosity during the holidays. 'The
joke was that Jonny's allowance was more than John's. John was kept on quite
a tight rein financially to begin with.' (Michael Chappell, who became John's
accountant soon after his eighteenth birthday, agrees with this assessment.)
Juliet never interceded, accepting that 'pocket money and allowances were
Victor's domain'. Distaste for his son might have inspired Victor's stringency,
although it seems plausible that it might have owed as much, if not more, to
a belated acknowledgement (never publicly voiced) that the tide of money
that had engulfed him at Eton had done him no good at all. Indeed, towards
the end of his life, he disclosed – to John Knight[17] – his regret that he had
not restricted John to a modest allowance for longer than he did.

The policy helped spur John into his first business venture, a discotheque.
'He did my eighteenth birthday,' remembers Stewart Johnston. 'Arrived with
all the kit, very big speakers and all the lights. He was quite good at it.'
Randle Siddeley, to whom John appeared rich enough, remembers the disco
(and a set of drums, installed in the nursery floor at Ickworth) but sensed that
John was as interested in being fashionable as in making money. If so, it
underscores what Stewart Johnston remembers about John in his final days
at Harrow: his apparent normality. 'Given the circumstances of his upbringing, he was straightforward, very normal, worked quite hard, was quite
bright.' It was much the same summary as delivered by John's housemaster,
John Leaf ('a thoroughly nice, well-mannered boy, not outstanding in any
way'). Leaf had, however, noticed one attribute that distinguished John from
his contemporaries: 'I have little doubt that he was a smoker... but, unlike
most boys, he was good at covering his tracks and was never caught.'

Unknown to Leaf, John broke other rules. Down below the Hill, in
Harrow town, next to the Underground station, he rented a lock-up garage.
It was here, during term-time, that he kept an Austin 1300 GT – a vivid
orange, a 'souped up Austin Sports', its windows tinted mafia-black. Back at

Ickworth, Randle Siddeley had become familiar with 'hell-raising trips' to the Lambtons in Newmarket ('lucky none of us had any nasty accidents'); Tommy Watson experienced these in Suffolk and at Harrow. 'I was terrified. I remember him missing the tailgate of a lorry by inches.'

It was a rare display of swagger. As those who were to meet him in the coming years would generally agree, he could never be mistaken for an Old Etonian, certainly not one of the 'successful Etonians [who had] learned the joys of privilege and practised natural authority without let or hindrance'. Harrow had not imbued him with impregnable confidence, nor had it stretched him athletically or intellectually. He would, ever after, seem more at ease with – and more stimulated by – sensory exploration than cognitive endeavour. Harrow had, though, both shaped him for and anticipated the role that he would develop in adulthood, a role which embraced the reputation for dodginess that Harrovians themselves enjoyed perpetuating, with the attendant suggestion that, 'for all their wealth, position, sophistication, and social style', they were, and knew they were, 'not quite "U".'

All the same, in the summer of 1972, he appeared an implausible candidate for disreputability, still less notoriety, just a sensible, level-headed if slightly effeminate young man: someone who had subconsciously heeded the conclusion of Sister Patricia's Sunday evening sermon four years earlier, with its quotation from Deuteronomy 30:19: 'I have set before you life and death, blessing and cursing: therefore choose life.'

* * *

It was a squeeze: three adult men in a Ferrari 308. Two of them shared the passenger seat, one sitting on the other's knee. It wasn't long until the screaming started. John had warmed up with vodka tonic ('he had about four'), knocked back in the American Bar at the Hotel de Paris, Monte Carlo. His companions, on the other hand, had still been sipping Perrier when he announced that they were off to dinner, their destination La Réserve, eight miles along the Basse Corniche at Beaulieu. It was doubtful that as prosaic an anaesthetic as alcohol could have negated the terror of the minutes that followed: a blur of blind corners and insane speed which could, at any moment, have ended in head-on collision and fatal immolation.

The man riding in slightly elevated position was soon noisily on the brink of hysteria. 'He was freaking,' remembers his fellow passenger, whose own silence was born not of contempt for the howls and whimpers being emitted above him, nor of lack of fear, but of bitterly won familiarity with John's driving. On this occasion, he concedes, things were worse for the man on top.

'It wasn't exactly a convertible, but it had a little section that came off. The top of the windscreen was about level with David's nose; he thought the top of his head was going to come off, like a boiled egg.'

David began yelling for mercy: the wrong tactic, as the man beneath him knew. 'I remember thinking, "Just shut up". The more David screamed, the more John would overtake coaches on corners – completely blind corners – on two wheels, just roaring, cackling with laughter.' They reached La Réserve alive. David, recalls his fellow passenger, was howling in shock and fury. 'I did completely agree: if you want to risk your life [that's fine], but don't risk your friends or the people in the car coming in the opposite direction. But that's the way John was: always pushing it, always pushing it.'

By then, the late 1970s, none of his intimates doubted it. A friend, who would share in a variety of John's boundary-breaking experiences, recalls the triumphal phrase habitually uttered after each return to Ickworth: 'I did the last stretch[18] at 120mph.' Speeding, particularly when taken to potentially suicidal or homicidal extremes, was a cause for satisfaction, a reminder to himself, and a demonstration to others, that rules were for little people.

It was a philosophy of which his solicitor, Roger Lane-Smith, would periodically be reminded, generally via urgent telephone call. 'He was always in trouble. He rang me up one day and said, "I've just had an incident with the Ferrari".' Elaboration was sought.

'Oh, I was coming up the M11 and there was a lot of traffic in front of me, and I got very, very irritated with all this traffic. I floored the accelerator, I just overtook everything, must have got up to 140 mph, then the police stopped me.'

Lane-Smith had heard worse. 'That's bad, John, but you know...'

'I was on the hard shoulder...'

Negotiating gridlocked traffic via the hard shoulder at twice the legal speed limit had obvious appeal, but even this dimmed in comparison with the special challenge that unfailingly greeted John at Ickworth, once the cattle grid had been crossed and the National Trust's 20 mph signs been confronted. A friend recalls the experience: 'The drive at Ickworth – 100 mph – with me in the car, screaming. In a Ferrari. This was when there were National Trust people wandering around – visitors – not at 4 a.m. People with dogs and children. He was completely bonkers a lot of the time. The more you screamed, the more he liked it. I learned very quickly not to say anything, rather like Cary Grant in *To Catch a Thief*, when Grace Kelly is driving him. That's what I used to do – grip my legs, grit my teeth and stare straight ahead.'

John Knight witnessed the accelerating pace of Ickworth life. Invited to dinner one night, he was still there – 'in the little Chinese Room, four or five of us' – when one of John's friends arrived from London. 'This chap said the police had been after him because he'd been doing 100 mph on what was then the A45. I remembered him as the sort of individual who'd be no good to John.'

John's friends have no truck with milksop criticism of that sort: they speak ill of each other with fluency and vehemence and some imagination: '—, a really vicious young queen, now a really vicious old queen...'; 'My understanding is that — possibly has unnatural affections for younger men – as did — ...we're talking considerably younger'; '— has been married for some years to a fellow junkie'; '— is a real operator: if you or I tried to do any of those things, we'd be taken off to prison'; 'You've got the social maggots...[and others] feeding him drugs'; 'That ghastly — ...a crook. He should never be allowed to work again'; '— was the biggest crook of the lot; he robbed John blind'.

They endured one another, explains Imogen von Halle, because John 'had a stately to offer and the rest of us didn't', (and those who had a stately coming to them still had parents to contend with). John insisted on standards commensurate with his status: guests' cars were washed during the course of the weekend, just as they had been in Victor's day. There was, adds Imogen von Halle, 'brilliant, wonderful food and wines and drinks, equivalent to those you'd find at a good restaurant'. Her brother, Tim von Halle, who moved into John's circle a year or two later, remembers him as a considerate, almost consummate, host. 'He was very good. He'd say, "In the morning, do you want to go riding? I won't be up but, if you do, go: I'll make sure the horses are there."' Riding was not always strictly equestrian: there were motorbikes for those who wanted them, or a chance to try out a car, possibly a Ferrari, or the green Rolls, the blue Bentley, the green Aston, the Lamborghini, the GMC ('known as a Jimmy. Had a lot of horse power. He used to leave the engine on; it would sit there, throbbing'), all of them bearing the Hervey coat of arms, a snow leopard leaping from each bonnet. The shoot was run with the same precision and brio as in the Victor era (John led the way, shooting peacocks), whilst there was always the chance to go racing at Newmarket – given added zest during the early 1980s, thanks to the success of John's horse Saxon Breck – arriving at the meeting by helicopter, quite possibly after taking what one of his closest allies categorizes as 'nasal refreshment'. By then, Ickworth's reputation was firmly established: it was, in the words of John's first business partner, Peter Geiger, 'an adult Disney'.

The advance from Austin to Aston had not been instantaneous; still less had it coincided with John's departure from Harrow in July 1972. Those meeting him that summer, as Imogen von Halle did, were far from overawed. She found his opinions conventional, his character unassuming, even nervous, as though he were slightly unsure of himself: 'trying to make an impression,' yet 'always aware of who he was'. He did not have to tell her: her father had known Victor and Pauline years earlier: Imogen and John had 'apparently been to the same children's parties in London'. The guests from those parties now re-coalesced as a group of eighteen-year-olds – John and Imogen, Jasper Guinness and Ned Cavendish, Christopher Nevill and Clarissa Baring, always (at that time) known as 'Crissa' – none of whom was bewitched by the Herveys' reputation or John's hereditary status.[19] 'He was just one of the crowd: not the leader of the gang, merely a member of it, pretty desperate to fit in. We knew he had more money than us, and he always seemed a bit grander, more pompous, but we took it as a bit of a joke.'

Peter Geiger viewed John from a different perspective. Four years his senior, a Cambridge graduate who had attended neither Eton nor Harrow, who lived neither in Chelsea nor Belgravia nor the country, Geiger[20] was, by 1973, a trainee at Arbuthnot Latham, a merchant bank whose unit trust division was run by a voluble, 6'4" baronet, Sir Hugh Trevor Dawson. Returning from lunch one day, Geiger noticed two young men enter the building: one he recognized as William Arbuthnot;[21] the other – 'very gawky, in a Seventies suit, which looked rather awful' – was, until then, unknown to him.

Though disinclined to forgive aesthetic dissonance, Geiger was prepared to make an exception where John was concerned; indeed, quite quickly he adopted a tutorial role. 'The thing about John,' he remembers, 'was that he was such a blank canvas. I think I was interesting because I had a Bentley, a 1955 S1 Fastback Continental. And I was interested in knowing someone who was an Earl. John had a title, an ill-fitting suit and, I think, a Triumph GT; I felt he should have a Bentley. He asked me to help him find one.'

It seemed likely that John could afford it. While he was still at Harrow, the *Daily Telegraph* had reported that he was to become life tenant of 'between 7,000 and 8,000 of some of the richest acres in East Anglia', valued at £4 million (£85 million today). 'Lord Jermyn's life tenancy involves about 55 per cent of the 15,000 acres of the Bristol estates, 10,000 acres of which are in Lincolnshire and the rest in Essex and Suffolk,' explained the *Telegraph*, before conceding that 'the actual income Lord Jermyn will receive has still to be worked out and will probably be limited until he is at least 21'. Although Peter Geiger successfully oversaw the purchase of John's first Bentley (a 1956

S1 Continental, two-door coupé), he became aware that John's finances were 'on a very short rein', one which could be loosened only via supplication to Victor and Trevor Dawson.

John's first London residence was, accordingly, unremarkable: a flat in the municipal mid-1930s pink brick of Dolphin Square, in Pimlico. 'It was utilitarian and non-palatial,' says Peter Geiger, who remembers a white plastic framed mirror and white Lucite drinks trays. Advancement to South Kensington – 18 Brompton Square – was achieved courtesy of Victor, who bought it and allotted his son the basement flat (the rest of the house being let on a fixed lease). Members of 'the gang' tended to congregate there before going out to dinner, despite misgivings about what one habitué remembers as its 'very hideous Seventies décor'. 'It was outfitted like an arab's place,' remembers Imogen von Halle: 'pictures which were bound to have come from Ickworth, gold taps in the bathroom. We thought it was terribly funny.' It was here that John would learn to shrug off inhibition.

Initially, however, he appeared content to mimic the rich middle-aged, his choice of restaurants, for instance, being 'more suited to somebody twenty years older, proper, old-fashioned restaurants [with] chandeliers, white damask tablecloths. He would spend a lot of money in the Mirabelle,' remembers Imogen von Halle. 'We were just eighteen-, nineteen-year-olds, giggling and drinking too much, always expensive wines.' John was generous but within sensible limits, 'not wanting to be regarded as the chequebook.'

The same measured courtesy was evident when at the wheel of the Bentley. Imogen von Halle remembers him 'driving extremely well, not fast'. A taste for developing his own language – 'franchement' was a favoured neologism – appeared the only suggestion of non-convention. In the summer of 1973, Victor and Trevor Dawson decided that John – no more than nominally employed by Arbuthnot Latham – was to attend 'some sort of crammer' in Switzerland. Unfortunately, the course chosen, under the aegis of Neuchâtel University, lasted no more than three or four months, conferred no diploma, still less degree, although it would, in future, encourage John to bracket Neuchâtel with Harrow in *Who's Who* and *Debrett's* as a place of his education. Peter Geiger joined him for his last fortnight there, driving out in his Fastback Bentley. He introduced John to someone Geiger *père* had been in business with. John was appreciative. Hesitant 'to accept Victor as his only role model' (in Geiger's opinion), he increasingly sought advice from 'the boy brought up in the house bought with "the perfume money"'. Indeed, it was Geiger's different perspective and circumstances, he believes, as well as his capacity for candour, that John found reassuring: so much so that, by 1975 he had appointed Geiger as sole executor of his will. 'Switzerland was the best time we had together,' says Geiger. 'John was very sweet, a very good friend... until he grew up.'

It is the sweetness that Maria Rawlinson remembers. Their friendship had deepened since childhood, to the extent that John was known and welcomed by various generations of her family. 'He was a fantastically kind person with my great-aunt and my grandmother. At drinks parties, he could have talked to anybody but he sat down, right down on his knees, and talked to them. I think he liked the fact that they were very warm to him. That's really how I remember my John. I always call him "my John". My great-aunt was very old when she died, and my grandmother was ninety-seven when she did; there weren't a lot of people to come to their funerals, but he came. My John took that trouble and care; I will never forget that, never.'

A contemporary from Harrow was treated with similar sensitivity. '[John] was the only school friend who wrote to me on the death of my mother,' he remembers. Their paths had by then already begun to diverge. On his last visit to Ickworth, John's old ally was dismayed by the palpable sense of conflict between father and son, even though it was less openly expressed than it had been a year or so earlier, perhaps because of the adjustment in John's status: from shunned schoolboy to publicly acknowledged heir. 'It was almost like two titans preparing for a sparring match. It was a great sadness to see [them] at such odds.' This was not, he believes, what John had sought. 'He was, in many ways, a kind, loving person who, presumably, found it very difficult when he couldn't engage with his father. I suppose that lack of engagement fuelled the rage.'

Guy Sainty, who by the early 1970s was regularly offering Victor advice about paintings, witnessed not rage but despair. Staying at Ickworth for a weekend, he and John were alone in the drawing room after dinner one night when John began to talk about himself and his father and mother, whilst simultaneously beseeching Sainty for advice. 'He suddenly burst into tears. I remember feeling desperately sorry for him.' They remained in the drawing room for twenty minutes, possibly half an hour. 'I can only remember the tenor of the conversation. Whatever it was [that John wanted to say], he was desperately mixed up and desperately wanted his father's love. I think his father did love John – and had no idea how to show it. [John] definitely needed help.'

He knew little of the detail of his father's life, or of his immediate family, his knowledge increasing only as his paternal line safely receded into the eighteenth and late seventeenth centuries. In the mid-1970s, he was still scurrying into position when Victor sat shirtless in his study, hoping to see if his father's back bore the scars of a flogging. Even though, by the early 1990s, he had learned the correct details of his father's crime and punishment, he appears to have known little more than that, and was certainly ignorant of the Cochranes' recent past. None of his intimates heard him mention Gwrych or his great-grandmother's tendresse for the Archbishop of Wales, still less John Rowley's bestial groans and brown-stumped teeth, or George Rowley's requirements for alcohol and prostitutes. These were subjects which few fathers would necessarily have relished discussing, even within the family, but Victor utterly denied their existence, filling the vacuum with a myth which his eldest son unquestioningly accepted. 'He was a highly successful businessman,' John said during an interview in 1991. 'Do you know he made his first million by the time he was 21?... I adored him because I admired his financial acumen.' Unaware that his father's biggest coup had been the defrauding of the Finnish Ministry of Defence, with a bonus via similar success with Finnish State Railways, John held him in awe, as well as fear, seeing him as a man of extraordinary exploits[22] and intimidating accomplishment. The false premise became the foundation for his future.

Yet catastrophic though that would prove, it could not explain the speed with which his relationship with his father now disintegrated completely. Peter Geiger detected the change of mood. 'To begin with, Victor was quite into me: he felt that I was quite a sensible influence.' Gradually, however, it began to dawn on Victor that Geiger's tastes – and his son's – were less red-blooded than his own. 'Victor had a traditional attitude towards homosexuality. I don't know if he saw me as a poofter but I suspect that he didn't like the thought that his son had those proclivities.'

Disquieting though this was, it need not have been fatal, especially if John in due course were to marry and father an heir. Instead, it was Victor's new romantic entanglement – and John's reaction to it – that led to rupture. 'John always used to say that the three pivotal things in his life were his mother leaving when he was very little; then Juliet leaving; then his father marrying Yvonne,' remembers an intimate friend. The pain of Juliet's defection was initially eased by Sanchia's consoling presence. 'She had a great sense of humour. Whenever they were all in Italy or Spain together, she had this special language, so everything had an 'a' on the end of it: "Howa mucha isa...?" It used to make John howl with laughter. She was outstandingly sweet, charming, adorable, loyal, lovable.'

John refused to accept that Victor might prefer to make Yvonne Sutton his next wife. Later, when he could no longer deny his mistake, he and Jonny

Ruane interpreted events to their own satisfaction, if not everyone else's. 'Jonny always said of Yvonne that Victor chased her round the typing desk, and she said, "Not unless you marry me". That's how Jonny put it. [He] and John were absolutely vitriolic about her.' Peter Geiger heard the same allegation directly from John.

Friends inevitably tended to take his side. However, Maria Rawlinson met Yvonne and was enchanted ('she was very, very sweet to me'), whilst Peter Geiger, although not disputing that Victor's third marriage triggered the estrangement of father from son, doubts that this was Yvonne's intention[23]. 'She was genuinely concerned with [John's] welfare,' he says. On one occasion, he adds, when he and Yvonne were alone for a while in Chapel Street, she asked him to use his influence to persuade John to 'try harder to get on with his father'.

The slender chance that John might have been won over expired with news of the marriage. Always most comfortable when communicating with his son from afar, Victor reached him, by telegram,[24] in a bar in Marbella, where he was in the company of a friend called Mark Byers. 'It read: "Have married Yvonne. Love Father." John picked up a glass and threw it at the mirror above the bar. He liked gestures like that.' There would be no rapprochement. John's accountant, Michael Chappell, speaks of 'a huge rift… which just got wider and wider'; for Kay Fisher, John's relationship with Yvonne 'was the nightmare', an assessment with which Roger Lane-Smith agrees. 'There was tremendous bad blood there. Yvonne,' he adds, 'hated John.'

Her detestation was a price that John was happy to pay. Whereas Juliet had shielded him from Victor's attacks, Yvonne saw no need to intercede. Worse, says Randle Siddeley, if she ever did so, she unfailingly allied herself to Victor. 'With Yvonne, Victor could never do anything wrong: Victor was perfect. She always took his side… she was clearing the way for her future succession.' John decided that all-out counter-attack was the best response. His chosen weapon was one he shared with Victor: belief in superiority by birth, the creed inculcated in him since infancy. References to 'that secretary' were delivered with an Olympian sneer, although Yvonne's status was revised downwards in succeeding years, to 'the under-secretary' or 'Miss Crimplene'. Carol Havers heard a variation. '"That awful girl," he'd say, "bit her nails in the top floor".' Peter Geiger suggests that 'it was worse than that: John always went on about her father being an accountant from Cheam'.[25] He remembers John remarking, at an earlier time, that Victor 'could be married off to your mother'. (Mrs Geiger was unattached at the time.) Geiger was amused.

'Given the upper class's feelings about Jewish immigrants, this was saying something.' John's hostility to Yvonne, he realized, was inspired – in part, at least – by embarrassment.

If possible, John coated each contemptuous aside with inventive malice, most famously with his explanation as to why he had not attended Victor and Yvonne's wedding: 'I don't go to office parties'. Even more rewarding were those occasions which offered a chance for John to wound his prey in public, such as an evening when King Leka and, more importantly, his Australian wife, Queen Susan,[26] were at Ickworth. 'John was looking at Yvonne and Queen Susan. He just said: "Where did you two meet? In the typing pool?"'

Victor, the supreme social segregationist, was paralysed, his response ('You mustn't take any notice of my ridiculous son') unable to convey a fraction of his fury; nor could he ever do so, not without admitting that Yvonne was defined by qualities quite distinct from her rank at birth. He needed no further incentive to distance himself – and his bride – from his malevolent and ungrateful heir.

The conflict between John's desire to belittle Yvonne and his need for his father's affection was one which he was never to resolve. Instead, he found refuge and welcome at his mother's house in Newmarket, where Sunday lunch became a ritual, almost a rite, observed with unforced devotion, to the surprise of at least one close friend. 'David Lean had this expression that the iron door closed [on] ex-wives or people who had been in his life: that was it. He wouldn't even say *bonjour*. John's was an unforgiving nature very much like that, so it seems extraordinary that he had such a good relationship with Pauline later on in his life, forgiving her for abandoning him – it's really not too strong a word – when he was young.'

As it was, John's feelings went far beyond forgiveness. 'He was closest to his mother: a key figure,' remembers Tim von Halle. The relationship flourished with the blessing of John's stepfather. 'Teddy Lambton was terribly nice to him; he was a charming man.' John was delighted by his younger half-brother, George, too. 'He wanted family: it meant a huge amount to him to have that family [feeling].' Yet had it not been for an unusually intense bond with his mother, it seems likely that he would have remained aloof. Something in Pauline sparked their belated connection: a warmth that he had never experienced before, a trace of theatricality, an acceptance that rules could (and sometimes should) be broken; the fact, in the nebulous yet apt phrase of Paddy Ireland, one of John's friends in later life, that 'she was sort of the one who got it'.

Ireland remembers Pauline as 'very sweet'. Almost all John's friends do;

some adored her. Peter Geiger recalls her as 'typically Thirties, vampy, often in dark glasses: she drank, she was fun, very good hearted'. To another friend she was 'an absolutely incredible character: drunk, eccentric, outspoken, out-going, [someone who] stood no nonsense'. All were intrigued by her relationship with Victor. She indulged one or two of them with the occasional disclosure (the revolver fired into the ceiling at the Bag o' Nails, perhaps, or his bedroom performance, to which she gave mixed notices) or made a general observation on their marriage (perfectly satisfactory, she said, until Victor became Earl Jermyn and incurably pompous). Her own background was less thoroughly reviewed. Some knew that her marriage to Victor had not been her first; others variously convinced themselves that she had been a barmaid, or had met him in a pub, or was the daughter of an East End boxer.

The rumours smelled of the street. In the opinion of one of John's friends, there was little that could have delighted him more: 'He was Byronic in the sense that Byron hung around with boxers and street people. He loved low-life.' Minnie Winn, a friend a generation older, who met him towards the end of the 1970s, sensed that he was unusually protective of Pauline: 'It was as if he were amending a wrong, trying to prove a point.' She believes that this was an implied rebuke to Victor, a demonstration that, though Victor had lacked the decency to treat Pauline properly, John would do so instead.

Perhaps in part it was. It had, however, been Pauline, not Victor, who had tired of their marriage. John arguably offered a truer clue to the origins of his attitude in an interview in 1991. 'I don't give a damn about the aristocracy,' he said. 'As far as I'm concerned I have a title which makes me an aristocrat, but I don't consider myself to be upper class and therefore better than anyone else. There's not a great deal of blue about my blood.'

The declaration was not as disingenuous as it sounded: if John's paternal lineage was authentically aristocratic, most of his maternal forebears were of Leveller stock. This was not apparent from Pauline's manner or appearance. She might not have been, as one of John's friends puts it, 'out of the handkerchief drawer', but she spoke Belgravia English, had married successive aristocrats (preceded, admittedly, by Mr Ames) and was wholly at ease with the grandees of the Turf, whose appetites for horseflesh, alcohol and adventure she shared. Her father, Herbert Cockson Bolton, had been neither a pugilist nor an East Ender but was born amidst the wool mills of Elland, north Yorkshire, in 1871, the son of Francis and Isabel Bolton. Francis – John's great-grandfather – was an educated man who had taken holy orders; unlike his clerical Hervey counterparts, however, he came from Luton, was a graduate of London University (newly established for the benefit of non-conformists denied admission to Oxford and Cambridge), and had been ordained by the Congregationalists, in whose service he moved from chapel to chapel in the north of England, from Elland, for instance, to Lancaster, where he remained until his death in 1898, leaving £446 6d.

Herbert, the younger of his two sons (there was also a daughter), eschewed an ecclesiastical career in favour of life as a commercial traveller, successively lodging in Moss Side, then in Longstone, Derbyshire, and Manchester. By 1901, he had acquired a wife, Eveline, two children, Norman, then six, and Effie, three, and was living at 47 Waterside, Spring Banks, in Marple, a small Cheshire town then easily distinct from nearby Stockport. He had prospered, having established himself as a manufacturer and printer, a trade to which he devoted himself for the rest of his professional life. By the time Pauline was born, on 23 October 1923, he was managing director of a company with offices at 2 Pemberton Row, London EC4. The following year, his name was listed in the London telephone directory for the first time, his residence given as 3 The Avenue, Willesden, NW6, a very substantial Victorian house in London brick. There was nothing here to suggest that John had East End antecedents, the only real connection with London being supplied by Herbert's wife Eveline, who was born there. She, though, was not Pauline's mother.

On 5 November 1985, an eighty-six-year-old woman called Lucy Gilbert died in Newmarket. Her final residence had been 6 Exning Road, a street of modest Victorian terraced houses not far from the more grandiloquently named Howard de Walden Way and George Lambton Avenue. Few of John's intimates ever met her; his wife did, however: 'She was a Cockney; John loved that.' Technically, the description is inaccurate. Lucy had been born on 29 April 1899, not within the sound of Bow Bells but at 59 Kingswood Road, Clapham, the daughter of William Child, a journeyman hatter,[27] and his wife, also Lucy (née Cross).

The circumstances in which the younger Lucy first became acquainted with Herbert Bolton, a man twenty-nine years her senior – he was fifty-three, and she twenty-four, when Pauline was born – are not on public record. What is apparent is that Lucy and Herbert were not married, at least not to one another, either then or ever after. Despite this, Pauline laid claim to her father's surname when signing the register at her marriage to Victor: proba-bly an accurate indication of the part he had played in her upbringing, since someone had evidently paid for her to receive an expensive education. Her advance appears to have come at the cost of a rapport with her mother, at least in the latter's dotage. 'They didn't seem to be very close,' remembers John's ex-wife, who visited Lucy Gilbert at Exning Road two or three times. The same, she adds, could not be said of Lucy and John, whose adoration was mutual.

Denied the chance for grandmotherly indulgence during John's childhood – even if Victor and Pauline had not divorced, it is difficult to envisage that Victor would ever have allowed his first mother-in-law across the Ickworth cattle-grid – Lucy had a trove of family lore to offer him later, all of it thrillingly at odds with the claustrophobia of his nannied youth. Her own journey had taken her from Clapham to Kennington to Leyton (119 Capworth Street, where she had given birth to Pauline). If that lacked East End credentials, she could reassure the older of her two noble grandsons that her father, William Child, had been born in Bethnal Green, as had his brothers Waller, Albert and Sidney (their other siblings, Alice, Henry and Herbert, had emerged in Hackney). Perhaps no story, however, matched that of her mother, the elder Lucy, whose family, the Crosses, had been farm labourers from Bridgwater, Somerset. In service at thirteen,[28] the elder Lucy had migrated to the capital within a decade, becoming one of six servants retained by Joseph Becraft, a restaurateur, at his residence, 2 Bartholomew Close, City of London. In 1894, Lucy secured her freedom (or a version of it) with marriage to William Child.

How much of this John heard from his grandmother remains a matter for conjecture. It is, though, arguably instructive that, however abominably he could (and did) abuse restaurant waiters and hotel managers, he treated his own staff with an affection and generosity that bordered on love, and did so until the end of his life; conduct which was rewarded by their unfaltering loyalty. When Lucy died, he did not consign her remains to a Newmarket church or municipal cemetery. In the small enclosure surrounding the Ickworth church (not to be confused with the parish church of Horringer, at the entrance to the Park) a headstone bears the following inscription:

Lucy Elizabeth Gilbert
29th April 1899 – 5th November 1985
Grandmother of the Marquis of Bristol

It was the most public and durable proclamation of kinship that John could make: a declaration that Lucy – and, by implication, his mother – deserved the same recognition and respect as any other member of his family.

A decade earlier, however, John had defined himself as a Hervey as narrowly as his nanny or his father would have wished, which eased the task of heaping scorn on Yvonne, as well as conforming to what his friends expected of him. One of them noticed that, at the basement flat in Brompton Square, each bar of soap bore a small blue sticker emblazoned with the Hervey motto: 'Je n'oublierai jamais'. He noticed, too, that the doors of John's Bentley were badged 'with coronets and all the rest of it, like Victor's'.

Far from moving beyond his father's shadow, John appeared to have accepted it as a natural boundary much as he accepted the burden of early 1970s fashion. 'He wasn't devastatingly good-looking nor was he frightfully magnetic, sexual or anything like that,' remembers Imogen von Halle, 'so he took great care how he dressed.' His hair was long; his jeans (pressed) were teamed with Gucci loafers. 'He wore cravats sometimes,' adds Imogen von Halle, 'from Turnbull & Asser.' Another friend, meeting John in the mid-1970s, was taken aback by his lack of sophistication, evident in the fact that 'he had never been out of Europe' and his nerviness when flying ('but he soon got over that').

After-dinner entertainment was locked in the same safe section of the West End as restaurants and shirt-makers, the two favoured nightclubs being Tramp or Monkberries, both in Jermyn Street. In as far as John strayed from these havens, it was to Connoisseur, a basement gambling club off the Fulham Road, patronized by the gang two or three times a week. None of them, with the definite exception of Ned Cavendish, was an ardent gambler, but that didn't matter to John or anyone else. 'He liked it because we all went,' remembers Imogen von Halle. 'He liked being part of the scene.'

The need to belong was yoked to what seemed an acute appetite for convention, particularly at Ickworth. 'We changed for dinner, usually black tie,' adds Imogen von Halle. 'This was when we were eighteen, nineteen, twenty, twenty-one. It seems preposterous now; it was quite normal then.' Formality did not preclude relaxation, however. Indeed, it was at Ickworth that John seemed most at ease, fooling around in the billiards room, 'screaming with laughter, but in the right way. Nobody had an inkling of what was going to happen.'

Peter Geiger agrees. By the end of 1974, he been sacked from Arbuthnot Latham by Trevor Dawson (seven years before the Stock Exchange ordered Sir Trevor's suspension), largely, he thinks, because his doubts about Dawson's business ethics had become known to Victor. It was then that Geiger and John decided to go into business together. The promisingly named Investment Motoring Company (the wording was Victor's; he also gave decorative advice: 'white-and-gold is always best') specialized in the provision of beautiful, ideally classic cars, and had its showroom on the Fulham Road. The two founders provided its capital, although in John's case this effectively meant that Victor did, with the agreement of trustees, the most significant of whom happened to be Sir Hugh Trevor Dawson (who resisted any temptation to cause difficulties). John's enthusiasm was obvious, even to the police, who, a week before the company opened for business in January 1975, observed him removing 'No Parking' signs from the pavement and loading them into a car. He explained to Bow Street magistrates that he had done so to allow cars in and out of the showroom, but was fined £20. It was his first court appearance, but one which might easily have involved almost any of his friends. 'You did what suited you – and you were entitled to,' remembers Imogen von Halle. 'Nobody else was entitled, but you were. There was definitely a lot of that.' *Tatler* magazine covered the company's launch party, an exuberant moment encapsulated in Crissa Baring's scrawl in the guest book: 'I want all the cars – now.'

Peter Geiger was a restraining influence, then and afterwards. He usually arrived at the showroom at 10.15 a.m. (John a little later). They lunched at Pizza Express on the Fulham Road, taking it in turns to pay. Despite the modest scale of their new enterprise, John enjoyed the transition from stock-broker's dogsbody to motor trade proprietor. 'He liked having the business; he liked driving nice cars. He wanted a secretary; he needed a secretary,' says Geiger, adding that John was probably 'dyslexic, undiagnosed'. His administrative requirements were variously met by Paula Ruane (Jonny Ruane's sister-in-law), Camilla Birtwistle, and Mrs Mance, 'a lady of a certain age' from Maidenhead, who later moved into 18 Brompton Square as John's social secretary. Sometimes the two partners would jointly invest in a car; at others, they would back their respective hunches and buy individually, sharing show-room space accordingly. As far as John was concerned, a car was almost naked unless emblazoned with flags and AA or RAC badges. This obsession was indicative of a profounder difference between them. 'John went for flash. He wanted to buy rubbish and tart it up,' remembers Geiger. 'I wanted to buy lovely, genuine, untouched, low mileage. He was a big advocate of Connollising – repainting leather. If done sensitively, it refreshes the leather, which I liked. I liked the signs of ageing.' John favoured a bolder, broad brush approach, so that the leather assumed 'the look and smell of a pantomime dame's make-up'.

John's 'rather preposterous idea of dealing' had economy of effort to commend it. That seemed to be the only way he knew: Geiger still remembers the astonished sense of victory he felt after convincing his business partner that a grey Bentley was worthy of sustained attention. 'He actually broke a sweat: spent an afternoon polishing.' Nevertheless, it was John, in part at least, who led the Investment Motoring Company to what Peter Geiger describes as its only spectacular profit. The car involved was a 1949 Rolls-Royce Silver Wraith with only 21,000 on the clock. Although 'quite frightening to drive', Geiger loved it and met half the purchase price of £2,750. John raised his share by really having a 'go at Trevor and Victor'. Geiger allowed him to set the resale price: £12,500. The Wraith sat in the showroom for a year, then a buyer paid – in full.

John was not overly concerned by the lack of similar successes. On his twenty-first birthday, he inherited 8,000 East Anglian acres, plus Ickworth and its paintings (many of them with 'absurdly optimistic attributions'), although these were, for a time, dispersed, along with every piece of furniture and almost every East Wing doorknob, courtesy of Victor's '£100,000 joke'. Jolted, John set about retrieving them from impending auction:[29] another grievance to set against his father's name. Their feud was a return to dynastic form, freshly respraying the Hervey name with bad blood, confirming prejudices within an older generation and kindling excitement within a younger one. John was becoming interesting. It was an invigorating discovery, one which in due course persuaded him that he, like his father before him, could reinvent himself – especially with press assistance.[30]

Initially, however, he struggled to express what he had so repeatedly been assured was innate superiority, other than by acquiring a Bentley and the gadgets which crowded 18 Brompton Square ('a kind of James Bond sort of flat', remembers one habitué). Imogen von Halle noticed the obsession with hi-fi ('always the latest'); Randle Siddeley did too, adding that John was hungry for 'every single gizmo, the latest stereo system, the latest computer system, everything', a trait which had been fully expressed in his room in Druries ('lots of gadgets; he always had the latest bit of kit'). Another friend remembers the radar detector fitted in the Ferrari, so convenient when 'doing the last stretch at 120mph'. Guests at Ickworth would, by the late 1970s, at some stage be distracted by a television screen of overblown dimensions; by the 1980s, they were treated to 'surround sound and all that stuff', although John's greatest love, says his last agent, 'was his Wurlitzer juke box in the billiards room'.

It was novelty and rarity, not utility, that invariably mattered. Possession of prototypical gadgetry conferred only minimal advantage, one which was likely to prove momentary, lasting only until the toy had been standardized and mass-produced or been speedily superseded. Briefly, though, John was ahead of the pack, and would be again as soon as he had fastened attention onto the latest Hammacher Schlemmer catalogue, 'Offering the Best, the Only, the Unexpected' ('stuff that you're never ever gonna need: sort of underwater telephones').

With his inheritance secured, however, John felt able to invest in something more substantial than a spiral of obsolescence. He settled for the *Braemar*, built in 1931, a twin-screw, teak-decked, 125-foot diesel yacht, with a range of 6,000 miles and a cruising speed of 12 knots. By the time John dispensed with her five years later, she was also equipped with a 750cc BMW motorbike, a Honda Trail bike, a 125 horsepower speedboat, internal telephones, an ice-maker, fridges, two deep freezes, a video library and a clay pigeon trap. His new solicitor, Roger Lane-Smith, accompanied him to Gibraltar when he took possession in late summer 1975. So did Imogen von Halle. '[John and I] both took suites at the Rock [Hotel], an unnecessary thing to do for two people aged 21. I think we were given a reception party by the Governor of Gibraltar.'

Although appreciative of the *Braemar*, Imogen was surprised by John's choice. 'It was odd because he wanted a gin palace; this wasn't a gin palace, but it did come with crew.' John recruited a captain ('a German: we were both petrified of him, John even more than me') and then sailed for Marbella, to which his Bentley had been sent ahead overland, in what would become routine procedure. Technically, remembers Imogen von Halle, their arrival in port was a breach of sanctions imposed by the Francoist regime in Spain. It was one of the smaller transgressions which would involve the *Braemar* in the coming years. More important than antagonizing the Spanish was the chance to put the *Braemar* on display, John having convinced himself that 'he'd bought the biggest boat on that part of the Mediterranean at that time'. This was a delusional assumption. Delightful though the *Braemar* was – 'beautiful, a classic motor yacht,' in the opinion of one guest – and though she could sleep eight – three twin cabins and two singles, with separate accommodation for her five-man crew – she was certain to face vulgar, modern competition. Marbella soon provided it. 'Another boat came in, *La Belle Hélène*,' remembers Imogen von Halle. 'It made us look like the tender. John was furious – furious in quite a jokey way, but also, I think, really annoyed.' It was an early indication of an inner equivocation: a self-awareness at variance with the role – created by Victor – which he had decided to play.

Although, as he now realized, the *Braemar* was liable to be trumped by younger pretenders, she was still a useful advertisement of Hervey style –

'there was a large crest painted on her funnel' – which, in turn, was a procla-mation of fearless expenditure, to be paraded across the Mediterranean and Caribbean. John assured friends that he had entertained himself during the inaugural trip from Gibraltar to Marbella by throwing overboard the fittings and possessions of the previous owners ('utter rubbish' says Imogen von Halle), so that the yacht's interior was ready to receive the attentions of Philip Geary ('a queen from Marbella'). There were Bergère chairs and a Regency drum table, Van Dycks ('quite effective copies, all with brass plaques stating: "Original held within the Marquis of Bristol collection at Ickworth"'), and a George II dining table. In the cabins, spotlights twinkled over greens and pinks. 'Typical John,' reflects his accountant, Michael Chappell. 'The interior decoration cost an absolute fortune.'[31]

It was not, though, solely on the inanimate that John now concentrated his largesse. Today, many of his most significant male lovers lead comfortable, orthodox lives, having tended to make their way in the worlds of art or prop-erty. 'They were always quite nice, well-mannered, soft-looking Englishmen,' remembers a friend of John's brother, Nicholas. One or two have married and successfully procreated. Generally speaking, they do not care to review the years – or months and moments – they spent in John's company, during which, in a number of cases, they gladly took the Jermyn shilling.

Sections of the press were soon confident of the young earl's preferences. 'Johnny has never gained a ladies-man reputation,' a report recorded in July 1975, when he was still two months short of his twenty-fourth birthday. Thereafter, readers received regular reminders about 'namby-pamby Earl Jermyn'. John gave no indication of dismay; Pauline felt unable to follow suit, assuring a newspaper, a decade later: 'All this stuff about my son being a confirmed bachelor is nonsense.' Imogen von Halle agreed. 'John was not overtly gay at the time, not at all. If anything, he was really nothing, asexual. There were rumours but we never believed them. We always thought it was because he wasn't having much luck with women, and it was perhaps easier for him to say he was interested in boys.'

This was not as perverse as it would subsequently appear, nor was it as absurd as it would have sounded to Henry Wodehouse who, at the age of seventeen, was startled to receive an invitation to shoot at Ickworth, despite not having seen John for a decade. 'The change was incredible... a slightly spoiled, arrogant little boy [had become] a very spoiled and extremely arro-gant and very effeminate late teenager. He had carefully coiffured hair and drank nothing but Crème de Menthe.' John's appearance, unhealthy though it seemed to Wodehouse, who was working on a farm at the time, fitted the experimental, epicene mood of the moment – '[David] Bowie, glam-rock and long hair'. In metropolitan circles, adds one of John's (male) lovers, experimentation went beyond the cosmetic. 'Anybody who didn't live through that period – from when he left school, 1972, until the early 80s – doesn't really understand it. It was between the invention of the Pill and the onset of AIDS. There was absolutely no problem about anything: if you wanted two girls, you had two girls; if you wanted a boy and a girl, you had them. It was absolutely extraordinary. The very nature of the decadence meant it was bound not to last. Inevitably, something awful was going to come along.'

After knowing Peter Geiger for two or three years, John indicated that he enjoyed bedroom variety. 'He said it didn't really matter whether it was with a female or male.' Years later, Pauline publicly reiterated a version of this on John's behalf. 'People say he's gay,' she told an interviewer, 'but he's actually bisexual.' A male lovers concurs. 'He certainly wasn't unattracted to women and certainly could, to use the vernacular, "do the business"; I don't think there was any problem. Like most people, he appreciated looks. It was just that he preferred men, boys, whatever, given the choice.'

John remained as adept at camouflage as he had been at Harrow. Some of those closest to him were, for example, unaware of his long, orthodox friendship with Dr John Martin Robinson,[32] and of his comparatively brief association with his black acquaintance Cecil. Even in New York, in the early 1980s, by which time it was harder to suspect him of heterosexuality, he did not, when in conventional company, veer towards stereotype. 'He was gay, but not camp,' in the opinion of an expatriate Englishman who met him at the time, 'and the friends with whom he seemed most comfortable were straight.' It is an opinion echoed by many, including Tim von Halle, a frequent visitor to Ickworth in the late 1970s and a periodic lodger at John's New York house the following decade, whilst Minnie Winn, a female friend a generation older, says that, 'If he was gay, he never thrust it into your face, never'.

This would have surprised other audiences, in whose company John extended his patois, a favoured neologism being 'twinkie' ('he is the most frightful twinkie'), an expression which, by the end of the 1970s, he was publicly parading on number plates (TWINK 1, TWINK 2), radiating joy in the distaste and occasional outrage that this caused.

Adaptability meant that he did not stoically embrace a life of celibacy. If the anguish witnessed at Ickworth by Guy Sainty in the early 1970s had been caused by confusion over his sexuality, it appeared to have been banished – or successfully suppressed – within a year or two, as Piers de Laszlo discovered. 'He wanted male crumpet on his boat,' remembers de Laszlo, who re-encountered John after leaving school. 'The deal was that I had to wear sawn-off shorts – and a pout – but I wouldn't be violated.' De Laszlo declined the invitation.

Before then, another Old Harrovian – again, two or three years younger than John – had come to his attention. Peter Henderson remembers the details with clarity and a degree of discomfort: a drive in the Bentley, drinks at 18 Brompton Square ('there was a coloured guy serving') and dinner in Knightsbridge. Henderson struggled to relax. 'We ended up in the dreaded François's.[33] I felt I was about to be propositioned by John. That wasn't my scene. So, when we got [there] – all my gang would have been there, male and female – I quietly said goodnight.'

Finding Harrovians a disappointment, John turned his attention to a rival stable, although, for a time, he was 'mad about' a friend called David Grigg, who accompanied him to the Fourth of June at Eton. By the mid-1970s, his half-brothers George and Nicholas were at school there. He had no doubt as to which of them would prove the more pliable ally. As a small boy, Nicholas had occasionally suffered from the attentions of John and his adolescent friends. 'He had a pretty miserable time with all of us,' says Randle Siddeley, adding that the younger Hervey's predicament was not eased by the fact that he was 'very immature' for an eight- or nine-year-old. 'He used to have a tricycle and really annoyed us cycling in and out of the room.' John, then about sixteen, opted for conclusive action. 'He said, "I've had enough", and threw it out of the window. It landed, crumpled, in pieces, in the garden. Of course, Victor got to hear of it – a major eruption.' At Heatherdown, he was 'rather a recluse', remembers a former master, whilst at Eton, in Martin Whiteley's house, his reputation as an oddity intensified. His intelligence was obvious, as were the rigidity of his sartorial tastes ('a blazer and cavalry twill trousers') and his disdain for the less couth of his contemporaries and their schoolboy practices. 'Nick didn't "mess" with anybody. The idea of making scrambled eggs or whatever the rest of us did was way beneath him,' recalls one of them. 'He'd have stuff sent in, put it all on account with the shop at Eton, Rowland's, and then invite people for tea.' Only in one arena did Nicholas (the diminutive 'Nick' would have caused him much pain) contentedly emerge into the light of common day. 'He wasn't sporty, but he was a big actor, loved that; very much played the Hervey.'

Sustained but trapped by unfaltering belief in his dynastic status, Nicholas stood in awestruck readiness to serve the only figures above him in the family hierarchy. Attempting to reconcile the interests of Victor and John would have tested the most supple of conciliators; for Nicholas – awkward, uncer-

tain, easily offended – the consequent friction must have been almost unbear-
able. But bear it he did, unquestioningly accepting the pre-eminence of the
Monarchist League, whose dinners he would later cross the Atlantic to
attend, yet also finding time to do the bidding for his older brother.

A visit to Eton yielded what John sought. Whilst out with Nicholas, he
spotted Robin Hurlstone, a senior boy in Whiteley's, 'very bright, rather
effete', who in the coming years was to discover that he was attractive to some
men and to women of extravagantly different ages. 'He looked at me and told
Nicholas: "that's the one I want",' Hurlstone recalled, many years later. 'I was
eighteen. He was twenty-one.' Hurlstone eventually moved into 18 Brompton
Square, whose interior was in due course attended to by George Renwick, an
Old Etonian and younger brother of a Northumberland baronet, though
better known as 'Mrs Renwick', who 'thought he was the second coming of
Nancy Lancaster and old John Fowler; he wasn't'. Untroubled by bourgeois
notions of restraint, Renwick 'spent John's money like water on his addiction
for ruched swags and draped tables'. Trophies included 'a towering four-
poster bed swathed in layers of thick brocaded curtains… a coat of arms set
into [its] upholstered bedhead, reminding you whom you were sleeping with
(in case you ever forgot)… plumes and a coronet tickled the ceiling from the
top of the canopy', all of it overseen by Hurlstone's portrait. Unfortunately, as
another visitor remembers, he 'had run out of money after John's bedroom. It
was hideous and cost an absolute fortune. There were two floors above that;
they had nothing spent on them.'

The glories of his bedroom did not tempt John into reclusion: on the
contrary, his social life intensified. 'Everybody would go for dinner, and then
– five, six nights a week – unless you were going down with a cold or something, you would go to a nightclub, which you would hit at about midnight.'
He and Hurlstone were regularly spotted by Jeremy Norman, another Old
Harrovian, who had followed in Sir Harry Mallaby-Deeley's footsteps by
acquiring Burke's Peerage, before venturing into territory beyond Sir Harry's
comprehension. The Embassy Club, at 7 Old Bond Street, had been patronized before the war by the Prince of Wales (subsequently the Duke of
Windsor) and after it by Prince Ali Khan; by the mid-1970s, its basement was
flooded and its owner bankrupt. Nevertheless, Norman sensed that the club
could be triumphantly resurrected, partly by making particular provision for
those who shared what he later described as his 'taste for young men'. Three
days of reopening parties were held in May 1978, initiated by a fashion show
attended by Margaret, Duchess of Argyll, Lady Diana Cooper and Bianca
Jagger. The club soon attracted what Norman described as a 'galaxy of

celebrities', amongst whom he identified Mick Jagger, Danny La Rue, Catherine Guinness (sister of Jasper, and at that time Andy Warhol's assistant), Pierce Brosnan and his wife Cassandra, Lionel Bart ('Aunty Li'), and Lords Bath, Hertford, Pembroke, Kenilworth and Montagu of Beaulieu, as well as 'public school boys out of bounds and models of both sexes and none' – and, of course, 'Earl Jermyn and his boyfriend Robin'.

Many of the Embassy's waiters would die of AIDS. So would Stephen Hayter, the club manager, remembered by Norman as 'an excellent and energetic promoter' and also as 'one of the most pernicious and evil individuals' that he had ever met, 'a sex and cocaine addict who used drugs to blackmail and control his friends and enemies'. John would later appoint Hayter to organize his wedding party, which might not have surprised Jeremy Norman, in whose opinion John's 'swine-like behaviour perfectly complemented his porcine appearance'.

Despite its attractions, the Embassy did not monopolize John's attention: he took in an establishment called Legends, and unearthed a new favourite, 'the most awful place, a huge place, by Centre Point, called Bangs: an enormous, gay night club – gay for two nights a week – [which] he always liked'. He was not always accompanied by Hurlstone. One evening at Monkberries, Imogen von Halle, still a regular visitor to Ickworth, noticed him at a nearby table. Amongst those sitting with him was a man – tall and noticeably good-looking – to whom she introduced herself. Soon they headed to the dance floor. 'We got on really well. I remember thinking, "There's absolutely no way he's gay".' She decided to ask, and was told that her conviction was correct. Eventually they returned to their table. John awaited them, speechless and 'smouldering with anger'. Moments later he flung his glass of crème de menthe into Imogen's face. 'Apparently I was stealing "his" chap. I left immediately – with the chap.' The incident, she says, was an example of how 'John was used to getting his own way, very much king of the castle, a lot more selfish, a lot more into everybody doing what he wanted to do.'

Certainly, he was, by the mid-1970s, confident in exercising droit de seigneur. 'He was always a predator, always had to go after what he wanted. Anybody who went after him never got him. He loved the chase, the seduction,' remembers Hurlstone, adding that the intensity and relentlessness of the pursuit could prove overwhelming. 'I'd had girlfriends from the time I was fourteen. John was not physically attractive; he was very, very shy, which he covered up by talking about money. But he had three things I love: humour, charm and vulnerability. He said, "I'd like you to come to dinner. Come to the Chelsea Rendez-Vous on 7th July".' At dinner, Hurlstone met two of John's friends, who addressed one another as 'dear' and referred to male friends as 'she' or 'Mrs'. Afterwards, the quartet progressed to a nightclub in Kensington High Street, 'known as the Sombrero but really called Yours & Mine'. John's other friends soon departed. 'I looked around. There were only men in the club. [John] said, "Oh, it's a gay club". I made my excuses and fled.'

The evening had been only a preliminary skirmish, however. Bombardment by telephone began. John's youthful quarry (an only child whose father had died two years earlier) still lived with his mother: soon she was fielding ten calls a day. When Robin fled abroad, John followed. The pursuit lasted a month, until his quarry's capitulation. Hurlstone found himself surrendering to 'a pathos that was enormously touching'. He recalls that John's charm, like Victor's, was of the most destabilizing kind. 'Charm and danger: very, very attractive to an eighteen-year-old who's been stuck in the public school system. He said I was the only person who could pick his lock... It has always reminded me of Anthony Blanche talking to Charles Ryder in *Brideshead*: "I warned you of charm... It spots and kills anything it touches. It kills love; it kills art; I greatly fear, my dear Charles, it has killed *you*."'

John's sexuality, with its trace of ambiguity, and Victor's six decades of misadventure were more than enough to ignite the richly satisfying theory that, after a couple of fallow centuries, 'the Hervey Gene' – the gene which determined any deviancy requiring explanation – had triumphantly resurfaced. Other forebears were of no consequence, not even the Lygons, whose talented ranks had included one homosexual for three successive generations.[34] Uninterested in analysing his appetites, or their origins, John preferred to satisfy them emboldened by the liberating power of alcohol. Henry Wodehouse witnessed the effects in 1973, when invited shooting at Ickworth. Driven there the night before the shoot by his older brother Edward, he remembers dinner in the dining room – just him, John and Edward – served by a white-gloved butler. He has no memory of what they ate, only that, by the end of dinner, he was badly drunk and his older brother, who was not staying for the shoot, arguably more impaired. The Wodehouses had arrived in a venerable Land-Rover: John insisted that Edward should borrow a suitable sports car in which to return home. Edward, then nineteen, hoping to become a racing driver, accepted and blazed back to Great Blakenham thirty miles away. Henry was shown to his room by Coles and advised to lock his door.

The seventeen-year-old Wodehouse did so. Half an hour later, the door was thumped and the doorknob rattled; a voice was raised in outrage. Wodehouse opened up. John stood in front of him, smoking 'an enormous cigar' and wearing 'a silk dressing gown, cravat, and fairly obviously not much else'. He carried two bottles, one of crème de menthe (empty), the other of cognac (half full). Swaying slightly, he leered at Wodehouse, thrust the bottle of cognac into his hands and demanded that they share a night cap. Then he lurched into Wodehouse's bathroom, where he lifted the lid of the cistern, extracted a full bottle of crème de menthe from within ('I knew I had hid a —ing bottle in here somewhere'), dropped the empty one into the bath, shattering it in the process, wished Wodehouse good night and departed.

The next morning, Wodehouse tottered downstairs with a brutal hangover. He was met by John ('clean shaven, bright as a button') wearing a very well cut, grey flannel suit. Wodehouse asked if the shoot had been cancelled.

'Don't be ridiculous. I always dress like this when shooting.'

It was then that Wodehouse realized that his host was still paralytic. In the first drive after an 11 o'clock break for alcohol (bull-shots rather than crème de menthe), John swung his gun enthusiastically at a hare, fired and hit Wodehouse, just below the right knee 'four pieces of shot, like four hornet stings'.

'Bugger, missed it.'

'No, you bloody didn't. You got me instead.'

'Oh, sorry, old boy, better luck next time.'

Fizzing with pain and rage – but aware that John was past the point of rational communication – Wodehouse spent the remaining three drives twenty yards behind the line of guns, out of immediate danger.

By 1977, Michael Chappell, John's accountant, had seen enough to become worried. Initially, he remembers, there had been 'too much [alcohol] at dinner, then it started spreading backwards', until the first drink of the day would be taken promptly at 11 a.m. (crème de menthe being ousted as solvent of choice by, successively, vodka and orange, then cointreau on the rocks, then vodka and grapefruit juice, although none of this precluded sustained infusions of Bloody Mary). Only the most intimate of friends were fully aware of the intensity of this routine. 'He was a chronic alcoholic, just couldn't go without a drink,' remembers one. 'Bloody Marys at eleven o'clock in the morning, then he'd be in a filthy temper, with an awful hangover.'

Ickworth regulars knew only that John was 'a drinker'. They felt no cause for alarm. 'It was a fun time, a very irresponsible time for lots of us.' Besides, his over-indulgence caused no surprise to those of his friends who knew his parents. In the words of one of them, who had seen Victor and Pauline in action, both were 'raging alcoholics'. Time on the *Braemar* had proved particularly educational. 'George [Lambton] and John would go to bed; Pauline and I would sit up and talk for hours, till four or five in the morning. She would drink a bottle of brandy, or more, and smoke three packets of cigarettes.' Pauline required assistance getting back to her cabin – 'then I'd undress her and get her into bed' – but full recovery would be achieved by the following morning, when she would be up by ten, 'as bright as a button'.

John would sustain his drinking as long as his liver would last. By the time it expired, however, he had for years been lifting his mood in a far less laborious manner. Although his relationship with drugs would come to define his public reputation and many of his private relationships, he did not, initially, exhibit particular hunger for them, nor pioneer their consumption, but allowed himself to be swept along in the company of friends. 'He first experimented with cocaine about 1973–74, when we all did,' remembers Imogen von Halle. 'Everybody else was doing it – everybody in the circle we mixed in. It was readily available. Chopping it up [on] mirrors and [snorting] it. It was the seventies and some of us had a little bit too much money,[35] and not enough to do. Speed was the other big drug.'

John was not an especially heavy user, although, in retrospect, there was an indication that he could become one. 'He always had the money to get the stuff. There were no brakes.' Not all of John's friends participated; others were pathfinders. 'Peter [Geiger] never took drugs; Nick [Somerville] never stopped.' One habitué of 1970s Ickworth argues that 'Nick-Knack' Somerville was 'always madly in love with John, in a non-physical way'. Somerville himself inspired more ambivalent emotions. 'I really hated him to begin with; I came round to him,' remembers one of John's lovers. '[He was] very charming, and I was very fond of him in a way, but he was just... the Machiavellian figure in the background.' Others remained impervious to his charm. 'Nick Somerville... Not nice,' says Michael Chappell. A female friend declares Somerville 'rotten through and through'. Nevertheless, by the mid-1970s Nick-Knack had become 'part of the furniture' in John's life. 'He was one of those people who, at the age of seventeen, look fifty, and who usually come into their own at fifty. He seemed to me to be fascinated by the perverse: drugs were bad and wrong and perverted – "*so let's do them*".'

The logic appealed to John, to the dismay of Randle Siddeley. 'Nick was a despicable creature, the most horrible, gruesome character.' Jonny Ruane, still John's closest friend, and still faithful to the pleasures of the bottle, repeatedly warned him against the twin attractions of Somerville and narcotic transgression. 'There would be Jonny [Ruane] telling him, "Don't...".' Almost always, attempted intercession was greeted by derision. Another friend, who developed and then conquered chemical addiction, insists that Somerville did not command complete dominion over his richer, younger friend. 'He felt slightly put out as John's group of friends [became] more international, and as he, Nick-Knack, descended into genteel poverty, not helped by his £50,000–£100,000-a-year drug habit.'

From within that international set, one of John's female friends noticed the intensity of the bond between Somerville and John, which meant so much to the older man. This friendship was a far more remarkable accomplishment than it would appear by the mid-1980s, when it seemed perfectly natural that Nick Somerville – Old Harrovian, Oxford scholar, husband of Tessa (granddaughter of Sir Christopher Musgrave, 6th Bt), City gentleman – should be the fixture at Ickworth shooting weekends that he had become. Although they had overlapped at Harrow, Somerville had been two years senior[36] to John and had been in a different house (Rendells), two factors which made any alliance between them highly improbable. Stewart Johnston, who recalls Somerville as 'a bit odd: a curious person', noted that 'he became more of a friend of John's after school'.

There was little or nothing in his appearance to commend him to John, who was always susceptible to good looks, especially in men. 'Nick was extremely small, squat, probably about 5'5",' remembers an acquaintance. 'He had a distinctly unattractive face, a bit like a frog: he wore glasses and was going bald... all at the age of twenty-one, twenty-two.' Nor did Somerville enjoy the advantages of aristocratic pedigree or money which John considered so redemptive. 'Nick wasn't "county",' adds the acquaintance, 'he wasn't anything.' His parents, Arthur and Hazel Somerville, weren't 'anything' either, according to the calculus by which Victor estimated social status, so there was no danger of their being sucked into the Ickworth orbit when they settled in Bury St Edmunds at about the time their son left Harrow. Their house – 38 Well Street – struck one of John's more metropolitan friends as almost painfully modest. 'I remember, at that age... being very shocked, in a bourgeois way... I had never in my life been somewhere like that. That sounds horrible.'[37]

Somerville did, however, offer John and others an entrée to a crowd of entertaining, intelligent Oxford men, amongst them Jasper Guinness, Connor Bradford, Julian Lynn Evans and Matthew and Sebastian Taylor. 'We were all targeted by Nick,' says says a female acquaintance. '[He] was a sort of Svengali, extremely bright, very entertaining, certainly a great friend of mine at that point. I remember him saying that the assets that are given out are nearly always fairly distributed, so, while you might not have looks, you might have personality or great charm. Before drugs had taken over, Nick was hugely amusing, very, very witty, could be utterly charming and could be slightly nasty in a seductive way.'

Other London girls, including 'Crissa' Baring, invested time in Oxford. So did John. 'He wanted a group to become part of, and this was a fun group,' explains one metropolitan female, adding that at first John, who invariably arrived by Bentley, tried to make up for what he lacked in conversational brilliance with 'the fact that he had a title and money'. But in Somerville's company that began to change. 'Nick made John laugh, and he made John feel secure. He fed his ego and fed [him] drugs. It was very often Nick who would turn up with the stuff. He loved it when people were taking drugs and encouraged them to do so. Heroin was considered, sad to say, fairly routine. He offered it to me more than once. Some people took it; I didn't. He was exactly the sort of person you warn your children against.'

Peter Geiger registered the dynamic between John and Nick-Knack. 'Somerville understood power,' he remembers. Somerville nurtured his protégé, interpreting the world for him and reassuring him of the preeminence he would enjoy in future, notably one evening when John looked out from the hamburger restaurant where they were having dinner to see someone urinating over his Bentley. 'John was not so much angry as confused,' Somerville recalled many years later. 'To him it was like making love on an altar. I said to him, "Look, John, in Oxford the only thing that counts is intellectual ability. One day you will be King and the centre of attention, even with the people who, at this time, do not care about material things." I was right. They turned out to be the very people who prostituted themselves for John.'

Soothed by alcohol and stimulated by narcotics, John began to assert himself in a manner which would have been unimaginable two or three years earlier. 'John could be funny too, could also be quick, poke fun at people, [although] not in the same quicksilver way as Nick,' remembers Imogen von Halle. 'He was a snob, but that was where he could be funny: [he would] stamp his foot, and say, "I'm the Earl Jermyn", and expect a table immediately. I'm sure we must have encouraged him.' ('Stamp!' became part of the private language, remembers Peter Geiger.)

At Ickworth, John made a point of ushering his guests inside the Rotunda whenever the mood took him, regarding it as his own property and voicing his disgust that it was open to the public. 'He was incredibly rude about [National Trust visitors],' remembers Imogen von Halle. His entourage offered support. 'Everybody was rude about them in every way. We all swore like mad. A lot of people didn't like us.' The validity of this assessment was especially apparent in London. John's cousin Catherine Rossdale remembers an especially challenging evening at a restaurant in Swan Walk, Chelsea, when he turned his derisive attention on fellow diners. By the second half of the 1970s, John had more or less perfected this technique, alternately lacerating staff or inviting them to join his table, which was invariably the scene of deranged and drunken argument. Anyone who voiced disgust was further antagonized via ostentatious pay-offs ('Give them a couple of hundred quid and tell them to **** off').

John's closest friends continued to see a side of him that blameless restaurant-goers never did: the capacity for courtesy and generosity, the sensitivity to others, traits completely at odds with the shrieking, bullying snob now frequently on public view. At Ickworth, he 'always drew people who looked a bit lonely, who were not fitting in, or not talking to anybody, into the conversation. He was very good like that, very sweet; he had a very, very good side.'

The descent into addiction was, in any case, not completed overnight, or even within a year or two. 'John struggled, from the summer of 1976 to the summer of 1977, to stop taking drugs,' remembers Hurlstone. 'I begged him to. At one point, I thought I was winning but then...

'John was snorting smack [heroin], snorting coke. I remember him bringing coke to Barbados. Sheer lunacy.' The yearning for drugs, and the discarding of sexual inhibition which they encouraged, competed with a fluctuating desire to resist them, as well as a more consistent desire to convince others that he had mastered the situation. Only precise orchestration could maintain the pretence. Peter Geiger observed the consequent compartmentalization of Ickworth life. From about 1976, there were shooting weekends, drug weekends and sex weekends, 'the drug addicts and queens phase'. Roger Lane-Smith was shepherded away from non-shooting weekends, a policy which enjoyed some success. 'When I first knew [John] I didn't notice that he was on drugs,' he acknowledges, 'but it became clear after four or five years that he was, [although] he would never openly admit it to me.' Even much later, when court appearances, custodial sentences and clinical treatment had shredded the last layers of a conventional façade, John did not indulge himself indiscriminately, for which Simon Pott, appointed agent at Ickworth in 1992, was grateful. 'He never, never took drugs in front of me. He knew that they were a thorough difficulty.'

If John's discretion owed something to the reassurance conferred by secrecy, it seems also to have stemmed from an undying consideration for his staff. Between 1973 and 1975, remembers Imogen von Halle, there had been no question of cocaine on silver salvers, later to become a staple of Ickworth legend, although this had partly been because 'nobody wanted to give their drugs to anybody else'. At the time, before John's investments extended much beyond the Bentley and Ferrari (and certainly not to the Hughes 500 Defender Helicopter), weekends were essentially passive, physical exertion being confined to the billiards room, as guests awaited the next alcoholic or narcotic shot. 'We hung around and did nothing. We knew that there was a swimming pool but no one would have used it. It wasn't like going to other friends, where it would be tennis and croquet. You didn't do that at Ickworth. Nobody did any of the normal things. It was never normal.'

Victor's old friends were periodically blended into the mix. Carol Havers remembers a shoot when 'a fairly ugly little man' was especially busy during lunch. 'He had a bottle of God knows what, drugs and things, and he would just disappear under the table. Very nasty individual. Not a nice friend. Not a good influence.' But Ickworth weekends retained vestiges of high-spirited innocence. Crissa Baring – 'very confident, mad, really good fun' and cheerfully experimenting on a number of fronts – often led the way. 'There was one shoot when she said, "Aren't you bored? Let's be pheasants",' remembers Imogen von Halle. 'So just before the next drive, we ran in front of the guns, flapping our arms, [shouting] "We're birds: shoot us".' Food fights were conducted with patrician vigour, 'all the food for the whole weekend, the whole lot' being expended in one particularly intense confrontation. Only with some difficulty did John dissuade the cook from submitting her resignation.

Above all, there was Ickworth itself. Imogen von Halle remembers the care with which John had repaired the fabric of the East Wing after Victor had torn out its light fittings and door handles. 'Ickworth was important to him. It was warm – lots of big houses weren't – and beautifully maintained, over-maintained in a way: the gold was a bit too gold. There were Da Vincis in the gents virtually. And John had inherited this thing of [having] crowns and coronets absolutely everywhere, the bigger the better. It was over the top. Absolutely wonderful.'

Its attractions, aesthetic and otherwise, and the attention that John generated in London, ensured that many hungered to see for themselves. Most were obliged to make do with the reports, or versions of them, that filtered back to London with the favoured few. Inevitably, though, the Ickworth guest list swelled. Hamish McAlpine, scion of the construction family, was an occasional visitor, as were Lords Neidpath[38] and Mancroft (the former a proponent of trepanning; the latter a convincing raconteur); so, more frequently, as the decade wore on, were Rupert Wace, a (heterosexual) art dealer; Mark Cecil, a junior doctor who had been a year or two below John at Harrow; Nick Ashley (the adopted son of a car auctioneer, who had graduated from Oxford before the Nick Somerville era and valiantly strove to match John's expenditure 'pound for pound'); Patrick Donovan, an Oxonian of a slightly later vintage; Marianne Hinton, an American heiress; Imogen von Halle's younger brother, Tim von Halle; and Dermot Verschoyle-Campbell, a few years older than the rest, a fearless drinker, 'a P. G. Wodehouse character who had a sort of charm – rather idiotic but fun – and swallowed his words'.

All enjoyed John's showmanship – of a kind that had been utterly beyond him when leaving Harrow a few years earlier. 'One of John's gifts, a very rare gift,' says Nick Ashley, 'was the ability to talk with a good vocabulary, good grammar – it didn't matter how stoned or drunk he was – and still sound plausible.' He was, adds another Ickworth regular, 'a master at telling derogatory stories about himself', whilst his observations at moments of apparent difficulty could be stimulating, the (inadvertent) shooting of a beater prompting the instruction: 'Put him on the game-cart then'.

'John was just a great deal of fun, very irreverent,' remembers a steadfast friend. 'While playing the role of the peer he actually thumbed his nose at it. That was kind of charming. I wasn't a lover; I didn't depend on him. He was a great person to party with.' Courtiers, he adds, jostled for favour. 'There were always two circles: inner and outer. [You] almost [felt] a superiority being in that inner circle.' Unfortunately, there were others who sought more tangible rewards, amongst them a 'most terrible sponger' whose sycophancy John appreciated – for a while. 'He was absolutely dishonest: [he would] borrow £100 and say, "I'll pay it back" with no intention of doing so.' The perpetual borrower was preferable to the visitor who came to be known as 'Klepto-****', who 'stole something strange, like a set of sheets, from Ickworth or Chatsworth. A strange person, very, very odd. Not to be trusted: little gold boxes on tables. Sexually, he was barricaded into the closet, which John always considered very funny. He subsequently trampolined out of it.' There was also persistent talk of an acquaintance who targeted cars rather than little gold boxes.[39] John's flat in Brompton Square was burgled, as was, a fortnight later, Imogen von Halle's in Lexham Gardens. 'The police were quite convinced it was somebody we knew in the group,' remembers Imogen, 'someone who knew that we spent the weekends away.'

John fortified himself against adversity with increasingly familiar tools. A new friend 'provided heroin to the upper classes at endless parties, held twice a week, at a flat in Kensington', thinking that 'the only way to get [John] was to keep him well fed on the old Henry or whatever it was called'. The edge to his behaviour, already evident in London restaurants and nightclubs, was exposed at an undergraduate party in Cambridge, where he hurled a carving knife through an open first-floor window. It embedded itself, blade first, in a pram in a neighbour's garden. 'There was a baby in the pram,' remembers a fellow guest. (The baby was unscathed.)

John's driving, now twin-fuelled by alcohol and narcotics, began to attract what would prove to be lifelong police attention. The Friday afternoon drive from London to Ickworth (via Baldock and Royston) held obvious challenges, especially after the pub stop on the A1 which always punctuated the journey. Tim von Halle remembers John's 246 Ferrari Dino being stopped three times in one trip; on another, following in the car behind, he saw 'a bag of substances' jettisoned without provoking police pursuit. Even the inevitable first driving ban (for three and a half years, notched up in a Bentley in March 1976 for drink-driving) failed to dent John's confidence, which was now also being projected via increasingly adventurous tailoring. A friend recalls meeting him first at Longchamp in 1977. '[John] was wearing a crème brûlée pinstripe suit, with huge lapels, incredibly tight fitting – like King Farouk – and shiny patent leather shoes with enormous buckles.' John's new acquaintance felt 'big embarrassment' at standing next to him. He lasted three minutes. 'Tony Lambton always said [John] looked like Liberace.' A year or two later, in Deauville, a fur coat of suspect provenance was added to his wardrobe. 'It was hideous,' remembers a Frenchwoman. 'Wolf or something.'

Armigerous detail, hitherto confined to the furnishings at Ickworth and Brompton Square, now migrated to John's person, a transition boosted by Robin Hurlstone who gave him a tie-pin shaped like a coronet. 'It was made by Theo Fennell for £1,000 [and] stolen in Fort Lauderdale by a taxi driver George Renwick picked up.' Its disappearance did not extinguish John's fondness for the motif.

Parading hereditary status was no longer enough, however. In the mid-1970s, John had spoken of a hovercraft project for 'hundreds of thousands of pounds: big money for the time'; towards the end of the decade, he was assuring friends that he intended to buy back the Rotunda from the National Trust. By 1978, Peter Geiger realized that this was a challenge beyond the scope of the Investment Motoring Company. '[John] had outgrown me. I showed him how to drive a Bentley; he drove away from me in a Rolls.'

Although they remained in touch, Geiger accepted their parting with a sense of relief, but not because he had seen the worst of John. Indeed, he appreciates in retrospect, that he saw 'good John': kind, vulnerable, more than a little lost, only once witnessing him in narcotic action, 'snorting lines on the *Braemar*'. Nevertheless, the showroom years had convinced Geiger that his friend was untroubled by scruple when commercial objectives were at stake. At the beginning of their friendship, John had presented him with one of the 'Liberty scrolls' with which Victor had hoped to lure Americans into buying worthless 4-foot square plots of Suffolk turf. A message was scrawled across it: 'Peter – One of the more successful cons! – John'.

Victor's weekly 'lessons' in the Ickworth study had left their mark. 'One of the things John admired about Victor was the way he was able to talk things up,' remembers Geiger. 'Being a conman meant you were frightfully clever: not necessarily breaking the law but being a cut above everyone else, a little sharper.' By the 1980s and 1990s, the trait would be brazenly advertised – to close friends, at least. One of John's favourite stories concerned a trip he had made, aged six or seven, to Harrods, where he had persuaded his nanny to buy a fabulous go-kart (a sports car in miniature, the largest item on display), promising that he had all the money needed in his piggy-bank at home. Nanny duly 'splashed out £50 or something, a fortune in 1960', returned to Ickworth to discover the true state of John's piggy bank ('he didn't have a penny in it') and was obliged by Victor to suffer the loss herself. In the 1970s, the proclamations of betrayal tended to be less brazen and less frequent, although one of his closest friends remembers glancing at the gold Rolex on John's wrist and repeating a maxim he had lately heard from Gianni Agnelli: '"Never trust a man who wears a gold Rolex". John roared with laughter.'

It became apparent that friendship was no guarantee of immunity against sharp practice. One (female) intimate sold her Mini through John; six months later, she was telephoned and reprimanded by its new owner, who accused her of irregularities concerning its paperwork. She was by then fully aware that John, as she puts it, 'loved a crook'. Imogen von Halle experienced a rougher ride. 'John sold me a Mini Cooper S, custom built, the first car I owned, in 1975. I was terribly proud of it.' Pride perished fast. 'Within about three weeks, it didn't work. I was simply furious, demanded my money back, said that he could have the car. But there was no deal: in those days, you didn't sue friends, you didn't take it any further, there weren't any [consumer] laws. He showed no shame at all. I only found out later from Peter [Geiger] that he'd known perfectly well that it wasn't [OK]. John would do the dirty on people without even knowing what he was doing. I don't think he had been brought up to understand that you didn't do that.'

Another potential victim proved more robust. By the mid-1970s, Roger Lane-Smith, a young solicitor from Manchester, was living in Dolphin Square, which was where he saw an Investment Motoring Company advertisement for a Bentley S3. John brought the subsequent sale to a successful conclusion; then, 'five hundred yards down the Fulham Road, the engine fell out. Roger went back, said he was going to sue. John said: "Don't do that – work for me".' Lane-Smith confirms that the Bentley had gone wrong 'in a very bad way' and that John sensed that it might be wiser to employ him than face him in court.

For the next two years they were engaged in 'absolute battles' with Victor, their objective being to extricate John from what one of his friends describes as 'Victor's supposedly unbreakable trusts'. These proved more fragile than their creator had hoped: 1,000 Essex acres were sold for about £1 million (£9.5 million today), approximately half of which, remembers Lane-Smith, was needed to pay Victor 'for the contents of Ickworth', which (with one or two exceptions) were not entailed. Although Victor repeatedly reprimanded John for 'depleting the resources of the marquisate', his authority for doing so was diminished by his own disposal of 7,000 family acres, a sale which helped fund his move to Monte Carlo and ensured that John would have to survive on 8,000 acres – little more than half Victor's own inheritance, and not much more than a quarter of the Hervey estates of only thirty years earlier.

Although, says Nick Ashley, Victor sweetened the pill by giving John £750,000, this had to be protected. 'He had to go non-resident; if he didn't, it would have cost a fortune in tax,' explains Lane-Smith, adding that, by 1978, John had decided, like his father, to take up residency in Monaco. 'The Ickworth lease went into the name of an offshore trust; John was fundamentally living [abroad] for the next four or five years. At first, he couldn't come [back] to the UK at all; thereafter, it was 90 days a year.'

Before his move, at the end of 1978, John extolled Monte Carlo's charms to Peter Geiger. Yet these pleasantries were soon eclipsed by a disquieting letter from Roger Lane-Smith. 'It said: "My client Lord Jermyn is suing you for having held out the prospect of profitability in the car trade".' Geiger asked John for an explanation. 'He said, "Oh, don't worry".' Nothing further happened, but the incident confirmed Geiger in his opinion that their time together had reached its natural conclusion.

Imogen von Halle had departed two years earlier. 'I didn't find it amusing any more. My brother did because he has never taken drugs, and never indulged in that lifestyle in any way.' It was a pattern that would recur for much of the remainder of John's life. Some, however, still catered loyally for his needs. Nick Somerville brought him Rupert Everett.

* * *

The flat was dazzling – a 'belle époque mirage', in Everett's phrase; 'more like a set', according to a French friend, 'an English-style Visconti set'; 'remarkable', remembers one of John's closest friends, 'the best thing George Renwick ever did'. Blue walls in the hallway led into a superb and overwhelming drawing room, 'about 40ft by 25ft', enriched by Louis XVI furniture, pictures from England, and *trompe-l'œil* panelling by Harry Gremillion, a muralist of real accomplishment. Some guests found their eyes drawn to the library ('I remember being incredibly impressed by the spines of the books. John said: "Haven't read 'em; bought 'em by the yard"'). Hospitality was unceasingly dispensed ('bloody Marys... anything you wanted'). The bedroom was most mesmerizing of all, a treasury of 'bordello red and gold'; 'incredible', remembers a French visitor, 'a four-poster bed, with a gold marquess crown above it'. The coronet, icon of John's adult life, had once toppled from its moorings (so he liked to say) when agitation within the four-poster reached an unusually intense crescendo.

The flat was also 'hugely impractical'. That scarcely mattered to John. High ceilings, wonderful proportions and decorative artifice contrived the illusion of unending space: what Victor had achieved at Ickworth, his son had repeated – in miniature, admittedly, but to great acclaim. The coup was pulled off in Paris, at 17 rue de Bellechasse, on the corner of Boulevard St Germain.

Monte Carlo had not been a success. Most of its residents were in competing stages of corporeal and emotional decay, Victor included, although it was, predictably, Yvonne who most excited John's attention. 'He hated her,' recalls a Frenchman then making John's acquaintance for the first time, adding that the Bristols' red Rolls ('white inside') was vividly identifiable. John's flat – in an anonymous modern block – had no charms; he had no friends; but he did have get-away vehicles at his disposal: a blue Bentley, later superseded by another (a dark grey Turbo), a Range Rover and, in due course, a Cherokee Chief Jeep. Special friends – lured in from London and, in one case, from Paris – tended to be confined to the intimate constrictions of the Ferrari, whose trajectory seared the Basse Corniche as John sought the vitality that Monte Carlo lacked, during jaunts to St Tropez or Cannes or Nice. Within months he had moved to Paris, though maintaining the fiction that he remained in Monte Carlo, thereby satisfying the tedious inquisitiveness of the Inland Revenue.

Adam Edwards, then working for a film company in Paris, remembers John's solution. 'He used to send his chauffeur, Foley, beetling down to Monaco in the jeep, to turn the lights on and off, run the heating bill up, use the telephone'. John was not alone in this – 'they were all doing it,' says Edwards, 'all the tax avoiders' – but he was alone in being able to count on Tom Foley, his Irish chauffeur. Remembered by John's last agent at Ickworth as 'utterly and totally faithful… a rather ageless person'; as 'deeply loyal' by Tim von Halle; as 'a darling, just lovely' by one of John's female employees, Foley had been taken on during the days of the showroom, first as chauffeur, remembers Peter Geiger, though soon as general factotum. To an extent, he performed the same role for his master that Juliet had for Victor: he put things right; when he could not, he made them better. In the end, recalls a Horringer villager, he was 'almost a father figure'.

It was Foley who drove the Bentley or Ferrari or Aston (plus 'all the toys' – bikes, guns, gadgets) to Germany (for shooting weekends) or the South of France or Jersey or Marbella or Porto Ercole (for more protracted leisure). It was Foley who, when John moved to New York, drove Tim von Halle, an occasional lodger, to his Wall Street office; Foley who, during nocturnal landings, guided John and the Hughes 500 down to Ickworth by torchlight; who was dispatched to retrieve guests or sent to buy what they required (red gumboots, for instance, for a last-minute female arrival); and Foley who drove one of John's friends to hospital for treatment after an accident. All was done without rancour or complaint. Too often careless of friendship, John treasured this association, most famously when Foley was banned from driving, after which, remembers Roger Lane-Smith, 'the chauffeur really did have a chauffeur'.

One of Foley's predecessors, Philips, recommended by Mrs Mance when John first lost his licence, had driven a Silver Shadow whilst John was at Brompton Square but had died in a car accident in Monte Carlo (unconnected, apparently, with his duties for John). A number of successors followed, until Foley became 'about the fourth or fifth driver over eighteen months'. Soon he was as indispensable as Coles, the 'marvellous old butler' at Ickworth (already well into his sixties when originally taken on by Victor). An admirer of the female form and an enthusiast for mid-morning refreshments ('Time for your medicine,' favoured members of staff were advised as he uncapped the whisky bottle), Coles 'adored John [and] saw everything'.

The tenor of John's reign was, though, more authentically represented by 'the chef [aboard the *Braemar*], who used to bring a caseful of knives every-where, which used to cause a lot of trouble' (but which could persuade the uninitiated – or the hostile – to attend to his master's wishes[40]); by novitiates from prison; by the secretary who neither typed nor knew shorthand; by the appointment, as agent at Ickworth, of those who had often (if not always) 'started out as [John's] lovers, then worked their way into business manage-ment'; and by a new and excitable butler who installed his boyfriend at Ickworth (inevitably described as 'the under-butler'). Amidst this household, its members recruited according to whimsical criteria, Foley emerged as lynchpin from Paris onwards, even though his time there was far from easy. 'He couldn't speak French, didn't know anyone there,' says one of John's closest friends, remembering that Foley was confined to a small room off the kitchen. 'It killed him.'

John's own predicament was little better. He had described Robin Hurlstone as 'the love of his life' to Imogen von Halle. Now Hurlstone decided that his future lay elsewhere, though he and John remained on good terms.[41] Needing entertainment and distraction, John found both in Rupert Everett. 'He was obsessed with Rupert for a bit,' remembers a female friend; another speaks wistfully of Everett in a diamond choker. Following their introduction courtesy of Nick Somerville, John had taken to dispatching Foley to the Central School of Drama (where Everett was studying) on Friday evenings. Arriving in a Bristol, Foley would hand its keys to the School's registrar, from whom Everett would collect them and drive down for a full weekend at Ickworth. Everett would later record that he, and other similarly impecunious members of John's court, were soon reduced to the status of vassals 'whether we liked it or not (and mostly we did)'. He contin-ued to make obeisance in Paris. 'Rupert Everett was staying there quite a lot, in the apartment,' remembers one of John's continental friends. 'He was very much helped by John, financially and more.' An English visitor remembers that Everett restrained himself from radiating gratitude, preferring to loiter 'in leather from head to toe, looking surly'.

In intervals between the young actor's appearances, John tried 'to break into the French aristocracy', as Anne-Muriel Bazin puts it. An eighteen-year-old ingenue in her first year at university, she had, understandably, never met anyone like John; nor, she felt, had the French nobility. 'I said that he had to be mysterious, playful. But subtlety and mystery weren't part of his make-up. He used to give huge dinners, splashing money around, very nouveau riche. What they said behind his back was absolutely appalling.'

John fared a little better with a Frenchman whom he had first encountered in Monaco. 'I introduced him to my very dear friend Ann of Bavaria, one of the last *salonnière* of Paris, extremely eccentric, cultivated, with a fabulous figure. Quite an alcoholic as well.' Admission to Ann's salon, adds the Frenchman, was not suffocatingly determined by social status, but by talent and qualities not susceptible to immediate analysis: there were, in consequence, established writers and publishers, members of the Academie Française 'and "characters". It was extraordinary, like a dream. John liked to go there very often.' The Frenchman was encouraged to invite Ann ('and most of her friends') to the rue de Bellechasse. 'He liked to have a room full of elegant people, to look at them, to see them around.' Determinedly mono-lingual, John exerted himself no further, adopting the role of young emperor requiring stimulation, rather than the assiduous host of Ickworth, relying on one of his vassals, Dermot Verschoyle-Campbell, to keep him abreast of developments amongst the natives. 'He liked Dermot because Dermot was very, very social: he did the rounds, he would [tell John what] was happening in the suburbs of Paris.'

However, when alone with the Frenchman John did open up, his subject invariably being himself and 'his problems'. The same tended to hold true aboard the *Braemar*, even in securely English company, as Nick Ashley had discovered, John 'in a white, Saturday Night Fever suit... being happy, like Duke Ellington, to let guests take solo spots'. After dinner a chosen favourite would be accorded the privilege of a private audience, during which his host would deliver a monologue, periodically interrupting himself to make 'offers of more nasal refreshment'.

Only with wheel or wallet in hand, and suitably dosed with 'refreshment', did confidence blaze through him. After begging to be taken to Maxim's Club by a member, an English friend, John rewarded him by drinking it out of Château d'Yquem. 'It was something like 1924 Yquem. He kept saying: "Only six bottles and they've run out". He loved doing things like that.' The Jeep was equipped with microphone and megaphone (the latter roof-mounted), remembers a lover who, like Everett, heard the squawks and shrieks John favoured *pour encourager les Parisiens* ('****ing collaborators. Get a ****ing move on'). The Range Rover, initially the only one in Paris, was dispensed with as soon as John noticed others in the city, but not before it had become woven into John's legend. The only passengers were Dermot Verschoyle-Campbell and one of John's platonic girlfriends.[42] They were in a comparatively narrow street when another car drew level, a difficult manoeuvre, remembers John's female friend, since John was, as usual, ensur-ing that the Range Rover laid proprietorial claim to the middle of the road.

'Some little Fiat or something pulled up beside [us] and a Mafioso type took a pot shot at the car out of the window. It was like something in a Buñuel film. I laughed; I can't remember if John did.'

A dedicated assassin would have been obliged to trail John far beyond Paris, notably to the Bahamas, a destination which established an enduring hold on his affections. During his first visit there aboard the *Braemar*, he secured sponsorship from members of the Lyford Cay Club, thereby enabling him to dock in the club's yacht basin. John liked what he found: a properly staffed clubhouse, an enclave of the Anglo-American rich, a number of whom were familiar to him by name (at the very least), like Trevor Dawson's sister, Pat Menzies. It offered obvious possibilities, amongst them the chance to sign bar chits in someone else's name (that of a member who had sponsored him) and to sink a golf cart in the club swimming pool, both activities which he would subsequently enjoy. First, though, he water-skied in the yacht basin where the water was still and smooth – a consequence, remembers an Old Etonian visitor, of 'a very, very strict five-knot limit'. Moments later, 'large, beautiful yachts were being bashed up against the jetties. He commented to somebody, "Well, it's the perfect place to water ski, because it's so calm".'

The 'mistake' was forgiven, although John was viewed with distaste, if not detestation, by the club's older generation, amongst whom those with adolescent (or slightly older) offspring voiced suspicions about the diversions available aboard the *Braemar*. 'The adults went into an absolute tailspin. We were forbidden from going on the boat, because, as all the parents said, it was filled to the funnels [sic] with drugs.'

Induction into recherché adult pleasures was a noisy process. After a series of disruptive nights John was instructed to remove himself. He complied at nightfall, the *Braemar* ('lit up like a cruise ship, with a string of lights from bow to stern, up one mast, across the next'[43]) departing down the narrow channel connecting the yacht basin, through the coral, to the Caribbean. Relief and self-congratulation at the clubhouse lasted until the following morning. 'He'd dropped anchor across the mouth of the channel, effectively blocking it, but he was out in open sea so no one could technically say he was breaking the law. That was all rather marvellous.' Sandro Corsini, whose father-in-law had helped arrange John's admission to Lyford Cay, and who would in subsequent years see John regularly in Italy, was impressed. 'There was an absolute back-up, all these American billionaires, people who never got impeded... For John it was a sport, the fun of getting people upset.' The American Navy, he believes, eventually persuaded him to move on.

A victim was not always required, however: sometimes it was enough to violate regulations, as when abstracting a (platonic) girlfriend from the American hospital in Neuilly, just as she emerged from a coma. 'John bribed the staff and took me out to Castels, said he'd have me back in Paris before anyone noticed, then chased after a Maltese waiter and left me sort of semi-conscious on a banquette.' Although bracketing her 'rescue' with what she defines as acts of 'operatic egotism', rather than ones of instinctive kindness, she scarcely thinks any the less of John for that. 'He always, always made me laugh... the theatre of John impressed me and charmed me.'

Adam Edwards similarly remembers 'a dramatic character... in dark glasses and silk ties' whose presence in Paris enriched it for others. 'He was fantastically good company, especially for me. I was living in Opera, by myself, in this sort of garret. Whenever I was bored, I would just wander down the Left Bank to see him.' Edwards's first meeting with John, effected by a former girlfriend living in Paris, had entailed an introductory treat. 'I was going to see *Death in Venice*. John, obviously, wanted to go and see *Death in Venice*, for about the 500th time I'd imagine. I got into his car with Lavinia [a pseudonym], shook hands, and he said, "Do you want a line of coke?" So we all bundled into *Death in Venice*, all refreshed. Afterwards we went to this extraordinary place. It was a perfectly respectable restaurant upstairs; then you went downstairs and it was a gay disco – carved bums on the wall, all that sort of thing.'[44] Edwards saw John regularly thereafter. 'He was always very generous, used to entertain everybody, any old flotsam and jetsam that came through.'

Old friends periodically bobbed their way to the surface, Clarissa Baring, for instance, appearing at a party held in the 16th arrondisement, where Edwards, who had arrived, accompanied by Amanda Nimmo, in his film company's Peugeot 605, 'mobbed John up for having a stupid great Jeep that couldn't go down the streets of Paris'. A while later, he and Miss Nimmo left. Once inside the 605, they heard an engine roar: Edwards remembers Amanda Nimmo screaming as John's Jeep hit the back of the Peugeot 'like a two-ton sledgehammer', then a blur of acceleration as the Jeep shot past. Yards later it stopped: John threw it into reverse and slammed at full throttle into the Peugeot's bonnet, which crumpled. 'It was like a cartoon – the headlights staring into the sky, steam coming out of the radiator. Poor old Amanda hurt her knee, actually.' John gave his victims a lift back to the rue de Belchasse where they were treated to a consolatory drink. The Peugeot, Edwards learned the next day, was a write-off.

Whilst enjoying the lack of police attention (drink-driving, remembers

Edwards, was a matter of well-practised routine), John was appreciative, too, of the broader freedoms conferred by life abroad. 'He was always happier out of England, said he only felt safe outside England,' recalls an intimate friend. 'He could be anything he wanted.' Lovers, notably but not exclusively Rupert Everett, were escorted to favoured clubs, where other associations – briefer but nevertheless concurrent – were formed. One evening, whilst in Everett's company, John persuaded a 'twinkie' whom he had long admired to accompany them back to No 17. His new acquaintance stipulated only one condition: that his sister should come too. John assented, and soon they had 'piled into the four-poster', only for John's bravado to evaporate, like that of 'a big dog... taken to the vet for an injection'. All four fell asleep until, a little while later, Everett was nudged awake by John, to find 'the brother and sister... hard at it'. Pausing only to decant a bottle of port, John was in his Ferrari minutes later, driving at breakneck speed towards the peripherique, naked beneath a fur coat, Everett at his side. 'We drove all the way to Florence,' Everett wrote, remembering that John managed 130 mph through the Mont Blanc tunnel. 'Finally, we sat... drinking coffee and laughing... but I could tell he was still upset about the boy. "I must admit," he said, "I'm Mrs Most Miffed".'[45]

The occasional rebuff from a 'twinkie' was almost the only curb on John's appetites; hence, in Paris, assert two of his intimate friends, 'everything began to go wrong'. Exile, with its invigorating sense of anonymity and consequent invulnerability – and its attendant threat of loneliness – spurred him into almost continuous indulgence. Sometimes this found comparatively benign expression, as when he rented a house in Deauville. 'We would drive from Paris with Jimmy Douglas, John Murphy and Dermot, perhaps eight or ten people in all for the weekend,' recalls a guest. 'It was great fun. John paid for the staff, who came with the house, including a very good chef. Everything [was] covered in cream and calvados.' John arranged for Pauline and his half-brother George to visit. '[Pauline] hadn't been [to Deauville] since the fifties,' remembers a friend who accompanied the Lambtons on the trip.

Anne-Muriel Bazin remembers nothing untoward other than a game of backgammon which concluded with her vanquished opponent ('a guy called Dermot Verschoyle-Campbell') throwing the board into the fire. Elements of normality lingered into the mid-1980s. In England, a couple – amongst the least moneyed but the very closest of John's friends – were delighted to be invited to join him on holiday in Italy; they insisted on paying for the flights ('really cheapo flights') as a small contribution. 'It meant leaving at the crack of dawn, with [John] staying the night before in our flat, sleeping on the floor.' He accepted without demur. 'There were a lot of times like that which were good.'

There were also moments of transgression innocuous enough to be safely discussed in front of Coles, as when, back at Ickworth, a protracted stint in a pub in Horringer threatened to make John, Tim von Halle, Christopher Nevill and Ned Cavendish late for Sunday lunch. 'We all had quite fast cars, but John was in a Range Rover. He said, "I bet you £50 I'll get home first".' The bet was accepted. Moments later, the Range Rover plunged off the road, down a track which was blocked by a five-bar gate: John smashed through it. The others stopped, joined moments later by the police. 'They had been chasing. We pointed out that we were on private land.' An explanation for the skid marks was still sought. None was forthcoming. 'Clear them up,' advised Ned Cavendish instead, 'like a good Indian tracker.' Ten minutes later, Coles, by then eighty or so, struggled to retain full control of the soup tureen as the young gentlemen recounted their adventure.

More often than not, however, John invested in transitory acquaintances. 'He didn't bother [to learn] even their names,' remembers a continental friend. 'They were just there for weekends, all in leather.' Recruited by inter-mediaries, they '[remained] hidden, then they would disappear'. Some very nearly disappeared forever in December 1980, when John organized a house party for twenty in Deauville, treating them to 'drugs, drink and foie gras'. On New Year's Eve, some of the party – a mixture of 'young English aristo-crats, strong silent Scandinavians, decorative models and girlfriends or fag-hags'– headed to a casino in nearby Cabourg, although John preferred to retire to bed with a Scandinavian boy. Returning from Cabourg, the casino party hit black ice: several of them were propelled through the windscreen and spent the next few days in Caen hospital. (Replying to those who asked the whereabouts of the missing house guests at breakfast next morning, the staff in the Deauville house offered a more conclusive denouement: 'Ils sont morts'.)

John, as events would show, was not a man to allow mishap to inhibit recreational interests. Nearly a year later, Adam Edwards was amongst the guests at his next Christmas party, held in a suite at Claridge's. 'All the cocaine was on the left-hand side of the mantelpiece, and all the heroin was on the right. In lines. You took whichever one you liked,' remembers Edwards, who had a present for John, 'a Dinky toy of a Peugeot 605 which I'd smashed with a hammer'. John seemed appreciative, although by now he knew what he appreciated most – the fireplace powder. Drugs, he had no doubt, worked for him, made him – and everything – better, conferred a magic against which no one – lover, twinkie, friend or even mother – could compete. By then his habit was dignified by the acquisition of 'a silver straw, two inch, two and a half inches, sort of ribbed silver, supposedly for some very short cocktail or something. Hallmarked, naturally, but with no coronet.'[46]

This routine was spiced by safaris to an establishment called Le Bronx, scene of abrasive homosexual activity, and another called Les Baindouches, 'very much a downtown sort of place: an ex-steam bath. The pools were dry...' Synthetic pleasures filled the void. Yet beneath the rapture of each narcotic moment and the over-excitement triggered by the pursuit of each fresh twinkie, beneath the 'odd mix of watchfulness and obstreperous confidence', it was just possible to sense a trace of self-disgust. 'I remember marching him into various churches in Paris or Rome,' says an intimate friend. 'It was like pulling teeth getting him to go inside, just to look at a Caravaggio. There was a kind of fear... that going in meant having to acknowledge your weaknesses... an aspect of, "I'm beyond redemption"... that if he confronted that idea in his head, it would just be too horrifying, so best to stay away.'

In the coming years, his actions often gave the impression that he was seeking punishment. 'I think sometimes John had a death wish,' says his accountant, Michael Chappell. 'If there were two ways of doing something – an easy way, which would have no repercussions, and a difficult way – John would always take the difficult way, knowing that the police or National Trust or somebody would be upset. He would get in his car knowing he was on drugs and that the chances of getting stopped were fairly high because he had a car that would stand out. Little things like that.'

Few of those enjoying John's hospitality in Paris concerned themselves with their host's psychology, however, unless sensing an opportunity to exploit it. One regular visitor to Paris, who was especially keen on the occasional day's racing at Longchamp, 'always had to be given money – 300 francs or so – which he never repaid'. More distressing was the acquaintance whom John for a time employed, who 'began forging John's signature on cheques and things'. Initially, the amounts involved were inconsequential, certainly too trivial to attract John's attention. Then his employee was tempted into escalation, writing cheques for sums too substantial to be missed. 'John found out. It was a really nasty little episode.'

There were others. Duncan Roy would later receive a fifteen-month sentence (at Knightsbridge Crown Court) for obtaining property and services by deception, but not before he had convinced John – and Ann of Bavaria who, he recalled, 'stank of whisky and cigarettes' and invited him to fondle one of her breasts, assuring him that it was 'as firm as a sixteen-year-old's' – that he was Anthony Rendlesham, son of Lady Rendlesham. (His introduction to John, he wrote in 1990, came via the unwitting Dermot Verschoyle-Campbell, whom he had encountered in Le Sept. Two of John's friends, mistrustful of his provenance, made inquiries: Lady Rendlesham had no son. The news was relayed to John, who trimmed Roy from his entourage and never spoke of him again. Loss of face failed, however, to persuade John to filter prospective guests with greater discrimination. 'Thirteen or fourteen people would turn up at a restaurant, and John would pay for them. If you spend money like that, people think you have a hundred times more than you have. Toy boys were taking his drugs and stealing his collar studs. He would complain about things being stolen off the dresser and so on.'

There were one or two diverting, non-thieving friends amongst the dross: Todd Bruno, an American whose professional life was the subject of prolonged conjecture;[47] another American, Cristina Zilkha, 'singer and sharp-tongued lyricist'; and Peter Bemberg, scion of an Argentinian family with immense interests in banking and property, who was much richer than John, which was rare if not quite unique. In addition, there were English favourites with whom John formed close (and more or less sequential) friendships, especially when Rupert Everett's burgeoning career began to draw him away from Paris: David Rocksavage[48] (who, like John, had moved from Monte Carlo, where he had been working for Rothschild's, to Paris), Hugo Guinness[49] (a holiday companion in Italy) and Crispin Vaughan (who, in 1982, would accompany John on the inaugural journey of the revived Orient Express). All were Old Etonians; all at least a year or two younger than John.

Rocksavage seemed especially ripe for John's friendship, partly because he lived in the same city (whereas Hugo Guinness, like Everett, visited from London), partly because he was six years John's junior. 'David was his protégé in a certain way,' says one of John's French friends, adding that Rocksavage frequently joined his fellow earl for weekends in Deauville. From time to time, John toyed with them all. 'Sometimes,' explains the Frenchman, 'John would be extremely kind and soft with people he respected.' At other times, he was less kind and 'very tricky'.

Then he met two men at whose exploitative genius he could only marvel: Andy Warhol and his business manager, Fred Hughes. He entertained them in Paris and London, and in return enjoyed what one friend remembers as 'many very funny lunches' at the Factory, Warhol's New York studio. The Hughes–Warhol artistry with numbers left the deepest impression. 'Fred was brilliant at getting money out of people, getting them to buy Andy's pictures,' recalls John's lunching companion. Warhol and Hughes helped influence the defection from Paris to New York in 1982, although there were other considerations, notably an 'inability to speak French very well, and a stubborn refusal to try to become better at it', and the fact that 1970s Paris was 'socialist, dead, recessioned, [its] buildings filthy'. 'The only thing they were good at, as John used to say, was the lighting.' New York was filthy too, but it was also 'probably the most exciting place in the world. It had this incredible energy that Paris didn't have: Xenon, Studio 54, the supermodel thing.' Other stimulation seemed likely to be more abundantly available too.

* * *

'Angie, darling, go to the bank and get $30,000. Get dressed. Tom, you're to drive: make sure you open the door for Angie. Come on, get dressed.'

The routine was always the same: preliminary instructions from John, who liked to see that Angela Barry looked right for the role ('six-inch heels and a little black number'); precise choreography by Tom Foley, who guided her to the back of the limousine (or whichever car John had decided on: 'there were hundreds of them') and then coaxed her through each performance:

'Come on, Angela, now, come on… you sit in the back, I'll put the hat on, I'll pretend I'm your chauffeur.'

'OK, whatever turns you on, Foley. Let's go for it.'

The drive was a short one: about a minute and a half from the house on Riverview Terrace to John's bank on Madison Avenue. Foley resumed directorial duty as he pulled into the kerb. 'Wait there. Don't get out until I open the door for you.'

Cash collection – invariably $30,000, never less than $10,000 – was a recurrent duty in Angela Barry's life as John's social secretary. They had met at one of his parties, to which she had accompanied her boyfriend. Prize specimens had been on view, Christina Onassis and Luis Basualdo amongst them; none was to Angela's taste. She had suggested they leave. When John heard, he insisted she sat next to him at dinner. She lasted five minutes. John asked why she was leaving.

'I don't like your friends.'

Conditioned by the users and greasers who constituted most of his court, John floundered. The next morning, however, the barrage of telephone calls began. It did not relent until a fortnight later when Angela finally agreed to meet him. John took her for dinner at Elaine's;[50] he took her out the next night too, and the next and the next and the next, four or five times in succession. Each evening creatures laying claim to varying degrees of friendship would join him, unbidden. 'They just sat there until he paid; none of them offered.' She told him that, if she went out with him in the evening, she would pay her own way.

Superficially, John's companion was 'just a typical Chelsea girl', as an older friend puts it, 'very glamorous, lots of fluffy blonde hair, big, big blue eyes – always up and bubbly'. The Liverpudlian accent, only partially eroded by time in London, suggested someone less easily reducible to stereotype. When John told her about his upbringing, she reciprocated with details of her own: the father she had never known or even met, the life in care ('to about 600 foster families'), work at Ronnie Scott's, then in Australia, then America. John sensed that this was someone whom he needed. He asked her to become his social secretary.

It was a full-time role ('booking restaurants, organizing helicopters, dinner parties and security'), fabulously well paid ('How much do you want?' John asked, 'you can have it'), requiring daily attendance at John's house, 3 or 4 Riverview Terrace, a cobblestone street unknown to most New Yorkers, just off Sutton Place, looking onto the East River close to the 59th Street bridge. Tall and narrow, its grandeur was accentuated by inventive use of a square of open space, barely more than ten feet across, separating it from the neighbouring house on whose exterior wall John erected a panelled mural of Ickworth.

Learning a fortnight after appointing her that she was unable to type, John instructed Angela to hire someone to do so on her behalf. Later he paid for her to attend evening secretarial school, insisting she share refreshments with him before each class – 'a glass of wine and a line of coke'. Her typing never progressed, but she remained at Riverview Terrace, becoming a member of John's family quartet: John himself, Foley and Pearl, the black cleaner, in her sixties, 'always stoned', thanks to her practice of easing the strain of housework by smoking an unending supply of joints.

There was one other to whom John was prepared to extend the familial embrace – Nicholas, his half-brother, by then enrolled at Yale where, dismayed by the lack of suitable dining clubs for gentlemen, he had founded one of his own, the Rockingham. His distinctive appearance ('always dressed as if for Henley') and priorities ('first, his own existence; second, his social life; third, anything academic'), as well as adherence to antediluvian routine ('at night he would always put his shoes outside his bedroom door, because he expected someone to clean them') ensured that Nicholas soon came to the attention of much of the university. 'He would normally make himself known to the professor,' remembers a friend, 'by walking up at the beginning of a seminar and [saying], "I am a pupil of yours; my name is Lord Nicholas Hervey".' Unfortunately, the failure of successive professors to appreciate the significance of his hereditary status, twinned with their inability to grasp the pre-eminence of the Monarchist League, led to irrevocable differences and Nicholas's consequent departure from Yale. Long before then, he had recruited to the Rockingham an assortment of extreme Texans, plutocratic Argentinians and international strays with rich connections. 'You had to be reasonably unusual and open-minded to accept someone like Nicholas as a friend,' recalls a contemporary. 'He was so eccentric, sometimes in a rather difficult way. He was quite good at deciding that you had given offence to him, his reputation, his honour, the honour of Lord Rockingham – you name it. Then he would sit down and write these *tomes* in very florid language, always on heavy Rockingham paper, [ending with] a string of Roman numerals for the day and date, even the time. In the old days, he would have challenged you to a duel at the drop of a hat, and would have been shot or stabbed in about ten minutes.'

It was an instinct for confrontation which John would, in due course, seek to harness. Yet even if willing to exploit his brother's eccentricity, and though almost as frequently exasperated by him as he had been in the Ickworth nursery, he was also aware of Nicholas's frailties – of his sense of perpetual outrage, his perplexity that others failed to see the world from his perspective. 'Nicholas was someone more to laugh at than with,' explains a Rockingham member. 'There were rather unfortunate times when we would mercilessly take the mickey out of him, just howling with laughter, and he just didn't get it.'

John did get it, and would, as a result become increasingly protective of the brother named as his sole heir in his will.[51] In 1982 and 1983, however, John was more intent on enjoying the Rockingham, already established as Yale's most celebrated and stimulating club, whose parties radiated genuine glamour (courtesy, in part, of Jodie Foster and Jennifer Beales, both then at Yale) and whose black-tie dinners often concluded with one or more young gentleman receiving treatment in Yale hospital. Initially held in Morys ('a serious Yale institution'), these entertainments later migrated to the ground floor of a handsome townhouse bought by Nicholas (assisted by five or six other members with useful trust funds) and transformed into a facsimile of a St James's club, with 'lots of leather seats and a series of portraits of unknown people, provided by Nicholas'; the latter, the largest investor, moved into what he referred to as 'his suite of rooms' on the first floor.

John's visits ('at least twice a term') assured the Rockingham of further acclaim. 'He'd show up in a limo, this Mercedes stretch, with Foley at the wheel, with a kind of entourage, including an English guy called Benjamin Clutterbuck, now a real estate dealer,' remembers a Rockingham veteran. 'Andy Warhol came a couple of times.' The New York set had the advantage of knowing what one of John's female friends describes as his desire for 'the wild side' – and his capacity for igniting it in others. 'A lot of people say John was a bad influence: he was, because around him we drank more, we took more drugs, we were outrageous. He did,' she adds affectionately, 'bring the worst out of people.'

The Yale boys learned quickly. 'When he was wicked and funny, it was pretty easy to laugh, as long as one wasn't too much of a puritan,' says one of them, recalling a dinner which John enriched by dropping Quaaludes into other people's drinks, and another at which he assured a Texan (brimming with confidence and alcohol) that if a tablecloth was removed with sufficient speed and strength everything above it would remain in position. Moments later, 'the best part of 150 glasses, plates, crockery and candlesticks' stormed into the air before shattering on the floor.[52] John was thrilled. 'He liked people to laugh with him, while encouraging other people to do vast amounts of damage.' There was also an evening which concluded with a lift in one of the Yale buildings shuttling from floor to floor, its doors periodically opening to disclose a black-tied figure slumped unconscious within. 'It was a friend of mine who John had given some lines. My friend thought it was cocaine; it was heroin.'

The young gentlemen of Yale were occasionally invited to parties in New York where John orchestrated his life with precision. Only rarely was he caught off guard, as he was by Guy Sainty, who by the early 1980s was living in Sutton Place. Neither was aware of the other's proximity until Sainty, returning home one day, had his attention diverted by 'a huge sort of fuss [as] this vast limousine arrived down the street'. He looked up to see John 'getting out with hordes of young men'. Sainty approached, asked how he was, and was invited to Riverview Terrace for a drink. He accepted: 'it was pathetic: hangers-on, awful people'.

For Tim von Halle's visits, however, John had ample warning, and reordered his life accordingly. 'The twinks,' remembers von Halle, 'were, in a way, kept on the side. Everything was segmented. I was segmented in normality.' In this context, normality might entail joining John for dinner with one of his newer acquaintances, Marianne Faithfull, who by then had abandoned the Shell Cottage at Carton for life in New York with her husband, punk guitarist Ben Brierley, whose marital status failed to diminish his popularity with other women, or Miss Faithfull's old friend Mick Jagger, whose photograph John inserted in an album next to the one of Warhol. By the same token, 'normality' ensured that von Halle never saw his fellow Old Harrovian, Jamie Blandford, whether at Ickworth (to which Blandford had been a very occasional visitor in the 1970s) or at Riverview Terrace or, later, at 11 South Eaton Place, the Belgravia house which John bought in the 1980s, where Blandford, says Angela Barry, was in evidence 'all the time'.

Anne-Muriel Bazin, who worked for John for two months in New York, found herself similarly insulated from experiences and people she might find distressing. When one of John's associates began saying disobliging things about her, John unhesitatingly and unequivocally interceded on her behalf. 'In that way,' she remembers, 'he was an extraordinary friend.' With Anne-Muriel in the house, John reverted to the more discreet narcotic practices of the early days at Ickworth. It took her some time 'to realize that the little brown bags that arrived [at Riverview Terrace] in the morning were not breakfast'.

The bags' contents absorbed much of John's attention, but he made time for business in a way which Anne-Muriel had never witnessed in Paris, though it had been whilst there that John had made his first major investment, a sheep station in Queensland. Roger Lane-Smith, who accompanied him to oversee its acquisition, remembers that, after about two hours' driving over the property, John, wearing 'a Gucci suit' for the occasion, had asked the Australian agent to explain where the boundaries lay and to estimate how long it would take to inspect everything he now owned. 'If you see it,' came the reply, 'you own it. I've been here eighteen months and I haven't see it all.' John approved. 'He liked it because it was big – 54,000 acres, I think, which was about 30 miles across,' remembers Lane-Smith, adding that John calculated that its size compared favourably with that of Bermuda, 'a statistic that impressed him'. The remainder of the inspection, John decided, would be conducted from the air.

Further acquisitions – 'one or two farms in Georgia in the States, one or two houses in Fort Lauderdale' – followed. 'He was trying to replicate outside the UK what he had inside the UK. There were big worries about the socialists, taxation, the Iron Curtain. People wanted to get their assets out and spread [them] around. It was his idea to buy something in Australia [and] America.' This could only be done by selling at home, a policy which caused unease to one of John's intimate friends, who was especially concerned to hear that land in Lincolnshire – 'incredibly valuable potato land', much of which was tenanted – was to go. 'I kept asking, "What happens when there are no more cottages?"' No answer came. The disposal, in 1980, of the bulk of the Lincolnshire estates, raised about £3 million.[53] Much of this was to be reinvested in property overseas; part of the capital, however, was used to generate additional income to meet John's living expenses, since it had been clear, from the late 1970s, that he 'wasn't going to be able to live on the income from the estates [he had inherited]'.

The strategy's success would depend partly on the rate of John's expenditure, and also on the return yielded by his Australian and American ventures. Roger Lane-Smith was hopeful: he judged his client to have 'quite a good business brain'. Anne-Muriel Bazin put it higher than that, believing John to be 'extremely capable of doing business', blessed with 'a very good brain, a very organized brain', her only reservation being that he never seemed to apply himself to work for long. One of Nicholas's Yale friends shared her admiration for John's acumen, categorizing him as 'extremely smart' and being especially impressed by the fluency with which he discussed his plans. Tim von Halle remembers weekends at Ickworth when John would discuss his business interests 'way into the middle of the night', occasionally jotting something down on the silver Asprey's pad which was forever at his elbow, the note often the precursor to a letter which would be talked into his dictating machine 'at two or three in the morning' and typed up the following day. Though conceding that John would have left failures unmentioned, von Halle gained the impression that his friend had made 'some quite wise investments'. But triumphs of that ilk would never sate ambitions fuelled by a need to emulate Victor's 'accomplishments'. The oil business held out the promise of rewards of the extravagance required, his entrée to it – specifically to the Murchison family – being effected whilst he was still in Paris, courtesy of Sebastian Taylor, one of the more purposeful of his friends.

When flying from Dallas to New York in the early 1960s, John Murchison and Clint Murchison Jnr had taken separate planes, minimizing the chance that neither would survive the flight; by the late 1970s, they had jets of their own. 'John Murchison always used to say, "Saddle up the jet – we're going to New York". John loved that.' Intent on 'saddling up' himself, he established Ickworth Exploration. A female New Yorker was doubtful of its prospects. 'It was all so opera bouffe. I remember [the business] cards vividly: there was a gold embossed oil derrick with a coronet on top of it.' By August 1982, however, it was being reported that an oil well in which John had a quarter share had 'obligingly started to gush black gold in Texas'. His partners were said to be the Murchisons, Sebastian Taylor and the Earl of Rocksavage. It was John, though, who was most lavishly praised: 'Having already protected his £5 million fortune by seeking tax exile three years ago in Monte Carlo, bachelor Jermyn has now multiplied this figure at least ten times.' John's fortune would be continuously recalibrated for the best part of the decade, though the emphasis on his financial flair never diminished, much to his delight, as one of his richest friends remembers. 'He loved it when they said he'd made millions.'

The press tried to keep abreast of developments. John, it was reported, had given a house-warming party for two hundred; he owned a Bentley, a brace of Rollses (one of which he shipped to Florida to coincide with inspection of his Fort Lauderdale properties), and an eight-seater, six-door Mercedes ('previously owned by Pope Paul VI and rock star Rod Stewart').

Fred Hughes was by now a fixture at Riverview Terrace, but there was room for others: Warhol, of course, but also Mick Jagger ('John loved having those two to dinner'), Christina Onassis and Luis Basualdo. There was usually time enough for enjoying the stretch Mercedes 600 SEL ('he'd cruise down to the West Village') but, if not, helicopters were booked ('to beat the traffic') for downtown excursions. Lunch was taken in Mortimer's, Le Cirque or Angus Montagu's favourite, the 21 Club. Angela Barry shuttled to and from Madison Avenue ($10,000 sometimes seemed the minimum required to see her employer through an evening). Recuperation followed in the Bahamas, in private houses (Richard Harris's on Paradise Island proving a favourite) or, occasionally, in England (John establishing himself as a dedicated patron of Concorde). It was a mark of his achievement that, 'even in Disco Manhattan', he stood out, abetted by the coronet tiepin, the misanthropic persona now actively cultivated (via, for example, the claim that watching those jumping to their deaths from the East 57th/58th Street bridge was 'a favourite diversion') and the provision of cocaine and heroin, usually 'consumed in small, cliquish groups' even in the Studio 54 VIP basement, but at Riverview Terrace 'catered like flowers'.

Clint Murchison Jnr lived at No. 1 Riverview Terrace, but it was to John that the *New Yorker* magazine devoted a profile. An English acquaintance understood why: John 'seemed a rare working model of excess'. The assessment was over-optimistic. John's entourage included 'le tout Eurotrash,' as well as the friend who maintained her cocaine habit through pregnancy (less distressing for her husband than it might sound, since he was not the father of her child). Beyond that constituency, however, 'a coterie of the wrong friends were appearing', says an English ally who, though sharing John's narcotic tastes, retained some capacity for discrimination. One lover (named

'Harvey: very pretty') 'worked' at Studio 54; another – 'a glorified rent boy: very manipulative, very clever' – at 'one of the big salerooms. A very, very ambitious boy. Always made his bosses fall in love with him; always got advanced very rapidly, used John and anybody [as] stepping stones.' This lover knew his worth; knew, too, how to pierce John's drug-nurtured self-confidence. 'There had been a famous suicide in New York of some pretty boy who'd had a very rich lover. This boy was found... He'd written "I'm not your Sin Angel" on himself with lipstick or Pentel or something. That was the phrase — — used. He left a note for John. It said: "I'm not your Sin Angel".'

Accompanied by one Sin Angel or another, John ventured into experimental areas, unseen by most of his friends but leaving clues to be glimpsed by Nicholas's Yale contemporaries, one of whom had been given (or had procured) a key to Riverview Terrace. This unconventional house guest treated friends to tours. 'In [John's] closet there were these handcuffs, [whose purpose] was clearly of a sexual nature.' There were also various videos, similarly of a 'sexual nature'. 'He fantasized about one of the young actors on the back of one,' remembers an English friend, whom John implored to track down his Ganymede 'and offer to fly him over to New York'. The English friend did as asked. 'The boy was tracked down and he was flown over; and he ended up stealing one of John's Old Master drawings from the wall.' John produced at least one video of his own, training the camera on himself (and himself alone) whilst in tumescent condition. The footage that followed was comparatively brief but graphic. The aberrant had become routine.

His narcotic needs were met, in part, by Fat Cynthia, dealer of choice for fashionable New Yorkers, her supply-chain staffed by 'East Coast boys, mules constrained to make runs to Mexico to pay off their debts', who tended to favour Slazenger tubes (designed to carry five or six tennis balls) for cocaine transport. 'John'd be amused by the stories, amused by the lengths people would go to,' recalls one erstwhile New Yorker, adding that John did not enjoy the transactional process of buying drugs, and invariably recruited 'someone else, like me' to buy on his behalf. However, he made an exception for Fat Cynthia, who leavened business with pleasure, operating from an apartment in Midtown ('85th Street or whatever'), then from a mews house 'down on Union Square, in the Village. The English of that time would all congregate there; John would arrive in his Mercedes 600. It was like going into a meeting with the Queen. You couldn't go in for $100 worth of coke, you had to go in with pretensions of taking tea.' There were no financial constraints for John, who 'bought colossal quantities'; there was much else for him to savour. 'She had these dead-eyed creatures around her, ranging from young catamites to old pansies.' John was able to place a double order: 'some athletic young boy he'd seen wearing chinos and tennis socks', plus cocaine, 'three quarters of which would be snorted by hangers-on. There was a menu, listed according to expense. The most expensive cocaine was "White Lady"; the cheapest was "Worker". John would have ten grammes of White Lady; I'd have two of Worker.'

It took its toll. One night, 'the most awful night', Angela Barry accompanied him to the opening of a new club, the Limelight, housed in a disused church. John selected a Rolls for the occasion; Foley was at the wheel. The drive was uneventful until, just before arrival, a car in front of them was involved in a collision, the impact from which propelled it into the Rolls.

John got out immediately. 'Look what you've done! You've really upset Foley!' The shriek was directed at the occupants of the other car.

Angela Barry followed him. 'John!' It was all she could manage. 'There were two dead bodies in the front, with blood on them. They were young, lovely people. One had gone through the windscreen. Somebody had hit them, killed them, and they'd bumped John's Roller. Foley was saying, "Fucking hell, what's wrong with that man [John]? They're dead."' John seemed detached, as if disengaging from a film which had ceased to appeal. 'He wanted to go into the nightclub. And he went in. He didn't care. Foley and I said we wanted to go home. It was just not on.'

The abrupt, distressing bifurcation of personality almost certainly had a pharmacological explanation. John's craving for drugs had already taken him to obsessive and inventive lengths: he had procured a toothpaste container 'hollowed out so you could unscrew the bottom and put your drugs inside', specially commissioned walking sticks whose intricate heads concealed discreet compartments, and carefully cobbled shoes ('I remember him saying, "That's a good idea: I'll have a [compartment] in my heel"'). But after a decade snorting cocaine and heroin, John no longer derived the same impetus and release from his habit; the solution, he had decided, lay in freebasing instead.[54] After one spree, he later recalled, he had spent ten days in his bathroom.

On 19 May 1983 two members of the Drug Enforcement Agency arrived on his doorstep at 7 a.m. Moments later, he was handcuffed, accused of international drug trafficking. Elsewhere, a British trio, Ben Brierley, Nick Cohn (screenwriter for *Saturday Night Fever*) and Frances 'Frin' Mullin (who had a flat in Cohn's townhouse), were simultaneously arrested. Foley alerted John's friends by telephone. John's mugshot and fingerprints were taken. Hours of questioning followed, first at a nearby DEA centre, then at the Federal Courthouse in Brooklyn, before he was allowed to return home. Within days, his New York bank, Morgan Guaranty, had warned him that he had until 30 June to make alternative arrangements; in Monaco his business licence was revoked. In Britain it was reported that a police surveillance team had seen him entering Mullin's flat; further evidence was said to come from recordings the police had made by tapping her telephone.

So began an uneasy time for a number of John's friends. 'I introduced Ben to John [who] thought that I had in some way betrayed him; I hadn't,' remembers an American whose name was shielded from public scrutiny (courtesy of potent family connections). 'Frin was the only dealer, [but] the DA's office [was] getting over-excited, thinking they had the new De Lorean[55] case because of the high profile of the people involved.'

Over-excitement was pardonable. John's dual identity – John Hervey/Earl Jermyn[56] – was a cause of unease and suspicion in the New York Police Department and the DEA, who noted his expansive way of life (invisibly financed, as far as they could tell) and his familiarity with Miss Mullin. Yet John, unwilling if not yet unable to visit a bank himself, was completely ill-equipped for a business whose currency was suitcases of street cash, its leading practitioners career criminals of frequently homicidal intent. 'It was absurd to say that he was a dealer. He wouldn't have known where to start,' explains a friend who, at the time, invariably procured drugs on his behalf. Within a month, the Federal authorities had reached the same conclusion and dropped the charges, although only after John had secured the services of a lawyer with 'mob connections'.

He then returned to Ickworth, but not before giving an interview. His difficulties with the American authorities had cost him $1 million, he said. But he could cope. He spoke of drilling reports (on four Louisiana wells), discussions with his Jersey bank and Queensland sheep station, immersion in the markets (the day before his arrest he had, he said, 'bought two gold contracts for £65,000 and invested £50,000 in sterling futures', as well as following a hunch which had persuaded him to put £25,000 on the FT All-Share Index) and his disdain for the plodding conservatism of fellow aristocrats. He had, he conceded, been a playboy until he was twenty-three, but had then become obsessive about preserving his inheritance, not for his own sake but for that of future generations, hence his willingness to apply himself to business and to pay a premium for expertise ('a quarter of a million dollars on tax advice in the last five years'). The effort had been worth it: he had tripled his inheritance. Now, though, his reputation had been tainted, detracting attention from his financial dexterity (his sixteen corporations, for example, 'quartered in such locales as Monaco, the Isle of Man... the British

Virgin Islands') to the suspicion that he had avoided a heroin-dealing charge on a technicality ('a smear that may follow me for ever').

John chose to recover in the Mediterranean, chartering a boat and summoning Nick Ashley and Clarissa Baring. Tranquillity proved elusive. Fistfuls of Rohypnol – seventeen-a-day – failed to deliver sleep. He instructed the skipper to dock in France, for a rendezvous with Foley and the latest Bentley. A crazed playback of the Limelight night followed, this time with John at the wheel, 'smoking, swigging Vodka Collins, snorting coke, making phone calls and fondling his twinkie's thighs'. Clarissa Baring's screams accompanied the collision when it came. Then John was out of the car, howling: 'You bloody fool, look what you've done to my fucking hub-caps.' A solitary, bloodied Frenchman lay on the ground, next to a shattered Mobylette; he lived. The frenzy appeared to have an almost cathartic effect: on the flight back to England, John assured Nick Ashley that he was 'never going to take heroin again… was going to find a suitable wife and prepare for a parliamentary career'.

Friends in England, and would-be friends, were soon much more absorbed by the resumption of full Ickworth service. The New York arrest had conclusively conferred on John the degree of disreputability and glamour commensurate with Hervey legend. Even more intoxicating, for handpicked favourites, was the chance to arrive at Ickworth by air, in John's newly acquired, extravagantly equipped Hughes 500 helicopter, considered (in aviation circles) to be the only such machine to have had a full auto-pilot installed. The cost of modification 'would have been huge', but it had the merit of allowing 'a less than fully functional pilot to sleep at the controls', a facility which would prove invaluable as John's flying career progressed.

Initially, though, he had little recourse to it, proving himself as capable at the controls as he was at the wheel, gaining his helicopter pilot's licence – a very appreciable achievement, Michael Chappell rightly emphasizes – under the tutelage of a Polish Second World War RAF veteran. His success in doing so suggested to one friend that the New York arrest had shocked him towards reform. '[He] was trying really hard,' she remembers. 'He'd decided that he wasn't going into a clinic – he'd play what he called mind-games if he did – but that he was going to be clean. If I had to pick the nicest time with John, it was then: you could actually see him as him. When we told him I was pregnant, he straightaway said, "All I want is to be a godfather".' She and her husband granted his wish. Later John joined them on holiday in Italy, where he put his showmanship to considerate use. 'I said I'd never been to Rome. He said, "Let's go to Rome for lunch tomorrow." So we flew off in a helicopter to Rome.' Three more people completed the holiday party: another friend of John's called Andy Pearce; Pearce's girlfriend; and the woman who had become John's wife.

* * *

News of the engagement had fascinated many of John's friends but appalled others, who feared that the prospective Lady Jermyn imperilled the continuation of the 'Adult Disney'. Candidates for her role had been mooted since John's late adolescence, speculation at one stage involving Christina Onassis, whom, he told Peter Geiger, he 'fancied the idea of marrying'. The emphasis had remained on the theoretical, John explaining to Angela Barry that he did not find Miss Onassis's intrinsic charms sufficiently compelling (even if her ownership of Olympic Airlines was considered to be one of them). The opportunity had been real enough, however, Christina assuring Angela that she 'really liked' John.

Ariane Leroux, John's childhood friend, was a possibility. 'She was in Monte Carlo when he was. She was sort of a girlfriend, but I don't think it lasted very long, although I think he saw her again.'[57] John's relationship with Gabrielle Coles, Nicholas's former nanny, had been more intense. She had accompanied him on holiday to the Bahamas in August 1978 and was, argues Randle Siddeley, 'the person John should have married. They were very, very close.' Events would suggest that in a sense she never left him.

Few others displayed any kind of staying power. 'The girls seemed to come and go,' says Imogen von Halle. 'Kirsten Blaize-Molony was one of them.' She, however, was particularly close to Nick Somerville, then became Ned Cavendish's first wife. Another was Maria Garton – blonde, memorably glamorous, 'almost too good to be true', ardently championed by her mother, linked to John by the press (with his blessing) but, though immensely fond of him in a sisterly way, untempted by him as a marital prospect.[58] 'I think Victor was keen to have her around as much as possible,' remembers Randle Siddeley, 'just to keep John away from [other options].'

Victor's views on another of John's favourites, Marianne Hinton, went unrecorded, though he would surely have approved of her financial pedigree (she owned, an acquaintance pointed out, 'a few percentage points of one of those Wall Street banks'). Whether John was at Ickworth or in London, in Paris or New York, Marianne was rarely far away. By 1979, the press spoke of her as his girlfriend. His intimates were less sure; so, it appeared, was John himself. At 17 rue de Bellechasse, there was an unusual painting above one of the doors: it was of Miss Piggy (a character from a children's television show,

The Muppets), John's nickname for Marianne, one which, while not strikingly gallant, somehow encapsulated the simultaneously affectionate yet antagonistic nature of their relationship. One of John's continental friends characterizes her as 'an extremely tough cookie', and observes: 'She wanted absolutely to marry him.' Minnie Winn, who saw John both in London and the Bahamas, sensed that Marianne 'would have been perfect: tall, commanding, very social, concerned with being a marchioness, always very elegant in an understated way. She wasn't about to be someone's handbag.' Winn concedes, however, that John tended to be drawn to fuller contours and less rigid souls, like those of Angela Barry. 'She was wonderful with him. I think she was a bit like Pauline in a way. At one stage John said to her, "We're so good together, why don't we get married?".' Much though she liked John, Angela Barry found the idea easily resistible. So did Tilly Dugdale. 'John wanted to marry her,' remembers Imogen von Halle. 'She came from the right sort of family,[59] was very attractive, bright.' Although John would later claim his intentions towards Tilly were playful,[60] one of his closest friends is adamant that that was not the case, adding that John's interest in the Dugdales extended to Tilly's cousin Eliza. But Tilly was his favourite. 'She's a sweet, smiley person. He was potty about her. Blondes were always his bag.'

Francesca Fisher fitted that requirement. She was also free-spirited, barely out of her teens, a teetotal vegetarian who had lived in Andalusia since the age of seven (though later attending the Rudolph Steiner school in Sussex), 'a really lovely girl', in Michael Chappell's estimation; 'absolutely beautiful, just so much fun, [with] a great sense of humour', in Sandro Corsini's. To another of John's heterosexual friends, Patrick Donovan, she was 'fantastic, always a ray of sunshine'. One evening in Porto Ercole, she had entered his bedroom, naked, to ask which of the two dresses she was carrying she should wear. It was a testing moment: both were 'perfect Alaïa dresses', recalled Donovan, whose girlfriend was with him at the time. John owed his introduction to Francesca to his friend Mark Cecil whom she had accompanied to Ickworth in the autumn of 1983;[61] John would remark later that he had married so as to father an heir. Later still, Francesca would say that he must have thought her perfect for his purposes: 'very naïve, very young, almost boyish'.

The couple's engagement in April 1984 – one of the least probable, the press implied, since that of the Dancing Marquess – prompted others to a similarly mechanistic interpretation. But scepticism felt by those closest to John soon faded. 'I think he really did love [her],' says Roger Lane-Smith

One of John's intimate male friends tends to agree. 'He surprised himself; I think he loved her. In the old Victorian sense, John wanted to do a good marriage.' That is too tepid an interpretation for one of John's closest female friends. 'I remember him ringing up at 6 a.m., saying that he'd bought a ring at Cartier [in New York]. He was so nervous. He adored her.'

There were times when Francesca felt that adoration. 'I felt very protected,' she later acknowledged, 'like a new toy.' It was an acute phrase, though delivered by someone who today disarmingly describes herself as 'a bit mad', an assessment with which John might have been inclined to agree when his fiancée announced that she was already married – in name, at least – to an American musician. John's astonishment rather puzzled her, remembers Sandro Corsini. 'She said, "Does that really count?" We said, "Well, yes, when you get married, it counts".'

A flurry of negotiation secured the necessary annulment, though not without transatlantic crossings, three months living on the Nevada side of Lake Tahoe[62] and help from Raymond Furnell, Provost of Bury St Edmunds Cathedral, an ecclesiastic of sympathy and sophistication. 'He liked coming to Ickworth,' remembers Francesca, 'liked all that.'

Her own instinct for adventure – and her indifference to convention – were gifts from parents who had not supposed their daughter destined for marriage into the aristocracy. Her father, Douglas, had, at various times, involved himself in property, interior design, antiques and antiquities, and restaurants (at one of which flamingo was on the menu, and where a chimpanzee had been recruited as a wine waiter). Her mother, Louisa, was a former model, whom Francesca characterizes as 'really cool', a quality which proved helpful on her first trip in John's helicopter. 'We had to land on the motorway because we ran out of fuel. My mother didn't really get too affected. The police came; they thought it was great.'

The generosity of Douglas Fisher's wedding present was indicative of his joy in his daughter's second match: enough marble to lay a floor over what had been the Ickworth swimming pool. Francesca was never to meet her father-in-law, which, she believes, was Yvonne's intention. One of John's former lovers, however, suggests that by then Victor would have had no desire to see his eldest son. If so, it was not an attitude he had held unwaveringly, as Guy Sainty explains. 'I remember talking to him when he thought John was being very clever… buying ranches in Australia. I think for a moment Victor was proud of him.'

Nothing would have thrilled John more. He yearned desperately for Victor's approval,[63] however ill he later spoke of him. Consciously or not, it was Victor whom he mimicked, whose traits and frailties now sometimes threatened to define him. No longer did he wear a grey flannel suit when shooting (any more than Victor, in later years, had retained the chalk stripe in which he had greeted Johnny Kimberley), but his addiction to 'the marquessate accoutrements' was as intense as Victor's had ever been. So were his obsession with money (and the pride in its acquisition by sharp practice), his craving for attention (ideally achieved by extravagant display), his preference for fantasy over reality (so gratifying that the gulf between the two could be obscured by manipulating the unwitting functionaries of the press), even his antipathy to opera and the concert hall (enthusiastic about the work of Elton John, Queen and Duran Duran, he never developed an appreciation for more extended composition).

Yet, as with Victor, his inadequate education and his distaste for sustained periods of application could not disguise charm and intelligence, both of which Simon Garnier, newly installed as the National Trust's operational manager at Ickworth, now experienced for the first time. 'He was absolutely charming and amusing and interesting, very knowledgeable; a very nice person to be with,' remembers Garnier, who was delighted to sanction use of the Rotunda for the wedding, as well as Hervey family silver which had been assigned to the Trust nearly forty years earlier. John, he adds, appeared 'very focused', much as he had to Nick Ashley and other friends in the year since his return from New York. Discovery of a sense of purpose had not extinguished familiar moments of self-parody or spasms of self-indulgence. 'I asked him if he would invite me to his wedding,' remembers one of Nicholas's Yale friends. Assured that he would be invited as long as he were 'particularly nice', the Yale man inquired if, when the time came, John would also pay for his flight to England from the States. 'He looked at me, [and said]: "Hmmm, for that, young man, you might have to bite the pillow, and think of your homeland".' The Yale man remained in America.

John's stag weekend, held at Ickworth a week before the wedding, afforded him the leeway he sought: he devoted half an hour of it to hovering in the Hughes 500 (over the Earl-Bishop's obelisk), accompanied by a twinkie, thereafter assuring Nick Ashley and others present that that would be 'absolutely the last time that he would go in for "that kind of thing"'. Twinkies were, accordingly, not in evidence on the wedding day, 14 September 1984, John contenting himself with a familiar medley of patrician junkies, Suffolk worthies, old friends and former lovers (principally Robin Hurlstone, whom he had telephoned, imploring his attendance). Francesca had been assured that she could invite whoever she wanted 'as long as they weren't Jewish or black'. (John, she felt, might not have been entirely joking, but he raised no objection to her father's attendance, nor indeed to her own, perhaps, as she points out, because her mother was not Jewish, 'so it doesn't count'.)

The service passed decorously enough, the congregation being limited to about thirty-five, all that could be seated in Ickworth church. Rain was falling as bride and groom emerged, led by Cara and Basil, John's Irish wolfhounds, but had eased by the time of the evening party. The guest-list was spangled with old allies like Jasper Guinness, and less intimate acquaintances like Dai and Vanessa Llewllyn, Bryan Ferry and Wayne Sleep. Under the cocaine-driven direction of Stephen Hayter, liveried footmen in costume wigs lined the drive, which was lit with flares. George Melly and the Joe Loss orchestra prepared to perform in a marquee for 400, which was linked by canopied walkway to the Rotunda. Each of those dining[64] received a miniature silver box engraved with the Hervey snow leopard. 'Francesca had changed into an incredible, shimmering, skin-tight, silver dress,' remembers Minnie Winn. 'It looked like mermaid's scales. Around her neck she had a huge rivière, which John had given her. She looked stunning: a little girl transformed into a star.' Nevertheless, Minnie Winn worried for her. 'She was sweet but you could see that she could be hurt.'

Francesca had felt at her most vulnerable immediately after John's proposal: her engagement ring ('emeralds with diamonds, from Cartier in New York; Foley collected it') had caused her particular unease. 'The first couple of weeks I thought, "Oh, my God, I'm not wearing it in front of Clarissa Baring and Marianne Hinton... they'll cut my finger off".' Anxiety resurfaced as she took her place at dinner. John had ensured that only his friends – none of hers – sat at the bridal table: Benjamin Mancroft, Patrick Donovan, 'Pickford' Sykes;[65] the women she found more daunting – Isabel Goldsmith, Clarissa Baring and Marianne Hinton – 'all of them wanting to stick a dagger in me'. (Marianne had, in fact, presented John with a pair of handguns, 357 Magnums, later used for 'target practice in the cellar, sometimes with dumdum bullets; one went through into the Rotunda, I think, through six layers of brick'.)

At another table, conversation turned to the terms of a trust, one of whose clauses stipulated that funds would only be released to John if he were married by his thirtieth birthday – 15 September 1984 – now just hours away. 'The speeches were mainly wishing John a happy birthday and congratulating him on his inheritance,' says Minnie Winn, who was intrigued by the style of the cake that now appeared. 'It was a helicopter, nearly three feet high. I said, "Why a helicopter? I would have thought it would have been a wedding cake." Someone said, "Forget the wedding – he's celebrating his fortune now".'

It was between 3 a.m. and 4 a.m. that Minnie Winn departed; by then John and what she terms his 'inner circle' had migrated to the East Wing. A little earlier, one of Francesca's allies had seen Nick Somerville gravitate towards the groom. 'I remember Francesca being distraught because Nick was shut away in a room talking to John. We were all distraught.' There are conflicting versions of what followed. Francesca recalled, twenty years later, that she had eventually found John after knocking on the door of an upstairs room: she had walked in to discover him and 'a group of friends' freebasing.

One of John's former closest friends remembers a slightly different sequence. In the early hours, he and Nick Somerville had joined John in the morning room. John locked the door behind them. There they remained, talking; there were no drugs. Eventually they heard the door being thumped. Francesca appeared.

John was the first to speak. He kept it brief. 'Fuck off.'

'I want to go to bed now, John.'

'Go to bed then.'

'John, it's my wedding night.'

'I love these two more than I'll ever love you.' John cackled: a sound his former lover had so often heard before. Then there were just two other sounds – Francesca crying and her retreating footsteps.

A few months later, John Knight had a chance meeting with Merri MacRae, a forthright woman who had never troubled to mask her distaste for Victor nor the sympathy and understanding she had for John, her much younger second cousin. He never forgot what she told him. 'She said: "Unless there's a baby soon, John won't live very long".'

* * *

Paul Foreman – Liverpudlian, car thief, charmer – led the way in the Cadillac ('coach lined in maroon and adorned with marquess's coronets', procured from Tatton Sykes), accompanied by Foley and a twenty-three-year-old called James; John, following in a Jaguar of cobalt blue, accompanied by a twenty-seven-year-old called Neil, drew level at successive traffic lights, at both of which he ran over, scrabbled at the Cadillac's tinted windows, and harangued one or more of its occupants ('James, the telephone is redirecting. Sort it out! I want to telephone you').

There was no Francesca, no Angela, no Clarissa, to witness the perform-ance, delivered en route from London to Ickworth, late in 1989. But there was

Jessica Berens,[66] to whom John had granted an interview, instructing her to arrive at his Belgravia house, 11 South Eaton Place, on a Friday afternoon, in readiness for a weekend in his company. Once inside, past the security camera and the brass plaque emphasizing that visitors would be admitted by appointment only, she was treated to 'the sight of cute young men in striped shirts skipping hither and thither'.

Later, at Ickworth, a bottle of scent was delivered to her room. The attached note read: 'Made by one of my companies. John.' Other subjects demanded her attention: divorce, addiction and, especially, La Moye Prison, from which John had been released at the end of April, after making Mr Foreman's acquaintance and serving two-thirds of a one-year sentence (for possession of 13 grammes of cocaine). During the course of the weekend, he addressed them all, often when slurping orange juice from a silver tankard and twitching 'like a fairground attraction', but only after first reviewing the disappearance of £3,500 worth of Theo Fennell ivory hairbrushes, the procedure for insuring £135,000 of jewellery, and how he had once tried to buy Simon Le Bon ('Mick Jagger told me I was mad not to').

Prison had not changed him ('it's designed for the lower classes really, isn't it?'), whereas cocaine had ('if you take [it] for ten years, your metabolism alters'); divorce had accorded him dietary freedom ('I hate avocados. Francesca ate avocados with everything. Repulsive. Mind you, I never wanted to eat Francesca either'). His appearances in the dining room were haphazardly connected to mealtimes, his passion ignited only by thoughts of his latest Rolls or Aston ('it doesn't know what's going to happen to it... painted dark green... red coach lining... TV... decanters... stereo'), though there were spasms of reflection too. 'I get bursts of pleasure from beauty. There was a fawn once that came into this house and I liked that, because it showed that people had emotions. My father had no emotions at all, really. In the end I've got my opinions but I don't know what the answers are.' Veering from incoherence to pretence to gentleness, this was John's staple performance, not just for journalists but also for old friends.

A year or so earlier, Peter Geiger and Imogen von Halle had met him for dinner in London. It was the first time Imogen had seen him for more than a decade. 'He was looking better than I'd expected – not dreadful, but definitely thinner. We went back for a nightcap in his house in Belgravia. It was a pleasant evening, really quite normal.' The wit of old was slightly blunted, but overall John appeared to have sustained less damage than several friends who were by then receiving much-needed clinical treatment. A winter weekend at Ickworth followed, prefaced by a warning from Peter Geiger that the occasion was likely to require significant effort from John and that they should, therefore, prepare themselves for 'all sorts of outcomes'.

Imogen noticed the installation of huge televisions and the development of John's video library. Throughout Saturday, however, there was little sign of him – and no sign of him at all as she and Geiger, Adrian Sassoon and 'a very young girl hosting [the weekend] with John' had drinks in the drawing room before dinner. 'Finally, at 9.30 p.m., I said, "Can you please serve dinner, with or without his lordship?"' A butler – no longer Coles – complied. Much later, John appeared; he left before his guests had finished eating.

The following day, Pauline joined them for lunch. John was not in evidence; Pauline did not seem too dismayed, unless her drinking masked anxiety. Soon she was 'absolutely plastered' and spilled red wine on the Aubusson carpet in the drawing room. John, who took his seat towards the end of lunch – which he did not see to its conclusion – was in much the same condition. 'He was so drunk – or whatever – that he sort of fell into his soup. He couldn't get a coherent sentence out.'

Imogen von Halle and Peter Geiger left shortly afterwards. 'The butler thanked us for coming; according to him, it was the most normal weekend they'd had for as long as he could remember.' It had been a dismaying experience but not a completely disastrous one, since both his old friends were aware that he was making an effort on their behalf, unsustainable though it had proved to be. An earlier effort had seemed destined to yield the novel and extraordinary reward of unstimulated contentment. 'When he got married to Francesca, he tried very hard to be the country aristocrat,' remembers Roger Lane-Smith. 'He did seem a much happier person.' The wife of one of John's closest friends agrees. 'He was really trying. Nick [Somerville] was off the scene completely. That was the very best time.' To Nick Ashley and others, the years 1983 to 1986, enriched by the Hughes 500 and Saxon Breck,[67] were the happiest of John's adult life. 'Not everybody,' says Tim von Halle, 'has had such a fun, interesting time in their lives. The flag was flying, the place was lit. It was magic. We'd fly to lunch with his mother – it was only about three minutes – land in her garden, flatten her roses. Her dogs – a St Bernard and lurchers – would scram across the heath.' Pauline, widowed in 1983, loved each needless, triumphal landing.

Bob Rush, recruited as head gardener in the same year, suffered bereavement in the most horrific of circumstances[68] within weeks of taking up his appointment. John reassured him that he could take as much time as he needed to recover; his salary would be paid regardless. It was a gesture, he discovered, which was entirely characteristic of his new employer's generosity. Even the National Trust was content, Simon Garnier willingly overseeing the rewiring of the East Wing, an intricate operation requiring the removal of the silk with which all its walls were dressed (and its reinstatement once the work was done).

The effort was not John's alone. Tim von Halle remembers Francesca as 'a great woman', the person who 'almost turned John'. Her husband had prolonged the test of the wedding night[69] into the honeymoon, the first leg of which was spent in an attic room at Gleneagles, where he experienced significant 'cold turkey' narcotic withdrawal symptoms, but mustered the strength to tell his bride to write the thank-you letters for their wedding presents. In Hong Kong and Antigua, he respectively whiled nights away, solo, in clubs of uncertain provenance and flew to New York on 'urgent business'. When Francesca followed a few days later, he telephoned her from London: 'Take Concorde home quickly – I haven't seen you all honeymoon.' During an interim leg in Australia, he invited friends to their hotel room in Sydney, but did offer evidence that he could enjoy time alone with his wife, when they visited the Queensland sheep station by plane.

It was in the air that John could really believe in himself. He was, one friend observed, 'an inspired pilot', always willing, as others discovered, to try manoeuvres unlisted in the instructor's manual. An occasional female passenger recalls a challenging return trip to Ickworth 'with the petrol warning light on, skipping over the pylons, [in] not brilliant visibility. We didn't make it to the H at the back of the house – we came down in the front.' Tim von Halle experienced a smoother ride to the Lake District to visit friends, nearing whose house John spotted that Windermere was speckled with windsurfers. Moments later, he was hovering low over the water, remaining there until none remained upright. An impromptu flight to Houghton Hall, David Rocksavage's Norfolk seat, was almost as rewarding, concluding with the Hughes 500 touring up and down the visitors' car park, its down-draught spraying gravel into car paintwork, until John found somewhere to 'park'.

He refined the procedure in Porto Ercole, repeatedly landing on the minute space next to the house he had rented, oblivious to neighbouring buildings as well as to trees and shrubs only feet from his rotor blades. 'It was the most extraordinary thing,' remembers Sandro Corsini. 'The neighbours never imagined that someone would have the guts to do something like that.' Friends dissuaded Corsini from flying with John again.

But no one could dissuade Francesca. After weekends at Ickworth, she and John flew to London each Monday morning, staying in hotels during the week, until the return on Friday. She remembers a London-to-Newmarket evening flight through impenetrable cloud. 'We couldn't see a thing, we were running out of fuel, and [John] knew that there was a lot of forest nearby. Because there were pylons, we had to be really careful.' Guidance was sought from air traffic control but none was forthcoming. John's – and Francesca's – version of being 'really careful' was then put into action. 'We couldn't see, so we just took a chance and landed, in a field, a ploughed field. We were fine. And you know what? I never got scared. I was too young to be scared. You don't get scared like that when you're twenty-one.' Nor did John at thirty. 'He was a good pilot; he loved it. It was exciting.' Plunging through cloud, with no inkling of what was below – a procedure, likely to prove fatal, which he periodically repeated – offered John proof that he could defy the odds, and could do so without the interference he tended to attract when, say, tackling the motorway hard shoulder at 140 mph. But his love for four wheels endured, especially when teamed with luxurious interiors (Wilton carpets were considered essential) and frenzied horsepower. It was a passion which led to the cliff-edge and beyond, remembers Sandro Corsini, who was awoken one night in Porto Ercole by a telephone call at 3 a.m.

John dispensed with preliminaries: 'You have to come: I don't speak any Italian. We need somebody to come and pick up the car.' When Corsini reached the scene, he saw Foley and some of John's friends; of John there was no sign. His car, a gold convertible Rolls, was in a precarious position, 'caught in some olive trees', with a 60 to 70-foot drop beneath it. John materialized an hour later, freshly showered, wearing a white scarf and 'a white bathrobe, with his coronet on it, and his crested slippers'. A team of mechanics, assisted by Foley, were by then attaching a recovery truck's cables to the Rolls in the hope of winching it back to safety. (Success was finally achieved by crane the following morning.) John was undismayed, mentioning that the Rolls was on loan, a temporary replacement for one of his which was being repaired. The incident made little impression on Francesca. 'We went for a drive – I don't remember where – and John went round a corner and slipped; I can't remember why.' The Rolls's front wheels had gone over the cliff edge. The only tricky moment, she adds, came when she opened the door to jump out ('the car nearly rolled'). She had soon put it all behind her. 'That sort of thing happened all the time.'

The bravura of John's performances continued to attract neophytes beyond his obvious sexual and narcotic constituencies. None revered him more than Gerald Carroll, remembered by Francesca for his vehement antipathy to drugs, his heterosexuality, his brand new tweeds, and his social discomfort in the company of John's patrician associates. Scion of a family which might fairly be considered the twentieth-century version of the Wythes,[70] Carroll soon established himself as an integral if improbable part of the Ickworth court. Nick Ashley, still at that stage trying to keep pace with John's expenditure, remembers Carroll's arrival in a Ford Escort; Tim von Halle remembers a Golf GTi. Both agree that the novitiate had soon advanced to a Lamborghini, the first step towards his acquisition of 'all the toys: a Bell Jet Ranger Helicopter, a Riva sprayed lacquer red, Bentleys, Ferraris'. There was sartorial progress, too, evidenced by a succession of Huntsman suits, though Carroll could never, allegedly, be persuaded to buy shoes of similar pedigree, although it was noted that his mother had invested in a gold ankle bracelet.

'Gerald Carroll desperately wanted to be John,' suggests one of John's younger friends. 'If John had monogrammed luggage, Gerald Carroll would have to [have it too].' It was an acute case of 'Bristolitis' – excruciating mimicry of John's mannerisms and expenditure. John revelled in his tutorial role, gratified by the zealousness with which Carroll responded to instruction that included advice about the composition of his coat of arms (this, John advised, should include Basil, John's Irish wolfhound, as an appropriate refer-ence to Carroll's Hibernian pedigree). 'He made John laugh,' remembers Francesca, adding that the three of them holidayed in Antigua together. 'He was a weird guy but nice: he wasn't in it for money or drugs, he was just impressed by John's courage.' John's new friend does not remember himself in such a subordinate role, describing himself as Ickworth's 'comptroller', a post he says he held for 'ten, twelve, fifteen years'. He adds: 'I kept John straight, as far as I could.' There were others who, if unable to emulate Gerald Carroll's abstemiousness, proved themselves bona fide friends, enjoying John for his own sake rather than feeding off his weaknesses. 'Ed Somerset [was] a very sweet, very lovely guy,' remembers Francesca. 'His wife was a very nice woman.[71] They were cool.'

Andy Pearce lacked Somerset's lineage but radiated similar style. By 1984, he was living in the ground floor flat at 74 Oakley Street, his Maserati parked outside. Gentle-natured, good-looking, a man with rockstar acquaintances (and a survivor of a ferocious mugging in Los Angeles a few years earlier), he was, remembers a former neighbour, 'charming, a delightful chap, never any bad behaviour, although a party animal'. The ground-floor flat, he adds, was devoid of alcohol but invariably littered with empty Coca-Cola cans. The following year, Pearce moved to 2 More's Garden, Cheyne Walk, lodging with Minnie Winn. John was a frequent visitor, possibly because of a joint business venture connected with Pearce's property interests. 'Andy's family had serious investments. Once he said to me, "John and I are equals finan-cially, but the amount of hangers-on he has..." It sickened him.'[72]

Unfortunately, Pearce had a problem of his own, his fondness for what he referred to as 'Cadbury's', a word he uttered in a mild, slightly mischievous tone, one which seriously under-sold the strength of the sweet in his palm: heroin. No attempt was made to disguise his habit, either from girlfriends ('Andy was beautiful but gone,' remembers one) or from Minnie Winn ('I kept saying, "You're killing yourself; stop it, stop it"').

John appeared to be in better shape, 'always very polite, correct. Arguably, that was his façade.' But in other company, cracks began to appear. John now attracted a new strain of hanger-on: those craving a fix of notoriety. Francesca particularly remembers 'a little guy with black hair, called "the Rat"' and his side-kick, 'Wiggy'. This pair, more formally known as Nigel Pollitzer and David Elias, were occasionally joined by another of Pollitzer's friends, Paddy McNally, at whose Verbier residence John and Francesca endured a difficult weekend. 'All they talked about was Fergie because she was going out with Andy [Prince Andrew]; it was such a big deal that Paddy had been her previ-ous boyfriend.' John took against McNally's house – 'he ripped it apart, and then we left' – but continued to see his new friends in London, particularly over lunch at a Chelsea restaurant, Foxtrot Oscar, from where he would return to Francesca 'coked up'.

Despite these lapses, she knew he was engaged in a battle he did not want to lose. 'He really tried.' At Ickworth, in particular, she could help. 'I can remember her going through rooms, chucking out drugs and all sorts of things,' says the wife of one of John's friends. Francesca herself recalls an especially productive sweep which ended with her putting 'three kilos of cocaine down the loo'. This did not endear her to John's friends, or even John himself. 'It was stopping his fun,' acknowledges her ally. But the Ickworth drugs war had greater significance than the curtailment of familiar pleasures.

In March 1985, John had succeeded Victor as 7th Marquess. He had long wanted children, recalls Michael Chappell, and shortly before his wedding had expressed his hope that they would benefit from his own filial experi-ences. 'I was acutely aware,' he explained, 'that when I was growing up my father was quite old and was never able to do any of the things with me that I'd like to have done as a child.' He was now in procreative mood; Francesca was not – and did not wish to be, at least until confident that John had got the better of his addictions. 'I wanted him to clean up for a few months,' is how she puts it. As long as he was at Ickworth, that seemed possible. 'He was fine the first year. It was when he [went] back to New York to sell his house that everything got really out of control.' She did not accompany him. 'He was only going for a few days but then he stayed quite a long time: long enough to do himself a lot of harm. A major binge.'

By the time of their holiday in Porto Ercole in August 1986, slightly under two years since their wedding, the Bristols' marital life had become sufficiently disjointed for husband and wife to travel separately. John arrived first. He was joined by an Italian friend, Enrico Recchi ('very rich; in the construction sector'); by an Englishman and his Swedish girlfriend; and by Andy Pearce, who, remembers one of the house-party, was 'in very bad shape, slurring [his words], falling all over the place, taking copious amounts of methadone – or other concoctions – and drinking. He was always a very, very heavy drinker.'[73]

Francesca, who was by then attracting attention from a Brazilian called Roberto Shorto, arrived a day or two later. None of the party – not only Pearce, of whom she was extremely fond – appeared to her to be benefiting from sea air or exercise. 'They were all high, all smacked out.' In other circumstances she might have coped, but there was a new difficulty for which she had no stomach: an additional house-guest, with 'a sailor's hat rakishly perched on his head looking like something out of a Fellini movie. John's current twink. [He and John] were taking all manner of drugs and sleeping together.' Francesca allowed her belief in her marriage to expire. 'They were sharing the double room, and I was put in the servants' quarters. At that stage I'd really had enough.' The house-party fractured. Enrico Recchi left for Rome; as did the Englishman and his Swedish girlfriend, and Francesca. In Porto Ercole, John concentrated on enjoying his remaining companions. But a day (possibly two days) later, the holiday came to a hideous end.

'DEATH RIDDLE AT MARQUIS'S VILLA'. The report accompanying the *Daily Mail*'s front page headline on 26 August recorded that Andy Pearce had died following what had at first seemed a banal accident. 'After lunch on Saturday,' explained Roger Lane-Smith, who had flown to Italy, 'he was walking along the corridor of the villa, slipped and fell.' Feeling unwell, he had gone to bed; everyone in the house had taken turns to watch over him. 'Suddenly, at night, his condition seemed to change. It was obvious that he had died in his sleep.' The following day, this was revised: the accident had happened at 9.45 p.m. on the Friday evening. Unnamed sources had by then spoken of Pearce's heroin and alcohol addictions. John commented: 'There are no drugs here. I know nothing about his heroin problem – nothing at all'. He added that he had spent most of the day in bed and had been having a bath when he heard that his friend had collapsed. Four days later, John made a further statement: he admitted, in the *News of the World*, that he had taken heroin. Drug-taking, John explained, was 'like brushing your teeth. You do it so often that you don't even notice.' The admission was layered in lies and contradictions. '[Andy Pearce] did not take drugs at my villa, nor did I, nor did anyone… I'm off drugs,' John said, insisting that that had been the case for four years. He and Andy Pearce, he now explained, had been out drinking when Andy had stumbled, fallen and hit his head. Francesca had left because 'she was just fed up with the fuss over Andrew's death. There's no rift.'

In the coming weeks, as the 'rift' could no longer be disguised, John would talk to the press of his hopes for a reconciliation. It was a soothing fiction. He had wept when Francesca walked out, aware that, without her, the mirage of family, stability and sanity could not be sustained. His better friends, including some who shared his taste for heroin, reserved their sympathy for her. 'As decadent as we might all have been,' reflects one of the Porto Ercole house guests, 'it just seemed incredibly unfair that John should be living this life in her face.' At Ickworth, Foley packed her clothes and dispatched them to her. Francesca did not ask for her engagement ring, which lay in the Ickworth safe. She proved well equipped for survival. Nearly twenty years later, she reflected that she had been lucky to have John 'on pretty good form' for as long as she had, a time when she felt loved and happy. She reiterates the point today, describing John as 'amazing'.

Three months after her departure, John was seen trying to make the acquaintance of Leo Ford, an American stripper, whom he had seen at Gay Night at the Hippodrome, a West End club. His choice of potential companion aroused little surprise, or disapproval, amongst his associates. Some of them, however, found the confusion surrounding Andy Pearce's death less easily assimilable. 'After Andy died, [John] became a pariah,' remembers a former female ally. 'I didn't see John after 1986, except once at a wedding, and I didn't speak to him then.'

Although others also disengaged, most accepted that Andy Pearce's death was caused by freakish ill luck (his fall being fatal only because of the damage he had sustained when mugged in Los Angeles a few years earlier). The Italian police ruled out foul play, a reassuring but ultimately superfluous detail for the more steadfast of John's friends.[74] None of that, however, could excuse or explain the obfuscation, and outright lies, that immediately followed the accident, nor gloss over a wretchedly misjudged attempt at flippancy. 'This has been the most miserable holiday I've ever spent,' he had told the *News of the World*. 'My best friend died, and now my Ferrari has broken down.' Andy's family told him to stay away from the funeral. New friends would accompany John on the final part of his journey.

* * *

Robert Ireland (always known as Paddy) was familiar with the sound of the Hughes 500. He did his best to ignore it now as he headed down the drive at Ickworth on a clear day, with the sunroof of his Fiat Uno pulled open. But the 500 did seem remarkably close. It was: more or less directly overhead, in fact, with John at the controls and his friend James sitting in the passenger seat beside him.

A moment later, the helicopter skids jolted against the Fiat's roof. A second blow sprayed the contents of the car ashtray upwards, against the windscreen and through the sunroof, though Ireland felt that most of it had gone up his nose. He kept the Uno on the road. 'I think he only banged the car twice. You just accepted it. That was normal.'

It was normal, too, during the high days of the late 1980s and early 1990s, that John should feast on cocaine, grab a shotgun and repeatedly fire it into the air whilst howling abuse at those members of the public who had paid to visit Ickworth's gardens ('****ING PEASANTS, ****ING NATIONAL TRUST'), and just as normal that those lunching with him should scarcely stir ('we just carried on: it was routine'). It soon seemed normal that his movements should become jerkier, 'his appearance sinister, his hair longer and oilier'; normal that he should have 'five suits made each week in materials more suited to soft furnishings'; that he should entertain 'frantically, seven days a week, as though he could not bear his own company'. It was normal that disdain for the fuel gauge should send the Hughes 500 plummeting from the sky into a ploughed field, as it did with Angela Barry onboard ('Where's the ****ing telephone?' shrieked John on reaching the nearest farmhouse, through which he stamped mud, oblivious of its owners); normal that a visitor (George Milford Haven) should be greeted by the news that John had blown the door off the fridge the night before (courtesy of the shotgun once more); normal that he should shatter furniture at Ickworth, much of it of little consequence (one piece, a commode, being mended 'four or five times: John actually had a good eye for smashing stuff that really wasn't that important'), though some of it precious if not priceless ('a portrait of Madonna and Child, or something like that, on a solid piece of lapis lazuli: unfortunately, that did get smashed'); normal, too, that he should become the object of police attention and should, in consequence, suffer periodic seclusion in clinics and prisons.

Most of this was accomplished in the company of a younger man. James Whitby had not followed his elder brother to Eton[75] but had, as a sixteen-year-old, been arrested outside the Chelsea Flower Show (he had drunk a bottle of vodka, was wearing his Che Guevara outfit and had an Uzi sub-machine gun slung from his shoulder). By the time he met John five years later, in 1987, he had developed expensive addictions to cocaine and heroin. His name curdles on the lips of many of John's longer established allies. 'Whitby? Oh, God, awful,' says Roger Lane-Smith; 'a drug-taking twink,' suggests Tim von Halle; 'the final straw, a complete bummer, one of life's spongers, [with] that sort of vacant stare,' says one of John's female friends. After John's death in 1999, Nick Ashley offered a different estimation. John had kept a companion, he said, 'in the same way that an eighteenth-century nobleman might have kept a marmoset: partly for his own amusement, but mostly for the irritation it caused the rest of the house'. Today he supplements that view by likening Whitby to a mastiff: always by his master's side.

Others detected the same fusion of mutual dependence and loyalty. '[James Whitby] had an appalling drug habit of his own, but I think he actually was a friend: he was certainly not a cause of John's problems,' remembers Michael Chappell, who continued to see John once every three months. Simon Pott, agent at Ickworth from 1992 onwards and consequently in almost daily contact with John (and Whitby), goes further. Whilst acknowledging that drugs were important to the relationship, he saw enough to convince him that Whitby's friendship was fierce and genuine and motivated by an affection which kept him at John's side through the years of John's bed-ridden disintegration.

James Whitby lays no claim to distinction or virtue during those twelve years, which he reviews with a measure of regret and a trace of innocence, seeing them as an updated version of *The Wind in the Willows*, its protagonists fuelled by cocaine and heroin rather than over-familiarity with the drinks tray. 'Toad ended up going off to jail, he was always getting the latest fast car. John really was Toad; Nick Somerville was Ratty.'

Inevitably, given John's consistent predilections, many, like Tim von Halle, categorized Whitby as a 'twink'. This was a misconception, if an understandable one. Whitby had a girlfriend, of whom he was fond; he reserved his passion for hard drugs. It was his willingness to procure them on John's behalf, and to enjoy them in John's company, that bonded him to his older friend. As Paddy Ireland, who was similarly enthralled, puts it: 'It was always about drugs.'

Leo Ford possibly reached much the same conclusion. Sixteen months after he had caught John's attention, his agent spoke to the *News of the World*. Collected by chauffeur-driven Bentley, the agent had been taken to South Eaton Place where John had talked incoherently about wanting to produce porn films with Ford in the leading role. Later, John had made his intentions clearer by telephone. A night in the stripper's company had followed, some of it spent at Blake's Hotel, South Kensington, and some of it at Heaven, one of John's pre-marital haunts. Cocaine was taken by both men in such quantities that John had felt obliged 'to send his chauffeur out for more'. Despite other intentions, he then lapsed into sleep. The night cost him £4,000 (Ford's fee), aside from drugs and hotel bills.

Although for a time in 1987 he became close to Peter Robinson (alias 'Marilyn'[76]), and though he would bond briefly with a young black friend, John's moments with Leo Ford offered an unerring gauge of preference and performance. If the supremacy of drugs in his affections ever faltered, prodigious consumption invariably precluded consummation. Even fleeting familiarity with Ickworth tended to make this apparent, as Peter Boitel-Gill, a former Army Air Corps pilot, discovered in June 1987 when contracted by Southern Aviation to act as John's co-pilot and flight-planner for a trip to the Paris Air Show. Arriving at Ickworth in the early evening, he learned that John was flying back from a party at Blenheim. Later, a butler headed to the helipad explaining that, on receipt of a wireless signal from the Hughes 500, he would illuminate the site for his lordship's benefit. It was after midnight by the time the signal was received; the landing, Boitel-Gill remembers, was 'enthusiastic and eventually successful'. John emerged, beaming, apologetic and charming, insisting that his guest should join him for a late supper. Boitel-Gill was supplied with a dinner jacket; John wore a white dressing gown. They were joined in the dining room by someone Boitel-Gill initially categorized as a good-looking adolescent of indeterminate sex (later confirmed as a male, 'Tintin' Chambers),[77] who accompanied them on the flight to Paris, which was delayed a day[78] by bad weather, a fortunate hiatus, given that, on the night of Boitel-Gill's arrival, John had not gone to bed 'in case he overslept'.

When they eventually got going, John piloted the Hughes 500 to Battersea heliport. He then departed to attend to some 'routine administration' at his London office, with Tintin in tow. Some time later, supported by his young friend, he lurched back, no longer fit for the pilot's role, although able to focus on Joan Collins, who had arrived at the heliport accompanied by a man Boitel-Gill identified as 'Bungalow' Bill Wiggins.

'Hello Joan, you old —.'

Miss Collins took John's greeting in imperturbable stride.

Slightly to Boitel-Gill's surprise, and certainly to his relief, he managed (with Tintin's assistance) to frogmarch John through Customs at Lydd, on the Kent coast, without prompting a baggage inspection. Strapped back into a rear seat for the remainder of the flight, John had been sick only once by the time they reached Le Bourget, but Boitel-Gill declined, on his behalf, an invitation to an immediate air show rendezvous with a vice-president of McDonnell Douglas at the company's 'hospitality chalet'.

At the Georges V (the penthouse suite), John recovered sufficiently to lower himself into the bath he had ordered Tintin to run. Half an hour later, water began oozing from beneath the bathroom door. Shouts from Boitel-Gill and Tintin went unanswered. The door was forced open by hotel staff; John was found – profoundly asleep but with his head above water, which continued to cascade over the side of the bath. Concluding that his new friends enjoyed 'a special relationship', Boitel-Gill asked Tintin to give John his regards, and took a flight to London.

By now, John's nose appeared 'to have taken on a life of its own'; his hands had become 'gnarled and twisted'. He adhered to nocturnal patterns or no pattern at all. 'Going down to give my daughter her breakfast I would see them all going up to bed,' remembers a female friend. What none knew, perhaps not even Jonny Ruane, was that in 1986 John had been told that he was grievously ill. 'He was too proud to talk about it,' says Nick Ashley who, like James Whitby, would not learn the diagnosis until much later. A third friend reflects that John 'knew he was not long for this world'.

From about the end of 1986 onwards, cocaine and heroin were no longer the delightful fixtures that they had been for thirteen years or so but mutated into crutch and cradle, life becoming insupportable without them: when, on the weekend of Jessica Berens's interview, Paul Foreman returned to London, despite being halfway to Ickworth, to collect 'paperwork', it was because John had realized to his horror that he had left his drugs in Belgravia. Planning was usually more rigorous, being conducted with patriotism ('we had people flying from London to the Bahamas with coke because "we like the coke in England" – well, "we prefer the heroin, actually"') and precision (courtesy, for example, of one of John's tailors with a helpful sideline: 'In every suit there was a gram of coke in the top left-hand pocket. That's why John had so many made'), although never with quite the finesse exhibited by one of John's friends and suppliers, Carlos Mavroleon[79] ('ridiculously methodical about his doses: knew to the nearest grain how much he should be taking of what').

When Mavroleon was not on hand, John coordinated things as best he could, on one occasion, when stranded without cocaine in Porto Ercole, issuing instructions that a horsebox at Ickworth be filled with electronic gadgetry and bits and pieces, and driven non-stop to Italy. On its arrival, he scrabbled through the contents, retrieved a Doobie Brothers cassette (loaded with cocaine, as required), then instructed the driver to return to Ickworth.

Consumption was relentless and immense, especially of cocaine. 'He would never buy less than three or four grams of coke at a time,' remembers James Whitby. 'Heroin, it was something like half a gram. But then the heroin took over because the body needed it: it was a physical dependency rather than a mental [one]. In the end, we were up to four or five grams a day of each – both of us. A huge amount of heroin.' Aside from Mavroleon and the accommodating tailor, John's requirements were met by, amongst others, Quintin Leatham,[80] an Old Etonian, and Lloyd, a West African who found it commercially advantageous to affect a Jamaican accent.

Other visitors to 11 South Eaton Place, the Belgravia house John acquired after Francesca's departure, were similarly variegated. Blandford, Pickford Sykes and the Rat put in appearances, as did others whose backgrounds were less gilded – not just Nick Somerville, who remained part of the furniture – but 'very, very dodgy guys in dressing gowns' who greeted Angela Barry when she arrived to open up the house each morning. 'By that stage,' she remembers, 'the sewer rats were coming in.'

This was the democracy of drugs, its participants united across divisions of class, race and geography, although John, unlike Blandford, spared himself from the brunt of negotiations, delegating the role initially to Nick Ashley and, latterly and enduringly, to James Whitby. 'He was usually in bed, asleep or with cold turkey; he just didn't want to be bothered,' remembers Whitby. 'He trusted my judgement; sometimes my judgement was wrong.' There were difficulties in the Bahamas ('I got shot at a few times. Yardies. Serious yardies') and mistakes in London ('I got ripped off twenty grand'). It seemed advisable to advance the security arrangements first trialled in New York. At Ickworth, four closed-circuit television cameras monitored the drive and other approaches to the East Wing, every inch of which was fitted with alarms, activated by laser; 11 South Eaton Place bristled with video cameras; a bomb-proof front door (four locks) led to an inner door with a two-way mirror and an additional lock (digital); a steel door ('with a mass of locks') secured John's bedroom. Grilles were fitted to all windows, which yielded an inadvertent bonus: 'You couldn't throw furniture through them,' remembers Whitby. John improvised, as Whitby was reminded when on the top floor discussing the acquisition of a Daimler with a dealer from the motor trade. 'I could see these plates – £250 plates – going past the window, then hear them smashing about three floors below.'

He knew what was happening: John was 'bleeping', the term they used for mania induced by sleep deprivation (itself induced by the ingestion of massive quantities of cocaine and heroin). 'When you've stayed up for so long, the body becomes hyperactive; it doesn't relax,' says Whitby, recalling that John had started 'bleeping' by the time he met him in 1987, generally for about two days at a time, before finally lapsing into sleep. Soon the bouts were more frequent and more frightening. 'He would be throwing furniture out of the window or smashing china or glass. I never slept when John was on a rampage. Yes, I was taking drugs as well but I couldn't sleep until he was asleep. I physically couldn't; I was just too scared to relax.' John's physiology was prone to fluctuation even on 'normal' days, with the result that the drive from Ickworth to Bury, once accomplished in about two minutes, now took a little longer. 'Every time he had a rush of heroin, the car would slow down from 180 mph to 30 mph; every time the coke dribbled down the back of his nose, he went from 30 mph to 180 mph. You felt you were in sort of... a steam catapult on an aircraft carrier, permanently being pulled backwards and forwards.' The Aston had been 'tweaked', adds Whitby, by Formula 1 specialists, Cosworth.

In the air, a delay now followed each lift-off whilst John paused for cocaine (snorted off his flight map), a stimulus thereafter regularly supplemented by shots of vodka Collins. 'He went everywhere with this bloody great drink dispenser. I don't think alcohol affected him very much, but that was probably due to the cocaine: coke and alcohol... I think they absorbed one another.' Nick Ashley was aboard for a flight from Battersea to Ickworth when John felt the need for something stronger. Hands off controls, fumbling in pockets, a gold cigarette case, foil 'covered with a brown, tarry substance': Ashley watched the sequence in disbelief which became intolerable, when, through his headphones, he heard 'a sharp, spluttering, sucking sound'. Asked what on earth he was doing, John replied, 'having a smoke', adding that he was then going to sleep. 'I'll shove it on autopilot,' he assured Ashley, in a voice which sounded (as it always did after he had been smoking heroin) as if he were inhaling helium. Listening to John snoring, and with London 1,800 feet below, Ashley decided that he, too, should seek comfort in 'a smoke'. About five minutes before reaching Ickworth, John came to, 'as if it were the most natural thing in the world'.

It became increasingly natural to find time for airborne smoking. Although John never attended the House of Lords (never even took his seat there), he did not ignore the Palace of Westminster entirely, piloting the Hughes 500 satisfyingly close to Big Ben on one occasion, then 'chasing the dragon'. Paddy Ireland, his passenger on that occasion, felt that, the occasional misjudgement aside, John was 'pretty much always in control'. In-flight disorientation did, however, become a problem. Roger Lane-Smith was aboard when John, though 'in no state to drive anything, let alone fly', managed the London–Suffolk flight, then began the final approach with confidence ('I know my own bloody house when I see it') and landed on the roof of the sugar beet factory in Bury. A trip to lunch with Pauline – a three-minute flight completed innumerable times before – involved diversion to a gathering of people on a lawn, some of whom John felt might be able to help clarify his position. It was a wedding party: hats, glasses, plates disappeared in the down-draught as guests fled inside ('all you could see were people looking out of windows, with terrified faces'). John weighed up the situation, decided not to alight ('Oh, perhaps we'd better not') and flew off.

At Ickworth, he experimented with the technique soon to be refined for use against the National Trust, hovering about ten yards from the window of an East Wing bedroom. 'The wind wash was quite something, and there was a hell of a lot of noise,' Whitby recalls, adding that the bedroom was occupied by Dominic Langlands Pearse, a comparatively new acquaintance, whose wife Frances (always known as 'France') was adored by John, who engaged her from time to time to do the East Wing flowers.

It was not the only respect in which he maintained standards. The shoot continued; so did the Christmas party. But these were paltry consolations to the National Trust. Simon Garnier, initially so charmed by John, now found their meetings dominated by lopsided discussion about his behaviour. 'He never really heard [what was being said]. Quite often he was looking out of the window.' The Trust caretaker logged atrocities from his Rotunda flat: the Hughes 500 landing in the Trust car park, or a Ferrari or Lamborghini breaking 100 mph down the drive, or the latest dispatch about the wolfhounds that killed and consumed chickens, cats, sheep and other dogs with some consistency (also occasionally leaving their mark on human flesh, although Bodie, John's Staffordshire Bull Terrier, arguably had the edge in all regards). Though unable to remember the caretaker by sight ('I might have set the dogs on him once or twice'), Whitby suspects that he found sleep elusive, thanks to the chaotic symphony from the East Wing's orchestra of fire-alarms, the most penetrating of them – triggered whenever an inner glass door was not properly secured – producing a sound impressively reminiscent of 'a Stukka dive-bomber'.

In London, Angela Barry endured the bedlam until the spring of 1988. 'It was just mad. I'd seen him spend in New York but not like this. It was spend, spend, spend: "Get me more of this!" Everything: hi-fis, speakers, cinema screens, gadgets. Stuff from Peter Jones, from Harrods. Non-stop.' One morning John stood on his doorstep. He was shouting, wearing what she describes as his 'nightie'; he appeared not to have slept for days. An address was bawled out: she was to go there, carrying the top hat he was handing her, then return with whatever she was given. Her proposed destination was a flat on an inner-city estate. She asked John if he thought she were mad, swore at him and walked to her car. Another senior member of staff ran the errand instead. John was still screaming as Angela drove away. It was the last time she saw him.

The parting was not without regret. Quite often, John had visited her in Ifield Road, near Earls Court. 'Before he went completely awful, he was very fond of me, and I was very fond of him. He'd come and chat in my grotty little bedsit – a bed, a gas fire, a little TV – all very jolly, all very basic.' There was no disdain for her surroundings, just gratitude for her friendship.

There were other moments when John tried to break the narcotic siege. During these he 'had a thought about marrying' Beatrice Versolato,[81] although the improbable relationship had faltered by the time of John's first imprisonment, which followed his arrival in Jersey on 8 June 1988 for what was intended to be a week's holiday. Aboard the Hughes 500 with him were Whitby, Dominic and France Langlands Pearse, Neil Thackeray (by then being described as John's business manager) and thirteen grams of cocaine, which was unearthed at Customs. It was over a fortnight before John was granted bail, on condition that he stayed at the Vermont Nursing Home, observed a 7 p.m. curfew, and submitted to treatment for cocaine addiction. On 15 September, his thirty-fourth birthday, he was seen enjoying pre-dinner drinks with friends at the Lobster Pot Restaurant, L'Etacq; bail was rescinded two days later.

The following month, on 6 October, he was jailed for a year for possession and importation. 'Very surprised'[82] by the length of his sentence, he coped well in La Moye Prison nonetheless, graduating from floor-scrubbing to serving food, and persuading the *Jersey Evening Post* that he was 'an ordinary, intelligent, sensitive man with a good sense of humour', a judgement it reached following interviews with various former fellow inmates.

He emerged on 28 April 1989, released early (like Victor) for good behaviour, apparently unscathed. Announcing that he had made £4 million 'buying and selling property in the North of England' whilst inside, he said it felt fantastic to be free and, when asked what he had learned about drugs, replied:

John with Teddy Lambton: 'A wonderful step-father to me... he used to take me hunting.'

John (back row, fifth right) in his second year in Druries, at Harrow. His first house master enjoyed selecting boys according to social status rather than academic attainment.

From 'pathetically lonely and unhappy little boy' at Harrow to 'very effeminate teenager'; John's progress was monitored by a 'curious' older boy, Nick Somerville, known as 'Nick-Knack' (bottom left corner).

David Grigg, 'Grigglet', (left), with Nick-Knack Somerville.
John's half-brother Nicholas is partly obscured on the far left.

John (centre) with Gabrielle Coles
and Peter Geiger at the launch of
the Investment Motoring Company.

Rupert Everett relaxing aboard the *Braemar*,
Lyford Cay, August 1978. (Maurice Gibb of
the Bee Gees was also present.)

John with Tim von Halle (left) and Nick-Knack.

John with
Nick-Knack
on the
Braemar.

John and Marianne Hinton ('Anybody who went after him never got him.'). On the left is Jonny Ruane, 'a really sweet, rather shy, crazy boy'.

Lord Nicholas Hervey (centre, seated) founder of the Rockingham, Yale's most stimulating club.

Left; *below right*: John with Francesca, attempting unstimulated contentment.

Andy Pearce: 'beautiful but gone'. Maria Rawlinson (née Garton): 'almost too good to be true'.

Left: John on his wedding day, on Saturday 14 September 1984, clinging to his wolfhound, Basil.

Above: Tweaked by Formula 1 specialists Cosworth, John's Aston was capable of 180 mph; when it slowed to 70mph, 'you felt you could get out and walk'.
Right: John with his mother, Pauline, in Jersey, June 1988: 'The person who mattered most'.

Farewell to Ickworth, June 1996. John pointed out that he had made his own money ('the accountants say it's £20 million') and spent it as he chose.

Leaving St Mary's, Paddington in February 1995, via the front entrance, a performance of 'magnificent defiance'.

John's old friend David Cholmondeley, Lord Great Chamberlain of England, attends the Queen at the State Opening of Parliament, November 1999.

'Don't carry them on your person'. In the next three or four years there were other occasional signs of the old splendour, memorably when pointing out the inconsistency of the Australian immigration department. 'Considering half your country comes from criminal stock,' he told its officials when facing deportation in April 1990, 'I find it extraordinary that you feel so strongly about criminals now.'[83]

In Porto Ercole, he booked a suite at the Pelicano, a hotel of the unremitting luxury and punishing expense that he always found reassuring, and additionally paid for rooms for a dozen friends whom he had invited to join him on a chartered boat. Sandro Corsini was among those who met the Pelicano party on board. 'We had a fantastic day on the islands,' he remembers. There would be a vintage finale.

Coming in to dock that evening, Corsini noticed quayside activity ('blue flashing lights, red flashing, yellow flashing: like a Christmas tree'). He peered through binoculars. As John emerged from his cabin, changed for entertainment ashore ('a pea green suit, coronet tiepin, hairdo a la Thatcher'), Corsini was able to report developments: 'Some mechanics are trying to figure out how to get your Testarossa on a flatbed... your Rolls is already on a flat-bed... policemen are walking around the BMW [motorbike].'

John cursed the manager of the Pelicano, muttered about the discovery of a bounced cheque, then recovered to ask Sebastian Taylor to bring him his American Express Card. Taylor complied. 'As the gangplank goes down, John throws the credit card onto the dock, and it skids across the street and magically flies right under the foot of the manager of the hotel.' The artistry of the gesture failed to placate the manager, who warned that a 30 per cent surcharge had been levied on John's hotel bill, now bloated by the cost of calling out tow-away lorries and police fines.

Apologizing insistently for the mistake, John allowed an imprint of his card to be made, watched the Pelicano's manager head back to the hotel, then returned to his cabin and telephoned American Express. 'He tells them to cancel all transactions – that his card has been stolen – and so the card is instantaneously annulled. He then puts Foley in the Rolls, a friend [in] the Testarossa, another [on] the motorcycle, and tells them to [make a] beeline for Monte Carlo "as fast as you can: get out of here". Those who stayed at Porto Ercole got off the boat, [which] immediately takes off for Monte Carlo.' 'This was pretty much the last straw, in terms of coming back to Italy,' adds Corsini, who concluded that John had intended that his cheque should bounce. 'It wasn't about the cost involved. He just loved the sensation of causing trouble.'

There had been other bad cheques, however, to Angela Barry, whose supplementary duties between 1986 and 1988 included cooking for South Eaton Place dinner parties and, in 1991, another to Blake's hotel, where John was additionally alleged to have 'damaged' his bed linen: the hotel's proprietor, Anouska Hempel, issued a writ against him for £1,358.52. It was one of a flurry.[84] But nothing inhibited him or his cohorts from talking expansively about his commercial success. The sale of ten manorial titles in 1988 had prompted Neil Thackray to remark that it had 'obviously' not been inspired by financial necessity; in 1991, John assured a journalist that he had nearly reached his goal of accumulating enough money to enable him to put Ickworth 'in trust for the next generation'. When, the following year, his estate management company went into voluntary liquidation, owing £43,884 to the Inland Revenue and £53,683 to about thirty-five creditors, Nick Ashley asserted that its collapse was 'in no way a reflection on Lord Bristol's financial position'.

Nick Somerville did his bit, too, assuring Jessica Berens that John had 'one of the most lucid and precise business minds' he had ever come across. If so, he struggled to convert brilliance into profit, partly because, as Roger Lane-Smith puts it and as Anne-Muriel Bazin witnessed in New York, 'he couldn't stay serious long enough to follow things all the way through'. Ignoring the Stock Market (contrary to what he had said publicly in 1983), his investments were in property. His record was patchy. He lavished money on Riverview Terrace before selling it at a healthy profit; the sheep station (sold to Gerald Carroll) yielded a return, as did the houses in Fort Lauderdale; the farms in Georgia 'he got out of without great gain', in Lane-Smith's phrase, whilst 11 South Eaton Place ('Bristol House') was put on the market for £400,000 in April 1990 but sold for a reported £300,000 the following year. The price reflected the shortness of its lease, which in turn indicated the shallowness of John's reserves. Had he doubled or trebled or quadrupled his inheritance, a Belgravia house with a longer lease would have been very comfortably within his means. There would certainly have been no need to sell during a slump, as he was forced to in 1991, nor would he have disposed of the *Braemar*[85] as early as 1980.

Three of his best friends had never been persuaded by his claims of financial brilliance. One of them, close to David Cholmondeley as well as John, knew that some schemes had inflicted disastrous losses. 'He put David into a lot of deals – pecan, kiwi fruit – [which] all failed. Cost David a lot of money.' The second friend says that all participants 'lost a fortune: millions and millions'. Failure left John's ambition undiminished. Indeed, it swelled further in discussion with Gerald Carroll,[86] whose self-belief 'engendered the idea that they were businessmen together, and could work wonderful business deals which would make them a lot of money'. The evidence suggested other-wise. 'The oil and gas exploration, the farming in Australia and America – we would hear stories about a farm in Colorado – all culminated in nothing.'

Smaller projects seemed similarly fated. Paddy Ireland remembers the arrival of a consignment of ties at South Eaton Place, one of a series of ventures for which John retained the services of Neil Thackray. 'The ties had palm trees on them', a design, he adds, which sent John 'into meltdown'. Plausible ideas did emerge in the 1990s, during what became known as 'the dash for cash': a golf course would be built at Ickworth (on land far from the house and park); a gym of unparalleled modernity would be installed in the East Wing, which would be converted into a hotel, with a flat (a penthouse was his preferred term) retained for John. But John had never cultivated allies in local government, while the National Trust was unlikely to prove receptive to his version of commercial innovation. None of the ideas came to fruition.

Here, John's reaction to his father's will was instructive. Victor, unsurprisingly, left his property to Yvonne. John, recruiting Nicholas's support, immediately challenged the will's validity, an indication not only of his enduring contempt for his stepmother but of his expectation of money by entitlement rather than accomplishment. By 1991, the battle, fought in the Monaco courts, had ended in entirely predictable and expensive defeat, the cost of which fell on Nicholas, who had delivered interminable telephone monologues to lawyers at ruinous expense.

Nevertheless, Nicholas continued to occupy a prominent position in John's thinking. As heir to the Fitzwilliam fortune (see Part Two 'Victor', p. 106), he was, potentially, far richer than his elder brother. John now proposed that he should become 'head of protocol' at Ickworth. 'Perfect for Nicholas. He loved all that pomp and circumstance,' reflects James Whitby, adding that John intended the position to be precursor to a redeployment of Fitzwilliam resources. 'John planned that Nicholas would basically take on the estate – buy it with the £100 million that he would have inherited. It would have all been tickety-boo.'

From John's perspective, it undoubtedly would have been: payment of millions in return for the nominal transfer of Ickworth to his heir-presumptive. Yet those who saw him with Nicholas argue that he also wanted to protect his younger brother. 'He was very fond of Nicholas,' remembers an intimate friend. 'He would have been very happy for him to have inherited, but I don't think any of us understood how bad Nicholas's problems were.' Since Yale, Nicholas had retreated further into a world of his own: he drove a Bristol (slowly yet with terrifying imprecision), considered it intolerable to travel anywhere without his humidor and decanter of port, and rejoiced in membership of his club, Brooks's. During 1989, he was frequently at Ickworth. Once, invited to inspect the estate, he took three hours to dress, selecting a suit and brogues. The tour did not go well. 'He scuffed his shoe: it was the only thing that concerned him,' remembers his guide that day. Gerald Harrison could sympathize. Appointed rector of Horringer in 1988, he was visited by Nicholas once a year. 'He made a gallant effort to take an interest [but] it was painful, absolutely painful. He would sit on the edge of the sofa, would have no idea of what to say.'

Eventually, in 1992, Nicholas was diagnosed as schizophrenic, like his first cousin once removed, John Rowley.[87] Unlike Rowley, however, he was permanently returned to 'the community' after treatment, his doctors confident that his condition could be controlled by medication. It was a decision which would prove tragically over-optimistic. In the same year, Nicholas was made bankrupt by the solicitors who remained unpaid after acting for him during the long and futile fight against Yvonne.

Yvonne temporarily switched her attack to John, whom she sued in October 1992 for nearly £100,000 (her own very significant costs from the courtroom battle). By then, however, John's situation was critical, his American Express card being good 'only for cutting things up', as Paddy Ireland puts it, the inescapable consequence of more than a decade during which his income had been dwarfed by expenditure of 'probably £1 million-a-year', in Roger Lane-Smith's estimate. Michael Chappell puts John's outgoings at about half that, but adds that problems were exacerbated by his taste for maintaining an immense overdraft. Periodic bank demands led him to rectify the situation by the only means available. 'He might sell something for a million.' Perhaps half of this would be swallowed by debt, 'then the Tax Man would take a share of it, so out of a million you might only see £300,000. By then, he'd already ordered a new Ferrari or a boat.'

The pattern of disposals was long established. Guy Sainty remembers selling three pictures on John's behalf in the late 1970s. Two of them were not especially valuable, but one, by José de Ribera, fetched about £100,000; today, reflects Sainty, it would be valued at £2.5 million. In 1987, John dispensed with two landscapes by Jakob Philip Hackert, originally acquired by the Earl Bishop; they went for £900,000. At about the end of 1992, Roger Lane-Smith and Michael Chappell gave their client a projection of his financial future: a graph showed that, at current rates of expenditure, he would be bankrupt by the year 2000 at the latest. The warning was regularly repeated. Each time the response was the same: John listened, then 'straightaway [bought] three new cars'.

After his release from prison in 1989, consumption had seemed one of the few recreational avenues open to him. His pilot's licence had been suspended on medical grounds (and would never be returned), his gun licence had been revoked (a consequence, in part, of an incident two years earlier, when Tintin Chambers had been remanded in custody, charged with removing a handgun from Ickworth, a 357 Magnum) and, as from January 1990, he had no driving licence (having been banned for three years for failing to provide a blood specimen), although this had inadvertently yielded a bonus, as he had just taken delivery of the first Aston Martin Virage, bought for £120,000. He sold it four weeks later for nearly £240,000, probably his greatest commercial coup since the sale of the Silver Wraith.

By 1991 his liver had abandoned its unwinnable battle with alcohol. Consigned to a Harley Street clinic for treatment for both drug addiction and alcoholism, he was delighted to spot his childhood friend Henry Wodehouse, by then running a private security firm (in which capacity he was overseeing protection for another patient). 'John immediately suggested we should go out for a drink,' remembers Wodehouse, who managed with some difficulty to persuade him that that would be inadvisable. It would be their last meeting. Thereafter John eschewed even his beloved vodka Collins. He also seemed, to Simon Pott, to do without food. 'He used to play with it; the dogs tended to help themselves from his plate, at the table.' Bedroom pleasures were by now entirely theoretical. 'He'd just get stoned,' remembers Paddy Ireland, 'and talk about twinkies.'

Death marched noisily alongside him. In May 1989, Enrico Recchi died crashing his plane ('a Second World War B52-type Catalina') during a storm at Turin airport. That August, France Langlands Pearse attended a summer party aboard a Thames riverboat, the *Marchioness*; she was one of fifty-one who drowned when it was rammed and sunk by a dredger. A year later, in August 1990, he lost his best friend, Jonny Ruane, in different but equally appalling circumstances. Ruane had begun to feel that life was too much for him. He sought oblivion in drink; he argued with John. 'He couldn't stand all the hangers-on [at Ickworth],' recalls a member of the Ruane family. 'They had a falling out.' A fortnight later, Ruane's wife Alice gave birth to their second daughter. Six weeks after that, he killed himself. His differences with John had never been resolved.

Comfort was found in familiar places: cars and drugs and the soothing absurdities of the Hammacher Schlemmer catalogue and Hollywood – especially the work of Arnold Schwarzenegger – though none of this distracted John from recruiting Nick Ashley (bankrupt and, by 1991, 'a pathetic figure', in his own estimation) to oversee a new automotive interest, 'buying old Rolls-Royce Silver Clouds and S Series and decapitating them'. John's intention was apparently to establish a museum of convertibles. Ashley noticed that one payment was made with a brick of forged US dollars, another with a dud cheque.

Altered circumstances failed to inhibit John's talent – and taste – for folie de grandeur, however. A new professional (entirely orthodox) acquaintance, arriving at Ickworth by Aston Martin (his first), was disconcerted to be told that there was something amiss with its engine. 'Just start your car, will you? Yes, I thought so. Sounds dreadful. Give Foley the keys.' Minutes later, the defective vehicle was entrusted to a driver, who was instructed to take it to a specialist in Somerset for retuning. The (unrelated) discussions between John and its owner proved protracted. At their conclusion, in the early evening, John's new acquaintance pointed out that he had to get home, a journey of several hours. John directed to him to a stretch limousine, emblazoned with the Hervey coat of arms: Foley would be driving him home. The beneficiary expressed thanks, then asked if John could recommend a suitable pub or restaurant en route? 'Thought of that. There's some chilled Chablis in the car, and some lobster sandwiches.' About a fortnight later, the Aston was returned to its owner, its engine retuned to concours condition.

John remained eager to save face in business, too. This tended to be an expensive process, Nick Ashley remembering that John delivered a cheque, deliberately post-dated, by hired limousine to 'Ernie of Birkenhead' because Ernie would feel more comfortable that way (the probable cost of the gesture, estimated Ashley, being £1,000). Commercial dealings with the north-east developed courtesy of Paul Foreman, who procured a number of cars from Liverpool on John's behalf, although these additions to the Ickworth fleet were never decorated with the Hervey coat of arms, an omission which aptly reflected the instability of Foreman's role at Ickworth. Doggedly loyal but illiterate ('he couldn't read the road signs, so not the greatest chauffeur'), he was fit, hungry for female companionship (of the most transitory kind), usually polite, though 'aggressive when drunk', once earning his dismissal for knocking out James Whitby. When on the pay-roll (he was reinstated two years later), Foreman had a room on the old nursery floor, as did Foley (though it was often used by Bob Rush, John's gardener, since Foley now had a cottage of his own), Paddy Ireland (if in residence) and Nick Ashley (directly above John's, whence at night emerged 'squawking monologues… in a tongue which bore no resemblance to any known language'). Close at hand were Malcolm, the butler, and his boyfriend Nathan. Whitby was on the mezzanine floor, as was Neil Thackray, although he was more often in London.

Visitors were rare, especially after John's gun licence was removed, a loss which persuaded him to let the shoot. Nevertheless, associates of recent vintage – Charlie Young (who also joined John on holiday), the Rat, Billy Johnson – occasionally appeared, as, very occasionally, did those of longer standing, like Sebastian Taylor, Mark Cecil and Pickford Sykes. This, at last, was John's Ickworth: no longer upstairs-downstairs, but one stairs – for good man, bad man, queen, junkie, beggar man, thief. Formality was nevertheless maintained, even on Sundays 'when you had a McDonald's presented to you by a butler on the best china'. Older members of the thirteen-strong staff were still addressed by their surnames, younger ones by Christian names.

At each trustees' meeting it was agreed that some of the staff must be laid off. Simon Pott would break the news to those who were to lose their jobs, explaining that circumstances were very difficult. 'They accepted this calmly,' he remembers, 'because they knew John would reverse it in the next ten minutes.' Calmness did not always prevail, however. Paddy Ireland was invited to 'sort John out' by various retainers who, though immensely fond of their master, sometimes struggled to make themselves understood to him. So did Ireland himself. 'You'd try and have a logical conversation with him but you couldn't really.'

The commitment to cocaine was exacting its toll, and it was a commitment, a choice – a point which John articulated whenever receiving treatment, as ill-health now frequently obliged him to do by the early 1990s, often at the Charter Clinic, Chelsea. 'He was very clever – and manipulative,' recalls a former member of staff. 'Drove the psychiatrist wild. He came up with all sorts of things about how cocaine isn't actually chemically addictive: it's habitually addictive. So he would say, "There's nothing wrong with me: I can stop tomorrow".' John demonstrated that this was not his favoured option. At about 7 o'clock on a summer's evening, he was discovered sitting in a car outside the clinic: cocaine was being administered to him by someone clinic staff took to be one of his drivers.

When not resisting treatment, he spent most of his time in London at a succession of grand hotels,[88] none of which sought to retain his patronage, their respective managements influenced by the damage that he inflicted, often inadvertently, as his coordination malfunctioned. James Whitby, who retreated each evening to his girlfriend's flat in Evelyn Gardens, South Kensington, remembers a bloodied hand endlessly imprinted on a white dressing gown 'as if he'd been silk screen printing', and 'a very white carpet' stained in a manner suggesting the sacrifice of 'a thousand blood-sucking insects'. By 1993, John was 'bleeping' almost continuously: 'up for five days, asleep for two, up for five'. Sleep when it came was akin to coma, a condition not without dangers. Calling on John on a winter morning, Whitby found his hotel room windows wide open. 'He was frozen: passed out cold.'

Ickworth at least assured him of safety, if not insulation from surprise. A meeting with an architect was interrupted when 'little white rocks' started landing on the plans under scrutiny. 'First of all, we looked up at the ceiling,' remembers Whitby. 'John thought: "Bloody hell, the roof's coming down again".' The white granules were plunging from a lesser height, however: from his nostrils, where cocaine, insufficiently well ground to permit ingestion, had coagulated and solidified. Even so, attendance at the meeting represented a triumph of sorts, since John now had difficulty prising himself from bed; once he had done so, he moved uncertainly, semi-paralysed. Simon Pott devised a routine with Malcolm, the butler, who would ring when 'Lord John' reached the stairs. In the next ten minutes, Pott would drive from his Bury office to Ickworth, by which time John would have wobbled down, to be delighted by what seemed to him his agent's entirely coincidental arrival.

Preparing for trips abroad inevitably required patience. 'John would say, "Right, we're going to the South of France",' remembers Paddy Ireland. A confusion of bookings and cancellations ensued; the entourage usually migrated about a fortnight later. The more prolonged of John's absences ought to have diminished household expenses. That was not always the case. James Whitby, who lived with his father during John's time in La Moye prison, says that it cost more to heat the East Wing during 1988–89 than in any other year, despite the fact that John was detained in Jersey from 8 June 1988 until 28 April 1989. Michael Chappell says that he has no memory of John's costs 'reducing dramatically', as they ought to have done. Other intimates noted an escalation in annual (conventional) expenditure. One of them says that, by the early 1990s, it had reached £300,000-a-year ('50 per cent more than his rental income'), much if not most of it inspired by professional fees, primarily resulting from litigation or criminal proceedings, even though Roger Lane-Smith disengaged John from as many court battles as possible.

There were also contentious redecorating schemes, £10,000 apparently being spent on 'having a cupboard painted with Disney characters'. John's drugs bill was rather more than this. Consuming eight grammes a day (between them) of both cocaine (£30-a-gramme) and heroin (£40–£50-a-gramme),[89] John and James Whitby needed over £200,000 to see them through each year. That figure was supplemented by frightening levels of ancillary expenditure: the endless new suits, the delivery of the Doobie Brothers tape ('hiring a guy to drive for three straight days'), courier fees for special delivery to the Bahamas. 'This is where it is possible that John spent £20 million on drugs,' reflects Whitby, 'not [just] on drugs but on all the ridiculousness that goes with them.'

Only a miraculous improvement in fortunes could stave off disaster. John hoped an old and intimate friend could achieve it: Crispin Vaughan, remembered by Michael Chappell as a 'very charming man: could charm the socks off you, whether you were female or male'; and by Simon Garnier as 'scrupulously polite, very protective of John Bristol'. Vaughan established himself in an office in Horringer, from where he attempted to see the proposed golf course through to fruition, as well as initiating orchid-growing on a significant scale. Neither yielded success; John's demands for cash, however, remained insatiable. In the absence of any other immediate solution, Vaughan suggested that his friend sell him Ruffin's Farm, a Victorian house standing in 20 acres of parkland. John agreed. 'Crispin came up with £150,000,' recalls Simon Pott, whom Vaughan had recruited as agent for Ickworth in 1992, 'and walked away with one of the more substantial houses on the estate.' Even for the early 1990s (probably 1993), this was a remarkable bargain. After spending money making improvements, Vaughan sold Ruffin's 'for about £500,000, really quite quickly, within a year, eighteen months'.[90]

Rather than sharing these windfall profits with John, Vaughan nursed grievances of his own: by 1995 he had begun proceedings against the estate. A resolution was achieved before matters reached court, though only at further appreciable expense to John's dwindling resources. Lurid stories now circulated in London: the East Wing, it was said, was being stripped of pictures and furniture which were sold via a network of runners and fences, each member of the chain rewarding himself with a percentage. John, it was added, was too enfeebled to intervene, lying bedridden in his room, in which a baby monitor had been installed by those keen to know the most felicitous moment to approach for more cocaine or 'Cadbury's'.

The rumours were not badly wide of the mark. John's expenditure could only be fuelled by what Nick Ashley called 'the fire sale of the century'. Disposals were unorthodox and, in some instances – not those involving

Ashley – seemingly criminal. 'There were secretaries writing John anonymous notes, left, right and centre, saying, "This guy's a crook",' remembers James Whitby, who agrees that activity in John's room was tracked by a baby monitor, but so as to ensure that he was not bleeding or freezing to death rather than for more self-interested purposes. Whitby's own favoured area of operations was the cellar, his prize discovery there being 'a lovely book of etchings' which Crispin Vaughan sold well on John's behalf.

Nick Ashley specialized in offloading acquisitions of more recent vintage, especially when left in charge of Ickworth. 'He wasn't invited to France,' remembers Paddy Ireland. '[During John's absence] a secretary would [say]: "We need to pay this bill", so he'd just start selling without John's authority.' Ashley, adds Ireland, had a talent for 'sell[ing] everything for the worst price… a beautiful customized motorbike [for example] for seven hundred quid'. James Whitby remembers stupendously expensive audio gadgetry being sold in Notting Hill for almost nothing, '[perhaps] three hundred quid. Unfortunately, that was a bit drug-induced. Nick Ashley had a bit of a problem at the time; not that I didn't.' Ashley, who was finally obliged to address his heroin addiction in 1993, makes the point that 'anything and everything was for sale, so long as there was a stack of pound notes at the end of the week'. Whitby and Ireland accept this, though the latter, in particular, remembers that John would 'freak out' after learning what had been sold.

Yet if this was premature tomb-raiding, it was tomb-raiding in which the prospective corpse was contentedly engaged. The disposal of parcels of land became a speciality. 'He was inclined to sell for cash,' remembers Simon Pott, 'so you never quite knew what had been sold.' The nerve displayed years earlier with the Silver Wraith was applied to 'the Thunderbird', a car whose beauty was matched by its fragility ('almost papier-maché'), a defect only fully appreciated after it had been bought in Ireland by Dominic Langlands Pearse. Forensically cleaned by Paul Foreman, it was artfully positioned behind 'about ten absolutely immaculate cars'[91] at the back of the garage. A prospective purchaser, assuming that it was in the same condition as neighbouring trophies, paid the asking price. The Thunderbird got beyond Horringer, but 'all four wheels fell off' as soon as it was driven in earnest.

John now developed his interest in art. 'He liked the idea of selling it,' explains Paddy Ireland, who recalls the departure of a Canova fireplace, under cover of darkness, by van, probably heading to Amsterdam. It was one of at least two fireplaces that John prised from the East Wing, one being sold – with the agreement of the National Trust – to a German buyer for £250,000 in 1992; the other – without Trust approval – ripped from his bedroom and subsequently spotted at a London antiques fair. John clung lovingly to the 'conmanship' which Victor had inculcated twenty years earlier: 'Oh, bloody idiots: it's not a Canova fireplace, it's school of Canova.' He reacted with glee and contempt when an expert (probably from Sotheby's) spent a week examining the East Wing's pictures, authenticating one in particular of dubious provenance ('Stupid idiot: my father had that done'). The triumphalism might have been premature. Late in November 1991 Sotheby's was obliged to withdraw an Ickworth picture from auction, after the publication of a story in the *News of the World*, which had itself been prompted by an anonymous tip-off pointing out that John's picture, purportedly seventeenth-century Dutch (catalogued as '*Farmyard Poultry* by a follower of Melchior d'Hondecoeter'), had actually been painted in 1986 in Florence, and bought for £250. John left Nick Ashley to explain the mistake on his behalf. 'He got it through his decorator a few years back,' reported Ashley.

It was another tip-off that led to John's second custodial sentence (and Nick Ashley's first). Amongst the new visitors who seeped into Ickworth following the disintegration of John's marriage was a bearded car restorer called Bruce Smith. His workmanship, remembers James Whitby, was impeccable. John was sufficiently appreciative to invite Smith to the Bahamas, to involve him with the proposed museum of Rolls convertibles, and to tell him the security code for every lock and alarm at Ickworth: 1-9-5-4, the year of John's birth. His new friend, hitherto unfamiliar with drug-taking aristocrats, tended to take what he was told at face value. 'Obviously, he thought there was a lot of money,' reflects Michael Chappell. In fact, by the early 1990s, the state of John's bank balance depended entirely on which part of his inheritance he had disposed of, and how recently. An unfortunately timed invoice might remain unpaid for months or be earmarked for oblivion.

Before long, he and Smith argued over money, Smith believing that he was owed plenty, John insisting that it was he who had been overcharged. He sued Smith for £134,000; Smith went to the police and engaged their interest with accounts of recreational activity at Ickworth. Soon afterwards, in 1992, John was charged with supplying cocaine and heroin. After the initial hearing, he returned to Ickworth, where Nick Ashley found him slumped in front of the television, his face awash with tears. It was a sight almost beyond Ashley's comprehension: this was the man who transcended the laws of aeronautics if not nature, the man whom for fifteen years he had revered and worshipped, the same John who now sobbed about his fear of jail.

Ashley, whose own drug dependency had still, at that stage, to be resolved, then attempted some freelance conflict resolution, arranging a meeting with Smith at which he suggested that John could be persuaded to drop his civil action – and find £10,000 to cover Smith's legal and accounting expenses – as long as Smith agreed to be an 'unsatisfactory witness' in John's forthcoming trial. Saying he would mull the proposal over, Smith returned to the police, who persuaded him to arrange a second meeting with Ashley – this time at a pub, the Golden Lion – wearing a concealed tape-recorder and microphone. The conversation that followed secured Ashley a three-month sentence for attempting to pervert the course of justice.

At about the same time as the Golden Lion rendezvous was underway, the police arrived at Ickworth, untroubled by John's security arrangements, thanks to Bruce Smith's assistance. They found a number of young people in the East Wing – guests, residents and John, who was out of bed – almost unprecedented – and carrying cocaine and heroin ('half an ounce of each'), which was placed in an evidence bag while the search continued. Possibly over-excited by their success, the police forgot the bag's whereabouts; one of John's less amnesiac friends retrieved it without detection. Several hours later, John was released from Bury police station; to his surprise (if not that of Ickworth allies), he faced no additional charges.

In July the following year, 1993, the charges of supplying cocaine and heroin were dropped. He was, however, convicted of possession, but was spared prison on condition that he commit himself to residential treatment for addiction. He stuck it out at the Charter Clinic until November, then discharged himself and made for the South of France, where he helped himself to such drugs as he desired, thereby guaranteeing his second prison sentence (of ten months), dished out at Snaresbook Crown Court on 6 December 1993, despite a remarkable performance by his barrister, George Carman. 'Until the age of thirteen,' Carman assured the court, 'Lord Bristol was not allowed to dine with his parents at all and was compelled on a daily basis to wear long white gloves. He has never spoken of these matters before.'[92]

John was taken to Brixton Prison, probably terrified, indisputably ill. Yet incarceration prolonged his life. He was immediately admitted to the hospital wing where, later, he had an ulcer surgically removed. Further hazards lay beyond the hospital wing, but John coped well, as he had at La Moye, and as he would again when transferred to Downview Prison, Surrey, to complete his sentence. Bolstered by specialist assistance from acquaintances of comparatively recent standing, he enjoyed a regular supply of money. 'He clearly needed to be protected,' says Simon Pott, who remembers a system of aliases ('one was "John Kent"') and intermediaries, the latter collecting funds from Ickworth 'so that [John] could be looked after'.

He submitted to the prison system's treatment programme for addiction and his health began to recover. So did his spirit. 'What on earth do you think I am?' he asked a journalist who heaped confectionery in front of him by way of thanks for an interview. 'Some kind of chocolate junkie?'

After five months, he was released; forty-eight hours later, he was re-arrested.

The police again acted on a tip-off. John was in the blue Bentley, with Foley at the wheel. Travelling with them were James Whitby and... Lord Nicholas Hervey. They had gathered at Nick Somerville's flat in Elizabeth Street, where Belgravia edges into the less conspicuous grandeur of Victoria coach station. 'We'd just left Nick Somerville's,' remembers Whitby, adding that John had spent his last fortnight in Downview ensuring that 'every single dealer of God knows what was ready to meet him on the outside'. Intending to head for Ickworth, they had gone about 200 yards when police forced them to a halt in Eaton Square. John passed a handkerchief to Whitby, who ran from the car, jettisoning a package as he did so. This was retrieved (as was Whitby) and found to contain 4.37 grammes of cocaine and a miniature bottle inside which was 0.41 grammes of heroin. Nicholas, who did not make a break for freedom, and who was not in possession of Class A drugs, 'was arrested because he happened to be there'.

Against the odds, sanity intruded into the legal process. Nicholas was not charged; John and Whitby were, but when they appeared at Horseferry Road magistrates' court in September, Roger Davies, the presiding stipendiary magistrate, sent neither to jail, sentencing them instead to two years' proba-tion, conditional on their attendance on an approved treatment programme. Both, by then, were registered drug addicts, entitling them to prescribed methadone and diamorphine, substitutes for heroin and cocaine. Neither John nor Whitby stuck too rigidly to the rules, as one of John's old friends noticed when visiting Ickworth for what proved to be the last time. 'I went down on a Friday. There were only two inhabitants; there was one servant. John was in bed. He had boxes of [prescribed] drugs, time-release diamor-phine, and street coke. He said: "Have a drink; I'll be right down".' By Saturday afternoon, John had still not surfaced. His old friend went up to say goodbye, then left Ickworth forever.

John would shortly follow. In February 1994, whilst he was in prison, the National Trust had indicated that it intended to terminate his lease on the East Wing, serving him with a notice of forfeiture, explaining that it had 'a statutory duty to safeguard its properties and visitors'. Although John weathered that first salvo, his position was rapidly deteriorating. A month later, with all other options extinguished, the remainder of the estate – 2,200 acres – was put up for sale. It sold for £3 million. If debts accounted for much of that (they did), John had the consolation that he was beginning to find a sort of equilibrium. Sustained by prescribed drugs (supplemented, insists James Whitby, by no more than 'a bit of coke now and then'), his 'bleeping' episodes diminished in duration and intensity, eventually ceasing completely.

A bout of extreme illness preceded this comparative recovery. At the beginning of 1995, he lay in bed, 'coughing, declining food and losing weight'. James Whitby was in America; Nick Ashley remained at Ickworth. Convinced that John was dying, he dialled 999 and sat in the ambulance as it rushed to hospital. Transfer to St Mary's, Paddington, followed. Reports filtered into the press. John weighed six and a half stone; five and a half; was unrecognizable; had lost two front teeth;[93] was in the Lindo Wing, under the care of an AIDS specialist, Dr William Harris. The junkie peer, the gay peer, the tragic peer was dying of AIDS.

After twelve days, John was strong enough to leave, but he was shrunken, wizened, diminished, a voodoo doll version of a self that no longer existed. Photographers staked out the hospital entrance. Nick Ashley stationed a car at the back, assuring John that he could slip away unseen. 'No,' came the reply, 'I will face them.' Shrouded in an overcoat, neck rattling inside a shirt collar now two, even three, sizes too big for him, traces of blood caked on to his lips, John walked out, unleashing a series of Olympian sneers, eyes ablaze in the flashlight storm: a performance, Nick Ashley remembered, of magnificent defiance.

He found the strength to tell James Whitby what Whitby instinctively knew. Although John had just survived pneumonia (as Simon Pott pointed out to the press), he now admitted that he had AIDS. 'The only thing I could do was give him a big hug and say, "We'll deal with it". I think a lot of the drug-taking, the massive drug-taking, was denial. Once he'd accepted it, he was quite well.' The sense of acceptance eased the parting with Ickworth. It came in June 1996, following a two-day sale, conducted by Sotheby's, at which John disposed of a 1964 Silver Cloud, a 1941 Cadillac, and more or less everything – paintings, silver, porcelain – that had dazzled and not infrequently bewitched guests since Victor treated the East Wing to his attentions more than thirty-five years earlier. Of 160 'problem pictures', each layered in varnish or dirt or both, the most intriguing, suggested an art correspondent, were a dozen 'Van Dycks' ('said by Sotheby's to be by his "circle"'), although the coronation portraits of George III and Queen Charlotte ('deemed studio') were 'hardly short of Ramsay at his best'.

John, looking much recovered from his previous public appearance, rose to the occasion. Spotting a Sotheby's employee eating a banana at the entrance to the East Wing, he spoke to Nick Ashley. 'Can you ask Dalmeny[94] to tell that man not to eat his lunch outside my house?' The proprietorial flourish marked the finale to a performance which had begun three months earlier with John's announcement that he was selling up: a decision influenced, he explained, by health – hereafter he would spend six months of the year in the Bahamas – and finance. Estimating that he had spent £350,000-a-year 'maintaining' the East Wing, he said that he wanted to lead 'a totally financially hassle-free life', but spoke, too, of his great sadness at leaving, even talking of a 'very happy childhood' spent at Ickworth.

To a journalist visiting Ickworth a few weeks later, he observed that he had made his own money ('the accountants say it's £20 million') and spent it as he chose. He had, he added, never been tested for AIDS (or HIV); he had never felt better. His inquisitor noted that, during silences in their conversation, John's breathing was disconcertingly audible; that he dragged his left leg when walking; that the East Wing was heated to a punishing temperature. After lunch, John selected a pair of black wraparound glasses and the Jimmy, the GMC left-hand Jeep, hit 100 mph down the drive, and rifled across the thirty miles to Cambridge to drop the journalist at its railway station. The reworking of autobiographical detail and the trademark cross-country sprint were not purely for amusement's sake. John's disintegration had, by then, twice been publicly dissected in court. At Snaresbrook, it was said that his estate and entire fortune ('something like £7 million') had been sacrificed to feed his addictions; at Horseferry Road, Ian Burton, the solicitor defending him, spoke of his client as 'an extremely sick man… a rather pathetic character'.

The portrayal was intolerable. Unable to match what he believed to be Victor's commercial brilliance, unwilling to broadcast his own doctor's diagnosis in public, he sought sanctuary in delusion. 'I bought back the furniture, didn't I, Simon? I held it together, didn't I? I've kept it going, haven't I?' Simon Pott heard the questions many times. He offered such reassurance as he could.

There was almost no one else left to listen. After the sale, which raised £2.3 million – twice as much as expected – John divided his time between the Bahamas and Suffolk, where initially he rented Chantry Farm in the village of Denston. An elderly couple there described him as 'the nicest neighbour they had ever had'. Then he moved into Little Horringer Hall, a farmhouse on what had until recently been his own estate. There was always a room for James Whitby (and, at Little Horringer Hall, for Tom Foley and Paul Foreman) but not for Nick Ashley. 'Publicly, I said that I had been "abandoned" by him,' Ashley wrote three years later. 'Privately, I acknowledged that I had deserted him because he had outlived his usefulness to me.'

One or two visitors came to call: Matthew Carr, brother-in-law of John's former secretary, Angela Carr, and a couple with Suffolk connections – Nick Somerville and his wife Tessa. Whitby recalls that 'Nick-Knack', of whom he was fond, was 'incredibly jealous of anybody occupying more time [with John]' than he did. But the person who mattered most had gone: Pauline died three months after John left Ickworth. Eight years earlier, she had flown to Jersey to stand beside him; she had visited him every three weeks in Brixton; she had never lost faith, perhaps partly because she shared his powers of imagination. In an interview a year before her death, she said that she and Victor had shared responsibility for looking after him following their divorce, adding that she had seen 'plenty of [John]' during his childhood, a claim contradicted by her own remorse (expressed in Antigua) and the congratulations she offered Juliet on confirmation day at Harrow. The same buoyant self-deception persuaded her to talk hopefully that he would marry, have a son 'and bring him up sensibly'. Almost until the end, John had lunch or dinner with her twice a week.

Without her, life was easier to bear in the Bahamas. Youthful triumphs were not repeated. There were, though, vestiges of glory. John maintained 'a red and green Mini-Moke, a Panther, all sorts of strange looking cars', and – a particular joy – the *Marquis8*, his Magnum motor yacht whose interiors were upholstered by Rolls-Royce 'in thick, cream leather', and whose exterior was painted red and green – 'his racing colours,' explains Michael Chappell. 'It made it unsaleable, because nobody else wanted a painted boat: they wanted white.' Nor did the Hervey coat of arms, emblazoned ('at least three feet high') on either side of the hull, necessarily help in that regard.

Grateful for these surviving toys, nursed by a forgiving climate, John lived quietly at a small rented property on Paradise Island. When he had holidayed there in the early 1990s, he had lured friends out from England, Roger Lane-Smith and Eliza Dugdale, Nick and Tessa Somerville, amongst them. Now, he saw no one aside from James Whitby, who scraped him up when he came off his moped or fell off the *Marquis8*, and a Bahamian resident, Sasha von Hoyningen-Huene, who had relished him in his pomp.

Once, by chance, in a bank in Nassau, he noticed a familiar figure; he put a hand on his shoulder. Sandro Corsini turned around. 'I was shocked. I hadn't seen him in about five years,' recalls Corsini. They sat down and talked. 'He told me he had chosen to end his life there, that he was happy being in the Bahamas. Then I accompanied him downstairs, and he went to the left, and I went to the right. I turned around and looked at him. He was very, very thin, very frail, walking with a cane; he had somebody he was leaning on. I knew that was it. It was like the ending of a movie.'

Back in England, as final preparations were being made for John's move from Denston to Little Horringer Hall, Simon Pott was telephoned one morning by the Angel Hotel in Bury. Lord Bristol was in difficulties: could he come and help? He arrived to find John's Porsche (its interior 'decked out in pink suede') parked on the pavement, straddling double yellow lines. John had reached the hotel where he, Pott, Roger Lane-Smith and another of his trustees were due to meet John Bidwell, the tenant of Little Horringer Hall. John was incapable of standing. 'He couldn't control his limbs. I had to carry him upstairs to the room where we were meeting.' Afterwards, Simon Pott removed his car keys ('he didn't know where his car was') and drove him home. But these incidents – when he had 'been on substances', as Simon Pott puts it – were rare.

No one would have held it against him had he relapsed early in 1998. By then, Nicholas had retreated to his top-floor flat in Redburn Street, Chelsea. He spent his days sleeping, heavily sedated; in waking moments, he was gripped by paranoia. A few months earlier, a Yale friend had taken him out to dinner. 'He showed me a letter he had sent to four people accusing them of being part of a conspiracy to defame him.' In the third week of January, the Yale man again took Nicholas to dinner ('to Benihana on the King's Road'). It was a depressing evening; 'in retrospect he was at his lowest ebb.' Nevertheless, Nicholas delivered a note of thanks to his friend's flat the following day. A week later, he hanged himself. His suicide note requested that 'Jerusalem' be sung at his funeral and ended, 'They got me.'

The funeral was held at Horringer church, the estate church now being in a state of disrepair. But it was at the latter, in the Hervey vault, that Nicholas would be interred. After the service, his friends and family walked the mile to Ickworth church, where they stood outside, awaiting the coffin. A car nosed its way into their midst. 'It was some kind of Rolls, I think. [John] was sitting in the back, with two guys.'[95] Ten, perhaps fifteen, minutes elapsed. John did not leave the car, although one of his friends briefly lowered a window. 'You could hear Madonna or something quite loud.' Nicholas's Yale friend edged closer: the tempo of the music thumping through closed windows was definitely not funereal.

When the hearse arrived, John emerged, propped up by 'a cane, and two friends either side of him'. Only then did he allow emotion to register: helpless sadness mapped across a raided face. Afterwards, a wake was held in the Rotunda. Juliet, who had just bidden farewell to her only son, was joined by Yvonne, who, three years earlier, had resisted Nicholas's offer to reach a settlement with his creditors.[96] Yvonne's three children were with her. '[John] stood on the side,' remembers the Yale man. 'He didn't really talk to anybody.' Nor did he stay long.

* * *

Almost a year later, John remained in bed for most of Friday the 8th and Saturday 9 January. That was not unusual. Christmas had passed quietly, as indeed had the whole of 1998, which had been notable only for the sale of the remainder of the East Wing lease (sixty-four years) to the National Trust, reportedly for a little under £100,000. Until then, John had continued to revisit Ickworth, if only to collect his post. He was comfortable at Little Horringer, with his wolfhounds, and James Whitby, Paul Foreman and Tom Foley (although, on that weekend in January, Foley was away in Ireland). Gabrielle Coles was also close at hand. 'He persuaded her to sell up in London and move into a house nearby, which he did up for her.' Gabrielle came in to cook for anyone who was at home at Little Horringer Hall.

On Saturday the 9th John wanted nothing to eat. He felt dizzy; his stomach ached. The next morning, Paul Foreman went into his bedroom: John was not breathing. Foreman made a valiant, futile attempt to revive him.

In the days that followed, John's obituaries were paraded across all the newspapers – and *The Economist*. The inquest was held in Bury, in mid-February. The coroner, Bill Walrond, announced that John's body had contained a cocktail of legal drugs and cocaine. Recording a verdict of 'dependence on drugs', he said: 'This is a particularly tragic case. But I suspect that Lord Bristol is as deserving of sympathy as he is of censure.'

His funeral, held in the Cathedral in Bury St Edmunds, was taken by Ray Furnell. Two hundred people and three television crews were in attendance. Furnell spoke of John's turbulent pilgrimage and troubled spirit, of his obduracy, wilfulness, impetuosity and lack of humility; also of his generosity, loyalty, considerateness, sensitivity and the intense devotion he inspired in his staff. Looking across the congregation, Furnell also remarked that there were those ('some of whom may be here today') who had 'abused his generosity, fed his weaknesses and bathed in his notoriety'. Randle Siddeley thought that he could identify one of them: Nick Somerville. 'John was his meal ticket. If it wasn't a prison sentence, we'd have done him in.'

John frequently chose a target from a different generation. At his worst and weakest, and even when some way from them, he blamed Victor for his fate. It was a tempting and understandable reflex, as Tommy Watson, his Harrow contemporary and East Anglian neighbour, acknowledges. 'If you have a father like Victor, it's bloody difficult to get anywhere: it doesn't give you the security, you haven't got the principles.' Many of the residents of Horringer would agree. At the time of John's death, one of them, a retired bank manager and former church warden, then in his nineties, spoke to the village's new rector, Brian Raistrick. 'He said, "If you'd known how he was treated as a child, how he was expected to behave as a child, you would understand even more".' It was a sentiment, Raistrick learned, shared by all 'who had known [John] for years, from childhood, not his friends but ordinary people. It wasn't even forgiveness; it was an understanding of what had happened.'

John deserved their understanding. His tragedy was that, almost until the end of his life, he shied away from accepting what had happened in the past, preferring instead to cast himself as its perpetual victim. Warped and damaging though his upbringing had largely been, it could be transcended, as he had demonstrated when finally overthrowing Victor's hierarchy at Ickworth, with its insistence that hereditary status was the primary determinant of a person's worth.

Unfortunately, John was, by then, in no condition to make progress on other fronts; in particular, to harness the flair with which he was enviably blessed in the automotive and aeronautical spheres. Here his showmanship, allied to his charm, could have yielded commercial reward and fulfilment, if never in quite the same orthodox, managerial manner as favoured by, say, Gerald FitzGerald, 8th Duke of Leinster, who had contended with an exacting upbringing of his own. It was for this reason that Tommy Watson, Michael Chappell and John Knight could never agree with George Lambton's generous verdict that John had 'made the most of his life'. In John Knight's words, it seemed, instead, 'to be a dreadful, wicked waste: something that should not be.' John had known this. 'You can buy something that is self-gratification,' he had told Jessica Berens, 'but self-gratification does not last long enough and it does not turn into happiness.'

A few weeks before he died, he telephoned Brian Raistrick, asking him to visit. 'I should think that happened on three or four occasions,' recalls Raistrick, whose appearances at Little Horringer Hall were unknown even to James Whitby, the mastiff who so rarely left his master's side. 'John'd let me in; there was no one else around.' The intelligence, which had slumbered undisturbed through Harrow and found only haphazard subsequent expression, had never died. Raistrick had been a Chief Examiner at the University of East Anglia and at Leicester University; his three sons had Oxbridge degrees. He was 'accustomed to mental sparring' as he puts it. 'I remember him saying, "I know what you're thinking about"'. I said, '"Of all the things you know, and all the things you don't, you certainly do not know [that]. You've invited me here; I'm here just to be here. John, you're no different from any other parishioner".' The message got home. 'We'd sit there for an hour, an hour and a half. [The] conversations [were] very wide-ranging. He had a very sharp mind, very sharp, very probing, searching.'

The detail of what passed between parish priest and parishioner remains their preserve. Brian Raistrick is able to say that John was utterly self-aware; that he had faced himself, accepted himself. He quotes Jeremiah 31:29: 'The fathers have eaten a sour grape, and the children's teeth are set on edge.'

Epilogue

Seven months after John's death, the National Trust announced its new plans for Ickworth: it was going to turn the East Wing into a hotel. Two months later, in October 1999, the Third Reading of the Lords Reform Bill was underway in the House of Lords when a bearded figure forced his way past Lord Boston of Faversham, vaulted onto the Woolsack (the seat from which successive Lord Chancellors had presided over centuries of lordly debate) and launched into a vivid and impassioned speech. 'Before us lies a wasteland: no Queen, no culture, no sovereignty, no freedom. Stand up for your Queen and country. Vote this treason down.'

Almost immediately, the interloper was escorted from the Chamber by Black Rod, General Sir Edward Jones; later he was identified as thirty-four-year-old Charles Francis Topham de Vere Beauclerk, Earl of Burford, who, as the son of a peer (son and heir, in fact, of Angus Montagu's occasional dining companion, the Duke of St Albans), was entitled to watch proceedings in the Lords but not to participate in them.

Burford had previously demonstrated his willingness to go his own way at Hertford College, Oxford (propounding the argument that his forebear, the Earl of Oxford, was the true author of Shakespeare's plays), and at Eton (he was obliged to leave after taking his housemaster's car for a drive along the M4, a misdemeanour exacerbated by the fact that he was fourteen at the time). His dramatic tastes were reflected in his choice of wife, Canadian actress Louise Robey, who had had bit parts opposite Arnold Schwarzenegger (in *Raw Deal*) and Tom Hanks (in *The Money Pit*). Interest in the couple was sustained when it emerged that Lady Burford had appeared naked in *Play Nice*, an erotic thriller.

Even the Burfords, though, proved unable to carry the day. The following month, on 11 November 1999, the House of Lords Act 1999, banishing hereditary peers from the Upper House, received the Royal Assent. There was a consolatory caveat, however: ninety-two would be allowed to remain, courtesy of a deal negotiated between the Labour government and the latest (last?) Cecil in the Lords, Robert Gascoyne-Cecil, Viscount Cranborne, Conservative leader in the Upper House, eldest son and heir of the 6th Marquess of Salisbury.[1] Neither the 8th Duke of Leinster nor the 13th Duke of Manchester was amongst the hereditary survivors; nor was the 8th Marquess of Bristol.

The fractures within the FitzGerald family remained. Gerald, the 8th Duke, who succeeded Edward in 1976, died aged ninety in December 2004 after declining into an amnesiac dotage. A reserved but kind man, it was typical of him that he should pay the transatlantic airfare for Rafaelle, the first of his stepmothers, when she needed to fly to America at the time of her mother's death. Yet Gerald could never reconcile himself to the existence of Adrian FitzGerald, his father's son by Yvonne Probyn. Adrian, whose parentage was acknowledged by *Debrett's* in 1998, does not hold out hope that he will ever be accepted by his family. This saddens Rosemary FitzGerald, who was unaware of his existence until interviewed for this book. The FitzGeralds, she says, are 'not a great family for gatherings. The whole business of life between my father and his father was, inevitably, impersonal. I would never have questioned [my father] about his feelings about Ed; it would not have led to a happy evening. Father [had] some things that he just [couldn't] bear. You have to understand that with an upbringing as curious as his, it [was] not surprising.'

The curious and the tragic continue to define recent FitzGerald history. The curators of San Simeon, Randolph Hearst's Californian castle to which twenty-one pantechnicons of family treasures were despatched more than eighty years ago, can find no inventory – nor records of purchase – of any FitzGerald possessions. However, on a visit to San Simeon in 1998, Conor Mallaghan, the current owner of Carton, spotted three pieces of silver bearing the FitzGerald coat of arms. It was also in California, in 2006, that the claim to the Leinster dukedom was revived, by an American builder, Paul Fitzgerald, son of previous claimant Leonard Fitzgerald. In May of that year, it was reported that the new Department of Constitutional Affairs, and Lord Falconer, the Lord Chancellor, would rule on the validity of his claim 'in the next two months'. Eleven months later, by which time the department had been renamed the Ministry of Justice, Lord Falconer delivered his ruling: he found in favour of Maurice, 9th Duke (Gerald's elder son), though granting the claimant leave to appeal to the House of Lords. At the time of writing, Paul Fitzgerald has yet to exploit that opportunity. He does not seek to perpetuate the story favoured by his father (namely, that Leonard's father had been Maurice, 6th Duke of Leinster, who, rather than dying in Craighouse in 1922, had emigrated after 'abdicating his title' in favour of Edward). Instead, Mr Fitzgerald maintains that he is the grandson of Desmond FitzGerald, who apparently did not die in the First World War but emigrated to Canada, travelling first class. This boldly ignores the fact that 'no life could be more straightforward, no death more reliably witnessed or precisely documented than Lord Desmond's'.[2]

The episode is no more than a side-show for Maurice FitzGerald, 9th Duke of Leinster – once employed as a head gardener (in a corporate capacity) by Robert Maxwell[3] – compared with the T.O.M. Fund, a charity financing bursaries for the specialist tuition of dyslexic children and adults. It takes its name from that of his only son, Tom, Earl of Offaly – the baby in the photograph showing four FitzGerald generations together – who died in a car crash in Ireland in 1997, aged twenty-three. The Montagus have been spared tragedy. Yet, in the guise of Alexander Montagu, 13th Duke of Manchester, they have suffered further vicissitudes. In July 1988, Alexander's first wife, Marion (née Stoner), remarked that their marriage had gone well until 'the spear-gun incident'. She had been moved to reminisce by Alexander's announcement that he was prepared to marry any woman willing to pay him £25 million. Like his great-grandfather and great-great grandfather, he had an American bride in mind: 'a lot of rich women would jump at the chance… to become a duchess'. He added: 'I'm hoping my father won't be around much longer, so the way will soon be open for me to become the 13th Duke.'

Marion pointed out that he would first have to divorce her. She said that Alexander had initially seemed 'a real gentleman'. Two months after their wedding on 17th January 1984, however, he had fired a spear-gun at her, which persuaded her to leave. In August the following year, Alexander was convicted of twenty-two charges of fraud (having obtained AUS$41,500 by deception). Sentenced to three years' imprisonment, he served nine months. He resurfaced in California in 1988, where his name cropped up in a divorce case involving Lia Belli and her husband, legendary American lawyer Melvin Belli (whose services Alexander's mother had tried to secure sixteen years earlier). That summer, an intruder broke into the Bellis' residence in San Francisco, firing two shots at Mrs Belli, missing both times. Alexander, who spoke freely in public ('I am so much in love with her. I have had a lot of girlfriends, but she is the only one who has really lit my fire'), was interviewed by police but was not detained. (Mrs Belli subsequently found domestic contentment with Prince Paul of Romania.) In May 1991, Alexander was convicted of fraud in a Brisbane court (he had hired a $16,000 car in one state and sold it in another) but was allowed to go free in view of the fact that he had spent eight months on remand. He progressed to Canada where he formed an attachment to thirty-eight-year-old retired stripper Katie Lynch (then working at the Backpackers Hostel, Vancouver); claimed to be fifty-second in line to the throne and a second cousin of the Princess of Wales; and was threatened with deportation for entering the country illegally. The following month, he announced that his title was for sale. 'I would prefer,' he said, 'to give it to someone who will use it properly.' This prompted one of his American trustees to write to an English counterpart, reflecting that, had Alexander's courtesy title not been inalienable – like all hereditary titles – 'someone else in the family would already have sold it'.

By 1993, he had fathered a son (also named Alexander), by a twenty-five-year-old American, Wendy Buford, whose father and mother were respectively a factory foreman and a waitress. The couple married a few months after Alexander Jnr's birth. 'This marriage is different,' said Alexander, who had continued his attempts to sell his viscountcy for £250,000 (as well as various of his father's lesser titles, for which he sought an additional £250,000). By 1997, however, he appeared to have reconciled himself to his aristocratic lineage, lavishly embossing his writing paper and envelopes with the Montagu coat of arms (in gold) and settling down as a 'house husband' while Wendy went out to work. Unfortunately, although the couple had a second child (a daughter, Ashley: Lady Ashley since her father's succession to the dukedom in 2002), the marriage did not endure, although it did survive peripheral exposure to the trial of Michael Jackson.[4] The divorce was rancorous, involving the imposition of a restraining order which, in turn, led to a dispute in 2007 which was resolved only by police intervention. Alexander, who is blessed with a bouncer's build and a boxer's face, alleged that the local constabulary had delivered a beating which left him bleeding badly; in consequence, he issued a lawsuit against the police for $100 million.

In the latter part of 2007, 'Lord Alex' (as he prefers to style himself in California) married Laura Ann (née Smith). Before meeting her, he had spoken of his desire to find someone 'confident and successful, with no problems'; someone, he explained, who 'can help mould me and better me. I do need to be bettered'. It was an assessment which suggested a self-awareness and candour that his father lacked. Louise, the third of Angus's wives, senses that her former stepson has simultaneously developed a financial acumen that her husband never managed. 'Two of the English trustees said that they were going to fly over to see him, travelling first class; Alexander said that he would come and see them, by himself, business class. He's learning.' He retains custody of his children by his second marriage, living with them in Newport Beach, a Los Angeles suburb, where his residence houses 'a television the size of a small car', 'Spy' cartoons of Victorian forebears, prints of Kimbolton, an edition of *Burke's Peerage* and the Montagu coronation robes. There is room for a tiara: by 2006, it had been ruled that Consuelo's jewels – the prospect of whose sale had nursed Angus through his lowest ebb – were Alexander's to do with as he chose. Consuelo's diamond choker necklace was plucked from the V&A and auctioned at Christie's in London for £131,200; two years later, more of the jewels went, this time in New York, again via Christie's, for $349,000. For the moment, however, the tiara remains in the family.

No similar windfall seems to be in the offing for the Herveys. On 8 October 1998, nine months after Nicholas's death, John drew up a new will. Unusually, it was not published in the aftermath of his own death but in August 2005, six and a half years later. He left a Jersey-based trust fund (or its residue) to his younger half-brother, Frederick (with the proviso that, should Frederick die, it was to pass to his older half-brother, George Lambton, instead); £25,000 ('or repayment of his mortgage, whichever the greater') to Tom Foley; and £100,000 (to be held in trust and 'distributed at £17,500 per annum') to James Whitby, who was also to receive any of John's property ('ie cottage/house or yacht') in the UK or overseas. There was no mention of his half-sisters, Victoria and Isabella.

The protracted delay in the will's publication reflected the complexity of Inland Revenue investigations. In the end, it transpired that John, who had sold the last of the estate for £3 million in 1994 and auctioned almost all the contents of the East Wing for £2.3 million two years later, had had nothing to bequeath.

The only property at Ickworth now definitively in Hervey hands is the estate church, which John bought for £2,000 just before his wedding.[5] According to one of the latter's closest friends, Frederick shares 'certain mannerisms – mannerisms that couldn't be mimicked by observation' – with his late half-brother, whose signet ring he wears. He is, adds this observer, 'a very sweet boy'. Much the same was once said of John, but Frederick, who stayed the course both at Eton and Edinburgh University, has immersed himself in the Estonian property market for nearly a decade, suggesting that he expects to earn his living by his own accomplishments, incrementally achieved, rather than via the sort of sensational coup that obsessed his father and brother.

His attitude impressed John Knight, who, towards the end of his long life, suggested that, with Frederick, there was 'a chance of restoration', not in the sense of immediately recovering control, still less ownership, of Ickworth or even just the East Wing, but in first retrieving, then strengthening, a squandered territorial connection.[6]

Frederick's sisters are less demonstrably concerned with their East Anglian connections, but seem well equipped for progress. More secular in their interests than the Herveys of the nineteenth and early twentieth centuries, they have displayed a precocious understanding that their courtesy titles are, in tandem with glamour and family notoriety, a perishable currency: chips to be cashed in as the price of admission to the celebrity arena. Isabella, who exhibits an athleticism arguably not in evidence in the family since the 1700s, became 'the face' of Playboy UK, an adult television channel, before establishing herself as a fitness guru, whilst Victoria's film work has taken her into the documentary field (in which capacity she has taken the opportunity of firing both a Glock and a Luger, although not into a pub ceiling).

It is apposite, if entirely coincidental, that Gwrych Castle is currently being restored not as a dynastic seat but, like Ickworth, as a hotel with 'over 90 luxury rooms, a world-class health & beauty spa, a fine dining restaurant and banqueting, wedding & conferencing facilities': the sort of setting favoured by the new senatorial order, whose supremacy was, by 2002, being acknowledged even by Lord Burford, who announced in March that year that he wanted to be known not by his courtesy peerage but simply as Charles Beauclerk.[7]

A decade earlier, the pretensions of that senatorial order had been advanced by the ennoblement of a pathological liar (championed by John Major[8]), despite the protestations of the Honours Scrutiny Committee, whose misgivings were speedily vindicated when the fledgling peer was later imprisoned for perjury. His fellow Conservative, Conrad Black (ennobled as Lord Black of Crossharbour), followed him behind bars in December 2007, receiving a six and a half-year jail sentence in the USA for mail and wire fraud, and for obstructing justice.

Two years earlier, the Labour government, which had successfully passed the House of Lords Act 1999, nominated four Labour Party donors for peerages. They included Barry Townsley, one of the two stockbrokers whose collusion with Victor's old friend, Sir Hugh Trevor Dawson, had been adjudged 'disgraceful' by the Stock Exchange, which had found Townsley guilty of 'gross misconduct'. Townsley withdrew his name from consideration after the House of Lords Appointments Commission expressed doubts about his suitability.

But Labour had more luck in 2008, raising Peter Mandelson to the peerage as Lord Mandelson of Foy in the County of Herefordshire and Hartlepool in the County of Durham, a decade after it had emerged that he had decided against declaring – either to Parliament or to his building society – that he was the recipient of an interest-free loan of £373,000 (extended to him by a fellow government minister, Geoffrey Robinson). In 2009, a number of his fellow Labour peers experienced difficulties. Lords Truscott and Taylor of Blackburn were suspended from the House of Lords for the remainder of the parliamentary session, after it was found that they had offered to amend government legislation in return for money, whilst Lord Ahmed of Rotherham was jailed for twelve weeks after admitting that he had sent text messages on his mobile telephone whilst driving his Jaguar along the M1, shortly before it ploughed into a stationary car, killing its driver. He served seventeen days before his sentence was suspended.

It is, however, Lord Watson of Invergowrie who most convincingly suggests that the new elite has developed the self-regard and advanced sense of entitlement of the old aristocracy without the intervening centuries of uneven service and sporadic self-sacrifice. Ennobled by Labour in 1997, Lord Watson pioneered the ban on hunting in Scotland but it was the night of 11/12 November 2004 at the Prestonfield House Hotel, Edinburgh, that brought his name to a wider public. After enjoying himself at dinner (marking the Scottish Politician of the Year awards), his lordship 'acted in a "hostile manner" towards a [hotel] porter' and requested more drink – a request to which hotel staff acceded, supplying him with a bottle of wine, although the bar was closed. A little while later, Lord Watson made another request for alcohol; this was refused. Shortly afterwards, at 2.15 a.m., he crouched 'at the base of a curtain in the hotel's main reception... The curtain burst into flames a few seconds later.' His lordship, it transpired, had ignited the curtains using matches he kept in his sporran, earning himself a sixteen-month jail sentence for wilful fire raising.

There is at least one precedent which suggests that the offspring of the new elite will not dutifully retreat into obscurity, despite being denied a seat in the House of Lords as of right. Besides orchestrating the destruction of gardens at Wentworth by open-cast mining (see Part Two, 'Victor', p. 107), Manny (later Lord) Shinwell fathered a son, Ernest. After wartime service in the Black Watch, Ernest embarked on eventful careers in property and finance, was invariably bankrupt and repeatedly imprisoned for fraud. By the late 1970s, he had been incarcerated once more, this time in Ford Open Prison. It was there, recalls a retired military gentleman who was detained at the same time, that 'he insisted on being called the Honourable Ernest, which drove the screws mad'.

On the other hand, one or two descendants of the new elite may entwine themselves with the more illustrious and durable of patrician families, rather in the manner that Jemma Kidd, a great-granddaughter of Sir Rowland Hodge, first baronet and convicted hoarder (see Introduction, p. 6), married the Earl of Mornington, eldest son of the Marquess of Douro, and grandson of the 8th Duke of Wellington, in 2005. (Adherents of the 'bad blood' school of dynastic history are likely to find comfort in the career of one of Sir Rowland's granddaughters, Vicki Hodge.[9]) Nevertheless, it seems doubtful that they will ever yield the same profusion of caricature characters who have recurred in the hereditary peerage, like the peer to whose memory his various wives and daughters remain in thrall years after his death. 'If he said this was blue,' says one of them, gesturing at a red fabric, 'I'd accept that it was blue, even though I know it's red.' A friend describes him as a 'brilliant man', asserting that he could, had he so chosen, 'have been Prime Minister'. A first cousin does not go that far, but concedes that his relation was 'a very attractive man', before adding, 'a psychopath, of course'.

It is here, in its repository of deformities and oddities and misfits, that the aristocracy and its stud books may perform an enduring service, helping to unlock the mysteries of heredity: why it is, for example, that studies suggest that inveterate liars have approximately 20 per cent more white matter in the prefrontal cortex of their brains (and commensurately fewer grey cells) than more honest men and women; or why criminals are more likely to have been the offspring of criminals (even if adopted into law-abiding families) despite the absence of any single 'criminal gene'. Perhaps it will provide evidence that what is currently deemed genetic drift – the 'lucky dip' of genetic inheritance – is less random than it appears. At the very least, it will offer an indelible reminder that a rigidly patrilineal interpretation of any single person or family is wholly inadequate.

'Class divisions have disappeared. It was thanks to the policies instituted by Attlee after 1945, particularly the welfare state. Most people, if you ask them what class they belong to, say "what the hell do you mean?".'

Lord Healey of Riddlesden,
interviewed by the Daily Telegraph, 24 January 2009

Notes

Part One – Edward

1. The 10th Duke of Argyll (1872–1949), the 5th Duke of Sutherland (1888–1963), and the restless, four-times married, indecently rich 2nd Duke of Westminster (1879–1953). All three, like Edward, were great-grandsons of George Leveson-Gower (subsequently Sutherland-Leveson-Gower), 2nd Duke of Sutherland.

2. Edgar Vincent (1857–1941), 1st and last Viscount D'Abernon, younger son of Sir Frederick Vincent, 11th baronet, was ambassador in Berlin from 1920 to 1926. His private secretary for his first two years in post was Josslyn ('Joss') Victor Hay, later the 22nd Earl of Erroll, who subsequently resigned from the Diplomatic Service, embraced (and, possibly, renounced) National Socialism, settled (perhaps not the right word) in Kenya, where he was horse-whipped outside Nairobi railway station by Major Cyril Ramsay-Hill (whose wife he later married) and was murdered on 24 January 1941.

3. His rebel status seems to have saved Carton from the fate meted out to countless of Ireland's great houses in 1922 when, according to family lore, 'armed men knocked on the door to warn its occupants that the house was to be burned to the ground… the butler asked them to wait a minute. [He then alerted] Lord Frederick Fitzgerald [who] took the portrait of Lord Edward off the wall and showed it to the terrorists saying, "Would you burn down the house where Lord Edward FitzGerald was born?" They left, leaving the house intact.'

4. Hubert was believed 'to have had countless children by a number of women,' remembered Peter Duncombe (6th Lord Feversham). 'One of them put in a claim for the title when I inherited – the late Colonel Harry Graham Duncombe.' (The claim was for the barony; the earldom expired in 1963.)

5. Churchill's opinion was widely shared. 'All Lord Feversham's daughters were beautiful – astonishingly beautiful,' recorded Lord Ernest Hamilton (seventh son of the 1st Duke of Abercorn), adding that the most beautiful was Hermione. 'As

a child of sixteen or so... her beauty was so dazzling as to be almost unbelievable. It was not only that she was divinely tall and absolutely flawless in shape,
feature and complexion – a very rare combination – but she also had on her face
that look of radiant goodness which, for some mysterious reason, is seldom seen
on the face of any except those doomed to an early death.'

6. Others hurriedly followed Lord Frederick's example, selling all their Irish hold-
ings, whether Anglo-Irish grandees like the Duke of Devonshire, the Marquess
of Lansdowne, Earl Fitzwilliam and Lord Leconfield, or those whose lands were
exclusively Irish, like the Earls of Ranfurly and Meath, and Lords Wicklow,
Fingall and Kilmaine.

7. In 1880, the Dukes of Sutherland (with £142,000, or about £140.5 million today),
Bedford (£225,000), Westminster (£290,000; £287 million today) and
Northumberland (£176,000) enjoyed annual incomes which the FitzGeralds
would never emulate, however adroitly they handled their affairs.

8. A number of Gerald's forebears shared his diminutive dimensions, including
George FitzGerald, 16th Earl of Kildare ('known as "the Fairy Earl" because of
his size') and Lord Edward FitzGerald, who was 5'5".

9. The boys also occasionally stayed with their maternal grandparents at Duncombe
Park, the family's Yorkshire seat. It was there, on an earlier visit, in 1894, that
Edward was only just rescued from a fire. His escape echoed an episode from
the thirteenth century: John, later the 1st Earl of Kildare, was still a baby when
fire swept through the FitzGerald stronghold, the Castle of Woodstock. The
FitzGeralds fled, returning to find John, unscathed amidst the castle's charred
ruins, being cradled by an ape, a pet which was usually chained up but which had
broken free during the fire. John later adopted monkeys as supporters in the
FitzGerald coat-of-arms.

10. Sir Fergus Graham's younger siblings were Richard, born 1896, and Daphne, born
1903.

11. Like Desmond, Edward was in the Revd H. T. Bowlby's house. Eton's Head
Master at the time was the Hon. Revd Edward Lyttelton, a vegetarian, who
'would pursue fads about hygiene, such as liking to sleep in the open air'.
Otherwise, there was little to unsettle Edwardian parents or guardians, certainly
not the school's disciplinary regime. During Edward's first year, the *Eton College
Chronicle* was engrossed in a debate about the merits of corporal punishment,
publishing a series of letters under the heading 'Floggers & Flogging'. 'A parent
who sends his son to Eton,' one correspondent reminded readers, 'does so on the
understanding that the Head Master will inflict corporal punishment on him if
he sees fit.' Warren Hill, which, a few years later, also educated the young Joss
Hay, is no longer in existence.

12. A granddaughter of Edward's third wife, Lady Caroline Tahany, née Cadogan,
1946–2008; third daughter of the 7th Earl Cadogan and his first wife, Primrose,
née Yarde-Buller.

13. Lady Marjorie Beckett (née Greville; a daughter of the 5th Earl of Warwick), had previously been married to the 2nd Earl of Feversham; she was also a mistress of Edward VII.

14. His Irish Guards records amount to two pieces of almost blank paper. His height – 5'9" – is included; so is the date of his resignation – 4 December 1912 – and his Commanding Officer's signature, but nothing else.

15. Rosa Lewis (1867–1952), daughter of a watchmaker-undertaker from Leyton in East London, assimilated patrician tastes whilst in service to Lady Randolph Churchill. After taking a lease on 81 Jermyn Street, in 1902, she mimicked them at what became the Cavendish. The hotel was divided into suites – an innovation – each one having its own bathroom and private dining-room. One of these suites was set aside for Edward VII, where he could 'give dinner parties and entertain his favourite ladies just as if he was in a friend's house, and Rosa would be there to cook for him and to see to all his requirements personally'. The 'Elinor Glyn' was named after Miss Glyn's bestseller, *Three Weeks*, detailing the seduction of a young man by a mature and resourceful woman. Her own engaging reputation was immortalized in doggerel: 'Would you like to sin/With Elinor Glyn/On a tiger skin?/Or would you prefer/To err/With her/On some other fur?'

16. The Cavendish's services and style endured into the next generation. Richard Boyle, 9th Earl of Shannon (born in 1924, thrice married), remembers how acquaintance with one of the hotel's maids helped him overcome his habitual antipathy to early morning tea. 'If they'd melted that girl,' he reflects, 'and poured her in liquid into that very tight black dress, it couldn't have fitted more perfectly.'

17. Horace de Vere Cole, an Old Etonian, was sometimes known as the World's Greatest Practical Joker (achieving particular acclaim by inspecting the Home Fleet at Portsmouth whilst in the guise of an Eastern potentate). By the time he died in 1936 – 'in seriously reduced circumstances in a remote district of France' – his young wife Mavis (whose sister was married to Neville Chamberlain) had abandoned him in favour of Augustus John.

18. Edward was accompanied by a brother officer from the Irish Guards. Like Edward, the third son of an Irish peer, Harold Rupert Leofric George Alexander, (1891–1969) rose to the rank of Field Marshal, and was ennobled as Lord Alexander of Tunis, though was always revered simply as 'Alex'.

19. Edward's grandfather had married a daughter of the Duke of Sutherland, his great-grandfather the daughter of an earl, his great-great grandfather had made do with the daughter of a baron of the first creation (although the bride's family had an old enough baronetcy), and his great-great-great grandfather had married the celebrated Emily, daughter of the Duke of Richmond. Younger sons had had to content themselves with lesser pickings, but even some of them had been matched with daughters of earls.

20. Nearly thirty years after this, at Edward's second wedding in December 1932, his

new wife was 'nearly knocked down' by photographers and reporters, as well as being 'overwhelmed by the sea of people' who cheered and shouted, 'God bless the bride'.

21. Sir Gavin Lyle, Bt (1941–), son of Sir Archibald Lyle, Bt, and the Hon Lydia Yarde-Buller.

22. Craighouse is today part of Napier, one of the newer universities. The authorities have removed its iron bars.

23. It is possible that 153 Morningside Drive was the postal address for Craighouse as a whole. There were, however, detached villas for the asylum's wealthier patients.

24. During grenade practice, the Padre, Father Lane-Fox, had thrown a defective grenade which exploded almost as soon as it left his hand, removing several of his fingers and blinding him in one eye. Desmond caught the full force of the explosion. Taken to Millicent Sutherland (No. 9 Red Cross) Hospital, he died within an hour. The obituary written by his grieving Eton house master said that he had died 'by an accident at Calais; not (as was first feared) through a careless mischance, but owing to a defective fuse in a bomb, while he was superintending regular practice . . . He was struck in the head and died without suffering.' Edward later heard a first-hand account from one of his brother's Guardsmen who had become a lift-man at the Dorchester.

25. Michael Estorick, author of *Heirs & Graces*.

26. Edward claimed that, whilst on guard, he routinely left the Tower of London to amuse himself elsewhere, telephoning before his return to 'ask for the password'. One night he forgot to do so. His Guardsmen, perfectly aware of his identity, refused to allow him back in, so he attempted to scale the Tower's walls at the point where the tide flows into Traitors' Gate. After nearly drowning – 'at times [the mud] was up to my waist,' Edward remembered – he was spotted by a passing barge and hauled aboard. The barge skipper waited two hours for the tide to rise, then manoeuvred the barge alongside the Tower, allowing Edward to climb the mast, slither along the gaff and drop down onto a wall. Edward's step-grandchildren heard slightly differently. 'We were told that another officer bet him that he couldn't swim the Thames and get into the Tower of London,' says one of them. 'He did it for money, and succeeded.' Edward stuck to his account in the *Sunday Dispatch*. The alleged episode was entirely in keeping with the way that he had chosen to live: combining a contempt for rules with a relish for demanding, sometimes desperate, physical action.

27. At one stage, in the 1930s, Edward was paid as 'a distinguished figure-head for a new sort of wrist watch, which was supposed to go on for ever, without being wound up'. He was not a success: at a promotional dinner in New York, he rose to his feet, made a 'delightful speech about nothing at all' and sat down, leaving the watch unmentioned.

28. Hearst's Californian castle, of which Bernard Shaw remarked that it was "the way God would have done it, if he had Hearst's money".

29. Edward was probably right. At the height of his powers, Arthur John Maundy Gregory (1877–1941) entertained lavishly at the Ambassadors Club, which he owned; numbered the Dean of Westminster, the Commissioner of the Metropolitan Police and a former Lord Chancellor (F. E. Smith, 1st Lord Birkenhead) amongst his key allies; and was making about £30,000-a-year. The Honours (Prevention of Abuses) Act 1925 persuaded him to diversify (he bought *Burke's Landed Gentry*; Sir Harry Mallaby-Deeley beat him to *Burke's Peerage*). But by 1932 he was in serious need of money. When he approached Lieutenant Commander Edward Billyard-Leake, DSO, and tried to sell him a knighthood, Leake reported him. At his trial, Gregory pleaded guilty, aware that he was to receive a £2,000-a-year pension on his release, paid by brewing and distilling interests. After serving a two-month prison sentence ('the lightest possible'), he moved to France, oscillating between Paris and Dieppe, and styling himself 'Sir Arthur Gregory'. He died in a German military hospital.

30. Hubert Bancroft Allen, (1856–1950), scholar of both Winchester and Brasenose College, Oxford, maintained 'a retinue of sick horses and donkeys' at the price of chronic insolvency. Following the death of his wife, he made Bert the sole beneficiary of his will: he left £139 17s 7d (gross). The net value of his estate was nil. He spent nearly forty years in neighbouring Cotswold parishes, including Stanway, and was a frequent visitor at Stanway House, Gloucestershire seat of the 9th Earl of Wemyss, who, as Lord Elcho, had been so close to Edward's mother Hermione.

31. All four took her at her word, and 'all of them,' observes one of her granddaughters, 'ended unhappy'. The eldest, Joan, married, successively, Loel Guinness, Prince Aly Khan (by whom she had a son, Karim, the current Aga Khan) and the 2nd Viscount Camrose; the second, Denise, made do with the 5th Lord Ebury, from whom she was divorced after fourteen bruising years; the third, Lydia, became Lady Lyle, and then Duchess of Bedford; the fourth, Primrose, did a twenty-four-year stint as Lady Cadogan, wife of the 7th Earl Cadogan, before that marriage, too, ended in divorce.

32. It was with her friends, the Headforts, that Jo dined with the Prince of Wales and the 7th Earl Fitzwilliam; it was with the Marchioness of Headfort alone – better known as former Gaiety Girl Rosie Boote – that she went yachting with Fitzwilliam, whose mistress Rosie was for many years.

33. Charles Gerald John Cadogan, now 8th Earl Cadogan, born 1937. Notable for being 6'6" and having size six feet.

34. After the death of her first husband, Lydia married Ian Russell, 13th Duke of Bedford, who had succeeded to the title (and death duties of £4.5 million) in 1953 after his father's death in a shooting accident.

35. Yvonne's great uncle, General Sir Dighton Probyn, had been awarded the VC,

and subsequently become Keeper of the Privy Purse to Edward VII, then Comptroller of the Household to Queen Alexandra; Yvonne's father, Colonel Percy Probyn, had won a DSO whilst serving in the Army Medical Corps.

36. It was almost certainly not Edward's only raid on his wife's property. One Christmas Jo gave her daughter Denise a treasured sapphire and diamond pendant. 'Granny had always had it; my mother was very moved,' recalls Richard Grosvenor. 'She then had it either cleaned or valued for insurance purposes.' The jeweller, Dibdens in Chelsea, had bad news: the sapphire had been replaced by cut blue glass.

37. Then controlled by William Cadogan, 7th Earl Cadogan (1914–97), who had good reason to view Edward's plight with sympathy: his own father, Gerald Cadogan, 6th Earl Cadogan (1869–1933), had died an undischarged bankrupt in 1933, an improbable accomplishment given his ownership of generous tracts of Chelsea.

38. Caroline Tahany – one of very few (perhaps the only person from outside the FitzGerald family) who not only knew Edward but who also encountered one of his direct descendants – was disinclined to give the allegation credence. 'Purely by chance, I met his grandson, Maurice Kildare [now 9th Duke of Leinster], at a dinner party,' she said. 'He is the absolute spitting image. It's very bizarre. It was like walking in and [finding that] Fitz was there.'

39. If a true reflection of the state of Edward's inheritance by the late 1960s, it suggests that the estate had been massively diminished in value. In 1922, when Edward succeeded as 7th Duke, it yielded an annual income of at least £21,000 – about £5.79 million today.

40. There seems little doubt that he would have done so, had he seen the letters. In 1973, Adrian's first wife, Colleen (née Cross), a florist from St Austell, just sixteen when they married the previous year, gave birth to a daughter, Kirsty. Informed by a newspaper reporter that he had become a grandfather for the fifth time, Edward expressed his delight, asking for the couple's address so that he could write to them. Adrian knew little of his father at the time. 'I have not told my father he is a grandfather again,' he said. 'Why should I? I have never had any contact with him. My mother lived in near poverty in a rented cottage in Tregony. She died on August 7 this year. My father was not informed. I can just remember my father when he used to visit my mother in London before she came to Cornwall. I would like to know if I have any claim to the estate as his son when he dies. I could certainly use some help now.'

41. Edward More O'Ferrall was one of Edward's first cousins once removed; his mother, Geraldine FitzGerald, was a granddaughter of the 4th Duke of Leinster.

42. According to the *Sunday Express* of 16 November 1975, he made a statement about the Irish troubles; according to records kept by the House of Lords Library, he never spoke.

43. Edward was aware of the claimant, remembers Richard Grosvenor, although

never especially concerned by his existence. His name was Leonard FitzGerald, and his case was exhaustively scrutinized in a book, *Heirs & Graces*, by Michael Estorick, published in 1982. Assisted by a specialist in family research, Estorick discovered that Leonard FitzGerald's father was really an expatriate soldier called Charlie Tyler. It is possible, though currently unproven, that Tyler was an illegitimate son of one of Edward's uncles.

44. The inquest heard that May had been living in a bungalow near Brighton with a public-school-educated burglar (called, improbably, Alan Allan). A verdict of accidental death was recorded.

45. By the rules of probate, most of this would have been allotted to Sir Harry's wife, Edith. When she died, in 1971, she left £37,762 17s (£37,655 9s 8d net).

Part Two – Victor

1. Albany was converted into a prison in the early 1960s and remains one today.

2. The third year was trimmed from his sentence for good behaviour.

3. One of Victor's second cousins, Brian O'Neill, younger brother of Lord O'Neill, was adjutant of the 1st Battalion Irish Guards which sailed for Norway for the Narvik campaign in May 1940. He was among those killed when the Battalion's troop ship was sunk by Heinkel bombers.

4. Moira Lister (1923–2007), South African-born actress who enjoyed enduring success in Britain, particularly on the West End stage. Reassuringly, from Victor's perspective, she was married to the Vicomte d'Orthez, a French Army officer and owner of a vineyard in Champagne.

5. 'I lay till near daylight,' recorded Augustus after one assignation, 'and performed wonders.' Two centuries later, the family risked publishing his diaries.

6. At about the same time, numerous 'Bristol Hotels' appeared across the Continent. Some of them benefited from the Earl Bishop's patronage; others attempted to do so by spurious association.

7. At the conclusion of a legendary dinner given for a number of his stoutest clergy after a rich living had fallen vacant, guests rose reluctantly to their feet to hear their host announce that he had decided how to determine who would secure the living: it would be the winner of a race, to be run immediately. The course devised by the Earl Bishop led them into a bog: none made it to the finish. 'The living was bestowed elsewhere,' recorded the Earl Bishop's biographer. 'The bishop, though hardly his guests, found the evening highly diverting.'

8. Suffering an attack of 'gout in the stomach', he was carried into a peasant's cottage, before being slung into a barn (his host having realized that he was a Protestant), remaining there for his final few hours. The British Minister in Naples arranged to have his body shipped home in a packing case, labelled as an antique. In 1817 a ninety-five foot obelisk was erected to the Earl Bishop's memory at Ickworth

by the people of Derry. The inscription records that, during his thirty-five years as their bishop, he 'endeared himself to all denominations of Christians'.

9. Sir Nicholas Hervey was Henry VIII's ambassador to the Holy Roman Empire; one of his sons was Knight Marshal to Queen Mary; and one of his grandsons, William Hervey, took part in the defeat of the Armada in 1588, the expedition against Cadiz in 1597, fought in Ireland, became an MP, was knighted, then raised to the peerage, receiving first an Irish title, then an English one, only to die without an heir.

10. Jean Taylor (née Bruce), 1892–1973.

11. In 1840, the tenants donated a pair of silver candelabra to the 2nd Marquess – a token, said the inscription from the Suffolk and Essex tenantry, of 'the kindness and liberality' which they had 'uniformly experienced', while their counterparts in the Herveys' Lincolnshire farms remarked that it represented 'a standing memorial of their attachment and gratitude for his noble act of generosity in the reduction of 20 per cent on their respective rents... during many years of extreme and unprecedented agricultural distress'. The 1st Marquess donated several plots of land in Brighton to charitable causes, one of them, of nine acres, helping to establish a boarding school for the daughters of the clergy.

12. At the end, the marriage existed 'only in the most formal of senses'.

13. Both Ballyscullion (demolished, unfinished, in 1813) and Downhill Castle (demolished in 1950), and the Earl Bishop's personal fortune were bequeathed to a cousin, Sir Henry Hervey Aston Bruce, 1st Baronet, who, in gratitude, extended his surname to Hervey-Bruce.

14. The Hon. Robert Erskine, born 1930, fourth and youngest son of Lady Marjorie Erskine, née Hervey (daughter of the 4th Marquess of Bristol) and Lord Erskine. Robert's older brothers – John, Alistair and David – were already at Ickworth, having been entrusted to their grandparents' care when their father was appointed Governor of Madras in 1934. An article in *Country Life* magazine in 1905 suggested that the circumference of Ickworth Park was eleven miles rather than nine.

15. Tessa Montgomery, elder daughter of Daphne du Maurier and Lieutenant General 'Boy' Browning, came to know Herbert in the 1950s through her first husband, Peter de Zulueta. In December 1952, Herbert had married Dora Emblin, widow of Don Pedro de Zulueta; she died three months later.

16. As sons of a younger son of a peer, Herbert and his brothers had no titles until the death of the 3rd Marquess (their uncle). Thereafter, Frederick succeeded as 4th Marquess, whilst his brothers enjoyed the style of younger sons of a peer (i.e. Lord Herbert, Lord Walter, Lord Manners).

17. Mr Wood lived in the East Wing only, leaving the Rotunda empty. The Herveys took advantage, slipping down to Suffolk when he was on his annual holiday, to spend a few weeks in the Rotunda's 'lofty rooms', their spirits, presumably, rising spontaneously higher.

18. The alleged starvation victim was Lord John Hervey (1841–1902), founder of the Horringer and Ickworth Men's Club, a Liberal, a magistrate, and a major in the West Suffolk Militia, who depended on a 'very small allowance' from his eldest brother. He died at the King's Head Hotel, Bungay; his death certificate attributed his demise to bronchitis and pneumonia.

19. Both C. S. Forester and Patrick O'Brien made liberal use of Cochrane's career as inspiration for their respective seafaring *romans-fleuves*.

20. After losing a battle to prevent the local council from building a new road near Gwrych, Winifred ordered her estate workers to axe all the trees on the disputed land. They obeyed.

21. The deal was struck by Douglas's father, the 11th Earl of Dundonald, and Lloyd Hesketh Bamford-Hesketh, Winifred's grandfather, and Robert, her father, who lacked little except for an heir. Lloyd had inherited his father's very appreciable fortune (significant deposits of coal, limestone and minerals enriched the family's 7,000 acres) in 1814. Five years later, he began work on Gwrych, married into the aristocracy in 1825 (his bride being Lady Emily Lygon, youngest daughter of the 1st Earl Beauchamp) and had the satisfaction of having Princess Victoria (subsequently Queen Victoria) to stay for a night in 1832.

22. Dr Edwards reciprocated by inviting Winifred to the Bishop's Palace, St Asaph.

23. His ejection reputedly followed his arrival, by yacht, in Liverpool Bay, accompanied by a mistress. Margaret Dundonald gives the legend little credit, explaining that her late husband, the 14th Earl of Dundonald, talked to her candidly about his family, but never mentioned that his grandfather had taken a lover. By 1912, Douglas had acquired Lochnell, a wreck of a castle in Argyll – 'bought to escape his wife,' according to the current Earl.

24. Marjorie's husband, Owsley Rowley, accused her of adultery with a Major Edward George Herris Clarke. When well into her nineties, Grizel (Lady Grizel Hamilton (1880–1976), widow of Hon. Ralph Hamilton, Master of Belhaven, killed in action 31 March 1918) demanded – and received – whisky and cigarettes from her nephew, Ian Cochrane, 14th Earl of Dundonald (1918–86), when he came to visit her in her nursing home.

25. Victor saw his stepfather frequently in London, and later took the chance to familiarize himself with more of the Isle of Wight than had been possible between 1939 and 1941. Their friendship deepened after his mother's death in 1955 and Sir Peter's second marriage the following year.

    Jean's reaction to Victor's imprisonment is not known. However, in 1933 her house in Mayfair – 65 Mount Street – was burgled. Fur coats and other belongings worth a total of £2,200 were stolen – significant losses, even for a rich woman. Nevertheless, she asked the magistrate to abandon the prosecution. One of the accused, David Hughes, described as a waiter of no fixed abode, had, she said, done odd jobs for her. Her request was refused.

26. The Archbishop is not held in high regard by the Cochranes. 'A clergyman wrote

to us, offering us some of her jewellery, if we wanted to buy it back,' recalls Margaret Dundonald. 'I would quite have liked to have bought it back, just because it was family, but Ian [her late husband, the 14th Earl] wouldn't have anything to do with it. He said, "They behaved disgracefully".'

27. When he died in 1883, Dora's grandfather, George Wythes, left £1,524,787, 10s 6d (£928,071,000 today), an intimidating sum which had enabled him to acquire two estates – Bickley Park in Kent, Copped Hall in Essex – without struggle.

28. The money was desperately needed. Although the 3rd Marquess was no longer letting out Ickworth when he died in 1907, he left just £3,506 – a sum which puts Dora's 'loan' into its true perspective.

29. Lord Manners, deaf and increasingly absent-minded towards the end of his life, was run over by a lorry carrying Italian prisoners of war through Horringer in December 1944, dying in hospital a few days later.

30. Brian O'Neill (1911–40), 2nd son of the 2nd Lord O'Neill, at Eton 1924–9; his younger brother Terence O'Neill (1914–90), at Eton 1927–32, Prime Minister of Northern Ireland 1963–9 (ennobled in 1970 as a life peer, Lord O'Neill of the Maine), and their first cousin, Con O'Neill (1912–88), son of the 1st Lord Rathcavan, at Eton 1925–31, Fellow of All Souls, British ambassador in Finland, 1961–3. The three O'Neills were, like Victor (their second cousin), great-grandsons of the 11th Earl of Dundonald.

31. All Etonians who are not King's Scholars (most of them, in other words).

32. Decades later, Shaughnessy (1916–2005) was chief scriptwriter and editor of *Upstairs, Downstairs*, a television series chronicling the lives of a fictitious patrician family, the Bellamys.

33. 'Messing' was, and is, the Etonian term for the custom of three or four boys eating together in a boy's room; Dame, similarly, is the designation for a house matron.

34. Parts of the letter, concerning Victor's life after Eton, were badly wide of the mark, but its description of 'swiping' – Etonian slang for birching – was authentic; and the school's records show that its author, Michael Parker, was one of Victor's contemporaries. They show, too, that there was a John Dyer at Eton at the same time. He died, unmarried, in 1940 of tuberculosis, aged twenty-six. His sister, Jackie Paravicini, had never heard of the alleged attack but points out that she was four years younger than her brother and therefore likely to have been spared details of a disturbing incident.

35. In 1937, Victor told a reporter that the figure was £2,000-a-year, but the true amount may have been £500, which was what Victor assured the reporter he was receiving by way of allowance in 1937. Or it may have been £750, the figure which Victor opted for at his trial, when he might have veered closer to the truth than usual. Even £500-a-year would have been far more than all but one or two of his contemporaries received. A decade later, Anthony Blond received £3-a-term at Eton, which he considered a 'rather good allowance'.

36. According to Henry Cadogan Hoare (son of Victor's first cousin, Rennie Hoare) a few thousand pounds were owed to tradesmen, while debts of more than £100,000 had been accumulated by a disastrous arms deal.

37. An alias possibly selected because Bellenger 'knew the name quite well'.

38. The two defendants from the Hyde Park robbery who received the cat also received severe prison sentences: seven years' penal servitude (with two years' hard labour, running concurrently) for Harley, and five years' penal servitude (with two years' hard labour, running concurrently) for Wilmer.

39. Owen Crosby Philipps, 1st and last Lord Kyslant, pointed out in *Who's Who* that he owned over 5,000 acres in Carmarthenshire and Pembrokeshire. A new prison uniform had to be specially made for him at Wormwood Scrubs.

40. Victor's first butler at Ickworth was Hanscombe. Jenkins, who succeeded him, died suddenly in 1970, to be succeeded in turn by Coles, a revered figure who survived long into the decreasingly orthodox era of Victor's eldest son, John, 7th Marquess of Bristol.

41. In 1931, there had been 1.3 million domestic servants in Britain; by 1951, only 250,000, and by 1961 just 100,000.

42. Michael Havers (1923–92), QC, Tory MP for Wimbledon from 1970 to 1987, was 'very ambitious' (his younger son's verdict). In the mid-1950s, he bought a cottage in Suffolk for £200 (it had no running water and no electricity) for weekend use, naming it 'White Shutters'; in the 1960s, he successfully defended Mick Jagger and Keith Richards when they appealed against a conviction for cannabis possession, and took them for lunch at the Garrick, the club where he would later enjoy convivial conversations with journalists during and after his stints as Attorney-General and Lord Chancellor.

43. Sir Eldon Griffiths says he remembers King Zog playing billiards in the basement, although, more probably, it was Zog's son, another Ickworth regular, King Leka, later to marry Susan Cullen-Ward, the daughter of a New South Wales sheep farmer. Zog died in 1961, three years before Sir Eldon became Victor's MP.

44. John Clotworthy Talbot Whyte-Melville Skeffington, 13th Viscount Masserene and 6th Viscount Ferrard (1914–92).

45. Ambassadors from Finland, Germany, Italy and Portugal all stayed at Ickworth during the 1960s.

46. Begun in 1720 by Thomas Wentworth, 1st Marquess of Rockingham, Wentworth Wodehouse's 200-yard East Front was marginally longer than the frontage later contrived at Ickworth (and almost twice that of Buckingham Palace). A nine-mile stone wall enclosed the park designed by Repton, its oaks planted in patterns replicating the troop formations at the Battle of Blenheim.

   In the 1930s, footmen, wearing the Wentworth livery, unwound balls of string when showing guests to their rooms along five miles of passages (in earlier years, coloured confetti had been used). Outside, the grass glittered with the coal dust which gusted in from the mines on which the family fortune depended.

47. The claim was made by Ann Parker Bowles (née de Trafford; 1918–87), whose uncle Raymund de Trafford was apparently in prison with Victor, for a time at least. Jeremy Monson, to whom Mrs Parker Bowles recounted the story, remembered it as follows: 'Raymund's mother somehow got him a jar of marmalade or strawberry jam. During the war, that was like gold dust in prison. Raymund offered him a spoonful and Victor Hervey then said, "If you don't give me half, I will report you". And Raymund said, "You wouldn't do that". [Victor] said, "I would" – and he did. Poor old Raymund certainly got some stick for it, lost a week's remission or something like that.'

48. His first cousin, Ian Cochrane (subsequently 14th Earl of Dundonald), was serving in the Black Watch; John, Alistair and David Erskine in the Scots Guards (Alistair was killed in action less than a month before VE Day); another cousin, the Master of Saltoun, also perished, serving in the Grenadier Guards in Italy. Shane (later the 3rd Lord) O'Neill was in the 8th Hussars, and his surviving younger brother, Terence, in the Irish Guards (their other brother Brian had been killed in Norway in 1940); Phelim O'Neill was a major in the Royal Artillery, whilst his brother, Con, was working in intelligence.

49. Nor was there any question of Frederick's surviving brother, Poor Old Herbert, enjoying an Indian summer at Ickworth. He was, remembered David Erskine, 'rather cut out' by Frederick, and spent the last nine years of his life, as 5th Marquess, in familiar obscurity at Basil Street, dying in April 1960. During that time, Victor was known by the courtesy title Earl Jermyn.

50. Hugh O'Neil, 3rd Lord Rathcavan, born 1939; his grandfather, the 1st Lord Rathcavan, 1883–1982, was Lady Jean Cochrane's first cousin.

51. Douglas Cochrane (1928–2007), a grandson of the 1st Lord Cochrane of Cults, 'never really [did] anything useful from 1951 onwards', in the opinion of his cousin, Vere Cochrane, the 4th and current Lord Cochrane of Cults.

52. Colonel John Jacob Astor (1886–1971) was the younger son of the 1st Viscount Astor, who had acquired Hever in 1903. In 1956, a barony was conferred on the colonel, who became the 1st Lord Astor of Hever.

53. John Wodehouse, 4th Earl of Kimberley (1924–2002).

54. Diana Seton would soon have reason to regret not marrying Victor, notwithstanding his subsequent criminal record and marital inadequacies. When a reporter from The People newspaper 'rediscovered' her in 1962, she was living in a Manchester slum (whose rent she could no longer afford), and suffering from advanced tuberculosis. She warned 'silly teenagers' and 'social butterflies' how easily even a well-bred girl could slide into disaster.

55. An Old Etonian, Derek Le Poer Trench was possibly a very distant kinsman of Victor's, though the validity of the connection is unlikely to be proved: several years ago, Charles Kidd, editor of Debrett's Peerage, embarked on a genealogical

study of the Le Poer Trenches but abandoned it after realizing that the family's appetite for spawning illegitimate offspring would require a lifetime's work.

56. Edward Lambton (1918–83), a grandson of the 2nd Earl of Durham.

57. William John Robert Cavendish, Marquess of Hartington (1917–44), elder son and heir of Edward Cavendish, 10th Duke of Devonshire (1895–1950), had married Kick Kennedy in May 1944. He was killed in action four months later.

58. Joseph P. Kennedy (1888–1969), bootlegger, blackmailer, fornicator and anti-Semite. Appointed American Ambassador to Britain in 1938, he expressed his eagerness to meet Hitler 'to bring about a better understanding between the United States and Germany'. He left London during the Blitz in favour of his country retreat.

59. Shinwell was broadly indiscriminate in his hostility towards the landed classes. Peter Fitzwilliam, then serving with the SOE, paid 8,000 guineas for a filly midway through the war – a record for the Newmarket sales – a detail which Shinwell, who had spent the First World War in Glasgow as a trades union official, included in a pamphlet entitled, *When the Men Come Home*: 'This sum represents about forty years' wages of what is commonly regarded as a well-paid workman. Need anything more be said?'

60. Certain of being blackballed by the clubs of St James's – a fate which appears to have befallen him at the Garrick, for which Michael Havers reportedly proposed him – Victor consoled himself elsewhere. In the year of his death, he claimed membership of the Eccentric, Hurlingham, Mark's, House of Lords Motoring, Guards Polo, Royal Worlington Golf, House of Lords Yacht, Royal Thames Yacht (categorizing his status there as 'courtesy member'), Monte Carlo Yacht, Monte Carlo Country and Monte Carlo Motor.

61. Victor and Juliet could be almost overwhelmingly generous, particularly to their house guests at Christmas and Easter. Carol Havers remembers 'lovely Limoges Easter eggs and all sorts of other small things, all individually wrapped and labelled, hand-written. [Victor] went to a tremendous amount of trouble.'

62. A conscious misspelling, as his eldest son's first business partner puts it.

63. To Victor's credit, he salvaged the marble floor, if not the fireplace, from 6 St James's Square, prior to demolition, and had it relaid in the hall at Ickworth.

64. There are still some residents of Horringer who talk of 'the old Marquess' – a reference to Frederick, not Herbert. Although Dora died in 1957, Victor did not move into Ickworth until three years later.

65. The *East Anglian Daily Times* put the price at £4 15s for a 2-ft square plot, equivalent to £103,000 per acre (or £2,772,400 today).

66. He had, he assured Moira Lister years later, retrieved $1 million before a mutiny erupted, but had yet to return for the rest.

67. Niklas Jensen-Eriksen suffered from none of these disadvantages when he embarked on a Ph.D. analysing Britain's export performance to Finland between

362 SPLENDOUR & SQUALOR

1957 and 1972. Noting that, even in 'the post-war seller's market' British suppliers had struggled to deliver products on time or 'even supply their Finnish customers at all', he detected two exceptions to the malaise: tractor sales and the performance of a British company long established in Finland but recently reinvigorated by new ownership: de Jersey & Co (Finland) Ltd. His findings became the basis for his book, *Hitting Them Hard? Promoting British Export Interests in Finland, 1957–1972* (Helsinki: Finnish Society of Sciences and Letters, 2006).

68. Frederick James Errol (1914–2000), last Baron Errol of Hale. Born Frederick Bergmans, he and his family had changed their surname in 1914; they had no connection with Josslyn Hay, 22nd Earl of Erroll.

69. O'Neill was sufficiently adroit an operator to survive: his continued advancement was dignified by a knighthood in 1962.

70. In the year of his death, he described himself as 'an expert on Central American affairs and adviser to Governments', and listed his recreations as yachting, shooting, antiques and beautiful women.

71. Her father was the 16th Earl of Huntingdon, hence her courtesy title.

72. Although Victor's bloodstream was usually enriched by alcohol, and although he enjoyed driving at speed, he received only one drink-drive ban (for a year, in April 1970; his friend, Michael Havers, defended him at Marlborough Street Magistrates' Court). It helped that he retained a chauffeur and, at one stage, a chauffeuse.

73. Juliet says her marriage to Victor effectively ended in 1971; they divorced the following year.

74. At Caxton Hall, on 12 July 1974, witnessed by Sir Michael and Lady Havers, and Yvonne's parents. When signing the register, Victor was in inventive mood. Calling himself Victor Frederick Cochrane – there was no mention of Hervey – he fictionalized his father's name as 'Robert Arthur Cochrane' (mentioning neither his true Christian name or surname) and persuaded Yvonne to dignify herself as 'Company Director'.

75. Whilst still Victor's secretary, Yvonne had enjoyed the attentions of 'an extremely handsome young man', son of the Chief Planning Officer for Suffolk. 'He squired her to a Cambridge Hunt Ball,' remembers an acquaintance. As a wife, she was so protective of her husband's past that, when in 2002 her son Frederick – the 8th and current Marquess of Bristol – visited David and Caroline Erskine, he asked them 'if they knew why his father had been in prison'. Three years later, Yvonne's younger daughter, Isabella, remarked that her father had been a 'very good man'.

76. Odd though Victor might have become, he retained enough charm to persuade Ian Gow, a young Tory MP, to become (by 1975) one of his son John's trustees. Gow subsequently became Parliamentary Private Secretary to Margaret Thatcher; he was murdered by the IRA in 1990.

77. Victor was persuaded to return some furniture by a girlfriend of John's who, hearing that he was in hospital in London, tracked him down and confronted him.

78. Michael Chappell suggests that Victor paid perhaps one hundredth of the tax he claimed to have done.

79. Juliet remarks that she is 'happy to say' that, during their marriage, 'Victor did not employ karate'.

80. Frederick's 'honorary godfathers' included Rached al-Mandi, who styled himself King of the Tunisians, and (would-be) King Ahmed Fouad of Egypt. Juliet remembers that Victor did not find it easy to discuss religion.

81. The Ickworth christening of Victor's elder daughter, Victoria, was similarly memorable. Despite receiving annual invitations to his Christmas parties, the Commanding Officers of local regiments declined to provide a guard of honour. 'In the end', says Isla Abinger, 'Victor got the boy scouts.'

82. Called Le Formentor, on Avenue Princess Grace.

83. Victor and Yvonne's third child, Isabella, was born on 9 March 1982.

84. Victor's pretensions certainly hinted that something was amiss. Two years before moving to Monte Carlo, he bought three thrones, which were deemed surplus to requirements by Cardinal Hume. Asked by a reporter whether he and his marchioness would be sitting on them, Victor declined to reply.

85. Trevor (as Sir Hugh was known), one of whose sons was handicapped, killed himself hours before one of his life policies expired on 15 February 1983. The Phoenix Assurance Company agreed to honour claims on all four of his policies, paying £137,500 to his widow. A Stock Exchange investigation later found that Trevor and his associates had generated profits for themselves 'on a very substantial scale' at the expense of the funds (and therefore the shareholders), for which Trevor was responsible. He would have been unable to have pulled this off, had it not been for the cooperation of stockbroker Barry Townsley, whose conduct, the Stock Exchange concluded, was 'disgraceful'.

Part Three – Angus

1. Some of William Ladde's nineteenth-century descendants propagated the fiction that their line could be traced from one Drogo de Monte Acuto, said to have come over with the Conqueror: all male Montagus have had 'Drogo' amongst their names since 1880. In the same way, the FitzGeralds, by employing genealogists tractable enough for their purposes, asserted that they were descended from a Florentine family called Gherardini.

2. The second Sir Edward's eldest son was ennobled as Lord Montagu of Boughton, the first of many Montagu titles. Some of these, including this barony (and another dukedom: Lord Montagu of Boughton's younger grandson was

made Duke of Montagu), perished within a couple of generations. Nevertheless, one of Lord Montagu of Boughton's great-great-great granddaughters married the 3rd Duke of Buccleuch, thereby weaving the Montagu name into that of another ducal household (the 9th Duke of Buccleuch, 1923–2007, was Walter Francis John Montagu Douglas Scott). In 1885, a barony was conferred on the 5th Duke of Buccleuch's 2nd son, who became the 1st Lord Montagu of Beaulieu (who reordered his name to Douglas-Scott-Montagu). The second Sir Edward's sixth son, Sydney, married Paulina Pepys (great aunt of Samuel), and fathered a son who was created 1st Earl of Sandwich.

3. The Castle was where Katherine of Aragon had been confined for the last three years of her life, 1543–46.

4. The title is often assumed to be an abbreviation of Godmanchester, twelve miles east of Kimbolton, but (as Brian Masters recorded in *The Dukes*) the patent roll of 1626 shows that 'Henry Montagu is quite clearly Earl of Manchester *in the county of Lancaster*... [perhaps Godmanchester] suggested "Manchester" to [Henry's] mind for want of any better alternative.'

5. One of five Parliamentarians who fled the Palace of Westminster, just before the king arrived with a body of musketeers, on 3 January 1642, to accuse them of high treason. Subsequently commander of the Parliamentary forces in the Eastern Counties by Cromwell, Edward initially performed creditably, taking Lynn-Regis and Lincoln, and coming to the assistance of Fairfax at York. But after participation in Cromwell's victory at Marston Moor in 1644, he 'subsided into inaction'; by the second Battle of Newbury in October that year, his 'lethargy [was] fatally conspicuous'. By one account, Cromwell 'hated him above all men, and desired to have taken away his life'.

6. Descendants of the 1st Earl by his first wife included three admirals in successive generations. Other descendants gave reputable service as soldiers or colonial administrators (a Crimea general and a Superintendent of the Ceylonese telegraph system amongst them); one, Eleanor Hervey (née Montagu), wrote a novel, *Snooded Jessaline*, as well as poetry. Many today live blamelessly in South Africa, a few in England, all linked to their kinsmen by name only, since the Manchesters have shown no interest in marrying Montagu cousins for many generations.

7. George, 4th Duke (1737–88), built a handsome town house in what became known as Manchester Square, though by 1797 the house had been leased to Francis Seymour-Conway, 2nd Marquess of Hertford. Today it is home to the Wallace Collection.

8. Always known as Harty-tarty, a nickname inspired by the fact that, until finally succeeding his father at the age of fifty-eight, he bore the courtesy title, the Marquess of Hartington. Reputed to have remarked that the happiest day of his life was when his pig won first prize at an agricultural show, he eventually married Louise in 1892 – two years after her first husband's death – and died sixteen years later. Louise, a 'raddled old woman', 'shuffled into an awe-

some old age... cover[ing] her wrinkles with paint, and her pate with a brown wig'.

9. His bride, in 1930, was Mildred Meux, a sixty-one-year-old widow, daughter of Henry Sturt, 1st Lord Alington. She had buried two previous husbands, Henry Cadogan, Viscount Chelsea (second son of the 5th Earl Cadogan), and Admiral of the Fleet, the Hon Sir Hedworth Lambton (later Meux), third son of the 2nd Earl of Durham. Of Mildred's five daughters, the eldest, Sibyl, married Charles Montagu's nephew, Lord Stanley (elder son of Edward Stanley, 17th Earl of Derby), and the third, Cynthia, Sir Humphrey de Trafford, 4th Bt. The younger of Sir Humphrey's two brothers, Raymond de Trafford (1900–1971), reputedly imprisoned at Camp Hill with Victor Hervey, enjoyed talking about his 'war wound', mention of which would prompt him to drop his trousers, preferably in female company. The 'wound' had supposedly been inflicted by Alice de Janzé at the Gard du Nord on 25 March 1927, although she had shot him in the chest. Sir Humphrey eventually offered him £10,000 if he would be castrated; Raymund replied that he would 'have one ball cut off and take £5,000'.

10. The housekeeper at Kimbolton reputedly felt obliged to buy tinned food and bottles of whisky with her own money – her wages remained unpaid – so that there was something to offer the duke's guests. Kim might have been comforted by the example of his friend, Moreton Frewen (aka 'Mortal Ruin'), who neglected to pay his servants as a matter of course, arguing that they preferred it like that, 'as it made them feel more part of the family'.

11. Between 1870 and 1914, more than one hundred peers' sons married Americans. 'An English peer of very old title is desirous of marrying at once a very wealthy lady,' ran an advertisement in the *Daily Telegraph* in February 1901, intended to catch the eye of lawyers acting for American heiresses. 'If among your clients you know such a lady, who is willing to purchase the rank of a peeress for £65,000 sterling, paid in cash to her future husband, and who has sufficient wealth besides to keep up the rank of a peeress, I should be pleased if you would communicate with me.'

12. Hopeful of placating his creditors, Kim used the English newspapers to announce his engagement to Mary Goelet (whose father had inherited $25 million); shortly afterwards, he issued a statement denying it (prompted by Miss Goelet's father, who had said that he would 'rather see his daughter dead than [become the] Duchess of Manchester'). Mary married the 8th Duke of Roxburghe instead.

13. Edward VII and Queen Alexandra enjoyed four days at Kylemore in 1904, causing the local railway station to be enlarged, redecorated and decked out with awnings and carpets. Aware that 'the food and wine had to be of the best', Kim sensibly forwarded the bill (approaching $150,000) to Mr Zimmerman. Eugene 'paid up like a man', though the 'only noticeable return he got from the specula-tion was the appointment of his ducal son-in-law as Captain of the Yeoman of the Guard', the apogee of Kim's public career. A 'displaced heart' prevented him

serving in the First World War, though he volunteered for both the army and the navy (to which he offered his yacht) before settling for a place with the Railway Transport Volunteers, and then 'a job in connection with the building of aeroplanes'.

14. Arriving in Monte Carlo with only eight louis, he converted it into 27,000 francs by putting it all on 22 (which came up three times in succession), and then, playing trente-et-quarante, into £30,000, a performance which, assisted by those of two other casino patrons, broke the bank.

15. His final years had been spent at Old Tiles, Sleaford, Sussex; he left £257 and ten shillings.

16. Tallulah Bankhead (1902–68), actress, delivered her more intense performances – epigrammatic and athletic – off-stage. The claim attributed to her that she had been raped in the driveway at home, aged eleven ('a terrible experience because we had all that gravel'), has yet to be authenticated; her last words ('Codeine... bourbon') are not in doubt. By the 1940s, her 'need to expose herself had begun to result in breaches of professional etiquette', but long before then she had prompted an MI5 investigation (into claims that she had performed indecent acts with half a dozen boys from Eton), had formed an attachment to Sir Francis Laking (1904–30), 3rd and last Bt, who reputedly died from drinking too much yellow Chartreuse (in fact, from diabetes and glandular dysfunction) and a more significant one to 'Naps', Napier George Henry Sturt, 3rd Lord Alington (1896–1940), a nephew of Lord Charles Montagu's wife Mildred.

17. A distance of six miles.

18. John Mayes, Dawn Gooderham and David Whiteman all presume that there must have been at least a maid and a cook at Park Lodge: 'Skipper' would not have cooked and cleaned for himself, still less for Angus.

19. Derby House subsequently became (and remains) the Oriental Club. Lord Charles left just over £278,000 (£58.8 million today), evidence of a lucrative stockbroking career, but, although he revised his will four times in the last five months of his life, he made no mention of Kim or Kim's sons, daughters or grandsons.

20. Initially, the War Office directed that it should be used as a field hospital; subsequently as a medical supply store. Finally, German POWs awaiting repatriation were housed in its mews and gatehouse.

21. Angus almost certainly did not see the albums from the late 1950s until the mid 1990s. They offered an awkwardly different version of events, which probably explains why, when on one occasion he made some of them available for limited public viewing, he wrapped a series of elastic bands around their pages, indicating that they were not available for inspection.

22. Mandy retired as a lieutenant, aged twenty-eight. Brampton Park, a fine Carolinean house, had come into the Montagu family by the 6th Duke's marriage to Millicent Sparrow. It is now an RAF base.

23. Mandy's roll-call of motoring difficulties included crashing in Stanhope Gardens, Kensington (the day before his wedding; his bride, whose knees were badly cut and bruised, limped slightly as she came down the aisle); seeing his car burst into flames on the Watford by-pass at Hendon; and, in January 1934, involvement in a fatal accident whilst racing from Brampton Park to Kimbolton, when his friend Lord Duncannon had careered down a hill and crashed. Duncannon and two of his passengers, an American, Albert Surprenant, and a Frenchman, Comte Clauzel, were flung from the car. Surprenant was killed. A verdict of accidental death was returned but the young Grey Duberly heard that Mandy, who had been well ahead in another car, had instigated the race. 'Mandy and the other men were much older [than Duncannon], who was only about nineteen [and] nearly got put in for manslaughter.'

24. 'They were terribly excited by her,' recalls Grey Duberly, adding that one of the estate workers ('very attractive') was also on the list. Louise additionally enjoyed visits from London gentlemen, although these arrangements were disrupted when the man who was to become her first husband, a Swiss called Herman Hofer ('a terrible man, always drunk'), interceded at an inconvenient moment; a brawl with one of Louise's admirers followed; so did detailed coverage in the popular press. The incident was not enough to dissuade Louise from marrying Hofer in 1936; they divorced in 1944. She died in 1948, in a Calcutta hospital, aged forty, having married twice, leaving £132.

25. During Edward's time as a crew member, the owner was shot dead whilst the Karma was berthed at Long Beach. 'I understood that [Edward] had killed somebody in America,' remembers Grey Duberly. 'That was what I was always told by my parents.'

26. Patsy Chilton had arrived in Kenya before the war, as the strikingly young wife of Dr Roger Bowles. On the evening of 23 January 1941, she enjoyed a drink with Lord Erroll and Diana Delves Broughton in the bar of the Muthaiga; hours later, her husband was examining Erroll's corpse.

27. Stead's devotion to his sister did not preclude him from conducting a very public, pre-war affair with the restless Louise Montagu.

28. Kylemore, bought by the hapless Eugene Zimmerman, the 9th Duke's father-in-law, was sold before 1935, probably after his daughter had secured her hard-earned divorce.

29. Barney Barnato (born Barnet Isaacs in Whitechapel) made a fortune in diamonds in South Africa, second only to that of Cecil Rhodes, but was lost overboard (probably thrown by his nephew Solly) whilst returning to England with his three children, including one-year-old Woolf (aka 'Babe'). Babe financed and ran the Bentley Motor Company, drove its cars to victory at Le Mans in three successive years, raced the Blue Train back to London from Paris (he won), boxed, skied, rode, shot, swam and played cricket and golf to a demanding standard, married three times and fought in both World Wars. He died, aged fifty-three, in 1948, after a minor operation.

30. Knockie was named as Nell's executor in her will, in which he is described as a retired company director and banker. 'He was a great man for picking up the handbags and glasses and things,' remembers Mary Fox.

31. Patsy Chilton described the suggestion that Nell would have been capable of performing as a wartime nurse as 'absolutely ridiculous'. Grey Duberly agrees, saying that Nell – never one to make light of a practical difficulty – was 'quite useless', though accepting that, when in uniform, she could have had a therapeutic effect on service morale.

32. Some of Nell's bequests to Angus were initially to be held in trust by Mandy. Her final alienation from Kim followed a bad car crash, in which part of his cheek was sheared from the bone. His girlfriend, pressing the loose flesh to his face, got him to hospital. At 2 a.m., Patsy Chilton received a message asking her to go to Kim at once. She learned that his face had been salvaged with remarkable success (only a small scar would remain). But Nell's reaction was almost demented. 'I won't tell you the word she used. She never forgave him.'

33. During the war, Kim had been removed from Hawtreys, his father's old prep school, and despatched to safety in America. Louise Manchester believes that he attended at least six schools whilst there, perhaps as many as eight.

34. With not untypical exaggeration, Mandy later claimed that it had taken six years to complete the house, during which time he and Kim had 'lived in a mud and wattle hut... and worked on the land from sun-up to sun-down', whilst also building a school for a hundred African children. Patsy Chilton knew differently. 'They didn't build the house; [they bought] an old farmer's house.' The school, she added, would have taken only 'a week to put up, if that'.

35. Jean Sclater Booth's former husband, George Sclater Booth, in due course became the 4th Lord Basing of Basing Byflete and of Hoddington. Neil, whose godfather was Mandy, succeeded him in 1983 but, as an American citizen, did not use the title.

36. Others – both children and adults – agreed. Dawn Gooderham's father, Charlie Waite, frequently returned from the estate farm to give reports of Angus in disruptive action; David Whiteman's older brother Ian, senior cub in the Kimbolton pack, smacked Angus 'because he just got so totally out of control'.

37. Current thinking suggests that 'IQ is approximately 50 per cent "additively genetic", 25 per cent influenced by the shared environment and 25 per cent influenced by environmental factors unique to the individual'. The genetic component is believed to become increasingly important with age, though 'factors unique to the individual' (e.g. Angus's time alone with Nell) play a role in determining IQ in adulthood.

38. Angus remembered the school fondly enough to take Louise to see it, only to find, on arrival on Anglesey, that it had been subsumed into a housing estate.

39. Gordonstoun did not require potential pupils to take Common Entrance, the

standard exam for admission to the public schools, but selected them by interview instead.

40. McComish went on to found his own school, Box Hill, Surrey. Its alumni include Prince Ernst of Hanover (1954–), who would now be king of England, if Salic Law, limiting the throne by male descent, prevailed here.

41. Gordonstoun's founder, Kurt Hahn (1886–1974), evolved an educational philosophy largely inspired by the first three chapters of Plato's *Republic*. After helping to found Salem, a private school in Germany whose purpose was to 'train citizens who would not shrink from leadership', and being imprisoned by the National Socialist government, he came to Britain. In 1934, he founded Gordonstoun, whose Platonic ethos was reflected in the terms 'Guardian' and 'Helper' (rather than head boy and prefect). Boys were required to join either the fire service, the coastguard watchers or the mountain rescue – life-saving duties which Hahn saw as the 'moral equivalent of war'.

42. The money was immediately disbursed. Not all of it was invested in hotels and restaurants. 'If he had sixpence left,' reflects Paul Vaughan, 'he would have given it to me, if I was in trouble.' Charles Lousada's venerable mother was a beneficiary receiving a present – usually a 'huge box of chocolates' – every birthday. 'I never reminded him,' says Lousada. 'If he came over here, he would always go and see her and say, "This is my best girlfriend".'

43. Driving back to Nairobi from the coast, Patsy Chilton and her husband spotted the Manchesters having a drink from 'a sort of mobile bar' in the boot of their car. They joined them for refreshments. Whilst there, the Mombasa–Nairobi train went past. 'Mandy said, 'You see those last three coaches? That is all my furniture going to our new house.'

44. Bridget Portsmouth (née Crohan), second wife of Gerard Wallop, 9th Earl of Portsmouth, 1898–1984.

45. Maundy Gregory's nemesis, Lieutenant Commander Edward Billyard-Leake, DSO. See Part One, 'Edward', p. 41, and endnotes, pp. 348, 349.

46. Like Mandy, Montrose (1907–92) was a great-grandson of the 7th Duke of Manchester. After Eton (where he reputedly bit Quintin Hogg, a future Lord Chancellor, whilst playing the Wall Game) and Christ Church, Oxford, he emigrated to Rhodesia (now Zimbabwe), served in the RNVR during the war (insisting that the crew of his ship, the *Ludlow*, spoke Gaelic), and returned to Rhodesia where he was successively Rhodesia's Minister of Agriculture and Minister of External Affairs and Defence. Following the Unilateral Declaration of Independence by its Prime Minister, Ian Smith, in 1964, Montrose resisted the Queen's appeal that her Rhodesian subjects should remain loyal to her government in London. He resigned from office in 1968, because he considered that Smith had become intolerably prone to compromise.

47. Four months earlier, Mandy had offloaded some of the family silver, much of it given to the 1st Duke of Manchester by William III. The sale, at Christie's, which

included two silver altar candlesticks, each weighing 445 oz and measuring over a yard in length, realized £4,513.

48. In 1957, Mandy said that he had emigrated to Africa because he could not afford to live in England. Had he and his trustees proved more alert, however, he could have leased the Castle and remained at Park Lodge or bought a more elegant house of a similar size.

49. Galitzyn's successor, a Colonel Robinson, reputedly tackled the cellars with similar enthusiasm. He left Kimbolton abruptly when an affair he was conducting with more vigour than discretion became public knowledge.

50. Whilst Fergus Rogers had been at Gordonstoun, his father had told him something of the 9th Duke's gambling problems. More significantly, on 24 March 1954, Edward Montagu, 3rd Lord Montagu of Beaulieu (1926–), had been sentenced to twelve months' imprisonment for acts of gross indecency with two RAF men.

51. Gordonstoun was redeemed from obscurity only by the fact that the dashing Prince Philip, Duke of Edinburgh, had once been a pupil there. The aristocracy knew it as the former family seat of the hapless Sir William Gordon-Cumming, 4th Bt (1848–1930), accused of cheating during a game of baccarat involving the Prince of Wales (later Edward VII) whilst a house guest at Tranby Croft. Gordon-Cumming later sued for slander – and lost.

52. On board HMS *Loch Fyne*, the Marines could buy one or two cans of beer each night but no more.

53. Lisa Gastoni, (1935–), Italian-born film actress, star of *The Runaway Bus* (and more).

54. She had changed her name from Hudson to Montagu by deed poll.

55. Angus's name duly appeared on the birth certificate; he was described as a public relations consultant. The mother was named as Trixeena Bertine STEL, formerly HUDSON, of 1A Douro Place, Kensington & Chelsea.

56. A former swimming champion, Esther Williams (1923–), star of (inter alia) *Dangerous When Wet*. 'All they ever did for me at MGM,' she later reflected, 'was change my leading men and the water in my pool.'

57. In roulette, the odds available are determined by how a player positions his chips on the table. At its simplest, this involves placing them on red or black. Angus preferred to cover blocks of numbers.

58. A member of the family suggests that there were moments of rapprochement, including one in the early 1970s when Mary was briefly in London. During her visit, Angus apparently went shopping with her, buying her a silver bracelet from Harrods.

59. Belli, a lawyer, had come to prominence by defending Jack Ruby, the Dallas bar owner who shot dead President Kennedy's assassin, Lee Harvey Oswald, on 24

November 1963. He had also acted aggressively and effectively for film stars like Errol Flynn and Mae West.

60. Edmundo Ros (1910–), acclaimed singer and drummer, in fact arrived in London in 1937.

61. *The Times* recorded the names of thirty mourners; Angus was not among them. Besides the three members of Nell's family – Mandy, Kim and her mother-in-law, Lady Kintore – only two of those present were titled, the Countess of Portsmouth, Nell's acquaintance from Kenya, and Lady Vestey.

62. Angus was, for a time, a rather half-hearted member of the 'In and Out', the Naval and Military Club.

63. The accident happened at night, between 12.30 a.m. and 1.30 a.m., on Saturday 27 November 1971, the *Evening Standard* reported later that day. Angus had been allowed to leave hospital after treatment.

64. Brian Joyles, by then in the Metropolitan Police force, heard Angus's name being mentioned 'on the periphery of what's known as a finder's fee fraud'. The case prompted Mandy to visit Scotland Yard. 'He was afraid,' recalls Mandy's solicitor, 'that Angus had got in with a very undesirable lot of people.'

65. In the early 1950s, Mandy had one of his occasional car accidents. 'The first person he asked for was Kim,' remembers Mary Fox. 'Kim was the one he wanted to come and get him out of the car.'

66. Name for Kenya's Asian shopkeepers.

67. Thomas Pitt Hamilton Cholmondeley, 4th Lord Delamere (1900–1979). The first of his three wives was Angus's kinswoman, Phyllis Montagu-Douglas-Scott, granddaughter of the 6th Duke of Buccleuch; the third, Diana Delves Broughton (former wife of Gilbert de Preville Colvile, and subsequently wife, then widow, of Sir Henry 'Jock' Delves Broughton, 11th baronet, who killed himself with a morphine overdose at the Adelphi Hotel, Liverpool, on 5 December 1942, six months after being acquitted of the murder of Joss Hay, 22nd Earl of Erroll, with whom Diana had been pursuing a very public affair). In 2009, Delamere's grandson Tom Cholmondeley was convicted of manslaughter in Kenya, following a fatal shooting on the family estate.

68. Mandy had no appetite for returning to England himself. When, in the mid 1960s, he decided to buy a secondary residence, he did so in America.

69. Now over 100 and dividing her time between Venice and California, the Dowager Duchess of Manchester declines to review her life with Mandy or her dealings with either of his sons. She is, however, keenly remembered. 'She had a coronet on her handbag,' recalls one of Angus's most orthodox friends, who lunched with her and Angus in London. 'She took away the half drunk bottle of wine, said, "I'll have that".'

70. Since when the Dukedoms of Newcastle (1988) and Portland (1990) have become extinct.

71. A courtesy peerage borne by the Duke of Manchester's eldest son; never conferred on younger brothers like Angus.

72. They were tenth cousins; Lord Montagu was Victor Hervey's fourth cousin once removed.

73. Angus assured Paul Vaughan that the Montagus bore the name Drogo 'because they were "descended from the Doges of Venice". There was no point in arguing.'

74. Whilst staying with Paul Vaughan in England, Maggie Sheerin drank a bottle and a half of Grand Marnier in an evening, collapsing in her bathroom at 2 a.m. She had staged a complete recovery by breakfast at 7 a.m.

75. Angus developed a useful record, attending the House of Lords on 15 occasions in 1985–6; 64 times in 1986–7; 101 times in 1987–8; 37 times in 1989–90; 29 times in 1990–91; 25 times in 1991–2; 135 times in 1992–3; 106 times in 1993–4; 109 times in 1994–5; and 42 times in 1995–6.

76. Richard Gerard Long, 4th Viscount Long (1929–), thrice married Old Harrovian, a Lord in Waiting (the House of Lords designation for a whip) 1979–97; Barbara Castle (1910–2002), daughter of a tax inspector from Yorkshire, Labour MP 1949–1977, created Baroness Castle of Blackburn (a life peerage) in 1990.

77. Angus's solitary Montagu first cousin, Roderick Montagu – Edward Montagu's only son – lived (and would die) in Canada. Angus never met him. His closest Montagu relations were fourth cousins (the 6th Duke of Manchester's descendants). From other branches of the family, he was equally estranged. Teddy Stanley, current Earl of Derby, knew of him only from newspapers; the 6th Earl of Gosford (1911–66) 'never mentioned him'; the Duke of Montrose says that his family were similarly aloof, the only evidence of kinship being a locket in his sister's possession. Containing a child's lock of hair, it is engraved with the word 'Kimbolton'.

78. Margaret, Duchess of Argyll (1912–93), daughter of George Whigham, a self-made Glasgow businessman, who was 'able to give her some fine earrings but *nothing* to put between them'. First married to an American, Charles Sweeny, by whom she had a son, Brian, and a daughter, Frances, who later married Charles Manners, 10th Duke of Rutland (1919–99). Immortalized by Cole Porter in his song, 'You're the Top' ('You're Mussolini/You're Mrs Sweeny/You're Camembert'), Margaret secured further recognition in 1963 with the divorce which concluded her second marriage to Ian Campbell, 11th Duke of Argyll (1903–73).

79. Jill and Frank Chamberlain, friends of Angela Wood, met Angus on holiday in Cyprus. They were charmed by him; back in England, he approached them for money. The Chamberlains had, however, by then been alerted by Angela Wood, from whose husband, Pat Wood, Angus had vainly sought a £10,000 loan in the mid-1970s. When rejected, Angus told anyone who would listen that he should have inherited Wornditch Hall, where the Woods were living, because he had

been Reuben Farley's godson. 'Pat had had to buy the place,' remembers Angela Wood, 'and he was [Farley's] wretched nephew.'

80. The jewels were '[a] diamond tiara, [a] diamond dog collar, [a] necklace with pendant of diamonds, pear-shaped diamond and emerald necklace, [and a] diamond and emerald pendant with jewel drop', worth hundreds of thousand of pounds today. They were to be held in trust, for the 'use and enjoyment' of her daughter-in-law, Helena. 'Use and enjoyment' would then continue in succeeding generations 'until the expiration of twenty-one years after the decease of the survivor of all persons living at my death who by possibility may succeed to the [Dukedom of Manchester].' There were twelve of 'these persons' alive at the time of Consuelo's death, all descendants of George Montagu, 6th Duke of Manchester. The oldest of them was fifty-five in 1909; the youngest, thirteen.

81. The 9th Duke reputedly made further attempts to release the jewels' capital value. 'Mandy showed me a photograph of the family diadem or tiara,' remembered Patsy Chilton. '[Pointing at] every huge diamond [was] an arrow saying, "paste", "paste", "paste". All the big stones had been picked out.' In fact, most survive.

82. The jewels were also used to secure a huge loan to meet the costs of Angus's Old Bailey trial in 1985, a process which would be repeated in America nine years later.

83. The waste-disposal scheme in the Republic of Ireland seems to have involved at least one 'top person', Charles Haughey, who, according to Louise Manchester, met Whitear for discussions. This was several years before Haughey, sometime Taoiseach (Prime Minister) of Ireland, was found to have pocketed at least 8.4 million Irish pounds from an assortment of cronies without informing the tax man.

84. Angus almost certainly did not know how to fly. He did, however, have a talent for striking up a rapport with cabin crew (remembers Kerry Cheeseman). In addition, as a young titled boy, flying home unaccompanied from Britain to Kenya, he would have been assured of special attention, which in those days could very easily have extended to an invitation into the cockpit. It is not impossible that, when almost senseless with alcohol and amphetamines, he suggested that he had a pilot's licence and would like to land the plane.

85. Drug-taking was never one of Angus's primary recreations, but he enjoyed it in the company of Kerry Cheeseman, whose narcotic experiences have been more or less comprehensive, heroin excepted.

86. This will come as a disagreeable surprise to Mr Whitear. 'I'm not involved,' he explains, 'never have been and never have wanted to be involved in anything whatsoever to do with the other side of the law.'

87. Required in franchise payments by the National Hockey League before the latter would recognize the fledgling club as a League member; if the club failed to meet

the 15 June deadline, it would lose $5 million which it had already paid as a deposit.

88. At 4 a.m. on his last night alive, Thomas attempted to visit the Ministry of Sound, a south London club owned by Jamie Palumbo, son of Lord Palumbo. Fuelled on Jack Daniels, cocaine and ecstasy, he was turned away after refusing to submit to a body search by bouncers. Police believed that he committed suicide, unhinged by fear and narcotics. Allegations about the IRA were never tested in court. Although several people had been arrested by the time Cheeseman jumped bail (and although all but two of the 301 bonds were recovered), no one was convicted. The trial of the four leading suspects was abandoned after it was decided that it would not be in the public interest to proceed.

89. Donald Bruce (1912–2005), Labour MP for North Portsmouth 1945–50, and MEP 1975–9, ennobled as Lord Bruce of Donington in 1974.

90. Murray de Vere Beauclerk, 14th Duke of St Albans, (1939 –), Hereditary Grand Falconer of England, Hereditary Registrar of the Court of Chancery, chartered accountant. He subsequently divorced his (second) wife Cynthia, and now lives quietly with Gill Roberts, his companion of many years.

91. A second cheque – also for $3 million and also bearing Angus's signature – has survived.

92. Mehta had appropriated £300,000 from the Britannia Building Society; he was additionally suspected of many similar irregularities, though these were difficult to prove since he declined to submit his accounts for the Law Society's annual inspection.

93. Angus and Michael Whitear's friendship had survived the collapse of Link: on 25 April 1992, they were amongst four signatories to an agreement involving Manchester Financial & Investments. This stipulated, inter alia, that a bank account would be opened 'through the Bank of Burmuda [sic] (New York) Limited'. Asked to testify on Angus's behalf, Whitear said that he would only be willing to do so on condition that he received a guarantee of immunity from prosecution. None was forthcoming from the federal authorities.

94. The longest was forty-one months.

95. Angus had, over the years, demonstrated his strength by doing one-armed press-ups in San Francisco, slinging a friend of Allan Warren's over his shoulder and carrying him into a Los Angeles restaurant, and by disposing of a Bedford mugger who mistook him for a vulnerable target (Angus effortlessly hurled him into the Ouse).

96. There may have been one more attack. After his release, Louise noticed that Angus's legs were badly scarred. 'I asked him how it had happened. At first he wouldn't tell me. Then he said somebody had thrown acid over him.'

97. Andrea counted Lord Runcie, Archbishop of Canterbury between 1980 and 1991, as what her son Joss describes as a 'personal friend'. He visited her in Kenya, and

took tea with her when she came to London.

98. Joss Kent shared his windfall with his half-brother and sister (his mother's children by her first marriage to Stuart Whitehead). It is quite possible that none of them will inherit the capital, since the trust will only 'terminate 21 years after the death of the last to die of the descendants of George V who [were] living on July 7th 1953 or of Consuelo Dowager Duchess of Manchester or King George V'. The last of Consuelo's descendants in that category was Angus; there remain, however, ten descendants of King George V who were alive on 7 July 1953: the youngest, Henry Ulick Lascelles, nephew of the 7th Earl of Harewood, was born on 19 May 1953. While he (or any of the other nine) are alive, the income of the trust will be divided between Joss Kent and his half-brother and sister – and, as Angus was so bitterly aware, his own children, Alexander, Kimble and Emma.

99. A small but useful bonus arising from his membership of the In & Out – The Naval & Military Club – slipped from his grasp in predictable manner. When the club moved from Piccadilly to smaller premises in St James's Square, some of the profit from the sale of the old building was distributed amongst members. Angus missed out because his subscription remained unpaid.

100. Alan Brodie, a stalwart of Bedford Rowing Club, stepped into the breach.

101. *Hello!* magazine resisted the temptation to publish the pictures.

102. Biba was not meant to be present, a detail Angus overlooked when he subsequently decried the report for alleging that his wife had been drinking gin and tonic. 'It was gin and soda!' he told Paul Vaughan.

103. Angus had owned an impressive gold watch (an Omega or a Rolex); it was not in his flat when he died.

104. Most, arguably all, of Angus's closest male Montagu relations, the descendants of George Montagu, 6th Duke of Manchester, seem as sturdily orthodox as Mandy was, one of them, a surgeon, serving in the Royal Navy during the war (and one of his sons later serving in the RAF); another emerging from Gordonstoun in rather better shape than Angus, subsequently gaining a law degree and serving in the Grenadier Guards.

Part Four – John

1. Carmel Lowndes (née McGuire) had been the second of Johnny Kimberley's six wives. Lowndes confessed to killing her (in 1992, in Spain) to her son by Kimberley, John Wodehouse (now 5th Earl of Kimberley). 'Always a lunatic,' remembers Kimberley's third son, Henry, Lowndes attempted to end his life in the same manner as Le Poer Trench; he failed. 'I think that, as he pulled the trigger, he lost his nerve so that it sort of creased his skull.'

2. Kay Fisher remembers a gang of children – all blessed with Hervey blood – 'playing together, riding, climbing trees', part of 'a lovely childhood at Ickworth', made no less lovely by holidays in Bognor.

3. Catherine Rossdale (born 1958), second daughter of David Erskine and his first wife Jean (née Campbell Douglas).

4. Maria's father had kept his distance from Victor in early adulthood. Like many others, however, he discovered that he was vulnerable to Victor's charm when encountering him in maturity. 'I think,' says Maria Rawlinson, 'my parents might even have joined the Monarchist League.'

5. The courtesy title by which John had been known since Victor succeeded as 6th Marquess of Bristol.

6. The dictates of the Ickworth nursery were not to be ignored. Janet Milford Haven remembers that Nicholas's nanny, in particular, 'wasn't riddled with fun: she was very tall, rather severe. When my boys [George and Ivar Mountbatten] went to Ickworth, they certainly behaved themselves.'

7. 'By the standards of the day, [Edwards] wouldn't have been very unusual,' recalls Harry Wyndham. Heatherdown's curriculum was similarly traditional, encompassing boxing, scripture classes on Sunday, and chapel twice a day on weekdays.

8. Harrovians were usually confirmed around the age of fifteen or sixteen.

9. After retiring from Harrow, Lillingston, who favoured a smoking jacket, an eye-patch ('after an unhappy accident with gunshot') and crème de menthe after dinner, became a housemaster at Millfield.

10. Sir Mark Thatcher (born 1953; at Harrow – Bradbys house – from 1967 until 1971), son of Baroness Thatcher (formerly Margaret Thatcher, on whom a life peerage was conferred in 1992) and Sir Denis Thatcher (created a baronet in 1991). He succeeded to his father's title on the latter's death in 2003.

11. A pseudonym.

12. A pseudonym.

13. As far as Randle Siddeley can remember, the weekly sessions in Victor's office were already established by the time John was sixteen.

14. Lady Phyllis MacRae (1899–1989), Victor's first cousin (daughter of Frederick and Dora).

15. The bond between John and Jonny Ruane was reputedly forged in their early teens, whilst pigeon shooting on the Ruanes' stud. The birds were racing pigeons. 'Both [their] fathers had a huge bill. At that point, they had to be friends,' says a member the Ruane family. 'They did terrible things together, things that bound them. They were very, very close friends, went through an awful lot.'

16. The Druries triumvirate – John, Beckett and Cayzer – enjoyed a better reputation than Blandford, says Peter Henderson. 'I can remember we all signed our Latin primers; he signed his "Sunderland", which he was at the time, and [said], "That'll be worth a lot of money one day". I can remember thinking, "You little shit".' Piers de Laszlo has a fonder memory. It is of Blandford standing in the middle of the school shop, showering the floor with change and shouting,

'Grovel!' (an injunction which, de Laszlo says, he and other less favoured Harrovians had no hesitation in obeying).

17. John Knight: see Part Two 'Victor' pp.80, 122.

18. The Newmarket bypass.

19. Jasper Guinness, elder son of Jonathan Guinness (now 3rd Lord Moyne) and grandson of Diana Mosley (née Mitford); Ned Cavendish, great nephew of the 9th Duke of Devonshire and younger brother of Hugh Cavendish (now a life peer, Lord Cavendish of Furness); Christopher Nevill, at the time still nephew of the 5th Marquess of Abergavenny, whose title he did not expect to inherit but which came to him in 2000; and Clarissa Baring, great-granddaughter of the 1st Earl of Cromer.

20. Peter Geiger, educated at University College School, London, and Trinity College, Cambridge, was a son of the empire – 'the merchant class of the Austro-Hungarian empire'. His maternal grandparents had fled from Vienna in 1938, taking refuge in Prague, then Paris, where his grandfather, virtually penniless, survived 'by selling perfumes out of a tray at entrances to the Metro'. They were interned after the fall of France. It was with the 'perfume money', as it was known in the family, that their daughter, Geiger's mother, and his father, a Jewish Hungarian former cavalry officer, born in 1897, bought 2 Marsh Lane, Mill Hill, in 1947. The house, which remained in the family until 2004, was 'prominently visible on the journey to Ickworth,' remembers Geiger, 'where Marsh Lane disgorges into the A1 at Apex Corner'.

21. Now Sir William Arbuthnot, 2nd Bt, having succeeded his father in 1992.

22. Victor's treasure-hunting expedition struck a particular chord. Signing a leaving photograph for a friend at Harrow, John scribbled the line: 'We'll go looking for the gold!'

23. Another friend suggests that Yvonne – at the outset, at least – tried to show John that she was on his side. 'She used to do his laundry,' he remembers, 'as a favour: wash his smalls, his unmentionables.'

24. John told friends that his father had used a similar technique for informing Sanchia. 'He sent her a post card, saying "Have married Yvonne",' remembers one of them, who later learned that Victor had sought advice from a financial adviser with a view to helping Sanchia. 'They were going to buy a lock-up garage, to give Sanchia an income: she had no money.' If a plan was formulated, it was never expedited. 'Sanchia just got dumped. There were no garages.'

25. Whatever his precise professional status (head buyer for C&A is also suggested), Yvonne's father, Tony Sutton, was delighted by her advance – a fact that he did not trouble to disguise from acquaintances in Beckenham, some of whom, like him, enjoyed playing snooker at the Beckenham Club. Tony's refrain, 'My son-in-law, the Marquess of Bristol', soon became familiar to those chalking their cues.

26. Queen Susan (1941–2004), née Susan Cullen-Ward, grew up in her native Australia, on a sheep station in New South Wales. She married King Leka (6'9" son of King Zog; crowned in 1961 in exile in Paris following his father's death) in 1975. In the early years of their marriage, the King was armed with two pistols, reputedly Colt .45s, although after he and Queen Susan were expelled from Spain in 1979 (police had discovered an arsenal of machine guns, rifles and pistols beneath their house in Madrid) he boarded the plane to their next place of exile (South Africa) with hand grenades dangling from his belt (Queen Susan carried a sub-machine gun). The royal couple later returned to Albania. Queen Sue was interred at the royal palace, just outside Tirana, in a grave next to her mother-in-law and late bridge partner, Queen Geraldine.

27. William's was a comparatively new career: five years earlier, at the time of his marriage, he had been a dairyman, an occupation in which his own father, James Child (John's great-great grandfather), of 19 Collingwood Street, Bethnal Green, had preceded him.

28. Lucy became the solitary general servant in the household of a young Bridgwater greengrocer.

29. Achieved by bidding anonymously, John claimed, with the help of an unsecured loan (for $3million) from the sixth bank whose help he sought. He failed to mention the girlfriend who had traced Victor to his hospital bed and shamed him into returning some of what had been removed.

30. Two of John's allegations – that Victor had sold his two hunters 'as dog meat' and had said that John was illegitimate – were amongst his most imaginative, say two of his closest friends.

31. The expenditure was not greeted with unanimous acclaim. One of John's old friends, a man of cosmopolitan experience, felt able to approve the original panelling but little else. He remembers the *Braemar*, a wartime hospital ship, as not the most restful of vessels. 'Very narrow. It rocked… pretty grim.'

32. John Martin Robinson: Maltravers Herald Extraordinary, and Librarian to the Duke of Norfolk.

33. Restaurant and bar on the King's Road, Chelsea, West London.

34. Henry Lygon, 5th Earl Beauchamp (1829–1866), 'had taken 'cures abroad as he struggled with homosexual leanings'. The predisposition of his nephew, William, 7th Earl Beauchamp (1872–1938), 'had been clear from an early age'; in 1931, he was hounded into exile by his brother-in-law Bend'or Westminster. His second son, Hugh (1904–36, Victor's cousin third once removed, 'an alcoholic wrestling with his own homosexuality'), was a bankrupt who found comfort in his horses and his two greyhounds, Luke and Dan. All, like John (and Victor), were directly descended from William Lygon, 1st Earl Beauchamp (1747–1816), whose youngest daughter, Emily, had married Lloyd Bamford-Hesketh.

35. Monitoring events from the Embassy Club, Jeremy Norman learned that (in

about 1978) cocaine cost about £50-a-gram – 'horrendously expensive' – more than twice Edward FitzGerald's weekly income of two years before.

36. Somerville arrived in summer 1966 and left in winter 1970.

37. The Somervilles had previously lived in Kent, their residence during their son's time at Harrow being in Herne Bay (97 Beltinge Road). Arthur Somerville left £30,000 when he died in December 1981.

38. Lord Neidpath (now 11th Earl of Wemyss and March, born 1948), son of the 10th Earl of Wemyss and March (whose grandfather, Lord Elcho, was occasionally said to be Edward FitzGerald's true father). A newly married couple, staying at Stanway, Neidpath's Gloucestershire seat, discovered whips and razor blades strewn across their pillows – so they assured a friend, Selina Hastings.

39. Amongst the belongings removed from John's flat were a set of agate-handled fruit knives, given to the 1st Marquess by Frederick the Great. The car thief's technique was said to have involved voluble and plausible discussion of an impending inheritance, a test drive and – some time later, when his 'inheritance' was secure – a celebratory lunch at Claridge's with two of the dealership team. In between times, he had asked for (and received) the Rolls's handbook. 'He got the key number, had a key made, ordered a table at Claridge's, asked where the car was going to be parked – in a mews behind Claridge's – waited for the dealership people to arrive, excused himself, went out, nicked the car, drove it for six months. In the end, he got bored of it, and put a notice in the back saying, "This car is stolen; please report it to Scotland Yard".'

40. The chef reputedly proved especially effective aboard a Miami-bound jumbo, interceding after John's party – four guests, plus 'bodyguard' and Foley – were warned that, unless they moderated their behaviour, the plane would be diverted to Bermuda, where they would be thrown off. 'If you're rude to my master,' the chef advised a steward, 'I'll cut your balls off.' The plane continued to Miami.

41. Hurlstone, never a drug-taker (then or now), told John that he must choose between him and drugs.

42. The girlfriend lived for a while at 17 rue de Bellechasse, in the tiny chambre de bonne, converted into a spare room, above and separate from the rest of the apartment.

43. It is said that John did not go quietly. 'The story goes – and there may be an element of exaggeration to it – that, as he cruised down the channel, he gave himself a 21-gun salute – he and two or three other homosexuals firing twenty-one cartridges into the air.'

44. This was Club 7 or 'Le Sept', says another of John's allies. 'It was the place that combined society and gays. You had Mme Pompadour – Claude Pompadour – and Jacques Laing and Frederique Mitterand.' Another celebrated public figure shed the conventional suit he wore during the daytime in favour of leathers and aviator goggles, and enjoyed kissing young men who caught his eye.

45. 'Mrs Most...' was a Dermot Verschoyle Campbell expression, remembers Peter Geiger.

46. John occasionally improvised. Adam Edwards remembers him indulging himself unhurriedly in the drawing room at 17 rue de Bellechasse, 'chopping [cocaine] out on the mantelpiece into two thin lines', and snorting it through a tautly rolled 100-franc note. In the late 1980s and the 1990s, he progressed to 'nice little gold tubes and things', says a younger acquaintance; when these were mislaid, as they tended to be, he made do with a £50 note.

47. Todd Bruno was often spoken of as being in the service of the CIA, though one of his friends recalls that his expertise lay in the field of white deer.

48. David Cholmondeley (at the time, the Earl of Rocksavage), born 1960, succeeded his father as 7th Marquess of Cholmondeley in 1990. 'Charming and sensitive... immensely handsome,' recorded James Lees-Milne in his diary on 5 August 1988. 'Billa [Wilhelmine Harrod; widow of Sir Roy Harrod] told us he was queer, on account of which he spent some years living in Paris. (Surely that can't have been right? Tax, more likely.)'

49. Hugo Guinness, born 1959, brother of Sabrina Guinness, kinsman of Sir Kenelm 'Tim' Guinness, 4th Bt.

50. Elaine's restaurant, a New York institution on 2nd Avenue.

51. Drawn up in 1975, with Peter Geiger as executor.

52. It was this incident that brought the Rockingham's association with Morys to a conclusion.

53. The new owner was 'this Marquess trustee company'.

54. A method by which heroin or cocaine is heated (typically on a spoon) and the resultant smoke inhaled. John, terrified of needles, never injected.

55. John de Lorean (1925–2005) was a brilliant engineer and a 'world-class conman' specializing in fraud, embezzlement, tax evasion and (almost certainly) cocaine smuggling.

56. Most New Yorkers, not just the police, struggled to come to grips with either. A message delivered by a hotel receptionist ('Foist name "Earl", last name "Joiman", resident in Monte Carlo') epitomized their confusion, remembers a Manhattanite, while the Brooklyn mechanics who fixed John's cars repeatedly inquired: 'Is Earl there?'

57. Selina Hastings confirms that the friendship endured. 'I met him once or twice with Ariane when she was in her early twenties. She would have a party and John was there.' (Ariane, long since married, declines to comment.)

58. Maria was the girlfriend who had traced Victor to his hospital bed and persuaded him to return some of the furniture he had removed from the East Wing. Her closeness to John had caused alarm to Nick Somerville and to her father, albeit for different reason. '[Somerville] didn't know I existed. When I met

him he said, "So you're the person who thinks she's going to be the next Marchioness of Bristol?"' Her father restricted himself to 'coughing and shaking his head' whenever John's name was mentioned.

59. Daughter of Sir William Dugdale, 2nd Bt, she was also John's fifth cousin, being, like him, one of the great-great-great-great grandchildren of William Lygon, 1st Earl Beauchamp (1747–1816).

60. John sent Tilly, then living in Australia, a sapphire and diamond necklace, with a note reading: 'I want you to marry me'. She declined his proposal and returned the necklace. 'I knew she would,' said John, who explained that he had 'got a really big kick out of it' since his intention had been to annoy her boyfriend.

61. Cecil had been Francesca's boyfriend at the time. A few months later, however, he stood aside in John's favour with perplexingly little resistance – or so it appeared to some of John's intimates. 'It was really extraordinary, sort of: "Oh, if you want her, have her",' remembers one of them. 'He would do anything to please John, or David [Rocksavage] for that matter.' It had been to Cecil that John had turned when seeking to keep the Murchisons entertained for a weekend at Ickworth. 'We must have some girls, find some girls,' John had told him. Cecil (remembers John's half-brother George Lambton) had obliged.

62. Angela Barry had been dispatched to buy a house, since residency there validated Francesca's divorce from her forgotten husband, Philip Jones.

63. Francesca remembers that John never saw his father from the time of their engagement until Victor's death in 1985. Yvonne has a different memory: it is of John visiting his father towards the end of his life, a successful meeting which concluded with John saying that he would return with 'books, tape cassettes and even Newmarket sausages'. But he never did. Yvonne added that Victor's dying words were, 'Have nothing more to do with that boy. He has been a permanent thorn in my side all my life.' He had then slipped into a coma and died.

64. These included Pauline, his half-brothers George and Nicholas, Juliet and Somerset de Chair, his best man, Jonny Ruane – to whom John had never been closer – Ruane's wife Alice, Tim von Halle and Sarah von Halle and Francesca's parents. All had earlier attended the wedding lunch in the East Wing.

65. Nicholas 'Pickford' Sykes, born in 1953, played the organ at the wedding service. His elder brother, Tatton Sykes, was engaged in protracted correspondence with John, who shared the ripest details with Francesca.

66. Jessica Berens (born 1959), granddaughter of 4th Lord Churston and great-granddaughter of Edward FitzGerald's third wife, 'Jo', née Smither.

67. John's horse, Saxham Breck, a grey gelding, enjoyed appreciable success in 1983. John reputedly told friends that he'd put £1,000 on it to win at Folkestone; it had, at odds of 20–1. But John, it was reported, had backed it through the Tote and won £48,700.

68. His daughter had been murdered in Ipswich.

69. John had finally reached their bedroom (Francesca recalled twenty years later) and grunted: 'S'pose I better consummate the marriage, Squidgy.'

70. The family fortune had been made in construction of supermarkets and service stations rather than railways, according to John's friends.

71. Caroline Somerset, née Davidson, daughter of Viscount Davidson (see Part Two 'Victor', pp. 95, 97); her husband, Lord Edward Somerset, was the second son of the Duke of Beaufort. By 1988, it was being noted that the Queen no longer stayed at Badminton, the Somerset family seat. The local vicar, the Revd Thomas Gibson, surmised that 'the police protecting the Queen would bring their sniffer dogs, which might detect the drugs the young people take'.

72. This was not the exaggeration it might have sounded. Certainly, in terms of cash, Andy Pearce was at least John's equal, leaving £500,000 at the time of his death, or about £1.8 million today.

73. Andy Pearce's apparent teetotalism in Oakley Street represented an attempt as 'to go through a clean period,' says this acquaintance. 'Otherwise he was drinking and out of it.'

74. An intimate friend, who experienced John's delight in tormenting those who loved him, points out that he was also the least violent of men. Panic rather than guilt explained the tangle of evasions and distortions of Porto Ercole: a month earlier, the New York trafficking charges from 1983 had been resurrected. They would, in time, be seen off, with the assistance of Tom Puccio, the attorney who had recently represented Claus von Bulow in a celebrated case.

75. Like Paddy Ireland, Whitby had been schooled at Milton Abbey.

76. A pop singer.

77. A month or two after the air show, John and Tintin were reported to have holidayed in Italy, where they met Lord and Lady Vestey. The latter inquired after 'the lovely Francesca'. John replied, gesturing at Tintin: 'I sacked her.'

78. During his unscheduled day at Ickworth, Boitel-Gill was entrusted to the care of someone who appeared to be John's private secretary – James Whitby, 'a tall, charming man who seemed to be able to handle John. [He] selected a Ferrari when John decided to go on a shopping spree. They returned laden with parcels a couple of hours later.'

79. Son of shipping magnate 'Bluey' Mavroleon, Carlos had briefly been at Eton, leaving it ('expelled for drugs') in favour of a London comprehensive where for two years he took 'a lot of LSD and indulg[ed] in 'industrial scale shoplifting'. His 'heroin-soaked body' was found in a hotel room in Peshawar on 27 August 1998.

80. Remembered by Whitby for his 'amazingly wealthy' girlfriends and for being simultaneously 'a very nice guy but *completely* ruthless', Leatham, who had managed two years at Eton, later sold an account of his dealings with John to the *News of the World*, and continued to trade in cocaine, heroin, crack and ecstasy,

sometimes supplying children as young as eleven or twelve, thereby financing his own £500-a-day habit, which contributed to his contraction of hepatitis C and AIDS, and his death, aged forty, in 2003.

81. Beatrice was almost certainly the girl whom Imogen von Halle and Peter Geiger met during their weekend at Ickworth. She had been introduced to John in summer 1987 in Porto Ercole by Charlie Young, a man of catholic friendships (they extended to the Duke of York). Like Francesca, Beatrice was very young (nineteen), blonde, pretty, rather sweet, and probably unaware of quite how recently Tintin Chambers had occupied the Hughes 500 cockpit. Soon she was at Ickworth almost every weekend, with the approval of her father, Italian businessman Adriano Versolato, whose services were retained by the Sultan of Brunei.

82. John's chequered history in New York was probably to blame. At an earlier hearing, Advocate David Le Cornu had pointed out that 13 grams of cocaine (whose street value was £1,625) might not have lasted his client his planned week's holiday. James Whitby was fined; Dominic Langlands-Pearce and his wife France both received short prison sentences the following year.

83. The fight against deportation ended in defeat in June 1990.

84. They included one for nearly £7,000, issued by his Jersey solicitors – to whom he had given an assurance that he would pay the legal fees of his cocaine case co-defendants, James Whitby and France and Dominic Langlands Pearse – and another, for £1,600, for work on an Ickworth estate cottage.

85. The *Braemar* had been sold in 1980 to Mike Batt, songwriter and creator of the Wombles, who recalls that the sea-trial – off Monte Carlo – revealed weaknesses in the hull and very significant engine problems. Roger Lane-Smith, who had witnessed the yacht emerge from dry-dock – with a hideous clashing of gears and smoke billowing from the engine – later remarked that, though he had seen John drive fast, he had never seen him shift the Ferrari quicker than he did as he made off to Paris with Batt's cheque in his pocket.

86. Carroll himself subsequently suffered a precipitous decline in his fortunes, seemingly presaged by the sale of his horse, Carroll House, in 1989, a decision he explained by saying that the horse 'didn't have a top gear'. It won the Prix L'Arc de Triomphe shortly afterwards.

87. The heritability of schizophrenia (in the West) is high: 'roughly 80 per cent, or about the same heritability as weight and considerably more than personality'.

88. After 'Bristol House' was sold, John briefly rented a two-bedroom flat off Gloucester Road, where he spent most of his time in the bathroom, before resorting to hotels.

89. Wholesale rather than street prices, the latter then being about £100 and £70 for a gram of heroin and cocaine respectively.

90. Ruffin's Farm for around £1.6 million in 2008.

91. In 1992, five of these were also sold: a 1973 V12 E-Type Jag, a 4.6 litre Chevrolet

Corvette, two Rolls-Royce convertibles and a 1949 Bentley Mark VI drophead coupé (coachwork by Park Ward). In all, they were expected to fetch around £150,000 at auction.

92. John had never spoken of them at all, as he later acknowledged: 'I just thought, who the hell is he talking about?' George Carman, QC (1929–2001), imaginative in court, was volatile at home, especially during his second marriage ('My father's repeated violence towards my mother,' recalled their son, 'included banging her head against the wall, threatening her with carving knives and punching her') when his enthusiasm for adultery was undermined only by his appetite for alcohol. According to George Best, liver transplant recipient and footballer, Carman was the greatest drinker he ever knew.

93. 'He lost one of his front teeth when he passed out and banged his face on a basin,' remembers one of his closest friends who visited from London. 'He lived nine months without replacing it.'

94. Harry Primrose, Lord Dalmeny, eldest son and heir of the 7th Earl of Rosebery.

95. James Whitby was not one of them: he was attending his own mother's funeral.

96. In November 1994 Nicholas had offered his creditors 7p in the pound; an offer which Yvonne rejected: 'If he thinks he can get away with that after all it has cost me in blood, sweat and money during seven years' litigation, he's got another thought coming.'

Epilogue

1. Cranborne did not succeed his father until 2003, but enjoyed a seat in the Lords (as Baron Cecil of Essendon), courtesy of a writ of acceleration. The agreement he reached with the Labour government had not been sanctioned by the Conservative Party leader, William Hague, who, on learning of it, sacked him. Accepting that his dismissal was well deserved, Cranborne reflected that he had 'rushed in, like an ill-trained spaniel'.

2. Desmond was buried at Calais on 5th March 1916: 'As he himself had expressly desired, there was no formal parade, but the whole Battalion... lined the road to his grave.' His remains lie in Calais Southern Cemetery, Plot A; Row Officers; Grave 5.

3. Robert Maxwell (né Hoch), MC, 1923–1991; Labour MP for Buckingham, 1964–1970. In later life, he developed a taste for his employees' pension funds, which he raided of £400 million, and for swimming solo, insisting that his youngest daughter's friends leave the pool at Headington Hill Hall, the house he rented from Oxford City Council, whenever he was about to take the plunge. He died after falling from his yacht, the *Lady Ghislaine*.

4. Mr Jackson (singer and devotee of reconstructive surgery, 1958–2009) faced charges of child molestation. Alexander appeared on American television,

explaining that he was, potentially, a prosecution witness. He was never called; Jackson was acquitted.

5. Tom Foley has a firmer hold on Hervey property, owning what Bob Rush, formerly head gardener at Ickworth, remembers was once 'a ramshackle ruin'. 'We were out on a shoot with Lord John,' adds Bob Rush. '"Foley," he says, "I'll have that built up for you into a nice little cottage." At the time, we took it with a pinch of salt but he did [have it restored]. It's a lovely little cottage.' The property is currently let; Tom Foley lives in north Norfolk, where he is in service to John's old and special friend David Cholmondeley.

6. Frederick might take encouragement from the St Clair-Erskines, Earls of Rosslyn. Peter St Clair-Erskine, the 7th Earl (born 1958), great-grandson of the 5th Earl who beggared the family (see Introduction, pp. 2–3), progressed through Eton and Bristol University, then joined the police. In 2003, he was appointed head of the Royal protection squad. Like Frederick Bristol, he retains ownership of his family's place of worship, in his case, Rosslyn Chapel, mention of which is made in *The Da Vinci Code*.

7. Lady Burford's reaction was not recorded: she had defected from the marital home fourteen months earlier, preferring to pursue opportunities with Cradle of Filth, a band then based near Ipswich in Suffolk. However, her estranged husband's decision drew support from Tony Benn (Anthony Wedgwood-Benn, born 1925, succeeded father as 2nd Viscount Stansgate in 1960, but disclaimed his peerage for life in 1963). After wartime service as a Pilot Officer in the RAFVR and as a sub-lieutenant in the RNVR, Benn put his redistributive beliefs into practice whilst having drinks at the London home of John Irwin, producer of an early current affairs television programme, *Free Speech* (later re-entitled *In the News*, following its transfer to ITV), on which Benn regularly appeared. 'That's where I lost my love of socialism,' recalls Irwin's son, Jonathan, 'because I found Tony Benn helping himself out of the silver cigarette case: putting handfuls of cigarettes into both pockets.'

8. Prime Minister 1990–97. Major sent his son James to Kimbolton School, albeit too late for James to encounter Alexander Montagu.

9. Born in 1946, Miss Hodge helped reacquaint Prince Andrew (subsequently the Duke of York) with civilian life following his service in the Falklands campaign. Later, she turned their eight days together to commercial advantage, firstly by selling photographs to the *Daily Mirror* and, a year later, by chronicling their friendship in the *News of the World*. Her financial acumen had already been evident during her rather lengthier association with John Bindon, a Londoner who had a number of claims to physical distinction (he said, for example, that he had been excused wearing a tie whilst at borstal because no shirt with a collar size big enough for him could be found). In 1976, he accompanied Miss Hodge to Mustique, where he allegedly entertained Princess Margaret, sitting next to her whilst wearing a T-shirt emblazoned with the slogan, 'Enjoy Cocaine'. Two years later, he killed John Darke at the Ranelagh Yacht Club, Fulham, stabbing

him nine times with a machete. He was acquitted of murder but died of AIDS, induced by heroin addiction, in 1993.

Sources

Comprehensive source notes, and some supplementary endnotes, can be found at www.blacksheeparistocrats.com. Dates of birth, marriage and death have invariably been taken from *Burke's Peerage and Baronetage* (1999) or various earlier editions of either the *Peerage* or the *Landed Gentry*, or *Debrett's Peerage*, or *Who's Who* or *Who Was Who*, or, in one or two instances, from *Burke's Royal Families of the World*, vol. I (Europe & Latin America).

Conversions of monetary values from an earlier era to that of today are courtesy of Professor William D. Rubinstein (Professor of History at the University of Wales, author of *Men of Property: The Very Wealthy in Britain since the Industrial Revolution* 2nd edn, (London: Social Affairs Unit, 2006) and *The Richest of the Rich* (2007), who has painstakingly and generously answered scores of questions put to him. His method, shared by other economic historians, is to calculate a sum in, say, 1900, as a percentage of the National Net Income of that year, and to work out the value of the same percentage for the National Net Income for 2007 (2007 being chosen because of the contraction in the British economy in the last two years). The figures produced are much higher than those solely reliant on any inflation index – and are, accordingly, far more credible. Sceptics might consider James Lees-Milne's diary entry for 9 June 1991, in which he recorded an assertion by Roy Jenkins, a former Chancellor of the Exchequer, that the money of 1941 could be converted to that of 1991 by multiplying by forty. Lees-Milne replied that a great-aunt of his had been living at No.5 Royal Crescent, Bath, with a cook, a parlour maid and a housemaid, on £600 per annum. Jenkins conceded that no one would 'get far on £24,000' in 1991.

If staff costs have accelerated far faster than the general rate of inflation, others have gone faster – and higher – still, the price of a house in South Kensington, London, rising by between 500 and 1,000 times since the early 1930s. So the Rubinstein 'method' of calculation, although necessarily an approximation, is that favoured throughout this book.

Similarly, the whole peculiar odyssey of compilation was undertaken with one guide never far from hand: David Cannadine's epic *The Decline and Fall of the British Aristocracy*, which maps out the landscape with unrivalled clarity, revealing to all but the wilfully purblind how, from about 1875 onwards, 'five centuries of aristocratic history and hegemony were irrevocably reversed in less than one hundred years'.

Introduction

Newspapers, magazines, periodicals
Observer ('Fall from grace' by Alex Duval Smith, 9 July 2009)

Books

Bence-Jones, Mark & Montgomery-Massingberd, Hugh, *The British Aristocracy*, London: Constable, 1979

Cannadine, David, *The Decline and Fall of the British Aristocracy*, London: Picador, 1992

Masters, Brian, *The Dukes: The origin, ennoblement and history of 26 families*, London: Blond & Briggs, 1975

Raymond, Derek, *The Hidden Files*, London: Little, Brown, 1992

Sutherland, Douglas, *The Yellow Earl*, London: Cassell, 1965

Sykes, Christopher Simon, *Black Sheep*, London: Chatto & Windus, 1982

Interviews

Gerry Farrell (first cousin twice removed of the 'Dancing Marquess'); Martin Selby-Lowndes; plastic surgeon who operated on Lord Shaftesbury; family friend of Lord Shaftesbury.

Edward

Newspapers, magazines, periodicals
Business & Finance magazine (Ireland); *Daily Express*; *Daily Mail*; *Daily Mirror*; *Daily News*; *Daily Sketch*; *Daily Telegraph*; *Eton College Chronicle*; *Evening Standard*; *Guardian*; *News of the World*; *Private Eye*; *Spectator*; *Sunday Dispatch*; *Sunday Express*; *The Times*.

Broadcast media

World in Action, 'The Dukes', 6 July 1965

Books

Asquith, Lady Cynthia, *Diaries 1915–1918*, London: Hutchinson, 1968

Barrow, Andrew, *Gossip: A history of high society, 1920–1970*, London: Hamish Hamilton, 1978

Bedford, John, Duke of, *A Silver-Plated Spoon*, London: Cassell, 1959

Cannadine, David, *The Decline And Fall of the British Aristocracy*, revised edn, London: Picador, 1992

Card, Tim, *Eton Renewed: A History from 1860 to the Present Day*, London: John Murray, 1994

Channon, Sir Henry, *Chips, The Diaries of Sir Henry Channon*, edited by Robert Rhodes James, London: Weidenfeld and Nicolson, 1967

Cullen, Tom, *Maundy Gregory: Purveyor of Honours*, London: Bodley Head, 1974

De Courcy, Anne, *The Viceroy's Daughters: The lives of the Curzon sisters*, London: Weidenfeld and Nicolson, 2000

Dooley, Terence, *The Decline of the Big House in Ireland: A Study of Irish Landed Families, 1860–1960*, Dublin: Wolfhound Press, 2001

Estorick, Michael, *Heirs & Graces: The Claim to the Dukedom of Leinster*, London: Weidenfeld and Nicolson, 1981

Fielding, Daphne, *The Duchess of Jermyn Street: The life and good times of Rosa Lewis of the Cavendish Hotel*, London: Eyre & Spottiswoode, 1964

Fingall, Elizabeth, Countess of, *Seventy Years Young: Memories of Elizabeth, Countess of Fingall*, Dublin: Lilliput Press, 1991

Kehoe, Elisabeth, *Fortune's Daughters: The Extravagant Lives of the Jerome Sisters: Jennie Churchill, Clara Frewen and Leonie Leslie*, London: Atlantic Books, 2004

Kipling, Rudyard, *The Irish Guards in The Great War: The First Battalion*, Staplehurst: Spellmount, 1997

Lacey, Robert, *Aristocrats*, London: Hutchinson and BBC, 1983

Leinster, Rafaelle, Duchess of, *So Brief A Dream*, London: W. H. Allen, 1973

Leinster, Duchess of, 'Memoir' (Duchess 'Jo', née Jessie Smither), unpublished

Masters, Brian, *The Dukes: The origin, ennoblement and history of 26 families*, London: Blond & Briggs, 1975

Mordaunt Crook, J., *Rise of the Nouveau Riches: Style and Status in Victorian and Edwardian Architecture*, London: John Murray, 1999

Sayer, Michael, *The Disintegration of A Heritage: Country Houses and their Collections, 1979–1992*, edited and introduced by Hugh Massingberd, Norwich: Michael Russell, 1993

Somerville-Large, Peter, *The Irish Country House*, London: Sinclair-Stevenson, 1995

Thompson, Douglas, *The Hustlers: An Explosive True Story of Gambling, Greed and the Perfect Con*, London: Sidgwick & Jackson, 2007

Tillyard, Stella, *Aristocrats: Caroline, Emily, Louisa and Sarah Lennox, 1750–1832*, London: Chatto & Windus, 1994

Trzebinski, Errol, *The Life & Death of Lord Erroll: The Truth Behind the Happy Valley Murder*, London: Fourth Estate, 2000

Archives

The National Archives at Kew hold some of Edward's army records, particularly those concerning his attendance, or non-attendance, at various medical boards; it also holds details of correspondence about the Leinster estate.

Interviews

Hilda Archer; Sir Richard Beckett; the late Lydia, Duchess of Bedford; Mark Bence-Jones; Laura Brouard, Assistant Archivist, Lothian Health Services Archive; Major Alastair Campbell of the Argyll & Sutherland Highlanders; Sir James Cayzer; Andrew H. Colquhoun, former head of Printed Books at the Imperial War Museum; Anna Cull; Hugo Deadman, former Senior Library Clerk, House of Lords; Dr Terence Dooley; Michael Estorick; the late Lord Feversham; Adrian FitzGerald; the late Brigadier Desmond FitzGerald; Lady Rosemary FitzGerald; Sir James Graham; Richard Grosvenor; Penny Hatfield, Archivist, Eton College; the Duke and Duchess of Leinster; Sir Gavin Lyle; the late and supreme Hugh Massingberd; Conor Mallaghan; Killoran Murrell; Andrew Orgill, Senior Librarian, Royal Military Academy, Sandhurst; Jeff Payne, Collections Registrar, Hearst Castle; the late Sir Edward Pickering, and his daughter, Louise Page; the Earl of Shannon; the late Lady Caroline Tahany; the late Earl of Wemyss and March; Lucy Warrack; Glyn Wright; and some who prefer to remain anonymous.

Victor

Newspapers, magazines, periodicals

Bury Free Press; *Country Life*; *Daily Express*; *Daily Herald*; *Daily Mail*; *Daily Mirror*; *Daily Sketch*; *Daily Telegraph*; *East Anglian Daily Times*; *Eton Chronicle*; *Evening News*; *Evening Standard*; *Isle of Wight County Press*; *Mail on Sunday* (particularly You magazine, interview with John Bristol); *News Chronicle*; *People*; *Private Eye*; *Star* (of 1941: not easily confused with its contemporary successor); *Sunday Dispatch*; *Sunday Express*; *Sunday Telegraph*; *Sunday Times*; *The Times*; *Tatler*.

Broadcast media

The Real Pink Panther: Lord Victor Hervey, Form Media/Channel 4, 2 March 2009

Books

Argyll, Margaret, Duchess of, *Forget Not*, London: W.H. Allen, 1975

Bailey, Catherine, *Black Diamonds: The Rise And Fall of an English Dynasty*, London: Viking, 2007

Baker, Mark, *The Rise and Fall of Gwrych Castle*, privately published, 2003

Barrow, Andrew, *Gossip: A history of high society, 1920–1970*, London: Hamish Hamilton, 1978

Cannadine, David, *The Decline and Fall of the British Aristocracy*, revised edn, London: Picador, 1992

Card, Tim, *Eton Renewed: A History from 1860 to the Present Day*, London: John Murray, 1994

Danziger, Danny, *Eton Voices*, London: Viking, 1988

De Courcy, Anne, *1939: The Last Season*, London: Phoenix, 2006

De-la-Noye, Michael, *The House of Hervey: A History of Tainted Talent*, London: Constable, 2001

Devonshire, Duke of, *Andrew Cavendish, Accidents of Fortune*, Norwich: Michael Russell, 2004

Erskine, David (ed.), *Augustus Hervey's Journal, The Adventures Afloat and Ashore of a Naval Casanova*, London: Chatham Publishing, 2002

Everett, Rupert, *Red Carpets and Other Banana Skins*, London: Little, Brown, 2006

Havers, Nigel, *Playing With Fire*, London: Headline Review, 2006

Hersh, Seymour, *The Dark Side of Camelot*, London: HarperCollins, 1998

Howson, Gerald, *Arms for Spain: The Untold Story of the Spanish Civil War*, London: John Murray, 1998

Howard de Walden, John Osmael, *Earls Have Peacocks*, London: Haggerston Press, 1992

Hyde, H. Montgomery, *Norman Birkett: The Life of Lord Birkett of Ulverston*, London: Hamish Hamilton, 1964

Jensen-Eriksen, Niklas, *Hitting Them Hard? Promoting British Export Interests in Finland, 1957–1972*, Helsinki: The Finnish Society of Sciences and Letters, 2006

Kimberley, John Wodehouse, *The Whim of the Wheel: The Memoirs of the Earl of Kimberley*, Cardiff: Merton Priory Press, 2001

Martin Robinson, John, *The Country House at War*, London: Bodley Head, 1989

Mulvagh, Jane, *Madresfield: The Real Brideshead. One Home, One Family, One Thousand Years*, London: Doubleday, 2008

Plomin, Robert, *Nature and Nurture: An Introduction to Human Behavioral Genetics*, Pacific Grove, California: Brooks/Cole, 1990

Pugh, Martin, *'We Danced All Night': A Social History of Britain Between the Wars*, London: Bodley Head, 2008

Ridley, Matt, *Nature via Nurture: Genes, experience and what makes us human*, London: Fourth Estate, 2003

Rowley, Peter, *Spoils of War: A Trans-Atlantic Tale*, Oakham: Fydell Press, 2005

Seymour, Miranda, *In My Father's House: Elegy for an Obsessive Love*, London: Simon & Schuster, 2007

Shaughnessy, Alfred, *Both Ends of the Candle: An Autobiography*, London: Peter Owen, 1978

Thomas, Donald, *Villains' Paradise: Britain's Underworld from the Spivs to the Krays*, London: John Murray, 2005

Ward, Zoe, 'The Herveys and Ickworth', unpublished manuscript

Waugh, Auberon, *Will This Do? The First Fifty Years of Auberon Waugh: An Autobiography*, London: Century, 1991

Archives and additional documentary sources

The Governor's log book, 1940, HMP Camp Hill

The Eton Calendar and the Eton Register

National Archives, both for Victor's criminal records and for his tussles with the Treasury and National Trust over the ownership of paintings

Suffolk Record Office, Bury St Edmunds, for details of the Ickworth estate and the 4th Marquess's dealings with his uncle, the 3rd Marquess

Interviews

Isla, Lady Abinger; Craigie Aitchison; Nick Ashley; Mark Baker; Branko Bokun; the late Roger Bray, former assistant governor, HMP Camp Hill, and the staff of HMP Camp Hill; Michael Chappell; Ben Cochrane; Denzil Cochrane-Newton; the late Douglas Cochrane; Douglas Cochrane (Earl of Dundonald); Lord Cochrane of Cults; Viscount Colville of Culross; Jinni, Countess Coreth; Viscount Davidson; Margaret, Dowager Countess of Dundonald; the late David Erskine, and Carol Erskine; Robert Erskine; Lady (Kay) Fisher; Peter Geiger; Sir Eldon Griffiths; Tim von Halle; Selina Hastings; Henry Hoare; Gerald Howson; Carol Hughesdon (formerly Havers); Richard Innes; the late Ronnie Kershaw; the late John Knight; Diana Lainson; Roger Lane-Smith; Janet, Marchioness of Milford Haven; the late Jeremy Monson; Lord Montagu of Beaulieu; Lady Montgomery of El Alamein; Johnny Paravicini; Pam Potter; Brian Raistrick; Lord Rathcavan; Catherine Rossdale; Peter Rowley; Guy Sainty; Brian Sewell; Randle Siddeley; Grizell Stewart (née Cochrane); Betty Stafford; Sir Michael Swinnerton-Dyer; Lady Juliet Tadgell; Jackie Tarrant-Barton, Secretary of the Old Etonian Association; the late David Williamson; and a number who prefer to remain anonymous.

Angus

Newspapers, magazines, periodicals

Bedfordshire on Sunday; Bucks Free Press; Daily Express; Daily Mail; Daily Sketch; Daily Telegraph; Evening News; Evening Standard; Guardian; Independent (the article 'Where is Cheeseman?' by Suzie Mackenzie, in the *Independent Magazine* of 14 December 1991, proved especially rewarding); *Independent on Sunday; Mail on Sunday; New York Times; News of the World; Observer; Sun; Sunday Dispatch; Sunday Telegraph; Tampa Tribune; The Times; Times & Citizen* (Bedford).

Hansard (25 November 1991) offered appropriate coverage of Angus's maiden speech.

Other media

The History of the Wallace Collection at <http/: www.wallacecollection.org>

BBC report, 2 March 2000, detailing MI5's investigations into Tallulah Bankhead

Books

Barnato Walker, Diana, *Spreading My Wings*, Yeovil: Patrick Stephens Ltd, 1994

Barrow, Andrew, *Gossip: A history of high society, 1920–1970*, London: Hamish Hamilton, 1978

Bence-Jones, Mark, and Montgomery-Massingberd, Hugh, *The British Aristocracy*, London: Constable, 1979

Brereton, H. L., *Gordonstoun, Ancient Estate and Modern School*, privately published (copyright Gordonstoun School, 1982)

Bret, David, *Tallulah Bankhead: A Scandalous Life*, London: Robson Books, 1996

Burkett, P. R., *Kimbolton Castle: The Guide* (especially for the extract of a letter from Vanburgh to the 4th Earl of Manchester, July 1707)

Cannadine, David, *The Decline and Fall of the British Aristocracy*, revised edn, London: Picador, 1992

Davie, Michael, *The Diaries of Evelyn Waugh*, London: Phoenix, 1995

Donaldson, William, *Rogues, Villains and Eccentrics: An A-Z of Roguish Britons Through the Ages*, London: Phoenix, 2002

Eliot, Elizabeth, *Heiresses and Coronets: The Story of Lovely Ladies and Noble Men*, New York: McDowell, Obolensky, 1959

Falk, Bernard, *The Way of the Montagues: Gallery of family portraits*, London: Hutchinson, c. 1947

Kehoe, Elisabeth, *Fortune's Daughters: The Extravagant Lives of the Jerome Sisters: Jennie Churchill, Clara Frewen and Leonie Leslie*, London: Atlantic Books, 2004

Lobenthal, Joel, *Tallulah! The Life and Times of A Leading Lady*, London: Aurum Press, 2005

MacColl, Gail, and Wallace, Carol McD, *To Marry an English Lord: The Victorian and Edwardian Experience*, London: Sidgwick & Jackson, 1989

Manchester, The Duke of, *My Candid Recollections*, London: Grayson & Grayson Ltd, 1932

Masters, Brian, *The Dukes: The origin, ennoblement and history of 26 families*, London: Blond & Briggs, 1975

Pearson, Hesketh, *The Pilgrim Daughters*, London: Heinemann, 1961

Raymond, Derek, *The Hidden Files*, London: Little, Brown, 1992

Ridley, Matt, *Nature via Nurture: Genes, experience and what makes us human*, London: Fourth Estate, 2003

Stratford, John, *From Churchyard to Castle, This History of Kimbolton School*, privately published (copyright Kimbolton School, 2000)

Walker, John (ed.), *Halliwell's Who's Who in the Movies*, 13th edn, London: HarperCollins, 1999

Waller, Maureen, *London 1945: Life in the Debris of War*, London: John Murray, 2004

Wheeler, Sara, *Too Close to the Sun: The Life and Times of Denys Finch Hatton*, London: Jonathan Cape, 2006

Additional documentary sources

Transcript of *USA v. Angus Charles Montagu* Case No. 95-65-CR-T-21E (13–15 March, 18–20 March and 6 June 1996)

Fax from Michael Whitear to Durgesh Mehta, 14 June 1991

Fax from Carl Tessier to Angus Manchester and Michael Whitear, 24 July 1991

Findings and Order of the Solicitors' Disciplinary Tribunal, 17 June 1993, chaired by Mr A. Gaynor-Smith, sitting with Mr D. E. Fordham and Lady Bonham-Carter; findings submitted, 12 August 1993

Letter from Durgesh K. Mehta to His Grace The Duke of Manchester and Michael Whitear, Esq, 7 May 1991

Memorandum drawn up by Montagu family trustee, 24 June 1991

Minutes of board meeting at Link International Limited, 21 May 1991

Interviews

Jane Bishop; Nora Butler; Keith Cheeseman; Kerry Cheeseman; the late Patsy Chilton; Ian Codrington; Karen Codrington; Jinny, Countess Coreth; Katie Crutchfield of the Human Resources Office, the House of Lords; Hugo Deadman, formerly Senior Library Clerk at the House of Lords; the Earl of Derby; Grey

Duberly; Helen Eldred (now Hutchinson); Bill Ewens; Rachel Fannen, Assistant Curator, Maritime Archives and Library, Merseyside Maritime Museum (repository of HMS *Conway* records); Alec Foster; Mary Fox; the late William 'Bill' Fuller; Dawn Gooderham; Cynthia, Countess of Gosford; the late Bill Green, Secretary, East Lancashire Branch, the Royal Marines Association; Mike Green; Peter Green; Lady Fiona Hannon; Captain John Hillier, editor, the *Globe & Laurel*; Madeleine Hindley; Pippa Isbell, Vice President, Public Relations, Orient Express; Brian Joyles; William F. Jung; Joss Kent; the Earl of Kintore; Charles Lousada; Louise Manchester; Lord Montagu of Beaulieu; the Duke of Montrose; Caroline Konig; John Mayes; Giles Remnant; the late Fergus Rogers; Graham Smith, of the Bedford Fire Brigade; Jane Steenson, Alumni Secretary, Gordonstoun School; the late Neil Sclater Booth (Lord Basing); Paul Vaughan; Allan Warren; Carol Waycaster; Olga Welton; Michael Whitear; David Whiteman; Willie Wong; Angela Wood; and a number who prefer to remain anonymous.

John

Newspapers, magazines, periodicals

Daily Express; *Daily Mail*; *Daily Star*; *Evening News*; *Evening Standard* (also in its brief guise as the *New Standard*) and *ES Magazine*; *Guardian*; *Harrovian*; *Jersey Evening Post*; *Mail on Sunday* (especially *You* magazine, 7 April 1991); *New York Times*; *News of the World*; *Observer* magazine (particularly 'The End of the Peer' by Anthony Haden-Guest, 22 January 2006); *Sunday Express*; *Tatler* (particularly, 'What's Up John?' by Jessica Berens, February 1990); *The Times*; *Today*.

Broadcast media

BBC report, 30 March 1999.

Books

Blond, Anthony, *Jew Made in England*, London: Timewell Press, 2004

Everett, Rupert, *Red Carpets and Other Banana Skins*, London: Little, Brown, 2006

Lees-Milne, James, *Ceaseless Turmoil: Diaries 1988–1992*, London: John Murray, 2004

Mulvagh, Jane, *Madresfield: The Real Brideshead. One Home, One Family, One Thousand Years*, London: Doubleday, 2008

Norman, Jeremy, *No Make-up: Straight Tales From A Queer Life*, London: Elliott & Thompson, 2006

Ridley, Matt, *Nature via Nurture: Genes, experience and what makes us human*, London: Fourth Estate, 2003

Sayer, Michael, *The Disintegration of a Heritage: Country Houses and their Collections*,

1979–1992, edited and introduced by Hugh Massingberd, Norwich: Michael Russell, 1993

Smith, Roly, *Yorkshire: Living Memories*, Salisbury: Frith Book Company, 2000

Tyerman, Christopher, *A History of Harrow School, 1324–1991*, Oxford: Oxford University Press, 2000

Interviews

Nick Ashley; Angela Barry; Mike Batt; Ann-Muriel Bazin; Peter Boitel-Gill; Francesca Bristol; Gerald Carroll; Michael Chappell; Sandro Corsini; Adam Edwards; Simon Garnier; Peter Geiger; Lady Fisher (née Lady Kay MacRae); Richard Grosvenor; Selina Hastings; Gerald Harrison; Carol Havers (now Hughesdon); Imogen von Halle; Tim von Halle; Robin Hurlstone; Paddy Ireland; Stewart Johnston; the late John Knight; George Lambton; Roger Lane-Smith; Piers de Laszlo; John Leaf; Rhidian Llewellyn; the Marquess of Milford Haven; Janet, Marchioness of Milford Haven; Simon Pott; Brian Raistrick; Maria Rawlinson; Catherine Rossdale; Kevin Ruane; Robert Rush; Guy Sainty; Randle Siddeley (Lord Kenilworth); Jackie Tarrant-Barton, Secretary of the Old Etonian Association; Lady Juliet Tadgell; the late Edmund Vestey; John Ward; James Whitby; Paddy Whitby; Minnie Winn; Henry Wodehouse; Harry Wyndham; and many who prefer to remain anonymous.

Epilogue

Newspapers, magazines, periodicals

Age; *Australasian Post*; *Daily Express*; *Daily Mail*; *Daily Telegraph*; *Evening Standard*; *Guardian*; *Mail on Sunday*; *Sunday Telegraph*; *People*; *Sydney Morning Herald*; *Tatler* (September 2007); *Vancouver Sun*.

Books

Donaldson, William, *Rogues, Villains and Eccentrics: An A–Z of Roguish Britons Through the Ages*, London: Phoenix, 2002

Estorick, Michael, *Heirs & Graces: The Claim to the Dukedom of Leinster*, London: Weidenfeld and Nicolson, 1981

Kipling, Rudyard, *The Irish Guards in The Great War: The First Battalion*, Staplehurst: Spellmount, 1997

Leinster, Rafaelle, Duchess of, *So Brief a Dream*, London: W. H. Allen, 1973

Additional source

The Commonwealth War Graves Commission

Interviews

Mark Baker; Adrian FitzGerald; Lady Rosemary FitzGerald; Jonathan Irwin; Duke of Leinster; Conor Mallaghan; Simon Pott.

Index